Nebraska
Symposium on
Motivation
1988

Volume 36

University of Nebraska Press
Lincoln and London 1990

# Nebraska Symposium on Motivation 1988

Richard Dienstbier
Ross A. Thompson

*Presenters*
Carol Z. Malatesta

Inge Bretherton

Carolyn Saarni

# Socioemotional Development

*Series Editor*
*Volume Editor*

*Associate Professor
of Psychology,
Long Island University*

*Professor of Child and
Family Studies,
University of Wisconsin–
Madison*

*Professor of Counseling,
Sonoma State University*

Carolyn Zahn-Waxler

*Chief, Section on Child Behavior Disorders, Laboratory of Developmental Psychology, National Institute of Mental Health*

Grazyna Kochanska

*Senior Staff Fellow, Laboratory of Developmental Psychology, National Institute of Mental Health*

Dante Cicchetti

*Professor of Psychology and Psychiatry, and Director, Mt. Hope Family Center, University of Rochester*

Ross A. Thompson

*Associate Professor of Psychology, University of Nebraska–Lincoln*

*Nebraska Symposium on
Motivation, 1988,* is Volume 36
in the series on
CURRENT THEORY AND
RESEARCH IN MOTIVATION

"The Library of Congress has cataloged this serial publication as follows:"
**Nebraska Symposium on Motivation.**
  Nebraska Symposium on Motivation.[Papers] v. [1]–1953–
  Lincoln, University of Nebraska Press.
    v. illus., diagrs. 22cm. annual.
  Vol. 1 issued by the symposium under its earlier name: Current Theory and Re-
search in Motivation.
  Symposia sponsored by the Dept. of Psychology of the University of Nebraska.

  1. Motivation (Psychology)

BF683.N4   159.4082   53-11655

Library of Congress

# Preface

The volume editor for this 36th edition of the Nebraska Symposium is Professor Ross A. Thompson. He assumed the major responsibility for drawing together the contributors to this volume and for the coaching and editing that was required to bring this volume to completion. My thanks to him for his extended efforts in nurturing this volume.

The Symposium series is supported largely by funds donated in the memory of Professor Harry K. Wolfe to the University of Nebraska Foundation by the late Professor Cora L. Friedline. This Symposium volume, like those of the recent past, is dedicated to the memory of Professor Wolfe, who brought psychology to the University of Nebraska. After studying with Professor Wilhelm Wundt, Professor Wolfe returned to this, his native state, to establish the first undergraduate laboratory of psychology in the nation. As a student at Nebraska, Professor Friedline studied psychology under Professor Wolfe.

We are grateful to the late Professor Friedline for her bequest, and to Mr. Edward J. Hirsch of the University of Nebraska Foundation for his assurance of continuous financial support for the series. Our thanks also to Vice Chancellor for Research John K. Yost and Chancellor Martin A. Massengale for their continued support of and interest in the Symposium.

RICHARD A. DIENSTBIER
*Series Editor*

# Contents

# Introduction

## Ross A. Thompson
*University of Nebraska–Lincoln*

*T*he term "socioemotional development" does not roll easily off the tongue, and thus it is a suitable addition to the professional vocabulary of psychologists. But it is useful to inquire what this agglomerated phrase really means and why it was chosen as the theme for the 1988 Nebraska Symposium on Motivation. Briefly stated, the study of socioemotional development concerns the intersection of emotional and social growth, and this includes an interest in how emotion is expressed in social contexts, the social elicitors of emotional expressions, the social construction of emotional experience and emotional understanding, the social ramifications of emotional reactions, and the effects of emotion on social behavior. When children learn, for example, that you smile and thank Aunt Nancy for the underwear she gave you for your birthday, it reflects progress in socioemotional development. When children begin fighting with their siblings while their parents are arguing, an important socioemotional phenomenon is involved. The influence of a baby's emotional expressions in parent-infant attachment also reflects a facet of socioemotional development (for each partner). A child's capacity to understand another's feelings, to experience moral affects like guilt or shame, to anticipate how parents will respond when she expresses anger or distress, or to regulate her own emotional arousal—all of these are aspects of socioemotional development. A concern with socioemotional development is also reflected in researchers' efforts to understand the consequences of maltreatment on young children, or the origins of depression, or the effects of congenital disorders on their social and emotional functioning. Thus the topic of socioemotional development is at once familiar, relevant, and important.

## EMOTION AND THE ORGANIZATION OF BEHAVIOR

There are other reasons this topic seemed appropriate for the symposium on motivation. First, the theme of socioemotional development is intrinsically motivational in nature, and current work in this field reflects an emerging view of emotions as significant contributors to the organization of biologically adaptive and psychologically constructive behavior throughout the life span. Contrary to traditional views of emotion as peripheral, disorganizing, or epiphenomenal, current views underscore the way emotional reactions organize valuable facets of behavior and personality from an early age. An important catalyst to this emergent view is evolutionary biology, which stresses the biologically adaptive value of emotional reactions in species evolution as social signals and self-regulatory mechanisms. Moreover, the view that emotions can be organizing as well as motivational is also consistent with a growing recognition of the early-emerging competencies of human young, for whom emotions are significant features of everyday experience. A third catalyst for this emergent view is work in social-cognitive development, in which researchers are discovering the significant roles emotion and emotional understanding assume in children's social information processing and strategies of social interaction.

This current view of emotions as motivational and organizing is reflected in all of the contributions to this symposium. Dante Cicchetti, for example, integrates emotive processes into the organizational perspective that guides his research on Down syndrome and maltreated children, and his studies with these two populations illustrate how congenital and experiential influences can alter the role of emotions in the organization of developmental processes. In my own chapter this view is reflected in our research on emotion and parent-infant attachment, which indicates that "emotional dynamics" regulate the organization of the baby's attachment behavior and leads to new questions concerning how emotion is itself developmentally regulated in ways that permit the ongoing integration of emotive processes into higher-order social, personality, and cognitive functioning. Taken together, these new perspectives on the motivational and organizational roles of emotion throughout development have led to a resurgence of research interest in emotional processes as researchers are beginning to discover the constructive functions of emotions in behavioral organization. The contributions to this symposium reflect and extend this perspective.

## SOCIOEMOTIONAL DEVELOPMENT AS AN INTEGRATIVE FIELD OF STUDY

Another reason for interest in socioemotional development, related to the foregoing, is that its study integrates diverse domains of developmental change. This is especially important for the field of developmental psychology, which tends to segment developmental phenomena into different content domains (eg., cognitive development, perceptual development, personality development) or into distinct chronological periods (e.g., infancy, childhood, adolescence). By contrast, the study of socioemotional development virtually compels researchers and theorists to think more integratively, drawing together diverse developmental processes that affect social and emotional functioning and linking these processes across different periods of the life span. In a sense this area fosters the reintegration of the whole person, in all its complexity.

For example, socioemotional reactions are necessarily related to cognitive functioning, insofar as certain intellectual skills are necessary to interpret and respond emotionally to social events, to reflect upon and manage one's emotional experiences, and to understand the emotional behavior of others. Socioemotional development is influenced by the growth of language and communicative skills because these skills influence the expression of emotion and how emotion is socialized. Genetic and hereditary processes assume a significant (though sometimes misunderstood) role in shaping the emergence of individual differences in socioemotional reactivity, and neurobiological changes with development alter the character of emotional behavior, especially in the early years. Furthermore, it is becoming increasingly apparent not only that socioemotional development is affected by allied changes in other developmental domains, but that the growth of emotion itself acts as a catalyst for growth in cognition, sociability, and other developmental processes. The growth of social skills, for example, is profoundly influenced by the development of emotional self-regulation in childhood, which includes a capacity to manage states of heightened arousal, understand display rules for emotional expressions, and appreciate one's own idiosyncratic emotive processes. Moreover, the links between socioemotional development and other developmental processes not only are bidirectional, but are also transactional, involving mutual influences that change over time. In a manner rare in developmental study, therefore, the consideration of socioemotional development integrates our thinking about the developing person.

This perspective is also reflected throughout the contributions to this year's Nebraska Symposium on Motivation. One way it is revealed is through the concern of several contributors with emotions and relationships and how they are mutually influential. Clearly, emotions are involved in social relationships throughout the life span—beginning with parents' responses to the cries of their newborn infants—but elucidating their developmental association is a challenging task. In a theoretical analysis, Inge Bretherton explores how early understandings of self and other are constructed out of the emotional quality of attachment relationships, and she argues that these "internal working models" have far-reaching implications for social and personality growth because of the way they organize self-awareness. Carolyn Saarni is likewise concerned with the links between emotions and relationships, but from a different viewpoint: she is concerned with how the skills of "emotional competence" arise out of the child's emotional experiences in relationships, arguing that emotional development is fundamentally linked to social interaction. In different ways, both Bretherton and Saarni argue that emotional development and social relationships are intertwined in the development of self-and other-understanding.

The integrative perspective is also revealed in a second way in this symposium: through a concern with emotions and personality development. Individual differences in personality organization are commonly portrayed in socioemotional terms (e.g., warmth, dominant mood, emotional stability), but the developmental role of emotion in personality has only recently received systematic attention. As a contributor to this task, Carol Malatesta offers a portrayal of personality organization focused on the concept of "emotion biases" that color perceptions, expressions, cognitive processing, and inter-personal transactions, and she outlines their developmental origins. In another chapter, Carolyn Zahn-Waxler and Grazyna Kochanska consider the origins of guilt in early childhood and the functional as well as dysfunctional roles of guilt arousal in personality, and in doing so they discuss the influence of child-rearing practices, social-cognitive understanding, and the emotional climate of the home on the development of guilt in childhood.

Zahn-Waxler and Kochanska also reveal another way the study of socioemotional development is integrative: it fosters multi-disciplinary thinking. In the subject populations they study as well as the implications they derive from research findings, Zahn-Waxler and Kochanska unite the concerns of developmental psychology with those of child clinical psychology and developmental psycho-pathology. The same is true of the contributions of Cicchetti, Mal-atesta, Bretherton, and (to a somewhat lesser extent) Saarni and Thompson. These contributors also draw on other cross-disciplin-ary analyses to elucidate the themes of socioemotional develop-ment: Saarni's chapter is deepened by anthropological perspectives, Malatesta draws on philosophical insights, and neurobiological sources add to Cicchetti's discussion. To truly understand the na-ture of socioemotional functioning, it seems, it is necessary to inte-grate insights from developmental psychology with a variety of al-lied fields, exploiting the cross-fertilization of ideas to elucidate this complex and significant developmental phenomenon.

## BROADER DEVELOPMENTAL ISSUES AND CONCERNS

Finally, a third reason this topic was selected for a symposium on motivation is that the study of socioemotional development invites us to consider a number of broader issues concerning development and emotion. What are the long-term effects of early influences? What can account for the consistency of individual characteristics from infancy to later life? Do early parent-infant relationships exert a formative influence on early personality—and if so, how? How does the study of normative developmental pathways provide insight into the origins of developmental psychopathology, and can the study of clinical population likewise provide perspective on normal development? In addition to touching on these classic *developmental* questions, contributors to this symposium also address fundamental questions concerning *emotion*. To what extent is emotional experience socially constructed? How do biological underpinnings of emotion affect mature emotional experience? Is emotion best studied as discrete phenomena (i.e., distinguishing emotions of anger, fear, sadness, and the like) or as a dynamic process? In both their theoretical formulations as well as in their research findings, contributors to this symposium offer perspectives on some of the issues that motivate the work of developmentalists and students of emotion.

ACKNOWLEDGMENTS

Over the years, the topics selected for the Nebraska Symposium on Motivation have reflected the changing interests and concerns of psychologists, and this year is no different. In organizing the first symposium to be devoted to a developmental theme in more than 10 years, I sought to invite contributors who not only could offer a state-of-the-art portrayal of some of the most exciting research in this field, but could also provide a prospectus for emergent issues and themes to come. I am grateful to this group of contributors for their excellent presentations and papers that more than fulfilled my hopes for the symposium. My only regret is that Joseph Campos, who enlivened the fall session of the symposium with a remarkable discussion of locomotion and its role in emotional and cognitive development, could not contribute to this volume.

I am also grateful for the assistance of colleagues and students at the University of Nebraska who contributed to the success of the symposium. Noteworthy among them is a cohort of graduate students who devoted a semester to studying the work of the symposium contributors with me before the speakers' arrival in Lincoln, and who contributed to the symposium with provocative questions (and answers). Students in our Developmental Research Group were also catalysts to this process. And not to be neglected are the thespians among our graduate student group, who enlivened the symposium with a parody of developmental research that will be long remembered.

Finally, I am grateful to the Nebraska Symposium Committee for inviting me to contribute a chapter to this volume at the time this symposium was in its genesis. This is a rare honor for an in-house editor. Taken together, this volume has been long in gestation, but like many developmental achievements, the outcome is satisfying. I hope you, the reader, will agree.

# The Role of Emotions in the Development and Organization of Personality

## Carol Z. Malatesta
*Long Island University*

*I*n this chapter I examine the case for considering emotions as central organizing axes for personality, thus confronting one of the oldest problems in psychology—the organization of behavior. The latter topic has long fascinated European psychologists, but it is a late-maturing interest among American psychologists, even developmentalists. However, within the field of developmental psychology there are two main lines of research that reflect the European emphasis on behavioral organization in recent decades. Piaget's work, and that of the Geneva school, was concerned with the structural properties of cognition. Research from this group has been focused chiefly on establishing the universality of cognitive structures and stages of development; there has been little interest in individual differences and issues of personality, and thus this work will not concern us further here. A second stream of European influence comes from the German and English ethologists; a direct offshoot, attachment theory, originally focused mainly on the "affectional tie" that binds caregiver and child but has since shifted to broader aspects of development, including sociocognitive and socioemotional sequelae of the attachment relationship.

I thank Klaus Grossmann and Ross Thompson for reading an earlier version of this manuscript and making valuable suggestions.

The European interest in underlying structure or organization can trace its roots back to early German *Strukturpsychologie* and Spranger's influential work *Lebensformen* (*Types of Men*, translated 1928). Spranger assumed, as did many other psychologists of his time, that once one understood certain basic organizational or structural aspects of an individual, one was in a position to understand and predict many other aspects of that person's functioning. Such a viewpoint appears to have a certain attractiveness for developmental psychologists, since the goal of much of our research is to predict future forms of behavior. If organizational constructs can be identified, the task of predicting behavior may be within easier reach— hence the organizational approach of this chapter.

First it is necessary to review some additional history concerning the fate of organizational views of personality as transported to American soil. In the United States, European ideas on the organization of behavior are identified with Gordon Allport's personalistic psychology and his use of the concept of traits. Allport defined a trait as a "generalized and focalized neuropsychic system (peculiar to the individual), with the capacity to render many stimuli functionally equivalent, and to initiate and guide consistent (equivalent) forms of adaptive and expressive behavior" (Allport, 1937, p. 295). In this definition Allport appears to be focusing on what one might regard as biases in perception and behavior, a point to which I shall return later.

Although trait theories of personality enjoyed popularity for some time, in the late 1960s and 1970s the concept of trait came under attack by theorists such as Walter Mischel, who argued that traits demonstrated little cross-situational stability. The antitrait position was subsequently weakened by other lines of evidence contradicting Mischel's claim. For example, Seymour Epstein (1980), in an incisive critique of the antitrait position, demonstrates high stabilities in a wide domain of behaviors when measures are aggregated over time or stimulus conditions. Evidence from within the developmental literature over the past decade also seems to challenge the antitrait position, including demonstration of stability in the dimensions of ego strength and ego resilience (Block & Block, 1980) and in certain aspects of temperament (Rothbart & Derryberry, 1981). Finally, McCrae and Costa (1984) have adduced robust evidence in favor of the stability of personality traits over years, even decades, in longitudinal studies of adults. It thus appears timely to examine the concept of trait as it relates to emotions and the ontogenesis of personality.

First a word about the use of the word *trait*. Although the term provides a common anchor point in thinking about individual differences, its vicissitudinous history gives us pause to consider whether using it here would be more a help or a hindrance. After much thought, I have decided that a more neutral, less emotionally freighted term that preserves Allport's original meaning would bridge the gap between those who favor the resurrection of the term and those who would like to inter the word for all time. Thus I will employ the term "biases" in behavior to refer to individual differences that show a degree of stability across time and situations and the term "emotional biases" to index emotion-based consistencies.

As already mentioned, the notion of underlying organizational aspects of personality has already entered the epistemology of developmental psychologists within the framework of attachment theory. However, although attachment theory is concerned with organizational aspects of behavior and can accommodate individual difference variables, it turns out to be an inadequate model of personality development, at least as the theory is currently formulated, because it lacks *both* comprehensiveness and specificity, or what Allport called "generalized and focalized" specifications of behavior. I believe that differential emotions theory, as originally proposed by Tomkins (1962, 1963) and elaborated by Izard (1971, 1972, 1977; Izard & Malatesta, 1987), can provide a complementary and perhaps enriched view of human personality development. In this chapter I discuss these two organizational views of personality development—attachment theory and differential emotions theory, in juxtaposition.

## Attachment Theory

The attachment concept evolved from research on the effects of "maternal deprivation" during the 1940s and 1950s. Rene Spitz's (1965) pioneering work documented the profound deterioration of infants separated from their mothers and reared in a foundling home or hospital. Although we now know that some of the effects he observed were due to stimulus deprivation as well as lack of a consistent caregiver, his work was influential in alerting professionals as well as the lay public to the potentially devastating effects of institutional rearing.

With the observations above in mind, John Bowlby, a British child psychiatrist, began formulating his ideas on attachment, which culminated in the three-volume work *Attachment and Loss* (1969, 1973, 1980). These volumes reflected his attempts to synthesize theory from psychoanalysis and ethology in trying to understand the young infant's response to separation and loss of the mother.

An American psychologist, Mary Ainsworth, applied some of Bowlby's ideas in her 1967 study of attachment in Uganda and, later, in Baltimore, Maryland, and in so doing launched two decades of research on the topic. Inge Bretherton's chapter in this volume summarizes much of this research, so I will only highlight a few points here. As Bretherton's chapter indicates, Ainsworth and her colleagues developed a laboratory procedure for assessing children's attachment, the "Strange Situation," and a classification system for rating the quality of attachment. Originally, three types of classification were distinguished: an A type, reflecting an "anxious, avoidant attachment," a B type, reflecting a secure attachment, and a C type, reflecting an "anxious, resistant" attachment. Thus, originally two anxious types of attachment were described; however, the practice of referring to C babies as anxious was subsequently dropped in favor of identifying them as "ambivalent." As research on attachment progressed, subclassifications were also distinguished, including a passive C2 subtype and an angry C1 subtype, A1 and A2 subtypes, and four subclassifications within the B group. According to Ainsworth, the differences in behavior distinguished by the classifications reflect individual differences in the level of inner organization. (Also see Bretherton, this volume, on "internal working models.")

Originally great pains were taken to distinguish between the attachment construct and personality constructs such as dependency. Attachment was to be viewed not as a personality configuration, but rather as an index of a biologically based, goal-corrected motivational system oriented toward maintaining homeostasis. Over the years, however, as research on the characteristics of A, B, and C children accumulated and as the attachment construct began to take on more and more traitlike qualities, the resemblance to personality constructs could not be ignored. Indeed, many workers seemed inclined implicitly to regard the A, B, and C typologies in the same way personologists have treated different personality types. For example, Sroufe (1979), in a discussion of individual personality development, noted that personality is closely linked with the outcome of attachment; individual differences in competence and styles of adaptation in later childhood are said to result from the kind of early affective bond experienced by the mother and infant.

According to Pervin (1975, p. 3), "Personality represents those structural and dynamic properties of an individual or individuals as they reflect themselves in characteristic responses to situations." Given this definition, and the stress on *uniqueness, consistency,* and *dynamic prediction,* attachment classifications may indeed qualify as personality constructs. First, they show a certain degree of *uniqueness* in organization, at least when initially measured. A cluster analytic technique employed by Lamb, Thompson, Gardner, Charnov, and Estes (1984) on five samples of infants tested in the Strange Situation demonstrated modest support for the claim that A, B, and C groupings summarize individual differences.

There is also some support for the stability of pattern over time (*consistency*), at least in terms of major attachment classifications. The first studies that examined the stability of classifications were able to demonstrate moderately good stability from 12 to 18 or 20 months; the latest research shows that patterns of attachment classification remain relatively stable from 12 months to 6 years (Main, Kaplan, & Cassidy, 1985).

Let us now examine the evidence for the *predictive validity* of attachment classifications. Recall that three major categories and eight subclassifications have been distinguished. First, there seems to be ample evidence for the utility of distinguishing between *securely attached* and *insecurely attached* infants; the "securely attached" category indexes the B group(s), whereas both A and C infants are regarded as insecurely attached, and many investigators combine those categories in analyzing follow-up data. Securely attached infants show less frustration in problem-solving situations, are more enthusiastic (Matas, Arend, & Sroufe, 1978), and generally demonstrate longer attention spans and more positive affect during free play (Main, 1973); they exhibit greater curiosity and more autonomous exploration and are more "ego resilient" (Arend, Gove, & Sroufe, 1979). In interactions with peers, they show greater social competence (Waters, Wippman, & Sroufe, 1979). In contrast, insecurely attached children exhibit less empathy and compliance with peers and teachers (LaFreniere & Sroufe, 1985), are more readily frustrated, whiney, and negativistic during problem-solving tasks (Matas et al., 1978), demonstrate a conspicuous breakdown in communication under stress (Grossmann & Grossmann, 1985), and are more negative toward peers (Pastor, 1981). (See Bretherton, this volume, for further distinctions between the secure and insecure groups.)

In summarizing this pattern of findings, one clear generalization we can make is that B children appear to be generally competent and emotionally healthy, whereas insecurely attached children show more maladaptive behavior and less general competence. As far as finer distinctions among the subtypes go, however, the picture is more clouded. Despite the early excitement over the prospect that attachment typologies might offer a unique predictive window on a range of theoretically relevant behaviors, such results have not been forthcoming. There has been almost no attempt to establish the predictive validity of the B subclassifications, and attempts to establish the discriminant validity of the A and C types have generally been unsuccessful. (But see some very recent research described by Bretherton, this volume.) Research on the predictive correlates of Strange Situation behavior typically has failed to identify reliable differences between the two groups (Lamb et al., 1984), and A versus C differences often fail to obtain even when they have been specifically tested (Ford & Thompson, 1985).

In light of the observations above, a number of writers have suggested that the Ainsworth typologies may not provide the best way of summarizing individual differences (e.g., Campos, Barrett, Lamb, Goldsmith, & Stenberg, 1983; Lamb, Thompson, Gardner, & Charnov, 1985). Though the classification system is able to make predictions about generally adaptive or maladaptive patterns of behavior in preschoolers and grade-school children based on their attachment classification (secure or insecure) at one year of age, the question that needs to be pursued is whether we can identify the uniqueness of individual children in other ways. Ideally, our grouping factor should have a broader, longer, and more specific predictive reach. It should enable use to say more precise things about children's future expressive behavior, their perceptual biases, how they might interpret ambiguous social events, their reactions to stressors, their ability to introspect about feelings, and so forth. It is not yet clear whether the predictive power of the A, B, C distinction (and subclassifications) can be enhanced by focusing on different aspects of behavior or more discrete behaviors, or whether the A, B, C grouping factor is simply not a sensitive enough way of clustering children for more than very limited predictive purposes. I believe that an analysis of individual emotional biases may augment the predictive power of early relationship ssessments.

In the following, I examine an array of data in support of the concept of emotional biases as organizers of personality and provide a model of the ontogenesis of distinctive emotional orientations. In brief, I suggest that individual differences in affective organization, acquired during the course of development, result in affect-specific biases in expressive patterns and idiosyncratic perceptual organizations. These affective biases, which appear to have a pervasive influence on a wide domain of individual and interpersonal behaviors, contribute to psychological continuities within individuals. It is also becoming clear that person-specific emotional organizations can be detected as early as the first year of life.

## Discrete Emotions Theory and the Ontogenesis of Emotional Biases

### TERMINOLOGY

Before I begin with an exposition of the theoretical model, I wish to specify how I intend to use certain terms. The operative framework for my model is a functionalist one embedded in a discrete emotions framework. I use the term functionalist as it was used in William James's time to describe a Darwinian or psychoevolutionary view that regards mental events as adaptive, goal-relevant acts, meaningfully studied in their natural biological and social contexts. Emotions clearly qualify as mental events, can be regarded as adaptive acts, and so can be treated within a functionalist context. My use of the term "discrete emotions" (sometimes called differential emotions) coincides with the typological (versus dimensional) approach within emotions theory. As such, I view emotions as entities that vary more than merely along a hedonic dimension or continuum of arousal; instead, my position is consistent with the view that there are a limited number of identifiable "primary" or fundamental emotions, each with distinctly different properties, including different functional properties.

## BACKGROUND

A major thesis of the model presented in this chapter is that emotions alter and order the phenomenological field of the individual in diverse and profound ways. Although this assertion may seem intuitively reasonable—even obvious—it is only recently that psychology has begun to take serious stock of what this might mean for a coherent psychology of behavior. The German émigré psychologist Felix Krueger originally suggested such a possibility in 1928 when he described emotion as occupying the most central aspect of personal experience. He noted that feelings "embrace or penetrate all other mental events in some way" (1928, p. 58) and, more important to my thesis, that mental events are deeply colored by the *quality* of the emotional experience.

More extended analyses, in which the implications are more fully spelled out, come to us not from psychology but from philosophy. Charles Fourier (Beecher, 1986), a 19th-century French utopian philosopher, constructed an elaborate taxonomy of personality types whose signal feature was that they were dominated by one or several recurring or "radical" passions. The presence of a particular personality/emotion configuration meant that a person would tend to behave in a relatively consistent way across a variety of situations. A relatively "pure" affect/personality type dominated by one passion (a "monogyne") was the "cabalist"—a calculating individual frequently drawn into conspiracies. More complex personality types, those dominated by two or more radical passions, also ex- isted. Fourier described Louis XIV as a "digyne" dominated by two passions—ambition and love. Henri IV was an even more complex personality, a splendid "tetragyne," ruled by friendship, love, ambi- tion, and romanticism.

A 20th-century philosopher, Martin Heidegger, has focused more on the *way* emotion (passion, mood) exerts its effect on behav- ior, specifically as a product of interaction with mind. Of course the earliest systematic hermeneutic of "states of mind" (a term used to refer to affects in early philosophic systems) dates back to Aristotle and the second book of his *Rhetoric*. However, the phenomenologi- cal interpretation of the affective life had not progressed very far by the first quarter of the 20th century, either within philosophy or in other relevant fields, as Heidegger observed. Writing in 1926, he pointed out that psychology had failed to fully appreciate the signifi- cance of mood; even the field of personology, which had taken the *individual* as its unit of study, had failed to come to terms with the emotions as pivotal *"existentialia"* of being human.

That has all changed in recent times, at least in psychology (al- though we tend to deal in "parameters" of emotion rather than *exis- tentialia*). Indeed, contemporary models of emotion, especially those that fall within the domain of differential emotions theory, share some of the assumptions and intuitions about the place of emotion in human life that Heidegger first explored half a century ago. As a historical footnote, I will examine the relevant aspects of Heidegger's theory before proceeding to his psychological suc- cessors.

In the work *Being and Time* (*Sein und Zeit*, 1926/1962), Heidegger takes up the nature of man's existential being-in-the world, or *Da- sein*. There is a particularly penetrating analysis of "mood" in this work, in which Heidegger anticipates a number of the assumptions and formulations of subsequent affect theory (e.g., Ekman, 1984; Izard, 1971, 1977; Plutchik, 1980; Zajonc, 1984). For example, he as- serted the primacy of emotion over cognition ("ontologically mood is a primordial kind of Being for Dasein, in which Dasein is disclosed to itself *prior to* all cognition and volition" [p. 175]). He also main- tained that mood is ever present ("we are never free of moods"; "when we master a mood, we do so by way of a counter-mood" [p.

175]). He believed that objective perception of the world was not possible; emotions or moods act as selective filters on the world, controlling perception and hence one's interpretation of reality ("the perceiving of what is known is not a process of returning with one's booty to the 'cabinet' of consciousness after one has gone out and grasped it" [p. 89]); "entities within-the-world 'matter' to [the individual] in a way which [his or her] moods have outlined in advance" [p. 177]).

During the 1940s and 1950s psychology experimented with a "new look" (Bruner, 1957; Klein, Schlesinger, & Meister, 1951). In the field of perception this took the form of interest in phenomena such as perceptual readiness and defense. Experiments undertaken at this time produced findings that can be taken as empirical support for some of the ideas Heidegger had proposed many years earlier. Specifically, this literature documented the way extracognitive faculties such as motivation affected perception. However, there was little attention to the way differential moods, as differential motivational states, might alter the content of perception in qualitatively different ways. It is likely that this ellipsis occurred largely because dimensional models of emotion, stressing activation level, arousal, and hedonic tone rather than qualitative differences among emotions, prevailed within psychology at that time.

*Being and Time*, however, had a good deal more to say on the subject of differential moods and their impact on human perception and information processing. Heidegger referred to moods as "modes of state-of-mind." Moods (or what we would call emotions) were held to organize and structure the total primary field of experience so that certain elements of one's life situation emerged as focal and others receded. Moreover, he recognized that the different modes or moods altered the nature of the phenomenological world in distinctly different ways. The emotion of *fear* is given extended treatment for illustrative purposes. "Fearing discloses [one's Being] as endangered and abandoned to itself." And one "sees the fearsome because it has fear as its state-of-mind. Fearing, as a slumbering possibility of Being-in-the world in a state-of-mind (we call this possibility 'fearfulness' [*Furchtsamkeit*]) has already disclosed the world, in that out of it something like the fearsome may come close" (p. 180). This excerpt contains three important points I wish to develop further: that different mood states render the psychological world in qualitatively different ways; that they have a pervasive influence on a wide domain of psychological functioning; and that when subsumed within the *personality*, moods may affect psychological functioning in more enduring ways (as they "slumber" within the personality).

Each of the foregoing notions finds some expression in contemporary theories of emotion, at least those having a typological and not a neofunctionalist approach. However, as I will show, neither philosophical systems nor contemporary psychological theory has explored in full the ramifications of the above theses for a theory of personality development. Here I take up the challenge. I propose a theory of personality development that is grounded in the assumptions of Fourier and Heidegger and in the theoretical formulations of differential-emotions theory. In brief, I argue that emotions function both as momentary affective states and as more enduring dispositions within individuals. I maintain that individuals develop emotional organizations in the course of growing up, that these emotional predispositions come to function in a traitlike way, and that they have a pervasive influence on a wide domain of individual and interpersonal behaviors. I believe that such a model of individual development will complement and enrich the work on emotional development that has already taken place within attachment theory and, moreover, that it may provide a more discriminating characterization of individual differences and a more discrete predictive developmental odel.

The notion that emotional dispositions play a prominent part in personality organization is not new within psychology, at least in recent times. It finds recognition in nearly every major emotions theory, although theorists differ in whether they attend to developmental questions. Since my own model shares with other theoretical systems certain assumptions about the role of emotion in personality organization, it will be helpful to summarize the other systems first, detailing areas of agreement and departure with the present model.

## Theories That Address the
## Role of Emotion in Personality

Among contemporary theories of emotion, we find five that propose a strong link between emotion and personality; coincidentally or not, they are all discrete emotions theories. Robert Plutchik (1962, 1980), for example, has proposed a psychoevolutionary theory of the emotions stressing the functional aspects of discrete emotions. Each of eight primary emotions is associated with a prototypic adaptive pattern; in the case of anger, for example, the adaptive pattern is destruction/removal of barriers to satisfaction. Plutchik's theory proposes that in humans, emotion mixtures represent conflict and may exist as stable personality traits. Plutchik suggests that emotional traits are produced by "persisting situations" but leaves unclear the mechanisms involved in transforming repetitive emotional experiences such that they then acquire the characteristic of structure. Do cues to the self play a part? What about the role of cognition? Plutchik tends to focus on responses rather than on feeling states and cognitive processes, and he does not explore the developmental implications of this theory.

In Silvan Tomkins's affect theory (1962, 1963), emotions represent the primary motivational system in humans. Subjective experience is a product of feedback from facial expressions, and it is this experience that spurs subsequent instrumental activity. According to Tomkins (1963), people organize their experiences of affects in accord with personal "affect theories." These are ideoaffective organizations that have two features: a tendency to scan incoming information for relevance to a particular emotion, and a set of strategies for coping with a variety of contingencies specific to that affect in order to avoid or attenuate it. Avoidance of negative affect is central to his ideas about personality development; it is "the repeated and apparently uncontrollable spread of the experience of negative affect which prompts the increasing strength of the ideo-affective organization" (p. 324). His formulations about personality types and development constitute a rich and provocative body of theory, one that is far too complex to summarize here. Rather, I limit my discussion to differences between Tomkins's formulations and my own model.

First, for Tomkins, particular affective organizations are at the service of avoiding or escaping negative affect. In contrast, I take a broader, psychoevolutionary point of view, noting the adaptive function of all affects, even negative emotions, and note that negative affective organizations may be embraced, especially in psychopathological states, rather than avoided, because of the adaptive functions they serve (Malatesta & Wilson, 1988). Second, I emphasize the social signal value of affect as well as the subjective feedback aspect, noting its critical value interpersonally and especially in early ontogenesis. Tomkins implies that ideoaffective organizations will have an influence on a broad spectrum of behaviors and that they fundamentally affect the "interpretation and disposition of information" (1963, p. 303). Here I take this intuitively appealing general principle and specify what it implies in terms of different classes of affective organization; I also specify domains of influence and a set of test conditions where the affective organizations will be manifest.

Lewis and Michalson (1983) have proposed a model of emotional development that is particularly focused on individual differences. In their view, personality consists of patterns of enduring emotional states. These traitlike patterns are characterized by two features: dispositions to act in certain ways given particular classes of events and at a certain level of intensity, and a tendency to perceive particular classes of events in certain ways. Lewis and Michalson do not indicate how these characteristics will vary as a function of the type of emotional organization, nor do they specify the conditions that will encourage their manifestation. However, they have developed scales that permit the discrimination of five different emotional profiles that reflect enduring emotional states in very young children. They have also adduced preliminary evidence in support of their concepts.

Ekman's (1984; Ekman, Friesen, & Ellsworth, 1972) neurocultural theory of emotion also makes allowances for individual differences in expression of emotion. Although there is a class of universal emotional expressions that appear to be biologically based, learning experiences contribute to individual differences in the expression of emotion, as evidenced in emotional traits and emotional disorders. According to Ekman (1984), an emotional trait such as hostility is manifest if a particular emotion, such as anger, appears chronically. In the case of emotional disorders such as depression or mania, the central emotion or emotions do more than recur frequently—they are said to "flood" the individual, being elicited with minimal or no overt provocation, and to be poorly modulated. They are also said to seriously interfere with fundamental life tasks. Ekman has not attempted to deal with the origins of individual differences in emotional traits.

Carroll Izard's differential-emotions theory (1971, 1977) represents another discrete emotions approach to the study of behavior. Compared with the foregoing theories, this theory is the most explicitly developmental in its orientation. Izard stresses both the social-communicative and self-cueing functions of differential facial expression and notes that facial expressions play a prominent role in parent-child communication and therefore in individual development. There are two formulations that speak directly to the link between emotion and personality: the notions of *affect thresholds* and *affective-cognitive structures*. For Izard, particular emotional organizations consist of "thresholds for the various emotions" (1977, p. 10). These are formed by an interaction between genetic makeup and individual social experiences. The repetitive experience and expression of emotion are said to establish particular kinds of responses from others. Over time, this interaction "inevitably produces distinct and significant personality characteristics" (p. 11). Affective-cognitive structures are traitlike psychological organizations of affect and cognition deriving from repeated interactions between a particular affect or pattern of affects and a particular set or configuration of cognitions. A complex affective cognitive structure, or structures may constitute an affective-cognitive orientation, a more global personality trait, trait complex, or disposition such as extroversion.

It is clear that Izard views emotions as constituting a fundamental component of personality and that individual differences in personality will have a great deal to do with differences in patterns of discrete emotions across individuals. However, he has not articulated a formal linkage between types of emotional organization and their developmental origins, nor has he specified where and in what form these organizations might be manifest in different domains of behavior, aspects that I develop here.

## The Present Model

A central assumption I make is that individuals are predisposed toward particular mood states. Our everyday language reflects a certain awareness that mood states are idiosyncratically organized within individuals. One commonly speaks of a somber, haughty, or hostile person. In the terminology of discrete emotions theory we would say that these people were organized around the primary affects of sadness, contempt, or anger. An emerging body of data suggests that these descriptions are correct. It is my theory that these emotional state predispositions accrue by and large from repetitive experiences that occur within certain social ecologies. It is important to qualify this claim. Although I will be emphasizing the *social* influences in emotional development, it goes without saying that biological factors are also consequential contributors to individual development (Zivin, 1986). Social influences ultimately impinge on a biological substrate, as when a parent reacts to the temperamental disposition of her child. For example, over time an inherently sensitive mother may be drawn into a more and more intrusive interactive style with a relatively unresponsive infant (Field, 1987), which may in turn create the conditions for anxiety and mutually avoidant behavior. I will have more to say about the role of temperament and other biological contributions to development in a later section.

In the course of their normal everyday social interactions, children learn to assign meaning to their emotional experiences. Certain emotional states occur often, are experienced in a salient fashion, become highly centered in experience, and become associated with self-feeling. I intend to show that when these patterns become consolidated over time, they can function in a traitlike way, acting as pivotal aspects of personality that can then influence a wide range of behaviors. Evidence for the existence of such patterns and an elaboration of the mechanisms by which experiences become dispositions follows.

In setting forth the present model, I first review my basic operating assumptions about the function of affect and its place in adaptation and development. Like many contemporary emotions theorists, including the ones cited above, I view emotions as part of an evolutionarily adapted behavioral system that promotes both species and individual survival. According to most neo-Darwinian ac-

counts, there are a limited number of primary or fundamental emotions (5 to 10, depending on the author), each with distinctive feeling
states, motivational properties, and behavioral patterns. Although
basic emotional programs appear to be hard-wired into the mam-
malian nervous system (Panksepp, in press), humans, and possibly
other primates, are capable of exerting instrumental control over the
behavioral expression of emotion. Most commonly this control
takes the form of intensifying or deintensifying the basic emotional
expression or qualifying it in some way; nevertheless, the fundamental patterns tend to be preserved so that emotional expressions
in one culture can typically be recognized by members of other cultures; in addition, each emotion pattern is associated with particular
feeling states (Ekman, 1973).

In this chapter I am especially interested in the signal value that
is inherent in emotional expression. To observers, different emotional expressions convey different kinds of information regarding
an individual's response disposition; for example, a rage expression
is often taken as a signal of impending attack, while a shyness expression signals retreat and the desire to be alone. To the person experiencing an emotion, another kind of signal is provided, one that
is informational and motivational as well. For example, the experience of anger organizes awareness of barriers to goals or sources of
frustration and mobilizes the body to prepare for energy expendi-
ture directed at eliminating the obstacle. The notion that emotions
provide crucial information to both the self and others is discussed
in greater detail in Izard and Malatesta (1987). Buck (1984) has also
discussed this concept, referring to the "read-out" and "read-in"
function of expressive behavior. In the present treatment I expand
upon these notions by specifying the nature of the signal value to
both the self and others in functional terms for each of 10 primary
emotions. Table 1 (adapted from Malatesta & Wilson, 1988) provides
a summary of these characteristics. For example, fear, as a signal to
the self, identifies threat and promotes flight or attack; as a signal to
others, it implies submission and typically has the adaptive consequence of warding off attack. The functional aspects of the various
emotions presented in this table have largely been culled from the
theoretical literature (e.g., Izard, 1971; Izard & Malatesta, 1987;
Tomkins, 1962, 1963); a few were supplied by Malatesta and Wilson
(1988) as reasonable inferences based on evolutionary theory. These

**Table 1**

Signal Properties of Emotions and Their Adaptive Functions

| Emotion | Elicitor | Function within the Self System | Function within the Interpersonal System |
|---|---|---|---|
| Anger | Frustration of goal | Removes barriers or sources of frustration toward goals | Warns of possible impending attack, aggression |
| Sadness | Loss of valued object; lack of efficacy | Reduces activity possibly forstalling further trauma) and conserves energy | Elicits nurture, empathy, succor |
| Fear | Perception of danger | Identifies threat; promotes flight or attack | Signals submission, wards off attack |
| Contempt | Perception of superiority | Organizes and sustains awareness and social position and dominance | Signals dominance to others |
| Shame / shyness | Perception that the self is the focus of intense scrutiny | Produces behavior that protects the self against further violations of privacy | Signals need for privacy |
| Guilt | Recognition that one has done wrong and the feeling that escape is not possible | Promotes attempts at reparation | Produces submissive postures that reduce likelihood of attack |
| Disgust | Perception of noxious substances/individuals | Repels noxious substances | Signals individual's lack of receptivity |
| Interest / excitement | Novelty, discrepancy, expectancy | Opens the sensory systems for information intake | Signals receptivity |
| Joy | Familiarity; pleasurable stimulation | Signal to self to continue the present activities | Promotes social bonding through contagion of good feeling |
| Surprise | Perception of novelty; violation of expectancy | Serves "channel clearing" function (Tomkins, 1962) to ready organism for new experience | Demonstrates naiveté of organism, protecting it from attack |

*Source*: Adapted from Malatesta & Wilson, 1988.

responses are given to immediate stimulus situations, but if elicited repetitively and within certain learning contexts, they can become incorporated into the personality, as described in a later section.

In my treatment of the functional aspects of emotions, I have chosen the term signal to emphasize that emotions carry information and convey messages. Unfortunately, the term also connotes a certain episodic quality or fleetingness. We tend to think of signals as either "on" or "off." In the case of emotion, this may be true only in a relative sense. Like Heidegger, I believe that some kind of emotion is always "on" when one is engaged with the world, at least in some form and at some level of intensity. (See Lewis & Michalson, 1983, and Izard & Malatesta, 1987, for similar views.) More important, I believe that low-level "background" emotion figures prominently in individual personality functioning and that different background affects can be found for different persons. In fact, most persons can identify their own background affect. Kurt Vonnegut, for example, in his autobiographical work *Palm Sunday* (1981), described for himself an "existential hum" of embarrassment that he felt pervaded his being.

To explore the idea of emotional dispositions, it may be helpful to make the distinction Ekman (1984) has made among the terms emotion, mood, emotional trait, and emotional disorder. Clearly, each of these terms connotes emotional events or emotion-related phenomena; the dimension along which they seem to vary is the degree to which they are situationally bound versus person bound. An episode of emotion seems more situationally bound than person bound, whereas an emotional disorder would be more person bound. Both emotional traits and emotional disorders show greater signs of embeddedness in the personality than an emotion or a mood. Here I will focus on the ontogeny of emotional traits, or what I call biases, and their role in personality. Elsewhere (Malatesta & Wilson, 1988) I discuss the development of emotional disorders. I regard emotional biases as stable emotional organizations that function flexibly in personality, whereas emotional disorders involve stable emotional organizations that function more rigidly and less adaptively.

Before proceeding to explore the issue of ontogeny, let us exam-

ine more closely what I mean by emotional biases and how they
might be manifest in behavior.

## The Concept of Emotional Biases

In general, personality traits are said to consist of broad dispositional tendencies that show stability over time and consistency
across domains (Levy, 1983; McCrae & Costa, 1984; Pervin, 1975). Although not all traits that have been nominated by psychologists
show all these features in as robust a fashion as their sponsors
would like, current consensus seems to be that the trait concept is
still viable, as mentioned earlier. A few traits such as extroversion
and neuroticism (Eysenck & Eysenck, 1985) seem fairly well established. More recently, in reviewing the literature of several large-
scale studies, McCrae and Costa (1986) have adduced evidence of
five central traits, the usual two of extroversion and neuroticism and
an additional three: openness, agreeableness, and conscientious-
ness. Although various emotions theorists have alluded to the likelihood that something like *emotional* traits also exist, this idea has typically not been elaborated or applied to the range of primary
emotions. Trait inventories exist for the individual emotions of anxiety (e.g., the Taylor Manifest Anxiety Scale) and hostility (e.g., the
Cook Medley Hostility Scale from the MMPI), but only Izard (1972)
has generated an emotional trait measure that covers the range of
primary affects. Nor have the necessary supporting data on interindividual difference and intraindividual stability in emotional traits
(biases) been assembled. I do so now, on the basis of the existing literature. I begin by identifying the domains in which emotional biases can be found; next I present data on the continuity of individual
differences with respect to emotional dispositions.

## Emotional Biases in Behavior

If, as I have proposed, emotional biases are organizational in nature,
they should be evident across wide domains of behavior. We would
expect them to be discernible in the areas of perception, behavior,

and information processing. In the following sections I present what data I have been able to adduce in support of the thesis in each of three areas. I summarize the data on adults and then on children; the data on adults are almost always more extensive.

## PERCEPTUAL BIASES

Early on, the German structuralists recognized that an individuals' personal characteristics influenced perception and that in fact they were indissociable from it. In William Stern's terms, *"Keine Gestalt, ohne Gestalter."* Now if, as I contend, people are organized around a particular emotion or emotions, it would be reasonable to expect that this emotional bias might also affect the accuracy with which they interpret the emotions of other people. We might expect that the bias would generally take the form of overattributing one's own emotional state to others. In fact, we find that there are two kinds of perceptual bias, corresponding to a perceptual readiness effect and a perceptual blindness effect. Tomkins and McCarter (1964) were the first to identify the two phenomena with respect to emotion. In a test of subjects' ability to judge the affective quality of a set of facial expressions of emotion, they found that most of the time the subjects were accurate in recognizing the emotional expression of the poser. But a good number of mistakes were also made, and an analysis of the patterns revealed that some subjects tended to wrongly ascribe a particular affect to photographs expressing some other type of affect; others failed to recognize a particular type of facial expression. More important, the subjects were intraindividually consistent.

A recent study by Toner and Gates (1985) not only has substantiated the perceptual biases of subjects in emotion-decoding tasks but, more critically, has been successful in linking subjects' judgment errors to personality. Scores on four specific "emotional traits" (fear, sadness, anger, and surprise) correlated positively with subjects' preference for the use of the corresponding labels when decoding a set of facial expressions. A similar phenomenon was found in a study of facial-emotion recognition among aggressive and undersocialized delinquents (McCown, Johnson, & Austin, 1985). Delinquents made more errors in affect recognition than nondelinquents, especially in the case of two emotions that are considered part of the hostile triad (Izard, 1972)—anger and disgust.

Evidence for the existence of these two perceptual phenomena in younger children has not yet appeared in the literature, although there have been any number of studies of children's ability to recognize facial expressions of emotion. Such studies have been more preoccupied with comparing children's accuracy rates with those of adults or in demonstrating that children get better at the task as they mature than in looking at the errors children make. I have hypothesized that under the right conditions idiosyncratic error patterns can be identified in children. As such, I am at present looking at children's attributions of emotion to Emde's (1984) I-FEEL pictures. These pictures consist of infants' unposed emotional expressions; they have been selected and validated for their signal ambiguity. For my purposes, the ambiguity is a crucial virtue of the stimuli. I am more interested in what is typically regarded as "error variance" in emotion-recognition studies than in the main effect of emotion category with respect to accuracy scores. Although my study is not yet complete, it is clear that children have perceptual biases just as adults do. The interindividual differences in this study are striking, even more so than in studies with adults. I do not know yet whether this is because background emotion exerts a stronger influence on children or whether it is owing to the *signal ambiguity* (and projective affordances) of the test stimuli.

## BEHAVIORAL BIASES IN EMOTION PRODUCTION (EXPRESSION)

In addition to perceptual biases, there are striking interindividual differences in expressive capacities. People vary in their ability to encode emotion-specific facial expressions. Although production biases have been noted in the literature for some time (Malatesta & Izard, 1984), systematic research documenting such biases and their relation to personality has only recently begun to emerge. Friedman, DiMatteo, and Taranta (1980) examined physicians' ability to express happiness, sadness, anger, and surprise to an imaginary patient while saying each of three affectively neutral sentences; they also administered personality tests. Other subjects also judged the physicians' accuracy of emotional communication. The investigators found that the physicians' ability to express sadness was linked with the personality trait of sadness, and the ability to express anger was linked to the trait of dominance. Another study, this time looking at error scores rather than rates of accuracy, uncovered a similar pattern of productive biases. Malatesta, Fiore, and Messina (1987) had a group of older adults take personality tests and produce five different emotional expressions that were then judged by naive raters. Examination of the pattern of errors raters made when judging the encoders' poses showed that each encoder subject tended to elicit a preponderance of errors in one or two particular affect categories; more important, the pattern of errors was linked, on an affect-specific basis, to emotional bias scores as rated by the personality tests. There was significant correspondence between raters' errors of emotion attribution and subjects' emotional bias for anger, sadness, guilt, and contempt, and marginally significant correspondence for joy and disgust. One other study also provides evidence of productive biases linked to personality. Jonas (1986) studied productive biases of Type A individuals, attempting to determine whether the impression of greater "hostility" in Type A's results from suppressed anger or from a surfeit of anger expression. Using an emotion-induction procedure as well as paper-and-pencil tests of hostility, she was able to determine that although Type A individuals were no different from Type B's on the hostility trait test and reported equal degrees of anger arousal following anger induction, analysis of their facial behavior revealed significantly less hostile emotional expression than Type B's, which she interpreted as suppression; ancillary data supported the interpretation that the production bias was specific to hostility.

Productive biases in children have been reported anecdotally for some time (Malatesta & Izard, 1984), but there has been virtually no systematic work in this area. Our own laboratory is currently engaged in using affect-laden wordless picture books to isolate verbal and nonverbal (expressive) biases in 4–5-year-olds. Although only 15 subjects have been run so far, we see clear preferences for types of emotional terms and expressions in individual children.

BIASES IN COGNITIVE PROCESSING

There are few studies that examine how emotional organizations might bias performance on cognitive tasks, although an analogue of the phenomenon exists in the literature on experimentally manipulated mood. Assumedly, an induced mood state would have approximately the same qualitative effect on information processing as an "endogenous" mood or an enduring background emotion.

What the literature shows is that induction of *happy* moods enhances creative problem solving and increases friendliness and optimism (Isen, 1984). Induction of *sadness* tends both to impair general performance and to promote a more yielding and conventional attitude and introspective stance, as assessed by personality tests (Isen, 1984; Messick, 1965). Thus far readers may not be very impressed. Isn't it possible that these effects simply reflect the difference between a positive hedonic tone and a negative one, rather than the effect of a differential emotion? In a set of studies reported by Bower (1981) concerning the *quality* of the cognitive production, there is evidence of a more emotion-specific effect. For example, mood manipulations of happy versus angry differentially affected verbal productions in tests of free association and in response to TAT cards. The biases were more than merely a bias toward "positive" versus "negative" productions; they appeared related to type of positive and negative mood—that is, joyous, ebullient associations and stories under the happy mood condition versus angry associations and violent stories under the angry condition. An even better test of the discrete emotions hypothesis would require studying the differential performance of subjects under *several* negative or positive mood inductions. This kind of study has rarely been performed. In our own laboratory we are at present examining how three experimentally induced negative moods (anger, fear, and sadness) affect the interpretation of vignettes depicting ambiguous events and interpersonal situations.

There is little in the literature on how mood affects cognitive performance or influences behavior in children that is germane to my thesis, mainly because the children's studies typically have contrasted only "positive" versus "negative" or "happy" versus control conditions. In the one study that did employ differential negative moods, the results are in accord with a differential emotions thesis. Nasby and Yando (1982) compared the learning performance of fifth-grade children following *sad* and *angry* mood inductions. They found that the sad mood induction condition impaired recall of positive information and did not improve recall of negative material. However, there was a *facilitative* encoding effect with anger; anger at the time of learning improved the later recall of negative information. This study illustrates that the effects of a sad mood are not simply those of "negative mood" and that different negative moods produce different effects.

This review should make it obvious that moods or emotional dispositions alter the nature of the phenomenological world in important and distinctive ways, in accord with a differential emotions prediction, although clearly much more confirmatory work needs to be done. The next question to raise is whether one can find evidence of enduring emotional dispositions in individuals. This addresses the issue of stability or continuity of behavior that is assumed by dispositional models of personality. Let us turn now to a survey of studies in which continuities in emotional variables have been investigated.

## Stability and Continuity in Emotions

Stability of behavior in particular emotional patterns has been found for adults as well as for children. In adults, individual differences in positive and negative affect have been found to be highly stable over several weeks (Epstein, 1980). There is also evidence of good intraindividual stability in terms of particular emotions. Epstein and colleagues (Epstein, 1980) have demonstrated highly stable patterns of *anxiety* as measured under authentic arousal conditions. Berry and Webb (1985) found stability coefficients ranging from .20 to .87 (with a median of .66) in a range of mood-related measures, including *cheerful, angry, anxious,* and *depressed* as measured over several nights before going to sleep. Longer-term stability coefficients have also been reported. The four-year test-retest correlation coefficient for *trait hostility* was found to be .84 (Williams, 1984).

Evidence of behavioral stability in measures related to emotionality is also found in children. First, it is important to point out that although "personality coefficients" from one developmental stage to another, especially from infancy to childhood, are generally low (Moss & Susman, 1980; Porter & Collins, 1982), when the measurements are centered on emotion-based behaviors the stability coefficients become more robust. Bronson (1970) found that *fearful* 1-year-old boys remained fearful when assessed at from 6 to 8 years of age. Lafreniere and Sroufe (1985) found that indexes of *affiliation, aggression, positive affect,* and *negative affect* in 4–5-year-olds showed significant stability measured across contexts and over time. Kagan and colleagues (Coll, Kagan, & Reznick, 1984; Kagan, Reznick, Clarke, Snidman, & Coll, 1984) have found that a measure of "behavioral inhibition," which appears to index *shyness* or *anxiety,* correlated .66 from the second to the third year and .50 from the second to the fourth year.

Children begin to show preferences for certain emotional expressive styles during infancy. A number of studies have shown stable individual differences in fear or wariness in infants. For example, Scarr and Salapatek (1970) found cross-situational and cross-temporal stability (at two-month intervals) in 6–18-month-olds in response to a variety of *fear* stimuli such as masks and placement on the visual cliff. Birns, Barten, and Bridger (1969) found that infants' *irritability* and *tension* were stable over four months. Rothbart and colleagues (Rothbard & Derryberry, 1981) have found significant stability for a dimension of positivity from 3 to 12 months by caregiver report and from 3 to 6 and 6 to 9 months in home observations.

In terms of discrete facial expressions of emotion, three studies involving the coding of various discrete emotions during infancy have found significant stability of individual differences for a range of emotions. Izard and colleagues (Izard, Hembree, Dougherty, & Spizzirri, 1983) obtained evidence of stability of sadness and anger expressions from 2 to 19 months, as measured during DPT inoculations. Hyson and Izard (1985) coded emotional responses during brief mother-infant separation at 13 and 18 months and found stability coefficients of .61, .90, .53, and .90 for interest, anger, blends (expressions with more than one emotional component), and total negative emotion. Malatesta, Culver, Tesman, and Shepard (1989) coded emotional expressions over a play and reunion episode at 2 ½, 5, 7½, and 22 months, and found significant correlations for surprise, sadness, anger, and total negative emotions from 2½ to 5 months, significant correlations for interest, joy, surprise, sadness, anger, knit brow, and total positive emotion from 5 to 7½ months, and significant correlations for anger, sadness, and total negative emotion from 7½ to 22 months.

In summary, there is a considerable amount of data on the stability of behaviors related to emotion in both adults and children. However, as Lewis and Michalson (1983) point out, the critical question for personality theory is not so much *whether* emotional dispositions are part of personality, since so much evidence to that effect already exists, as *how* the personality structures themselves come into being and what they consist of. In the next section I consider the processes and mechanisms that underlie such behavioral continuity.

## Mechanisms Contributing to Continuity

The obvious candidates to consider when examining the origins and mechanisms involved in behavioral continuity in emotional dispositions are (1) biologically based influences such as genetic and constitutional differences, and (2) socialization influences.

### BIOLOGICAL INFLUENCES

There is a fair amount of evidence that there are early, built-in, constitutionally rooted behavioral biases in emotional organization. The very existence of continuities in emotional dispositions during *infancy* (as noted in the review above) strongly suggests that emotional dispositions are not forged exclusively out of the material of social interaction and cognitive development. However, we do not know how strong the biological influences might be, since most of the studies cited above began assessments well beyond the neonatal period, increasing the likelihood that social influences could be contributing to the effects. Nevertheless, I regard it as quite likely that genetic and constitutional influences are part of the equation with respect to the origins of emotional dispositions. These early biases are sometimes referred to as temperament traits (Goldsmith & Campos, 1982; Rothbart & Derryberry, 1981), and it is assumed that they have an enduring impact on subsequent personality develop-ment. However, there is a fair degree of consensus that tempera-mental biases are not immutable (Buss & Plomin, 1984; Goldsmith & Campos, 1982; Thomas & Chess, 1977). More important, tempera-ment is seen as interacting with environmental forces rather than ruling them imperiously. I do not intend to review the extensive lit-erature on temperament and its contributions to development in this chapter but will concern myself mainly with social influences.

ENVIRONMENTAL INFLUENCES

In this section I focus on aspects of the child's social environment and the ways they contribute to personality formation. A good deal of contemporary research has convincingly demonstrated that in-fants are exquisitely sensitive to the emotional signals of others. The work on social referencing described by Campos during the present symposium is a case in point. The work of Cohn and Tronick (1983) and Haviland and Lelwica (1987) on infants' emotional responses to simulated states of maternal depression, anger, and joy is also ger-mane. This same body of work indicates that infants have an active response to the emotional behaviors of others. I believe it is helpful to view children's emotional responses to these kinds of social input as forms of environmental adaptations or coping strategies (see also the chapters in this volume by Cicchetti, Thompson, and Saarni). Table 1, presented earlier, indicates the adaptive function of each emotion with respect to *self*-evaluation and regulation as well as re-latedness with *others*. Let us consider one of these emotions. Sup-pose an older sibling, uneasy about her own status in the family since the birth of her younger brother, repeatedly approaches the unwanted baby with threatening face and gestures. The infant's sense of himself as *endangered* causes him to avert his gaze and with-draw into his blanket to escape further visual exposure to the fright-ening stimuli. If the sibling persists he may emit a frightened cry, which will likely elicit the rescuing intervention of the caregiver. Thus the fear response brings about subsequent behavioral change in self and other that ultimately proves adaptive in ameliorating the situation. From a functionalist perspective, all emotional responses are ordinarily adaptive in that they help individuals organize their experience and behavior in a coherent way to deal with a variety of motivational goals; moreover, they provide information about the individuals' needs to others who might intervene in their behalf. However, even though each affect has a fundamentally adaptive purpose, in the course of development some affects can come to dominate the personality. These response predispositions become part of what makes each personality unique (a sanguine, sociable person versus a haughty person, for example). And because we are talking about *emotional* dispositions or biases, which are organizational in nature, they will have a rather pervasive influence on consciousness and behavior; they will be domain-*pervasive* rather than domain-*specific*.

The next question to address is, How do certain emotions come to dominate in a person's response repertoire? In the following section I consider this question at length, focusing extensively and fairly exclusively on socialization variables. Furthermore, I continue to emphasize a functionalist perspective. I propose that a functional analysis of expressive behavior is critical to understanding how individuals become organized around certain affects and why these affective structures are maintained. I will pursue the task developmentally, beginning with the period of infancy.

## The Ontogeny of Emotional Biases in Infancy

In thinking about the forces involved in the development of early emotional dispositions in infants, I find it helpful to draw upon concepts that were originally elaborated by two of our field's earliest systematic infant observers—John Watson and Rene Spitz.

In his important and somewhat neglected work *The First Year of Life*, Spitz (1965) articulated a genetic field theory, in which he stressed the importance of recognizing that early emotional development is forged in a *relational* context. Healthy emotional development depends on subtly tuned, reciprocal, affective communication between caregiver and infant. The emphasis on relational aspects of emotional development appears as well in Karl Buhler's (1929) notion of "gegenseitige Steurung" or mutual accommodation and in

John Bowlby's original work on attachment. The relationship emphasis today is embodied in, and most closely associated with, contemporary attachment theory and research. However, as I indicated in the introduction to this chapter, attachment theory says little, at least directly, about the nature of particular, that is, discrete emotion, affective organizations. Here is where a concept from Watson becomes useful.

It was in a paper entitled "Emotional Reactions and Psychological Experimentation" (Watson & Morgan, 1917) that Watson first staked his claim to three innate emotional reactions in infants—fear, rage, and love. All other emotions and emotional patterns were said to be acquired through learning. Within the same paper, in a set of early formulations that eventually led to his experiments involving the conditioning of fear, he also mused about how certain emotions could come to monopolize a subject's response repertoire. He noted that "so far no one has tried explicitly to introduce the illuminating concept of habit formation into the realm of emotions" (p. 168). He did admit, however, that the psychoanalytic idea of *Uebertragung* (transference) came close to the concept, although it had been applied to only one emotion, that of affection. That is, the transference phenomenon described the condition wherein the affection a patient felt for a parent spread, or was generalized, to another unrelated person, the psychoanalyst. Watson proposed that the same thing could occur for other emotions and thus established the theoretical groundwork for his experiments on the conditioning and transference (generalization) of fears. Although Watson's work emphasized the learning of an emotional habit in a nonsocial context (assisted by laboratory manipulanda), it is probably safe to assume that the more ordinary context for learning emotional patterns is a social one. But it is the notion of "habit formation in the realm of emotions," or what we might term emotional habit strengths, that is germane to our discussion of emotion traits.

With the foregoing concepts in mind, I wish to show how particular emotional patterns or habit strengths can develop and become consolidated within relational contexts, as part of an adaptive accommodation, and can occur as a function of a variety of learning situations besides classical conditioning.

I begin by examining the case for the existence of emerging emotional biases in infancy. But first a note on the appropriate test conditions for their detection. Elsewhere (Malatesta & Wilson, 1988) I have reviewed studies indicating that emotional organizations are more likely to be evident under conditions that tax the individual's adaptive capacities. As such, they are most salient when the child is experiencing some degree of stress. One of the most commonly used paradigms in contemporary research on socioemotional development is that of the "strange situation"; recall that this entails exposing the child to series of graded stressors, including an unfamiliar environment, approach of a stranger, and the leavetaking of the caregiver. Although the strange situation procedure is engineered to disclose the quality of attachment between infant and parent, a molecular analysis of particular behaviors occurring within the separation and reunion episodes of the strange situation reveals that certain classification subtypes may overlap somewhat with particular discrete emotional organizations. In the following treatment I explore the existence of these organizations as disclosed during assessment of attachment. I also go beyond the specification of personality *types* to identify *antecedent conditions* from which differential emotional biases, as environmental adaptations, may accrue.

I begin with three negative emotional organizations that can be observed in the context of stressful encounters, in this case during the separation and reunion episodes of the strange situation. Although we will draw upon patterns revealed in the strange situation, the use of these data for exposing emotional organizations is merely opportunistic. Intrinsic to the strange situation paradigm is the very test condition (stress) that facilitates disclosure of emotional organizations. In the ensuing analysis, I am less concerned with the ABC typologies of attachment quality that can be identified through this procedure than with what is revealed about emotional organizations. As we shall see, children differ in how readily they react with anger, sadness, or fear when they experience distress. I hasten to add that I do not intend the following analysis to *replace* the relational one described within attachment theory but rather mean to *supplement* it with a finer-grained description of individual difference with respect to emotional organizations.

## THE FEAR ORGANIZATION

Although Ainsworth's classification system originally referred to both A and C categories as reflecting "anxious" attachments, the pattern of emotions displayed by these groups of children, especially during reunion, is quite differentiated. In fact, it is the differential response of *anger* versus *avoidance* that permits the determination of differential attachment classification. A children do not show the angry, resistant behavior shown by children in the C group, especially those in the C1 subgroup. Instead, A children show avoidant behavior, and some, predominantly A2's, show approach-avoidance conflict when the mother returns after separation, often approaching her only to veer away at the last moment. This behavior pattern seems to conform to a fear-dominant behavioral orientation, at least as assayed under stress conditions. The behavior pattern is reproducible both within and across Ainsworth sessions (Bretherton, 1985) and appears to be a stable part of the child's emotional organization.

Now, based on what we know about the provocations to fear and the ensuing responses, we can begin to speculate about the origins of the fear organization in infancy. According to Table 1, fear is typically elicited when the self is experienced as endangered. The fear then activates flight or attack. What kinds of stimuli might young infants experience that would engender a sense of the self as endangered, and what might their flight or attack patterns look like? On the basis of accumulated literature, it appears that the primary provocations for fear in young infants reside in strange, abrupt, or unusual events and intense, uncontrollable stimulation (see Malatesta, 1985, for a review). The question for my analysis is whether insecurely attached A-type children (or some subset of them) show evidence of a history of exposure to such experiences. I also ask whether it is likely they have experienced these kinds of conditions chronically enough to have affected their personality organization. Several studies seem to indicate that this may in fact be the case. Belsky, Rovine, and Taylor (1984) observed mothers and infants at home when the infants were 1, 3, and 9 months old and assessed attachment at 12 months. A composite measure of maternal interactive behavior (including level of stimulation/arousal, vocalization, attention and three-step contingent exchange) during the early months was found to predict attachment classification, with A-type children having received the highest levels of stimulation and arousal. In a similar vein, Langhorst and Fogel (1982) found that the frequency and intensity of avoidance in the strange situation was inversely correlated with maternal tendency to decrease activity when their 3-month-olds averted their gaze in face-to-face interaction. Isabella (1987) also found that avoidant A children had experienced high levels of intrusive stimulation earlier in infancy, as measured by patterns and rates of maternal vocalizations to their infants.

Data from my own laboratory tend to confirm the picture above (Malatesta, Grigoryev, Lamb, Albin, & Culver, 1986; Malatesta et al., 1989). We found that extremely high rates of maternal facial contingency (immediate facial expression changes in response to infant changes) during face-to-face play in early infancy, a pattern that seems to index an overstimulating style, predicted avoidance and A classification a year later, although not all A children had high-contingency mothers. What kinds of emotional responses do such children display in the context of such aversive encounters, in the short run as well as in the long run? In our study we found that high contingent responding on the part of the mother was an intraindividually stable aspect of behavior as assessed during three face-to-face interaction sessions taped when the infant was 2½, 5, and 7½ months old; not so surprisingly, we found that the infants of these mothers showed a decline in smiling over the course of the three sessions. We hypothesize that this response may be part of an early escape mechanism; infants who fail to smile are presumably not very rewarding to mothers, so that in time there may be a mutual turning away. Interestingly, a more active behavioral avoidance of the mother is a key feature of A children during a later stage of development (as measured during the reunion episodes of the strange situation). It is also interesting that although avoidance of the caregiver is the striking feature during the laboratory session and presumably indexes "anxious" attachment (or what we might also construe as a conditioned fear of the caregiver), the emotional profile when observed in the home is also mixed with aggression (Cassidy & Kobak, in press). This mixed pattern is entirely consistent with theoretical predictions derived from our functionalist analysis; both *flight* (avoidance) and *aggression* are the predicted responses to fear arousal. In terms of long-term sequelae, Bates, Maslin, and Frankel (1985) found that the more children avoided proximity to mothers at reunion at 13 months, the more they were seen by observers as having anxiety problems two years later.

## THE ANGER ORGANIZATION

Certain infants display a proneness to anger in their day-to-day interactions with others, especially under stress. The Ainsworth system tends to classify children who display substantial anger during the reunion episodes of the strange situation into the C1 subtype. These infants are said to show an *anxious-resistant* pattern of attachment, as originally described. However, a key aspect of the behavior that results in C1 classification is strong proximity/contact seeking mixed with conspicuous *anger* and rejection. This behavior is reproducible both within and across Ainsworth sessions; I assume this represents a primary anger organization, although the necessary cross-situational validation, involving testing in other contexts, remains to be done. Because of what a functional analysis reveals about the eliciting conditions for anger and the adaptive function of the response (see Table 1), we can hypothesize that the anger behavior of the C1 child results from chronic (repetitive) frustration of goals early in life, with the angry behavior directed at the frustrating agent. According to experimental work by Stenberg and colleagues (Stenberg, 1982; Stenberg, Campos, & Emde, 1983), infants as young as 7 months, and possibly younger, are able to discriminate and identify persons who act as frustrating agents.

## THE SADNESS ORGANIZATION

Another pattern of emotional organization is seen in the passive C2 subtype of the C classification. During *reunion*, these infants show a tendency to cry rather than approach and to cry passively when put down. A study of the emotional responses of children to the *separation* episodes of the strange situation conducted by Shiller, Izard, and Hembree (1986), consisting of microanalytic coding of facial expressive behavior, revealed that A, B, and C children did not differ in the amount of anger they displayed during this portion of the procedure; however, C children, who were primarily C2 types in this study, showed more sadness than the other groups, suggesting that a sadness-prone pattern was more diagnostic of this particular group. In terms of possible antecedents, the work of Howes, Hokanson, and Loewenstein (1985) with adults and of Cohn and Tronick (1983) with infants, documenting the ready contagion of depressed affect between interactants, suggests that the sadness-prone children identified by Shiller et al. (1986) may have been exposed to a natural history of depressed maternal affect. Alternatively, they may have experienced other kinds of unresponsiveness, as work on failure-to-thrive syndrome infants indicates (Bradley, Casey, & Wortham, 1984) and from what we know about the antecedents of learned helplessness (Seligman, 1975). Interestingly, mothers of C children have been described as being less involved with their infants and less responsive than other groups of mothers and somewhat flat in affect (Ainsworth, Blehar, Waters, & Wall, 1978; Lyons-Ruth, Connell, Zoll, & Stahl, 1987).

In the foregoing analysis I have concentrated on the ontogenesis of fear, anger, and sadness organizations. To break the monotony of negative emotional organizations, let us pause to consider a more positive organization. Securely attached B children are said to show more *positive affect* than insecurely attached A or C children, as noted earlier. They are well adapted to their environment in that interactions with caregivers and others are typically cooperative and harmonious.

From a functionalist point of view, A and C children may be well adapted to their particular niches as well, in terms of dealing with their caregivers, although they may appear maladapted in other contexts. For example, as Schneider-Rosen and colleagues (Schneider-Rosen, Braunwald, Carlson, & Cicchetti, 1985) point out, children of abusing parents who show A attachment and an avoidant pattern of behavior may be behaving quite adaptively. The fear organization and avoidance behavior serve to keep the child out of reach of the abusing parent.

The notion of "functional adaptation" is a key aspect of my

analysis of emotional organizations. It also explains why seemingly maladaptive behavior patterns develop in children and why they may be maintained over time. Above, I considered four emotional organizations in infants. A functionalist analysis would summarize the patterns in the following way: *Fear* motivates escape and avoidance behaviors and thus reduces the chances for harm. In young infants, avoiding the mother protects them from overstimulation. It may also protect older children from actual physical abuse. Mothers of A children have been described as demonstrating covert hostility (Cassidy & Kobak, in press; Lyons-Ruth et al., 1987). The fear reactions of children, with the submissive content that fear postures convey, may help such mothers keep hostile impulses in check. Because the fear response in this context is adaptive for both mother and child, we can presume that these kinds of behavioral responses to one another will continue to be enacted and that the fear organization in the child will undergo consolidation over time. *Anger* reactions organize behavior directed at overcoming obstructions to goals; they also notify social agents that frustration is experienced. Angry crying in infants can and often does enlist caregiver attention and behavioral interventions (Wiesenfeld & Malatesta, 1982); with this kind of reinforcement, angry responses are likely to persist over time. *Sadness*, according to our functionalist analysis, elicits nurture, empathy, and succor. In fact, in a study of young adults' reactions to different photographs of infant affective expressions, Stettner and Loigman (1983) found that the modal response to sadness expressions was the desire to "cuddle and hug." *Positive affect* (as in the joy expression) is said to promote social bonding; we have already seen that children whose behavioral pattern is typified by positive affect (B children) tend to have harmonious social relationships.

The patterns of emotional organizations highlighted above can be discerned as early as the first year of life. These patterns in some sense typify individual children and distinguish one child from another. To simplify matters at the service of exposition, I focused earlier on emotional organizations that were typified by the prominence of one or another particular discrete emotion. In fact it is likely that the situation is far more complex, and it may be helpful to think of emotional organizations as comprising response *hierarchies* (Malatesta et al., 1987), with certain emotions higher on the response hi-

erarchy than others. Thus one way of viewing emotional organizations is from the perspective of "ipsative stability" (cf. Emmerich,
1968), in which it is the *pattern* of relationships among different personality features within the individual, or in this case among different emotional predispositions, that tends to be preserved over occasions. One particular emotion may tend to dominate, although
other emotions that are relatively high in the response hierarchy
may be activated as well, in interaction with certain situational demands or provocations.

The concept of emotional dispositions, whether rendered in the
form of a particular dominating emotion or in terms of a pattern of
several emotions, captures the idea of emotional biases as described
earlier. We find that such biases are evident in young infants, as detected within studies of children's reactions to strange environments and separation from caregivers. It is assumed that emotional
organizations will also be readily detected in other stressful or challenging situations, although this remains to be verified by future research.

A note on the relationship between attachment classification
and emotions typologies is warranted at this juncture. Although in
this section as well as earlier I have drawn from the literature on attachment to cull emotional organizations, I do not regard emotional
organizations as synonymous with attachment constructs. Still,
there is obviously some overlap in that the classification typology
uses affective signals, among other data, to distinguish the different
classes of attachment. Classification criteria that distinguish A
babies from B and C babies include a general absence of emotional
distress during separations, a lack of greeting and overt positive affect when the mother returns, and in many cases active avoidance;
C1 babies are distinguished by angry and emotionally ambivalent
behavior. Some researchers (e.g., Belsky & Rovine, 1987; Connell &
Thompson, 1986; Frodi & Thompson, 1985; Thompson & Lamb,
1984), in addition, have shown that children's responses to separations and reunions can be reliably characterized along other emotional dimensions, such as latency to become distressed and the
general intensity of emotional response. Another point of similarity
between contemporary attachment theory and the present analysis
of the ontogenesis of emotional biases involves the concept of mu-

tual accommodation within relationship contexts. What is particularly interesting is that emotion typologies seem to be more discriminating predictors of behavioral problems or emotional organizations later on than are attachment classifications. For example, Bates et al. (1985) have found that attachment classification at 1 year did not predict behavior problems of anxiety and hostility at 3 years very well, but a behavioral measure of *avoidance* as coded by an independent observer and maternal reports of *unsociability* (consisting of negative reaction to new people and likely indexing social *anxiety*) did predict subsequent anxiety problems.

Let us return to the notion that emotional organizations observed in infancy are forged within the context of relationships. It is probably not accidental that some of the best data supporting the notion of emotional biases were first detected within the context of attachment assessment. A key feature of the assessment procedure involves challenging the child's felt security by temporary separation from the primary caregiver (in the strange situation procedure). As the child's experiential horizon expands with further development, other important relationships will also be established, thereby allowing for further consolidation of emerging emotional organizations, given that basic relational elements are repeated within the new relationship, *or* for divergence from the earlier pattern if the experiences are quite different. This notion allows us to resolve what appears to be a problem for the emotional disposition position: namely, the observation that a child's attachment classification status may be altered as a function of the particular caregiver (mother, father, alternative caregiver) with whom the child is tested (Grossmann & Grossmann, 1981; Main & Weston, 1981; Sagi, Lamb, Lewkowicz, Shoham, Dvir, & Estes, 1985). If emotional dispositions and attachment classification are somewhat overlapping, as it appears from the foregoing analysis, and if, as I assert, emotional organizations represent somewhat stable aspects of individual difference even during infancy, different classifications (and hence different emotional profiles) under the differing test conditions seem to engender a paradox.

However, once again the notion of emotional dispositions as embedded within response *hierarchies*, and the importance of relational elements, seems to come to our rescue. A child's attachment classification status, as well as emotion profile as assessed with the mother, may be divergent from that assessed with the father owing to the strength of patterns of mutual accommodation with each parent, which may vary with the prominence of certain relationship histories; differential amount of stress engendered by separation from the two attachment figures, requiring differential amounts of adaptive (emotional) response; and differential cognitions (appraisals, expectations) about the person available for support. Although Shiller et al. (1986) found that anger is the prototypical response of infants when they are separated from their mothers, patterns of anger expression vary from child to child (Cassidy & Kobak, in press). Avoidant children are said to "mask" their anger, assumedly because they have been punished for its expression earlier in life, with anxiety eventually superseding and replacing the original experience of anger. However, if the discriminative stimuli that elicit anxiety and suppression of anger are absent (as in the absence of one caregiver and presence of another) anger may break through and temporarily overtake the anxious organization. Thus a discrete-emotions analysis combined with a relationship analysis serves to resolve an apparent paradox and highlights the likely complexity of emotional organizations.

Let us turn now to a discussion of the ontogeny of emotional biases beyond infancy. Because of the relative dearth of literature on aspects of socioemotional development beyond the first few years of life, my treatment of the ontogeny of emotional biases will be more limited.

## Ontogeny of Emotional Biases Beyond Infancy

There is some evidence that emotional organizations developed in infancy are carried forward in time. I have already summarized some of the data on stability of individual differences in various emotional expression patterns. Here I include sources not previously mentioned. The evidence is drawn mainly from follow-up studies of children whose attachment status was assessed at least once during early infancy. In general, there is significant stability of attachment classification over time, even into the sixth year of life (Main et al., 1985). Because of the somewhat overlapping nature of attachment classification subtypes and certain emotional patterns, we might expect to find evidence within this literature concerning the preservation of early emotional dispositions. Indeed, some such evidence does exist. Cassidy and Kobak (in press) view the avoidant behavior of A infants as "masking" an underlying anger. On the basis of several studies they review, they contend that masked anger exhibited in the presence of caregivers continues to typify these children at later developmental periods. In contrast, as discussed previously, I hypothesize that anxiety is the prevailing emotional state of these children, with anger as a secondary feature. As Bates et al. (1985) have shown, avoidant behavior in infancy predicts anxiety problems in preschool. Moreover, the very existence of suppressed affect suggests an underlying anxiety. In any event, it appears that this aspect of emotional behavior—that is, a neutralization of affect—is carried forward in time. Thus the pattern of behavior (avoidance, neutralization) seen earlier in infancy continues to be a feature of the emotional organization of at least some A children. The *aggressive response* displayed by A infants in the home *also* has an analogue during the preschool years. Sroufe (1983) reports that these children show both distance from and aggression toward their caregivers in preschool. In addition, insecure boys, especially A children, exhibit more hostile and antisocial behavior toward their peers (Erickson, Sroufe, & Egeland, 1985).

Children who are classified as showing the C attachment pattern during infancy in the strange situation procedure have also been shown to display behavioral continuity beyond early infancy. In preschool, C children tend to show either an easily upset, angry profile *or* extreme passivity, submissiveness, and withdrawal (LaFrenier & Sroufe, 1985). Although such observations are based on global ratings rather than detailed, discrete emotion coding, it appears that these two groups of children are showing patterns that are continuous with the anger-dominant and sadness-prone emotional patterns discerned in C subgroups during infancy. Obviously much more confirmatory work remains to be done in this area, but these initial findings appear to support the emotional organization thesis.

Of course not all children show such cross-temporal stability, either in their attachment classification or in their pattern of emotional expression. In the following section I consider the mechanisms through which emotional organizations that are established during infancy undergo either further consolidation or modification and alteration developmentally.

## Mechanisms Involved in the Development of Emotional Biases

Let us first consider the mechanisms that are likely to prevail in early infancy, some of which will continue to operate in later developmental periods.

### LEARNING PRINCIPLES: GENERAL MECHANISMS

Among the hypothesized processes presumed to mediate the socialization of emotion, classical conditioning, operant conditioning, and observational learning appear to be the most likely candidates in cognitively immature, preverbal infants (Lewis & Michalson, 1983; Malatesta & Izard, 1984).

**Classical conditioning.** The conditioning of fear in "little Albert" by J. B. Watson was the first laboratory demonstration that emotional reactions could be classically conditioned. This experiment also demonstrated that emotional reactions could undergo spontaneous generalization; over time, Albert's fear reactions were elicited by a broader range of stimulus events.

**Operant conditioning.** In more recent times, a series of experimental studies of the reinforcement and extinction of infant expressive behaviors (reviewed by Campos et al., 1983) have demonstrated that the emotional behaviors of young infants are responsive to environmental contingencies and can be altered on a short-term basis. Seminaturalistic observational studies have indicated that mothers behave in ways that can modify children's expressive behavior more permanently. Analysis of data derived from video-recorded mother/child interactions has demonstrated that maternal behavior in response to infants' and children's emotional behaviors is nonrandom, contingent, and repetitive (Denham, 1985; Malatesta & Haviland, 1982; Malatesta et al., 1986). There are apparently long-term sequelae of certain patterns. In one study of the relation between early maternal facial contingency patterns and subsequent infant development (Malatesta et al., 1986), we found that the contingency of maternal facial responses to infant emotional expressions predicted increases in infant positivity and expressiveness from 2½ to 7½ months.

**Observational learning and imitation.** In the course of face-to-face interaction with their mothers and other individuals, infants are repeatedly exposed to well-articulated expressions of emotion. Thus they have ample opportunity to observe the form and pattern of various emotional expressions and to imitate or match them. A review of the experimental literature of infant imitation (Malatesta & Izard, 1984) indicates that young infants are capable of matching elements or whole facial expressions of models with similar expressions of their own. Long-term exposure to modeled expressions appears to materially affect subsequent expressive development. For example, in a study of the facial behavior of mothers and infants in face-to-face interaction (Malatesta & Haviland, 1982), we found that members of different mother-infant pairs shared commonalties in how they used their facial muscles, both in their discrete facial movements and in their preference for certain categorical expressions; moreover, the strength of the correlations between the mothers and infants for types of facial movement increased from 3 to 6 months. The older the infant, the more similar were its facial expressions to those of its mother. In a more recent study (Malatesta et al., 1986), we found that high rates of maternal modeling of joy and interest to infants at 2 ½ months of age were associated with increases in infant joy and interest at 7 ½ months.

In summary, there is evidence that infants' emotional expressive behaviors are influenced by the basic learning principles of classical conditioning, operant conditioning, and observational learning. Given the repetitive aspect of mothers' emotional expressive displays during face-to-face interaction with their infants, and given the nonrandom nature and contingency of these patterns, it is likely that substantial entrainment of infants' emotional disposition occurs during this time. It is easy to see how emotional patterns in infants could be readily shaped by general learning theory principles alone. However, there is evidence that additional learning principles, perhaps specific to the emotion system, may exert similarly powerful effects—those of contagion and emotion induction (Haviland & Lelwica, 1987).

## LEARNING PRINCIPLES SPECIFIC TO THE AFFECT SYSTEM: CONTAGION AND EMOTION INDUCTION

*Emotion contagion* has been described as taking on the emotional state of a person through exposure to his or her emotional behavior (Izard, 1977). *Emotion induction* refers to an emotional response that may or may not involve taking on the same state experienced by another person; it may consist of a contagious matching response *or* a different emotional response that occurs as a form of self-regulation in the face of emotional stimulation (Haviland & Lelwica, 1987). Infants appear to be highly sensitive to the emotional states of others and to be affected by them in ways that alter their own emotional states. For example, Cohn and Tronick (1983) have shown that 3-month-old infants will show fleeting positive expressions, and then protest, in response to simulated maternal depression; these initial responses may be self-regulatory or directed at altering the response of the other. Subsequently, however, the brief smiles and longer angry/distressed cries give way to what appears to be a contagion of the depressed affect as the infants eventually turn away and withdraw.

In a study of endogenously depressed mothers and their infants during interaction, analysis disclosed that infants had already adapted to the depressed behavior of their mothers and showed signs of having developed their own depressed style of interacting (field, 1984). In an experimental study, Haviland and Lelwica (1987) found differentiated emotional responses in 2½-month-olds to maternal simulation of anger, sadness, and joy. Maternal *sadness* simulations resulted in infants' inhibition of anger expressions and a significant increase in mouthing responses (which are possibly self-soothing attempts), accompanied by downcast eyes. *Anger* simulations resulted in a significant inhibition of interest expressions and an increase in anger expressions, as well as an increase in no-movement responses (possibly a freezing reaction indexing fear), accompanied by sideways gaze aversion. In response to their mothers' *joy* expressions, infants showed a significant increase in their own joy expressions. Haviland and Lelwica emphasize that the infants' responses to their mothers' emotional expressions consisted of more than simple motor mimicry devoid of feeling content. The responses involved both change in expression and change in state (as indexed by the entire pattern of response).

Finally, Cummings, Iannotti, and Zahn-Waxler (1985) showed that 2-year-old children exposed to angry, argumentative behavior of adults displayed more aggression (apparently from the spread of anger) toward a peer following exposure than they did before the exposure. A similar study with 4–5-year-olds (Cummings, 1987) also found a general trend for an increase in verbal aggression following such exposure, and some children admitted to feeling angry after the experimental condition. However, at this older age children showed differentiated responses to the anger displays of others; some attempted to intervene, some withdrew, and others engaged in aggressive behavior with peers. We can regard these stylistic differences as reflecting different modes of self-regulation; they may be related to particular histories of mutual accommodation and differentiated emotional coping strategies.

From the description above we see that the affective expressions of others are potent social inputs for infants. In certain circumstances infants are affected in ways over which they have little voluntary control (as in the case of classical conditioning and contagious responding to pathological states of caregivers). It is also obvious that infants are capable of a fair degree of active incorporation of expressive styles (imitation) and active adaptation or self-regulation in response to affect induction. However, active resistance to negative affect induction seems to break down in the face of prolonged and repeated exposure to strong affective stimuli (see chapters by Cicchetti and by Zahn-Waxler, this volume).

## THE ROLE OF COGNITION AND LANGUAGE

As we move beyond infancy, other mechanisms and processes will reinforce or modify emerging emotional organizations. During the preschool years the increase in linguistic competence and representational/memory capacity expands the area of potential social influences as well as the range of opportunities for self-regulation.

As cognitive processes mature, much of the raw emotional behavior that is seen in infancy takes on greater subtlety and modulation. This capability is promoted through mechanisms of symbolic representation (Izard, 1971) and self-regulation (Fischer, Shaver, & Carnochan, in press).

Fischer et al. (in press) have addressed the cognitive processes that may be involved, using a novel multistage perception/appraisal model. What is unique about this particular model is that it is both developmental in nature and concerned with general processes as well as individual differences. Moreover, unlike other "cognitive" models of emotion, it permits *emotional experiences* to play an important role in the ontogenesis of emotions. According to the model, emotions are processed differentially at each developmental stage as different kinds of appraisal capabilities become available to the child. Emotions are said to begin with the perception of notable change, followed by evaluative appraisal related to "concerns" or implicit goals; if events interfere with goals, they are appraised negatively and negative emotion (negative action or action tendencies) results. With the development of self-monitoring capabilities, emotions are processed through an additional appraisal loop, and children become able to exercise self-control of action tendencies. At this juncture emotional action tendencies become the events to be appraised, "causing an emotion about an emotion" (Fischer et al., in press, p. 11) or an emotion loop. For example, an appraisal of frustrated goals may lead to anger; however, if experience has taught that angry behavior is severely punished, fear may result instead, leading to a suppression of anger. As experiences are repeated and development proceeds, children develop complex emotion loops that may be activated readily and automatically; they also acquire emotion-related concerns, which function at an organizational level and affect the nature of subsequent interactions and appraisals in emotion-specific ways. (See Fischer et al., in press, for a further elaboration of the theory.)

How do such "emotion loops" evolve over time? Social experiences, of course, are of prime importance, especially if they occur repetitively. It is during social interaction that children learn to "appraise" or assign meaning to their emotional experiences and develop self-conscious awareness of their emotional states. This emerging capacity is assisted by the contingencies they experience between their own immediate emotional states, on the one hand, and the nonverbal and verbal responses they elicit from interactants, on the other. In normal development the child's state, reflected in expressive behavior, is perceived, interpreted, and commented upon by the caregiver, both behaviorally and verbally—by contingent facial expressive responding (Malatesta & Haviland, 1982; Malatesta et al., 1986) and verbal commentary that reflects upon the nature of the child's state. Over time, these inputs sensitize the child to emotional cues and provide the necessary linkages in consciousness between emotional states and behaviors. For the most part, the parental verbal commentary reflects the child's actual behavioral state. However, particular parents may show a *restricted range* of comments about feeling states overall, or they may *selectively* label certain states and not others, or they may *mislabel* certain states (Lewis & Michalson, 1983), thereby shaping the child's "cabinet of consciousness" about feeling states in idiosyncratic ways. Dunn, Bretherton, and Munn (1987), for example, found that there are stable individual differences in the way caregivers talk to their children about emotions. Significant individual-difference dimensions that showed stability included the total number of maternal utterances about feeling states, the proportion of maternal conversation turns concerned with feeling states, and the frequency of maternal causal statements about feeling states. Interestingly, when children's emotional language was evaluated at 24 months, child feeling-state utterances were positively correlated with maternal feeling-state utterances and feeling-state conversation turns at 18 months.

The particular shape that the child's consciousness about emotional states takes will conceivably have a profound impact on subsequent development, affecting, as it will, various cognitive functions, including perception and appraisal, encoding, memory, interpretation of information, and attributions. Elsewhere, (Malatesta & Wilson, 1988) I have described the recursive and sustaining relationship between affect and cognition in terms of emotional organizations. In brief, I maintain that emotional organizations are typically accompanied by congruent cognitions. For example, to experience *fear* is also to entertain cognitions about the threatening nature of events or objects as well as cognitions related to escape and avoidance possibilities. In such a state of heightened fear sensitivity, one is more likely to detect the fearsome properties of events and objects, both those that are immediately dangerous and those that can be construed as potentially dangerous. Having identified a "real" source of fear, one concludes that one's fearfulness is justified, thus setting the stage for subsequent fearful appraisal of the world.

A good illustration of this principle can be found in a recent study by Dodge and colleagues (Dodge, Pettit, McClaskey, & Brown, 1986). These researchers examined the relationship between social-information processing and social behavior in children. A sample of teacher- and peer-identified aggressive children were found to be more likely than matched nonaggressive peer controls to attribute hostile intentions to a peer provocation, to access aggressive responses to this stimulus, and to behave aggressively when provoked. They were also more likely than average children to receive negative and ignoring peer responses when they attempted to enter a group, thus probably reinforcing their sense of needing to screen the world for hostile intentions in others.

The aggressive children in the Dodge et al. (1986) study seem to display an affective organization around the primary emotion of anger; what is notable is that this disposition affects a range of relevant behaviors and that the behaviors themselves seem to sustain the organization. We assume that children can acquire affective organizations around other emotions, with similar interpersonal consequences. Alternatively, they may develop a more balanced, integrated kind of emotional organization where no single affect dominates (cf. Tomkins, 1963). It will be a challenge to future research to identify different kinds of emotional organizations and their manifestations and to specify the environmental conditions that give rise to them.

## Summary and Conclusion

In this chapter I have attempted to introduce a model of personality development that emphasizes the important contribution of emotional experiences, specifically differential emotional experiences. I have suggested that in the course of development children acquire affect-specific emotional organizations that then influence the way they subsequently engage the world. The attachment literature has led in establishing that early, formative social interactions with caregivers affect, in consequential ways, the nature of the subsequent parent-child bond and the child's social competence and cognitive skills. The discrete-emotions analysis undertaken here suggests it may be informative to learn more about the specific types of emotional exchanges that go on between infants and their caregivers. From this we may be able to understand more about differential personality development.

In this chapter I also attempted to establish the case for the existence of emotional biases in adults and to show that these emotional biases appear to have rudimentary counterparts in infants and young children. I suggested that differential emotional biases are acquired developmentally in the context of differential social ecologies that elicit and emphasize certain emotions over others. Several mechanisms were proposed to account for the consolidation of emotional biases over time, including social learning principles, contagion and self-regulation, language, and the formation of cognitively mediated emotion loops.

Once these kinds of ideoaffective organizations (Tomkins, 1963) or affective-cognitive structures (Izard, 1977) that are embodied in emotional organizations have taken shape, they tend to be self-sustaining without further "emotion socialization" from caregivers and other family members, although the wider social environment may continue to reinforce emotional biases, as is evident in the Dodge et al. (1986) study. Does this mean that emotional organizations established early in life will resist subsequent change? I suggest that cognition and feeling experience are capable of contributing to *either* further consolidation of emotional organizations and their dominance in personality and behavior *or* the forging of a new developmental path. Although emotion and cognition tend to sustain one another within emotion organizations, experience teaches that one can discover one's own "modes of states of mind" and deploy this information in the service of enlightened self-management (although there may be limitations on this ability, especially if the organization is of the more inflexible form found in psychopathology [Malatesta & Wilson, 1988]). As we learn more not only of how children think about emotion (Harris, 1983; Harris, Olthof & Terwogt, 1981) but of how they feel about it and what they make of their subjective experiences, we may learn more about how children can and do take charge of their own emotional ontogeny beyond childhood.

It is a curious fact of the history of developmental psychology that we have focused on a restricted definition of "cognition," and a decathected one at that, in our study of child development. Piaget's theory of genetic epistemology, which has had a tremendous influence on child psychology, is a theory of the way children learn to *objectify* the world. But cognitions, in interaction with emotions, also play a role in the way children and adults *subjectify* the world. In a thought-provoking paper delivered at the most recent meeting of the Society for Research in Child Development, Vandenberg (1987) noted that developmental psychology has tended to ignore critical ontological issues. He believes that genuine consideration of such issues would have a transforming impact on the field. Indeed, developmental psychology might well profit from expanding its horizons by adding a genetic *phenomenology* to that of genetic epistemology.

In taking away a lesson from philosophy, we in psychology can perhaps return the favor. Fourier and Heidegger tended to focus on the individual to the exclusion of the broader social ecology in the construction of meaning. In Heidegger's terms, individuals are thrown into the world as orphans; a fundamental ontological task is to make meaning out of a meaningless world. It is developmental psychology's contribution to draw attention to the fact that making meaning is a process of co-construction. And as we are now more keenly aware, the co-construction of meaning is a unique, dyad-specific and affect-imbued project that is forged in early relational contexts.

## REFERENCES

Ainsworth, M. D. S. (1967). *Infancy in Uganda: Infant care and the growth of love*. Baltimore: Johns Hopkins University Press.

Ainsworth, M. D. S., Blehar, M. C., Waters, E., & Wall, S. (1978). *Patterns of attachment: A psychological study of the strange situation*. Hillsdale, NJ: Erlbaum.

Allport, G. W. (1937). *Personality: A psychological interpretation*. New York: Holt, Rinehart & Winston.

Arend, R., Gove, F., & Sroufe, L. A. (1979). Continuity of individual adaptation from infancy to kindergarten: A predictive study of ego-resiliency and curiosity in preschoolers. *Child Development, 50*, 950–959.

Bates, J. E., Maslin, C. A., & Frankel, K. A. (1985). Attachment security, mother-child interaction, and temperament as predictors of behavior-problem ratings at age three years. In I. Bretherton & E. Waters (Eds.), Growing points of attachment theory and research (pp. 167–193). *Monographs of the Society for Research in Child Development, 50* (1–2, Serial No. 209).

Beecher, J. (1986). *Charles Fourier: The visionary and his world*. Berkeley: University of California Press.

Belsky, J., & Rovine, M. (1987). Temperament and attachment security in the strange situation: An empirical rapprochement. *Child Development, 58*, 787–795.

Belsky, J., Rovine, M., & Taylor, D. G. (1984). The Pennsylvania infant and family development project: III. The origins of individual differences in infant-mother attachment: Maternal and infant contributions. *Child Development, 55*, 718–728.

Berry, D. T. R., & Webb, W. B. (1985). Mood and sleep in aging women. *Journal of Personality and Social Psychology, 49*, 1724–1727.

Birns, B., Barten, S., & Bridger, W. (1969). Individual differences in temperamental characteristics of infants. *Transactions of the New York Academy of Sciences, 31*, 1071–1082.

Block, J. H., & Block, J. (1980). The role of ego-control and ego-resiliency in the organization of behavior. In W. A. Collins (Ed.), *Development of cognition, affect, and social relations* (Minnesota Symposium on Child Psychology Vol. 13, pp. 103–130). Hillsdale, NJ: Erlbaum.

Bower, G. H. (1981). Mood and memory. *American Psychologist, 36*, 129–148.

Bowlby, J. (1969). *Attachment and loss: Vol. 1. Attachment*. New York: Basic Books.

Bowlby, J. (1973). *Attachment and loss: Vol. 2. Separation: Anxiety and anger*. New York: Basic Books.

Bowlby, J. (1980). *Attachment and loss: Vol. 3. Loss: Sadness and depression*. New York: Basic Books.

Bradley, R. H., Casey, P. M., & Wortham, B. (1984). Home environments of low SES non-organic failure-to-thrive infants. *Merrill-Palmer Quarterly, 30*, 393–402.

Bretherton, I. (1985). Attachment theory: Retrospect and prospect. In I. Bretherton & E. Waters (Eds.), Growing points of attachment theory and research (pp. 3–38). *Monographs of the Society for Research in Child Development, 50* (1–2, Serial No. 209).

Bronson, G. W. (1970). Fear of visual novelty. *Development Psychology, 2*, 33–40.

50

Bruner, J. S. (1957). On perceptual readiness. *Psychological Review, 64*, 123–52.

Buck, R. (1984). *The communication of emotion.* New York: Guilford Press.

Buhler, K. (1929). *Die Krise der Psychologie.* Jena: Gustav Fischer.

Buss, A. H., & Plomin, R. (1984). *Temperament: Early developing personality traits.* Hillsdale, NJ: Erlbaum.

Campos, J. J., Barrett, K. C., Lamb, M. E., Goldsmith, H. H., & Stenberg, C. (1983). Socioemotional development. In M. M. Haith (Ed.), *Handbook of child psychology: Vol. 2. Infancy and developmental psychobiology* (pp. 783–916). New York: John Wiley.

Cassidy, J., & Kobak, R. (in press). Avoidance and its relation to other defensive processes. In J. Belsky & T. Nezworski (Eds.), *Clinical implications of attachment.* Hillsdale, NJ: Erlbaum.

Cohn, J. F., & Tronick, E. Z. (1983). Three-month-old infants' reaction to simulated maternal depression. *Child Development, 54*, 185–193.

Coll, G. C., Kagan, J., & Reznick, J. S. (1984). Behavioral inhibition in young children. *Child Development, 55*, 1005–1019.

Connell, J. P., & Thompson, R. (1986). Emotion and social interaction in the strange situation: Consistencies and asymmetric influences in the second year. *Child Development, 57*, 733–745.

Cummings, E. M. (1987). Coping with background anger in early childhood. *Child Development, 58*, 976–984.

Cummings, M. E., Iannotti, R. J., & Zahn-Waxler, C. (1985). Influence of conflict between adults on the emotions and aggression of young children. *Developmental Psychology, 21*, 495–507.

Denham, S. A. (1985). *Maternal emotional responsiveness and its relation to toddlers' social-emotional competence and expression of emotion.* Paper presented at the biennial meeting of the Society for Research in Child Development, Beverly Hills, CA.

Dodge, K. A., Pettit, G. S., McClaskey, C. L., & Brown, M. M. (1986). Social competence in children. *Monographs of the Society for Research in Child Development, 51* (2), 1–80.

Dunn, J., Bretherton, I., & Munn, P. (1987). Conversations about feeling states between mothers and their young children. *Developmental Psychology, 23*, 132–139.

Ekman, P. (1973). Cross-cultural studies of facial expression. In P. Ekman (Ed.), *Darwin and facial expression: A century of research in review* (pp. 169–222). New York: Academic Press.

Ekman, P. (1984). Expression and the nature of emotion. In K. Scherer & P. Ekman (Eds.), *Approaches to emotion* (pp. 329–343). Hillsdale, NJ: Erlbaum.

Ekman, P., Friesen, W. V., & Ellsworth, P. (1972). *Emotion in the human face.* New York: Pergamon.

Emde, R. (1984, April). *Collaborative history of a standard technique for interpreting Infant Facial Expressions of Emotion from Looking at Pictures (I-FEEL Pic-*

*tures)*. Paper presented at the International Conference on Infant Studies, Los Angeles.

Emmerich, W. (1968). Personality development and concepts of structure. *Child Development, 39*, 671–690.

Epstein, S. (1980). The stability of behavior: II. Implications of psychological research. *American Psychologist, 35*, 790–806.

Erickson, M. F., Sroufe, L. A., & Egeland, B. (1985). The relationship between quality of attachment and behavior problems in preschool in a high-risk sample. In I. Bretherton & E. Waters (Eds.), Growing points of attachment theory and research (pp. 147–166). *Monographs of the Society for Research in Child Development, 50* (1–2, Serial No. 209).

Eysenck, H. J., & Eysenck, M. W. (1985). *Personality and individual differences.* New York: Plenum Press.

Field, T. (1984). Early interactions between infants and their postpartum depressed mothers. *Infant Behavior & Development, 7*, 527–532.

Field, T. (1987). Affective and interactive disturbances in infants. In J. Osofsky (Ed.), *Handbook of infant development* (2nd ed.) (pp. 972–1005). New York: John Wiley.

Fischer, K. W., Shaver, P., & Carnochan, P. (in press). From basic- to subordinate-category emotions: A skills approach to emotional development. In W. Damon (Ed.), *Child development today and tomorrow*. San Francisco: Jossey-Bass.

Ford, M. E., & Thompson, R. A. (1985). Perceptions of personal agency and infant attachment: Toward a life-span perspective on competence development. *International Journal of Behavioral Development, 8*, 377–406.

Friedman, H. S., DiMatteo, M. R., & Taranta, A. (1980). A study of the relationship between individual differences in nonverbal expressiveness and factors of personality and social interaction. *Journal of Research in Personality, 14*, 351–364.

Frodi, A., & Thompson, R. (1985). Infants' affective responses in the strange situation: Effects of prematurity and of quality of attachment. *Child Development, 56*, 1280–1290.

Goldsmith, H. H., & Campos, J. J. (1982). Toward a theory of infant temperament. In R. N. Emde & R. J. Harmon (Eds.), *The development of attachment and affiliative systems* (pp. 161–194). New York: Plenum Press.

Grossmann, K. E., & Grossmann, K. (1981). The mother-child relationship. *German Journal of Psychology, 5*, 237–252.

Grossmann, K. E., & Grossmann, K. (1985, July). *From attachment to dynamics of relationship patterns: A longitudinal approach*. Paper presented at the biennial meeting of the International Society for the Study of Behavioral Development, Tours, France.

Harris, P. L. (1983). Children's understanding of the link between situation and emotion. *Journal of Experimental Child Psychology, 36*, 490–509.

Harris, P. L., Olthof, T., & Terwogt, M. M. (1981). Children's knowledge of

emotion. *Journal of Child Psychology and Psychiatry and Allied Disciplines,*
22, 247–261.

Haviland, J. M., & Lelwica, M. (1987). The induced affect response: Ten-week-old infants' responses to three emotion expressions. *Developmental Psychology, 23,* 17–104.

Heidegger, M. (1962). *Being and time.* New York: Harper & Row. (Original work published 1926 as *Sein und Zeit*).

Howes, M. J., Hokanson, J. E., & Loewenstein, D. A. (1985). Induction of depressive affect after prolonged exposure to a mildly depressed individual. *Journal of Personality and Social Psychology, 49,* 1110–1113.

Hyson, M. C., & Izard, C. E. (1985). Continuities and changes in emotion expressions during brief separation at 13 and 18 months. *Developmental Psychology, 21,* 1165–1170.

Isabella, R. A. (1987, April). *The origins of infant-mother attachment: An examination of interactional synchrony during the infant's first year.* Paper presented at the biennial meeting of the Society for Research in Child Development, Baltimore.

Isen, A. A. (1984). Toward understanding the role of affect in cognition. In R. Wyler & T. Srule (Eds.), *Handbook of social cognition* (pp. 179–235). Hillsdale, NJ: Erlbaum.

Izard, C. E. (1971). *The face of emotion.* New York: Appleton-Century-Crofts.

Izard, C. E. (1972). *Patterns of emotions: A new analysis of anxiety and depression.* New York: Academic Press.

Izard, C. E. (1977). *Human emotions.* New York: Plenum Press.

Izard, C. E., Hembree, E. A., Dougherty, L. M., & Spizzirri, C. L. (1983). Changes in facial expressions of 2 to 19 month old infants following acute pain. *Developmental Psychology, 19,* 418–426.

Izard, C. E., & Malatesta, C. Z. (1987). Perspectives on emotional development: I. Differential emotions theory of early emotional development. In J. D. Osofsky (Ed.), *Handbook of infant development* (2nd ed.) (pp. 494–554). New York: John Wiley.

Jonas, R. (1986). *A component analysis of the emotionality of type A behavior pattern.* Unpublished doctoral dissertation, New School for Social Research.

Kagan, J., Reznick, J. S., Clarke, C., & Snidman, N., Coll, G. C. (1984). Behavioral inhibition to the unfamiliar. *Child Development, 55,* 2212–2225.

Klein, G. S., Schlesinger, H. J., & Meister, D. E. (1951). *Psychological Review, 58,* 96–112.

Krueger, F. (1928). The essence of feeling. In M. Reymert (Ed.), *Feelings and emotions: The Wittenberg Symposium.* Worcester, MA: Clark University Press.

LaFreniere, P. J., & Sroufe, L. A. (1985). Profiles of peer competence in the preschool: Interrelations between measures, influence of social ecology, and relation to attachment history. *Developmental Psychology, 21,* 46–69.

Lamb, M. E., Thompson, R. A., Gardner, W., & Charnov, E. L. (1985). *Infant-mother attachment.* Hillsdale, NJ: Erlbaum.

Lamb, M. E., Thompson, R. A., Gardner, W. P., Charnov, E. L., & Estes, D. (1984). Security of infantile attachment as assessed in the "strange situation." *Behavioral and Brain Sciences, 7*, 127–147.

Langhorst, B., & Fogel, A. (1982, March). *A cross-validation of microanalytic approaches to face-to-face play*. Paper presented at a meeting of the International Conference of Infant Studies, Austin.

Levy, L. (1983). Trait approaches. In M. Hersen, A. E. Kazden, & A. S. Bellack (Eds.), *The clinical psychology handbook*. New York: Pergamon Press.

Lewis, M., & Michalson, L. (1983). *Children's emotions and moods*. New York: Plenum Press.

Lyons-Ruth, K., Connell, D. B., Zoll, D., & Stahl, J. (1987). Infants at social risk: Relations among infant maltreatment, maternal behavior, and infant attachment behavior. *Developmental Psychology, 23*, 223–232.

Main, M. (1973). *Play, exploration and competence as related to child-adult attachment*. Unpublished doctoral dissertation, Johns Hopkins University.

Main, M., Kaplan, N., & Cassidy, J. (1985). Security in infancy, childhood, and adulthood: A move to the level of representation. In I. Bretherton & E. Waters (Eds.), Growing points of attachment theory and research (pp. 66–106). *Monographs of the Society for Research in Child Development, 50* (1–2, Serial No. 209).

Main, M., & Weston, D. R. (1981). The quality of the toddler's relationship to mother and to father: Related to conflict behavior and the readiness to establish new relationships. *Child Development, 52*, 932–940.

Malatesta, C. Z. (1985). Developmental course of emotion expression in the human infant. In G. Zivin (Ed.), *The development of expressive behavior: Biology-environment interactions* (pp. 183–219). New York: Academic Press.

Malatesta, C. Z., Cullver, C., Tesman, J., and Shepard, B. (1989). The development of emotion expression during the first two years of life. *Development, 50* (1–2, Serial No. 219). *Monographs of the Society for Research in Child Development*.

Malatesta, C. Z., Fiore, M., & Messina, J. (1987). Affect, personality, and facial expressive characteristics of older people. *Psychology and Aging, 2*, 64–69.

Malatesta, C. Z., Grigoryev, P., Lamb, C., Albin, M., & Culver, C. (1986). Emotion socialization and expressive development in preterm and full term infants. *Child Development, 57*, 316–330.

Malatesta, C. Z., & Haviland, J. M. (1982). Learning display rules: The socialization of emotion expression in infancy. *Child Development, 53*, 991–1003.

Malatesta, C. Z., & Izard, C. E. (1984). The ontogenesis of human social signals: From biological imperative to symbol utilization. In N. Fox & R. Davidson (Eds.), *The psychobiology of affective development* (pp. 161–206). Hillsdale, NJ: Erlbaum.

Malatesta, C. Z., & Wilson, A. (1988). Emotion/cognition interaction in personality development: A discrete emotions, functionalist analysis. *British Journal of Social Psychology, 27*, 91–112.

Matas, L., Arend, R., & Sroufe, L. A. (1978). Continuity of adaptation in the second year: The relationship between quality of attachment and later competence. *Child Development, 49,* 547–556.

McCown, W., Johnson, J., & Austin, S. (1985, June). *Inability of delinquents to recognize facial affects.* Paper presented at the British Psychological Society's International Conference on the Meaning of Faces, Cardiff, Wales.

McCrae, R. R., & Costa, P. T., Jr. (1984). *Emerging lives, enduring dispositions.* Boston: Little, Brown.

McCrae, R. R., & Costa, P. T., Jr. (1986). Clinical assessment can benefit from recent advances in personality psychology. *American Psychologist, 41,* 1001–1003.

Messick, S. (1965). The impact of negative affect on cognition and personality. In S. S. Tomkins & C. E. Izard (Eds.), *Affect, cognition and personality* (pp. 98–129). New York: Springer.

Moss, H. A., & Susman, E. J. (1980). Longitudinal study of personality development. In O. G. Brim & J. Kagan (Eds.), *Constancy and change in human development* (pp. 530–595). Cambridge: Harvard University Press.

Nasby, W., & Yando, R. (1982). Selective encoding and retrieval of affectively valent information. *Journal of Personality and Social Psychology, 43,* 1244–1255.

Panksepp, J. (in press). The neurobiology of emotions: Of animal brains and human feelings. In H. Wagner & T. Manstead (Eds.), *Handbook of psychophysiology.* New York: Plenum Press.

Pastor, D. L. (1981). The quality of mother-infant attachment and its relationship to toddler's initial sociability with peers. *Developmental Psychology, 17,* 323–335.

Pervin, L. (1975). *Personality: Theory, assessment, and research.* New York: John Wiley.

Plutchik, R. (1962). *The emotions: Facts, theories, and a new model.* New York: Random House.

Plutchik, R. (1980). *Emotion: A psychoevolutionary synthesis.* New York: Harper & Row.

Porter, R., & Collins, G. (Eds.). (1982). *Temperamental differences in infants and young children* (Ciba Foundation Symposium No. 89). London: Pitman.

Rothbart, M. K., & Derryberry, D. (1981). Development of individual differences in temperament. In M. E. Lamb & A. L. Brown (Eds.), *Advances in developmental psychology* (Vol. 1, pp. 37–86). Hillsdale, NJ: Erlbaum.

Sagi, A., Lamb, M. E., Lewkowicz, K. S., Shoham, R., Dvir, R., & Estes, D. (1985). In I. Bretherton & E. Waters (Eds.), Growing points of attachment theory and research (pp. 257–275). *Monographs of the Society for Research in Child Development, 50* (1–2, Serial No. 209).

Scarr, S., & Salapatek, P. (1970). Patterns of fear development during infancy. *Merrill-Palmer Quarterly, 16,* 53–90.

Schneider-Rosen, K., Braunwald, K. G., Carlson, V., & Cicchetti, D. (1985). Current perspectives in attachment theory: Illustration from the study of maltreated infants. In I. Bretherton & E. Waters (Eds.), Growing points of attachment theory and research (pp. 194–210). *Monographs of the Society for Research in Child Development, 50* (1–2, Serial No. 209).

Seligman, M. E. P. (1975). *Helplessness*. San Francisco: Freeman.

Shiller, V. M., Izard, C. E., & Hembree, E. A. (1986). Patterns of emotion expression during separation in strange-situation procedure. *Developmental Psychology, 22*, 378–382.

Spitz, R. (1965). *The first year of life: A psychoanalytic study of normal and deviant development of object relations*. New York: International Universities Press.

Spranger, E. (1928). *Types of men: The psychology and ethics of personality*. New York: Johnson Reprint.

Sroufe, L. A. (1979). Socioemotional development. In J. D. Osofsky (Ed.), *Handbook of infant development* (pp. 462–516). New York: John Wiley.

Sroufe, L. A. (1983). Individual patterns of adaptation from infancy to preschool. In M. Perlmutter (ed.), *Minnesota Symposia on Child Psychology* (Vol. 16). Hillsdale, NJ: Erlbaum.

Stenberg, C. (1982). *The development of anger facial expressions in infancy*. Unpublished doctoral dissertation, University of Denver.

Stenberg, C., Campos, J., & Emde, R. (1983). The facial expression of anger in seven month old infants. *Child Development, 54*, 178–184.

Stettner, L. J., & Loigman, G. (1983, April). *Emotion cues in baby faces as elicitors of functional reaction choices*. Paper presented at the biennial meeting of the Society for Research in Child Development, Detroit.

Thomas, A., & Chess, S. (1977). *Temperament and development*. New York: Brunner/Mazel.

Thompson, R. A., & Lamb, M. E. (1984). Assessing qualitative dimensions of emotional responsiveness in infants: Separation reactions in the strange situation. *Infant Behavior and Development, 7*, 423–445.

Tomkins, S. (1962). *Affect, imagery, consciousness: Vol. 1. The positive affects*. New York: Springer.

Tomkins, S. (1963). *Affect, imagery, consciousness: Vol. 2. The negative affects*. New York: Springer.

Tomkins, S., & McCarter, R. (1964). What and where are the primary affects? Some evidence for a theory. *Perceptual and Motor Skills, 18*, 119–156.

Toner, H. L., & Gates, G. R. (1985). Emotional traits and recognition of facial expressions of emotion. *Journal of Nonverbal Behavior, 9*, 48–66.

Vandenberg, B. (1987, April). *Development within an existential framework*. Paper presented at the Society for Research in Child Development, Baltimore.

Vonnegut, K. (1981). *Palm Sunday*. New York: Delacorte Press.

Waters, E., Wippman, J., & Sroufe, L. A. (1979). Attachment, positive affect, and competence in the peer group: Two studies in construct validation. *Child Development, 50*, 821–829.

Watson, J. B., & Morgan, J. J. (1917). Emotional reactions and psychological experimentation. *American Journal of Psychology, 28*, 161–174.

Wiesenfeld, A. R., & Malatesta, C. Z. (1982). Infant distress: Variables affecting responses of caregivers and others. In R. Gandelman, L. Hoffman, & H. R. Schiffman (Eds.), *Parental behavior: Its causes and consequences* (pp. 123–139). Hillsdale, NJ: Erlbaum.

Williams, R. B. (1984, March). *Psychological concomitants of cardiovascular disease in the elderly.* Paper presented at the NIMH Conference on Mental Health Aspects of Physical Disease in Late Life, Bethesda, MD.

Zajonc, R. B. (1984). On the primacy of affect. *American Psychologist, 39,* 117–123.

Zivin, G. (1986). Processes of expressive behavior development. *Merrill-Palmer Quarterly, 32,* 103–140.

# Open Communication and Internal Working Models: Their Role in the Development of Attachment Relationships

Inge Bretherton
*University of Wisconsin–Madison*

## Introduction

*T*he recent shift of attachment research away from an almost exclusive focus on infancy and toward a much greater emphasis on other periods of the life span has led to provocative new discoveries. Not only have these discoveries begun to shed light on attachment as a lifelong and transgenerational phenomenon, they have also lent renewed importance to certain aspects of the classical work on attachment in infancy. Findings from Ainsworth's Baltimore study (Ainsworth & Bell, 1969; Bell & Ainsworth, 1972; Blehar, Lieberman, & Ainsworth, 1977; Stayton & Ainsworth, 1973) had already shown that individual differences in mothers' sensitive responsiveness to their infants' signals during the first three months of life were associated with different mother-infant communication patterns during the last three months of the first year. The new findings demonstrate that communication patterns in secure and insecure attachment relationships differ not only in infancy, but in childhood and adult-

Support from the MacArthur Foundation Network for Childhood Transitions is gratefully acknowledged. I would also like to thank Robert Hinde for helpful comments on this manuscript.

hood. Secure relationships, it turns out, go hand in hand with the partners' ability to engage in emotionally open, fluent, and coherent communication, both *within* attachment relationships and *about* attachment relationships. Insecure relationships, by contrast, seem to be characterized by selective ignoring of signals, as well as by certain forms of incoherence and dysfluency when discussing attachment relations.

In this chapter I review the significance of these new findings for attachment theory. I will begin with a brief account regarding the conceptual links between a caregiver's sensitive responsiveness to an infant's signals, the development of open communication patterns, and the child's ability to construct adequate representations or working models of self and other in the attachment relationship (Bowlby, 1969, 1973, 1980). I will then summarize findings from the recent empirical studies of infants, toddlers, kindergartners, adolescents, and adults that corroborate the theoretical account developed in the first section. In the next section I will show how the concept of working models in attachment theory can be enriched through ideas derived from related theoretical perspectives: from new insights about representational processes, from recent findings in social-cognitive development, and from the classical literature on the social self. I believe that ideas from these domains, when incorporated into attachment theory, will allow us to ask some new questions about the healthy and pathological development of internal working models and the intergenerational transmission of attachment patterns.

## Maternal Sensitivity and Internal Working Models

In her first study of infant attachment in Uganda (Ainsworth, 1967), but especially in the subsequent Baltimore study (summarized in Ainsworth, Blehar, Waters, & Wall, 1978), Mary Ainsworth discovered that a mother's sensitive, appropriate responsiveness to her infant's signals during feeding, physical contact, infant distress, and face-to-face play in the course of the first three months, far from spoiling the baby, actually led to a more harmonious (secure) attachment relationship by the end of the first year of life. Mothers who were characterized as very sensitive during the early months had infants who, during the last quarter of the first year, cried less but had a larger communicative repertoire, were more obedient, and enjoyed close bodily contact more, although they demanded it less often. Moreover, 1-year-olds with sensitive mothering behaved differently from insensitively mothered infants in a laboratory situation known as the "Strange Situation" at 1 year of age. It is because infants' behavior during this procedure was correlated with mother-infant communication patterns at home that it later became a short-cut method for assessing the quality of infant-mother attachment.

The Strange Situation consists of a standard sequence of one introductory and seven 3-minute episodes in which mother, baby, and a stranger participate. The sequence of episodes is described in Table 1. Of special importance in this assessment are the two separation/reunion sequences. It turned out that sensitively mothered infants (as assessed during feeding, crying, holding and face-to-face play), tended in the reunion episodes of the Strange Situation to approach the mother readily, to seek interaction or contact with her, to derive comfort from this interaction or contact, and then to return to exploring the toys. These infants were labeled secure (group B). Insensitively mothered infants either avoided the mother upon her return (snubbed her by turning or walking away or by refusing to interact) or responded ambivalently (expressed a desire for proximity and contact combined with angry, resistant behavior). The patterns of insensitivity shown by mothers of avoidant and ambivalent babies differed. Mothers whose babies avoided them on reunion in the Strange Situation (group A) tended to provide less affectionate holding during the first three months and frequently rejected bids for close bodily contact during the last quarter of the first year. In conversations with the observer, these mothers also mentioned their dislike of close contact with their babies. Mothers of ambivalent babies (group C), by contrast, were inconsistently sensitive at home and frequently ignored their babies' signals. They did not, however, reject close bodily contact (Ainsworth & Bell, 1969; Ainsworth, Bell, & Stayton, 1974; Ainsworth & Blehar, 1971; Blehar et al., 1977). More recently, Main and Hesse (in press) have identified a fourth group of infants termed insecure-disorganized (group D) who are difficult to classify into one of the three categories defined by Ainsworth et al. (1978). The insecure-disorganized classification

**Table 1**
The Strange Situation Procedure

| Episode | Duration | Partici-pants[a] | Events |
|---------|----------|------------------|--------|
| 1 | 30 sec | M, B, O | O shows M and B into the room, instructs M on where to put B down and where to sit. O leaves. |
| 2 | 3 min | M, B | M puts B down close to her chair, at a distance from the toys. She responds to B's social bids but does not initiate interaction. B is free to explore. If B does not move after 2 minutes, M may take B to the toy area. |
| 3 | 3 min | M, B, S | This episode has three parts. S enters, greets M and B, and sits down opposite M without talking for 1 minute. During the 2nd minute, S engages M in conversation. S then joins B on the floor, attempting to engage B in play for 1 minute. At the end of this episode, M leaves "unobtrusively" (B usually notices). |
| 4 | 3 min | B, S | S sits on her chair. She responds to B's social bids but does not initiate social interaction. If B becomes distressed, S attempts to comfort B. If this is not effective, M returns before 3 minutes are up. |
| 5 | 3 min | M, B | M calls B's name outside the door and enters (S leaves unobtrusively). If B is distressed, M comforts B and tries to reengage B in play. If B is not distressed, M goes to sit on her chair, taking a responsive, noninitiating role. At the end of the episode M leaves, saying "Bye-bye; I'll be back." |

| 6 | 3 min | B | B remains alone. If B becomes distressed, the episode is curtailed and S enters. |
| 7 | 3 min | B, S | S enters, comforting B if required. If she cannot comfort B, the episode is curtailed. If B calms down or is not distressed, S sits on her chair, taking a responsive role as before. |
| 8 | 3 min | M, B | M returns (S leaves unobtrusively). M behaves as in episode 5. |

[a]O = observer; M = mother; B = baby; S = stranger.

is given to infants who display a combination of strongly avoidant *and* resistant reunion behavior or who show a variety of disorganized behaviors (sudden stilling in the midst of a greeting, very fleeting fear responses as the mother returns, and other behaviors that do not make sense in the context in which they occur). Much less is known about this group, and unlike the ABC classifications, the disorganized-disoriented behavior pattern still remains to be validated against home observations during the first year of life. As we will see later, however, parents of infants classified into group D are known to differ in a number of ways (for further details see Main & Hesse, in press).

At this point the definition of maternal sensitivity deserves further clarification. Ainsworth et al. (1974) termed mothers sensitively responsive or simply sensitive if they noticed their infants' signals, interpreted them accurately (by taking the infants' perspective), and then responded reasonably promptly and appropriately. The criteria for judging the accuracy of parental interpretation and the appropriateness of parental responding were not precisely specified but can be derived from some of the basic assumptions underlying attachment theory (Bowlby, 1969). According to attachment theory, infants are preadapted to a caregiver who responds to their attachment behaviors as bids for comfort, soothing, and protection but who also permits and supports autonomous action and exploration. Where a caregiver fairly consistently interprets security seeking as overly demanding or as unimportant or too often restricts the baby's desire for independent exploration, the infant's attachment behavior will not be effectively assuaged, nor will eagerness to explore be

appropriately fostered. This has important sequelae for the development of communication patterns in attachment relationships. Not
only are insensitively mothered infants prevented from reaching
their immediate goals, but they also repeatedly receive the implicit
messages "I do not understand you"; "your communications are not
meaningful or important" (see also Stern, 1977, for extensive discussions along similar lines).

In discussions of this topic it is often overlooked that insensitivity is not necessarily indexed by unpleasant, mean, or nasty maternal behavior. Rather, insensitivity implies that the caregiver is not
reading and supportively responding to the infant's states or goals.
It is thus insensitive to deny a distressed or fearful infant the solace
of bodily contact (rejection), but it is equally insensitive to insist on
affectionate physical contact when the infant is deeply engrossed in
exploration (interference).

## FROM COMMUNICATION PATTERNS TO INTERNAL
## WORKING MODELS

Although both caregiver and baby contribute to reciprocal transactions from the beginning, findings from the Baltimore study indicate
that in the early phases of development the caregiver's sensitivity to
the infant's signals appears to be more influential in setting the tone
of the relationship than are infant characteristics such as temperament (Ainsworth, 1984). However, as memory and information-processing capacities improve, the infant gradually assumes a more active part in upholding emerging transactional patterns. Instead of
moment-to-moment reciprocal responsiveness, transactions toward the end of the first year are increasingly based on the infant's
developing representations or, as Bowlby terms them, internal
working models of self and caregiver in the attachment relationship
(Bowlby, 1969, 1973, 1980). Because new interactions are assimilated
to representations of past interaction patterns, an infant who has too
often been rebuffed by the caregiver and has consequently become
reluctant to seek or accept comfort is, according to this formulation, not likely to become immediately responsive when the caregiver suddenly becomes more sensitive (for example, at the end of
a prolonged illness). This in turn may make it more difficult for the
caregiver to remain sensitive. Conversely, if the caregiver has
been consistently sensitive, the infant's expectations are not

likely to change because of fairly infrequent lapses in responsiveness.

Internal working models of self and attachment figure(s) as defined by Bowlby (1969, 1973) are dynamic representations that predict and interpret the partner's behavior as well as helping one plan one's own response. Bowlby derived the term from the writings of Craik (1943), a psychologist involved in the design of intelligent rocket guidance systems. Craik suggested that organisms that carry a small-scale model of reality in their heads are thereby enabled to choose among alternative courses of action and to react to anticipated situations before they arise.

Bowlby, elaborating on this idea, postulated that within an individual's internal working model of the world, working models of self and caregiver in the attachment relationship are especially salient (for further elaboration see Bretherton, 1985, 1987). Building on Piaget's theory of sensorimotor development, Bowlby speculated that internal working models of self and caregiver are constructed out of the actual transaction patterns between the partners. For that reason, internal working models of self and of caregiver complement each other. If the caregiver has acknowledged the infant's needs for comfort and protection and respected the infant's need for independent exploration of the environment, the child is likely to develop an internal working model of self as valued and self-reliant. Conversely, if the parent has frequently rejected the infant's bids for comfort or for exploration, the child is likely to construct an internal working model of self as unworthy or incompetent.

Clinical studies reviewed by Bowlby (1973) further suggest that the *insecure* child is likely to develop at least two mutually inconsistent working models of the caregiver. One working model—accessible to awareness and discussion—represents the parent as good and the parent's rejecting behavior as due to the "badness" of the child. The other model—defensively excluded from awareness—represents the hated or disappointing side of the parent. Bowlby (1985, citing Cain & Fast, 1972) attributed this split in working models to contradictions in what the parents tell the child and what the child experiences. Research reviewed in the next section suggests, however, that it may not be necessary for the contradiction to be communicated so overtly. A caregiver's disavowal or discounting of an infant's communicative signals leads to the elimination of specific topics from reciprocal, mutually validating communication. It appears that the resulting partial, biased, and distorted communication patterns can in and of themselves lead to a disassociation between conscious and unconscious internal working models of self and attachment figure (see also the review of Stern, 1985, for similar ideas). To put it differently, lack of open communication between attachment partners may be associated with restricted flow of information about attachment issues not only *between* partners, but *within* each partner's representational system (Bowlby, June 1987, personal communication). Empirical evidence for such an interpretation comes from recent studies that will be reviewed in the next section.

## Review of Studies: Caregiver Sensitivity, Communication Patterns, and Internal Working Models

Two types of studies will be reported. The first type, so far almost exclusively restricted to infant-parent and toddler-parent attachments, contrasts the communication patterns of secure and insecure dyads *within* attachment relationships. In the second type of study the focus is on how a person communicates *about* attachment relationships. Studies of the second type are based on projective methods and interviews, administered to a variety of age groups ranging from young preschoolers to kindergartners, young adults, and parents.

### INFANTS

Our understanding of communication patterns in attachment relationships has taken a significant step forward through several painstaking analyses of parent-child interactions by Klaus and Karin Grossmann. Their findings allow us to pinpoint with much greater specificity how the communication patterns of secure and insecure dyads differ. In the first analysis Grossmann and Grossmann (1984) examined tape-recorded maternal and infant vocalizations during two-hour home observations when the infants were 2, 6, and 10 months old. They identified three maternal conversational styles that they termed tender, lighthearted, and sober. The tender style was characterized by an intermediate tempo of speech, many expressions of quiet pleasure, very few directives, no impatience or tension, a strong tendency to respond to infant vocalizations promptly but without being overly dramatic, and a sort of even attentiveness, together with prompt, generous soothing in a very calm tone of voice. The lighthearted style was associated with a fast tempo of speech, frequent and sometimes extreme variability in loudness and pitch, much laughing, mock surprise, a frequently demanding voice quality, and intermittent, often delayed responsiveness to the baby's vocalizations. The sober style was characterized by a relatively slow tempo of speech, fewer and short utterances, an uneven rate of responding to the baby, long reaction time, and somewhat delayed soothing, at times accompanied by signs of resignation.

These maternal communication styles were significantly correlated with global ratings of maternal sensitivity made independently but concurrently from narrative reports of mother-infant interactive behavior at home during the same three ages, as well as with the baby's propensity to vocalize (excluding fussing and crying). Babies whose mothers had sober or tender conversational styles tended to increase their vocalizations from 6 to 10 months, whereas babies of lighthearted mothers decreased their vocalization frequency. Cross-indexing of maternal conversation styles with Strange Situation classifications indicated that 50% of the mothers of secure babies, but only 11% of the mothers of avoidant babies and 10% of the mothers of ambivalent babies, used the tender style. The lighthearted style was employed mainly by mothers whose infants were classified as avoidant or ambivalent. Interestingly, the sober style was common in all three groups (38% secure, 50% avoidant, and 55% ambivalent). Thus maternal communication styles predicted attachment classifications for many, but not all, infants in the sample.

In a second analysis, Escher-Graeub and Grossmann (1983) examined infant-parent communication patterns during a laboratory play situation (not the Strange Situation) at 12 and 18 months. Parents of infants classified as secure in the Strange Situation ignored only 4% of the signals addressed to them, as contrasted with 18% for parents of avoidant infants. Moreover, parents of avoidant infants joined them in play as long as they were in a positive mood but tended to withdraw when the infants showed evidence of negative feelings. By contrast, parents of secure infants joined in when their infants signaled that they were at a loss but watched quietly when the infants did not need them.

In a third analysis, Grossmann, Grossmann, and Schwan (1986) examined communicative behavior in the Ainsworth Strange Situation itself. They focused on infant-mother communication during those three episodes of the Strange Situation when mother and baby are alone together (the low-stress initial mother-baby episode and the two high-stress reunion episodes). Only secure and avoidant infants were included in this analysis (the number of ambivalent infants was very low). It turned out that attachment classifications were associated with specific communicative behaviors during the mother-baby episodes of the Strange Situation. These findings do not, of course, provide external validation for the classifications, but they illustrate more precisely how the communication patterns of insecure dyads differ even in the Strange Situation (note that the classifications are based on infant behavior alone). Twelve of the 16 secure infants engaged their mothers in "direct communication" (by eye contact, facial expression, vocalization, and showing and giving of objects) during the initial mother-baby episode (see Table 1), whereas only 12 of 24 infants classified as avoidant did so. During the reunion episodes the difference widened. Thirteen of the 16 infants classified as secure communicated directly, while only 7 of 24 infants classified as avoidant did so. In the second reunion episode, 15 out of the 16 secure infants, but only 11 of 24 avoidant infants, communicated directly. Moreover, secure infants never stayed away from the mother when their mood was negative, and although some infants classified as avoidant did engage in direct communication, they did so only when they were in good spirits. Infants classified as avoidant tended not to signal to the mother when they were distressed, nor did they seek close bodily contact. With fathers the results were essentially equivalent. On reunion a high proportion of infants classified as secure communicated with him directly, whereas only a few of the infants classified as avoidant with him did so.

A set of important conclusions can be drawn from the three analyses. The way parents respond to their infants' communications modifies the patterning of emotional expressiveness in the infants as well, affecting the developing transactional patterns and hence, according to the theory, the internal working models of both partners (see also Grossmann & Grossmann, in press). In particular, easy flow of communication between partners or—to use Emde's (1983) term—continued mutual emotional availability seems to require that the parents not selectively discount signals of distress.

TODDLERS

A study by Matas, Arend, and Sroufe (1978) illustrates both partners' contribution to open or inadequate communication patterns in attachment relationships beyond infancy. Twenty-four-month-old toddlers who had earlier (at 18 and 12 months) been classified as secure or insecure in the Strange Situation were presented with problem-solving tasks in a laboratory playroom with their mothers present. One of the tasks was difficult enough to require help from an adult. Secure toddlers first attempted to solve the task on their own and did not ask for their mothers' assistance until they got stuck. Their mothers respected the toddlers' autonomy and did not try to intervene as long as the children were still trying to solve the task independently. When secure toddlers did request help, however, their mothers were ready to provide it and were effective in doing so. Effective assistance, as defined in this study, required that the mother pay attention to the child's cues and help the toddler to achieve at least part of the solution alone. In insecure dyads the children tended to whine, and the mothers tended not to offer help.

In a series of clinical case reports, Lieberman and Pawl (in press) have recently described several inadequate attachment communication patterns in highly disturbed toddler-mother dyads. In these dyads the mothers had been unable to convey their availability as secure haven (protection) or as secure base (fostering safe exploration). One resulting attachment pattern was associated with insufficient maternal protection and discounting of security-seeking behavior. In response, the toddlers showed excessive danger seeking or recklessness; that is, they tended to wander off without checking back to the mother and therefore frequently got lost, or hurt in the course of exploration. However, they became intensely anxious when it was their mothers who left them. A second pattern consisted of unpredictable punitiveness in the mothers coupled with excessive danger fleeing in the children. Danger-fleeing toddlers showed restriction of affective range, withdrawal from social interaction with unfamiliar persons, frozen vigilance, and suppressed exploration. It looked as if these children were using self-restraint as self-protection in response to their mothers' inability to serve as a secure base. The third pattern was seen in dyads where clinically depressed mothers were able to retain positive interest in their children. The children tended to show precocious competence, expressed through the child's overconcern for the mother, a phenomenon akin to the compulsive caregiving found in pathological mourning (Bowlby, 1980). A precociously competent child is overly solicitous of the mother's welfare, especially in situations where one would expect the child to need the mother, not vice-versa. In these dyads the child takes on the role of attachment figure, consoling the mother at separation ("don't be sad, Mommy") but frequently refrains from expressing his or her own painful and anxious feelings.

In a second clinical study, Radke-Yarrow, Cummings, Kuczynsky, and Chapman (1985) undertook careful observations of mother-child communication patterns over almost three days in a homelike laboratory situation, comparing well and clinically depressed mothers. They were able to show that mothers diagnosed with bipolar depression answered their 2- to 3-year-olds' social bids with often unpredictable and hence meaningless or confusing affective responses. This made it impossible for toddlers to experience acknowledgment, affirmation, or understanding of their own signals. In this situation—unlike the Grossmanns' studies—the mothers' insensitivity was not selectively focused on signals of distress but seemed randomly distributed over many signals. In an adaptation of the Strange Situation procedure, most of these toddlers showed evidence of strong avoidance combined with strong ambivalence (that is, they were classified as avoidant-ambivalent).

PRESCHOOLERS

We now move to studies whose primary focus is communication *about* attachment relationships, whether through stories, pictures, or interviews. The interpretation of the findings is based on the hypothesis that an individual's ability to discuss attachment issues openly and coherently depends on the adequacy of that individual's internal working models of self and other in attachment relationships. Where defensive information processing has disrupted or distorted communication patterns between attachment partners, the construction of adequate internal working models is also impeded, making the open and fluent discussion of attachment issues difficult.

Bretherton, Ridgeway, and Cassidy (in press) undertook a study of 37-month-olds' attachment story completions. They used family figures (mother, father, two children, and grandmother) along with simple props. Each of five story beginnings (spilled juice, hurt knee, monster in the bedroom, separation, reunion) was acted out with the family figures and props, followed by an invitation to the child to "Show me and tell me what happens next." Children seemed able to understand this task ell.

Building on prior findings with 6-year-olds by Kaplan (1984) and Cassidy (1988), Bretherton et al. developed a classification system for the 3-year-olds' story responses. Children were classified as secure on the basis of the attachment story-completion tasks if they addressed the story issues with little hesitation and invented adequate resolutions (for example, in the hurt knee story, the parent picked up or hugged the child and/or put on a Band-Aid; in the reunion story, the child tended to smile as the car with the family figures returned, to eagerly "drive" it home, to enact greetings between family members, and often to make the reunited family go for a ride together). Children were classified as insecure-avoidant if they produced story resolutions only after many prompts, if they responded with "don't know" or with avoidant or irrelevant completions. They were classified as insecure-disorganized if they enacted somewhat bizarre story endings (after the reunion the family has a car crash). An actual separation-reunion procedure, conducted at the same age, was classified by Cassidy without knowledge of the story classifications (using a system for 3- to 4-year-olds developed by Cassidy, Marvin, & the MacArthur Attachment Workgroup, 1987). The concordance between the secure/insecure classifications in both assessments was highly significant. However, the type of insecurity (resistant, avoidant, disorganized) could not be predicted across procedures.

## KINDERGARTNERS

In a study of 6-year-olds and their parents Main, Kaplan, and Cassidy (1985) found that representational assessments of attachment were related to attachment patterns assessed in a separation-reunion procedure at 6 years *and* in the Strange Situation in infancy. The sample included approximately equal numbers of children classified as secure, insecure-avoidant, and insecure-disorganized in infancy.

In this study, part of the six-year phase of the Berkeley longitudinal study, the children's ability to express their thoughts about attachment issues and to communicate within the attachment relationship was assessed in a subsample of 40 families. Children's responses were observed in the following procedures: (1) presentation of a picture set involving mild and severe separation scenes, adapted from the Klagsbrun and Bowlby (1976) version of the Hansburg (1972) separation anxiety test for adolescents; (2) presentation of a family photograph; (3) children's drawings of the family; and (4) parent-child conversations upon reunion after a one-hour separation. Analysis of the data showed:

1. Six-year-old children classified as secure with their mothers in infancy gave coherent, elaborated, and open responses to the pictures showing mild to more stressful parent-child separations. The secure subjects also tended to volunteer information regarding their own separation experiences. Subjects judged as insecure-avoidant with their mothers in infancy described the children in the separation pictures as sad but could not say what the pictured child could have done in response to separation. Subjects classified as disorganized/disoriented (Main & Hesse, in press) were usually completely silent or gave irrational or bizarre responses (Kaplan, 1984).

2. Six-year-olds judged secure with their mothers at 12 months of age responded to a family photograph presented during separation from the parents by looking at it, smiling at it, and commenting on it, whereas subjects judged insecure-avoidant with their mothers in infancy turned away from the photograph, dropped it, or handed it to the examiner. Subjects who were insecure-disorganized with their mothers at 12 months showed depressed affect or became disorganized in response to the photograph (Main, 1985).

3. In response to a request to draw a picture of their families, 6-year-olds classified as secure with mother in infancy depicted family members as close but not clinging to each other. Figures were well individuated, and not all of them were smiling. Arms tended to be held out in an embracing position. By contrast, drawings by subjects earlier classified as avoidant with their mothers had—according to Kaplan and Main (1985)—an aura of falseness, with all family members bearing similar smiles and with greater distance between family members. Figures tended to be armless. Drawings by subjects judged to have disorganized/disoriented attachments to their mothers in infancy showed a mixture of elements observed in the drawings of secure and avoidant children but were bizarre in a number of ways. Strange marks were added, and unfinished objects or figures were present. Parts of the work were sometimes scratched out. In addition, cheery elements such as hearts and rainbows were added to the setting without making sense within the overall design (see Kaplan & Main, 1985).

4. Discourse patterns during mother-child reunions at 6 years of age were systematically related to earlier Strange Situation classifications with the same parent. Dyads classified as secure in infancy were fluent in discourse and discussed a wide range of topics. Dyads classified as avoidant in infancy were restricted in discourse, emphasizing impersonal topics (focusing on activities or objects), showed little topic elaboration, and asked questions that were rhe-

torical or had yes/no answers. Dyads classified as disorganized/disoriented in infancy were dysfluent, with much stumbling and many false starts. The focus of the conversation was on relationship topics (not activities or objects), with the child steering the conversation (Strage & Main, 1985).

A second set of results regarding kindergartners comes from a study by Cassidy (1988). Fifty-two children and their mothers were seen twice, in sessions one month apart. During each of the two sessions a separation-reunion procedure was used to assess the quality of the child-mother attachment, and a puppet interview and story completion task concerning the child's view of self in the attachment relationship were administered to each child in the mother's absence. Data from both sessions were combined. In the puppet interview, subjects judged to be secure on the basis of reunion behavior with the mother tended to represent a positive picture of the self, but many were also able to acknowledge less than perfect aspects of the self. Insecure-avoidant children tended to depict the self as perfect without mentioning interpersonal relationships, insecure-ambivalent subjects showed no clear pattern of responses, and insecure-controlling subjects tended to make excessively negative statements about themselves. In Main et al.'s (1985) Berkeley study the insecure-controlling classification at 6 years of age was associated with the disorganized classification in infancy.

In the story procedure, children were asked to use a doll family to complete six story beginnings in which self-esteem, family conflict, and outside threat were enacted in the context of the mother-child attachment relationship. Secure subjects tended to present the doll protagonist as someone worthy, with a warm, supportive relationship to the mother. Insecure-avoidant subjects, on the other hand, portrayed the doll protagonist as isolated or rejected; insecure-ambivalent subjects showed a variety of different responses that did not cohere in a recognizable pattern. Finally, insecure-controlling subjects tended to involve the doll protagonist in violent, hostile, negative, or bizarre behavior, enacting a disorganized relationship to the mother.

## ADULTS

Three studies will be discussed. The first two (Main, 1985; Kobak & Sceery, 1988) were based on the Berkeley Adult Attachment Interview, which probes for an individual's recollections of childhood attachments. In the third study Bretherton, Biringen, Ridgeway, Maslin, & Sherman (1989) used a parent-child attachment interview designed to elicit information about the parent's internal working model of self and child in the attachment relationship.

The Adult Attachment Interview was developed by George, Kaplan, and Main (1984) as part of the Berkeley Social Development Project. It was designed to provide insight into an adult's current thoughts and feelings about childhood attachment experiences by asking questions such as: "Could you give me five adjectives that describe your relationship with your mother/father? . . . Now could we talk about what made you choose these adjectives?" "When you were upset as a child what did you do?" "Did you ever feel rejected as a child . . . and why did your parents behave as they did?" Adults were also asked whether they felt that childhood experiences with their parents had influenced their adult personalities. The interview protocol was evaluated as a whole, with special attention given to its internal coherence and organization. For example, it was noted whether a person's global statements and recall of specific incidents were internally consistent or contradictory, and whether a person made many statements claiming not to remember specific events while painting an idealized global picture of the parent. The emphasis was not so much on content (Did the person report happy or unhappy memories?), as on whether the person could readily access and coherently discuss experiences, ideas, and feelings surrounding attachment issues. The interviewer sought to elicit information regarding attachment in an abstract, general sense as well as descriptions of specific relationships. Three patterns of responding were discovered: *secure-autonomous; dismissing of attachment;* and *preoccupied with attachment*. Interview protocols were classified as secure-autonomous if the adult valued attachment, whether with parents or with others, and was at ease in discussing the influence of early attachment relationships on his or her own personality. A further criterion was an ability to describe specific attachments with some objectivity, regardless of whether a secure or insecure childhood was recalled (most, but by no means all, of the adults classified as secure autonomous reported secure childhoods). Interview protocols were classified as dismissing if the adult said that attachment relationships were of little influence, concern, or value and if there were many inconsistencies (especially idealized global statements accompanied by reports of contradictory specific incidents or inability to remember specific incidents). Adults were classified as preoccupied with attachment issues if they described themselves as lacking in autonomy and seemed to be engaged in unsuccessful and unreasonable struggles at pleasing parents. Preoccupied adults seemed unable to give overall impressions that summarized the relationship, although they were able to bring up a very large number of specific childhood memories. The content of these memories was often conflictual.

The Adult Attachment Interview was first administered to the mothers and fathers of children who participated in the Berkeley Social Development Project. The sample of families was drawn from a larger pool for whom infant Strange Situation classifications were known, with participation limited to those parents who had not experienced traumatic family events such as divorce or long hospitalizations (Main et al., 1985). The interview, which took from 45 minutes to 1½ hours, was administered separately to both parents while the child was being observed in another room. When the interview classifications of the parents were matched with the Strange Situation classifications of their infants, it turned out that secure-autonomous adults tended to have infants classified as secure, dismissing adults had infants classified as insecure-avoidant, and preoccupied adults had infants classified as insecure-ambivalent. Finally, parents of infants classified as disorganized in the Strange Situation tended to bring up issues related to unresolved mourning for a childhood attachment figure (Main & Solomon, in press; for replication of these results see Eichberg, 1987, and Grossmann, Fremmer-Bombik, Rudolph, & Grossmann, in press).

Inspired by Main's (1985) findings, Kobak and Sceery (1988) administered the Berkeley Adult Attachment Interview to 53 first-year college students. The same three major response patterns Main discovered (secure-autonomous, dismissing, and preoccupied) were identified. Students classified into each category were then compared with respect to a variety of other assessments. In peer ratings, young adults classified as secure-autonomous scored significantly higher on social adjustment than the preoccupied and dismissing groups. More specifically, the autonomous group adults were rated as lower on negative affect and higher on social relatedness, insight, achievement motivation, and ego-resilience. Interestingly, the pattern of self-report findings differed somewhat from the peer ratings. The autonomous and dismissing groups resembled each other in terms of self-esteem, and only the preoccupied group scored lower than the secure group. Kobak and Sceery (1988) explain this result in terms of defensive processes that may have caused the dismissing (avoidant) group to deny personal weaknesses that were nevertheless perceived by their peers (akin to the results of Cassidy's study with 6-year-olds).

In a third study of adults, Bretherton et al. (1989) administered the Parental Attachment Interview to 36 mothers of 25-month-olds for whom Strange Situation classifications were available. Instead of focusing on a mother's attachment relationships in her family of origin, this interview centered on her attachment relationship with the child. The interview began with a discussion regarding the mother's feelings and thoughts during the period around the child's birth. The mother was then asked to choose five adjectives to characterize her child and to elaborate on her choice in terms of specific incidents. Descriptions of child and maternal behavior in emotional situations (happy, angry, fearful, painful) were also requested. In the next section of the interview, mothers were asked to describe situations that required negotiations about attachment-autonomy issues (conflicting goals) and separation issues (bedtime, substitute care). One intergenerational question was also included ("In what way is the relationship you have with your child similar to or different from the relationship you had to your own mother?"). The interview ended with the mother's thoughts about her future relationship with the child. Interview protocols were evaluated as a whole by applying a scale assessing insight/sensitivity. This scale was significantly related to attachment measures at 18, 25, and 37 months. Preliminary analyses also show that it may also be possible to match the avoidant and ambivalent types of insecurity in the child with different maternal response styles to the interview.

## SUMMARY

The findings from the observational studies of parent-infant or parent-toddler interactions, and from interview and storytelling studies with preschoolers, kindergartners, and adults paint a remarkably consistent picture. The observational studies conducted with infants and toddlers indicate that in relationships in which the child's attachment or autonomy signals consistently go unheeded or are consistently misread there will be interference with the balance between attachment and exploratory behavior as described by Lieberman and Pawl (in press) and interference with open parent-child and child-parent communication because defensively excluded material cannot participate in error-correcting feedback. Attachment theory would further lead us to predict that inadequate communication patterns are likely to give rise to inadequate internal working models of self and attachment partner.

Studies with preschoolers, kindergartners, and adults, based on projective material and interviews, support the conclusions drawn from the interactional studies. Secure children, parents, and young adults are able to communicate about attachment issues with ease and to discuss attachment relationships coherently without necessarily insisting that they or their attachment figures are perfect. By contrast, insecure-avoidant children and adults (those dismissing of attachment) tend to defend themselves against closeness by processes that restrict the flow of ideas about attachment relationships intrapsychically and interpersonally. They tend to give an aloof and nonempathic impression. At the same time, they have a strong tendency to idealize parents or themselves when giving general statements without being able to illustrate these global judgments with autobiographical memories (the memories may be absent or may contradict the generalizations). The third major pattern is characterized by ambivalence to reunion in infancy and by preoccupation with conflictual attachment issues in adulthood. The corresponding patterns for children have not been as easy to pinpoint. In a fourth group, the underlying problem in the adults seems to be unresolved mourning for a childhood attachment figure. Infants of these parents were classified as disorganized/disoriented during the Strange Situation. At 6 years of age the same children were overly controlling of the relationship—using either a caregiving or a punitive mode of interaction with the parent in the separation-reunion procedure (Main & Cassidy, in press). It is important to note, however, that disorganization in thought about attachment did show up the children's responses to projective tests at 6 years of age.

Taken as a whole, the empirical findings reviewed in this section also allow us to understand more clearly how *parents'* internal working models of attachment relations may indirectly (through communicative signals) influence the development of their children's working models. Even before their infants are born, parents have working models of themselves as parents and of the unborn infant (Zeanah, Keener, Stewart, & Anders, 1985). On the basis of Main's findings (as well as clinical writings to be discussed in the next section), we may speculate that these anticipatory parental working models of the infant are strongly influenced by the parents' experiences in childhood, although later relationship experiences and other factors are also likely to play a role. When the parent encounters the actual infant, these anticipatory working models are imposed on the new relationship, but they must be corrected and fine-tuned to fit the individual baby's temperament and needs. This will be relatively easy if the new parents' internal working models are coherent, well organized, and easily accessible to awareness with a minimum of defensive exclusion. It will be much more difficult if the parents' internal working models are inadequate, not easily accessible to awareness, and therefore not easily adaptable. In this case parents will not be able to interpret the actual infant's signals appropriately. Sensitive parental responsiveness, as defined by Ainsworth (Ainsworth et al., 1974), requires that the parent be ready to take the baby's perspective, to notice what the baby's goals are, and to respond to them empathically. Without adequate internal working models of self as parent in relation to a specific infant, the parent could not provide appropriate empathic feedback or validate the infant's signals; and without this feedback and validation, the infant's budding working models are likely to become biased, distorted, and inflexible from the outset. This line of reasoning suggests that "good enough" parental sensitivity is directly involved in the adequacy of the infant's emerging working models.

Whereas the new research on attachment from infancy to adulthood offers us a coherent framework for conceptualizing the development of attachment at the representational level, much further work remains to be done on how working models are organized, how they develop, and how they change (see also Thompson, in press). Toward this end, we can draw on useful ideas from several other fields of study that will be discussed in the second major section of this chapter.

## Elaborating the Construct of Internal Working Models

Four topics will be covered. First, I will consider in more detail how recent studies of representational processes might help us understand the structure and functioning of working models. Second, I will examine studies of social cognition with a view to better understanding the developing complexity and organization of working models. Third, I will discuss the question of a unified working model of self in the context of different relationships, using the framework of classical writings on the social self. I will conclude the chapter by considering structural change in working models in light of theories of therapeutic change.

As previously noted, Bowlby's view of representation as internal working model was inspired by an insightful book, *The Nature of Explanations* (Craik, 1943). Craik offered a conceptualization of representational processes that emphasizes their dynamic, structural, and functional qualities:

> By a model we thus mean any physical or chemical system which has a similar relation-structure to that of the process it imitates. By "relation-structure" I do not mean some obscure nonphysical entity which attends the model, but the fact that it is a physical working model which works in the same way as the process it parallels. . . . . If the organism carries a "small-scale model" of external reality and of its own possible actions within its head, it is able to try out various alternatives, conclude which is the best of them, react to future situations before they arise, utilize the knowledge of past events in dealing with the present and future, and in every way to react in a much fuller, safer and more competent manner to the emergencies which face it. (p. 61)

Interestingly, psychoanalysts from Freud onward have advanced ideas that presuppose a theory of representation based on internal models or simulations, although none of them went on to develop such a theory in a systematic way. For example, Freud (cited in Hartmann, 1958) described thinking as an *experimental action* using small quantities of energy. Likewise, Hartmann contends that "in higher organisms, *trial activity* is increasingly displaced into the interior of the organism, and no longer appears in the form of motor action directed toward the external world."

Along similar lines, psychoanalytic object relations theorists seem to conceptualize representations of self and other as internalized chunks of experienced relationship patterns. For example, Sullivan (1953) speaks of "personifications of mother and me" and of "me-you patterns." Fairbáirn (1952) proposed the notion of internal (love) objects and associated portions of the ego, Sandler and Sandler (1978) mention "interactions between self and object representations" that make unconscious dialogues with love objects possible, and Kernberg (1976) talks of self-object-affect units (positive or negatively toned interaction schemas) that become the basis of self and object representations. In advancing the idea that an individual constructs internal working models of self and attachment figure, Bowlby was therefore not alone among psychoanalytic thinkers.

## EVENT REPRESENTATION AND SCRIPT THEORY AS RELATED TO INTERNAL WORKING MODELS

The concept of an internal working model requires a representational system that operates with event- or agent-action-object structures rather than with static images, concept hierarchies, and logical operations alone. Piaget's (1954, 1951) explanation of sensorimotor development seemed to have the makings of such a theory. By acting on the world the world the infant was said to develop schemas into which related experiences could subsequently be assimilated, but which could also be refined or accommodated so as to better fit external reality. This approach might have been carried over into a representational theory whose primary building blocks are actions on objects and interactions with people. However, in his studies beyond the sensorimotor period, Piaget ceased to be interested in the representation of events or interpersonal interactions (figurative representation), devoting his energies primarily to clarifying the development of operative thinking (logico-mathematical mental processes dealing with time, space, causality, and conservation of quantity). Though highly important, operational thought cannot in and of itself explain the human ability to simulate the external world internally. Recent theories with roots in Craik's (1943) propositions about working models, and in Bartlett's (1933) prior work on the role of schemas in memory can, however, make a helpful contribution toward sharpening the concept of working models.

Johnson-Laird (1983)—quite independently of Bowlby—rediscovered Craik's (1943) writings about representational processes conceived as mental working models and brought the term into wider circulation among cognitive scientists. Taking an evolutionary perspective that is very congenial to attachment theory, Johnson-Laird pointed out that mental models afford an organism considerable survival advantage by permitting both insightful and foresightful behavior. The more adequately these models can simulate relevant structural-causal relationships found in the external world, the better the potential planning and responding capacity of an organism (see also Mandler, 1986). Humans and the higher primates differ from other animals not only in their ability to construct more complex working models of the physical and social world, but in their capacity to create internal working models of themselves, including (at least in humans) their own and their partners' representational processes. It is this ability that underlies the development of reflective self-awareness, of perspective taking, and of the capacity for intersubjectivity, to which I will turn in the next section.

In work with adults, Johnson-Laird and his colleagues discovered that reasoning is affected by task content (Johnson-Laird, Legrenzi, & Legrenzi, 1972; Wason & Johnson-Laird, 1972). If a problem is presented within a concrete familiar framework that facilitates the construction of a mental model of the problem situation, the subject's inferential performance is very much better than if reasoning must rely on abstract symbolic information alone. Johnson-Laird (1983) hypothesized that the required mental models are constructed, tested out, and revised in working memory from elements (people, objects) and relations (spatial, temporal, causal) stored in the long-term knowledge base. Note that Johnson-Laird is using the term mental model in two senses: as structures in short-term and long-term memory. His research, however, is primarily concerned with the construction of working models in short-term memory. The structure of knowledge stored in long-term memory is not extensively discussed, although Johnson-Laird seems to imply it too is model or schema based.

In contrast to Johnson-Laird, theorists building on Bartlett's (1933) work (Mandler, 1979, 1983; Nelson & Gruendel, 1981; Nelson & Ross, 1982; Schank, 1982; Schank & Abelson, 1977) focused most of their efforts on defining the schematic structure of long-term memory. They postulated that the representational system consists of mental structures called *event schemas* or *scripts* that summarize skeletal information about recurring similar events. An event schema or script is a sequential structure with "slots" for specific agent roles, for action sequences motivated by specific goals and emotions, for recipients of actions, and for locales. Relevant scripts are "instantiated" or called up when the person experiences familiar events, and they help predict what may happen next. Note that, like Johnson-Laird, Schank does not explicitly distinguish between schemas held or constructed in short-term memory and those held in long-term memory, although he seems to imply such a distinction in his notion of script "instantiation" wherein a schema in long-term memory is called up if it fits the current situation.

Schank (1982), in a revised formulation of early script theory (Schank & Abelson, 1977) further refined his earlier ideas. He now argues that information derived from episodic or autobiographical memories is reprocessed, partitioned, cross-indexed, and summarized into a variety of different schema categories, each of which preserves some aspect of the spatial-temporal-causal structure of experiences in the external world. Only some of these structures order mini-event representations into coordinated longer event sequences (such as the "script" of going to a restaurant or putting a baby to bed); others summarize information from similar mini-events (e.g., all feeding situations regardless of context), and yet others generalize across different event sequences (e.g., all caregiving routines). Schank's new conceptualization deliberately blurs the distinction between episodic and semantic memory originally proposed by Tulving (1972, 1983) and substitutes multiply interconnected hierarchies composed of schemas that range from being very experience near to being very general and abstract. These hierarchies are constructed and continually revised and refined on the basis of new input (for related ideas see Nelson, 1986).

Although event schemas at all levels of abstraction are open to revision, the extent of possible restructuring is restricted because old schemas guide the processing of new information. Past encoding (memory) determines how the next similar experience is decoded (processing). Unexpected events, if noticed, are registered as exceptions. Moreover, because information from an experienced episode will be parsed in many ways, the resulting data are fed into schemas at many levels. These parsing and ordering processes can thus explain how events experienced with attachment figures can affect what I have called normative working models of the caregiving role (as opposed to a specific parent) that are part of a person's knowledge base on working model of the world.

Although Schank was not concerned with biased or incomplete processing, I propose that his revised theory of event representation can also shed new light on defensive phenomena. If portions of autobiographical memories enter into cross-referenced schemas at many hierarchical levels, it is possible to see how material that has been defensively excluded from recall as an autobiographical memory might still influence schema formation at other levels. Moreover, once the lines of communication within an individual's representational system are broken, biased or incomplete processing is bound to follow because existing schemas guide processing of new experience (Erdelyi, 1985).

**The development of event representation.** Early studies on event representation and scripts were restricted to adult subjects, raising the question whether these theories could be extended downward to children, perhaps even to infants. Evidence shows that this is feasible.

Recent studies of infant memory have documented that cued recall of motor acts is possible as early as 3 months (e.g., Rovee-Collier & Fagan, 1981; Rovee-Collier & Lipsitt, 1981). Based on these results, Stern (1985) has postulated that infants may register routine interaction sequences with a caregiver as generalized episodes that represent *small coherent chunks of lived experience, storing sensations, goals, affect, and actions by self and other in a temporal-physical-causal relationship*. Stern calls these generalized memory structures RIGs, (representations of interactions that have been generalized) in analogy to Nelson's concept of GERs (generalized event representations; see Nelson & Gruendel, 1981). To avoid conceptual confusion, however, note that Stern's use of the term representation in this context is nontraditional and does not imply recall memory.

RIGS storing and guiding the processing of attachment experiences would be interactive events such as cuddling or molding to a warm body and being cuddled, or looking into another's eyes and feeling soothed. Stern hypothesizes that RIGs are accessed whenever a familiar self-with-other episode recurs, suggesting that RIGs might be the sensorimotor basis for the construction of representational interaction schemas that can be imaged or verbalized independent of action. The notion of RIGs is supported by studies showing that infants anticipate another person's behavior in context. For example, Izard (1978) reported that 8-month-old infants cringe in fear while their arms are being prepared for an injection and subsequently refuse to interact with the nurse responsible for the unpleasant experience. At this age infants also display anticipatory smiles during peek-a-boo games *before* a playmate reappears from behind a cloth (Sroufe & Wunsch, 1972) and anticipatory distress when an attachment figure prepares to depart (Piaget, 1954).

With the onset of representation, toddlers demonstrate in their pretend play and language that information about everyday events is available to them in schematic form. In pretending, infants reenact events from everyday life, beginning with single acts such as sleeping or eating performed on themselves and progressing to complex sequenced acts that include others (people or dolls) as actors and recipients (see Bretherton, 1984, for a review). The ability to encode simple events in language develops concurrently (e.g., Shore, O'Connell, & Bates, 1984; Greenfield & Smith, 1976).

By 3 years of age, children's event schemas can be investigated more formally by asking them to describe routine events such as having dinner or attending a birthday party. Nelson and Gruendel (1981) found that the 3-year-olds they interviewed showed a remarkably good grasp of the order in which the action sequences of routine events take place. This was especially true when event sequences were causally related (e.g., the candles on the birthday cake must be blown out, and it must be cut before it can be eaten). Interestingly, autobiographical memories of an everyday event (such as eating dinner last night, not eating dinner in general) could not easily be elicited. Three-year-olds tended to produce dinner scripts instead of talking about a specific dinner episode. At this early age, an event had to be truly extraordinary (going to the circus for the first time) to be recalled as an episodic or autobiographical memory. Moreover, young children did not seem to require a large number of exposures to an event in order to construct a schema of it (Fivush, 1984; Price & Goodman, 1985). Indeed, when children expect an event to be repeated (like going to school), they seem to use the impersonal "you" and the timeless present tense usually reserved for scripts even to describe the first day at school ("and then you do reading or something"; Fivush, 1984). The major difference between older and younger children was that the older ones invariably described more actions. In addition their statements tended to be more probabilistic (they reported what might, but need not happen;

Fivush & Slackman, 1986). Older children were also better at correcting script-based stories that had out-of-order action sequences. Four-year-olds merely tended to leave out the misordered actions on retelling the stories, while the 5-year-olds reinserted them in the appropriate places or transformed them to make better sense (Hudson & Nelson, 1983).

**Event schemas and working models of specific relationships.** Until now, studies of event representation have been concerned with normative findings (how human of all ages process event information). It may therefore not be immediately obvious how these insights could apply to individual differences in internal working models of self and caregiver in a specific attachment relationship. This issue is easily resolved, however, when we consider that nothing in these theories precludes the idea that an individual develops schemas of interaction with specific partners and that these schemas can be arranged in a hierarchy.

In this connection I have found Epstein's (1973, 1980) notion of the self-concept especially useful. Epstein contends that the self-concept (internal working model of the self) is best understood as part of an individual's theory of reality. A self-theory, according to Epstein, consists of several hierarchically organized postulate systems into which new experiences are assimilated. Epstein's formulation is strikingly close to Bowlby's notion of complementary working models of self and attachment figure (Ricks, 1985). A person with high self-esteem "in effect carries within him a loving parent, one who is proud of his successes and acceptant of his failures," whereas the person with low self-esteem "carries within him a disapproving parent who is harshly critical of his failures" (Epstein, 1980, p. 106). Translating Epstein into the language of event representation, we can now conceptualize working models of self and parents as related schema hierarchies derived from actual parent-infant and parent-child transactions (see also Markus, 1977). On the lowest level would be interactional schemas that are very experience-near ("When I hurt myself, my mommy always comes to comfort and help me"). Above this level would be more general schemas ("My mommy is usually there for me when I need her") that subsume a variety of lower-level schemas of need-fulfilling events with the mother. Somewhere near the top of the hierarchy would be both "My mother is a loving person" and "I am loved," in turn subsuming a variety of general schemas. Note that I am advocating not a tri-level system, but one with multiple levels of unknown number. I *am* proposing that we go beyond a notion of working models as composed of a two-level system based on autobiographical (episodic) and general (semantic) memory. To think of internal working models of self and attachment figure as multiple-level schema hierarchies will, I think, make the concept more amenable to detailed study.

Questions that remain to be addressed concern how these working models may increase in complexity and internal coherence with development. These questions will be addressed in the next two sections.

## INTERNAL WORKING MODELS AND SOCIAL COGNITIVE DEVELOPMENT

Two questions about the development of internal working models of the self and of attachment figures are of special interest. The first concerns the increasingly complex psychological information about self and other that comes to be built into working models (see also Thompson, in press). The second question regards the notion of working models as hierarchical organizations of interpersonal schemas as it applies to children (see also Harter, 1983).

**Understanding self and other (developing a theory of mind).** Bowlby (1969) proposed that the infant is prepared from birth to interact with a human caregiver who responds appropriately to the infant's signals. On the basis of research then available, he postulated that newborns do not yet have a capacity to distinguish one caregiver from another, but that discriminating responsiveness develops during the first six months and prepares the way for attachment proper between 7 and 9 months of age, when disruptions of the bond become much more disturbing (Yarrow, 1967). At the same time, infants master intentionality, means-end relations, and object permanence, all of which are prerequisites for constructing internal working models of self and caregiver in the attachment relationship.

Acquiring these working models ultimately enables the toddler to enter into what Bowlby has called a goal-corrected partnership with the caregiver in which both members of the dyad can negotiate plans regarding attachment and autonomy (see also Greenberg & Speltz, in press). Bowlby did not venture speculations about the young infant's sense of self, or about precursors to internal working models.

*Infancy (0–9 months).* Since 1969 there has been a surge of interest in infant perception, social cognition, and language acquisition that permits us to develop empirically grounded working hypotheses about the young infant's social understanding. Stern's review of that research (1985) led him to advance a theory about the development of the sense of self and of interpersonal relatedness that is very compatible with attachment theory, although it originated from his interest in mother-infant play rather than from consideration of the mother as an emotional support system. Stern cites empirical research in support of the view that even newborn infants can begin to extract self-invariance and other-invariance from the stream of experience, invalidating the traditional notion (e.g., Mahler, Pine, & Bergman, 1975; Piaget, 1951) that there is ever a period during postnatal life when self and external world are completely confused. I will not review Stern's careful account of infants' sense of *core self, core other,* and *core relatedness.* Instead, I will concentrate on the latter part of the first year when psychological understanding of self and other seems to take a giant leap.

*The intersubjective infant (9–14 months).* A developmental spurt around 9 months of age enables infants to realize—at some rudimentary level—that inner experiences, attention, intentions, and affective states can be shared with another person (e.g., Bretherton, McNew, & Beeghly-Smith, 1981; Feinman, 1982; Klinnert, Campos, Sorce, Emde, & Svejda, 1983; Trevarthen & Hubley, 1979).

For example, 9-month-olds reliably and easily follow their mothers' line of regard (Scaife & Bruner, 1975), whereas such shared reference is only sporadically observed before 9 months. At the same time infants begin to follow their mothers' pointing gestures, although this ability is still fairly limited at 9 months (Murphy & Messer, 1977). A related change occurs in the function of emotion signaling. From 6 to 9 months of age infants respond to an adult's negative facial-vocal displays with frowning, crying, or sobering, in-

terpreted by Charlesworth and Kreutzer (1973) as emotional resonance to the adult's signals. After about 9 months, however, infants
seem to understand that a partner's emotional expressions can convey information about a third event. A 10-month-old is much less
likely to approach a remote-controlled robot if the mother frowns
when the child looks up to reference her face than if she smiles
(Campos & Stenberg, 1981; Feinman, 1982). During the same period
of development, Bates, Camaioni, and Volterra (1975) observed the
onset of intentional communication. In 9- to 12-month-olds such intent is inferred from a variety of behaviors, such as looking back and
forth from a pointed-at object to a person (as if making sure that the
partner is attending to the signal), substituting one gesture for another if the first gesture does not work (known as repair of failed
messages), and ritualizing previously instrumental gestures (e.g.,
using a noninstrumental brushing-aside motion to indicate an object is not wanted).

This newfound ability to share interest in or affect about a joint
topic has also been observed in studies of mother-infant play. Nine-
month-olds, but not younger infants, can use a toy as the topic of interaction with the mother and begin to show sophisticated understanding of maternal instructions. When mother demonstrates how
a peg is to be inserted into a bottle by repeatedly lifting the peg in
and out of its mouth, the infant—rather than copying this motion
literally—tries to drop the peg into the bottle (Trevarthen & Hubley,
1979). Along similar lines, Ross and Kay (1980) found that in turn-
taking games with an unfamiliar adult companion 12-month-olds re-
sorted to a variety of strategies for reviving reciprocal games. In the
Ross and Kay paradigm the adult "stopped playing the game" for 10
seconds after smooth turn taking had been established. Infants responded to this interruption by looking back and forth from adult to
toy, by partially or fully retaking their own turn and then waiting, or
by holding up their hands to invite a turn from the adult (in object
exchange games). These signals occurred almost exclusively during
game interruptions. The infants also watched the adult playmate's
face more during interruptions, whereas during the normal phases
of the game they looked more at her hands and at game-related objects. The data provided by Ross (1980) revealed that all infants had
several of these strategies at their disposal. In view of the variety of

behaviors infants used to reinstitute interrupted games, it makes sense to assume that they expected the partner to understand their signals.

In sum, infants' affective, vocal, and gestural communications seem intended to attract the addressee's attention and direct it to topics of mutual interest. At the same time infants begin to understand others' communications to them as messages. Bretherton and Bates (1979) suggest that the most parsimonious explanation for these phenomena is to assume that by the end of the first year infants have acquired a rudimentary "theory of mind" or ability to impute mental states to self and other (see Premack & Woodruff, 1978) and further, that they have begun to understand that one mind can be interfaced with another through conventional or mutually comprehensible signals.

The phenomenon of maternal affect attunement that emerges concurrently with intentional intersubjectivity is interpreted by Stern (1985) as the caregiver's response to these changes in the baby's psychological understanding. Before 9 months, mothers tend to imitate their babies' behavior literally. After 9 months mothers match the affective information carried in the temporal beat, the intensity contour, the duration or spatial shape of the baby's behavior, but they often do so in a different modality than the infant employs. For example, a mother may attune to her baby's fast, energetic, joyful up-and-down arm movements by recreating the same affect through fast, undulating, energetic, and joyful vocalizations (see Stern, 1985, for further details). Stern suggests that such cross-modal reverberations focus the infant's attention on the intersubjectively shared affect rather than on joint action.

Individual differences in affect attunement are important factors in the developing relationship. Some mothers consistently "underattune" or "overattune" to certain infant behaviors, falling short of or exaggerating their infants' affect in their attunement to it. If done consistently, this may undermine infants' ability to pay attention to their own inner states. Indeed, consistent overattunement (exaggerated "overdone" attunement to infant behavior) can, as Stern sees it, become a form of emotional theft, where mothers model for their infants how and how intensely they ought to feel, as opposed to affirming how the infants do feel. By contrast, maternal failure to attune to particular states at all means that these states will remain isolated from the interpersonal context and may be experienced as something that cannot be shared. For Stern, maternal attunement thus plays an important role in infants' developing ability to engage in open emotional communication.

The fit between Stern's theoretical formulations and the Grossmanns' findings on parent-infant communication in secure and insecure attachment relationships is striking (Escher-Graueb & Grossmann, 1983; Grossmann & Grossmann, 1984; Grossmann et al., 1986). The lighthearted mothers described by Grossmann and Grossmann are, in Stern's terminology, engaged in overattunement. The mothers of insecure-avoidant infants described by Escher-Graueb and Grossmann seem to be engaging in nonattunement to stressful signals. Furthermore, Stern's arguments need not be restricted to affect attunement but can easily be extrapolated to other forms of communication between mother and infant.

*The verbal stage (early development).* This account brings us to the onset of language. Although the intentional attention-getting and directing signals from the preverbal stage continue to play a crucial role, inserting single words into gestural message structures can lead to more precise interfacing of minds (for a review see Bretherton, 1988).

Infants' capacity for intentional intersubjectivity becomes even more striking once they have acquired a variety of object names and relational words (such as all gone, more, and uh-oh). Greenfield and Smith (1976) found that toddlers tended to use these two types of words differentially. If mother and child had already established a focus of joint attention, the children commented on the action component of the situation with a relational word. If a joint topic of attention had not yet been established, the infants labeled the object first (see also Scollon, 1979). This culminates, about the middle of the second year, in the ability to engage in simple conversations about absent objects and people in which one partner supplies the topic while the other comments on it (Bloom, 1973).

In light of the level of psychological understanding implied in toddlers' management of communicative situations, it is perhaps not surprising that by 18 months some of them begin to label internal states in appropriate contexts. The earliest explicit references are to hunger, pain, disgust, ability, volition, and moral approval. This ability, along with the acquisition of the shifting pronouns (you and I), mushrooms during the third year (Bretherton et al., 1981; Dunn, Bretherton, & Munn, 1987; Kagan, 1981). Concurrent developments are the capacity to express empathy toward distressed others (e.g., Zahn-Waxler, Radke-Yarrow, & King, 1979; for a review see Thompson, 1987), to use dolls as active partners in symbolic play (Bretherton, O'Connell, Shore, & Bates, 1984; Wolf, Rygh, & Altshuler, 1984), and to recognize the self in a mirror (Lewis & Brooks-Gunn, 1978). Bretherton and Beeghly (1982) have attributed this shift to a gradual transition from an implicit theory of mind to a more explicit one. Although this transition makes deeper relations with others possible, the acquisition of verbal labels for inner experiences also has its dangers. Stern (1985) points out that some experiences of core and intersubjective relatedness cannot easily be recreated on the verbal level. In addition, verbal children may be offered interpretations of events that do not coincide with their own experience of them (see also Bowlby, 1973), leading to intrapsychic contradictions between verbal working models that are accessible to conscious reflection and nonverbal working models that may become defensively excluded from awareness.

*Transition to early childhood (2–3 years).* The proposition that children in the second year begin to entertain a more explicit theory of mind was initially based on findings obtained through mothers who were trained to record their children's utterances about internal states in everyday contexts (Bretherton & Beeghly, 1982; Ridgeway, Waters, & Kuczaj, 1985). These results were subsequently corroborated through direct observation of family conversations in the home (Dunn et al., 1987).

Bretherton and Beeghly (1982) found that by 28 months a majority of their sample of 30 children used a fairly rich vocabulary to discuss internal states. Almost all talked about perceptions, sensations, physiological states, and volition/ability. About two thirds of the sample labeled at least some emotions. Only a few children used terms referring to moral judgment (except for the ubiquitous good/bad distinction), and utterances about cognitive processes were even rarer, although these become more common after 30 months (Shatz, Wellman, & Silber, 1983). There was a tendency for the 28-

month-olds to attribute internal states to themselves before they imputed them to others, but the lag was very slight. In addition, many of the children were able to converse about past or anticipated states.

Perhaps most intriguing, in terms of internal working models, was the finding that toddlers made causal statements about internal states. "Causal" in this context does not mean that the utterances invariably contained causal connectives like "so," "because," or "if," but means that they referred to internal states in causally related sequences ("Grandma mad [because] I wrote on wall"). Hood and Bloom (1979) provide detailed justification for interpreting such utterances as causal. Three types of causal statements about internal states occurred: utterances about the events or actions that precede or cause a particular state; utterances about negative states as motivators or causes of subsequent behavior; and utterances explaining an emotion in terms of a related mental state or in terms of behavioral/expressive correlates (e.g., "Katie not happy face, Katie sad"). The underlying causal notion in the last type is the logical inference "Katie looks unhappy; this makes me think she must be sad." Data from a project by Radke-Yarrow and Zahn-Waxler (1973) corroborate and extend the earlier findings (see Bretherton, Fritz, Zahn-Waxler, & Ridgeway, 1986, for a review).

Finally, there is evidence that 2- to 3-year-olds are able to impute emotions and intentions to themselves, dolls, and playmates in make-believe play as well as to manipulate parents' and siblings' feeling states (Dunn et al., 1987; Wolf, Rygh, & Altshuler, 1984; reviewed in Bretherton et al., 1986).

Although some investigators (e.g., Shatz, 1983) have questioned whether it is advisable to use the term "theory of mind" in describing toddlers' speech about internal states, Wellman (1988) concurs that such a case can be made for 2 ½-year-olds. Not satisfied with Premack and Woodruff's (1978) simpler definition, Wellman proposed that three criteria must be met before one may impute an explicit theory of mind to an individual. First, the individual must have basic constructs or categories for defining reality; second, these basic constructs or categories must be organized into a coherent system of interrelationships; and third, the individual must have developed a causal-attributional framework of human behavior. Do young children have a theory of mind in this sense?

Wellman's criteria are met by some of the 28-month-olds in the Bretherton and Beeghly (1982) study. For example, some of the children distinguished real from nonreal ("Is that monster real?" "It's only pretend"), some defined one mental state in terms of another (looking unhappy = sadness), and many talked about causes and consequences of such mental states as emotions (sad, happy, scared, mad) and physiological states (e.g., hunger, thirst, and disgust). Furthermore, in a study of mental verb acquisition, Shatz et al. (1983) were able to demonstrate that utterances that distinguish between reality and internal states become quite frequent during the second half of the third year.

By 3 years of age more formal questioning techniques can be attempted, yielding even more persuasive data. In his interviews of 3-year-olds, Wellman found that they knew a real cookie could be touched, whereas a thought cookie could not (or could be touched only "with my dream hands"). When asked about absent objects as opposed to "pictures in your head" (Estes, Wellman, & Wooley, in press), children aged 3, 4, and 5 years gave different reasons for their inability to touch a real but absent object ("because it's not there") and a thought object ("it's not real"). These findings demonstrate that young children have categories for distinguishing mental from nonmental phenomena, thus satisfying Wellman's first criterion for a theory of mind. In addition, Wellman's 3-year-olds defined mental states by recourse to other mental states ("it's like dreaming"; "people can't see my imagination"), satisfying his second criterion. With respect to the third criterion, a causal explanatory framework, Wellman directs our attention to social cognitive studies of emotional understanding (see Bretherton et al., 1986, for a review). For example, Trabasso, Stein, and Johnson (1981) have shown that children as young as 3 years can produce plausible causes and consequences for a variety of positive and negative emotions (see also Farber & Moely, 1979). Studies of intentionality (Shultz, 1980) have extended our information beyond the emotional realm. For example, 3-year-olds are expert at distinguishing acts that someone meant to perform from mistakes, reflexes, and passive movements. Moreover, the children seemed to think of intentions as causes of behavior. Based on this and similar evidence, Wellman (1988) reasons that 3-year-olds seem to be engaged in the same interpretive enterprise as older children and adults. They do not seem to hold a stimulus-response or mechanistic theory of human behavior. On the other hand, 3-year-olds' theory of mind is more limited than that of older children or adults in a number of important respects.

*Early childhood (4–6 years).* Further progress in children's psychological understanding is dependent on changes in their conception of mind (Chandler & Boyes, 1982; Wellman, in press). The younger child seems to have a theory of mind as a container that holds information. Implicit in much of children's reasoning about cognitions and feelings after 4 years of age, however, is a theory of mind as a processor that construes and interprets information (Perner, 1988).

What are the differences between 3-year-olds' and 4- to 5-year-olds conceptions of mind? Only 4-year-olds are able to ascribe false beliefs to another person. After they have been allowed to glance inside a matchbox filled with candy, 4-year-olds (but not 3-year-olds) will correctly predict that an uninitiated child would wrongly guess its contents to be matches. Along similar lines, after observing another child inspect the inside of a cardboard box, 4- to 5-year-olds give that child credit for knowing the box's contents even though they themselves are still ignorant of it (Wimmer, Hofgrefe, & Perner, 1988). In both cases only the older preschoolers are able to grasp that their truth is not necessarily another child's truth. In addition, 4- to 5-year-olds are able to discuss changes in their representations (what they used to think and what they now think; Gopnik & Astington, 1988) and can give explicit explanations of the appearance/reality distinction. A sponge painted to simulate a rock is now described as "really and truly a sponge" that "looks like a rock to my eyes" (Flavell, Flavell, & Green, 1983). Three-year-olds cannot make this double description.

In the domain of emotional understanding parallel changes occur. Four- to 5-year-olds realize that two children who receive the same gift can feel differently about it (Gove & Keating, 1979). They are also able to reconcile two conflicting emotional cues, such as a child's unhappy expression during a normally happy event such as a birthday party (Gnepp, 1983).

Perner (1988) explains these developments in children's theory of mind by recourse to Johnson-Laird's (1983) view of mental models. Young infants, he suggests, have mental models but cannot yet manipulate them out of context (presentation). Toddlers, by contrast, can rearrange components of mental models (elements and relations holding between them) to create alternative realities, as in pretending, or to predict the future as in anticipation (representation). To achieve this the toddler must be able to do something analogous to copying models and parts of models stored in long-term memory into a working space where they can be manipulated on a trial basis without permanently altering the representational system itself (see also Leslie, 1987, for similar ideas). At about 4 years of age an additional ability, metarepresentation, comes into play. Older preschoolers do not just manipulate alternative models of events, they construct mental models of belief states *about* events: they manipulate mental models of mental models.

After about 7 years of age, further developments in the capacity for metarepresentation (complex forms of conceptual perspective taking) have been observed. Older children are able to think not only about what the other believes or thinks, but about what the other may be thinking about them (Miller, Kessel, & Flavell, 1970). This requires an ability to create and manipulate a mental model of two individuals' belief states about each other. The capacity to construct mental models of mental models also seems to underlie children's ability to understand and respond strategically to others' deceptive intentions in hiding/guessing games (Shultz, 1980), to understand second-order false beliefs (Perner & Wimmer, 1985), and to realize that others as well as the self can be deliberately fooled about what the self feels (Selman, 1981). The same holds for 7- to 9-year-olds' understanding that negative feelings can spill over into subsequent interactions with blameless individuals (Harris, Olthof, & Terwogt, 1981; see also Harris, 1983) and that similar outcomes (success or failure) will be evaluated quite differently depending on the psychological causes assigned to them (Weiner, Graham, Stern, & Lawson, 1982).

Improvements in metarepresentation should lead to enormous improvements in a child's capacity to interpret the motivations and intentions of attachment figures and to forecast, explain, and influence their behavior. So far, however, little is known about the reciprocal effect that social cognitive development and attachment quality have on each other. The only relevant study was undertaken by Marvin and Greenberg (1982), who found that when a mother and her 4-year-old negotiated a plan about her departure from a laboratory playroom, the child did not become distressed during separation. Whether negotiation took place was, in turn, related to the child's performance in a conceptual perspective-taking task. From other studies, there is evidence that such correlations are reflections not just of the child's IQ but of the quality of the parent-child relationship (Light, 1979). Clearly, much further research is needed in this area.

In view of what is now known about children's social understanding, it appears vital that researchers attend to it closely in designing studies of attachment at the representational level. For example, there is evidence that preschoolers have a tendency to blame themselves for their parents' divorce (Wallerstein & Kelly, 1975) and frequently believe that the absent parent does not love them anymore (Neal, 1983). Such misunderstandings are likely to occur even in previously secure parent-child relationships if the child cannot engage in sufficiently high levels of metarepresentation. Moreover, the false initial interpretations may persist unless they are discussed with the child at later stages in development.

**Evidence for the hierarchical structure of working models.** Empirical evidence about the hierarchical organization of working models (discussed in an earlier section) can be gleaned from studies in which children were asked to describe themselves and specific others. The findings are somewhat surprising, in light of preschoolers' fairly sophisticated understanding of false belief, intentions, and emotions reported in the previous section. Perhaps the seemingly discrepant results are due to differences in task difficulty. The previously cited social cognitive studies about emotional and conceptual perspective taking are based on the analysis of situations. By contrast, when children are requested to describe self, friend, or parent they must themselves recall and organize a complex body of information rather than analyze a specific hypothetical event; the former is a more difficult task.

Consistent developmental changes have been noted in how children responded to requests to describe specific children and adults whom they liked or disliked. Livesley and Bromley (1973) reported that 7-year-olds tended to portray these individuals in terms of behavior, possessions, and physical appearance rather than abstract psychological traits. When psychological or evaluative labels were used, they were extremely general (such as "he is very nice"). By 8 years of age, however, children increasingly mentioned differentiated traits and dispositions (instead of merely "nice," others are now "considerate" or "helpful"). In spite of this progress, statements still tended to be strung together in list fashion without conveying a coherent personality description ("He does silly things and is very stupid. He has brown hair and cruel eyes"). It was only after 13 years of age that young people attempted to integrate the available information into coherent descriptions reflecting an individual's uniqueness: "She is always very sensible and willing to help people. Sometimes she gets a bit cross but that doesn't last long and soon she is her normal self" (p. 222).

Damon (1977) observed a similar developmental shift in interviewing children about their best friends. Up to about age 7, children tended to characterize best friends in terms of behavior or very simple traits: "someone who plays with me" or "someone who gives me toys," "someone who is nice (or fun)." However, children over 7 years of age mentioned more abstract concepts such as helping and trusting one another as well as preferred personality traits. Finally, adolescents described best friends as persons who understand one another, share their innermost thoughts and feelings and secrets, and help each other with psychological problems (see also Selman, 1980). Suggesting further differentiation, Rosenberg (1979), in a study of 10- to 18-year-olds, pointed out that the trait labels used by preadolescents tend to focus on character traits (honest, brave) or temperament (lose my temper). By mid-adolescence, individuals incorporate interpersonal traits (friendly, shy) into their statements. Finally, 18-year-olds describe an inner world of attitudes, emotions, wishes, and secrets.

Children's conceptions of self develop along similar lines. Self-descriptions also start out with concrete statements about behavior, appearance, and possessions and progress to abstract, well-organized statements about personality and relationships in adolescence. For example, when Bannister and Agnew (1977) questioned children about differences between themselves and others, they found that 5-year-olds focused on physical features or activities, whereas 9-year-olds mentioned personality traits such as "I'm not quiet," "I have different thoughts." Likewise, in Guardo and Bohan's (1971) study of self-identity in 6- to 9-year-olds, 6-year-olds recognized themselves as distinct human individuals in terms of behavior and appearance. By 9 years of age children realized that their identity rested not only on physical appearance and behavior but also on feelings and attitudes.

Greater integration of seemingly incompatible trait descriptions has also been observed with development, whether children are talking about self or others. For example, Harter (1982) found that preschoolers were unable to understand that a person could have two contradictory traits at the same time—that is, be smart in some respects and dumb in others. Livesley and Bromley (1973) recognized the same tendency for one-sided descriptions in 7-year-olds, for whom self and others were either all good or all bad. By 8 years of age children did allude to contradictory traits, but they merely juxtaposed them without integration ("sometimes he is good and sometimes he is bad"). Only adolescents wove contradictory information into one coherent picture ("she is very reserved, but once you get to know her she is exactly the opposite"). Selman (1980) and Hand (1981) corroborate the Livesley and Bromley findings. Specifically, Hand reported that young children are unable to comprehend how the same person can be both nice and mean, but that adolescents use the concept of intentionality to create a plausible integration of both traits.

The child interview findings I just reviewed suggest that internal working models of self become more differentiated and hierarchically integrated with development, but one must not therefore conclude that young children rely exclusively on concrete behavioral categories in thinking about self and others. As noted above, in reasoning about situations rather than describing personalities, children show considerable understanding of their own and others' thoughts and feelings at an early age. Nevertheless, in terms of what is directly accessible to conscious reflection out of context, working models seem to develop from very simple hierarchical structures during the preschool period into considerably more complex, multi-layered, differentiated, multiply connected hierarchies at adolescence. This suggests that working models should become more difficult to reorganize and reconstruct after adolescence, an issue that needs to be resolved by research (Bowlby, 1973; see also Sroufe, in press).

## INTERNAL WORKING MODELS AND THEORIES OF THE SOCIAL SELF

The classical literature on the social origin of the self (Baldwin, 1911; Cooley, 1902; James, 1890; Mead, 1934) is concordant with Bowlby's (1969) view that internal working models of self and of attachment figures develop out of interpersonal transactions. However, the earlier writers tended to focus on the self or "me" as based on the viewpoint of others (Cooley's looking-glass self). Only Baldwin held the more modern view that concepts of self and other are mutually interdependent, each reciprocally influencing the other. This is in line with current theories of cognition that emphasize that children are not passive receptors but active processors of information. Earlier writers on the social self also share Bowlby's view that a sense of self-worth should be correlated with how well the self is accepted by others.

There are, however, two issues addressed by the classical writers that have not yet been sufficiently considered in recent theorizing about attachment at the representational level. These regard the unity of the self and the construction of what I have called normative working models.

For James (1890) the "me" (working model of self) was not a unified structure but a composite. Because social relations are the origin of "me," James speculated that individuals had to have as many social selves as there were people who carried images of them in their minds and groups of people they cared about. There could be discordant splitting or harmonious integration of the different "mes" (or working models of self in relation to different others), but there was never just one self. In a previous paper (Bretherton, 1985) I asked a related question: How can we conceptualize the internal working model of the self in a child who has a secure relationship with one parent and an insecure relationship with the other? Bowlby (1973) made provision in his theory for discordant working models about the self in the *same* relationship, one defensively excluded and one accessible to awareness, but the question of different "mes" in different attachment relationships has yet to be worked out. The few relevant findings are somewhat contradictory. Some studies report less favorable child outcomes when the relationship to both parents is insecure and intermediate outcomes if the relationship to one parent is insecure while that to the other is secure, suggesting some sort of averaging process (Main & Weston, 1981). Other studies (Main, Kaplan, & Cassidy, 1985) have shown that internal working models of self as assessed in projective tasks at 6 years of age are more closely related to earlier and concurrent attachment security with the mother than with the father. Finally, clinical case studies (Gustafson, 1986) suggest that individuals with unintegrated selves may waver back and forth between working models of self derived from the relationship with the father and with the mother, giving rise to inconsistent behavior that may be incomprehensible to a partner.

Mead (1934) took James's propositions about the integration of different selves a step further. The ability to view the self as object requires that individuals take the role of the other toward themselves or, to use the language of mental models, that they be able to construct models of themselves as viewed by a partner (metarepresentation). This is similar to Cooley's notion of the looking-glass self. Mead, however, unlike the other writers, proposes that there are two developmental stages to this process. First, children learn to take the role of several *particular* others. This ability manifests itself in pretend play, where children are continually taking the attitudes of those who control and nurture them. The second stage, not yet considered by attachment theorists, begins when children learn to participate in rule-governed games that require participants to take the attitude of the group (or generalized other) toward the self. When children participate in a game, each must be ready to take the attitude of everyone else in that game (to see themselves from the stance of all the participants). Furthermore, they must also understand the relation of all the game-related roles to each other. Thus, in taking the attitude of the group toward the self, the individual incorporates the rules of society and integrates the multiple selves that originated in different dyadic relationships with others into a whole unified self. The representational processes whereby this is achieved are not specified in detail; only their outcome is given: an understanding of self and other in a system of relationships. Individuals at this level of understanding should therefore be able to construct normative models of the role of child and parent within the family context (see Byng-Hall, 1985).

We have not even begun to reflect on how to incorporate these ideas into attachment theory, although some of Main's (1985) findings on secure-autonomous adults with insecure childhoods could benefit from a conceptual differentiation of working models representing specific relationships, those representing a person's stance toward attachment relations in general, and those representing a person's understanding of societally shared working models. One would, of course, have to postulate that these are not completely separate models but are part of an interconnected hierarchy, so that higher-level concepts of attachment in general will feed back on the individual's working models of self and other in specific attachment relationships. The theories regarding mental models and event representation laid out in the section on representational processes can begin to provide a conceptual framework for this enterprise.

## Concluding Remarks: Developmental Change and Therapeutic Change in Attachment Relationships

I began this chapter by acknowledging the ethological and psychoanalytical roots of attachment theory. On the basis of ethological thinking, Bowlby interpreted the child's tie to a specific attachment figure as a protective device that enhances survival. So strong is the propensity to become attached that a human child will form an attachment relationship even with a quite inadequate caregiver.

Unfortunately, ethological thinking cannot shed as much light on the psychological aspects of attachment. To account for attachment from the internal, subjective point of view, Bowlby drew on psychoanalytic object-relations theory by introducing the concept of internal working models of self and attachment figure(s), postulating that qualitatively different attachment relationships will lead to qualitatively different working models. Further refinement of these ideas was possible by linking the quality (organization and coher-

ence) of these representational models to the quality of communication in attachment relationships. Work reviewed in an earlier section
has demonstrated that dyadic communication patterns in insecure
and secure dyads differ as early as 1 year of age. Secure parent-infant
dyads are characterized by open emotional communication, whereas
insecure dyads selectively restrict and ignore specific signals, especially signals of distress. In childhood and adulthood, the difference in
communication patterns is reflected not only in how attachment partners communicate with each other, but in whether they can talk *about*
attachment-related issues with emotional openness.

A major advantage of the communication perspective on attachment (pursued by Bretherton, 1987, as well as Grossmann & Grossmann, in press) is that it allows us to understand more clearly the
fundamental ways internal working models differ in secure and insecure attachment relationships. In secure relationships, signals are
mutually acknowledged, allowing for an open flow of emotional information between the partners. As long as this continues, internal
working models of self and other in relationship can become more
complex and be easily updated, at the same time as they become
more integrated and unified. The developmental progression in coherence and integration of the self that is described in the literature
on the development of social understanding (reviewed in the second section of this chapter) is remarkably congruent with what has
been discovered about *secure* individuals at corresponding developmental stages.

The developmental literature is much less helpful in conceptualizing *insecure* attachment relationships. It appears that the infant
whose signals are consistently ignored or misunderstood does not
simply construct an increasingly complex and integrated working
model that realistically reflects the interactions of self and others in a
mutually unsatisfying attachment relationship. Two processes seem
to prevent this. First, the caregiver in such a relationship does not
provide sufficient meaningful feedback to the child's signals (possibly on the basis of his or her own distorted working models), and
second, defensive processes prevent the child from adequately representing parental insensitivity. This line of reasoning suggests that
internal working models developed in insecure attachments not
only are less coherently organized from the beginning, but are also
less likely to become more integrated even as metarepresentational

processes emerge in development. This is so because new information is always processed in terms of existing schemas. To revise and update working models of self and other in insecure attachment relationships is hence a much more difficult feat than it may appear at first. If the arguments just presented are correct, reconstruction of working models cannot be achieved by "lifting repressions" or removing barriers that allow well-encoded but hitherto inaccessible information to come into conscious awareness. Something much more akin to complete reorganization and reinterpretation will be necessary.

## THE TRANSFORMATION OR RECONSTRUCTION OF WORKING MODELS DERIVED FROM INSECURE ATTACHMENT RELATIONSHIPS

Research by Main et al. (1985), Morris (1980), and Ricks (1985) has shown that adults who can give coherent reports of very painful childhood experiences tend to have secure attachment relationships with their own children. In other words, intergenerational transmission of attachment patterns is avoidable, and organizational change in working models of insecure relationships is possible. All short-term longitudinal studies of attachment in infancy, toddlerhood, and childhood have similarly documented changes from insecure to secure attachments and vice-versa, with the proportion of changed attachments small when family circumstances remain fairly constant (Main & Weston, 1981; Wartner & Grossmann, 1987; Waters, 1978) and greater when the family experience is disrupted by stressful life events (Thompson, Lamb, & Estes, 1982; Vaughn, Egeland, Sroufe, & Waters, 1979). More specifically, positive changes have been noted in cases where a mother who has had little social support acquires a stable partner (Sroufe, 1988).

What is missing so far is an explanation of the processes that mediate changes in attachment quality and hence in internal working models. Because subjects in longitudinal studies are not normally seen at frequent enough intervals, investigators must resort to intelligent guesswork in explaining observed changes in attachment quality. Clinicians, on the other hand, have made it their business to understand the processes that bring about change in an individual patient's internal world. Admittedly, clinical data are generally insufficiently systematic to qualify as empirical studies. Nevertheless, some of the insights derived from clinical work may eventually be helpful in the study of relationship changes in everyday situations.

Different schools of therapy use their own terminology, but a remarkable consensus emerges (Gustafson, 1986): A trusting, empathic relationship with a therapist who respects the patient is the first prerequisite for reconstructing internal working models. In the language of attachment theory, an empathic therapist provides the secure base from which the patient can explore his or her internal world and thus go on to create revisions of old working models (Bowlby, 1985): "Our role is in sanctioning the patient to think thoughts that his parents have discouraged or forbidden him to think, to experience feelings his parents have discouraged or forbidden him to experience, and to consider actions his parents have forbidden him to contemplate."

Peterfreund (1983), a psychoanalyst who has espoused Bowlby's notion of internal working models, suggests that therapeutic empathy is nothing other than the ability to enter emotionally and cognitively into another person's internal working models of attachment relationships and of the world. Working models are useful in therapy, Peterfreund points out, because they are experience-near representations that reflect the full richness, strength, depth, vividness, subtlety, and complexity of human thought and feeling. Although many of the processes involved in the activation of working models go on outside awareness, Peterfreund argues that specific processes associated with working models that *are* consciously accessible can be enlisted to assist the clinician in generating images, emotions, fantasies, even nonverbalizable sensorimotor interaction schemas that will provide helpful insight into the patient's working models, always in conjunction with error-correcting feedback from the patient. When other clinical theorists suggest that the therapist should use the patient's own language (Balint, 1968), discover what the patient's representational models of change are (Guidano & Liotti, 1983), or provide a "holding" environment (Winnicott, 1965), they are alluding to the same phenomena as is Peterfreund.

Where theorists of therapeutic change differ is in their view of how actively the therapist should intervene to help the patient accomplish this goal. Some (e.g., Bowlby, 1985) recommend that the therapist's stance be primarily supportive and responsive; others (e.g., Sullivan, 1953) advocate that the analyst challenge the patient's maladaptive interpersonal patterns more directly. In systemic family therapy, all these notions are taken a step further. Instead of coming to understand the working models of one person, the therapist has to understand the working models of the whole family— their scripts and interaction rules (Byng-Hall, 1985). Empathy and acknowledgment of what is positive about the family, known technically as "joining," play a role in this. If the family members feel connected to the therapist, change in working models may be accomplished by co-constructing new views of attachment relations within the family. Alternatively, a therapist may attempt to set up new interaction patterns not previously tried by the family. This experiential technique does not appear to require insight in order to engender relationship change, but the result is the same: changed working models.

I believe that the processes of empathic understanding (sensitive responsiveness), combined with exploration of and cognitive or experiential challenge to a person's inadequate working models, need not be limited to professional therapeutic situations. They can and do occur spontaneously in close friendships or marital relationships, especially during normal psychosocial transitions (courtship, transition to parenthood) or stressful life events. They may even occur in ongoing attachment relationships between parent and child, if a highly stressed parent begins to receive more adequate social support. Whether severely inadequate, rigid, and outdated working models of attachment figures and self can be restructured *only* within a close trusting relationship, as the clinical evidence suggests, is an important topic for future research.

## REFERENCES

Ainsworth, M. D. S. (1967). *Infancy in Uganda: Child care and the growth of love.* Baltimore: Johns Hopkins University Press.

Ainsworth, M. D. S. (1984, April). *Adaptation and attachment.* Paper presented at the International Conference on Infant Studies, New York.

104

Ainsworth, M. D. S., & Bell, S. M. (1969). Some contemporary patterns in the feeding situation. In A. Ambrose (Ed.), *Stimulation in early infancy* (pp. 133–170). London: Academic Press.

Ainsworth, M. D. S., & Blehar, M. C. (1971, April). *Developmental changes in the behavior of infants and their mothers relevant to close bodily contact.* Paper presented at the biennial meeting of the Society for Research in Child Development, Minneapolis.

Ainsworth, M. D. S., Bell, S. M., & Stayton, D. (1974). Infant-mother attachment and social development. In M. P. Richards (Ed.), *The introduction of the child into a social world* (pp. 99–135). London: Cambridge University Press.

Ainsworth, M. D. S., Blehar, M. C., Waters, E., & Wall, S. (1978). *Patterns of attachment: A psychological study of the strange situation.* Hillsdale, NJ: Erlbaum.

Baldwin, J. M. (1911). *The individual and society.* Boston: Goreham.

Balint, M. (1968). *The basic fault: Therapeutic aspects of regression.* London: Tavistock.

Bannister, D., & Agnew, J. (1977). The child's construing of self. In J. Cole (Ed.), *Nebraska symposium on motivation* (pp. 99–125). Lincoln: University of Nebraska Press.

Bartlett, F. C. (1933). *Remembering: A study in experimental and social psychology.* London: Cambridge University Press.

Bates, E., Camaioni, L., & Volterra, V. (1975). The acquisition of performatives prior to speech. *Merrill-Palmer Quarterly, 21,* 205; P1–226.

Bell, S. M., & Ainsworth, M. D. S. (1972). Infant crying and maternal responsiveness. *Child Development, 43,* 1171–1190.

Blehar, M. C., Lieberman, A. F., & Ainsworth, M. D. S. (1977). Early face-to-face interaction and its relation to later infant-mother attachment. *Child Development, 48,* 182–194.

Bloom, L. (1973). *One word at a time.* The Hague: Mouton.

Bowlby, J. (1969). *Attachment and loss. Vol. 1. Attachment.* New York: Basic Books. (2nd rev. ed., 1982)

Bowlby, J. (1973). *Attachment and loss. Vol. 2. Separation.* New York: Basic Books.

Bowlby, J. (1980). *Attachment and loss. Vol. 3. Loss, sadness and depression.* New York: Basic Books.

Bowlby, J. (1985). The role of childhood experience in cognitive disturbance. In M. J. Mahoney & A. Freeman (Eds.), *Cognition and psychotherapy* (pp. 181–200). New York: Plenum Press.

Bretherton, I. (1984). Representing the social world in symbolic play: Reality and fantasy. In Bretherton I. (Ed.), *Symbolic play: The development of social understanding* (pp. 3–41). New York: Academic Press.

Bretherton, I. (1985). Attachment theory: Retrospect and prospect. In I. Bretherton & E. Waters (Eds.), Growing points of attachment theory and research (pp. 3–35). *Monographs of the Society for Research in Child Development, 50* (1–2, Serial No. 209).

Bretherton, I. (1987). New perspectives on attachment relations: Security, communication, and internal working models. In J. Osofsky (Ed.), *Handbook of infant development* (pp. 1061–1100). New York: John Wiley.

Bretherton, I. (1988). How to do things with one word: The ontogenesis of intentional message making in infancy. In M. Smith & J. Lock (Eds.), *The emergent lexicon* (pp. 225–260). New York: Academic Press.

Bretherton, I., & Bates, E. (1979). The emergence of intentional communication. In I. Uzgiris (Ed.), *Social interaction and communication during infancy* (pp. 81–100) (New Directions for Child Development, No. 4). San Francisco: Jossey-Bass.

Bretherton, I., & Beeghly, M. (1982). Talking about internal states: The acquisition of an explicit theory of mind. *Developmental Psychology, 18*, 906–921.

Bretherton, I., Biringen, Z., Maslin, C., Ridgeway, D., & Sherman, M. (1989). Attachment: The parental perspective. *Infant Mental Health Journal*.

Bretherton, I., Fritz, J., Zahn-Waxler, C., & Ridgeway, D. (1986). Learning to talk about emotion: A functionalist perspective. *Child Development, 57*, 529–548.

Bretherton, I., McNew, S., & Beeghly-Smith, M. (1981). Early person knowledge as expressed in verbal and gestural communication: When do infants acquire a "theory of mind"? In M. E. Lamb & L. R. Sherrod (Eds.), *Infant social cognition* (pp. 333–373). Hillsdale, NJ: Erlbaum.

Bretherton, I., O'Connell, B., Shore, C., & Bates, E. (1984). The effect of contextual variation on symbolic play development from 20 to 28 months. In I. Bretherton (Ed.), *Symbolic play* (pp. 271–296). New York: Academic Press.

Bretherton, I., Ridgeway, D., & Cassidy, J. (in press). The role of internal working models in the attachment relationship: Can it be assessed in 3-year-olds? In M. Greenberg, D. Cicchetti, & E. M. Cummings (Eds.), *Attachment during the preschool years: Theory, research, and intervention*. Chicago: University of Chicago Press.

Byng-Hall, J. (1985). The family script: A useful bridge between theory and practice. *Journal of Family Therapy, 7*, 301–305.

Cain, A. C., & Fast, I. (1972). Children's disturbed reactions to parent suicide. In A. C. Cain (Ed.), *Survivors of suicide* (pp. 93–111). Springfield, IL: Charles C. Thomas.

Campos, J. J., & Stenberg, C. R. (1981). Perception, appraisal and emotion: The onset of social referencing. In M. E. Lamb & L. R. Sherrod (Eds.), *Infant social cognition* (pp. 273–314). Hillsdale, NJ: Erlbaum.

Cassidy, J. (1988). The self as related to child-mother attachment at six. *Child Development, 59*, 121–134.

Cassidy, J., Marvin, R. S., and the MacArthur Attachment Workgroup. (1987). *Attachment organization in three- and four-year-olds: Coding guidelines*. Unpublished manuscript, University of Virginia.

Chandler, M. J., & Boyes, M. (1982). Social cognitive development. In B. Wolman (Ed.), *Handbook of developmental psychology* (pp. 387–451). Englewood Cliffs, NJ: Prentice-Hall.

Charlesworth, W. R., & Kreutzer, M. A. (1973). An ethological approach to research on facial expressions. In P. Ekman (Ed.), *Darwin and facial expressions* (pp. 317–334). New York: Academic Press.

Cooley, C. H. (1902). *Human nature and the social order*. New York: Charles Scribner's Sons.

Craik, K. (1943). *The nature of explanation*. Cambridge: Cambridge University Press.

Damon, W. (1977). *The social world of the child*. San Francisco: Jossey-Bass.

Dunn, J., Bretherton, I., & Munn, P. (1987). Conversations about feeling states between mothers and their young children. *Developmental Psychology, 23*, 132–139.

Eichberg, D. (1987, April). *Quality of infant-parent attachment: Related to mother's representation of her own relationship history*. Paper presented at the biennial meetings of the Society for Research in Child Development, Baltimore.

Emde, R. N. (1983). The pre-representational self and its affective core. *Psychoanalytic Study of the Child, 38*, 165–192.

Epstein, S. (1973). The self-concept revisited or a theory of a theory. *American Psychologist, 28*, 404–416.

Epstein, S. (1980). A review and the proposal of an integrated theory of personality. In E. Staub (Ed.), *Personality: Basic aspects and current research* (pp. 82–131). Englewood Cliffs, NJ: Prentice-Hall.

Erdelyi, H. M. (1985). *Psychoanalysis: Freud's cognitive psychology*. San Francisco: W. H. Freeman.

Escher-Graeub, D., & Grossmann, K. E. (1983). *Bindungssicherheit im zweiten Lebensjahr-die Regensburger Querschnittuntersuchung* (Attachment security in the second year of life: The Regensburg cross-sectional study). Research Report, University of Regensburg.

Estes, D., Wellman, H. M., & Wooley, J. D. (in press). Children's understanding of mental phenomena. In H. Reese (Ed.), *Advances in child development and behavior*. New York: Academic Press.

Fairbairn, W. R. D. (1952). *Psychoanalytic studies of the personality*. London: Tavistock.

Farber, E. A., & Moely, B. F. (1979, March). *Inferring others' affective states: The use of interpersonal, vocal and facial cues by children of three age levels*. Paper presented at the biennial meeting of the Society for Research in Child Development, San Francisco.

Feinman, S. (1982). Social referencing in infancy. *Merrill-Palmer Quarterly, 28*, 445–470.

Fivush, R. (1984) Learning about school: The development of kindergartners' school scripts. *Child Development, 55*, 1697–1709.

Fivush, R., & Slackman, E. (1986). The acquisition and development of scripts. In K. Nelson (Ed.), *Event knowledge: Structure and function in development* (pp. 71–96). Hillsdale, NJ: Erlbaum.

Flavell, J., Flavell, E. R., & Green, F. L. (1983). Development of the appearance-reality distinction. *Cognitive Psychology, 15*, 95–120.

George, C., Kaplan, N., & Main, M. (1984). *Adult attachment interview for adults.* Unpublished manuscript, University of California, Berkeley.

Gnepp, J. (1983). Children's social sensitivity: Inferring emotions from conflicting cues. *Developmental Psychology, 19,* 805–814.

Gopnik, A., & Astington, J. W. (1988). Children's understanding of representational change and its relation to the understanding of false belief and the appearance-reality distinction. *Child Development, 59,* 26–37.

Gove, F. L., & Keating, D. (1979). Empathic role-taking precursors. *Developmental Psychology, 15,* 594–600.

Greenberg, M. T., & Speltz, M. L. (in press). Attachment and the ontogeny of conduct problems during the preschool years. In J. Belsky & T. Nezworski (Eds.), *Clinical implications of attachment* (pp. 177–218). Hillsdale, NJ: Erlbaum.

Greenfield, P. M., & Smith, J. H. (1976). *The structure of communication in early development.* New York: Academic Press.

Grossmann, K., Fremmer-Bombik, E., Rudolph, J., & Grossmann, K. E. (in press). Maternal attachment representations as related to patterns of infant-mother attachment and maternal care during the first year. In R. A. Hinde & J. Stevenson-Hinde (Eds.), *Relationships within families.* Oxford: Oxford University Press.

Grossmann, K. E., & Grossmann, K. (1984, September). *The development of conversational styles in the first year of life and its relationship to maternal sensitivity and attachment quality between mother and child.* Paper presented at the Congress of the German Society for Psychology, Vienna.

Grossmann, K. E., & Grossmann, K. (in press). The wider concept of attachment in cross-cultural research. *Human Development.*

Grossmann, K. E., Grossmann, K., & Schwan, A. (1986). Capturing the wider view of attachment: A reanalysis of Ainsworth's Strange Situation. In C. E. Izard & P. B. Read (Eds.), *Measuring emotions in infants and children* (Vol. 2, pp. 124–171). New York: Cambridge University Press.

Guardo, C. J., & Bohan, J. B. (1971). Development of a sense of identity in children. *Child Development, 42,* 1909–1921.

Guidano, V. F., & Liotti, G. (1983). *Cognitive processes and emotional disorders.* New York: Guilford Press.

Gustafson, J. P. (1986). *The complex secrets of brief psychotherapy.* New York: Norton.

Hand, H. (1981). *The development of concepts of social interaction: Children's understanding of nice and mean.* Unpublished doctoral dissertation, University of Denver.

Hansburg, H. G. (1972). *Adolescent separation anxiety: A method for the study of adolescent separation problems.* Springfield, IL: Charles C. Thomas.

Harris, P. L. (1983). Children's understanding of the link between situation and emotion. *Journal of Experimental Child Psychology, 36,* 490–509.

Harris, P. L., Olthof, T., & Terwogt, M. M. (1981). Children's knowledge of emotion. *Journal of Child Psychiatry and Psychology, 22,* 247–261.

Harter, S. (1982). Children's understanding of multiple emotions: A cognitive-developmental approach. In W. F. Overton (Ed.), *The relationship between cognitive and social development*. Hillsdale, NJ: Erlbaum.

Harter, S. (1983). Developmental perspectives on the self-system. In E. M. Hetherington (Ed.), *Handbook of child psychology. Vol. 4. Socialization, personality and social development* (pp. 275–385). New York: John Wiley.

Hartmann, H. (1958). *Ego psychology and the problem of adaptation*. New York: International Universities Press.

Hood, L., & Bloom, L. (1979). What, when, and how about why: A longitudinal study of early expressions in causality. *Monographs of the Society for Research in Child Development, 44* (2, Serial No. 181).

Hudson, J., & Nelson, K. (1983). Effects of script structure on children's story recall. *Developmental Psychology, 19*, 625–635.

Izard, C. E. (1978). Emotions as motivations: An evolutionary-developmental perspective. In R. A. Dienstbier (Ed.), *Nebraska symposium on motivation* (pp. 163–200). Lincoln: University of Nebraska Press.

James, W. (1890). *The principles of psychology* (Vol. 1). New York: Henry Holt.

Johnson-Laird, P. N. (1983). *Mental models*. Cambridge: Harvard University Press.

Johnson-Laird, P. N., Legrenzi, P., & Legrenzi, M. S. (1972). Reasoning and a sense of reality. *British Journal of Psychology, 63*, 395–400.

Kagan, J. (1981). *The nature of the child*. Cambridge: Harvard University Press.

Kaplan, N. (1984). *Internal representations of separation experiences in six year olds: Related to actual experiences of separation*. Unpublished master's thesis, University of California, Berkeley.

Kaplan, N., and Main, M. (1985, April). *Internal representations of attachment at six years as indicated by family drawings and verbal responses to imagined separations*. Paper presented at the biennial meetings of the Society for Research in Child Development, Toronto.

Kernberg, O. (1976). *Object relations theory and clinical psychoanalysis*. New York: Jason Aronson.

Klinnert, M. D., Campos, J. J., Sorce, J. F., Emde, R. N., & Svejda, M. (1983). Emotions as behavior regulators: Social referencing in infancy. In R. Plutchik & H. Kellerman (Eds.), *The emotions. Vol. 2. Emotions in early development* (pp. 57–86). New York: Academic Press.

Kobak, R. R., & Sceery, A. (1988). Attachment in late adolescence: Working models, affect regulation, and perceptions of self and others. *Child Development, 59*, 135–146.

Leslie, A. M. (1987). Pretense and representation: The origins of "theory of mind." *Psychological Review, 94*, 412–426.

Lewis, M., & Brooks-Gunn, J. (1979). *Social cognition and the acquisition of self*. New York: Plenum Press.

Lieberman, A. F., & Pawl, J. H. (in press). Disorders of attachment in the second year: A clinical developmental perspective. In M. Greenberg, D. Cicchetti, & E. M. Cummings (Eds.), *Attachment during the preschool years: Theory, research, and intervention*. Chicago: University of Chicago Press.

Light, P. (1979). *The development of social sensitivity*. Cambridge: Cambridge University Press.

Livesley, W. J., & Bromley, D. B. (1973). *Person perception in childhood and adolescence*. New York: John Wiley.

Mahler, M. S., Pine, F., & Bergman, A. (1975). *The psychological birth of the human infant*. New York: Basic Books.

Main, M. (1985, April). *Adult mental organization with respect to attachment: Related to infant strange situation attachment status*. Paper presented at the biennial meetings of the Society for Research in Child Development, Toronto.

Main, M., & Cassidy, J. (in press). Categories of responses to reunion with the parent at age 6: Predictable from infancy and stable over a one-month period. *Developmental Psychology*.

Main, M., & Hesse, E. (in press). The insecure disorganized/disoriented attachment pattern in infancy: Precursors and sequelae. In M. Greenburg, D. Cicchetti, & E. M. Cummings (Eds.), *Attachment during the preschool years: Theory, research, and intervention*. Chicago: University of Chicago Press.

Main, M., Kaplan, K., & Cassidy, J. (1985). Security in infancy, childhood and adulthood: A move to the level of representation. In I. Bretherton & E. Waters (Eds.), Growing points of attachment theory and research (pp. 66–104). *Monographs of the Society for Research in Child Development, 50* (1–2, Serial No. 209).

Main, M., & Solomon, J. (in press). Procedure for identifying infants as disorganized/disoriented during the Ainsworth Strange Situation. In M. Greenberg, D. Cicchetti, & E. M. Cummings (Eds.), *Attachment during the preschool years: Theory, research, and intervention*. Chicago: University of Chicago Press.

Main, M., & Weston, D. (1981). The quality of the toddler's relationship to mother and father: Related to conflict behavior and readiness to establish new social relationships. *Child Development, 52*, 932–940.

Mandler, G. (1986). *Cognitive psychology*. Hillsdale, NJ: Erlbaum.

Mandler, J. H. (1979). Categorical and schematic organization in memory. In C. R. Puff (Ed.), *Memory organization and structure* (pp. 259–299). New York: Academic Press.

Mandler, J. H. (1983). Representation. In J. H. Flavell & E. M. Markman (Eds.), *Handbook of child psychology. Vol. 3. Cognitive development* (pp. 420–494). New York: John Wiley.

Markus, H. (1977). Self-schemata and processing information about self. *Journal of Personality and Social Psychology, 35*, 63–78.

Marvin, R. S., & Greenberg, M. T. (1982). Preschoolers' changing conception of their mothers: A social-cognitive study of mother-child attachment. In D. L. Forbes & M. T. Greenberg (Eds.), *Children's planning strate-*

110

*gies* (pp. 47–60). (New Directions for Child Development, No. 8), San Francisco: Jossey-Bass.

Matas, L., Arend, R. A., & Sroufe, L. A. (1978). Continuity and adaptation in the second year: The relationship between quality of attachment and later competence. *Child Development, 49*, 547–556.

Mead, G. H. (1934). *Mind, self, and society*. Chicago: University of Chicago Press.

Miller, P. H., Kessel, F. S., & Flavell, J. H. (1970). Thinking about people thinking about people thinking about . . . : A study of social cognitive development. *Child Development, 41*, 613–623.

Morris, D. (1980). *Infant attachment and problem solving in the toddler: Relations to mother's family history*. Unpublished doctoral dissertation, University of Minnesota.

Murphy, D. J., & Messer, D. J. (1977). Mothers and infants pointing: A study of gesture. In R. H. Schaffer (Ed.), *Studies in mother-infant interaction* (pp. 323–354). New York: Academic Press.

Neal, J. (1983). Children's understanding of parental divorce. In L. Kurdek (Ed.), *Children and divorce* (pp. 3–14) (New Directions for Child Development, No. 19). San Francisco: Jossey-Bass.

Nelson, K. (1986). *Event knowledge: Structure and function in development*. Hillsdale, NJ: Erlbaum.

Nelson, K., & Gruendel, J. (1981). Generalized event representations: Basic building blocks of cognitive development. In M. E. Lamb & A. Brown (Eds.), *Advances in developmental psychology* (Vol. 1, pp. 131–158). Hillsdale, NJ: Erlbaum.

Nelson, K., & Ross, G. (1982). The general and specifics of long-term memory in infants and young children. In M. Perlmutter (Ed.), *Naturalistic approaches to memory* (pp. 87–101). San Francisco: Jossey-Bass.

Perner, J. (1988). Developing semantics for theories of mind: From propositional attitudes to mental representation. In J. W. Astington, P. L. Harris, & D. R. Olson (Eds.), *Developing theories of mind* (pp. 141–172). New York: Cambridge University Press.

Perner, J., & Wimmer, H. (1985). "John thinks that Mary thinks that . . .": Attribution of second-order beliefs by 5- to 10-year-old children. *Journal of Experimental and Child Psychology, 39*, 437–471.

Peterfreund, E. (1983). *The process of psychoanalytic therapy: Models and strategy*. Hillsdale, NJ: Analytic Press (Erlbaum).

Piaget, J. (1951). *The origin of intelligence in children*. New York: International Universities Press.

Piaget, J. (1954). *The construction of reality in the child*. New York: Basic Books.

Premack, D., & Woodruff, G. (1978). Does the chimpanzee have a "theory of mind"? *Brain and Behavioural Sciences, 1*, 515–526.

Price, D., & Goodman, G. S. (1985, April). *Preschool children's comprehension of a recurring episode*. Paper presented at the biennial meeting of the Society for Research in Child Development, Toronto, Canada.

Radke-Yarrow, M., Cummings, E. M., Kuczynsky, L., & Chapman, M. (1985). Patterns of attachment in two- and three-year-olds in normal families and families with parental depression. *Child Development, 56,* 884–893.

Radke-Yarrow, M., & Zahn-Waxler, C. (1973). *Developmental studies of altruism.* NIMH Protocol, Clinical Project No. 73-M-02, J00.111.

Ricks, M. H. (1985). The social transmission of parenting: Attachment across generations. In I. Bretherton & E. Waters (Eds.), Growing points of attachment theory and research (pp. 211–227). *Monographs of the Society for Research in Child Development, 50* (1–2, Serial No. 209).

Ridgeway, D., Waters, E., & Kuczaj, S. A. (1985). The acquisition of emotion descriptive language: Receptive and productive vocabulary norms for 18 months to 6 years. *Developmental Psychology, 21,* 901–908.

Rosenberg, M. (1979). *Conceiving the self.* New York: Basic Books.

Ross, H. (1980, April). *Infants' use of turn-alternation signals in games.* Paper presented at the International Conference on Infant Studies, New Haven, CT.

Ross, H. S., & Kay, D. A. (1980). The origins of social games. In K. Rubin (Ed.), *Children's play* (pp. 17–32). San Francisco: Jossey-Bass.

Rovee-Collier, C. K., & Fagan, C. W. (1981). The retrieval of memory in early infancy. In L. P. Lipsitt (Ed.), *Advances in infancy research* (Vol. 1, pp. 225–254). Norwood, NJ: Ablex.

Rovee-Collier, C. K., & Lipsitt, L. P. (1981). Learning, adaptation, and memory. In P. M. Stratton (Ed.), *Psychobiology of the human newborn* (pp. 147–190). New York: John Wiley.

Sandler, J., & Sandler, A. (1978). The development of object relationships and affects. *Journal of Psycho-Analysis, 59,* 285–296.

Scaife, M., & Bruner, J. S. (1975). The capacity for joint visual attention in the infant. *Nature, 253,* 265–266.

Schank, R. C. (1982). *Dynamic memory: A theory of reminding and learning in computers and people.* Cambridge: Cambridge University Press.

Schank, R. C., & Abelson, R. P. (1977). *Scripts, plans, goals and understanding.* Hillsdale, NJ: Erlbaum.

Scollon, R. (1979). An unzippered condensation of a dissertation on child language. In E. Ochs & B. B. Schieffelin (Eds.), *Developmental pragmatics* (pp. 215–227). New York: Academic Press.

Selman, R. L. (1980). *The growth of interpersonal understanding.* New York: Academic Press.

Selman, R. L. (1981). What children understand of the intrapsychic processes. In E. K. Shapiro & E. Weber (Eds.), *Cognitive and affective growth* (pp. 187–215). Hillsdale, NJ: Erlbaum.

Shatz, M. (1983). Communication. In J. H. Flavell & E. M. Markman (Eds.), *Handbook of child psychology, Vol. 3. Cognitive development* (pp. 841–889). New York: John Wiley.

Shatz, M., Wellmann, H. M., & Silber, S. (1983). The acquisition of mental

112

verbs: A systematic investigation of the first reference to mental state. *Cognition, 14,* 301–321.

Shore, C., O'Connell, B., & Bates, E. (1984). First sentences in language and symbolic play. *Developmental Psychology, 20,* 872–880.

Shultz, T. R. (1980). Development of the concept of intention. In W. A. Collins (Ed.), *Minnesota symposia on child psychology* (pp. 131–164). Hillsdale, NJ: Erlbaum.

Sroufe, L. A. (1988). The role of infant-caregiver attachment in development. In J. Belsky & T. Nezworsky (Eds.), *Clinical implications of attachment* (pp. 18–38). Hillsdale, NJ: Erlbaum.

Sroufe, L. A. (in press). Relationships, self, and individual adaptation. In A. J. Sameroff & R. N. Emde (Eds.), *Relationships and disturbances in early childhood: A developmental approach.* New York: Basic Books.

Sroufe, L. A., & Wunsch, J. P. (1972). The development of laughter in the first year of life. *Child Development, 43,* 1326–1344.

Stayton, D. J., & Ainsworth, M. D. S. (1973). Individual differences in infant responses to brief everyday separations as related to other infant and maternal behaviors. *Developmental Psychology, 9,* 226–235.

Stern, D. (1977). *The first relationship: Infant and mother.* Cambridge: Harvard University Press.

Stern, D. N. (1985). *The interpersonal world of the infant.* New York: Basic Books.

Strage, A., & Main, M. (1985). *Attachment and parent-child discourse patterns.* Paper presented at the biennial meetings of the Society for Research in Child Development, Toronto.

Sullivan, H. S. (1953). *The interpersonal theory of psychiatry.* New York: Norton.

Thompson, R. A. (1987). Empathy and emotional understanding: The early development of empathy. In N. Eisenberg & J. Strayer (Eds.), *Empathy and its development.* Cambridge: Cambridge University Press.

Thompson, R. A. (in press). Construction and reconstruction of early attachments: Taking perspective on attachment theory and research. In D. P. Keating & H. Rosen (Eds.), *Constructivist perspectives on atypical development and developmental psychopathology.* Hillsdale, NJ: Erlbaum.

Thompson, R. A., Lamb, M. E., & Estes, D. (1982). Stability of infant-mother attachment and its relationship to changing life circumstances in an unselected middle-class sample. *Child Development, 53,* 144–148.

Trabasso, T., Stein, N. L., & Johnson, L. R. (1981). Children's knowledge of events: A causal analysis of knowledge structure. In *The psychology of learning and motivation* (Vol. 15, 237–282). New York: Academic Press.

Trevarthen, C., & Hubley, P. (1979). Secondary intersubjectivity: Confidence, confiding, and acts of meaning in the first year. In A. Lock (Ed.), *Action, gesture and symbol* (pp. 183–229). New York: Academic Press.

Tulving, E. (1972). Episodic and semantic memory. In E. Tulving & W. Donaldson (Eds.), *Organization of memory* (pp. 382–403). New York: Academic Press.

Tulving, E. (1983). *Elements of episodic memory*. New York: Oxford University Press.

Vaughn, B., Egeland, B., Sroufe, L. A., & Waters, E. (1979). Individual differences in infant-mother attachment at twelve and eighteen months: Stability and change in families under stress. *Child Development, 50,* 971–975.

Wallerstein, J., & Kelly, J. (1975). The effects of parental divorce: Experiences of the preschool child. *Journal of the American Academy of Child Psychiatry, 14,* 600–616.

Wartner, U. G., & Grossmann, K. (1987). *Stability of attachment patterns and their disorganizations from infancy to age six in South Germany*. Unpublished manuscript, University of Virginia.

Wason, P. C., & Johnson-Laird, P. N. (1972). *Psychology of reasoning: Structure and content*. Cambridge: Harvard University Press.

Waters, E. (1978). The reliability and stability of individual differences in infant-mother attachment. *Child Development, 49,* 483–494.

Weiner, B., Graham, S., Stern, P., & Larson, M. E. (1982). Using affective cues to infer causal thoughts. *Developmental Psychology, 18,* 278–286.

Wellman, H. M. (1988). First steps in the child's theorizing about the mind. In J. Astington, P. Harris, & D. Olson (Eds.), *Developing theories of mind* (pp. 64–92). New York: Cambridge University Press.

Wimmer, H., Hofgrefe, J., & Perner, J. (1988). Understanding of informational access as source of knowledge. *Child Development, 59,* 386–396.

Winnicott, D. W. (1965). *The maturational processes and the facilitating environment*. New York: International Universities Press.

Wolf, D. P., Rygh, J., & Altshuler, J. (1984). Agency and experience: Actions and states in play narratives. In I. Bretherton (Ed.), *Symbolic play: The development of social understanding* (pp. 195–217). New York: Academic Press.

Yarrow, L. J. (1967). The development of focused relationships during infancy. In J. Hellmuth (Ed.), *Exceptional infant* (Vol. 1, pp. 227–242). Seattle: Special Child.

Zahn-Waxler, C., Radke-Yarrow, M., & King, R. (1979). Childrearing and children's prosocial initiations towards victims of distress. *Child Development, 50,* 319–330.

Zeanah, C. H., Keener, M. A., Stewart, L., & Anders, T. F. (1985). Prenatal perception of infant personality: A preliminary investigation. *Journal of the American Academy of Child Psychiatry, 24,* 204–210.

# Emotional Competence: How Emotions and Relationships Become Integrated

## Carolyn Saarni
*Sonoma State University*

## Introduction

*T*he idea of emotional competence was first brought to my attention by the sociologist Steve Gordon (1989), who used the term in reference to how children understand emotions in the context of social demands placed on them, so that they become socialized into the culture's valued emotion-meaning systems. Gordon and others, including myself, contend that children learn the emotional behaviors, norms, and symbols of their culture (or subculture) as unintended consequences of social interaction. Gordon's theoretical position is that of a social constructionist—a position I am also disposed toward—and consistent with that position, he sees children as active creators of their emotional life. Thus he states, "Having understood the cultural meaning of an emotion, children become able to act *toward* it—magnifying, suppressing, or simulating it in themselves, and evoking or avoiding it in other people" (1989, p. 324). Gordon firmly embeds emotional experience in relationships and

I would like to express my appreciation to Jane Weiskopf and Michael Crowley for their assistance in two of the studies described in this chapter. Partial support for the preparation of this work was contributed by the Spencer Foundation and the National Science Foundation.

emphasizes the social *process* aspects of emotion in ways that developmental psychologists have been reluctant to investigate explicitly.

Using Gordon's discussion of emotional competence as a starting place, I have expanded the meaning of emotional competence to refer to the demonstration of self-efficacy in the context of emotion-eliciting social transactions. Although concise, this definition is more complex than it first appears. Bandura's (1977) definition of self-efficacy is used here to mean that the individual has the capacity and skills to achieve a desired outcome. When the notion of self-efficacy is then applied to emotion-eliciting social transactions, we are talking about how people can respond emotionally yet simultaneously and strategically apply their knowledge about emotions and their expression to relationships with others so that they can negotiate interpersonal exchanges and regulate their emotional experiences as well.

Self-efficacy has also been linked with self-esteem (e.g., Harter, 1982), and self-esteem is implicated in such an umbrella construct as emotional competence. But I foresee a chicken-and-egg problem here: Which comes first, emotional competence or high self-esteem? If they are correlated but one does not "cause" the other, does something else bring about their concordance? My hunch is that as one develops the skills of emotional competence one also feels better, which reinforces or validates self-esteem and confirms competence in some situation. The more one feels that one's self-esteem is resilient, I suspect, the more willing one becomes to risk one's as yet untested competence in some new situation. If the situations we are referring to are social ones, then resilient self-esteem will facilitate trying out new interpersonal negotiation strategies. Resilient self-esteem also makes the job of regulating emotional experience easier because it reduces anxiety about self-evaluation (cf. Thompson, this volume).

What follows are my attempts to synthesize both empirical data and theoretical positions in order to identify the skills and capabilities that are significant for the progressive development of emotional competence. After enumerating these components and skills of emotional competence, I shall use several excerpts from popular children's literature to illustrate more vividly what varying degrees of emotional competence might look like. (I suspect that many novelists are ahead of psychologists in creating the emotional-cultural scripts we are only beginning to understand from a scientific viewpoint.) Then I shall try to map out the theoretical context for the concept of emotional competence and its relation to models of how emotional organization develops. A likely mediator of emotional development and emotional competence is the individual's naive theory of emotion, which I will also discuss. Last, I shall return to the eleven components and skills noted below and elaborate on each relative to empirical research conducted by myself and others.

## Components and Skills of Emotional Competence

1. Awareness of one's emotional state, including the possibility that one is experiencing multiple emotions, and at even more mature levels, awareness that one might also not be consciously aware of one's feelings owing to unconscious dynamics or selective inattention.

2. Ability to discern others' emotions, based on situational and expressive cues that have some degree of cultural consensus as to their emotional meaning.

3. Ability to use the vocabulary of emotion and expression terms commonly available in one's (sub)culture.

4. Capacity for empathic involvement in others' emotional experiences.

5. Ability to realize that inner emotional state need not correspond to outer expression—either in oneself or in others.

6. Awareness of cultural display rules.

7. Ability to take into account unique personal information about individuals and apply it when inferring their emotional state, which may be discrepant from cultural expectations for what would commonly be experienced in some emotion-eliciting situation.

8. Ability to understand that one's emotional-expressive behavior may affect another and to take this into account in one's self-presentation strategies.

9. Capacity for coping adaptively with aversive or distressing emotions by using self-regulatory strategies that ameliorate the intensity or duration of such emotional states (e.g., "stress hardiness").

10. Awareness that the structure or nature of relationships is in

part defined both by the emotional immediacy or genuineness of expressive display and by the degree of reciprocity or symmetry within the relationship; for example, mature intimacy is in part defined by mutual or reciprocal sharing of genuine emotions, whereas a parent-child relationship may entail asymmetric sharing of genuine emotions.

11. Capacity for emotional self-efficacy: individuals view themselves as feeling, overall, the way they want to feel. That is, emotional self-efficacy means that one accepts one's emotional experience, whether unique and eccentric or culturally conventional, and that this acceptance is in alignment with one's beliefs about what constitutes desirable emotional "balance." In essence, one is living in accord with one's *personal* naive theory of emotion when one demonstrates emotional self-efficacy.

## Illustrations from Children's Literature

The following excerpts from Beverly Cleary's *Ramona and Her Father* (1975; which received a Newberry award as an outstanding book for elementary-school children) illustrate 7-year-old Ramona's understanding (as portrayed by Cleary, of course) of her own emotional state, its antecedents, its consequences, and particularly of how she *embeds* another's (her father's) emotional response in her prior emotional transactions with him. In her imagination Ramona effects a series of transactions that lead her into misery and dejection. Ramona has been virtually harassing her father to stop smoking; he is currently unemployed, and the family's emotional milieu has been tense.

> Mr. Quimby continued to smoke, and Ramona continued to worry. Then one afternoon, when Ramona came home from school, she found the back door locked. When she pounded on it with her fist, no one answered. She went to the front door, rang the doorbell, and waited. Silence. Lonely silence. She tried the door even though she knew it was locked. More silence. Nothing like this had ever happened to Ramona before. Someone was always waiting when she came home from school.

Ramona was frightened. Tears filled her eyes as she sat down on the cold steps to think. Where could her father be? She thought of her friends at school, Davy and Sharon, who did not have fathers. Where had their fathers gone? Everybody had a father sometime. Where could they go?

Ramona's insides tightened with fear. Maybe her father was angry with her. Maybe he had gone away because she tried to make him stop smoking. She thought she was saving his life, but maybe she was being mean to him. Her mother said she must not annoy her father, because he was worried about being out of work. Maybe she had made him so angry he did not love her anymore. Maybe he had gone away because he did not love her. She thought of all the scary things she had seen on television—houses that had fallen down in earthquakes, people shooting people, big hairy men on motorcycles—and knew she needed her father to keep her safe. . . . She put her head down on her knees and cried. Why had she been so mean to her father? If he ever came back he could smoke all he wanted, fill the ashtrays and turn the air blue, and she wouldn't say a single word. She just wanted her father back, black lungs and all.

And suddenly there he was. . . . Ramona wiped her sweater sleeve across her nose and stood up. She was so glad to see her father and so relieved that he had not gone away, that anger blazed up. Her tears became angry tears. Fathers were not supposed to worry their little girls. "Where have you been?" she demanded. "You're supposed to be here when I come home from school! I thought you had gone away and left me." (Excerpted from pp. 103–108)

Ramona's emotional contortions involve a number of the emotional components and skills listed above. She is aware of her own emotional state (fear) and makes attributions about her father's emotional state that include believing he is angry with her *because she was mean to him* when she *should not have been mean, because he was worried* about his unemployment; that is, he did not deserve her "meanness" in a reciprocal sense. She takes into account unique personal information (his unemployment) and tries to apply it to her relationship with her father. She contemplates modifying her emotional-expressive behavior around his smoking, and when her misery is interrupted by his return, she quickly terminates her distressed vulnerability by becoming righteously angry. We can only guess whether young readers of this book comprehend the emotional roller coaster that Ramona experiences and whether it mirrors internal processes they go through. As I will argue later, much of what Ramona experiences and understands about emotions is accessible to many children 6 to 8 years old; however, for our present purposes the vignette also anchors the notion that emotional experience is firmly embedded in relationships, whether present or past.

A second excerpt is from Barthe DeClements's *Nothing's Fair in Fifth Grade* (1981). An overweight child, Elsie, has been mercilessly teased by her classmates. As she makes progress with her diet, her clothes become loose, and one day her skirt falls down as she stands in front of the class. She flees to the bathroom, and the teacher asks Jennifer, the protagonist, to go and check on her.

> Elsie was slumped against the wall at the end of the sinks. Her head was tipped back and her face tilted up. Tears were streaming from her eyes, but she didn't bother to brush them away. One hand hung at her side. The other still clutched her skirt. She looked sad and hopeless and alone.
>
> I had never thought of Elsie as a human being. Just a fat girl. "Are you O.K.?" I asked her. "Mrs. Hanson wanted me to see if you're O.K." Elsie closed her eyes. The tears dripped from under her eyelids. I stood there for a while. "I'll go get a safety pin from Mrs. Hanson so you can pin up your skirt." Elsie didn't answer. . . .
>
> When I returned to Elsie, she still had her eyes closed. I held out the pin. "Here. You can fix your skirt." Elsie didn't seem to hear. She slid down the wall to the floor and sat there in a huge lump, her head drooping over her lap, tears falling onto her skirt. . . . I sat down on the floor beside her. "Elsie, it isn't that bad."
>
> "What do you care?" she asked.
>
> "Well, I don't want to see you cry."
>
> "Then get out of here."
>
> "No. Hey, Elsie, come on. Let's fix your skirt. . . . The kids will forget about this in a couple of days."

"So what?" Elsie's tears started coming again. "They all hate me. You hate me too."

"No, I don't, Elsie. I did, but I don't now. I guess I didn't think about your having feelings." (Excerpted from pp. 49–51)

This vignette demonstrates the beginning of empathic responsiveness combined with the protagonist's attempts to ameliorate a previously negative relationship with Elsie. The character Elsie had been viewed as one *whose feelings did not count,* and therefore her classmates showed little emotional competence in their interaction with her; that is, they did not attribute emotional states to her, they did not consider how their taunts could be the antecedents for her sadness, nor did they use culturally approved display rules in their exchanges with her. This does not mean that Elsie's classmates did not possess these skills, but they did not use them vis-à-vis Elsie. However, Jennifer's vivid exposure to Elsie's dejection and sadness has the expected emotion-confronting effect on her: she responds to the intense emotion Elsie displays and is prompted by her empathic feelings to try to negotiate a different sort of relationship with Elsie, who is now perceived as a human being *with feelings that do count.*

Another excerpt, from Beverly Cleary's *Mitch and Amy* (1967), illustrates the dissociation of emotional state and expression for the sake of strategic self-presentation. The situation involves Alan, a local bully, who harasses Mitchell and eventually destroys his homemade skateboard and sends him running home in humiliation.

The two boys coasted to a stop at the curb beside Mitchell. "Hi there, kid," said Alan.

"Hi." Mitchell did not much care to be called *kid* by a boy who was only one grade ahead of him in school.

"Look at his little skate board," scoffed Dwight, who was noted not only for his battery-powered eraser, but for the number of times he had been sent to the principal's office.

"Did you build it all by yourself?" Alan wanted to know. Mitchell could see he was trying to act big because he was with a junior-high-school boy.

"I have a boughten one at home," said Mitchell, indignant at the way he was being treated. "I just wanted to see if I could make one that would work."

"I bet," said Alan.

Mitchell's stomach suddenly tightened as if it were clenched into a fist. "Well, I do have a real one at home," he said defiantly.

No one spoke for a moment. Dwight pulled a cigarette out of his shirt pocket, tapped it on his wrist, and stuck one end into his mouth. Mitchell watched, fascinated. "You're not old enough to smoke," he said.

"Who says so?" Dwight squinted as he struck a match and held it to his cigarette. "Yes, who says so?" echoed Alan. . . .

Dwight flicked out the match and took a deep puff on the cigarette. Mitchell could not help watching while Dwight's face grew red, his eyes watered, he spluttered, and was finally forced to give in to an embarrassing fit of coughing.

Mitchell managed not to laugh out loud, but he could not keep the corners of his mouth from quirking. Old Dwight wasn't as big as he thought he was. . . .

"What's so funny?" demanded Alan, embarrassed and angry because the boy he had been imitating looked ridiculous.

"Old Dwight," said Mitchell, "That's what's funny. . . ."

Dwight struggled for breath, which seemed to make Alan madder. Before Mitchell realized what the other boy was doing, Alan had picked up the homemade skate board and was pounding it with all his strength against the bus-stop sign. . . . Then Alan turned on Mitchell with menace on his face. "Start running," he ordered. . . . Mitchell realized there was only one decision he could make and that he had to make it now. He turned and ran. . . .

Mitchell held back tears of humiliation, but he could not keep his heart from pounding with exertion and fury. Let them laugh. There were just a couple of no-good bullies. (Excerpted from pp. 23–27)

Cleary aptly describes the social processes of self-presentation gone awry, with embarrassment the result (experienced by the bullies Dwight and Alan). The vignette also captures how children respond to what they think others' reactions will be (Mitchell manages not to laugh out loud), but when Mitchell reveals a limited amount of mirth at Dwight's fumbling, the story presents *unexpected* social consequences: Alan's reaction of vengeful aggression when he believes his dominance is threatened. Alan's emotional competence is rather obviously limited: He escalates milder negative feelings such as embarrassment into full-scale fury (see skill 9); he is not especially articulate about emotions, nor is he sensitive to emotional states or antecedents in others. Empathy is presumably not one of his strong points.

With these examples I trust readers have a concrete grasp of the more obvious aspects of emotional competence and may also intuit its more subtle components and skills. My intention with these vignettes is also to lay the foundation for my emphasis on emotions as inextricably connected to social relations (Saarni, 1989). It is no accident that authors of children's books portray emotional experience as part of social transactions: we may have a biological base or "skeleton" for our emotions, but social experience, whether conveyed by the media or in real-life interpersonal exchange, provides the "flesh and blood" for the full range of complexity of emotional experience. That growth in complexity of emotional experience is what I am interested in, and it is also represented in the construct "emotional competence."

## Theoretical Context for the Concept of Emotional Competence

Some years ago I sketched out a sequence of steps that I argued represented a model for the differentiation of emotional experience (Saarni, 1978). I will elaborate it here and then discuss it relative to Lewis and Michalson's (1983) components approach to emotion, to Leventhal and Scherer's (1987) model for emotional development, and to Fischer, Shaver, and Carnochan's (1988) skills approach to emotional development. Lewis and Michalson's lucid structural approach helps clarify several concepts in emotion; the two developmental approaches were selected because they both take a stage or sequential approach toward emotional development—as does my model. After preparing this theoretical foundation, I shall link it to the development of emotional competence.

PROPOSED MODEL FOR THE DIFFERENTIATION OF
EMOTIONAL EXPERIENCE

Although a number of theories exist for "explaining" how emotion
processes work (see Lewis & Michalson, 1983, for a review), there
are few explicit models for the development of emotion. The major
conceptual influences on developmental views of emotion are derived from psychoanalytic or object relations theory, evolutionary
views, social learning, or a Piagetian cognitive developmental perspective. My approach reflects a strong contribution from cognitive
developmental theory, especially in that I have adopted a sequential
approach (earlier development is integrated within subsequent developmental processes), and I also endorse the "dialectic dynamics"
of assimilation and accommodation as useful ways to understand
how developmental change comes about. For the sake of brevity, I
shall use as my format a modified outline, and the progression
should be thought of as beginning with birth and extending to early
adulthood.

I. Biology of affective experience
   A. Infants in the first month of life have been observed to demonstrate a rich patterning of expressive behavior in facial, vocal, and
   postural channels that is accompanied by varying degrees of
   arousal. These emotion-related behaviors as well as other non-
   emotion affective behaviors (e.g., gustatory reactions) are assumed to be reflexively activated (Emde, Gaensbauer, & Harmon, 1976).
   B. These expressive channels show considerable, perhaps spontaneous, behavioral variation, which suggests a physiological
   competence for their expression, but the competence is not yet
   linked to specific eliciting criteria for consistent performance as
   *emotional experiences*. (This is a controversial point; the relevant arguments are reviewed by Malatesta, 1985.)
   C. Behavioral synchrony with others in some expressive channels is
   observable (e.g., contagion crying with other babies' crying, not
   with the infant's own taped crying, Martin & Clark, 1982; and
   mouth and tongue movements, Burd & Milewski, 1981).
   D. Gradually these reflexive expressive behaviors become coordi-

nated into an assortment of simple emotions that are activated by increasingly specific situational releasers or antecedents. An operant connection between expressive pattern and internal sensory feedback may also be part of this gradual partitioning. By 3 to 4 months of age infants demonstrate greater responsiveness to stimuli that is under their contingent control (e.g., Watson & Ramey, 1977) and to social exchanges, with both of these developments affecting subsequent emotional development in very significant ways.

II. Coordination of emotion and expression

A. The infant develops self-awareness (Lewis & Brooks-Gunn, 1979), which provides for awareness of its own emotional reaction.

B. As the infant's evaluation of emotion-eliciting events becomes more complex, there is a simultaneous increase in the range and kinds of emotional experience.

C. As the infant becomes increasingly active and intentional (e.g., Kaye & Fogel, 1980) in its impact on the social and physical environment, emotional states are linked to and coordinated with encoding specific expressive patterns both for instrumental purposes and for figuring out the emotional meanings of ambiguous situations (as in social referencing).

D. The infant now expressively signals its emotional experience to others in order to affect their behavior toward itself.

E. Constructing, maintaining, and synchronizing emotional-communicative exchanges becomes a goal in itself.

III. Representational elicitors of emotion

A. The development of symbolic schemes allows for a fluid extension of experience forward and backward in time. Now the child can anticipate incentive events (i.e., emotion-eliciting events) as well as store memories of past incentive events. As a result, young children (1–2 years old) can anticipate their emotional experience, based on memory of how they responded emotionally in the past.

B. The young child's fantasies (e.g., nightmares) can become the incentive events for eliciting changes in emotion.

C. Representation-mediated anticipation of others' psychological and behavioral reactions toward the child can elicit emotional experience (e.g., anxiety, excitement).

D. Representation-mediated anticipation of others' psychological and behavioral reactions begins to influence the child's expressive behavior (as with display rules and instrumentally managed expressive behavior).

E. Communication with others extends and elaborates the child's evaluation of emotion-eliciting events.

F. Communication with others extends and elaborates children's consciousness of their own feelings.

IV. Cognition about emotion and emotion as an elicitor of other emotions

A. By 6–7 years of age deliberate manipulation of expressive behavior for social-communicative goals is readily accomplished, if sufficient motivation is present.

B. By middle childhood children begin to infer that the emotional experience and the expressive behavior of others are influenced by their anticipation of one's own psychological and behavioral reactions (including emotional expressiveness) to them.

C. Preadolescents can begin to step outside of their emotional experience and objectively reflect on it as long as they are not in the midst of an emotional crisis (e.g., Harris & Lipian, 1989).

D. Adolescents acquire awareness of their own emotion cycles: emotion A becomes an elicitor for emotion B (e.g., a person may feel anxious and simultaneously be aware that anxiety may interfere with performance; the initial anxiety then becomes compounded by a secondary anxiety about feeling anxious to begin with—and the individual continues to be aware of these two layers of mutually influencing and perhaps reinforcing anxiety). (Adapted from Saarni, 1978, pp. 371–372)

Although more than 10 years have passed since I drafted this sequence of steps for the differentiation of emotional experience, I find that it is still an adequate general description of the major changes characterizing emotional development. But during this past decade our knowledge about emotional development has vastly expanded in terms of recognizing the complexity involved in the steps noted above. In the years since I drew up this sequence, Lewis and Michalson's (1983) landmark volume *Children's Emotions and Moods* appeared, which certainly provided a wealth of detail concerning the developmental trajectory of emotion in infancy and early childhood. But of particular interest here is their introduction of a clearly articulated components approach to understanding emotion in general, which is described below.

## LEWIS AND MICHALSON'S COMPONENTS OF EMOTION

Lewis and Michalson divide emotion into five components that are also those aspects of emotion that are most often studied and referred to. (If nothing else, their components approach promotes ease of communication about the vague yet complex concept of emotion.) Their five components can be thought of as occurring in a sequence of action or time, yet they emphasize that *initiation* of an emotion can occur at any point in their model. Below is a brief discussion of these components with additional commentary regarding their social-developmental implications. Overlaps between my sequence of emotional differentiation and the description of the components are also noted.

The first component is *emotional elicitors*. These refer to situational features that people appraise and that provide the stimulus for emotional responses. However, emotional elicitors need not always refer to external situations; they can also be internal events that elicit emotional responses (e.g., emotion A can function as an elicitor for emotion B). A common example of this emotion cycle in North American culture occurs when hurt feelings become the incentive or eliciting stimulus for feeling angry. (Whether awareness accompanies this emotion cycle depends on what degree of abstract self-reflection has developed, such as in stage IV above.) From a developmental perspective we must bear in mind that what constitutes an emotional elicitor at one age need not function similarly at another age, owing to changes in cognitive appraisal or social expectations, or owing to simple physical maturation. Socialization clearly affects what becomes culturally or idiosyncratically defined as an emotional elicitor. Families may also socialize their members into responding emotionally to some situations in a way that is idiosyncratic or even contrary to what the majority culture would expect. For example, children growing up in violence-prone, abusive homes may come to associate anger and aggression with love. Thus, at its simplest level this component of emotion is relevant to how the infant comes to anticipate feelings; for example, we begin to see unfocused anticipatory responses such as whimpering outside a doctor's waiting room when the last visit included an injection. At a progressively more complex level, emotional elicitors are acknowledged and explicitly verbalized. Still more sophisticated is the individual who reflects on emotional elicitors as embedded in patterns of emotion cycles—the grist for much of insight-oriented psychotherapy.

The second component is *emotional receptors*. This aspect of emotion has received relatively little attention. Emotional receptors are best thought of as biological processes that occur in conjunction both with anatomical structures in the nervous system and with neurochemical transmitters that aid communication within and across physiological processes. Emotional receptors function as the interface between the nervous system and emotional elicitors. They are the "first contact" or signal detectors for whether and how something is to be responded to emotionally. We do not really know if social processes influence emotional receptors directly; however, it is conceivable that socialization can modulate some aspects of an individual's emotional receptor system, such as arousal level. An interesting speculation is whether temperament is involved here (Strelau, 1987) as well as such processes as "blunting" and "sensitization" as described by Miller and Green (1985), which regulate the intensity of felt emotion as one copes with stressful events.

The third component, *emotional states*, also refers to body changes. They differ from emotional receptors in that they follow or result from activity in the emotional receptors. Emotional states are normally biochemical, neurological, and physical in nature, and they refer to characteristic patterns of somatic activity that are typically associated with basic categories of emotional responding. For example, when fear is induced, we may respond with a characteristic pattern of increased perspiration, capillary constriction, and gastrointestinal activity. Emotional states appear to be reflexively activated in early infancy, but they tend to be global in nature; their partition into more specific and identifiable emotion patterns emerges perhaps as early as 3–4 months of age (see, for example, Malatesta & Izard, 1984). Social processes may not affect emotional states directly, but social influence apparently does occur indirectly. Support for this indirect influence of social experience on emotional states may be found in research conducted by Ekman, Levenson, and Friesen (1983), who determined that facial expressions of emotion (which reflect central nervous systems activity) affect the autonomic nervous system through a hypothesized feedback system. Since social experience definitely influences emotional-expressive behavior (discussed below), emotional state changes are also likely to be affected via neurological feedback from the patterning of skeletal muscles used in the socially influenced expressive behavior.

*Emotional expression* is the fourth component and is readily available for study because it is generally observable. Emotional-expressive behavior is evident across all the nonverbal channels of communication (e.g., facial expression, body gestures, vocal qualities), but social processes probably influence most the channel of facial expression. It may well be that part of our human adaptation is the ready facility with which we can monitor and modify our facial expressions for assorted social goals (e.g., Ekman, 1985). No wonder then that facial expression should be so greatly influenced by social processes, for cultural meanings, expectations, and social relationships are all invested in the "interaction rituals" that we lead with our faces (see also Goffman, 1967).

This component is repeatedly evident in my model for emotion differentiation because expressive behavior constitutes the primary mode of emotional communication among individuals. Given my premise that emotions and social relations are developmentally inseparable (see also Saarni, 1989), the component "carrying" the communicative aspect in Lewis and Michalson's approach to emotion will receive relatively greater emphasis in my model of emotion differentiation.

The last component of emotion described by Lewis and Michalson is *emotional experience*. This refers to the subjective experience of emotion; it requires a concept of self in order to reflect upon and interpret what one is experiencing; generally, both situational factors and emotional state and expressive responses will be taken into account as one makes sense of one's emotional experience. Developmentally, it also requires some degree of competence with emotion words and concepts used in one's culture. Considerable developmental research has been undertaken with a focus on emotional experience (see Saarni & Harris, 1989). Much of it has been concerned with age differences in children's articulation of what sorts of situations, emotions, and expressions tend to go together in North American and Western European cultures. Cross-cultural research shows us that variability exists in "emotional scripts" (see Gordon, 1989; Lewis, 1989) and in the lexicon available for describing emotional experience (e.g., Lutz, 1985; Miller & Sperry, 1987). The overall generalization one can make is that young children (3–4 years of age) across assorted cultures are remarkably competent at linking common situations with the emotional responses expected in their culture (e.g., Russell, 1989; Stein & Trabasso, 1989). (A cautionary note here: Children may consistently anticipate a particular emotional response that differs from what adults would have expected; this is due to differences in age roles. See Lewis, 1989, for further details.) To sum up, social processes influence this last component, emotional experience, by influencing how we formulate our implicit or naive theories of emotion; that is, how we make sense of our feelings reveals the impact of socialization, whether it stems from our families, our peers, social institutions such as schools, the media, or our culture in general. I will return to the topic of naive theories of emotion later in this chapter.

Lewis and Michalson's components approach to emotion is not a developmental model for how emotion differentiates; however, their descriptive approach is useful for my model of emotion development. Specifically, their five components suggest that we may want to look at different aspects of emotion as possibly having different developmental "timetables." Different aspects of emotion may also be differentially modifiable by environmental influence (e.g., the emotional expression and emotional experience components). Given my emphasis on the social context in emotional development, interesting questions may be raised about how social relations work to influence the different components of emotion yet yield an integrated emotion system within the individual.

LEVENTHAL AND SCHERER'S MODEL FOR
EMOTIONAL DEVELOPMENT

Leventhal and Scherer (1987) bravely jumped into the controversy surrounding the relative primacy and independence of emotion and cognition, a controversy largely associated with Zajonc (1980, 1984) and Lazarus (1982, 1984), who represent the two "polarized" positions. Essentially Leventhal and Scherer concluded that the controversy was a superficial one by proposing that emotion processes are relatively simple in the first weeks of life but become more complex with maturity and eventually emerge as a "dynamic, multilevel emotion processing system" (p. 3). Their model borrows some of its metaphors from information processing, and thus they talk about adult emotional experience as reflecting a hierarchy of levels of organization: (1) The *sensorimotor level* is the most basic and probably innate set of emotion processes; it is presumably present at birth. (2) The *schematic level* is the bridge between sensorimotor processes and the next highest level. The schematic level appears to consist of templatelike prototypes of emotional experience, which refer to distinctive combinations of situational antecedents, emotion states, and emotion expressions (sometimes called *scripts* by others, e.g., Lewis, 1989). (3) The *conceptual level* is the highest level in the hierarchy, yet apparently it is reached as early as the second to third year of life. Its chief prerequisite is the ability to invoke memories about emotion so that emotional responses are viewed within a longer time frame. Self-awareness is also a prerequisite, since reflection upon the self's experience, including emotional experience, is at the core of being able to abstract properties of emotion antecedents, states, and expressions and map them onto new experience "in the continued development and updating of the individual's emotional life" (p. 13).

Operating within these three levels of emotion processes is a system of hypothetical "checks" that the infant or adult carries out to evaluate the meaning of an external or internal stimulus. However, the "checks" system is also ontogenetically organized: (a) The sensorimotor-level emotion processes can presumably access only the first two checks, which scan for novelty and intrinsic pleasantness in stimuli ("This is interesting" and/or "I like it!"). (b) The schematic-level emotion processes begin to permit goal significance checks ("I want this"), and (c) the conceptual level emotion processes allow for more subtle goal or need evaluations ("This is risky, but I think I really want it" or "I feel ambivalent") as well as coping potential checks and norms- or self-compatibility checks ("I can get through this"; "I'm polite"; "I'm intense"). One still makes use of the more "primitive" kinds of stimulus checks or evaluations (novelty and pleasantness of stimuli) on the conceptual level.

Leventhal and Scherer's model is consistent with my proposed sequence of emotional differentiation. Their sensory motor level appears to be very similar to my first "stage," namely, the biology of affective experience. Their schematic level appears similar to my hypothesized gradual partitioning of affects into simple emotions that are operantly linked to situational antecedents, expressive patterns, and internal sensory feedback. Their conceptual level, which is very broad indeed, appears to begin with my second "stage," which starts with self-awareness and proceeds to constructing, maintaining, and synchronizing emotional-communicative exchanges as a goal in itself. My third and fourth "stages" seem to represent more advanced aspects of Leventhal and Scherer's conceptual level of emotion processes. For example, their coping check is related to my proposed step in the sequence of emotional differentiation that refers to emotional cycles. If the full richness of some emotional experience is processed at the conceptual level, then one would also be considering how one copes. Coping is implicated in emotion cycles (where emotion A elicits emotion B), because one may cope with threat or vulnerability by becoming, for example, angry and aggressive. As Folkman and Lazarus (1988) rightly point out, coping changes appraisal processes and thus mediates the subsequent emotion cycle. In the preceding example, if one appraises a threatening individual as having violated a "rule," this appraisal will typically contribute to one's feeling angry. Coping also suggests a meta-level approach to emotion: one has values or motives about emotions—one is motivated to avoid feeling humiliated or values the emotion of pride.

Both emotion models described so far (Lewis and Michalson's and Leventhal and Scherer's) pay lip service to social processes, but neither gives them as much emphasis as does my proposed model of emotional differentiation. Given this emphasis on social processes, my definition of emotional competence as the demonstration of self-efficacy in emotional-eliciting social transactions incorporates the proposed model of emotional differentiation: emotions are simultaneously the "fuel" and the "destination" in our interpersonal relationships. Lewis and Michalson's components model is strictly a structural one and was not intended to be viewed as a developmental model. Indeed, in other sources Lewis similarly emphasizes the social foundation for the development of emotion processes (Lewis & Michalson, 1985; Lewis & Saarni, 1985; Lewis, 1989). Leventhal and Scherer's model is an individual and intrapsychic model of emotional development. Their model does not necessarily preclude a greater emphasis on the social processes that are embedded in emotional development; rather, they have focused their model-building efforts on developmental changes in the internal organization of emotion without much regard for the social *system* in which children develop.

## FISCHER, SHAVER, AND CARNOCHAN'S SKILLS APPROACH TO EMOTIONAL DEVELOPMENT

Fischer et al. (1988) have adapted an earlier skills approach to cognitive development proposed by Fischer (1980) and integrated that approach with recent research and theory on the development of emotional experience. They also draw heavily on the idea of *prototypes* (Schwartz & Shaver, 1987) to describe the constellations of emotional states, behaviors, and controls that people develop to represent various kinds of emotional experiences. Such prototypes are hierarchically organized and provide a script that is integrated with cultural content for how to anticipate antecedents to emotions, how to respond emotionally (including physiological, cognitive, and expressive responses), and how to cope with them (defined as self-control procedures; Schwartz & Shaver, 1987). For example, my prototype for anger includes an eliciting antecedent of intent to harm, but I may monitor or control my expressive response depending on how I feel about the instigator or the risks to me in expressing my anger. A subordinate aspect to my hierarchically organized prototype for anger could include, for example, resentment if I were to chronically suppress angry feelings toward someone or to avoid that person.

The hierarchical organization of emotion prototypes permits a tripartite division of emotional experience into (a) a superordinate level consisting of a simple dichotomy between positive and negative emotional valence, (b) a middle level of relatively simple "basic" categories of emotions (e.g., anger, happiness, sadness, fear), and (c) a final extensive level for the many subordinate emotions derived from the basic emotion categories (e.g., from anger would come irritation or resentment, from happiness would come contentment, from sadness would come disappointment, from fear would come worry, and so forth). This hierarchical organization lends itself to a developmental model with the superordinate division being first to appear and probably innate, the middle level of basic emotion categories appearing next and probably also innate, and the last level being already well established by middle childhood but undergoing further complex changes at various times throughout one's development, depending on constraints imposed by socialization and cultural context.

Interwoven with this hierarchical organization of emotion prototypes is Fischer's concept of a psychological skill, which is defined as "essentially a scheme or procedure for controlling variations in behavior in a context," which is another way of saying that one can change one's behavior within contextual constraints. The emphasis here is on the notion of *control* schemes: depending on the stage of development, one can operate on one's actions (reflexive and sensorimotor), one's representations, and eventually one's abstractions and thus systematically effect changes. The model is clearly one that emphasizes cognitive structure in emotional experience. Assuming I have appropriately understood this amalgamated model of emotion prototypes and cognitive skills as a description for how emotions develop and differentiate, then apparently the young infant first acts reflexively, indicating a processing of negative or positive emotional valence. Subsequently the developing infant begins to respond in a sensorimotor mode and actively displays the "basic" emotion categories. However, within this sensorimotor mode (called a "tier" in Fischer's model) there is further development in that the infant begins to show behaviorally that it distinguishes between its own basic emotions and emotions experienced by others. With the advent of representational skills this repertoire of basic emotions is freed from the limitations of sensorimotor action and can be combined with representations about other events, such as social relations. Representational skills thus permit the sorts of elaborations need to derive some of the subordinate constructed emotions. Finally, upon acquiring skills of abstraction, the developing child (or adolescent by this point) can manipulate complex sets of derived emotions and make connections across emotion categories, across social categories, and across whatever other categories may be relevant to emotional experience. With the most advanced level of abstract skills, one can presumably maneuver through systems of prototypes (which are themselves systems), taking into account simultaneously the various antecedents, responses, and self-control procedures of multiple emotion prototypes. (When I try to think of an example of the latter, all I can come up with is what we psychologists are proposing as *models* for emotion, and somehow emotional experience seems lacking in all this cool contemplation.)

I have not done justice to Fischer's cognitive skills analysis, which entails a complex system of levels-within-tiers of cognitive manipulations; see Fischer (1980). With that apology I shall go on to compare the Fischer et al. skills approach to emotional development with the model I presented that emphasizes social and communicative processes in emotional differentiation.

The skills approach to emotional development has considerable overlap with my "stages" of emotional development: my stage I is very similar to Fischer et al.'s reflexive tier, stage II to their sensorimotor tier, stage III to their representational tier, and stage IV to their abstraction tier. Indeed, Fischer et al. and I also use similar terms to introduce these four stages or tiers. The skills approach to emotional development permits a rigorous and more finely detailed approach to emotional differentiation when the entire levels-within-tiers model is applied, but similar to Leventhal and Scherer's model, it does not address the mutually influencing role that relationships play in emotional development. I see the young infant as endowed with considerable innate reflexive emotional response systems, but I also emphasize that an infant's reflexive emotional responding is not occurring in a social vacuum. Rather, it occurs in intense and intimate relationships, and because of that the young infant's reflexive emotional responding is socially influenced from the beginning of life, even as it also influences caregivers' emotional responding.

Perhaps what is occurring in early infancy is the meshing of several biological reflexive systems, so that the emotion reflexive system is from birth interactive with the perceptual processing system that facilitates orientation toward human sensory information (e.g., preference for human faces, staring at eyes, turning toward voices, quieting at a human touch). Intriguing (and controversial) is the research that has documented the capacity of very young infants to mimic or synchronize some of their facial expressive behaviors with those of a familiar adult (Meltzoff & Moore, 1977). Obviously such a skill, reflexive in origin as it appears to be, is going to have communicative impact on caregivers, and as any parent can attest, even nonsynchronized smiles from very young babies elicit considerable attention and emotional responding from the parent.

In the second stage of emotional differentiation and similarly in Fischer et al.'s second tier, the focus is on sensorimotor involvement in emotion processes. Combined with the development of self-awareness (also manifested in sensorimotor activity) in the second half of the first year, the 6- to 12-month-old infant shows a rich and often playful repertoire of coordinated emotional-expressive behaviors that can be used strategically to influence other people's behavior toward the infant. "Games" of turn-taking in emotional-expressive behavior are now sought out by the infant as activity goals in themselves. For example, some readers may recall how often their babies threw an object from the crib and the parent retrieved it, perhaps in the mouth, crawling on all fours and enacting wildly expressive behavior while pretending to be a dog (or whatever). The baby, laughing uproariously, just could not get enough of this routine and would promptly throw the object onto the floor again. "Peek-a-boo" games are another (and perhaps more common) emotional-expressive game played by infants in this age group, and again they appear not to tire of the routine. To sum up, the construction, maintenance, and synchronization of the the infant's own emotional-expressive behavior with that of another person (with whom the infant is closely involved or very familiar) is a hallmark in the differentiation of emotion in infancy. It signals to us that the infant possesses a number of emotional competencies that it can use to promote its efficacy in social transactions (such as getting a parent to act repeatedly in an entertaining and foolish-looking manner). But it also means that the infant's emerging mastery and self-concept are influenced, one hopes favorably, by being able to intentionally influence others to respond emotionally to its own emotional signals in a fashion that is functional and adaptive.

Stage III emphasizes representational ability in emotional differentiation, and Fischer et al.'s skills approach also views the development of representation as a key ingredient in the growing complexity of emotional experience. In my emphasis on social construction, I regard developing representational skills as helping children acquire *expectancies* about how others will respond to them psychologically and behaviorally. Being able to entertain such generalized expectancies, which are representations, allows children to try to monitor their emotional-expressive behavior to prevent negative expectancies from being fulfilled or to promote positive ones.

Socially shared fantasies such as playing "house" or "Batman" become eliciting events for emotional experiences, as do unique personal fantasies such as imaginary playmates. Imaginary playmates are good examples of how the young child can use forms of social communication in an internal dialogue that fosters some emotional responses or permits coping with emotions experienced outside the imaginary relationship. (I remember my own imaginary playmate very well: her name was Eileen, and she lived in the forest high up in the Berkeley hills; she could fly and, of course, got to do all sorts of things that I was not allowed to do. She was both an exciting and a comforting figure and was with me from about age 3 to 5. This was a stressful period, I suspect, because two siblings were born in rapid succession during that time.)

By middle childhood children have a fairly good understanding that one's facial expression does not have to coincide with how one is feeling (Saarni, 1979a; 1989). Thus they can represent the likely internal states of another person, even though that person may not be providing expressive cues to the internal emotion. From the standpoint of cognitive developmental prerequisites for understanding the distinction between appearance and reality, Harris and Gross (1988) have found that even a few 4-year-olds can appreciate that the "appearance" of the facial expression may be discrepant from the "reality" of the internal emotional state, although by age 6 this understanding is better and more reliably articulated.

Television is an interesting pseudosocial medium that may actually promote this representational differentiation between inner state and outer emotional expression, and given the many hours even very young children apparently watch it, we may be underestimating how influential television is in structuring emotional experience. The technology of television permits interesting and rapid juxtapositions of characters' facial expressions and subsequent interpersonal transactions. The camera can cut from character to character, highlighting their facial expressions, and such close-up shots are generally congruent with internal state. Then the camera can back off and pan the whole set or group of people, who now display incongruent facial expressions. Such camera zooms and retreats repeatedly demonstrate characters' dramatic emotional-expressive shifts and are visible in "Sesame Street" characters as well as in hero figures of the "Wonder Woman" genre. (However, I think only the villain on the "Smurfs" shows such expressive dissemblance.)

Family comedy shows often contain a conflict between two or more characters that centers on their misinterpretation of someone's emotional experience, often owing to these incongruities in emotional state and expression. But such family shows can also portray emotional state and expression-consistent behavior when the characters still manage to misinterpret the *representational* antecedents of one another's emotional states. For example, I sat through a rerun of the program "Webster" in which little Webster appears very sad to his adoptive parents, gives away all his toys, and generally mopes around the house. His mother misattributes the cause of his emotional display and believes that he is rejecting *her* because she is an inadequate adoptive parent. Webster thinks *he* is being rejected by her and therefore is responding with predictable sadness. Eventually they straighten things out, but the point here is that the interpretations given to another's emotional behavior become part of a communication exchange, with the interactants reciprocally dovetailing their representations of what they think the other is feeling and thinking about them. As a result, rapid shifts in emotional-expressive behavior take place that are especially likely to occur in facial expressions. In real life these shifts may be extremely rapid, but video technology allows for their emphasis and thus may help young children comprehend (a) that what one sees may not be what is being felt; (b) that causes of feelings can be different for different characters, and (c) that how characters feel about each other—their relationship to one another—affects what they show about their emotions and how they interpret others' emotional-expressive behavior.

To sum up, the developmental emergence of representational skills greatly expands the subtlety of emotional experience, and communication with others elaborates still further children's representations of emotion-eliciting events, including their ability to recognize that others' representations can constitute emotion-eliciting events, whether for oneself or for another. Communication with others also elaborates and refines children's consciousness of what they are feeling, perhaps in the sense of helping them acquire derived subordinate emotions as proposed by Schwarz and Shaver's emotion prototype analysis (1987).

My fourth hypothesized stage of emotional differentiation has considerable overlap with the fourth tier in the Fischer et al. model for a skills approach to emotional development. Whereas I propose as the defining feature of this last stage "cognition about emotion," Fischer et al. emphasize the ability to manipulate cognitively and behaviorally whole systems of action, feeling, and control, which I think captures the sort of conceptual complexity available to the individual in this most mature stage of emotional development. The capacity to apply multiple insights and awarenesses to one's emotional experience also opens the door to subtle involvement in complex webs of social relationships. When I reflect on psychotherapy's use of psychological insight into one's emotional malaise as a primary path toward change, I see clients "working through" (with regard to their relations with others) the multiple systems of action, feeling, and control proposed by Fischer et al. Clients presumably then attempt to use this abstract understanding to attain a greater sense of autonomy and acceptance of their emotional life.

The ability to think abstractly and juggle multiple systems and categories simultaneously would also be involved in older children's emergent understanding that even as they are trying to anticipate another's emotional response to them, the other is doing a similar sort of thinking routine. Readers may feel a bit dizzy trying to keep track of knowing that one's self-presentations also have to take into account others' awareness of one's own self-presentational strategies and that they are using that awareness in their own self-presentations. Therefore allow me to give an example drawn from an adolescent and his family whom I know well. After experiencing his parents' divorce in early childhood, Matt had recently moved in with his father, who remarried a year later. A child was subsequently born, another son. Consider the multiple systems of relationships and multiple self-presentation strategies Matt had to take into account: a new brother, a renewal of his relationship with his father, entering a new school, and forging a relationship with his stepmother, who also happened to be very beautiful and not much older than he was (21 and 14, respectively). Each of these relationships overlapped with the others; each relationship also entailed multiple sets of feelings, which in turn overlapped with the feelings involved in the other relationships. For example, not many of the girls Matt met in his new school were as attractive as his stepmother, yet she was obviously off limits, even though she was much more present in his life than the girls at school. Matt's eventual choice of emotional controls and self-presentational strategies was to be as obnoxious as possible to his stepmother, lavish his love on his baby brother, avoid closeness with his father, and become very peer oriented. Had he been able to examine reflectively what he was doing and recognize it from a metasystems perspective, he might have realized that his odious behavior toward his stepmother was perhaps in part reaction formation, but was also a self-presentation guaranteed to alienate her and to contribute to her reacting to his disagreeable behavior by becoming the classic "wicked stepmother." Matt could then use her negative behavior to create feelings of distance and alienation from her. The "winner" here may have been the innocent baby brother whom everybody adored, but the anguish in this blended family is by no means unique (see, for example, Visher & Visher, 1988). (Fortunately the stepmother sought counseling and worked very hard to form an alliance with her stepson, which proved successful.)

What intrigues me about the complexity found in this last stage of emotional differentiation (although there may be more stages after this fourth one) is how its metasystems perspective affects the implicit or naive theory of emotion by which each of us operates. A naive theory of emotion may be operative by the time we acquire representational skills, and young children do seem to have acquired "internal working models"—if I may borrow a phrase from attachment research (see Bretherton, this volume)—of what basic emotional experience is "supposed" to be about. They can nominate typical antecedents of emotions, they can identify basic prototype emotions from facial expressions, they possess a simple emotional vocabulary, and they know that what they feel is not necessarily what someone else feels. So what happens when one develops a truly abstract metasystems perspective on emotional experience? Does it delay the spontaneity of emotional response or bleach the subjective intensity of emotion experience? Or, to the contrary, does it permit more occasions for spontaneous and intense feeling, because one can appreciate all the more the mazelike or house-of-mirrors subtlety of so much more interpersonal entanglement? I do not have an answer, but on that note I shall turn to a brief discussion of the concept of naive theories of emotion, for I think it is central to the notion of emotional competence put forward in this chapter because it mediates between emotional development and emotional competence.

## Naive Theories of Emotion

"Naive" is used here to mean that we are talking about the layperson's set of assumptions about emotion rather than what a scientist or psychotherapist might have in mind. "Theories"—and I specifically use the plural—is used here to represent hypotheses individuals hold to explain how emotion works or functions. Naive theories of emotion are significant for the concept of emotional competence for several reasons, but perhaps foremost to emphasize the cultural and developmental relativity of emotional competence. Thus, one's naive theory of emotion will vary depending on one's culture; similarly, it will vary depending on one's stage of emotional differentiation. To make the matter even more complicated, I think that one's naive theory of emotion also reflects unique family influences such as children of alcoholics seem to experience (Ackerman, 1983). Finally, depending on one's naive theory of emotion (which will reflect cultural, familial, and developmental influences), one may experience certain limits in one's emotional competence. People have varying "profiles" of emotional competence, and it is possible that for a given individual some social transactions will also elicit more emotional competence, while the dynamics of other social exchanges elicit less.

Cultures (or families, for that matter) socialize their members according to a variety of descriptors of emotional experience and have different assumptions about what constitutes normative emotional responding. It follows that what one believes or takes for granted about emotions and feelings will affect how one's emotional competence manifests itself. For example, if one's cultural or familial model of emotion precludes being able to take into account that someone's emotional response can be disproportionate to or incongruous with an eliciting event because of some unique viewpoint, then one cannot interact with this individual from that perspective. Instead, one might avoid the person or label her or him crazy, possessed, or whatever. Thus one's social efficacy would be limited, and one could not negotiate with insight into the person's emotional experience.

Can we summarize any general qualities that characterize a naive, but widely shared, theory of emotion in Western culture? There appear to be such summaries available, judging from work undertaken by D'Andrade (1987), Lutz (1987), and Weiner (1987). I will discuss each of their positions in turn.

## D'ANDRADE'S FOLK MODEL OF THE MIND

D'Andrade has presented a comprehensive hypothetical description of what North American and probably Western European folk models of the mind entail. The folk model of the mind refers to what ordinary people would call commonsense understanding of internal states. More specifically, D'Andrade states that the folk model of the mind consists of perceptions, beliefs/knowledge, feelings/emotions, desires/wishes, intentions, and will/self-control. I will focus on his discussion of feelings/emotions as reflecting a generalized naive theory of emotion.

Based on interview data with high-school and college students,

D'Andrade (1987) proposes the following descriptors for a North American folk model of feelings and emotions, which is tantamount to a generalized naive theory of emotion: (1) emotions may have either external or internal causes; (2) one is generally aware of what one feels, although one may be confused; (3) emotions can be directed at specific objects (e.g., fear of lightning) or at propositions (e.g., fear about the possibility of nuclear holocaust); (4) the self appears generally to be the passive experiencer of emotion (e.g., "deadlines make me anxious" or "the faculty meeting bored me"), but the self can become an agent when the verb *feel* is used with an emotion word or phrase as in "I feel relieved at meeting my deadlines"; (5) emotions are not considered to be under direct control— one must distract oneself from the emotion-eliciting event by thinking or doing something else; (6) emotions are referred to by *mass* nouns rather than by *count* nouns; the former do not have a defined number and the latter do (e.g., one can have great sadness but not six sadnesses); (7) feelings can be experienced as blends of more than one emotion; (8) emotions or feelings underlie desires or "action tendencies"; (9) emotions are thought to cause involuntary visceral reactions; (10) feelings and beliefs are mutually influencing; and (11) feelings and emotions generally "fit" the eliciting event, but they can be disproportionate to or incongruous with the nature of the event.

What is evident in D'Andrade's summary of a Western folk model of emotion is that it is not especially social or interpersonal in perspective. However, one might argue that its intrapsychic emphasis is accurate for describing Western folk models of the mind insofar as North Americans pride themselves on their "rugged individualism" and the like.

## LUTZ'S ETHNOTHEORIES OF EMOTION

Lutz (1987) presents an alternative non-Western view of a naive theory of emotion that emphasizes social roles and relationships in conjunction with emotional experience. She uses the term *ethnotheories of emotion* to describe "a fundamental and ubiquitous aspect of psychosocial functioning. They are used to explain why, when, and how emotion occurs, and they are embedded in more general theories of the person, internal processes, and social life" (p. 291). She also comments that though ethnotheories of emotion may be highly abstract, they more often function as implicit and pragmatic guidelines for daily social-emotional exchange. Thus, for example, for the Ifaluk islanders (the society Lutz studied in the western Pacific) to figure out which emotional response fits the situation, they must take into account the social status or rank of each of the individuals involved, their history of relationship, and whether any other third parties might be involved in the consequences of actions taken. She describes the Ifaluk as believing that emotions experienced by one person can lead directly to another's experiencing an emotion, with the result that people are held responsible for causing the emotions others experience. Lutz refers to this as emotional symbiosis, and perhaps we see something similar to it in North America when we hear a person say, "*You make me* so mad."

Lutz also takes into account in her ethnotheory of emotion two kinds of goals: action tendency goals and disclosure or attribution goals. The former kind is readily understood as the motivating value of an emotion in terms of its likelihood of leading the experiencer to some course of action. Disclosure or attribution goals refer to the degree of social acceptability implied by an emotion term when one discloses that one is experiencing some emotion or has attributed some emotion to oneself. For example, consider the social acceptability differences in North American culture for admitting that one has experienced guilt as opposed to shame (the former has connotations of moral rectitude whereas the latter seems to imply wallowing in a private hole of misery). Lutz properly notes that both action tendency goals and disclosure goals are fluid in the sense that they are affected by whether it is oneself or others experiencing the emotion, by what social statuses are involved, and by what situational constraints may exist.

Last, Lutz notes that ethnotheories of emotion are inconsistent, incomplete, ambiguous, not shared by all members of a culture or subculture, and may be undergoing continual reconstruction or modification. On one hand, Lutz's perspective has great appeal, for it is dynamic and open ended; on the other hand, it is a viewpoint that is difficult to translate into scientific methods of observation and description. However, its fluidity does fit with what I am proposing with the construct of emotional competence, and her approach does mesh well with my emphasis on emotions in interpersonal contexts. Specifically, the skills of emotional competence are variable, as in the idea I mentioned earlier of uneven "profiles" of emotional competence. Emotional competence can also "expand" in the sense of enhanced maturity and insight, perhaps brought about by dealing with a difficult experience, or "contract" in the sense of regression (see, for example, Harris & Lipian, 1989).

## WEINER'S NAIVE THEORY OF EMOTION

The last perspective on naive theories of emotion focuses on attributions and beliefs that function as tacit rules for describing the connections between particular emotions and particular thoughts. This view has been proposed by Weiner and his associates (Weiner, 1987; Weiner, Amirkhan, Folkes, & Verette, 1987; Weiner & Handel, 1985). Weiner views the expression of emotion as an important *cue* others use to infer not only the emotional state but also what sorts of accompanying attitudes and self-attributions are likely to have been involved in bringing it about. For example, if a student reveals anger (as opposed to sadness) when a teacher returns a paper with a low grade, then others will infer that the student believes the teacher was unfair and that the student's self-esteem may be unaffected by the grade. On the other hand, the student who responds to a low grade with sadness and dejection is likely to be perceived as also experiencing reduced self-esteem and feelings of low ability. Students responding with guilt over low grades may also experience reduced self-esteem but would be perceived as having devoted little effort to their academic performance because of the way they responded emotionally.

As a social psychologist, Weiner is interested in the interpersonal transactions that are affected by the naive theories of emotion interactants hold. In one fascinating developmental study that investigated beliefs about how to prevent another person from getting angry (Weiner & Handel, 1985), children were given vignettes in which a social engagement was broken for reasons that were either controllable ("you decided to stay home and watch TV") or not con-

trollable ("you got sick"). Even young children (5 years) were atten-
tive to the controllability issue as a prime determinant of whether
the recipient of the excuse would get angry. They clearly realized
that revealing a controllable reason for breaking an engagement
would be more likely to provoke anger. The naive theory about anger demonstrated in this research has to do with the link between intentionality and controllability: if one has control over some course
of action and intentionally follows that course, even though it goes
against some social contract, then the individual with whom one
made the social contract is likely to become angry, and this will generally be viewed as *justifiable* anger in North American culture. In
contrast, if one did not have control over some action or did not intend the action to occur, yet a social contract is broken, then the individual with whom one made the contract is likely to be disappointed. Becoming angry instead will be viewed as *unjustified* in our
culture.

Weiner's work on attribution of emotion in the context of controllability, locus, and stability of events raises important questions
about the process of socialization of emotion, such as which aspects
or components of emotion are most influenced by socialization and
how directly or indirectly socialization actually affects emotion (see
Lewis & Saarni, 1985). Given this melting pot of beliefs, attributions,
emotions, and social contracts or expectations, emotional development would have to proceed in a mélange of interpersonal exchange *and* emotional experience. Thus we come back to the emphasis on communication and relationships in my model of
emotional differentiation and the necessity for grounding the concept of emotional competence in emotion-eliciting social transactions.

In concluding this section on naive theories of emotion, I think
that my set of "skills" of emotional competence also reflects a naive
theory of emotion *in interpersonal contexts*. Many of these skills appear in D'Andrade's, Lutz's, and Weiner's work (e.g., ability to discern others' emotions, ability to use the emotional lexicon of one's
culture). What they do not appear to address are those skills concerned with empathic responsiveness, self-presentational strategies, coping with aversive emotions, and the notion of emotional
self-efficacy. My set of emotional competence skills is also not necessarily exhaustive; as Lutz rightly points out, ethnotheories of emo-

tion are open ended and can be modified or constructed further, whether by individuals or by subcultures. In addition, I can only guess at the cross-cultural applicability of my proposed set of emotional competence skills, and my guess is that probably the first nine or ten skills do have a fair degree of cross-cultural generalizability. Although this statement may constitute a caveat, I shall now turn to a discussion of each of the skills of emotional competence and briefly summarize a developmental study or two that illustrates the particular skill in question.

## Skills of Emotional Competence

**1. Awareness of one's emotional state and of the possibility of multiple emotions, and awareness that one may be "unaware" of one's feelings.** This skill builds upon basic or biologically predisposed patterns of emotional response, but in order for awareness of one's emotional response to occur, a sense of self must have developed: The young child must be able to cognitively apprehend that it is the self that is feeling something. Judging from research undertaken by Brooks and Lewis (1975) on infants' self-recognition in a mirror and further theoretical elaboration by Lewis and Brooks (1978), a very young infant (perhaps under 6 months) *has* emotional states but does not experience a conscious *awareness* of the emotional state. Lewis and Brooks stipulate that the infant must develop first an existential self (self as agent or subject) and then a self as object (also called the categorical self) in order to have the capacity to know that the self is experiencing an emotion. We can begin to infer that pre-verbal infants are aware of their emotional experience when they show reliable intentional behaviors to sustain or invite events (many of which are social transactions) that produce pleasurable emotional states (see also Lewis & Michalson, 1983). Our inference of their awareness is on even firmer ground when we see infants evaluate events and persons present before expressing a distinct emotion. Social referencing is a good example of this, and infants as young as 10–12 months demonstrate such strategies as looking to their mothers' emotional-expressive behavior when faced with a stranger (or some other emotionally ambiguous situation) as a guide to their own emotional reaction (Feinman & Lewis, 1983; Sorce, Emde, Campos, & Klinnert, 1985). By age 2, many toddlers are able to verbalize simple feeling states and can describe anticipatory affective states such as liking or wanting something; and as "terrible twos" they are especially adept at articulating what they do *not* want to do.

Awareness of experiencing multiple emotions or contrasting emotions (as in ambivalence) is a development that may appear as early as 5–6 years of age (Stein & Trabasso, 1989) or not until late childhood (Harter & Whitesell, 1989), depending on one's criteria and methods of eliciting such understanding. Stein and Trabasso examined 5–6-year-olds and determined that at this age children could readily describe people who made them feel good *and* bad or whom they liked *and* did not like. However, Stein and Trabasso caution that this does not mean that children *simultaneously* feel conflicting feelings: rather, they first focus on one situation to which they attach values and attributions, respond emotionally to its impact on them (e.g., "I don't like her because she took my Halloween candy"), and then focus on another situation with its accompanying values and attributions and respond emotionally to its impact (e.g., "But I like her when she plays with me"). Thus ambivalence for Stein and Trabasso is a *sequential* process with different appraisals attached to the different or polarized emotional responses, and they suggest that this process is the same for adults, just much more rapid.

Harter and Whitesell (1989) are concerned with children's cognitive construction of their own emotional experience (readers should note the connection here to naive theories of emotion), particularly when multiple emotions are involved. They focus on the cognitive developmental prerequisites for understanding the simultaneity of multiple emotions embedded in a situation or relationship and use Fischer's (1980) skills theory as their organizational framework (see also Harter, 1986). Not until there is access to "representational mappings" (Harter's level 3) would the child be able to integrate opposite-valence emotions (happy and sad) about different targets that co-occur in a situation (e.g., "I'm glad I get to live with my dad, but I'm sad about not being able to live with my mom too"). And in level 4 the child (now probably a preadolescent) can simultaneously integrate opposite-valence emotions about the same target (e.g., "I love my dad, even though I'm mad at him right now"). Harter and Whitesell acknowledge that what may occur as we experientially integrate contrasting emotions about the same target is a rapid oscillation between the multiple emotion-eliciting aspects of a relationship or situation. Perhaps an appropriate metaphor here is the kaleidoscope: as one turns the tube the brilliantly colored chips of glass merge rapidly from one pattern into another, but the series of complex designs retains a structural relationship to the prior patterns— until one shakes the thing hard.

I cannot describe an empirical study relative to knowing that one may not be consciously aware of some emotion, but clinical anecdote suggests that acting-out behavior in children and adolescents may "mask" a depression. Similarly, a general malaise may be consciously evident, but it may be hard for someone to pinpoint more specific emotions because to zero in on those specific feelings one must also evaluate the eliciting events, which is likely to evoke still more negative emotions. For example, a husband feels mildly despondent but does not know why; with the support of counseling he realizes he is bored to death with his wife, whom he politely avoids confronting because his boredom is presumably not her fault and to initiate a separation would imply some character deficiency on his part. Therefore he feels trapped or in limbo and may even wish he had never undertaken therapy and found out about all his different and specific feelings. Other clinical suggestions for selective inattention to emotions, yet accompanied by an awareness that one is avoiding something, may occur in instances of procrastination (I have some personal familiarity with this one) and possibly even in the precipitating anxiety that precedes bulimic excesses or drug abuse. Socialization within the family very likely contributes to the development of such emotion-avoidant patterns and the use of emotion-numbing coping methods such as are found in chemical dependency. Indeed, we see occurring across generations both addictive behaviors (Ackerman, 1983) and patterns of family violence, which are also often accompanied by chemical dependency (Saunders, Lynch, Grayson, & Linz, 1987).

**2. Ability to discern others' emotions.** At a rather young age children are able to act pragmatically vis-à-vis others' emotional-expressive behavior, which suggests that they both discern others' emotions and can use others' emotional-expressive behaviors as reference points for guiding their own emotional response (reviewed in Michalson & Lewis, 1985). By age 2 they can also show by means of a matching process that they understand the verbal labels for the facial expressions of six basic emotions, although they could not produce the verbal labels for the facial expressions themselves (Lewis & Michalson, 1985). These same 2-year-olds also demonstrated a limited degree of understanding about which situation was likely to elicit which emotion (between 25% and 71% were able to choose the appropriate facial expression for the happy, sad, and surprised situations). By age 4 children can nominate the sorts of situations that "go together" with a simple set of emotions (Barden, Zelko, Duncan, & Masters, 1980). Their accuracy in decoding facial expressions of basic emotions is good, with only a little confusion of the negative emotions, and by school entry at age 5 to 6, children reliably distinguish among the negative facial expressions as well (reviewed in Camras, 1985).

Strayer (1986) has also documented that by age 5–6 years children are able to provide reasonable determinants for emotions experienced both by the self and by others. She also examined several thematic shifts in situational determinants of emotion such as impersonal versus interpersonal attributions, achievement themes, the role of fantasy, and degree of agency or control. Older children (7–8 years) made more use of interpersonal and achievement themes than did the younger children (5–6 years), and, interestingly, there were no significant differences in explanations given whether the emotion was experienced by the self or by somebody else.

Several investigators have gathered data suggesting that children who have emotional problems, or who have been abused, show deficits in understanding links between facial expression and emotion, in producing facial expressions, and in discriminating emotion expressions (Camras, Grow, & Ribordy, 1983; Feldman, White, & Lobato, 1982; Walker, 1981). Do children who are exceptionally socially competent show an enhancement of understanding emotion and expression linkages? A study undertaken by Walden and Field (1988) suggests that preschoolers who obtained high sociometric peer preferences as play partners also tended to be better at discriminating among emotional facial displays and to demonstrate high spontaneous expressivity (though they did not excel in posed expressions). Another study undertaken by Edwards, Manstead, and MacDonald (1984) with somewhat older children demonstrated a similar relationship: Children's sociometric rating was positively related to their ability to recognize facial expressions of emotion.

We can conclude that this particular skill of emotional competence is initiated at a relatively early age and the degree of sophistication is influenced by the relative adequacy of social relationships experienced by any given child.

**3. Ability to use the vocabulary of emotion and expression terms commonly available in one's (sub)culture.** Based on maternal reports, Bretherton and Beeghly (1982) concluded that verbalization of emotion-related language typically first appears at about 20 months of age and increases rapidly throughout the subsequent year. Ridgeway, Waters, and Kuczaj (1985) undertook a study to produce norms on the rank order in which emotion-related and body-state vocabulary terms were likely to emerge in the age range from 18 months to 6 years. They also used parental reports, and their sample size ($N =$ 270) was considerably larger than Bretherton and Beeghly's ($N =$ 30). From an initial pool of 518 emotion-related terms, they selected a subset of 125 terms that were most frequently encountered. The 10 earliest acquired words within this subset of 125 words were (in order of difficulty): sleepy, hungry, good, happy, clean, tired, sad, afraid, busy, and quiet. The 10 latest acquired words, again in order of difficulty, were: gay (as in happy), insecure, weary, rejected, carefree, at ease, envious, tense, dominant, and aroused. Certainly one point to be made here is that their set of norms provides us with an excellent resource for designing research materials with appropriate word use relative to the age groups we intend to study. But their ranked set of 125 emotion and body-state words also shows us that children as young as 3–4 years of age have considerable comprehension of emotion vocabulary. Words like relaxed, uncomfortable, and cooperative were thought by parents to be comprehended by more than half of all 3-year-olds in the study. Given a redundant stimulus situation that fits such sophisticated terms, it may well be that preschoolers do understand the approximate meaning of these words when they are used in context.

Another study relevant to this skill of emotional competence is an ethnographic analysis of the emotion language used by three little girls in a South Baltimore community (Miller & Sperry, 1987). The girls were all about 2½ years old and resided with their single mothers, who were economically stressed (receiving public assistance). Miller and Sperry present a rich set of data showing that these little girls were remarkably competent at using the emotion language of their particular community or subculture. In this community emotion language was especially elaborated for situations involving aggression and self-defense. Thus, although the children did not often use classic emotion terms like "angry," they did use aggression terms (e.g., bite, hit) in appropriate contexts that indicated their aggression was an outcome of feeling angry. They were even able to make false accusations of naughty behavior by other children to justify aggression against them. The justification for aggression was that if one needed to defend oneself—if one was "attacked"—one was justified in feeling angry. However, this applied only to the interaction among children: the little girls were not supposed to show anger toward adults, much less be aggressive against them, even if the circumstances were similar to those eliciting justifiable anger and aggression among their child peers.

Lutz (1985) describes the acquisition of emotion vocabulary among Ifaluk children with special attention to highly *contextualized* words such as *nguch*, which among adults is associated with contexts of tedium, lack of alternatives, and weariness. Among children (8 to 13 years) Lutz found that children contextualized this word to refer to how one would feel in a variety of situations, such as physical discomfort from heat or walking, tedium from being alone, or the performance of repetitive chores. "Boredom" does not quite get at the meaning of *nguch*, because we lack reference to specific contexts for homing in on the emotional communication uses of such a word. But for the Ifaluk child, skillful use of such words in the appropriate contexts for communicating how one feels signifies one's connection to others, for if one communicates that one feels *nguch*, then the other will respond (given the emotional symbiosis that Lutz described for this culture), and as a result, one's *nguch* is likely to be relieved by the response.

**4. Capacity for empathic involvement in others' emotional experience.** For describing this aspect of emotional competence I have drawn heavily upon the work of Strayer (1989), whose interpretation of empathic development similarly emphasizes the social context in which children experience emotions, in this case, the vicarious experience of *others'* emotions. She makes an important developmental distinction between an empathic response that essentially is derived from the young child's focus on the emotion-eliciting *events* that are affecting another (e.g., watching child A hit child B and becoming distressed about witnessing the event) as opposed to an empathic response that stems from *participation* in the emotional reaction of the affected individual (e.g., showing distress upon seeing a child cry without having seen the precipitating event). The former event-focused empathy relies on a rather concrete cognitive awareness of what sort of situations "cause" emotions; the latter participatory empathy requires cognitive awareness of others' internal states. Thus Strayer does include cognitive developmental complexity in her assessment of empathy, because representations, whether of emotion-eliciting events or emotion-experiencing people, determine the quality of the empathic response. Furthermore, what can elicit an empathic response in children or adults will depend heavily on what sorts of representations they are capable of.

Using a rating scale called the Empathy Continuum, Strayer examined children's (ages 5 to 13) attribution of emotions to themselves upon watching dramatic video episodes. She found age differences indicating that the youngest children tended to attribute happiness to themselves more often than negative emotions; older children demonstrated the opposite pattern. The older children were responding in a more "empathically accurate" way to the sort of emotional experiences portrayed in the video scenarios. What is interesting here is that the 5-year-olds were accurate in reporting the negative emotions experienced by the characters in the video scenarios, but they differed from the older children in attributing emotion to *themselves* when asked how they felt upon watching the video dramas.

Gender differences also occurred in what kinds of emotions children attributed to the self while watching the videos. Girls more often reported sadness and fear than did boys, who in turn more often reported angry responses than did girls. Strayer interpreted these sex differences as reflecting the nature of sex-role socialization and the effect of cultural display rules (see below) on what children were perhaps willing to report.

Another developmental trajectory described by Strayer is the change from overidentification with or "engulfment" by the circumstances surrounding another's emotional experience to a more mature sharing in another's emotion. The former entails a blurring of self/other boundaries; the latter maintains an awareness that while one may feel much as the affected person does, one is in fact not in the same situation. She poses the question whether young children's self-reports of happiness after watching video characters feel distressed are actually a way to control dysphoric emotions and thereby reduce the risk of engulfment in the fear-producing stimuli.

The excerpt from *Nothing's Fair in Fifth Grade* near the beginning of this chapter is a good illustration of how attending to a person's emotional experience as opposed to the eliciting events, leads to empathy. The protagonist, Jennifer, is moved to an empathic response upon witnessing Elsie's unrelenting sadness, even though Jennifer had been one of the perpetrators in the circumstances leading to Elsie's distress (e.g., teasing and ridiculing). She changes her belief about Elsie's being somewhat less than human to one that defines Elsie as a person with feelings: "I guess I didn't think about your having feelings," and from that point on in the book Jennifer forges a different and more empathic relationship to Elsie. In terms of emotional competence, I think empathic responsiveness may be one of the most significant components for promoting social bonds among people and fostering prosocial behavior. Without empathy as a component of emotional competence, one could conceivably demonstrate all the other "skills" of emotional competence in a Machiavellian or even sociopathic fashion.

**5. Ability to understand that internal state need not correspond to external expression.** Based on their collective social-emotional experiences over time, infants learn to synchronize their emotional states and expressive behavior relative to an eliciting situation. But by the preschool years, if not earlier, young children also learn how to introduce discrepancies between their internal state and their external expressive behavior. Perhaps the earliest form of this discrepancy is the *exaggeration* of emotional-expressive behavior in order to gain someone's attention (a trivial injury becomes the occasion to howl loudly and solicit comfort and attention); parents are likely to think that this occurs in the second year, if not earlier. More systematic observational research supports this anecdotal view: Blurton Jones (1967) reported that children aged 3–4 in a free-play situation were more likely to cry after injuring themselves if they noticed someone looking at them; they were less likely to cry if they thought they were unattended.

*Minimization* may be the next to appear; it consists of dampening the intensity of emotional-expressive behavior despite one's feelings. Socialization is likely to be highly influential here, such as when we admonish children to tone down their rambunctious behavior or control their upset feelings. *Neutralization* describes the adoption of a "poker face," but it is probably relatively difficult to carry off, and indeed, Ekman and Friesen (1975) suggest that *substitution* of another expression for what one genuinely feels is probably a more successful strategy.

In an early study (Saarni, 1979b) I interviewed elementary-school children about when and why they would conceal their own feelings of hurt/pain and fear. Most referred to avoiding embarrassment or others' derision for revealing vulnerable feelings. Getting attention, making someone feel sorry for you, and getting help were also among the reasons mentioned for dissembling emotional-expressive behavior. Significant age differences appeared only when children were questioned about when it would be appropriate to express one's genuine feelings, and older children (10–11 years) were likely to cite many more such occasions than younger children—suggesting that they perceived the expression of emotion, whether genuine or dissembled, as a regulated act. The older children were more likely to refer to the degree of affiliation with an interactant, status differences, and controllability of both emotion and circumstances as contextual qualities that affected the genuine or dissembled display of emotion. (In a study now under way we are systematically examining these contextual effects.)

Relative to children's learning that others may not be revealing how they really feel, Harris and Gross (1988) found that by age 6 children understood that an interactant can have a mistaken belief about someone's internal emotional state, that a dissembled facial expression can significantly contribute to this mistaken belief, and that such dissembled emotional-expressive behavior stems from trying to protect oneself or maneuver a situation to one's advantage.

This skill of emotional competence permits fluidity in social interaction that clearly can be used to promote self-efficacy in interpersonal transactions. Whether one is trying to protect one's vulnerability or enhance some advantage, being able to monitor emotional-expressive behavior strategically is adaptive (see also Saarni, 1989).

**6. Awareness of cultural display rules.** Display rules are essentially predictable social customs for how to express one's feelings appropriately (Ekman & Friesen, 1975). All cultures have display rules, but obviously they vary considerably in content and application. As summarized by Shennum and Bugental (1982), in North America children gradually acquire *knowledge* about when, where, with whom, and how to express their feelings behaviorally. They also need to have the *ability to control* the skeletal muscles involved in emotional-expressive behavior. Last, they need the *motivation* to enact display rules in the appropriate situations.

In a study with elementary-school children I investigated knowledge of such cultural display rules and also examined expectations about what motivated story characters to use them (Saarni, 1979a). Four stories were used, with accompanying photos of children acting out the story line: (a) receiving a disappointing gift from an aunt, (b) setting off the school fire alarm and being caught by the principal, (c) showing off on skates or skateboard and then falling down, and (d) being bullied by another child at school. In the final photograph, the protagonist's face was averted from the camera, and the children were asked to tell how the character felt and then to select from a set of four full-face portraits of different facial expressions the way the person would look in this situation. No sex differences were found, although age differences did occur: older children were more likely to spontaneously nominate facial expressions that did not match the actual feeling of the protagonist. With interview prompts, this age difference diminished somewhat. When we asked why protagonists would not look as they felt, four broad categories of motives were established: trouble avoidance (most frequently mentioned), relationship factors (e.g., "she looked that way so her aunt would feel OK"), maintenance of self-esteem (e.g., "he didn't want to get teased"), and reference to norms (e.g., "you should be polite"). The last category was used only by the oldest children (10–11 years).

In another study I conducted, children were observed trying to monitor their expressive behavior in order to meet the cultural display rule of "look agreeable when someone gives you a gift, even if you don't like it" (Saarni, 1984). The children, who ranged from 6 to 11 years old, attended a parochial school that had explicit expectations for conduct; thus they were more likely to be "motivated" to carry out this particular display rule. The children met individually with an ostensible market researcher, did a small task, and then received candy and money. This first session provided baseline data for their expressive behavior upon receiving a desirable gift. A couple of days later they returned to do another task, and this time were presented with a grab bag of wrapped gifts. They received dull and inappropriate baby toys for their effort. The videotapes of their unwrapping the baby toys and having to interact with the market researcher provided the following results: 6-year-old boys were uniformly negative in their expressive behavior; the youngest girls and both boys and girls of 8–9 years frequently demonstrated what was categorized as transitional behavior; and the oldest children (10–11 years), especially the girls, were most likely to express positive behavior toward the market researcher despite receiving a dumb baby toy.

Socialization clearly influences the adoption of cultural display rules, and in another recent study I sought to investigate which contextual factors socialization processes might be most reactive to (Saarni, 1987). Children in three age groups (7–8, 10–11, and 13–14 years) responded to seven cartoon vignettes featuring a same-sex, same-age protagonist who displayed genuine emotion in the presence of either the mother or the father. The subjects were asked to select a likely parental reaction to the emotional display of the child protagonist, and the four options of parental reaction ranged from most accepting to most controlling, presented in random order. After making their choice of parental reaction, the children were asked to justify it. Four of the cartoon vignettes contained story themes in which the protagonist's genuine emotional display could make another person vulnerable (e.g., Grandmother serves an unappetizing-looking casserole, and the child's display of disgust could hurt her feelings). The other three stories contained themes in which the child protagonist might become more vulnerable by displaying genuine emotion (e.g., showing one's fear about being bullied). There were no developmental differences in how this contextual feature (who might be made vulnerable by the display of genuine emotion) was taken into account by the subjects. An overwhelming majority at all ages selected rather controlling and restrictive parent reactions to the stories involving someone else at risk for becoming vulnerable and justified their choice of parental reaction by stating either that it was rude to act this way or that the child should change his or her behavior because the other person might get hurt, be upset, or become embarrassed. For the vulnerable-child stories there was more variability, but most children anticipated an accepting, even empathic, parental response to the vulnerable child. They most frequently justified these parental reactions by saying that the parent was concerned with how the child felt.

The same cartoon stories were given to a sample of parents (Saarni, 1988). Their selections of parental reactions and justifications mirrored the children's choices very closely. Interestingly, whereas the children's data had not revealed any significant sex differences, the adults' data did: if the story protagonist was a boy and he was made potentially vulnerable by displaying his genuine emotional state, then the adults expected he would receive a controlling parental reaction to his display. They expected girls in a vulnerable position to receive accepting parental reactions. Since the boys in our sample did not anticipate parents' reacting this way to boys in an emotionally vulnerable position, this difference in perspective makes for some interesting speculation about a clash in socialization expectancies.

In this context it should be noted that Fuchs and Thelen (1988) found that older boys did not anticipate they would reveal sadness, a vulnerability-disposing emotion, to their parents (although if they did, they would more likely reveal it to their mothers). Fuchs and Thelen used a mood-induction procedure (vividly recalling a specific emotion-eliciting situation) and then asked the children to rate the degree of understanding expected from their mothers or fathers if they revealed this feeling (sadness, anger, and happiness). Then they also rated the likelihood of their actually communicating the induced feeling to their mothers or fathers. That the boys in their sample did not especially believe they would communicate sadness to their fathers, whereas the boys in my sample did expect fathers to be supportive and comforting to sons in distressing situations may stem from the very different methods involved and the questions such methods raised. For example, we do not know what situations the boys imagined in order to induce sadness in themselves, and thus we do not know whether it was something about the situation and their remembered emotion that led them to anticipate that their fathers would be unsupportive. In contrast, in my study the situations were described in detail, with accompanying pictures. Fuchs and Thelen's subjects also were directly imagining the reactions of expressing genuine sadness to their own fathers; my subjects were asked about likely parental reactions to hypothetical characters (whether they projected the likely reactions of their own fathers is unknown). Of course regional sampling differences may also exist: Fuchs and Thelen's children were from the Midwest, where expectations for emotional self-control may be greater; my sample was from California, a region notorious for its "insufficient" inhibition.

**7. Ability to take into account unique personal information in understanding others' emotional experience.** The most relevant studies for more fully describing this feature of emotional competence were conducted by Gnepp and Gould (1985) and Gnepp and Chilamkurti (1988) and recently theoretically elaborated in Gnepp (1989).

Gnepp and Gould examined whether children (aged 5 to 10) could use information about a story character's past experience (e.g., being rejected by one's best friend) to predict how the character would feel in some new situation (e.g., subsequently meeting the best friend on the playground). Not unexpectedly, the youngest children were more likely to use the current situational information to infer what the character was feeling (e.g., she would be happy at seeing her best friend), and older children were more likely to infer the character's emotional state by taking into account the prior experience (e.g., she would feel sad upon seeing her best friend). An interaction also occurred between the hedonic tone (positive/negative) of the emotion and the use of personal information: if the story character experienced a negative *emotion* at Time 1 but encountered a commonly assumed positive *situation* at Time 2, then children were more likely to use prior personal history information when inferring how the character would feel at Time 2. Gnepp (1989) suggests that children must first recognize what a person's perspective was at Time 1 and then apply that inferred perspective from Time 1 to Time 2 to come up with the atypical emotional response.

In an analogous investigation Gnepp and Chilamkurti (1988) presented stories to elementary-school children and adults in which characters' personality traits were systematically described as either negative or positive. The story characters then had some experience befall them, and the children were to infer the characters' emotional reaction to this new experience. Older children and adults were more likely to take into account the prior trait information in inferring the emotional response of the characters in the new situation. The younger children (6-year-olds) were less consistent in doing so, but a number were able to take personality trait information into account when inferring how someone might respond emotionally even when the reaction might be atypical for the eliciting event.

These two investigations show us that by school entry children are on their way to superimposing multiple frames of reference across time intervals to predict or infer other people's emotional responses. In this research no distinction was made between emotional state and emotional-expressive behavior; the assumption was that children would infer emotional state. Whether children could also infer what sort of expressive behavior would be displayed, and whether it would be congruent with an atypical internal emotional state or with the consensually defined "typical" emotion response to the situation, was not part of the focus of these studies. In terms of social efficacy, being able to take into account these multiple frames of reference in making good guesses about how someone else is likely to react emotionally is strategic and functional. It is strategic, because one can negotiate social transactions with considerably more finesse. It is functional, because it promotes relationship bonds and facilitates "depth" of communication; that is, one's communication is more accurate and incisive with an individual whose atypical emotional reaction can be understood as highly probable, *given the personal knowledge one has about that individual.*

**8. Ability to understand that one's emotional-expressive behavior affects another and to take this into account in one's self-presentation strategies.** This skill of emotional competence builds on the prior ones: (a) knowing that internal emotional state and expressive behavior can be incongruent and (b) being able to take into account personal, unique information about others when inferring their emotional states. For example, if someone knows I find faculty meetings achingly boring and that I tend to daydream during them, but that person must get me to attend to some task at hand in such a meeting, then managing his or her emotional-expressive behavior strategically might make a lot of sense. The speaker could adopt a more lively set of facial expressions (instead of the dull ones usually in evidence at such meetings), speak in a vital fashion (instead of the monotone most frequently heard), and use hands and body to accentuate speech (instead of the usual motoric inhibition). I might then wake up and actually pay attention!

Support for this skill of emotional competence from a developmental viewpoint can be found in studies undertaken by Carlson, Felleman, and Masters (1983) and by McCoy and Masters (1985). In the Carlson et al. study, 4–5-year-old children viewed slides of other young children displaying assorted emotional states, and their accuracy of emotion judgment was ascertained. They were then asked whether, if *something* could change how the child felt, they would want it to and whether, if *they* could change how the child felt, they would want to. As expected, targets feeling a negative emotion were selected by the subjects to have their feeling states changed, while those feeling happy were not (some children suggested intensifying the happiness). When they themselves were to be involved in the change of emotion, children were more willing to endorse changing the target's emotion than if some external cause were to do so. Although this study tells us preschoolers apparently recognize that they can play a role in influencing someone's emotional state, we do not know their reasoning for *why* this might be desirable or strategic. They were not asked to justify their responses or to nominate reasons for how or why they might be influential in changing another's emotional response. In any case, it is possible that preschoolers could not articulate such justifications.

McCoy and Masters (1985) remedied this ambiguity in a study in which 5–12-year-olds were interviewed in response to a series of slides depicting other children displaying assorted emotions. Accompanying stories were either social or nonsocial in nature, and the emotional state of the child was explicitly stated. The subjects were then asked, "What could you do to make [character's name] not feel [affect given]?" Depending on the emotion in question, children nominated intervention strategies that appeared to require managing one's emotional-expressive behavior; for example, nurture was nominated to alter sadness and anger, and aggression was suggested to change happiness. Nurturing behavior would entail a variety of expressive behaviors in the brow (perhaps sad looking) and mouth region (perhaps smiling slightly) along with an appropriate vocal tone, while aggressive behavior would include frowns, absence of positive expressions, threatening vocal tone, and gestures. The developmental difference in this study was that older children suggested more social and verbal nurturing strategies, which would presumably involve the expressive behaviors noted above. The 5-year-olds were more likely to suggest material nurturing strategies to alleviate someone's sadness or anger (e.g., give the sad person some candy).

Although this study has a number of other complex findings, for our purposes what is important is that school-age children can readily articulate ways to alter someone's affective state. Older children were more likely to suggest *interpersonal* strategies, and if they had been interviewed further about how one would *look* during these interpersonal interventions, this research might have shed light on their awareness of how their emotional-expressive behavior would need to be managed.

Research on adults' self-presentation has a long history (re-

viewed by Tedeschi, 1981; Tedeschi & Norman, 1985) and has recently been linked to coping with stress (Laux, 1986). Laux connects
emotional well-being directly with self-presentation, because if we
manage our self-presentation (and thus our emotional-expressive
behavior) to preserve our self-esteem in some threatening or otherwise stressful situation, then we will have coped more effectively
with that situation and will emerge from it *feeling better*. Thus self-
presentations that are simultaneously coping efforts can be oriented
toward changing the "person-environment transaction" and can
also have an emotionally relieving effect (see also Lazarus & Lanier,
1978).

From an emotional competence standpoint, self-efficacy in difficult interpersonal situations can be promoted (a) if we are aware that
our emotional-expressive behavior influences another's response,
and (b) if we then strategically try to manage our emotional-expressive behavior vis-à-vis the other so that the other will respond in a
way we deem desirable. In research still being analyzed, we asked
children to nominate how a story character's expressive behavior
should change to have a different effect on a target (e.g., How
should Jack look when Grandmother serves an unappetizing casserole if he doesn't want his mother to be upset with him for hurting
Grandmother's feelings, even though he feels disgust at the pecu-
liar-looking food?). Despite this convoluted three-person entanglement and the need to coordinate multiple frames of reference, preliminary data analyses showed remarkably few developmental
differences: 6–7-year-olds typically gave the same suggestion as 11–
12-year-olds; namely, the child should conceal his disgust. Other
strategies were also nominated: push the food around on the plate,
feed the dog under the table, pretend to have a violent coughing fit,
and so forth. Children are evidently very cognizant of how to maneuver through social situations, adapting both emotional-expressive dissemblance and situational strategies for promoting self-efficacy.

Does this same facility appear in children who differ from normally developing children? Adlam-Hill and Harris (1988) found that
emotionally disturbed children of average intelligence showed a distinct deficit compared with their nondisturbed peers in understanding that internal emotional state and external expressive behavior

can be incongruent. As a consequence, such children were also less likely to think that story characters would modify their facial expressions if showing how they really felt would hurt another's feelings. Adlam-Hill and Harris speculate about why this deficit occurred and suggest that emotionally disturbed children may not understand how to protect others' feelings, may not be motivated to do so, or may not even predict that the display of genuine emotion can affect another in the first place.

Hayes and McDonald (1988) examined another apparent deficit in children's understanding of the impact their emotional-expressive behavior has on others. They investigated the emotional and social behaviors of normal preschoolers toward several handicapped children who were placed in the preschool as part of the school system's attempt to mainstream special populations of children. Hayes and McDonald focused on the normal children's reactions to two little girls who had spina bifida and thus had difficulties in locomotion, had erratic bowel and urinary functioning, were small for their age, and had shunts to control hydrocephalic swelling. Their observational data collected over a year's time showed that the normal preschoolers responded to the two girls as if they were objects: they tended not to address them directly but would ask adults in their presence questions *about the child* that normally would have been asked directly of a same-aged peer. Some of their attributions to the two children were along the lines of "they must still be babies"; other attributions were startling in their apparent belief that the two girls were somehow not human; for example, one girl to another: "You're not allowed to stand on Debra" and "Does Debra have teeth?"

While Hayes and McDonald did not focus on emotional-expressive interactions between the normal and the handicapped children, the emotional behaviors of the two spina bifida girls did attract attention and even some faint attempt at comforting. However, relative to our discussion here, we do not know if the children were aware of how they might be affecting their disabled peers' emotional states. My guess is that they were not, but most likely because they were only 4 years old. It would be interesting to observe older children with mainstreamed disabled peers and see if they are aware that they manage their emotional-expressive behavior around such children so as not to hurt their feelings. Or perhaps they would not, if they continued to demonstrate some degree of objectification similar to the preschoolers and did not attribute the same kinds of emotional experience to disabled individuals as they would to nonhandicapped peers. The excerpt from *Nothing's Fair in Fifth Grade* cited at the beginning of this essay also captures this objectification and its resulting callousness toward the target child as somehow less than human.

**9. Capacity for adaptive coping with aversive or distressing emotions**. This "skill" of emotional competence is extraordinarily complex, for it entails consideration of an individual's developmental history that includes quality of attachment relations (e.g., Grossmann & Grossmann, in press; Main, Kaplan, & Cassidy, 1985), temperament (e.g., Thomas, Chess, & Birch, 1968), and access to a social milieu that facilitates coping with stress (i.e., consider the differences for children growing up in a refugee camp in Lebanon versus children growing up in North American suburbia). I am not going to address these challenging issues (but see Thompson, this volume); rather, I shall try to elaborate on this aspect of emotional competence by briefly discussing Weiner and Graham's (1984) notion of controllability and by commenting on studies by Harris and Lipian (1989).

The attribution of controllability is part of Weiner and Graham's (1984) model for emotional experience in which the emphasis is on individuals' search for causes of their emotional experience. The other two major attributional categories Weiner and Graham describe are locus (essentially the distinction between internal and external source of influence) and stability (likelihood of recurrence). Weiner and Graham posit that helplessness is one of the key outcomes when individuals attribute the causes of their experience both as uncontrollable and as based in an external source or locus. When the locus is internal and yet uncontrollable, shame is the emotional outcome (see also Zahn-Waxler, this volume). Another outcome when a situation is viewed as both uncontrollable and external is the use of a different coping strategy to promote a desirable situation or avoid an undesirable one—namely, second-guessing those who are perceived to be in control (see again Zahn-Waxler, this volume). On the other hand, when individuals do feel they are in control of emotion-eliciting events and are the source of influence, they are more likely to experience positive emotions and a sense of self-efficacy.

When I apply this attributional perspective that emphasizes controllability, source of influence, and likelihood of recurrence to children's efforts to cope with their own negative feelings, I come up with several possibilities, which are noted below. Each is followed by a statement in parentheses that suggests how Weiner and Graham's viewpoint might characterize the coping attempt.

(a) Children endure the negative emotion for a short time and then distract themselves by attending to another situation. (The child is in control, the source of influence is external, and the child seeks to minimize the recurrence of the negative emotion by leaving or avoiding the negative emotion-eliciting situation.)

(b) Children attempt to redefine the emotion-eliciting situation and thereby feel a less intensely negative emotion. For example, fear is reduced to apprehension by focusing on thoughts such as "well, this shot will keep me from getting a terrible disease," or an altogether different emotion is evoked, as when one feels hurt or scared and then becomes angry upon further reflection. (The child is in control, the source of influence is internal, namely, self-reflection, and recurrence is limited.)

(c) Children redefine the emotion they are experiencing; for example, "I'm not scared, I'm mad!" (The child is in control, the source of influence is internal, and recurrence is limited.)

(d) Children attempt to ameliorate the intensity of the negative emotion by managing their emotional-expressive behavior in a more positive way; for example, "whistling in the dark" when afraid, smiling through tears. (The child is in control, the source of influence may be both internal and external, and recurrence may be problematic.)

(e) Children endure the negative emotion for a short time but cope by ventilating it on a safe target; for example, the family dog gets hit when they actually want to hit their parents. (The child has only limited control, the source of influence is mostly external, and recurrence is unknown.)

(f) Children sublimate the negative emotion either through psychosomatic illness, through dissociation, or by means of another compensating activity; for example, my imaginary playmate of early childhood was in a sense a dissociative compensating activity for not receiving the attention I might have wanted when the births of two siblings preoccupied the family, and I also managed to develop an assortment of mysterious respiratory allergies during that time. (The child is for the most part not in control, the source of influence is external, and recurrence is problematic.)

Although I do not have empirical data to support these attributions of control, source of influence, or recurrence likelihood for the way children cope with aversive emotions, they appear in a few instances to be embedded in Harris and Lipian's work (1989). Harris and Lipian investigated children's understanding of emotion while they were undergoing a stressful experience. They interviewed children 6 and 10 years of age who had been briefly hospitalized (with neither chronic nor life-threatening illnesses). Compared with non-hospitalized healthy children, the hospitalized children did show an apparent regression in the maturity of their thinking about emotion. Of interest were the responses given to one of the interview questions: "Say you were ill and you felt sad [or whatever emotion the child had mentioned to describe his or her feelings at the beginning of the interview]. Is there anything you could do to change the way you felt, to change the feeling of being sad?" Approximately similar proportions of the healthy and hospitalized 6-year-olds could nominate a strategy (44% and 40%, respectively). However, while all of the healthy 10-year-olds could nominate a strategy, only 36% of the hospitalized 10-year-olds could think of something to do that would affect their emotional state for the better. Most of the hospitalized children were quite pessimistic about how they were feeling. The sorts of strategies nominated by the children, regardless of health status, to change negative feelings tended to fall into two broad categories: 6-year-olds suggested concrete distractions (e.g., "I would go and play with my friend") with virtually no elaboration, and 10-year-olds tended to suggest "mentalistic" strategies such as "do something to boost my morale" that included both distraction and some explanation of a psychological mechanism that would ameliorate the negative emotion. Thus, when asked directly what *they* could do to change emotions, children suggested the first coping strategy from my list above. A provocative question that Harris and

Lipian address is why so few of the older hospitalized children nominated *any* strategy for change. Their argument is that once a negative emotional state is firmly established, cognitive biases come into play that effectively screen out alternative frames of reference that the older children might have been capable of had they been in happier circumstances. Interestingly, hospitalized children especially lack control over their environment.

Harris and Lipian also interviewed a sample of boys (aged 8) entering boarding school for the first time concerning their feelings of loneliness. They asked similar questions about emotion, but this time they asked the children whether, if they wanted to cheer themselves up, they could do so simply by smiling. Only about 25% thought this would be an effective strategy, but when they were asked if they could cheer themselves up by thinking about something else, 77% of the boys affirmed this as a useful strategy. These responses indicate that children hold a naive theory of emotion in which redirecting one's thoughts will lead to different emotions, even if the situation cannot be changed. From Graham and Weiner's point of view, such redirection of thoughts for seeking emotional relief implies an internal locus and limited controllability, and the likelihood of recurrence would perhaps be dependent upon the effectiveness of the former two attributes. The cognitive deficit or slippage was not observed in these boarding-school boys, perhaps because admission to these boarding schools was much valued by the boys and their families. Thus, although these boys were in a situation that was not especially under their control, their emotional state was not as acutely negative as that of the hospitalized children, who appeared to demonstrate the cognitive distortions such negative states can bring about.

The preceding research, conducted in England, is related to Miller and Green's (1985) assumption that "the selection or avoidance of particular kinds of information while coping with aversive events" (p. 264) is closely linked to the effectiveness of such coping. They propose that according to the "blunting hypothesis," individuals reduce the aversive aspects of a stressful situation that are *not* under their control by cognitively avoiding them or psychologically withdrawing (as in intellectualization). If the situation *is* under their control, then monitoring it is more instrumentally useful, even though it induces greater emotional arousal.

Thus, if one monitors the situation closely *and* does not have control over its course or duration, one will maximize one's sense of upsetness and distress. If one distracts oneself or psychologically reduces the potency of incoming information about a situation over which one has no control, one will maximize one's sense of well-being (or at least not suffer as much). Indeed, the boarding-school boys in Harris and Lipian's work appeared to do just that: they suggested it was best not to think about missing Mom, the dog, or one's room at home but instead to think about positive things.

Monitoring does produce vigilance and thus sensitizes people to information about threatening aspects of a situation. The older hospitalized children in Harris and Lipian's research appeared to experience this: they were cognitively sophisticated enough to appreciate more of the threatening aspects than the 6-year-olds, who did not differ much from nonhospitalized 6-year-olds. Perhaps as a consequence, they got themselves into a vicious cycle: as they monitored more, they became more and more distressed, and their cognitive biases toward selecting pessimistic information tended to be reinforced, which in turn probably encouraged more monitoring.

Emotional competence, as reflected in coping with aversive emotions, will need to take into account this interaction of adaptive use of monitoring or blunting and the degree of control an individual has over a situation. We are virtually ignorant in our knowledge base when it comes to combining this perspective with patterns of attachment relations, temperament, and social milieu in individual developmental histories.

**10. Awareness that the nature of relationships is in part defined by degree of emotional immediacy and by degree of emotional reciprocity or symmetry.** Very little research has investigated this aspect of emotional competence from a developmental perspective; however, an adult literature does exist, and readers are referred to Patterson (1984) for a review of relevant issues and to Bradbury and Fincham (1987) for an analysis of emotional symmetry among married couples. A couple of studies with children that address this issue indirectly are discussed below.

Mendelson and Peters (1983) examined whether children took knowledge of relationship into account when predicting the emotions communicated in a dyadic interaction. Only 13–14-year-olds consistently used relationship structure (e.g., friend/not friend, parent/not parent) to make sense of how both hostile and affectionate behaviors were communicated. Children at ages 9–10 took into account only hostile behavior in their predictions, and affectionate exchanges were not much used to discriminate transactions that differed by how close the relationship was.

In a recent study (Saarni, 1988), I investigated children's beliefs about how others are likely to react when one presents an "emotional front," that is, when one dissembles emotional-expressive behavior so that one's genuine emotional state is not directly revealed. The children were in three age groups: 6–7, 10–11, and 13–14 years. They first answered a series of questions about four photo-accompanied vignettes, and the pattern of responses varied considerably according to context. What is relevant here is that when responses were coded for whether children viewed the interpersonal consequences of the emotional front as positive or negative, several significant age effects occurred. For example, the two older groups of children believed it would produce desirable consequences if they dissembled disappointment over an unwanted gift from an aunt (e.g., "her feelings won't be hurt"), whereas dissemblance toward a bully would be ineffective—bullies are presumably not deterred by a tough emotional front. The youngest children had a more negative view of dissembling to an aunt; their responses focused on the story character's not getting the desired birthday present. They also believed that dissembling to bullies would produce positive outcomes (e.g., "then he won't keep on bothering you"). Greater experience with bullies may have produced more cynicism among the older children. Across age groups a majority of children thought it would be a good thing to dissemble hurt when falling down after showing off on skates or a skateboard, and children at all ages also thought the outcome would be negative for having set off the school fire alarm, despite presenting a front of innocence to the principal.

When asked what the interpersonal outcome would be if the story characters showed their real feelings (appropriate photos of genuine facial expressions were than shown), significant age differences occurred for the fire alarm and the bully stories. Older children thought the outcome would be more positive if one showed one's apprehension to the principal (one could cut one's punishment losses, so to speak, by admitting the misdeed); younger children expected mostly negative consequences. For the bully story, more of the older children believed the outcome would be highly negative if one expressed one's genuine fear; more of the younger children thought there could be positive consequences such as "someone might help you if they see you are afraid." Across age groups, children thought the interpersonal consequences would be negative if one revealed genuine disappointment to a misguided aunt or expressed hurt after showing off and then injuring oneself.

The children were next asked a series of questions about whether they would be more likely to reveal genuine feelings to an adult (excluding parents) or a peer, why that would be so, and what would likely happen to a child who almost always presented an emotional front versus a child who almost always expressed genuine emotions. Whereas there were no sex differences in the preceding set of results, the responses to these questions did reveal a significant age × sex interaction. In particular, the two older groups of girls preferred peers as targets of genuine emotion and tended more often to justify that preference by saying adults were not trustworthy or would not understand. Generally, however, children justified their preference for either peers or adults as recipients of genuine emotion by most often appealing to the trustworthiness, sympathy, or quality of relationship (e.g., "your friends understand you better" or "adults wouldn't make fun of you").

When asked what would happen to the child who almost always expressed genuine feelings versus the one who almost always dissembled, 57% of the children (across ages) felt that the former would be socially rejected, although a few children thought that such a child would at least obtain "emotional relief," would be perceived as honest, and could even be popular. For the chronic dissembler, children had largely negative reactions: such a child would be disliked, perceived as emotionally maladjusted or as isolated and impenetrable (hard to get to know). An example from an eighth-grade girl expresses vividly the expectations about such a child: "If she kept everything inside her all the time, she'd consume all her anger, jealousy, whatever, and then one day she'd explode, commit suicide, and get emotionally disturbed." (This may be the "volcano theory" of emotion regulation.)

Children obviously think that either extreme, "letting it all hang out" or chronically adopting an emotional front, is maladaptive and not sensitive to interpersonal relationships. The body of data from this research also indicates that children evaluate how emotions are communicated in relation to the nature of the relationship between interactants and in relation to social goals or motives. Naive theories of emotion are also readily discerned in the children's beliefs, whether the facetious reference above to the "volcano theory" or the need to save face in some situations (e.g., hurting oneself after showing off) or to allow another to save face (e.g., one's misguided aunt choosing such a poor birthday gift). While this study did not investigate children's views of reciprocity or symmetry in relationships (and I am not aware of any study with children that does so directly), the ready acknowledgment of interpersonal consequences that are *contingent* on emotional-expressive behavior suggests that children do implicitly use notions of reciprocity in some of their expectations (e.g., "I won't show how I feel so that you won't have to experience a negative feeling"). This contingency was also evident in the research I described for the sixth emotional competence skill of awareness of cultural display rules.

**11. Capacity for emotional self-efficacy: individuals view themselves as feeling, overall, the way they want to feel.** The last skill of emotional competence to be considered brings us back to naive theories of emotion. When we accept our emotional experience as appropriate for ourselves and the circumstances, we are also implicitly living in accord with our naive theory of emotion. We may be unhappy or restless or distraught, but we can still judge these emotional states as appropriate to both self and situation and feel that they serve our interests in an adaptive manner. This is not to say that we want to go on feeling miserable or whatever; rather, we view our emotional response as justified and believe others would concur if they shared our perspective. Individuals with a capacity for emotional self-efficacy also know how to cope with aversive emotional states by regulating their intensity, duration, and frequency. They do so with the belief that they will generally be effective in such regulation and can tolerate and cope with negative emotions.

Depressed people, such as the sample of mothers described in Zahn-Waxler's contribution to this volume, may feel justified in their emotional response of sadness and hopelessness, but their efficacy in coping with negative emotional states is poor. Similarly, battering husbands may view their anger as "justified," but their sense of efficacy in coping with anger and aggression is also poor (Saunders, Lynch, Grayson, & Linz, 1987). Indeed, most depressed people would rather not feel depressed, and most battering husbands would rather not feel that their anger is *out of control*. Perhaps this is the key issue for emotional self-efficacy: one feels relatively in control of one's emotional experience from the standpoint of mastery and positive self-regard. One does not feel overwhelmed by the enormity, intensity, or complexity of emotional experience, nor does one react by inhibiting, distrusting, or "damping down and numbing it out." Issues of emotion regulation are relevant here, as is the question whether some kinds of emotion regulation are dysfunctional and ultimately maladaptive (see Thompson, this volume).

Clinical psychologists have typically been more concerned with the kind of thinking presented above than have developmental psychologists, and it is not immediately evident how developmental psychologists would empirically investigate children's emotional self-efficacy. Assessment of self-concept and perceived competence are relevant and have implications for emotional self-efficacy (see Harter, 1982, 1986; Piers & Harris, 1984). However, what intrigues me is the idea of how children recognize that some sort of integration or *balance* is important in one's emotional life: both negative and positive feelings have their place, as does the expression of both genuine and dissembled emotional displays in emotional exchanges with others. When emotional self-efficacy is examined from this viewpoint of developing a sense of balance between two courses of action or emotional valences, then a couple of developmental studies become relevant for discussion.

The first study was carried out by Harter and Whitesell (1989), who interviewed children 9 to 12 years old about whether experiencing two opposite-valence feelings (happy/sad or happy/mad) created an internal conflict. They found that only about 50% of the chil-

dren (across ages) reported conflict. Children who said there was little or no conflict made statements such as the following: "If I am really happy, the mad feeling just sort of fades and gets covered up by
the happy" or "The sad feeling is there, but it's not really controlling
how I feel." For the children who did report an internal conflict,
however, the relative intensity of the two opposite-valence emotions was a major contributor. If the two feelings—for example, mad
and happy—were reported as having relatively the same intensity
or if the negative emotion was rated as more intense than the positive one, conflict was more likely to be reported. Conflict was infrequently mentioned if happiness was experienced as more intense.
Harter and Whitesell go on to suggest that negative emotions will be
rated as highly intense (and therefore will "overpower" positive
emotions) if they occur within a close relationship, such as between
parent and child, and particularly if an expectancy is contradicted.
The child then feels a severe sense of betrayal or loss, leading to intense anger or sadness, respectively. There is no conflict over how
one feels; the negative feeling simply surpasses any positive emotion the child may also feel toward the parent.

Emotional balance in Harter and Whitesell's work appears to refer to having a mixture of feelings, but overall the positive ones pre-
dominate. How children come to be able to regulate their internal
emotional experience so they can reliably and over the long term
produce more positive than negative emotional states is related to
their unique developmental histories and to their ability to cope
with aversive emotions as discussed under the ninth emotional
competence skill.

As part of the study described earlier in which children's beliefs
about the interpersonal consequences of dissemblance were examined (Saarni, 1988), I also asked children how they thought they
achieved a sense of *balance* between expressing their genuine feelings and dissembling how they felt. Their responses were coded according to five categories that ranged from saying something utterly
tangential or answering with a concrete example (e.g., "one time I
fell off my bike, and I didn't cry,") to providing what we called "integration-plus" responses. This last category was reserved for explanations that connected both an elaborated context (e.g., "it would
depend on whether it was someone I knew well or if there was a

whole group of people around") *and* consideration of the emotion it-self (e.g., "if I felt very strongly, and it was really important to me"). Not surprisingly, age differences were pronounced, with the big jump occurring between 7–8 years and 10–11 years in terms of giving elaborated contextual responses. However, it was the 13–14-year-old girls who were most likely to give the "integration-plus" responses.

Thus, balance in this study had to do with coming to terms both with how one felt and with how one perceived the interpersonal situation. The oldest girls seemed to be saying that one had to respect one's feelings *if they were important* and therefore express them, even if the interpersonal consequences were less than desirable. From the standpoint of emotional self-efficacy, regard for one's emotional experience may begin to overlap with an ethical evaluation of what gave rise to these important feelings such that they are perceived as having a nearly obligatory quality to their display.

## Conclusion

I have focused on studies I am familiar with that demonstrate positive instances of emotional competence. There are many, many investigations I could have included that would have documented emotional *in*competence on the part of children and adults. Chemical dependency among preadolescents, teenage pregnancy, eating disorders, affective disorders, conduct disorders, posttraumatic stress syndrome resulting from sexual and physical abuse, and so on could all be described to show what goes awry when emotional development becomes maladaptive and distorted and the child's emotional competence is limited. Just as I contend that emotional competence is grounded in social interaction, so too is emotional incompetence: abusive or emotionally absent parents are prime contributors, but also bearing some of the responsibility are societal agents such as violent television programming, family-destructive policies, and inadequate housing, among others (see Bronfenbrenner, 1986).

My intent has also been to continue to strengthen the view among developmental psychologists that emotions are most productively studied from the vantage point of their occurrence in social contexts. This is not to deny our biological heritage relative to emotion, but rather to emphasize that if our focus is on *development*, we cannot ignore the way the assorted consistencies and inconsistencies of interpersonal relationships are fundamental to how emotional experience differentiates.

In summary, I have compared several models of emotional development, highlighting the importance of social transactions and communication in emotional differentiation. Naive theories of emotion were also described and proposed as the link between emotional differentiation and emotional competence. Last, I presented eleven skills of emotional competence with both supporting research and commentary about where gaps exist in our research base on children's emotional development.

REFERENCES

Ackerman, R. J. (1983). *Children of alcoholics: A guidebook for educators, therapists, and parents* (2nd ed.). Holmes Beach, FL: Learning Publications.

Adlam-Hill, S., & Harris, P. L. (1988). Understanding of display rules for emotion by normal and maladjusted children. Unpublished manuscript, Oxford University, England.

Bandura, A. (1977). Self-efficacy: Toward a unifying theory of behavior change. *Psychological Review, 84,* 191–215.

Barden, R. C., Zelko, F., Duncan, S. W., and Masters, J. C. (1980). Children's consensual knowledge about the experiential determinants of emotions. *Journal of Personality and Social Psychology, 39,* 968–976.

Blurton Jones, N. (1967). An ethological study of some aspects of social behavior of children in nursery school. In D. Morris (Ed.), *Primate ethology* (pp. 347–368). London: Weidenfeld & Nicolson.

Bradbury, T. N., & Fincham, F. D. (1987). Affect and cognition in close relationships: Towards an integrative model. *Cognition and Emotion, 1,* 59–87.

Bretherton, I., & Beeghly, M. (1982). Talking about internal states: The acquisition of an explicit theory of mind. *Developmental Psychology, 19,* 906–921.

Bronfenbrenner, U. (1986). A generation in jeopardy: America's hidden family policy. *Developmental Psychology Newsletter*, Fall issue, Washington, DC: Div. 7 of the American Psychological Association.

Brooks, J., & Lewis, M. (1975). Mirror-image stimulation and self-recognition in infancy. Paper presented at the meeting of the Society for Research in Child Development, Denver, CO.

Burd, A., & Milewski, A. (1981). Matching of facial gestures by young infants: Imitation or releasers? Paper presented at the meeting of the Society for Research in Child Development, Boston, MA.

Camras, L. (1985). Socialization of affect communication. In M. Lewis & C. Saarni (Eds.), *The socialization of emotions* (pp. 141–160). New York: Plenum Press.

Camras, L., Grow, G., & Ribordy, S. (1983). Recognition of emotional expressions by abused children. *Journal of Clinical and Child Psychology, 12,* 325–328.

Carlson, C., Felleman, E., & Masters, J. C. (1983). Influence of children's emotional states on the recognition of emotion in peers and social motives to change another's emotional state. *Motivation and Emotion, 7,* 61–79.

Cleary, B. (1967). *Mitch and Amy.* New York: William Morrow.

Cleary, B. (1975). *Ramona and her father.* New York: William Morrow.

D'Andrade, R. (1987). A folk model of the mind. In D. Holland & N. Quinn (Eds.), *Cultural models in language and thought* (pp. 112–148). New York: Cambridge University Press.

DeClements, B. (1981). *Nothing's fair in fifth grade.* New York: Viking.

Edwards, R. E., Manstead, A. S., & MacDonald, C. J. (1984). The relationship between children's sociometric status and ability to recognize facial expressions of emotion. *European Journal of Social Psychology, 14,* 235–238.

Ekman, P. (1985). *Telling lies.* New York: Norton.

Ekman, P., & Friesen, W. (1975). *Unmasking the face.* Englewood Cliffs, NJ: Prentice-Hall.

Ekman, P., Levenson, R., & Friesen, W. (1983). Autonomic nervous system activity distinguishes among emotions. *Science, 221,* 1208–1210.

Emde, R., Gaensbauer, T., & Harmon, R. 1976). Emotional expression in infancy: A biobehavioral study. *Psychological Issues, 10* (Whole No. 37).

Feinman, S., & Lewis, M. (1983). Social referencing and second order effects in ten-month-old infants. *Child Development, 54,* 878–887.

Feldman, R., White, J. B., & Lobato, D. (1982). Social skills and nonverbal behavior. In R. Feldman (Ed.), *Development of nonverbal behavior in children* (pp. 259–277). New York: Springer-Verlag.

Fischer, K. W. (1980). A theory of cognitive development: The control and construction of hierarchies of skills. *Psychological Review, 87,* 477–531.

Fischer, K. W., Shaver, P., & Carnochan, P. (1988). From basic- to subordinate-category emotions: A skill approach to emotional development. In W. Damon (Ed.), *Child development today and tomorrow.* New Directions for Child Development, No. 40. San Francisco: Jossey-Bass.

Folkman, S., & Lazarus, R. S. (1988). Coping as a mediator of emotion. *Journal of Personality and Social Psychology, 54,* 466–475.

Fuchs, D., & Thelen, M. (1988). Children's expected interpersonal consequences of communicating their affective states and reported likelihood of expression. *Child Development, 59,* 1314–1322.

Gnepp, J. (1989). Children's use of personal information to understand

178

other people's feelings. In C. Saarni & P. L. Harris (Eds.), *Children's understanding of emotion* (pp. 151–177). New York: Cambridge University Press.

Gnepp, J., & Chilamkurti, C. (1988). Children's use of personality attributions to predict other people's emotional and behavioral reactions. *Child Development, 59,* 743–754.

Gnepp, J., & Gould, M. (1985). The development of personalized inferences: Understanding other people's emotional reactions in light of their prior experiences. *Child Development, 56,* 1455–1464.

Goffman, E. (1967). *Interaction ritual.* Garden City, NY: Doubleday.

Gordon, S. L. (1989). The socialization of children's emotions: Emotional culture, competence, and exposure. In C. Saarni & P. L. Harris (Eds.), *Children's understanding of emotions* (pp. 319–349). New York: Cambridge University Press.

Grossmann, K. E., & Grossmann, K. (in press). Attachment quality as an organizer of emotional and behavioral responses. In P. Marris, J. Stevenson-Hinde, & C. Parkes (Eds.), *Attachment across the life cycle.* London: Basil Blackwell.

Harris, P. L., & Gross, D. 1988) Children's understanding of real and apparent emotion. In J. Astington, P. L. Harris, & D. R. Olson (Eds.), *Developing theories of mind* (pp. 295–314). Cambridge: Cambridge University Press.

Harris, P. L., & Lipian, M. (1989). Understanding emotion and experiencing emotion. In C. Saarni & P. L. Harris (Eds.), *Children's understanding of emotions* (pp. 241–258). New York: Cambridge University Press.

Harter, S. (1982). The Perceived Competence Scale for children. *Child Development, 53,* 89–97.

Harter, S. (1986). Cognitive-developmental processes in the integration of concepts about emotions and the self. *Social Cognition, 4,* 119–151.

Harter, S., & Whitesell, N. 1989). Developmental changes in children's understanding of single, multiple, and blended emotion concepts. In C. Saarni & P. L. Harris (Eds.), *Children's understanding of emotion* (pp. 81–116). New York: Cambridge University Press.

Hayes, A., & McDonald, N. 1988). Children's views of their disabled peers: The absence of affect? Paper presented at the meeting of the International Congress of Psychology, Sydney, Australia.

Kaye, K., & Fogel, A. (1980). The temporal structure of face-to-face communication between mothers and infants. *Developmental Psychology, 16,* 454–464.

Laux, L. (1986). A self-presentational view of coping with stress. In M. Trumbull & R. Appley (Eds.), *The dynamics of stress* (pp. 233–253). New York: Plenum Press.

Lazarus, R. S. (1982). Thoughts on the relations between emotion and cognition. *American Psychologist, 37,* 1019–1024.

Lazarus, R. S. (1984). On the primacy of cognition. *American Psychologist, 39,* 124–129.

Lazarus, R. S., & Lanier, R. (1978). Stress-related transactions between person and environment. In L. A. Pervin & M. Lewis (Eds.), *Perspectives in interactional psychology* (pp. 287–327). New York: Plenum Press.

Leventhal, H., & Scherer, K. (1987). The relationship of emotion to cognition: A functional approach to a semantic controversy. *Cognition and Emotion, 1,* 3–28.

Lewis, M. (1989). Cultural differences in children's knowledge of emotional scripts. In C. Saarni & P. L. Harris (Eds.), *Children's understanding of emotion* (pp. 350–373). New York: Cambridge University Press.

Lewis, M., & Brooks, J. (1978). Self knowledge and emotional development. In M. Lewis & L. Rosenblum (Eds.), *The development of affect* (pp. 205–226). New York: Plenum Press.

Lewis, M., & Brooks-Gunn, J. (1979). *Social cognition and the acquisition of the self.* New York: Plenum Press.

Lewis, M., & Michalson, L. (1983). *Children's emotions and moods: Developmental theory and measurement.* New York: Plenum Press.

Lewis, M., & Michalson, L. 1985). Faces as signs and symbols, In G. Zivin (Ed.), *The development of expressive behavior* (pp. 155–180). New York: Academic Press.

Lewis, M., & Saarni, C. (1985). Culture and emotions. In M. Lewis & C. Saarni (Eds.), *The socialization of emotions* (pp. 1–17). New York: Plenum Press.

Lutz, C. (1985). Cultural patterns and individual differences in the child's meaning system. In M. Lewis & C. Saarni (Eds.), *The socialization of emotions* (pp. 37–53). New York: Plenum Press.

Lutz, C. (1987). Goals, events, and understanding in Ifaluk emotion theory. In D. Holland & N. Quinn (Eds.), *Cultural models in language and thought* (pp. 290–312). New York: Cambridge University Press.

Main, M., Kaplan, N., & Cassidy, J. (1985). Security in infancy, childhood, and adulthood: A move to the level of representation. In I. Bretherton & E. Waters (Eds.), *Growing points of attachment theory and research* (pp. 66–104). *Monographs of the Society for Research in Child Development, 50* (Serial No. 209, Nos. 1–2).

Malatesta, C. (1985). Developmental course of emotion expression in the human infant. In G. Zivin (Ed.), *The development of expressive behavior* (pp. 183–219). New York: Academic Press.

Malatesta, C., & Izard, C. (1984). The ontogenesis of human signals: From biological imperative to symbol utilization. In N. Fox & R. J. Davidson (Eds.), *Affective development: A psychobiological perspective.* Hillsdale, NJ: Erlbaum.

Martin, G. G., & Clark, R. D. (1982). Distress crying in neonates: Species and peer specificity. *Developmental Psychology, 18,* 3–9.

McCoy, C., & Masters, J. C. (1985). The development of children's strategies for the social control of emotion. *Child Development, 56,* 1214–1222.

Meltzoff, A., & Moore, M. K. (1977). Imitation of facial and manual gestures by human neonates. *Science, 198,* 75–78.

Mendelson, R., & Peters, R. D. (1983). The influence of relationship knowledge on children's interpretations of social behavior. Paper presented at the meeting of the Society for Research in Child Development, Detroit, MI.

Michalson, L., & Lewis, M. (1985). What do children know about emotions and when do they know it. In M. Lewis & C. Saarni (Eds.), *The socialization of emotions* (pp. 117–139). New York: Plenum Press.

Miller, P., & Sperry, L. (1987). The socialization of anger and aggression. *Merrill-Palmer Quarterly, 33*, 1–31.

Miller, S. M., & Green, M. L. (1985). Coping with stress and frustration: Origins, nature, and development. In M. Lewis & C. Saarni (Eds.), *The socialization of emotions* (pp. 263–314). New York: Plenum Press.

Patterson, M. L. (Ed.). (1984). *Nonverbal intimacy and exchange*. Special issue of *Journal of Nonverbal Behavior*. New York: Human Sciences Press.

Piers, E., & Harris, D. (1984). *Piers-Harris children's self-concept scale*. Revised manual. Los Angeles: Western Psychological Services.

Ridgeway, D., Waters, E., & Kuczaj, S. (1985). Acquisition of emotion-descriptive language: Receptive and productive vocabulary norms for ages 18 months to 6 years. *Developmental Psychology, 21*, 901–908.

Russell, J. A. (1989). Culture, scripts, and children's understanding of emotion. In C. Saarni & P. L. Harris (Eds.), *Children's understanding of emotion* (pp. 293–318). New York: Cambridge University Press.

Saarni, C. (1978). Cognitive and communicative features of emotional experience, or Do you show what you think you feel? In M. Lewis & L. Rosenblum (Eds.), *The development of affect* (pp. 361–375). New York: Plenum Press.

Saarni, C. (1979a). Children's understanding of display rules for expressive behavior. *Developmental Psychology, 15*, 424–429.

Saarni, C. (1979b). When *not* to show what you think you feel: Children's understanding of relations between emotional experience and expressive behavior. Paper presented at the meeting of the Society for Research in Child Development, San Francisco, CA.

Saarni, C. (1984). An observational study of children's attempt to monitor their expressive behavior. *Child Development, 55*, 1504–1513.

Saarni, C. (1987). Children's beliefs about parental expectations for emotional-expressive behavior management. Paper presented at the meeting of the Society for Research in Child Development, Baltimore, MD.

Saarni, C. (1988). Children's beliefs about emotion. Paper presented at the meeting of the International Congress of Psychology, Sydney, Australia.

Saarni, C. (1989). Children's understanding of strategic control of emotional expression in social transactions. In C. Saarni & P. L. Harris (Eds.), *Children's understanding of emotion* (pp. 181–208). New York: Cambridge University Press.

Saarni, C. (1988). Children's understanding of the interpersonal consequences of dissemblance of nonverbal emotional-expressive behavior. *Journal of Nonverbal Behavior, 12*, 275–294.

Saarni, C., & Harris, P. L. (Eds.). (1989). *Children's understanding of emotion.* New York: Cambridge University Press.

Saunders, D., Lynch, A., Grayson, M., & Linz, D. (1987). The inventory of beliefs about wife beating: The construction and initial validation of a measure of beliefs and attitudes. *Violence and Victims, 2,* 39–55.

Schwartz, J. C., & Shaver, P. (1987). Emotions and emotion knowledge in interpersonal relations. In W. Jones & D. Perlman (Eds.), *Advances in personal relationships* (Vol. 1, pp. 197–241). Greenwich, CT: JAI Press.

Shennum, W., & Bugental, D. (1982). The development of control over affective expression in nonverbal behavior. In R. Feldman (Ed.), *Development of nonverbal behavior in children* (pp. 101–121). New York: Springer-Verlag.

Sorce, J., Emde, R., Campos, J., & Klinnert, M. (1985). Maternal emotional signalling: Its effect on the visual cliff behavior of one-year-olds. *Developmental Psychology, 21,* 195–200.

Stein, N. L., & Trabasso, T. (1989). Children's understanding of changing emotional states. In C. Saarni & P. L. Harris (Eds.), *Children's understanding of emotion* (pp. 50–77). New York: Cambridge University Press.

Strayer, J. (1986). Children's attributions regarding the situational determinants of emotion in self and others. *Developmental Psychology, 22,* 649–654.

Strayer, J. (1989). What children know and feel in response to witnessing affective events. In C. Saarni & P. L. Harris (Eds.), *Children's understanding of emotion* (pp. 259–289). New York: Cambridge University Press.

Strelau, J. (1987). Emotion as a key concept in temperament research. *Journal of Research in Personality, 21,* 510–528.

Tedeschi, J. (1981). *Impression management theory and social psychological research.* New York: Academic Press.

Tedeschi, J., & Norman, N. (1985). Social power, self-presentation, and the self. In B. Schlenker (Ed.), *The self and social life* (pp. 293–322). New York: McGraw-Hill.

Thomas, A., Chess, S., & Birch, H. G. (1968). Temperament and behavior disorders in children. New York: New York University Press.

Visher, E., & Visher, S. (1988). *Old loyalties, new ties: Therapeutic strategies with stepfamilies.* New York: Brunner/Mazel.

Walden, T., & Field, I. (1988). Preschool children's social competence and production and discrimination of affective expressions. Unpublished manuscript. Vanderbilt University, Nashville, TN.

Walker, E. (1981). Recognition of emotions in facial expressions by emotionally disturbed children and nondisturbed children. *Psychology in the Schools, 16,* 119–126.

Watson, J. S., & Ramey, C. (1977). Reactions to response contingent stimulation in early infancy. *Merrill-Palmer Quarterly, 13,* 219–228.

Weiner, B. (1987). The social psychology of emotion: Applications of a naive psychology. *Journal of Social and Clinical Psychology, 5,* 405–419.

Weiner, B., Amirkhan, J., Folkes, V. S., & Verette, J. (1987). An attributional analysis of excuse giving: Studies of a naive theory of emotion. *Journal of Personality and Social Psychology, 52,* 316–324.

Weiner, B., & Graham, S. (1984). An attributional approach to emotional development. In C. Izard, J. Kagan, & R. Zajonc (Eds.), *Emotions, cognition, and behavior* (pp. 167–191). New York: Cambridge University Press.

Weiner, B., & Handel, S. (1985). A cognition-emotion-action sequence: Anticipated emotional consequences of causal communications and reported communication strategy. *Developmental Psychology, 21,* 102–107.

Zajonc, R. (1980). Feeling and thinking: Preferences need no inferences. *American Psychologist, 35,* 151–175.

Zajonc, R. (1984). On the primacy of affect. *American Psychologist, 39,* 117–123.

# The Origins of Guilt

Carolyn Zahn-Waxler
and Grazyna
Kochanska
*National Institute of Mental Health*

*A*t some point in develop-ment, children begin to internalize cultural rules and expectations regarding appropriate interpersonal behavior. Rules that first were established by the parent become part of the child's own standards and values. This process of internalization is also known as conscience development, and guilt commonly is seen as a mediator of conscience. The root of the word conscience, *conscire*, in fact, means "to be conscious of guilt." Guilt has several definitions. One refers to factual culpability for a crime; this aspect of guilt versus innocence is determined through a system of laws in most cultures and is judged in courtrooms. Behavioral scientists have been more interested in the experiential and behavioral components of guilt, that is, the feelings of remorse and acts of reparation that accompany real or imagined wrongdoings, and their functions and consequences in people's lives. Throughout history vivid and eloquent descriptions of guilt have been present in literature, religion, and philosophical writings, but only recently has guilt be

We thank Marian Radke-Yarrow, who has been a coinvestigator on several of the NIMH research projects described here, for sharing her keen insights and for her support of the work described. We also thank Jean Mayo for assistance in preparing the manuscript.

come a topic for scientific study, and relatively few empirical data are available to explain the origins and development of this emotion.

The goals of this chapter are to review what is known about guilt in children by examining existing theories and empirical data; to review a program of research on the development of guilt; and to integrate research with theories pertaining specifically to guilt and more generally to the role this emotion plays in social interactions, personality development, and psychopathology. We place major emphasis on the early etiology of guilt, attempting to define adaptive and maladaptive forms in development and to identify contributors to variations in the different patterns shown.

People vary in their capacity for remorse, the situations that provoke feelings of wrongdoing in them, the ways they express the emotion, and how functional or destructive it is in their lives. Disturbances in guilt have been linked with various forms of psychopathology and psychiatric disorders (American Psychiatric Association, 1980). The ease with which sociopaths exploit and manipulate others reflects deficiencies in their capacity for empathy and guilt. The delusions and hallucinations of schizophrenics often reflect themes of persecution and attack and of intense guilt that is sometimes projected onto others. Excessive and inappropriate feelings of responsibility and self-blame are also linked with other emotional disorders such as depression, an affective disorder in which there are prolonged periods of sadness and inability to experience pleasure. Depression has both vegetative signs (e.g., lack of energy, disturbances in eating and sleeping patterns) and psychological symptoms (e.g., feelings of guilt and worthlessness). The intensity of guilt and associated cognitions of being pervasively unworthy, blameworthy, and responsible for the problems of others typically seem out of proportion in the depressed person. Guilt may contribute to, as well as index, some forms of affective disturbance; hence knowledge of its early precursors might aid in understanding the later development of problems in which guilt plays a role.

The concept of guilt has had a complex history in research with children, stemming in part from its dual relevance to moral development and to different conditions of psychopathology. Causal connections between moral internalization, guilt, and the development of neuroses were proposed in psychoanalytic theory (Freud, 1958), but conceptualizations of guilt as moral and mental health constructs have proceeded along separate paths. Developmental research has concentrated on guilt as a moral dimension that has an adaptive function. Dysfunctional features of guilt, emphasized in clinical theories, have received less emphasis in empirical research. A developmental psychopathology perspective (Cicchetti, this volume; Rutter & Garmezy, 1983) provides an approach for studying, simultaneously, adaptive and maladaptive forms of guilt. Developmental psychopathology differs from other areas of child development in its strong focus on individual differences. Much of child development research has addressed the developmental progressions that occur in all normal children. Although knowledge of universals is fundamental to understanding developmental process, it does not necessarily provide the most useful strategy for understanding patterns of healthy versus problematic development. In developmental psychopathology the focus is on the multiple processes and pathways by which early patterns of adaptation evolve to later patterns of adaptation, considering both biological characteristics of children and the environments in which they develop. Studies of high- and low-risk populations, usually longitudinal in design, characteristically are used to identify these different patterns. We have studied children from populations in which the meaning and functions of guilt might be expected to differ, in order to understand the different ways this emotion develops.

## Guilt: Theories, Perspectives, and Research

Theories of guilt and the developmental research generated by these theories are reviewed here. These include discrete emotions theory, psychodynamic, learning, and cognitive theories, as well as perspectives that have evolved from these more formal theories. The approaches vary in whether guilt is characterized as innate or learned, as functional or problematic, and as a state or a trait (personality characteristic). Theories also differ in whether affective, behavioral, or cognitive components of guilt are emphasized. There is variation in emphasis, too, in the types of guilt examined (e.g., guilt over aggression, sex, relationships, achievement, self-actualization) and in the particular antecedents of guilt (e.g., cultural factors, temperament, religious orientation, child-rearing and discipline practices). Finally, the theories differ with regard to when in development children are viewed as fully capable of experiencing and expressing guilt.

Different dynamics or motives for guilt are hypothesized in different theories. Three general conceptualizations of guilt may be distinguished. The first one, most clearly represented in classic psychoanalytic theory, is guilt conceived as a response to one's own unacceptable impulses. Its origins may be traced to a child's early experiences, when feelings of hostility or sexuality, or both, toward the parents become repressed owing to fear of punishment and of loss of parental love. Those unacceptable impulses are turned inward, various defense mechanisms are erected to prevent awareness of them, and the resulting guilt often has an irrational, primitive, and distorted quality.

In contrast to this view of guilt as primarily driven by the negative forces within the self, a different process has been suggested, particularly in the work of Hoffman (1982). In his model, guilt may develop very early as a result of the child's emotional arousal and sensitivity to others' distress. The emphasis here is not on the defensive dynamics, but rather on empathic concern over others. During the course of development, early emotional distress following others' distress evolves into guilt feelings and becomes closely interwoven with empathic and prosocial feelings.

Both of these guilt mechanisms have developmental roots in affective experience; there is, however, another type of guilt that is primarily cognitively based and not present in early development. Guilt feelings are aroused by perceived violation of one's own personal standard of conduct. This dynamic has been a focus of objective self-awareness models (Wicklund, 1975). According to these theories, when one's attention is focused on oneself in the act of objective self-awareness, one's personal standards of conduct (e.g., being helpful, being considerate, being a moral person) are activated. One then evaluates one's behavior in terms of adherence to one's personal standards; failure to act according to the standard brings feelings of guilt. This model assumes that several developmental tasks have to be accomplished, such as forming fairly complex representations of self, gaining the ability for self-reflection, and learning to analyze the outcomes of one's actions and compare them against personal standards. Each of these models assumes different developmental courses and socialization antecedents, different instigating conditions, and different qualities of guilt feelings (e.g., rigidity versus flexibility, distortion versus realistic quality, etc.).

## DISCRETE EMOTIONS THEORY

Guilt is viewed as one of the fundamental emotions in discrete emotions theory (Izard, 1977). In this theory, discrete emotions are viewed as constituting the primary motivational system for human beings. Each of the fundamental emotions has an inherently adaptive function and has the following components: an innately determined neural substrate, a characteristic facial expression or neuromuscular expressive pattern, and a distinct subjective or phenomenological quality. Other systems also are involved (e.g., cardiovascular, endocrine, and respiratory systems). Guilt is one of the more difficult emotions to characterize because it does not have a clear expressive component. Darwin (1872/1965) pointed out that gaze aversion and stealthy looks sometimes are indications of guilt. He described a guilty expression following a misdeed of his 2½-year-old as "an unnatural brightness in the eyes and an odd affected manner, impossible to describe." Izard has noted too that the other negative emotions have more distinct facial expressions than guilt, though in guilt the face sometimes takes on a heavy look.

Guilt, like other fundamental emotions, emerged through evolutionary-biological processes, its adaptive functions being to prevent waste and exploitation. In this view, feelings of responsibility and desire to make amends for wrongdoing have survival value—for individuals and relationships and, in a more long-term sociobiological sense, for societies and civilization. According to Izard (1977) guilt is the main affect in conscience because it checks aggressive impulses and encourages people to make reparation, hence restoring social harmony. Fear, in contrast, motivates escape from the source and subsides at a safe distance from threat of harm. Others (e.g., Eibl-Eibesfeldt, 1971) also have proposed a biological or genetic basis for ethical norms and a sense of personal responsibility. Guilt is one of the few emotions that many people believe is unique to humans, though some have argued that canines are capable of this emotion (see the work of Black, Soloman, and Whiting, described in Mowrer, 1966). And recently, displays of affection following acts of aggression have been observed in primates. These displays are not unlike what would be described in humans as reparative gestures.

**Guilt and temperament.** If the capacity for guilt is innate, are there also biologically determined individual differences in this emotion? There are proponents of the views that criminality, aggressiveness, and failure to feel remorse following wrongdoing are constitutionally determined (e.g., Mednick, Gabriell, & Hutchings, 1984). Or it is possible that other constitutional factors, such as temperament, might mediate guilt patterns. Dienstbier (1984), for example, has suggested that individuals with different temperaments might develop different emotion-attributional styles and levels of guilt. According to Dienstbier, a child who is temperamentally prone to high levels of emotional tension is also likely to feel intense discomfort and distress following a transgression. This tension is likely to be experienced as coming from inside, and therefore an attribution linking the tension with the transgression is likely. On the other hand, a child with only a slight tendency to experience negative emotional tension is likely to "condition" poorly and therefore inspire harsh socialization practices, intended to inhibit future transgression. This in turn provides salient external stimuli, to which the emotional response of the child can easily be attributed. Therefore, Dienstbier claims, the child who is vulnerable to tension will develop increasingly internal attributions, while the "unperturbable" child will form increasingly external attributions.

There is some evidence for individual differences in conditioned fear responses and avoidance learning in adults. Psychopaths, who appear remarkably guilt-free, have difficulty in learning to inhibit punished responses in conditioning studies and in learning from such experiences (described in Bandura & Walters, 1963). These studies demonstrate individual differences in conditionability but are less clear in identifying the reasons. For example, although temperament is thought to reflect constitutional, innate characteristics of organisms, research on temperament has not typically been conducted to rule out socialization influences. A prospective, developmental approach might help to illuminate characteristics of young children and their environments that produce individual differences in capacity for guilt.

**Guilt, personality, and psychopathology.** Guilt has been studied mainly in situational contexts, with relatively little emphasis on its role as an enduring trait or personality characteristic. Malatesta (this volume; Malatesta, in press) has applied a discrete emotions approach to personality development, suggesting that individual differences in affective organization, acquired during the course of development and socialization, result in affect-specific biases in expressive patterns. These patterns influence individual and interpersonal behavior and contribute to continuities that can be viewed as emotional traits or personality dimensions within individuals.

Within this framework Malatesta has characterized adaptive and pathological forms of emotional biases and the associated cognitions for each of the emotions. For guilt, the elicitor is recognition of wrongdoing. The signal and adaptive functions of guilt include promotion of attempts at reparation. A submissive posture may also reduce the likelihood of attack. In pathological forms guilt may be deficient or excessive. Excessive guilt appears in some forms of depression, in which the person thinks he or she has done wrong and should be punished. Deficiencies in guilt take two forms. Underdeveloped guilt appears as sociopathy, in which individuals think they can do no wrong and feel no discomfort over wrongdoing. Guilt that is warded off through dynamic mechanisms of conflict and defense appears as paranoia, and projection is common; the individual believes the other has done something wrong and should be punished. Malatesta has presented hypotheses regarding developmental pathways by which child characteristics and experiences in childhood contribute to the evolution of discrete emotions (such as anger and sadness) into traits or biases. In this chapter, Malatesta's framework is extended to explore conditions under which different types of guilt develop in children and evolve from discrete emotions to personality traits.

PSYCHODYNAMIC THEORIES OF GUILT

**Psychoanalytic theory.** In Freudian theory guilt was believed to emerge in the context of the development of the basic structure of personality. In this view, conscience evolves as sexual and aggressive impulses are tamed and children internalize a sense of proper conduct. The young child experiences many frustrations, some caused by the parent, and this produces hostility toward the parent. This hostility is held in or repressed because of anxiety about anticipated punishment and fears of loss of love and abandonment. The child thus adopts the parents' rules and prohibitions and also develops a generalized motive to emulate the parents' behavior. Moreover, the child adopts the parents' capacity to punish violations. And in assuming these capacities the hostility becomes directed inward. This self-punishment is experienced as painful guilt feelings. The child tries to avoid guilt by following the internalized prohibitions and by defending against awareness of impulses to engage in forbidden thoughts or actions. Much of this was thought to occur in the context of identification with the same-sex parent, between the ages of 4 and 6.

Psychoanalytic theory gave rise to several empirical studies of socialization of conscience. Allinsmith (1960) examined the hypothesis that severity of guilt feelings expressed by young adolescent boys should be related to harsh treatment in infancy (early weaning, severe toilet training). The severity of guilt was measured by the use of projective stories depicting transgressions; early socialization practices were reconstructed from maternal interviews. The findings were ambiguous; severe early practices were related to low or moderate, but not high, guilt, and the relation also depended on the type of transgression used to elicit a projective response. However, in two other studies inspired by the psychoanalytic theory some evidence was found that indeed severe weaning did relate to intense guilt feelings (Heinicke, 1953; Whiting & Child, 1953). Hoffman (1971) examined the relation between guilt and identification with the parent in seventh-grade children. None of the guiltlike phenomena (guilt feelings, confession, and acceptance of blame) related to identification with the parent (although some relations were found for other aspects of moral development). In summary, the empirical evidence for some of the classical psychoanalytic hypotheses regarding the development of guilt is mixed and inconclusive.

Socialization studies based on psychoanalytic theory may have placed too much emphasis on the literal severity of early practices (toilet training, weaning) as antecedents of fear-based guilt. However, the basic symbolic message about children's anxiety over loss of parental love and their experience of jeopardized self-worth in relation to the parents' withdrawal of love may have captured well the developmental dynamics of intense fear-based guilt. This idea has reemerged and has received some empirical support in more recent studies of socialization of moral internalization (to be reviewed in a subsequent section on learning theory and socialization approaches to guilt).

**Neopsychoanalytic perspectives on guilt.** Several theorists (see review by Friedman, 1985) questioned Freud's emphasis on hate, fear, and threats of punishment (and the general notion of the "inner policeman") as the driving forces that underlie guilt. Melanie Klein (1975) was one of the first to emphasize guilt and the desire or "drive" to make reparation as deriving from love rather than from hostility, self-interest, and fear. She conceived of two stages of superego development that later became identified as paranoid and depressive positions. In the first stage aggressive fantasies against the parents arouse anxiety about retaliation. In the second stage, guilt over aggressive and destructive impulses is not an internalized fear of retaliation for these impulses but rather an independent and primary motive to repair the harm.

Modell (1965, 1971) proposed that guilt has an underlying altruistic motive. It results from genuine caring and love for others, which in some circumstances can be quite dysfunctional. He emphasized concepts of survivor guilt and separation guilt. Survivor guilt refers to problems experienced later by survivors of disasters, who come to believe that remaining alive is a betrayal of the dead. Modell extended this concept to include more subtle forms of survival and disaster, for example, children of living "victims" (usually parents) whose lives are marred by problems, distress, and conflict. "Separation guilt" refers to the belief that evolving one's own autonomy and having a separate life will damage or destroy the parent. Both forms of guilt result from the belief that by pursuing normal developmental or life goals one is harming a significant other. Hence these goals must be renounced in order to maintain ties to the parents and avoid feelings of guilt.

Guilt may result from behaviors that are perceived as disloyal to the parent or that hinder, worry, or sadden the parent (Friedman, 1985). Friedman notes that children often accept responsibility for parents' problems and moods because of egocentrism and feelings of omnipotence as well as empathy. Parents may reinforce this perceived omnipotence by claiming that the child is capable of determining the parents' fate. Repeated experience of blame in childhood may lead to feelings of culpability and unworthiness later in life, leaving one vulnerable to blame.

Most psychodynamic approaches are based on a relationship perspective, with guilt arising when there is an imbalance between the needs and goals of the self and those of significant others. As with discrete emotions theory, the research base is meager. Information on guilt is derived from clinical wisdom and retrospective patient reports and some studies of child-rearing practices (see Hoffman, 1970a). There are problems, too, with an approach that attempts to explain universal processes by focusing on case histories of psychiatric patients. For example, guilt may be linked developmentally with fear, hostility, and aggression in people with particular emotional problems but may have quite different origins in others. Yet the psychoanalytic tradition has provided hypotheses and stimulated research on discipline practices that might explain certain patterns of individual differences in conscience and guilt. It has been influential as well in its implications for the differential development of feelings of responsibility in males and females.

**Perspectives on gender and guilt.** Freud tied the formation of the superego or conscience to castration anxiety and to eventual resolution of the Oedipus complex. Because women were deprived of this experience, he concluded that women's superego was compromised: it was never "so inexorable, so impersonal, so independent of its emotional origins as we require it to be in men." Freud concluded that women "show less sense of justice than men, that they are less ready to submit to the great exigencies of life, that they are more often influenced in their judgments by feelings of affection or hostility" (1925/1961). In social-cognitive theories of moral development (Kohlberg, 1976), high levels of conscience similarly are linked to impersonal, abstract ideals that are guided more by reason than by emotion. Gilligan (1982) has argued that Kohlberg's stage theory relegates women to a lower level of moral reasoning because their definitions of self and morality are more integrally tied to their relationships with others. Research findings do not unambiguously document sex differences in levels of moral reasoning (Baumrind, 1986; Walker, 1984), but there are indications that female children and adults are more interpersonally sensitive than males. For example, females more than males emphasize the importance of relationships in situations of interpersonal conflict and distress (Zahn-Waxler, Kochanska, Krupnick, & McKnew, 1990), accurately interpret others' emotions (see review by Hall, 1978) and psychological defenses (Chandler, Paget, & Koch, 1978), and report empathic experiences (Eisenberg & Lennon, 1983). Such sensitivity to the emotional states of others might render females more vulnerable than males to feelings of guilt—for example, when empathy for another's plight is so pervasive that one begins to feel (causally) responsible.

Although theories predict that males will have more severe and more highly developed consciences than females, almost all of the empirical evidence is in the opposite direction (Hoffman, 1975), especially when empathy and restraint from aggression are used to index conscience. Many studies report stronger guilt, particularly guilt over aggression, in women than in men (e.g., see review by Frodi, Macaulay, & Thome, 1977). The evidence is less consistent with children. Hoffman (1975) found sex differences in guilt and moral internalization favoring girls. Opposite effects, however, are sometimes obtained (e.g., Thompson & Hoffman, 1980), and still other studies (e.g., Chapman, Zahn-Waxler, Iannotti, & Cooperman, 1987) report no sex differences. Gender differences in guilt may evolve slowly or sometimes may take different forms in children: for example, well-documented sex differences in empathy (more in girls) and physical aggression (less in girls) may sometimes index early guilt. Gender differences also may be more evident in patterning than in amount. In two studies of 2-year-olds (Cummings, Hollenbeck, Iannotti, Radke-Yarrow, & Zahn-Waxler, 1986) aggression was positively correlated with reparative behaviors in girls but not in boys. This research is consistent with the literature on adults and suggests that anger and aggression may be particularly guilt-inducing for girls.

Gilligan's conceptualization of sex differences in moral development has precedents in the work of Chodorow (1978) and Lewis (1979, 1980). Both Chodorow and Lewis linked guilt and moral development to broader aspects of personality development, identity formation, and the definition of the self. Chodorow describes female identity formation as taking place in a context of ongoing relationship, since "mothers tend to experience their daughters as more like, and continuous with, themselves." Similarly, young girls experience themselves as like their mothers, thus fusing processes of attachment and identity formation. In contrast, "mothers experience their sons as a male opposite," and boys, in defining themselves as masculine, separate their mothers from themselves and in doing so cut short "their primary love and sense of empathic tie." For this reason male development involves a "more emphatic individuation and a more defensive firming of ego boundaries." Girls emerge from this period with a basis for empathy built into their primary definition of self in a way that boys do not.

There is research evidence that socialization efforts are directed toward having girls establish closer affective ties than boys. Moss (1974) observed that mothers and fathers both spent more time getting their infant girls to smile. They also used more affection terms when addressing girls than boys. Block (1973) found that parents reported more insistence on control of feelings and expressions of affect for their boys, while for girls greater emphasis was placed on maintaining close emotional relationships, talking about problems, and showing physical affection. This emphasis on interpersonal connections may become problematic when individuation is viewed as a major marker of healthy development, rendering females vulnerable to dependency, guilt, and fear of hurting others. Mothers do report less enjoyment and more worry in raising girls than boys (Susman, Trickett, Iannotti, Hollenbeck, & Zahn-Waxler, 1985), suggesting that close connections also may sometimes be marked by more negative, critical, guilt-inducing interactions.

Lewis (1979, 1980) emphasized similar themes in her conceptions of gender differences in guilt and shame. Women grow up more oriented toward connection and loving others as a central value in their lives, while men come to value the aggressive behavior required to meet their responsibilities for earning a living within a competitive economic system. Women are more prone to the shame of "loss of love," while men are prone to guilt for the more frequent transgressions the exploitative world requires of them. These gender differences in moral functioning are viewed as linked to sex differences in forms of mental illness as well. Women are more subject to depression, which Lewis argues is a disorder that results from a failure of high ideals of devotion to others. Depression is diagnosed two to three times as often in women as in men.

Research on early regulation and socialization of emotions in boys and girls would provide needed information on how these patterns of sex differences may develop. It would be valuable to focus on emotions of anger as well as empathy and guilt. If girls are encouraged not to express anger, these feelings may be held in and experienced as guilt and other forms of internal distress. Because girls learn early to value relationships and intimacy and because anger creates distance between people, they may also learn early to suppress anger. Adults respond differently to expressions of anger in male and female infants and preschool children. Adults are more likely to misinterpret anger in their preschool girls than boys (Feinman & Feldman, 1982), perhaps because they do not wish to see it or perhaps because young girls express anger with greater ambiguity than boys. Many caregivers may discourage their girls from expressing anger, even in infancy. These differential messages to boys and girls are often conveyed in subtle yet powerful forms, and caregivers may not be conscious of their actions (Saarni, this volume). For example, mothers are more likely to frown when their female infants express anger but to show concern/empathy in response to male infants' anger displays (Malatesta & Haviland, 1982). Such communications to females (which may signal or imply rejection and withdrawal of love) may help to establish very early the message that anger poses a threat to relationships. Despite societal changes, women are more involved than men in acts of caregiving in intimate relationships. The caregiving role requires a deeply ingrained sense of personal responsibility for resolving interpersonal distress and problems (which could become the high ideals of devotion to others

Block refers to). Anger in girls may be less tolerated by their mothers because it will interfere with later caregiver functions. One way to heighten a sense of responsibility for the welfare of others is to induce guilt and anxiety for angry expressions and interpersonal aggression.

## LEARNING THEORY AND SOCIALIZATION APPROACHES TO GUILT

Socialization approaches were prominent in the 1950s and 1960s and generated much of the existing empirical research on individual differences associated with conscience development and guilt in children. This work has been reviewed elsewhere (e.g., Hoffman, 1970a, 1983; Lickona, 1976; Staub, 1979), and interested readers are referred to reviews for extended summary and integration of research on how guilt is learned. Psychoanalytic theory and learning theory both have generated frameworks for studying the socialization of conscience and guilt. Social-learning theorists tried to avoid terms like guilt and moral internalization, since these refer to internal psychological states that are difficult to anchor in observable behavior. Rather, the initial attempt was to explain and study similar phenomena using different concepts and procedures. In social-learning theory, classic learning concepts (e.g., of reward, punishment, extinction, generalization, and discrimination) and paradigms (e.g., conditioning, avoidance learning) were extended to interpersonal and social phenomena, including conscience development and guilt (Bandura & Walters, 1963). The ability to refrain from deviation in the absence of external controls was demonstrated with animals in early studies using learning paradigms. For example, puppies showed strong resistance to temptation in a study by Black, Soloman, and Whiting (described in Mowrer, 1966).

Mowrer (1966) identified common concepts in psychoanalytic and learning theories by linking the psychoanalytic concept of anxiety with the concept of conditioned fear and the notion that behaviors associated with the termination or reduction of anxiety are reinforced. More specifically, according to Mowrer, the execution of a deviant act involves a sequence of response-produced cues, each providing sensory feedback. A painful stimulus (punishment) may occur at various points in the sequence and so lead to the relatively direct association of a fear response with the response-produced cues occurring at the time of punishment. If punishment follows transgression, fear will be associated with stimuli accompanying the deviant act. If punishment occurs earlier, it should be associated with the preparatory responses and the emotion of fear and should be more effective in preventing deviation.

Studies of the socialization of guilt originating from both psychoanalytic theory and learning theory have focused on the timing and severity of punishment, the specific discipline techniques used, and the quality of the affective relationship between parent and child. The studies deriving from a psychoanalytic tradition have used mainly naturalistic research designs and have emphasized the effects that different manifestations of parental power, authority, and discipline have on children's guilt. The studies deriving from social learning theory have been more laboratory based, using such experimental manipulations as variations in punishment, adult nurturance, and explanations regarding wrongdoing (induction).

Parental discipline techniques in response to children's transgressions typically have been grouped into categories of power assertion, love withdrawal, and induction (Hoffman, 1970a, b). Power assertion refers to the threats or use of physical punishment, deprivation of privileges or material objects, and use of force to control the child's behavior. Love withdrawal consists of direct but nonphysical expression of anger or disapproval when the child transgresses (e.g., ignoring the child, turning away, refusing to communicate, expressing dislike, threatening separation). Induction refers to techniques in which the parent provides information or gives reasons or explanations when requesting a change in behavior, in order to help the child gain insight or understanding. Other-oriented induction explicitly points out the implications of the child's behavior for another person (e.g., "that makes Johnny sad when you laugh at him").

Hoffman (1970a) has reviewed naturalistic studies of these discipline techniques in relation to several measures of internalization: resistance to temptation, guilt, internal versus external orientation, and confession. Power assertion was associated with low levels of moral development and guilt, induction was associated with high levels of moral development, and love withdrawal was related to guilt as well, but less consistently than was induction. Typically, findings were stronger for mothers' discipline practices than for fathers'. Some of these patterns have been replicated in laboratory-based studies in which adult discipline practices are experimentally manipulated. For example, use of cognitive structuring (Aronfreed, Cutick, & Fagan, 1963) or attributions focusing on the child's feelings about transgression (Dienstbier, Hillman, Lehnhoff, Hillman, & Valkenaar, 1975) are like inductions/explanations and have been shown to produce guilt and self-criticism in children.

Despite findings from Hoffman's review indicating less consistency in the effects on guilt of love withdrawal, than of induction, there are other indications of its potency. There is some evidence that love withdrawal may contribute to the inhibition of anger (described in Hoffman, 1970a), and inhibition of anger could be seen as a reflection of guilt. Laboratory research and more recent naturalistic studies not included in Hoffman's original review identify positive associations between love withdrawal and children's moral functioning as seen in measures of guilt, self-criticism, and reparation (e.g., Zahn-Waxler, Radke-Yarrow, & King's [1979] naturalistic study of 2-year-olds, Grusec's [1966] laboratory study of children, and Karylowski's [1982] work on self structure and violation of personal standards in adolescent girls).

Love withdrawal and induction may result in different *kinds* of guilt, as is illustrated in research by Hoffman (1970b). He distinguished two types of children: humanistic-flexible children, who expressed concern over harm done to others, and conventional-rigid, who expressed concern over violation of institutionalized norms. Humanistic-flexible children experienced guilt mostly as a result of awareness of harmful consequences for another person (empathy-related guilt). Conventional-rigid children experienced more guilt as a response to their own impulse arousal, and their guilt tended to have a harsh superego- and ego-alien quality, with more primitive, unconscious, extreme, and intense fears expressed in their guilt themes. These two kinds of guilt clearly correspond to the empathy-based and psychoanalytically based conceptions of guilt, respectively.

Socialization antecedents of the two types of guilt were different. Matter-of-fact induction by the parent was found to be more frequent in children whose guilt had empathy-based dynamics. Parents of conventional-rigid children, compared with humanistic-flex-ible, were found to frequently use techniques that, in fact, conveyed that the child's transgression jeopardized parental love. That is, parents used love withdrawal and inductions that highlighted the harmful consequences the child's act had for the parent. They also used more "ego attacks," communicating their diminished view of the child's worth. Hoffman (1983) has argued that, to experience empathically based guilt, the child has to receive the message that harm has been done as well as what it means for the other person. Further, the child needs to experience low to moderate discomfort in this context. Techniques that produce too high arousal (e.g., love withdrawal) will interfere with the child's processing of the inductive component of the discipline and will result in a different kind of guilt.

The role of parental love and affection was investigated in several studies, and a cumulative review of this literature (Hoffman 1970a) indicates positive associations of parental warmth with conscience and guilt in children. For example, in an early study by Sears, Maccoby, and Levin (1957) and in later studies by Burton, Maccoby, and Allinsmith (1961) and Zahn-Waxler et al. (1979), parental warmth and affection, as opposed to rejection, were found to be conducive to the child's development of conscience in general and guilt in particular. These findings have been corroborated by social-learning theorists in experimental studies in which warmth and nurturance have been manipulated. One reason for the inconsistent effects of love withdrawal on guilt and conscience may be the wide range of backgrounds of nurturance and rejection onto which love withdrawal techniques are imposed. That is, the effects of love withdrawal may interact with the existing levels of nurturance/rejection of the caregiver. Grusec (1966) reported that high nurturance and contingent reinforcement promoted development of self-criticism only when used in combination with withdrawal of love. Withdrawal of love was varied by the experimenter's saying the child's act made her "unhappy" or "disappointed." Another related reason for inconsistency in findings on relations between discipline practices and guilt is that specific disciplinary techniques are not studied within the broader context of the parent's personality, affective style, and emotional problems.

## SOCIAL-COGNITIVE THEORIES OF GUILT

Social-cognitive theory leads to the expectation that guilt develops during the early elementary school years and beyond. Guilt is viewed as a conscious process, in which a well-developed self structure is required for the reflective self-awareness and self-critical function that is part of guilt. This is consistent with the type of guilt described earlier, based on objective self-awareness (Wicklund, 1975). Cowan (1978) has argued that guilt emerges during the stage of concrete operations in Piaget's theory of social-cognitive development. Guilt is viewed as a self-judgment, based on internally held standards. Self-judgment cannot occur until a child can adopt a perspective on the self. Several factors may combine to establish guilt as developing fairly late in childhood: increases with development in the discrepancy between actual and ideal self; the increase in role-taking (understanding others' perspectives as it concerns self-evaluation); a view of self as subject and cause; and the emergence of autonomous moral standards. Young children may feel bad or ashamed, but they do not engage in explicit negative self-evaluation. Similar arguments have been used to explain the emergence of depression late in childhood. Cicchetti and Schneider-Rosen (1986) have suggested that because children younger than age 11 or so have neither a well-developed superego nor a fully integrated ego or self system, one should not expect to see guilt feelings in depression in infancy and early to middle childhood. Increases with age in the symptom of guilt in depression (particularly around adolescence) have been identified in studies of childhood depression (Garber, 1984; McConville, Boag, & Purohit, 1973; Ushakov & Girich, 1972).

In addition to cognitive limitations that may prevent young children from experiencing guilt, there are also, in social-cognitive theory, important differences in socialization experiences that characterize the different developmental periods. Piaget (1932/1965) described a shift during the early elementary-school years from a morality of constraint (based mainly on interactions with authority figures) to an autonomous morality based more on interactions with peers. Under the morality of constraint, the child is guided by the parents' rules. Right and wrong are defined in terms of conformity to parental commands. But in peer interactions the child learns

through experience that cooperation is motivated by respect between equals and by solidarity in coordinating activities for mutual
benefit. These latter conditions are seen as particularly conducive to
children's internalization of moral standards and feelings of remorse
for wrongdoing and concern for others, as they come to learn how
their behaviors affect their (relationships with) friends and playmates.

There have been relatively few longitudinal or cross-sectional
studies of age changes in guilt. The work that has been done has focused mainly on social-cognitive processes, and children's guilt has
been measured through verbalizations obtained from interview and
semiprojective procedures. These studies provide some indications
of increases with age in frequency and maturity of guilt responses.
This corresponds to increases with age in empathy and altruism (see
review by Radke-Yarrow, Zahn-Waxler & Chapman, 1983). In two
studies (Chapman et al., 1987; Zahn-Waxler, Kochanska, et al.,
1990), verbal guilt responses (e.g., statements of remorseful feelings, reparative behaviors) were found to increase with age during
the early school years. Thompson and Hoffman (1980) used semiprojective procedures describing explicitly wrongful acts to first-,
third-, and fifth-grade children. They found developmental changes
in children's reasons for guilt: older children showed more concern
for the victim and used internal justice principles, while younger
children feared detection and punishment. Graham, Doubleday,
and Guarino (1984) found that younger children expressed guilt
over uncontrollable or accidental outcomes, while older children en-
dorsed guilt for controllable outcomes involving intentionality.

Covell and Abramovitch (1987) studied understanding of emotion in the family by looking at children's attributions of parents'
happiness, sadness, and anger. Children ranged in age from 5 to 15.
Most children, regardless of age, believed they could alter maternal
emotion. The younger children, more than older children, were
likely to attribute maternal emotions to themselves, that is, to view
themselves as the cause of their mothers' emotions, especially anger. This suggests a greater sense of responsibility on the part of
young children than the pattern of findings from other studies indicates. This may reflect egocentrism in younger children—their guilt
experiences may be influenced by an immature understanding of
personal causality, confusing instances in which they are genuinely

culpable for parental distress and anger with instances in which they are not truly to blame. However, it may also reflect the reality of their frequent experiences with parental discipline and anger. Contrary to traditional Piagetian and Kohlbergian social-cognitive viewpoints on the development of guilt relatively late in childhood, very young children may experience guilt. What they may lack are sufficiently developed cognitive structures and verbal skills to articulate these experiences in ways that can be measured through the interview, projective, and moral reasoning procedures typically used to assess guilt and moral functioning. (Evidence for this position is reviewed next.)

RECENT THEORETICAL PERSPECTIVES ON THE EARLY DEVELOPMENT OF GUILT

The preceding formulations differ considerably on how guilt is conceptualized, acquired, and expressed. In psychodynamic and cognitive approaches very young children have not been viewed as "moral" beings or as capable of full-fledged internalization. Emotions theory, however, hypothesizes that the primary discrete emotions emerge during the first year of life (Izard, 1977), with only a few of the more complex emotions or blends (e.g., sympathy, guilt, jealousy) evolving later, in the second year. Recent research suggests that children as young as 2 years have already acquired an appreciation of moral standards and that this is a universal process, apparently "built into" the organism (Kagan, 1984; Radke-Yarrow & Zahn-Waxler, 1984). Hoffman (1982) and Emde and his collaborators (Emde, Johnson, & Easterbrooks, 1987) have presented views of children in the earliest years of life as capable of guilt that is not solely fear based and reflexive to the commands of parents. These perspectives are reviewed here, along with data that have been emerging during the past two decades on the social and emotional competence of very young children. These studies document a remarkably sophisticated repertoire of affect expression and social skills that many young children bring to their relationships with others, suggesting that feelings of responsibility for others (e.g., empathy and guilt) are present very early in childhood.

**Research on early social-emotional competence.** There are indications in the literature (Zahn-Waxler & Radke-Yarrow, 1982) that children as young as 2 years show emotional distress and reparative behaviors following acts of wrongdoing and also prosocial behavior when they are bystanders to another's distress. Early evidence of internalization, or children's adoption of parental roles, is also suggested by research on toddlers' enactments of parents' social patterns, emotional expressions, and discipline practices (Kuczynski, Zahn-Waxler, & Radke-Yarrow, 1987).

Several studies have documented turn taking, reciprocity, sharing, and cooperation between toddlers (e.g., Eckerman, Whatley, & Kutz, 1975; Mueller & Brenner, 1977). Young children engage in conflict and conflict resolution (Hay, 1984) and understand and use simple rules to guide social interactions (Bakeman & Adamson, 1986). Toddlers negotiate and try to justify behavior in disputes (Dunn & Munn, 1987). Many of these behaviors are expressed in the context of sibling and peer interactions. Hence the peer environment Piaget hypothesized to be particularly conducive to moral development may become operative well before the early elementary-school years.

Almost as soon as children begin to talk, they talk about their own feelings, and shortly thereafter they describe emotions and inner states of others as well (Bretherton, Fritz, Zahn-Waxler, & Ridgeway, 1986), sometimes in "appropriate" evaluative or moral terms (e.g., "good," "bad," "not nice"). In experimental studies, when role-taking or perspective-taking tasks are made simple, preschool children are able to put themselves in the place of another person. By the age of 2, children demonstrate self/other differentiation (Zahn-Waxler, Chapman, & Cummings, 1984). Self-awareness emerges in the second year, as evidenced in the child's self-recognition in video images and mirrors and in the use of personal pronouns (Amsterdam, 1972; Lewis & Brooks-Gunn, 1979; Schulman & Kaplowitz, 1977).

These patterns of social competence and simple role taking are preceded still earlier in development by nonverbal indicators of social skills in infants during the first year of life. Reciprocal social dialogues, sometimes referred to as affective attunement and shared meaning (Stern, 1985; Trevarthen & Hubley, 1979), are seen in normal infants even in the first six months. When caregivers are asked to disrupt these dialogues in experimental studies by acting depressed and withdrawn, showing a "still face" (Cohn & Tronick, 1983; Tronick & Field, 1986), infants try to reengage the mother (i.e., repair interactions) and show patterns of disorganization when they do not succeed. By the end of the first year, the ability to share interest and to cooperate in toy play emerges in mother-child interaction. Some rules about communication—about how to initiate, maintain, and terminate social interactions—operate even before language. Thus young children have a primitive understanding that others also are agents or "selves," motivated by affect and intention (Bretherton et al., 1986). Cumulatively, these studies support the notion that children in the first years of life are endowed with the cognitive, behavioral, and social-emotional competencies necessary to experience/express empathy and guilt. Young children may provide as well as receive physical and emotional gratification—caring for others as well as being cared for. The capacity for a sense of responsibility for others and accountability in relationships means that the capacity for guilt could be present in the earliest years of life.

**A psychoanalytic reformulation of early moral development.** Early psychoanalytic notions of moral development in terms of superego formation stressed the internalization of the "don'ts" (prohibitions) and 4–6 years of age as a time during which emotional conflict needed to be resolved before significant expressions of conscience and guilt could appear. However, theories of internalization have expanded to include infancy and toddlerhood and the "dos" (Emde et al., 1987). This change has been motivated in part by the burgeoning literature just reviewed. Also, according to Emde, 1–3 years of age is a time when motivational conflict is first internalized and when affectively meaningful rules and standards are formulated within the context of specific caregiving relationships. The toddler becomes willful and learns to say no. Correspondingly, parental concerns increasingly become those of teaching and discipline as well as nurturing.

The end of the first year of life is typically considered the time when parents begin to exert socialization pressure. They begin to perceive their children as responsible or capable of rudimentary regulation of their actions and start setting limits and expectations for their behavior. In the child, two conflicting developments occur: the increased capacity for self-regulation results in greater ability to comply with the caregiver's demands (Kopp, 1982; Vaughn, Kopp, & Krakow, 1984), but the emerging autonomy and the acquisition of social skills also results in resistance to parental pressure (Wenar, 1982), as evidenced by the child's use of negotiation, refusal, and other forms of noncompliance (Kochanska, Kuczynski, Radke-Yarrow, & Welsh, 1987; Kuczynski, Kochanska, Radke-Yarrow, & Girnius-Brown, 1987). It is likely that these conflicting developments result in inner motivational conflicts and that many early forms of guilt experiences are associated with the child's transgressions and misbehaviors, violating everyday parental demands. It is also likely that these feelings develop in the context of early discipline encounters, particularly following the child's noncompliance. Parents' use of reprimands, punishments, or explanations is likely to contribute to the child's emotional discomfort.

The emergence of self-awareness at this time also brings a new level of emotional organization. A new set of patterned emotional responses seems to emerge as self-awareness develops, which Emde et al. (1987) have termed "the early moral emotions." Several of these responses imply the child's awareness of a problem and, increasingly, of conflicting intentions. The "early moral emotions" include positive affect, sharing, and pride; shame; and "hurt feelings" (which may be viewed as a possible forerunner of guilt). "Hurt feelings" have been observed to occur in the context of a prohibition from the parent. The child "looks hurt or pained," possibly showing elements of sadness, anger, and "pouting," which in turn might be an early index of self-criticism. Empathy may be yet another "early moral emotion."

**Hoffman's theory of development of guilt.** Hoffman (1982) was the first to articulate a theory about the early development of guilt in children. He has focused on guilt over harming others, which he views as socially beneficial and as having rational, rather than irrational, motives. He suggests that the motive base for guilt is empathic distress and hypothesizes that true interpersonal guilt may be due to the conjunction of an empathic response to someone's interpersonal distress and awareness of being the cause of that distress. Guilt is viewed as having three components: affective, cognitive, and motivational. The affective component is the painful feeling of dissatisfaction with the self because of the harmful consequences of one's actions. The motivational component refers to the urge to undo the harm or make reparation. The cognitive dimension includes the awareness that others have independent inner states and the awareness that one has caused harm.

Developmentally, guilt over physical action occurs first, then guilt over inaction or omission, then guilt over contemplating a harmful act. Guilt can occur only after children become aware of others as separate physical entities from themselves (about the end of the first year). At first children may feel they are at fault because their actions co-occur in time and space with another person's signs of distress. Young children are especially likely to feel confused about the cause of the distress and sometimes feel something like guilt, even if they are totally innocent.

As children become more aware of the effects of their behaviors, true interpersonal guilt (around the age of 2) becomes possible. For example, when a child physically harms another, the victim's cues, usually a cry or a pained look, may elicit a guilt feeling. Often the child's manner appears genuinely contrite and sympathetic rather than fearful. As the child becomes aware that others too have inner states, guilt over hurting people's feelings should become a possibility. At about the same time, the child may also be developing the cognitive capacity to experience guilt over inaction. Finally, when children become aware that other people have their own existence and personal identity—in late childhood or early adolescence— they can begin to feel guilty over the harmful effects of their actions or inaction beyond the immediate situation (e.g., guilt about the less fortunate). Hoffman's developmental theory was based mainly on informal observations, but the research of others just reviewed, and to be discussed in a subsequent section, supports the hypothesized early appearance of empathy and guilt.

In Hoffman's view, empathy and guilt are the major prosocial motives, since they may transform another's pain into one's own discomfort and make one feel partly responsible for the other's plight whether or not one has actually done anything to cause it. Although empathic distress is a prerequisite for the development of guilt, guilt can become largely independent of its empathic origins. Hoffman hypothesizes that humans are "wired" for empathy from birth. The reflexive crying of infants in response to the cries of newborns may reflect an early form of emotional arousal in relation to another's emotions. This may in turn be a precursor or rudimentary form of empathy. If humans are biologically predisposed to be responsive to the distress of others, and if it is sometimes difficult early in development to distinguish self from others and self as cause versus bystander to another's problems, there may be a tendency, from early on, to become causally implicated in the distress and problems of others—regardless of actual culpability.

## CONDITIONS OF PSYCHOPATHOLOGY AND RISK ASSOCIATED WITH GUILT: ATTRIBUTIONAL MODELS OF DEPRESSION

A decade ago Izard (1977) noted that despite the role of guilt in psychopathology, it has not been the subject of much research, perhaps because theories of psychopathology frequently do not treat guilt as a separate, distinct motivational variable. In recent research on other topics (e.g., conditions of risk and stress), guilt and related constructs have emerged as central foci. These include, for example, research on the role of guilt in cases of sexual abuse and rape, depression, holocaust survivors, eating disorders, and stress-related physical disorders (e.g., Janoff-Bulman, 1979; Lamb, 1986; Leckman et al., 1984; Rose & Garske, 1987). There also has been increasing interest in the effects on children of marital discord and divorce (Emery, 1982) and other parental problems (such as alcoholism and emotional illness in the parent) in which children may come to feel responsible for the family problems.

Excessive guilt, as noted earlier, is a major feature of depression in adolescents and adults. Before adolescence, guilt is not a significant component of depression in children (e.g., Garber, 1984; Kovacs & Paulauskas, 1984). However, in a study of attributions of 8- to 13-year-old children (Seligman, Peterson, Kaslow, Tanenbaum, Alloy, & Abramson, 1984), children who attributed bad events to internal ("it's my fault"), stable, and global causes were more likely to report depressive symptoms than were children who attributed these events to external, unstable, and specific causes. The depressive attributional style predicted depressive symptoms six months later.

Because guilt may contribute to as well as index some forms of depression, and because there is evidence for familial aggregation and intergenerational transmission of depression, understanding the origins of the disorder may be advanced through study of factors that contribute to the early development of key symptoms of the disorder (e.g., guilt). A variety of factors have been implicated in the etiology of depression, several of which might be seen as simultaneously relevant to the development of guilt *and* depression. They have included absence or loss of a caregiver (Bibring, 1953; Bowlby, 1980); the development of insecure attachments to caregivers and the failure to develop autonomy and an adequate sense of self (Miller, 1981); exposure to deviant child-rearing practices that might make the child feel sad, helpless, confused, or self-deprecatory, such as inconsistent parental behavior (Anthony, 1975; Davenport, Adland, Gold, & Goodwin, 1979), emotional unavailability, parental derision and censure, failure to nurture, and rejection (Crook, Raskin, & Eliot, 1981); inadequate social supports in times of stress and distress (Davenport et al., 1979); and biological vulnerability or genetic predisposition toward affective illness (Cadoret, 1978; McKinney, 1977; also see review by Meyersberg & Post, 1979).

Guilt and depression have been most explicitly linked in models of the development of depressogenic attributional styles (Beck, 1979; Seligman, 1975). Two different attributional approaches to depression have been proposed. In Seligman's (1975) learned-helplessness model, helplessness, a major symptom of depression, develops when organisms learn that there is no contingency between their responses and outcomes. When they learn that events are uncontrollable, they show cognitive, motivational, and emotional deficits that parallel the hopelessness and futility of depression. In the reformulated attributional theory (Abramson, Seligman, & Teasdale, 1978) significant features (and possible causes) of depression are the attributions people come to make about the reasons for negative events; that is, that the self is responsible and these self-attributions are stable, global, and consistently internal. Beck's (1967) cognitive model of depression postulates that depressives have negative cognitive sets and interpret interactions within the environment as instances of failure. The depressive is likely to assume personal responsibility for events with negative outcomes, thereby producing feelings of guilt, self-blame, self-deprecation, and dejection. Abramson and Sackheim (1977) argued that the merging of Seligman's original learned-helplessness model and Beck's cognitive model results in the potentially paradoxical situation of individuals blaming themselves for outcomes that they know they did not cause and over which they have no control: that is, How can one feel so responsible and so helpless at the same time?

A number of possible "resolutions" of the paradox have been offered by Abramson and Sackheim (1977). The most likely and perhaps self-evident explanation offered, given that self-blame and helplessness are both symptoms of depression and have been found in research to covary (Seligman, 1975), is that depressives hold "inconsistent" beliefs about their impotence and omnipotence. The more interesting question is why and how the attributions and the apparently contradictory beliefs *develop*. In subsequent sections we consider in greater detail conditions of childhood that would contribute to the simultaneous development of beliefs of omnipotence, responsibility, and impotence, and consider their theoretical links to guilt and depression.

## The Development of Guilt in Children

We have studied guilt in children from both a developmental and a psychopathology perspective.[1] The following questions have been considered: When does guilt emerge, and how can it be measured? Does it take different forms in different children? Can adaptive and maladaptive forms that result in different developmental trajectories or pathways be identified early in development? How does guilt relate to other emotions? How is guilt learned or socialized? Children have been studied in two age periods: the early to middle elementary school years, when most theorists have argued that guilt develops, and the first years of life, when we argue that the groundwork is laid for different patterns of guilt later in development. We have found evidence for guilt in both time periods and have identified different developmental trajectories for adaptive and maladaptive patterns. We review these studies in some detail to indicate

1. This work was supported by the National Institute of Mental Health and the John D. and Catherine T. MacArthur Foundation Network on the Transition from Infancy to Early Childhood.

more specifically the questions asked, the methods used, and the results that have led to these inferences and generalizations. (Findings described here, all statistically significant, are elaborated in the other publications cited).

Guilt is very difficult to study; it is not an emotion that has a clear expressive component. What may appear to be direct expressions of guilt—for example, apologies, confessions, behavioral attempts to undo "wrongs"—sometimes may have other motives. Moreover, guilt may be indexed in ways that do not appear at first glance as guilt; for example, strong convictions about never hurting others, excessive empathy, fears, physical symptoms, and compulsions (hand washing). Most of the research has been on children's "sins of commission"—thoughts, feelings, and actions that accompany or follow acts of wrongdoing. But in addition to children's misbehaviors, there are the "sins of omission" (children's failures to do the right thing or to deal with problems not of their making but for which they feel responsible). We have attempted to study both types of guilt—over real and imagined wrongdoings, in situations of interpersonal distress and conflict.

The methods used included semiprojective procedures or story narratives containing themes of interpersonal conflict and distress; psychiatric interviews with children; observations of children's reactions to naturally occurring problems that they cause or witness in others; observations of children's reactions to simulated problems of others; and experimentally arranged "mishaps." A variety of research methods and designs were used and replication studies were conducted in order to yield generalizable conclusions. Longitudinal studies permitted both analysis of developmental progression and patterns of individual continuity/discontinuity over time. In studies of reparative behaviors, acts explicitly requested by the caregiver were not included in analyses.

We have studied guilt in children from populations in which the meaning, functions, and dynamics might be expected to differ, hence for whom there might be different developmental pathways. Children of well and depressed mothers have been compared in several of the studies. Children of depressed caregivers were expected to show more guilt and responsibility for the problems of others than children of well mothers. As we indicated earlier, guilt is a common feature of clinical depression. In conjunction with other symptoms of the disorder such as feelings of helplessness and fatigue, guilt may make caregivers unusually sensitive to issues of suffering, blame, and responsibility. This sensitivity, in turn, could be communicated to children in a variety of ways that might make them prone to maladaptive patterns of guilt. Ordinary tasks and responsibilities become overwhelming, and caregivers may seek others, including their children, with whom to share the burdens. Depressed mothers, more than well mothers, experience guilt and irritability in their relationships with their children (Belle, 1982; Weissman & Paykel, 1974), so the child is in close proximity to these emotions. Depression is part of a more global family "climate" of distress and conflict (Gotlib & Hooley, 1988; Radke-Yarrow & Kuczynski, 1983). Repeated exposure to this affective environment (to a sad caregiver and the conflict between parents that often accompanies depression) may increase the likelihood that children will feel responsible for negative events simply by being there. Through processes of contagion or conditioning, distress may become generalized, and children may feel globally as well as specifically responsible for bad things that happen. More particularly, they may come to feel they have caused the parent's depression.

Other socialization practices and discipline methods also may encourage maladaptive guilt in children of depressed mothers. Depressed mothers, more than well mothers, make negative attributions about their children during mother-child interaction (Radke-Yarrow, Belmont, Nottelmann, & Bottomly, in press). Depressed mothers report more use of guilt- and anxiety-induction procedures in conjunction with expressing disappointment in their children (Susman et al., 1985). Guilt may be learned through parental modeling of negative attributional styles ("it's my fault"). Seligman et al. (1984) reported that mothers who attributed bad events to internal, stable, and global causes had children with similar self-attribution patterns for negative events. Because depression often is characterized by social withdrawal, these caregivers may sometimes be less involved and less emotionally available. Hence their children may be more likely to experience love withdrawal, which, as we noted earlier, is related to guilt in children.

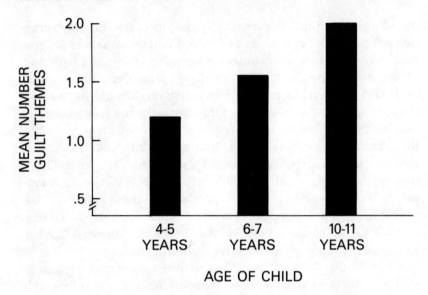

FIGURE 1. Age changes in guilt themes: normative patterns.

## GUILT IN OLDER CHILDREN

A sample of 64 children ranging in age from 4 to 10 years, from normal volunteer families, was studied (Chapman et al., 1987). Our research interests were in how children's responses to victims in distress changed as a function of age and in whether children's altruistic behaviors in these situations (e.g., help, comfort, sharing) could be predicted from their interpretations in hypothetical situations of interpersonal distress and conflict, especially their interpretations reflecting themes of guilt and empathy. Children's altruistic behaviors were observed during several staged mishaps: a kitten that needed to be taken out of its cage and fed, an adult who injured her back, and a crying infant in need of a bottle.

Children's interpretations in hypothetical situations were obtained from eight stories, illustrated with photographs, in which someone experienced distress or conflict in the presence of another child. The story child was either the cause of the problem or a bystander and either helped or did not, depending on the story. Spontaneous comments were noted, and then interview probes were used to explore interpretations of motives and feelings of the story character. For instance, in one story sequence two children fight over a bike; one pushes the other and then makes up. Guilt was coded if the research participant indicated that the aggressor felt sorry or engaged in additional reparative behaviors. Stories were based on situations established as within the life experiences of even the youngest children studied. Since children could attribute different thoughts and feelings to story characters, their attributions were assumed to reflect underlying motives to some extent.

Consistent with psychodynamic and social-cognitive theories of moral development, expressions of guilt, empathy, and altruism were more prevalent in older than in younger children in both hypothetical and real distress situations. Increases with age in guilt themes are indicated in Figure 1. In addition, children who expressed more empathic, altruistic, and guilt themes in the stories also were very helpful toward real distress victims, with guilt being the strongest predictor of actual prosocial behaviors. Thus it may not be just the tendency to feel the same emotion as the other person (empathy) that guides prosocial behavior, but a more broadly based disposition to feel responsibility for another person's well-being. The guilt themes evoked in this sample by these story procedures appeared to have an adaptive function and may reflect empathy-based guilt as described by Hoffman.

Because of our interest in maladaptive forms of guilt, we modified the narrative story procedure to elicit more frequent and varied expressions of concern over wrongdoing (Zahn-Waxler, Kochanska, et al., 1990) and interviewed 87 5- to 9-year-old children of depressed and well mothers. Mothers in this and subsequent studies of maternal depression were screened with the SADS-L interview (Schedule for Affective Disorders and Schizophrenia—Lifetime Version), using Research Diagnostic Criteria (Spitzer & Endicott, 1978). (Coders were not informed of the mothers' diagnoses.) The research questions concerned how guilt patterns changed as a function of age and how they related to psychiatric assessments of guilt. This time four stories were used. In addition to the object struggle used earlier (bike fight), the following situations were presented: an angry mother leaves the home, and her child watches the departure through the window; a sibling swings his hand near the baby in the crib (and there is ambiguity about whether he is about to hit or pat); and a mother cries on the telephone while her child watches.

In addition to the direct guilt themes scored in the preceding study, more indirect, primitive, less self-reflective expressions of concern or involvement were identified in the current stories. Typically in earlier research, circumscribed definitions of guilt as a conscious, explicit, action-oriented and/or self-critical reaction have been used (e.g., apologies, acknowledgment of wrongdoing, remorse, and clear reparative behaviors). But within a psychoanalytic framework, any of a large number of painful experiences that follow real or perceived transgressions (including nightmares, accidents, and unrealistic fears of external punishments) have been viewed either as expressions of guilt or as defensive manifestations of guilt (see Hoffman, 1970a). We coded bizarre, violent, unrealistic, or extreme elements in the narratives, or signs of vulnerability, hypersensitivity, or tension, and termed them "distortions." For example, a child would say "the mother is crying because the father is killed, and cars kept running over the father, even the ambulance (and the mother and boy watched from the bedroom window)"; or "the mother's leaving home because the boy wouldn't eat his peas"; or "the mother's crying because a plant bit her." Thus the modified semiprojective procedure yielded two dimensions or levels of guilt—one conscious, explicit, and functional (e.g., "she was wrong and she said 'sorry'") and the other more indirect and extreme, possibly representing fear-based guilt or a defense against unacceptable impulses.

Guilt patterns in children of well and depressed mothers differed, suggesting different developmental pathways or trajectories. Younger children of well mothers showed quite low levels of direct, explicit guilt and empathy in these hypothetical situations of interpersonal conflict and distress, but the frequency of these themes increased markedly with age during the early school years. This replicates the developmental findings in the preceding study and again is consistent with psychodynamic and social-cognitive theories of moral development about when guilt develops. Children of depressed mothers, however, did not fit this normative pattern: their explicit guilt and empathy themes were somewhat higher at the younger ages than for children of well mothers, and they showed no increases with age across the span of development studied here.

(See Figure 2.) When empathy and guilt scores were combined to represent high involvement in others' interpersonal distress and conflict, an interaction was observed: younger children of depressed mothers showed significantly *more* involvement in hypothetical situations of interpersonal conflict and distress than children of well mothers, while the opposite pattern obtained for the older age group.

There were other indications that the dynamics, meaning, and expression of guilt differ for the two populations. Children of depressed mothers showed more extreme elements in their story narratives (66% of the children) than children of well mothers (29%). These distortions typically indicated that children's representations

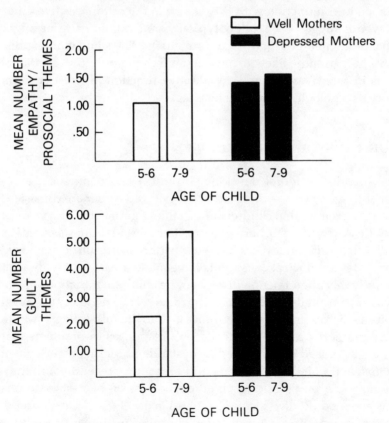

FIGURE 2. Age changes in guilt and empathy themes in children of well and depressed mothers.

of interpersonal distress and conflict were exaggerated, complex, and lacking in direct resolutions of problems. They may be a way of diverting painful feelings in problem situations, hence indexing a qualitatively different form of guilt. These studies of school-age children thus identify individual differences in adaptive and maladaptive guilt, both of which may originate earlier in evelopment.

This study also indicates the usefulness of multiple procedures for measuring guilt. In a separate psychiatric interview in which a number of problem areas were assessed, children were asked about a variety of situations in which they perceived themselves as at fault versus not at fault. There were increases with age in guilt scores for children of both depressed and well mothers. However, when viewed in conjunction with the data from the semiprojective interview, this suggests that phenotypically similar guilt patterns might have quite different motives and functions. The same guilt expressions may be more likely to have an underlying primitive, irrational basis in a risk sample and an adaptive function in children from more psychologically healthy families.

GUILT IN YOUNGER CHILDREN

The theories of moral development and research on social-emotional competence in young children reviewed earlier are consistent with the premise that children are capable of guilt in the first years of life. Research that supports this position and identifies systematic individual differences in children's patterns of guilt is reviewed here. Methodological constraints have made it particularly difficult to study this phenomenon in very young children. Situations of distress and wrongdoing do not occur frequently or regularly, so direct naturalistic observations are difficult. Our initial strategy was to have mothers observe their children's responses to problems that they had caused or witnessed as bystanders. Mothers were given extensive training in observing and reporting procedures, in individual and group sessions, and the reliability of their observations was assessed (Radke-Yarrow & Zahn-Waxler, 1973; Zahn-Waxler & Radke-Yarrow, 1982). A replication study using similar procedures was conducted, and a laboratory study of 2-year-olds was done in which a series of mishaps was staged (Barrett & Zahn-Waxler, 1987).

The mishaps were based on maternal reports of common problems during this age period, obtained from the original study (e.g., the child spills something, a toy breaks, or the child accidently hurts the mother). Such events were found to elicit reparative behaviors in most children in the home and laboratory.

A normal volunteer sample of 24 mothers and their children provided normative data on developmental patterns of guilt (reparative behaviors) and altruism (prosocial behaviors). Children were followed longitudinally between the ages of 1 and 2½ years. Mothers observed their children's responses to others' negative emotions (e.g., sadness, pain, fatigue, anger), and they also simulated emotions in the children's presence. Mothers narrated their observations into tape recorders, describing the emotion and how it was expressed, the circumstances of the event, the child's affective, verbal, and behavioral responses to the emotion, and the mother's (and others') responses to the child. Two classes of events were observed: those where the child was a bystander to someone else's emotions (e.g., child sees father crying), and those where the child caused emotion (e.g., child hits and hurts sibling). Home visits were also made periodically: mother-child interaction was observed, and an emotion was simulated by the home visitor.

Developmental changes are presented in Figure 3 that shows transitions in children's prosocial behaviors under three conditions: when the child caused another's distress, and when the child observed distress under natural conditions or under simulated conditions. Developmental patterns are similar under the three conditions. There are increases in altruistic and reparative acts with age, particularly in the last half of the second year of life (Zahn-Waxler & Radke-Yarrow, 1982). Children help, share and sympathize with, and comfort victims in distress, and they begin to attempt different solutions when one does not work. The developmental patterns recently have been replicated with another sample of 27 children (Zahn-Waxler, Radke-Yarrow, Wagner, & Pyle, 1988). These prosocial behaviors often indicate sophisticated pragmatic understanding of others' emotional states by young children (Saarni, this volume). Exemplars or prototypes of altruistic reactions have been described in other publications (e.g., Zahn-Waxler & Radke-Yarrow, 1982). Illustrations of remorseful, reparative, and guilt-like behaviors are provided in Appendix A.

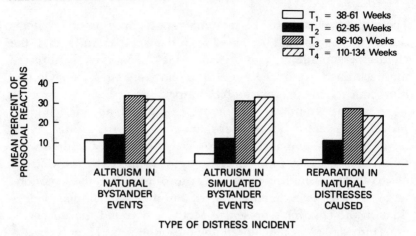

FIGURE 3. Age changes in children's prosocial reactions (altruism and reparation) in response to problems they have witnessed or caused.

Appendix A contains a variety of examples of concern, anxiety, remorse, reparation, and/or acknowledgment of responsibility in situations where the child has harmed others or caused distress. The examples are intended to illustrate the different patterns of reaction observed in 24 children between the ages of 1 and 2½ years. They were excerpted from narrative reports of trained mother-observers. A variety of types of reparative behaviors can be seen: direct help; indirect help; sharing; physical comfort, soothing, and affection; verbal sympathy; verbal apologies. Often there is affective involvement, and children are described as anxious, worried, concerned, remorseful. Some reparative behaviors appear perfunctory and devoid of feeling. Sometimes the links between reparative behavior and emotional concerns are clear (e.g., stated fears of loss of parental love). Occasionally children demonstrate explicit awareness that their (reparative) behavior could change another's emotional state (e.g., "Now are you happy?"). Self-punitive behaviors also are present. Internalized reactions become more evident as children develop the capacity to recall past occasions where they brought harm to others. It is not uncommon for their reparative behaviors to be closely linked to the continuation of injurious acts. In other words, there is aggression as well as guilt, and hence ambivalence or uncertainty in the child's reparative intentions. Often the child's emotionality and reparative behavior are "encouraged" by a variety of disciplinary acts from the caregiver, but it is uncommon for caregivers to explicitly request reparation (or provide explicit examples of how to undo harm). Although it cannot be readily discerned from the individual examples, examining the entire array of incidents for each child revealed dysfunctional patterns of overarousal for some of them.

As we noted, developmental progressions in children's prosocial acts were similar both for problems they caused and for those they witnessed in others. When children help someone they have injured, this is conceptualized as reparation for wrongdoing and hence a sign of conscience or guilt. When they observe others' distress, the same behaviors are interpreted as altruism or empathy. Since young children sometimes have difficulty distinguishing between harm they cause and harm they observe, early forms of altruism and conscience sometimes overlap. In fact, altruistic and reparative behaviors were highly correlated in these young children (Zahn-Waxler et al., 1979). Thus this may be a time in development when children are particularly vulnerable to developing feelings of responsibility for problems not of their own making. There was evidence that 2-year-old children who were prone to think they had caused distress in others showed developmental continuities in this pattern, suggesting long-lasting implications of these early confusions. Several children had initially shown "misplaced self-responsibility" as toddlers (Zahn-Waxler et al., 1979). These were children who sometimes responded as if they had caused distress when in fact they had not. Upon seeing their mothers cry, for example, they would ask apologetically, "Did I make you sad?" or "Sorry, I be nice." Thus they were likely to implicate themselves explicitly as causes of another's problem or, at least, to question their causal role. These children were also more likely than children who had not shown this pattern to produce guilt themes five years later in laboratory assessments (Cummings et al., 1986).

Even though children frequently behave similarly whether they cause or simply witness another's distress, there are other indications that they often respond quite differently, and hence that they discriminate between the two types of situations (Zahn-Waxler & Radke-Yarrow, 1982). For example, children show more distress and

more aggression when they have caused distress than when they
have witnessed it (see Figures 4 & 5). Often the aggression is a continuation of the distress they initially caused. Also, children make
more active efforts to understand harm they have witnessed as bystanders than harm they have created (e.g., by asking questions or

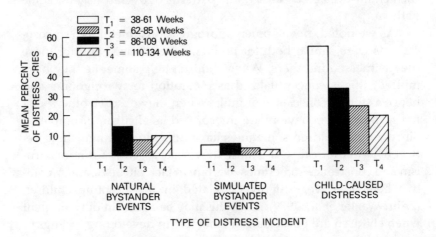

FIGURE 4. Age changes in children's emotional distress in response to
problems they have witnessed or caused.

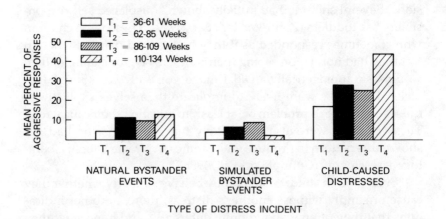

FIGURE 5. Age changes in children's aggression in response to problems they have witnessed or caused.

engaging in hypothesis testing). This suggests that they would sooner avoid dealing with problems they have caused, or that they already know why someone is distressed when they have caused it. Moreover, many mothers treat situations where children cause and witness distress quite differently, hence helping them to make this discrimination (Zahn-Waxler et al., 1979). We consider next socialization practices that may contribute to different levels and types of guilt in children.

## SOCIALIZATION OF GUILT

Messages from parents about what behaviors are valued and appropriate begin very early in the child's life. Some of the communications are conscious and explicit, but many socialization practices are carried out with little self-awareness or reflection (Saarni, this volume). With regard to moral development, the following environmental factors have been identified as possibly relevant: the specific discipline practices parents use to communicate to their children the nature and consequences of acts of misbehavior (e.g., techniques of induction, power assertion, or love withdrawal); the quality of the caregiver's affective relationship with the child (e.g., nurturing versus non-nurturing); the more general emotional climate of the home, including the affective states of the parents (e.g., high levels of anger, sadness, or tension conveyed in parental disharmony, depression, or anxiety states); attitudes, values, and philosophies about child rearing, especially in domains conducive to the development of guilt (e.g., aggression, sex, interpersonal relationships, achievement, and separation/individuation); attributional styles of parents (e.g., acceptance versus projection of blame and responsibility onto others); and cultural and religious differences. We assume that these dimensions affect not only children's specific behaviors but also their interpretations of interpersonal situations, as well as their feelings and emergent views about the self as good or bad, as valued or not respected. The different dimensions of socialization interact and overlap in complex ways (and also may interact with the child's temperament as well). In our research we have examined some of these influences.

**Maternal discipline practices and nurturance.** The literature reviewed earlier indicated that induction and love withdrawal were both associated with high guilt, while power assertion was associated with low guilt. Our research with mothers of very young children (1 ½ to 2 years old) are consistent with this generalization. Moreover, mothers who frequently used these techniques also tended to be empathic and sensitive in observed interactions with their children. To elaborate, mothers who frequently explained to children the consequences their actions have for others and their causal roles in situations of misfortune had children who were likely to make reparation for wrongdoing (Zahn-Waxler et al., 1979). The effect was strongest when explanations were accompanied by emotion and by implied threats to the relationship, such as evaluative comments and general statements of principles that conveyed high maturity demands and possibly unrealistic expectations (e.g., about *never* hurting other people). The maternal techniques that predicted children's guilt and reparative behaviors also predicted altruism in bystander situations, suggesting that the effects of discipline generalize. That is, discipline practices may influence not only children's responsibility for their own acts, but a more general responsiveness to the feelings of others.

Explicit love-withdrawal techniques associated with reparative behaviors in children were particularly likely to secure compliance. (Love withdrawal consisted of separations imposed by mothers following misbehaviors and statements regarding separation; e.g., "I don't want to be near you when you act like that.") Love withdrawal led to both more avoidant responses by the child *and* attempts to reunite or make up with the parent (Chapman & Zahn-Waxler, 1982). This suggests that when love withdrawal is a common disciplinary practice, high levels of ambivalence and tension may motivate young children's attempts to maintain interpersonal connections. Consistent with the Freudian view, excessive use of parental love withdrawal could lead to exaggerated feelings of responsibility and other neurotic symptoms in children rather than to the development of a more mature moral orientation. There were suggestions (though not statistically verifiable owing to the small N) that qualitatively different types of guilt were already emerging, which corresponded closely to different types of parental discipline. One form of guilt reflected levels of arousal and responsibility appropriate to the circumstances and appeared to result from moderate levels of more matter-of-fact, other-oriented parental induction. The other form of guilt appeared excessive, resulting from more extreme attempts to induce empathy and fear.

Mothers' use of other forms of love withdrawal and possibly guilt induction has been reported even earlier in development (Zahn-Waxler & Chapman, 1982). It was common for some mothers to highlight their very young children's behaviors involving harm to persons (in this case, to the mothers themselves) through distress vocalizations, facial or bodily expressions of pain and sorrow. These processes of "see how your behavior hurts me" may be a nonverbal precursor of guilt induction. Although our initial research did not focus on conditions of psychopathology, emotional illness in a parent (e.g., depression) may, for reasons noted earlier, incline caregivers toward increased use of these techniques and hence lead them to induce more (extreme) guilt in their children.

**Parental moods/emotional climate.** The parent's use of discipline and expression of emotions toward the child (e.g., expressions of warmth or coldness) do not occur in a vacuum. They occur in the context of yet broader rearing environments or "social climates" (Lewin, Lippitt, & White, 1939; Radke-Yarrow, 1977; Radke-Yarrow & Kuczynski, 1983), which may be conceptualized as "rearing influences at a distance" and operationalized in terms of the emotional experiences of and between other persons in the young child's world—that is, the immediate family environment. We focused mainly on the affective state of the parents (e.g., depressed versus well) and to a lesser degree on the affective relationship between them (e.g., discordant versus harmonious), since associations between marital discord and depression in women are common. A recurring theme in the literature on divorce and marital discord concerns both the children's conduct problems and the unrealistic sense of responsibility for their parents' problems they sometimes feel (Emery, 1982). Tensions between spouses may also be experienced by the children, who may sometimes try to help solve the problems. The effects on children of parental conflict may be heightened if one of the caregivers also acts sad and helpless in the situation. We have found that even at a very early age, children are negatively aroused emotionally by exposure to conflict and distress in others. Moreover, repeated exposure to conflict results in response patterns that may begin to crystallize into enduring emotional styles.

In our first longitudinal study of young children's responses to others' emotions, high- and low-conflict families were identified based on the number of arguments mothers reported having with their spouses. Children's reactions to parental fights were compared when they were 2 years old (Cummings, Zahn-Waxler, & Radke-Yarrow, 1981). The conflicts consisted mainly of verbal arguments, though there was occasional pushing and husbands sometimes threw things (e.g., hurling food at the dinner table) or were self-punitive (e.g., slamming a fist into the wall). Wives were more inclined to express anger as sadness; for example, "I was so furious, I just burst into tears." Children from high-conflict homes became more emotionally aroused; that is, they expressed more anger and distress in these situations. And they intervened more than children from low-conflict homes—trying to get the parents to stop, to comfort one of them, or to get them to make up (see Figure 6). When children from high-conflict homes responded, it was not uncommon for them to show all the patterns simultaneously by becoming upset,

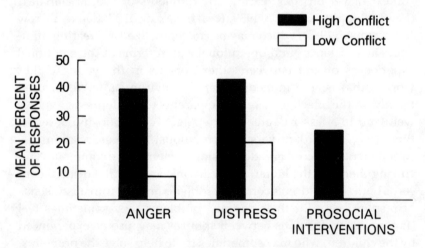

FIGURE 6. Two-year-old children's reactions to high and low conflict between parents.

angrily scolding the aggressor, and comforting the perceived victim. Frequent exposure to conflict may sensitize children to assume precocious responsibility for others' problems.

This sensitization process also was observed in an experimental study of 2-year-olds who observed a simulated verbal argument between two unfamiliar adults (Cummings, Iannotti, & Zahn-Waxler, 1985). Children's emotions and behaviors with a playmate were observed under these conditions of background anger and compared with their reactions to friendly interactions between adults. The children experienced identical procedures in a second session two weeks later, and a replication sample experienced one exposure to background conflict. Children showed high distress during the fight when compared with the condition of friendly interaction, and this effect became more pronounced following the second quarrel. Similarly, children showed high levels of aggression in peer play following the adult quarrel, and this effect became more pronounced after the second quarrel.

The children from high- and low-conflict homes in the initial study were seen again several years later, and there were similar developmental changes for both groups. By the early school years, children generally intervened in parental fights with greater dispassion and effectiveness (Cummings, Zahn-Waxler, & Radke-Yarrow, 1984). Most often, the older children tried to end the fight, reconcile angry partners, and comfort the distraught parent. These patterns of conflict resolution appeared adaptive because children no longer looked so upset. But these high levels of responsibility may lead to or index excessive guilt and role reversal as the child repeatedly takes the role of caregiver, mediator, or peacemaker. This in turn may reflect problematic enduring patterns or styles of coping with others' problems, especially for children from high-conflict homes who assumed these roles so early in life.

Our studies of younger children are consistent with existing research (see review by Parke & Slaby, 1983), indicating that anger and aggression, as well as the more prosocial behaviors we have observed, are stimulated by exposure to background conflict and observation of others' aggression. Distress and conflict in others may trigger preexisting internalizing or externalizing orientations and may trigger both patterns simultaneously in some children. While the anger may become less apparent in many children as they grow older, it still may be experienced, though sometimes masked or expressed in other ways. Aggressive impulses may become internalized, expressed as anger toward the self, or externalized and displaced in expression. One by-product might be patterns of guilt related to hostility in complex ways.

Emotional dysregulation and atypical patterns of involvement in situations of interpersonal distress and conflict also were found in a longitudinal study of a small sample of 5- and 6-year-old boys from high-conflict homes, where one parent had a history of bipolar depression (Zahn-Waxler, Mayfield, et al., 1988) and most spouses had unipolar depression. As toddlers the children were observed to have many socioemotional problems (Zahn-Waxler, McKnew, et al., 1984; Zahn-Waxler, Cummings, & Chapman, 1984). They were insecurely attached to their caregivers and showed problems regulating anger and aggression. The children found it difficult to share and to take the perspectives of others. In follow-up assessments, these children continued to show problems with empathy and aggression. In laboratory assessments they were lacking in insight or empathy in some domains. However, they also were unusually sensitive to conflict they observed in others and were able to generate a high number of problem-solving strategies in conflict situations. Sometimes these were strategies that involved "keeping the peace" (sharing with an aggressor and submissiveness or acquiescence).

In another laboratory study of 46 2-year-old children, offspring of unipolar depressed mothers often appeared to be especially well behaved. This conclusion is based on observations from sessions in which children interacted primarily with a same-age peer, but also with the mother and an unfamiliar adult (Cummings et al., 1985; Zahn-Waxler, Cummings, Iannotti, & Radke-Yarrow, 1984). Seminaturalistic and experimental conditions were designed to stimulate and challenge children, to elicit a range of responding for assessing individual differences in regulation of emotions and social competence. Children who had mothers with unipolar depression were more likely than children of well mothers to become preoccupied and upset when exposed to conflict and distress in others. Also, they were less likely to engage in acts of physical aggression toward their playmates (see Figure 7). These and other behavior patterns

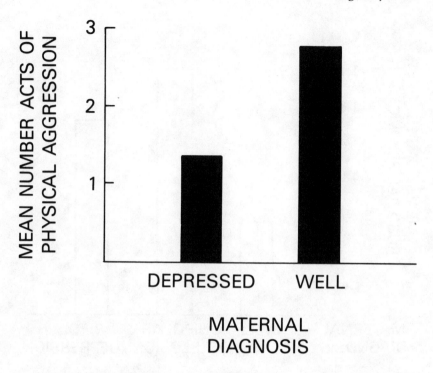

FIGURE 7. Aggression toward peers in 2-year-old children of well and depressed mothers.

suggested that toddlers with depressed mothers seemed already to have learned to treat others carefully. They appeared to suppress negative emotions, were polite in the face of frustration, and tended to make appeasement gestures. This heightened sensitivity suggests the early learning of high levels of accountability in social interactions with others, which may in turn reflect guilt.

In another study, young children's tendencies to assume responsibility for their mothers' problems were assessed in an interaction situation. Two- and 3-year-old children's reactions to depressed and well mothers' simulations of sadness were observed. A standard situation was used in which the mother and child, seated together, looked through a book of pictures of infants expressing various emotions. After they completed the series, the mother was asked to return to a photograph of a crying baby and to show her

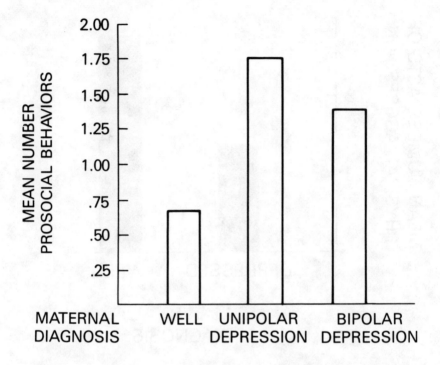

FIGURE 8. Two- and 3-year-old children's prosocial behaviors toward well and depressed mothers.

own sadness and concern. This provides information about how the mothers portray sadness, how the child responds, and the dynamics of their interaction. Children of unipolar and bipolar depressed mothers made more frequent ($F$ [2, 83] = 4.22, $p <$.025) and more different types ($F$ [2, 83] = 5.98, $p <$.004) of comforting reactions than children of well mothers (see Figure 8), indicating an extreme quality to their empathy and the assumption of too much responsibility in this situation.

Informal observations of the mothers suggested differences between depressed and well mothers. In simulations of sadness, well mothers would typically show the child the picture of the sad baby and comment on or explain the baby's sadness in an empathic but nonperseverative manner. Depressed mothers tended to bypass the infant's sadness and focused quickly on their own sorrow and problems (e.g., "I'm sad because the car broke and I have so much house-work to do"), and/or to identify their children as the cause of their sadness (e.g., "It really makes me sad when you don't obey"). These latter patterns can be viewed as forms of guilt induction. Some de-pressed mothers became so caught up in expressing despair that they were unable to bring the episode to resolution. This too could contribute to patterns of anxiety, ambivalence, and overinvolve-ment in the child.

Several studies, then, indicate that young children become overinvolved in the problematic emotions and emotional relation-ships of their caregivers, in ways that suggest they feel responsible and concerned. These feelings of accountability in specific situations may, over time, become established ways of handling difficult situa-tions that generalize to other settings. Although the behaviors and emotions shown by these children do not always conform to tradi-tional definitions of guilt (explicit concern, remorse, or reparation in situations of wrongdoing), we hypothesize that deep concerns about interpersonal conflict and harm brought to others come to be felt by children as "sins of omission" or failures in themselves. In other words, these children come to believe they could and should be doing more for their parents; and these feelings of obligation gen-eralize into stable coping patterns as they continue to try to make things right but often fail because they cannot effectively solve par-ents' problems. In Malatesta's framework (this volume), affect-spe-cific biases toward excessive or unrealistic guilt become enduring features of personality organization. Unrealistic guilt is likely to oc-cur when unrealistic expectations are conveyed to children. We have focused here on guilt that may result from failure to relieve chronic stress and distress in significant others.

**The Role of Child-Rearing Attitudes and Values.** We examined the extent to which guilt induction was a component of depressed and well mothers' child-rearing philosophies. The Block Child-Rearing Q-Sort was used to assess parental attitudes, beliefs, and values. The instrument covers four broad domains of child rearing: how positive and negative emotions are expressed, handled, and regu-lated within the child and in parent-child interaction; how parental rules and authority are conveyed, and specific discipline techniques and control strategies used to achieve socialization goals; the parent's ideals and goals regarding the child's aspirations and achievements; and the values regarding the child's development of autonomy and separation/individuation.

Depressed and well mothers were compared (Susman et al., 1985). Mothers with current major depression were especially likely to endorse guilt-inducing techniques in conjunction with anxiety-induction techniques (e.g., belief that their children should be made aware of maternal sacrifice, worry about bad and sad things that will happen as children grow up, belief that punishment is inescapable if children are bad) and to express feelings of disappointment in the children. These orientations expressed by depressed mothers were associated with other rearing values: depressed mothers more than well mothers were concerned with the impressions their children made on others but, paradoxically, were relatively unlikely to encourage their children to do their best. They also expressed difficulty in letting children make decisions, were overprotective, and tried to suppress children's vigorous (sometimes aggressive) questioning of some authority figures. These latter values appear to index the parents' difficulty in accepting the developing autonomy and individuation of their children. These attitudes and values, in conjunction with guilt- and anxiety-induction techniques, might be expected to foster guilt and low self-worth in children. Feelings of being blameworthy, responsible, and helpless have, as noted, been linked with depression.

## Discussion and Conclusions

We have reviewed theories and research on the development of children's propensity to experience and express concern over real and imagined wrongdoings. There appear to be at least two periods in children's development that are important for moral internalization: the first years of life and the early to middle elementary-school years. The tasks of adolescence (firm establishment of separation/individuation, adult identity, and relationship formation) undoubtedly present another (as yet unstudied) "critical period" for moral growth, especially as it interfaces with mental health concerns. Depression and conduct disorders, for example, become more prevalent in adolescence and begin to approximate more closely adult forms of internalizing and externalizing disorders. There are many biological, cognitive, and psychological factors that contribute to these changes (e.g., Rutter, 1988). Psychological symptoms associated with these disorders (e.g., excesses and deficiencies in guilt and the closely related feelings of worthlessness, blameworthiness, and low self-esteem) become increasingly apparent at this time.

Our discussion focuses on the two earlier periods of development that have received more attention in research and theory. There are striking changes with age in the elementary-school years in children's expressions of guilt and conceptualizations of moral issues. These developmental transitions indicate that this period represents a special time for moral growth and hence for the establishment of more mature awareness of issues of responsibility, wrongdoing, and blame. But the emphasis in theories and research on uniform processes of change during the elementary-school years has obscured other realities. For example, important aspects of moral development occur much earlier in development, and there are different adaptive and maladaptive patterns and hence different developmental pathways. Research has documented that feelings of remorse, reparative behaviors, and the capacity to make primitive attributions of the self as being "at fault" begin in the first years of life. Individual differences are apparent, some of which reflect appropriate understanding of one's causal role in the problems of others. Other patterns appear more dysfunctional. We have identified one form of dysfunctional guilt that appears as empathy gone awry or as overgeneralized acceptance of responsibility for others' problems. This can be linked in part to specific socialization experiences, such as overinvolvement with an unhappy parent. Here we consider some models and processes that might help to explain different developmental patterns.

We did not begin our research with a strong commitment to a given theoretical approach. Rather, we began with an interest in a particular psychological phenomenon, an important universal experience that appears to distinguish humans from other animals—namely, the capacity to feel responsible or at fault. We used various theories from research and clinical work to guide selection of research procedures and designs that would permit intensive and extensive empirical examination of children's perceptions and reactions in potentially guilt-inducing situations. Some of these studies were designed in the tradition of earlier research, to examine children's reactions to situations of wrongdoing. However, major emphasis also was placed on studying children's assumption of responsibility for problems that were not of their own making. We incorporated a longitudinal approach into some of the research designs, and continuity or stability in guilt patterns over time was identified not only during the first years of life but into the period of school transition as well (Cummings et al., 1986).

Our cumulative research findings and those of others indicate that any one theoretical focus is inevitably too narrow. A compelling articulation of the ontogeny of guilt requires the perspectives of psychodynamic, social-cognitive, emotions, and socialization theories and perspectives that stem from these theories. The capacity for guilt *is* innate and universal; its modes of expression *are* learned. Some forms are affectively driven (e.g., empathy-based guilt, anxiety- or fear-based guilt), while other forms require advanced symbolic and representational skills (e.g., self-reflection, role taking). Guilt has both adaptive and pathological forms that may begin early in development, and may be present at different levels of awareness that are more or less accessible to the organism. The more "unconscious," primitive aspects are more difficult to identify and measure, but they are important to study for the additional understanding they yield about different developmental pathways.

The patterns of continuity over time in guilt raise a broader set of issues that have not been addressed comprehensively in existing theories. They concern how guilt becomes part of an enduring personality pattern. That is, How does the experience of guilt change from a thought, feeling, or action tendency evoked in a particular situation to a more "chronic," stable set of characteristics that are reliably triggered by particular experiences, then to a still more internalized response pattern that becomes part of an underlying "core" of the personality? We have taken the position that repetitions of exposure to particular emotion-arousing experiences early in life may function to produce stylized guilt orientations. But many other experiences may produce guilt, and repeated exposure to others' distress may have other consequences as well. What is needed are broader theoretical models within which to incorporate the existing data and to generate new research questions about the more enduring nature of guilt under a greater variety of background conditions.

We describe here perspectives we have found useful for considering how guilt may evolve from a "state" to a "trait" expression within the organism over time, and also for how patterns of guilt may be perpetuated across generations. An organizational approach provides a framework for attempting to understand continuities and discontinuities in development and to delineate different developmental pathways or trajectories (Cicchetti, this volume; Cicchetti & Schneider-Rosen, 1986). Perpetuation of guilt across generations can be explored within the context of more broadly based theories of internal working models and intergenerational transmission of social interaction patterns (Bowlby, 1979; Bretherton, this volume; Main & Goldwyn, 1984). We review these perspectives and consider their implications for the development and perpetuation of different guilt patterns.

In the organizational approach, the qualitative reorganizations characteristic of development are conceived as proceeding in accord with an orthogenetic principle (Werner, 1948). The organism moves from a relatively diffuse and globally undifferentiated state, by means of differentiation and hierarchical integration, to a state of greater articulation and organized complexity. (See Cicchetti, this volume, for elaboration of this position.) Very young infants are conceived of as relatively psychologically undifferentiated from their environments. They are governed mainly by physiological processes, and their actions are bound closely to particular stimulus conditions. Thus temperamental and biological rather than cognitive factors play the largest role in guiding their behavior. As development proceeds, however, infants and children play a greater role in "constructing" experience; therefore cognitions and cognitive styles begin to be increasingly important in determining adjustment and adaptation. With this differentiation children develop greater flexibility in responding to their surroundings and become able to substitute various means for obtaining a desired goal. Children's increased ability to communicate and to understand others also would be expected to make them more responsive to (and influenced by) different socialization experiences. In other words, different environmental demands and constraints would become increasingly important.

In the organizational view, healthy development is defined in terms of competencies organized around a sequence of stage-salient tasks. Competence at one period of development paves the way for competence at the next time period. Pathological development is conceptualized in terms of developmental arrests or unsuccessfully resolved stage-salient developmental tasks. During the first two to three years of life, three major stage-salient tasks with respect to social-emotional development have been described: achieving regulation of physiological states (0–3 months); constructing and maintaining an effective attachment relationship with the caregiver (6–18 months), and establishing a sense of autonomy from the caregiver (18–30 months) through exploration and learning how to act as a causal agent in the environment (effectance motivation as described by White, 1959). Developmentally, guilt and empathy (both reflecting feelings of discomfort and responsibility in relation to others) emerge during this period of attachment to and separation from the caregiver. Whether these emotions initially take healthy or maladaptive forms seems inextricably linked to the quality of the attachment relationship with the caregiver, how attachments are established, maintained, and generalized to other relationships, and how individuation is achieved.

During the first year of life, children are emotionally aroused by the emotional problems of others, whether or not they have caused the distress. This emotional disorganization or disruption begins to diminish during the second year of life as children's cognitive and behavioral repertoires expand and they begin to show more planful and purposeful behaviors, attempting to deal with problems and to "repair" interactions or situations. Their emotional expressions become more controlled or regulated and more suggestive of remorse as they attempt to "undo" problems or make things right. This pattern of development fits the characterization of progression, described in an organizational perspective, of moving from a state of diffuse, undifferentiated arousal to greater differentiation, purposefulness, and complexity. This is a period of rapid flux and growth. Children are likely to have a confused understanding of their causal role in others' problems at this time. Also, socialization agents begin to hold children accountable and communicate their expectations for responsible behavior in a variety of ways. Thus this becomes a time when perturbations in the system might result in different developmental pathways and developmental arrest might occur, either because of vulnerabilities within the organism or because of environmental factors.

Some perturbations in development may result from organismic or constitutional factors. For example, autistic children have been characterized as having extreme difficulty from the first years of life in identifying or responding to others' emotional needs. They often are described as expressing minimal distress when they have been injured and as remaining aloof and avoidant in interpersonal interactions. They may be constitutionally incapable of experiencing intense guilt. Differences in temperament also may influence the ways children process their own and others' emotional circumstances, and hence their capacity for guilt. Impulsive, fearless children might have difficulty discerning their causal role, whereas inhibited, shy children might be particularly vulnerable to feelings of responsibility.

The environments in which children are reared also are differentially conducive to the development of guilt. Cultures, religions, and ethnic groups vary in how and to what extent they attempt to invoke guilt and responsibility. Parents differ in the implicit and explicit techniques used to induce internalization and accountability, and the emotional climates in which these messages are conveyed differ as well. Parents also vary in what they define as moral problems and emotional issues and in whether and how they intervene when children misbehave. As parents begin to hold their children accountable and to exert significant socialization pressures, during the second year of life, this becomes a particularly important period for examining exactly how their affective communications and discipline strategies contribute to individual differences in guilt in children. Parents who become very highly aroused over children's transgressions may induce similar emotion in their children. This may effectively "hold" children at a more primitive, undifferentiated level of high arousal long after it is developmentally appropriate. Developmental arrest might also be produced by an overly didactic, intellectualized parental approach that discourages young children from experiencing the initial arousal that may be critical in early phases of development of guilt. These parents may not be sufficiently aroused themselves to induce the feelings of distress in their children that are precursors of empathy and guilt. Or parents may planfully or unwittingly elicit other emotions counter to internalization of responsibility through excessive harshness, anger, and fear induction. For example, some parents variously censure, ridicule, deny, ignore, or take pleasure in the pain of others and communicate these attitudes and feelings to their young children.

We have considered environmental conditions conducive to overarousal, that is, that incline children toward experiencing too much distress, fear, and responsibility, too early in development, regarding their own and others' problems. This overarousal may result *both* in fear-based, primitive, and irrational guilt (in the Freudian sense) and in (excessive) empathic guilt that is focused on the plight of others. Several of our studies of children (particularly young children) with parents who are in conflict or experiencing emotional problems indicated patterns of overinvolvement—that is, patterns that reflect excessive concern for both self *and* other. This preoccupation and involvement occur at a time in development when children have not yet established the necessary cognitive and behavioral skills and emotional maturity to deal effectively with feelings of responsibility and guilt. Often these children are confronted with more than optimal levels of distress. They are "required" to assume a role beyond their natural capabilities that in turn may interfere with the development of normal levels of guilt and responsibility. Children who become overinvolved may, in addition to experiencing guilt, also develop tendencies to defend and protect themselves against the painful environment and their own distress. Thus, over time they sometimes may turn away or show ambivalence. Little is currently known about why some children develop avoidant, rejecting, or angry patterns while others remain committed to helping parents with their problems and yet others struggle and alternate the ways in which they cope.

High levels of emotional arousal and involvement in others' problems very early in development may pull children away from other stage-salient tasks or alter how these tasks are resolved. For example, it is difficult to regulate emotions and physiological states, to form secure attachments, and to begin to construct a broader, more expanded social environment when the caregiver is dysregulated, insecure, and in need. Children who become overinvolved in their parents' emotional problems may be deprived early in development of play experiences with peers, experiences that have been shown to help children develop important social skills (e.g., of negotiation, cooperation, and positive affect sharing).

This early overinvolvement that appears to result from repeated exposure to chronic distress (to more than normal "doses" of suffering) is conducive to the development of more enduring guilt patterns. One model that aids in understanding the later pathological effects on development of early overexposure is elaborated by Meyersberg and Post (1979). They describe work demonstrating that an organism that has become sensitized by repeated exposure to externally imposed noxious stimulation (for example, to shock) will later respond (for example, with epileptic seizures) to smaller doses of shock than were initially required to elicit a response. Eventually no shock is required and the responses appear spontaneously. Reasoning by analogy, they have discussed ways some forms of aversive psychological stimulation might operate similarly. In the case of children from emotionally disturbed families, it may take relatively little emotional disturbance in their environments later in life to trigger distress and dysregulation of emotion because of their greater and earlier than normal exposure to negative emotions. Or no apparent external stimulus may be required, since the pattern has become so internalized (possibly through conditioning processes). Goodwin and Jamieson (in press) have argued that early sensitization may help to explain the depressive episodes that emerge "out of the blue" in some adults. Our own work begins to elaborate some of the specific early experiences that might sensitize or "predispose" children toward experiencing some of the core features or symptoms (e.g., guilt) of depression. What may appear, later in development, as overreactions to somewhat stressful situations may result from depressogenic personality patterns that have antecedents in early experiences in which the child was overwhelmed with feelings of responsibility.

For some children, acute sensitivity to distress may bode well for later development, and they may be able to use this as a constructive coping pattern. Exposure to an emotionally distressed parent does provide numerous opportunities for empathic involvement and heightened interpersonal sensitivity. Beardslee and Podorefsky (1988) have recently studied resilient adolescents of affectively ill parents who show high levels of empathy, role taking, and interpersonal maturity. Research is needed to determine why some children cope especially well, others are unaffected, and still others are at risk for later overinvolvement, guilt, and depression. The complexity of this issue often was reflected in children's themes of sensitivity and overinvolvement in our research on their interpretations of interpersonal distress and conflict in hypothetical situations. For example, one 5-year-old child of a very depressed mother said she wished she had not seen the picture story about the sad mother because it upset her. She then said that the mother was crying because some robbers had come to the house and stolen her best lights, and that the robbers also had called her a bad mother. The child said that the mother wasn't really a bad mother, though. This child's sensitivity to the mother's depression (i.e., helpless, vulnerable and robbed of light [vibrancy and energy?]), and her protectiveness toward the mother define a complex pattern of responsibility and commitment not commonly seen in children with healthy caregivers. But ambivalence is conveyed in the child's interpretation as well.

We have focused on children with a depressed caregiver as one of several possible ways of considering how different socialization experiences might help to differentiate the development of normal guilt from neurotic or excessive guilt or guilt that is associated with defensive processes. Children with a depressed caregiver (usually the mother) may be at increased risk for assuming too much responsibility for others' problems for several reasons reviewed earlier: in summary, because of the pervasive environment of negative affect and adult helplessness that they experience, as well as the specific guilt-induction practices their parents use and the experience of failing to meet standards and hence of disappointing the parent. They are also exposed to the modeling of negative attributional styles (i.e., "it's my fault"). And because the depressed parent may more often be emotionally unavailable, love withdrawal may be experienced more commonly by these children. These experiences, in conjunction with the parents' stated difficulties in permitting their children to separate and develop autonomy, seem simultaneously to encourage the development of guilt, helplessness, and low self-worth (all correlates of depression). And these qualities in children become linked as well to the assumption of a caregiver role early in development. This model of "parent as perpetrator" is too narrow in some respects because it fails to take into account the many reasons or causes for maternal depression (e.g., societal constraints, spouse with unacknowledged problems) that lead to the depressogenic, guilt-inducing practices. For the child, however, this is a moot point because he or she experiences mainly the interactions and relationship with the depressed caregiver. Hence, for the child this is the main arena of influence.

Children's overinvolvement in caregivers' distress potentially provides insights regarding the origins of the "depression paradox" (Abramson & Sackheim, 1977), that is, the "conflicting" characteristics of helplessness and responsibility experienced by depressed individuals. Many children in a relationship with a troubled parent may both attempt to create a more effective parent and come to believe that they have caused the damage. That they cannot, for the most part, help the parent must inevitably lead to feelings of helplessness, futility, and failure. But children's belief that they can or should change their parents' behavior must lead to feelings of omnipotence that are intermittently reinforced when they do succeed in making the parents feel better. Our data have indicated that many of these very young children have elaborate repertoires for taking care of the parents' needs, even in the face of their own unmet emotional needs. By definition, these children are unable to resolve the problem yet accept an important causal role. It is not surprising that they show emotion dysregulation and come to form, in Seligman's terms, global, internal, and stable attributions of responsibility for negative events—that is, to feel unrealistic responsibility for "all the misery in the world."

The assumption of very high levels of responsibility that could lead simultaneously to feelings of omnipotence and impotence, making the child vulnerable to guilt and perhaps to later depression as well, may also help to perpetuate guilt and depression across generations. Children exposed to overwhelming distress in others are

likely to feel the suffering intensely and to feel burdened. Conditions of burden can create feelings of self-sacrifice, victimization,
and martyrdom in adults, which sometimes lead in turn to exaggerated expressions of injury and the need to include others in the suffering. It is reasonable to assume that children are similarly affected.
Like the attribution theorists, we believe that in some forms of depression guilt is not simply a correlate of the disorder but plays a
causal role. Unlike the attribution theorists, we emphasize the importance of childhood experiences (e.g., repeated experiences with
guilt and distress) that may contribute later in development to a de-
pression-prone personality. Guilt has sometimes been referred to as
the gift that keeps on giving. Views of the self as unworthy and ways
of relating to others that develop during childhood may carry over
into adulthood and affect adult relationships, including parent-child
relationships, hence perpetuating these social patterns across generations. And there is evidence for intergenerational transmission of
depression as well. A number of mechanisms (biological, genetic,
environmental) have been implicated in the transmission process.
Because feeling bad about oneself, unworthy, and pervasively responsible for bad things that happen are so integral to depression,
understanding the origins of maladaptive, excessive guilt may help
us understand the transmission of depression as well.

Our interest in intergenerational transmission of guilt (and its role
in depression) began several years ago in informal observations of families that we studied. For example, one intelligent, articulate, and well-
educated woman, who was in the sample of mothers trained to make
detailed observations of their children's and their own reactions to
emotional distress, had as one major goal *not* to inflict guilt on her
child. She described her own mother as highly guilt inducing and did
not wish to perpetuate that pattern and process. She showed warmth
and empathy toward her child on many occasions. She was armed
with childhood educational materials and strategies for child-rearing
and discipline practices that would not be guilt inducing. Ironically,
but perhaps not surprisingly, this mother used guilt-induction practices more than most of the other mothers, repeatedly emphasizing
how much the child's behavior hurt her. Moreover, her child already
appeared guilt-ridden by age 2.

Later we learned that the mother experienced depression. The

guilt induction conveyed in the frequent expressions of love withdrawal, anger, disappointment, and high expectations she directed
toward her child were probably linked to her more pervasive affective problems and associated feelings of lack of self-worth. The
mother did not believe in physical punishment, but love withdrawal
was common. It took both physical and verbal forms (e.g., leaving
the room or sending the child to her room, and statements such as "I
don't want to be near you when you act like that") and was typically
expressed in an emotionally charged manner. Love withdrawal, recall, consists of direct by nonphysical expressions of anger or disapproval when the child transgresses (by ignoring the child, turning
away, refusing to communicate, expressing dislike, threatening separation).

Through complex processes of modeling, contagion, and guilt-
inducing discipline practices, the child appeared to have developed
early vulnerability to feelings of guilt. Also, there were indications
that she "practiced" the same behaviors as her mother, used them
effectively against the mother, and incorporated them into her repertoire of coping skills. The way the child expressed guilt and used
guilt-inducing strategies early in development suggested enduring,
crystallized reactions that could readily be carried into maladaptive
interactional patterns later n.

By age 2 the child sometimes would become visibly shaky and
emotionally out of control if she caused harm to others. These occasions were well internalized, since she would verbally recall them
days and weeks later. She had an extended and sophisticated repertoire of reparative behaviors that she used frequently. At the same
time, she could be combative, manipulative, and controlling. For example, at 124 weeks the child was scolded for going into the refrig-
erator. The child responded with anger, saying, "I don't want to talk
to you. I go to my room, I slam the door, good-bye," thus having internalized a distancing mechanism to use in emotional encounters.
The reaction bears a remarkable likeness to what would be labeled as
love withdrawal if used (albeit in a somewhat more subtle form) by
an adult.

Five years later similar patterns were in evidence in both mother
and child. Observers noted warmth and caring in the relationship in
home observations. But again the mother was preoccupied with the

burdens imposed by her own mother, especially her mother's high expectations for children's assuming household responsibilities at an early age. The mother in our sample had made certain that she did not literally repeat this pattern (she did not assign household tasks, chores, etc., because "children should have time to be children"). But symbolically she continued to reenact the pattern through her unusally high expectations for responsible behavior in other domains, for example, for interpersonally appropriate behavior. And she expressed extreme disappointment when those expectations were not met. Similarly, the child continued to experience considerable guilt and to engage in guilt induction. During a car trip when the child was misbehaving toward her younger sibling, the mother threatened and raised her voice, but to no avail. She stopped the car and spanked the child (unusual for her), and they drove home in silence. The mother then said that she was not looking forward to their family vacation at the beach because it would mean being in the car with the children and being upset because they couldn't behave, and that she would rather stay home. The child responded in kind, saying that she hoped the mother wouldn't come, that it would indeed be nicer if the mother stayed home, because she always made them eat dinner and go to bed on time; moreover, she said that they would have more fun without her and that she hoped her mother would get sick and die. The mother's response was to go to her bedroom and lie down. Several hours later the child came in and asked if it had made her mother feel bad when she said all those mean things. The mother replied that it did make her feel sad but that she understood the child didn't know what to do with her angry feelings. The mother intellectualized the incident, interpreting the child's ability to ask questions about how and why people feel the way they do as reflecting the development of an ever-finer sensitivity toward people. The mother appeared quite unaware of the repetition of her own childhood experiences, which we view as placing her child at risk for perpetuation of patterns of guilt, blameworthiness, and a depressogenic style.

Concepts of intergenerational transmission of parental (social) behavior have been common in anecdotal case reports in research (as above) and in the clinical literature for some time, but they have been in disrepute in scientific circles. There are serious methodological problems in attempting to demonstrate that particular childhood experiences "cause" one to behave in particular ways in later adult interactions with other adults and with one's own children. And there has been little attempt to delineate the precise mechanisms involved. The longitudinal, prospective designs required to address the issues fully are unlikely to be conducted. Recently, however, a number of empirical studies, particularly in the areas of attachment and maltreatment, have lent scientific credence to the notion that there is intergenerational continuity in the quality of parental behavior (see Main & Goldwyn, 1984, and Ricks, 1985, for descriptions of research designs and procedures used). This view was explicit in Bowlby's theory of attachment (Bowlby, 1979), which in turn was derived from the idea, central to Freud's developmental theory, that an individual's childhood relationships with parents affect later close relationships, including adult love relationships and parent-child relationships—and hence that specific adaptive and maladaptive patterns are "passed on" to the next generation. (Also see Bretherton, this volume, for a review of this literature.)

According to Bowlby (1979), a child whose parents are available and supportive will construct a representational model of self as able to cope but also as worthy of help. Conversely, a child whose parents are consistently lacking in responsiveness, who threaten abandonment or who actually abandon the child, will tend to build a representational model of the self as unworthy and unlovable. Main and Goldwyn (1984) have studied the internal working models of individuals that may perpetuate rejection and child abuse across generations. They have been able to predict the mother's rejection of her infant from her representation of her own experiences with rejection. They also have identified the development of abusive and rejecting characteristics in young abused children, similar to those of the parent. The work of Main and her colleagues has elevated clinical concepts with intuitive appeal to scientific constructs with specific hypotheses to be tested.

It will be important, however, in subsequent research to consider in greater detail different kinds of maladaptive parent-child interaction that result in different maladaptive patterns of intergenerational transmission, and the different kinds of distorted internal representations that are associated with, or contribute to, these patterns that are "passed on" from one generation to the next. For example, the overinvolvement, enmeshment, and codependencies that are emphasized in some parent-child relationships (and that we have seen in our research) differ markedly in many ways from the distancing and levels of anger that are associated with repeated patterns of rejection in physically maltreating families. Yet rejection is implicated in both styles. The effects of rejection would be expected to differ depending upon whether it is part of a broader internalizing or externalizing orientation (or a complex mix of the two). In each of these types of insecure relationships, anger and affection have gone awry, but in different ways. In other words, parental rejection and difficulties in attachment can be expressed through anger and abuse or can be expressed in ways that are not physically abusive (e.g., love withdrawal) and can be simultaneously associated with attempts to keep closely connected to the child. Depressed caregivers, for example, are sometimes characterized both as sad and withdrawn and as critical and overinvolved (Belle, 1982; Weissman & Paykel, 1974). This particular combination of characteristics may expose children to experiences with being both pushed away and drawn in and hence result in frequent attempts to take care of their mothers' needs. When children are exposed to parents who are both abusive and depressed, their problems and the intergenerational patterns will be particularly complex.

Main and Cassidy (1988) have described a type of insecure attachment relationship of children to their mothers referred to as compulsive caregiving, where children tend to the mothers' needs in what would typically be construed as anxiety-provoking situations for children (separation). The concept of the "parentified" child is common in the clinical literature, and Bowlby (1980) earlier described compulsive caregiving as a response to parental loss. Main and Cassidy have identified two subtypes of children who precociously attempt to assume authority and control, one reflecting harsh, directive behavior and the other reflecting tender and solicitous reactions toward the mother. We have seen similar patterns in the offspring of depressed caregivers, and we hypothesize that these are linked with attachment relationships that are problematic in other respects.

In short, we agree that an internal working model of the self as unworthy and unlovable is likely to result from parental rejection and threat of abandonment, as Bowlby and Main have argued, but the consequences and forms will differ depending upon the level of distancing and the way it has been achieved. The concept of self as unworthy is connected to several other views of the self that will differ depending upon the precise nature of early experiences. For the circumstances we have emphasized, the concept of self as unworthy also becomes connected to the concept of self as helper and as responsible for meeting the needs of others. Females may be particularly likely to be drawn into this role for reasons outlined earlier. The intergenerational pattern of caregiving reproduced by overinvolvement may be fragile and brittle and hence may break down under the considerable stresses of actual caregiving that occur in adult life. When frustration and anger cannot be expressed appropriately and directly (and when physical maltreatment is unlikely to occur), excessive acceptance of blame (guilt) and nonphysical blaming of others (guilt induction) may be a logical consequence. Future research on intergenerational transmission of social patterns might effectively focus on the outcomes for later relationships in general, and guilt in particular, of specific patterns of emotional expression that characterize early parent-child relationships, such as whether there is a predominance of anger or of sadness in the parent's expressions or whether there is a mix of these emotions. It would also be important to examine these affective patterns in the broader context of the familial affective environment, the predominant discipline practices used, and the type of attachment relationship between parent and child.

Although empirical evidence is accumulating to suggest intergenerational consistency in maladaptive patterns of social interactions and relationships, it is important to bear in mind that much of the research to date has been done with populations in which the likelihood of finding consistencies between parents and offspring is maximized. Similarly, it is important to note that continuities that apparently do exist may derive to a significant degree from family *interactional* patterns and belief systems to which parents and offspring mutually contribute. With regard to our own research, not every child of every guilt-ridden, depressed mother shows excessive guilt. Nor would we expect them all to show similar patterns in adulthood. We need to learn more about why some children, more than others, participate in the patterns and, moreover, to learn what factors contribute to intergenerational change as well as what developmental processes lead to change.

We have attempted to place the construct of guilt into a broader scientific framework—one that emphasizes the importance of studying this effect in the context of enduring relationships. A major goal has been to use research on guilt to illustrate in specific ways how a developmental psychopathology perspective may be used to investigate the origins of emotional problems, to speculate about factors that contribute to the continuation of disturbance during development, and finally to speculate about how patterns may persist within families across generations. There are many conditions (of parenting and development) other than those considered here that contribute to children's *experience with failure to live up to expectations*—and hence to the increased likelihood that low self-esteem and guilt will develop. Parents may not know what is appropriate for children of different ages; their expectations may be unrealistic; they may be insensitive to the child's capacities and needs because of their own needs (which may or may not reflect psychopathology). Although poor self-concept and maladaptive guilt are not totally overlapping constructs, they share many common features and probably share similar socialization histories as well. Ultimately, understanding guilt will require better understanding of how the self system develops.

The inability to master developmental tasks may be a major contributor to low self-esteem and to consistent views of self as at fault or blameworthy. This process could occur in different domains, at different points in development, and need not necessarily be linked initially to moral concerns or relationship or mental health issues (e.g., it could be linked to failures in intellectual achievement, in athletic prowess, and so on). Although behavioral scientists distinguish between moral and nonmoral domains (e.g., aggression is a moral issue, etiquette and achievement are not), parents do not always make similar distinctions and may induce guilt over "breaches" or failures in any of these arenas.

Our research has emphasized conditions conducive to normal guilt and to excessive or distorted guilt. Research is needed on precursors of cruelty and of antisocial and sociopathic behavior—that is, where there is a profound deficit in the ability to experience anxiety over anticipated wrongdoing or remorse following transgressions. This has been less studied, perhaps for fear of inappropriate labeling of young children. We have, however, seen young children who seem callous toward suffering in others and uncaring about their acts of aggression. It would be valuable to learn more about conditions that foster or deter these problematic patterns.

APPENDIX A

These expressions of concern, anxiety, remorse, reparation, and/or acknowledgment of responsibility in situations of wrongdoing or accidental harm are representative of 24 children's reactions to distress they have caused in others. Examples are excerpted from mothers' observation reports of their 1 to 2½-year-olds' behavior.

*61 weeks*—Child is pounding with cup and accidentally hits father hard in the nose. (Father gives loud "ouch.") Child drops cup, looks very serious, leans forward to father for a kiss. (At 81 weeks when child accidentally kicks father and father responds similarly, child immediately gives him a big hug and pats him.)

*62 weeks*—Child repeatedly turns milk cup upside down. (Mother starts to hit child's hand but then takes the cup away and calls her a bad girl.) Child whines and calls herself "bad."

*69 weeks*—Child hits cat with beads. (Mother scolds and verbally prohibits.) Child stops immediately, pats cat, and says "nice, nice," but rather quickly begins to pound cat again.

*74 weeks*—Child makes a mess on floor and parent reprimands ("Oh no, bad girl"). Other parent reassures and begins to clean mess. Child frowns and looks worried, taps finger on wet spot. Takes cloth mother hands her and wipes at spot.

*75 weeks*—Child bangs head against mother's face in excess of affection. (Mother restrains, verbally prohibits, and explains, "that hurts.") Child says "kiss, kiss" and kisses mother. Then bangs head on mother again and says, "hurting, hurting." (Mother acknowledges and verbally prohibits.)

*75 weeks*—Child pulls hair of another child and hits her on face. (Mother becomes angry, scolds, and explains why it was bad.) Mother leaves room and child follows her saying "me," pulling own hair, and hitting self in face. Then returns to playmate, kisses her, and plays nicely for quite a while. Later the fight erupts again.

*81 weeks*—Child accidentally hits baby-sitter. Child says "sorry, Sally," pats her on forehead and gives her kiss.

*83 weeks*—Child accidentally pulls mother's hair. (Mother says "ouch, that hurt!") Child looks at mother with worried expression and immediately strokes mother's hair and pats her shoulder.

*86 weeks*—Child writes on sofa with indelible pen. Mother and father express horror ("How could you?" etc.) but do not yell. Child bursts into tears, starts screaming "I want Mommy," then throws arms around mother. He starts wiping at sofa with hands and says, "I clean up pencil."

*92 weeks*—Child pinches mother. (Mother expresses pain and orally reprimands.) Child hugs her, smiles, and says, "Now are you happy?"

*93 weeks*—Child throws favorite doll very hard out of crib, slamming it into toy chest and looking defiant, then looks at doll and says sympathetically (looking sad) that "baby" is crying. (Mother says, "You probably hurt her.") Child asks mother to get doll, hugs it, says, "Baby hurt foot," then kisses foot, sings, rocks, wraps doll in blanket and tries to give it bottle.

*98 weeks*—Mother is angry with child's whining and scolds. He bursts into tears and says, "Mommy, I love you; do you love me?"

*101 weeks*—Child throws tantrum. (Mother spanks her and sends her to her room.) Sibling tells child to "go give Mommy a kiss and tell her you're sorry." Child comes into room and says "sorry," then tries to cuddle with mother, sobbing profusely.

*104 weeks*—Child pulls cousin's hair. (Mother tells her not to.) Child crawls to cousin and says, "I hurt your hair; please don't cry," then gives her a kiss.

*106 weeks*—Child is hurt. He comes to mother and tells her that playmate bit him because he pushed her into wall (confession or acknowledgment of responsibility).

*107 weeks*—Child hurts friend at nursery school. (Teacher asks her if she can do something to make the friend feel better, and she brings other child toy.) The next day she points to her mother's eyes and says, "Tears, Mary had tears, I pushed Mary off chair, I sorry." Child wanted mother to take her to school that afternoon to say she was sorry. (Also at 102 weeks, child verbalized regret; "Hurt—sorry—sorry Grandpa; hurt him," over having hurt her grandfather two weeks earlier.)

*109 weeks*—Child bites playmate. (Mother explains, scolds, is judgmental, comforts playmate, tells child to say she is sorry.) Child does say sorry, with all the emotion of a wet fish. Later she says "sorry" with a little more sympathy in her voice, in presence of playmate's mother. And later she tells her father, "Pam cry, I bad."

*115 weeks*—Child pushes plant over, ruining it and creating mess on floor. (Mother yells, explains, tells him he's bad.) He goes to kitchen and brings mother a lollipop. (At first glance this reparative behavior may appear egocentric—what would soothe the child—but this particular mother had an affinity to sweets!)

*128 weeks*—Child hits playmate. (Mother explains how playmate feels, says she will not allow hitting, and tells him he can't play with others until he plays nicely.) Child says he wants to be nice, and he is.

250

REFERENCES

Abramson, L. Y., & Sackheim, H. A. (1977). A paradox in depression: Uncontrollability and self-blame. *Psychological Bulletin, 84*(5), 838–851.

Abramson, L. Y., Seligman, M. E. P., & Teasdale, J. D. (1978). Learned helplessness in humans: Critique and reformulation. *Journal of Abnormal Psychology, 87*, 49–74.

Allinsmith, W. (1960). Moral standards: II. The learning of moral standards. In D. R. Miller, & G. E. Swanson (Eds.), *Inner conflict and defense.* New York: Holt, Rinehart & Winston.

American Psychiatric Association. (1980). *Diagnostic and statistical manual of mental disorders* (3rd ed.). Washington, DC: Author.

Amsterdam, B. K. (1972). Mirror self-image reactions before age two. *Developmental Psychology, 5*, 297–305.

Anthony, E. J. (1975). The influence of a manic-depressive environment on the developing child. In E. J. Anthony & T. Benedek (Eds.), *Depression and human existence.* Boston: Little, Brown.

Aronfreed, J., Cutick, R. A., & Fagan, S. A. (1963). Cognitive structure, punishment and nurturance in the experimental induction of self-criticism. *Child Development, 34*, 281–294.

Bakeman, R., & Adamson, L. B. (1986). Infants' conventionalized acts: Gestures and words with mothers and peers. *Infant Behavior and Development, 9*, 215–230.

Bandura, A., & Walters, R. (1963). *Social learning and personality development.* New York: Holt, Rinehart, & Winston.

Barrett, K. C., & Zahn-Waxler, C. (1987). *Do toddlers express guilt?* Society for Research in Child Development, Abstracts.

Baumrind, D. (1986). Sex differences in moral reasoning: Response to Walker's (1984) conclusion that there are none. *Child Development, 57*(2), 511–521.

Beardslee, W., & Podorefsky, D. (1988). Resilient adolescents whose parents have serious affective and other psychiatric disorders: Importance of self-understanding and relationships. *American Journal of Psychiatry, 145*(1), 63–69.

Beck, A. T. (1967). *Depression: Clinical, experimental and theoretical aspects.* New York: Harper & Row.

Beck, A. T. (1979). *Cognitive therapy and the emotional disorders.* New York: Times Mirror.

Belle, D. (1982). *Lives in stress: Women and depression.* Beverly Hills, CA: Sage.

Bibring, E. (1953). The mechanisms of depression. In P. Greenacre (Ed.), *Affective disorders.* New York: International Universities Press.

Block, J. H. (1973). Conceptions of sex role: Some cross-cultural and longitudinal perspectives. *American Psychologist, 28*, 512–526.

Bowlby, J. (1979). The making and breaking of affectional bonds. *British Journal of Psychiatry, 130*, 201–210, 421–431.

Bowlby, J. (1980). *Attachment and loss: Vol. 3. Loss: Sadness and depression*. New York: Basic Books.

Bretherton, I., Fritz, J., Zahn-Waxler, C., & Ridgeway, D. (1986). The acquisition and development of emotion language: A functionalist perspective. *Child Development, 57,* 529–548.

Burton, R., Maccoby, E., & Allinsmith, W. (1961). Antecedents of resistance to temptation in four-year-old children. *Child Development, 32,* 689–710.

Cadoret, R. J. (1978). Evidence for genetic inheritance of primary affective disorder in adoptees. *American Journal of Psychiatry, 135*(4), 463–466.

Chandler, M. J., Paget, K. F., & Koch, D. (1978). The child's demystification of psychological defense mechanisms: A structural and developmental analysis. *Developmental Psychology, 14,* 197–205.

Chapman, M., & Zahn-Waxler, C. (1982). Young children's compliance and noncompliance to parental discipline in a natural setting. *International Journal of Behavior and Development, 5,* 81–94.

Chapman, M., Zahn-Waxler, C., Iannotti, R., & Cooperman, G. (1987). Empathy and responsibility in the motivation of children's helping. *Developmental Psychology, 23*(1), 140–145.

Chodorow, N. (1978). *The reproduction of mothering*. Berkeley: University of California Press.

Cicchetti, D., & Schneider-Rosen, K. (1986). An organizational approach to childhood depression. In M. Rutter, C. E. Izard, & P. B. Read (Eds.), *Depression in young people: Clinical and developmental perspectives*. New York: Guilford Press.

Cohn, J., & Tronick, E. (1983). Three-month-old infants' reaction to simulated maternal depression. *Child Development, 54,* 185–193.

Covell, K., & Abramovitch, R. (1987). Understanding emotion in the family: Children's and parents' attributions of happiness, sadness, and anger. *Child Development, 58,* 985–991.

Cowan, P. A. (1978). *Piaget with feeling: Cognitive, social and emotional dimensions*. New York: Holt, Rinehart & Winston.

Crook, T., Raskin, A., & Eliot, J. (1981). Parent-child relationships and adult depression. *Child Development, 52,* 950–957.

Cummings, E. M., Hollenbeck, B., Iannotti, R., Radke-Yarrow, M., & Zahn-Waxler, C. (1986). Early organization of altruism and aggression: Developmental patterns and individual differences. In C. Zahn-Waxler, E. M. Cummings, & R. Iannotti (Eds.), *Altruism and aggression: Biological and social origins*. New York: Cambridge University Press.

Cummings, E. M., Iannotti, R. J., & Zahn-Waxler, C. (1985). Influence of conflict between adults on the emotions and aggression of young children. *Developmental Psychology, 21*(3), 495; P1–507.

Cummings, E. M., Zahn-Waxler, C., & Radke-Yarrow, M. (1981). Young children's responses to expressions of anger and affection by others in the family. *Child Development, 52,* 1274–1282.

Cummings, E. M., Zahn-Waxler, C., & Radke-Yarrow, M. (1984). Developmental changes in children's reactions to anger in the home. *Journal of Child Psychology and Psychiatry, 25,* 63–74.

Darwin, C. (1965). *The expression of the emotions in man and animals.* Chicago: University of Chicago Press. (Original work published 1872)

Davenport, Y. B., Adland, M. L., Gold, P. W., & Goodwin, F. K. (1979). Manic-depressive illness: Psychodynamic features of multi-generational families. *American Journal of Orthopsychiatry, 49,* 24–35.

Dienstbier, R. A. (1984). The role of emotion in moral socialization. In C. Izard, J. Kagan, & R. Zajonc (Eds.), *Emotions, cognition and behavior.* New York: Cambridge University Press.

Dienstbier, R. A., Hillman, D., Lehnhoff, J., Hillman, J., & Valkenaar, M. C. (1975). An emotion-attribution approach to moral behavior: Interfacing cognitive and avoidance theories of moral development. *Psychological Review, 82,* 299–315.

Dunn, J. & Munn, P. (1987). Development of justification in disputes with mother and sibling. *Developmental Psychology, 23,* 791–798.

Eckerman, C. O., Whatley, J. L., & Kutz, S. L. (1975). Growth of social play with peers during the second year of life. *Developmental Psychology, 11,* 42–49.

Eibl-Eibesfeldt, I. (1971). *Love and hate: The natural history of behavior patterns.* New York: Holt, Rinehart & Winston.

Eisenberg, N., & Lennon, R. (1983). Sex differences in empathy and related capacities. *Psychological Bulletin, 94*(1), 100–131.

Emde, R., Johnson, W. F., & Easterbrooks, A. (1987). *The do's and don'ts of early moral development: Psychoanalytic tradition and current research.* In J. Kagan, & S. Lamb, (Eds.), *The emergence of morality.* Chicago: University of Chicago Press.

Emery, R. E. (1982). Interparent conflict and the children of discord and divorce. *Psychological Bulletin, 92,* 310; P1–330.

Feinman, J. A., & Feldman, R. S. (1982). Decoding children's expressions of affect. *Child Development, 50,* 710–716.

Freud, S. (1953). Inhibition, symptoms and anxiety. In J. Strachy (Ed. and Trans.), *The standard edition of the complete psychological works of Sigmund Freud.* London: Hogarth. (Original work published 1926)

Freud, S. (1958). *Civilization and its discontents.* New York: Doubleday Anchor Books.

Freud, S. (1961). Some psychical consequences of the anatomical distinction between the sexes. In J. Strachy (Ed. and Trans.), *The standard edition of the complete psychological works of Sigmund Freud* (Vol. 19). London: Hogarth Press. (Original work published 1925)

Friedman, M. (1985). Toward a reconceptualization of guilt. *Contemporary Psychoanalysis, 21*(4), 501–547.

Frodi, A., Macaulay, J., & Thome, P. R. (1977). Are women always less aggressive than men? A review of the experimental literature. *Psychological Bulletin, 84*(4), 634–660.

Garber, J. (1984). The developmental progression of depression in female children. In D. Cicchetti & K. Schneider-Rosen (Eds.), *Childhood depression* (New Directions for Child Development No. 26). San Francisco: Jossey-Bass.

Gilligan, C. (1982). *In a different voice: Psychological theory and women's development*. Cambridge: Harvard University Press.

Goodwin, F. F., & Jamieson, K. (in press). *Manic-depressive illness*. New York: Oxford University Press.

Gotlib, I., & Hooley, J. M. (1988). Depression and marital distress: Current status and future directions. In S. Ruck (Ed.), *Handbook of interpersonal relationships*. New York: John Wiley.

Graham, S., Doubleday, C., & Guarino, P. A. (1984). The development of relations between perceived controllability and the emotions of pity, anger, and guilt. *Child Development, 55*, 561–565.

Grusec, J. (1966). Some antecedents of self-criticism. *Journal of Personality and Social Psychology, 4*, 244–252.

Hall, J. A. (1978). Gender differences in decoding nonverbal cues. *Psychological Bulletin, 85*(4), 845–; P1857.

Hay, D. F. (1984). *Social conflict in early childhood* (Annals of Child Development, 1). Greenwich, CT: JAI Press.

Heinicke, C. M. (1953). *Some antecedents and correlates of guilt and fear in young boys*. Unpublished doctoral dissertation, Harvard University.

Hoffman, M. L. (1970a). Moral development. In P. H. Mussen (Ed.), *Handbook of child psychology* (Vol. 2) (3rd ed.). New York: John Wiley.

Hoffman, M. L. (1970b). Conscience, personality, and socialization techniques. *Human Development, 13*, 90–126.

Hoffman, M. L. (1971). Identification and conscience development. *Child Development, 42*, 1071–1082.

Hoffman, M. L. (1975). Sex differences in moral internalization and values. *Journal of Personality and Social Psychology, 32*(4), 720–729.

Hoffman, M. L. (1982). Development of prosocial motivation: Empathy and guilt. In N. Eisenberg (Ed.), *The development of prosocial behavior*. New York: Academic Press.

Hoffman, M. L. (1983). Affective and cognitive processes in moral internalization. In E. T. Higgins, D. Ruble, & W. Hartup (Eds.), *Social cognition and social development: A sociocultural perspective*. New York: Cambridge University Press.

Izard, C. E. (1977). *Human emotion*. New York: Plenum Press.

Janoff-Bulman, R. (1979). Characterological vs. behavioral self-blame: Inquiries into depression and rape. *Journal of Personality and Social Psychology, 37*(10), 1798; P1–1809.

Kagan, J. (1984). *Establishing a morality: The nature of the child*. New York: Basic Books.

Karylowski, J. (1982). Two types of altruistic behavior: Doing good to feel good or to make the other feel good. In V. J. Derlega & J. Grzelak (Eds.),

254

NEBRASKA SYMPOSIUM ON MOTIVATION 1988

*Cooperation and helping behavior* (pp. 397–413). New York: Academic Press.

Klein, M. (1975). *Love, guilt and reparation and other works: 1921–1945.* New York: Delacorte Press/Seymour Lawrence.

Kochanska, G., Kuczynski, L., Radke-Yarrow, M., & Welsh, J. D. (1987). Resolutions of control episodes between well and affectively ill mothers and their young children. *Journal of Abnormal Child Psychology, 15*(3), 441–456.

Kohlberg, L. (1976). Moral stages and moralization: The cognitive-developmental approach. In T. Lickona (Ed.), *Moral development and behavior: Theory, research and social issues.* New York: Holt, Rinehart & Winston.

Kopp, C. B. (1982). Antecedents of self-regulation: A developmental perspective. *Developmental Psychology, 18,* 199–214.

Kovacs, M., & Paulauskas, S. L. (1984). Developmental stage and the expression of depressive disorders in children: An empirical analysis. In D. Cicchetti & K. Schneider-Rosen (Eds.), *Childhood depression* (New Directions for Child Development No. 26). San Francisco: Jossey-Bass.

Kuczynski, L., Kochanska, G., Radke-Yarrow, M., & Girnius-Brown, O. (1987). A developmental interpretation of young children's noncompliance. *Developmental Psychology, 23*(6), 799–806.

Kuczynski, L., Zahn-Waxler, C., & Radke-Yarrow, M. (1987). Development and content of imitation in the second and third years of life: A socialization perspective. *Developmental Psychology, 23*(2), 276; P1–282.

Lamb, S. (1986). Treating sexually abused children: Issues of blame and responsibility. *American Journal of Orthopsychiatry, 56*(2), 303–307.

Leckman, J. F., Caruso, K. A., Prusoff, B. A., Weisman, M. M., Merikangas, K. R., & Pauls, D. L. (1984). Appetite disturbance and excessive guilt in major depression. *Archives of General Psychiatry, 41,* 839–; P1844.

Lewin, K., Lippitt, & White, R. K. (1939). Patterns of aggressive behavior in experimentally created "social climates." *Journal of Social Psychology, 10,* 271–299.

Lewis, H. B. (1979). Gender identity: Primary narcissism or primary process? *Bulletin of the Menninger Clinic, 43*(2), 145–160.

Lewis, H. B. (1980). "Narcissistic personality" or "shame prone superego mode": Some theoretical implications of differing formulations. *Comprehensive Psychotherapy, 1,* 59–80.

Lewis, M., & Brooks-Gunn, J. (1979). *Social cognition and the acquisition of the self.* New York: Plenum Press.

Lickona, T. (Ed.). (1976). *Moral development and behavior.* New York: Holt.

Main, M., & Cassidy, J. (1988). Categories of response to reunion with a parent at age 6: Predictable from infant attachment classification and stable over a 1-month period. *Developmental Psychology, 24*(3), 415–426.

Main, M., & Goldwyn, R. (1984). Predicting rejection of her infant from mother's representation of her own experience: Implications for the abused-abusing intergenerational cycle. *Child Abuse and Neglect, 8,* 203–217.

Malatesta, C. (in press). Emotion/cognition interaction in personality development: A discrete emotions functionalist analysis. *British Journal of Social Psychology*.

Malatesta, C., & Haviland, J. (1982). Learning display rules: The socialization of emotion expression in infancy. *Child Development, 53*, 991–1003.

McConville, B. J., Boag, L. C., & Purohit, A. P. (1973). Three types of childhood depression. *Canadian Psychiatric Association Journal, 18*, 133–138.

McKinney, W. T. (1977). Animal behavioral/biological models relevant to depressive and affective disorders in humans. In J. G. Schulterbrandt & A. Raskin (Eds.), *Depression in childhood: Diagnosis, treatment and conceptual models*. New York: Raven Press.

Mednick, S. A., Gabriell, W. F., & Hutchings, B. (1984). Genetic influences in criminal convictions: Evidence from an adoption cohort. *Science, 224*, 891–894.

Meyersberg, H. A., & Post, R. M. (1979). A holistic developmental view of neural and psychological processes. *British Journal of Psychiatry, 135*, 139–155.

Miller, A. (1981). *Prisoners of childhood: The drama of the gifted child and the search for the true self*. New York: Basic Books.

Modell, A. H. (1965). On having the right to a life: An aspect of the superego's development. *International Journal of Psychoanalysis, 46*, 323–331.

Modell, A. H. (1971). The origin of certain forms of pre-oedipal guilt and the implications for a psychoanalytic theory of affects. *International Journal of Psychoanalysis, 52*, 337–346.

Moss, H. A. (1974). Early sex differences and mother-infant interaction. In R. C. Redman, R. M. Richart, & R. L. Vande Wiele (Eds.), *Sex differences in behavior*. New York: John Wiley.

Mowrer, O. H. (1966). *Learning theory and the symbolic processes*. New York: John Wiley.

Mueller, E., & Brenner, J. (1977). The origins of social skill and interaction among play-group toddlers. *Child Development, 48*, 854–861.

Parke, R. D., & Slaby, R. G. (1983). The development of aggression. In P. H. Mussen (Ed.), *Handbook of child psychology* (4th ed.) (Vol. 4). New York: John Wiley.

Piaget, J. (1965). *The moral judgment of the child*. New York: Harcourt, Brace. (Original work published 1932)

Radke-Yarrow, M. (1977). *Emotions in the lives of children* (Bulletin of the National Institute of Mental Health). Washington, DC: U.S. Department of Health, Education, and Welfare.

Radke-Yarrow, M., Belmont, B., Nottelmann, E., & Bottomly, L. (in press). Young children's self-conceptions: Origins in the natural discourse of depressed and normal mothers and their children. In D. Cicchetti & M. Beeghly (Eds.), *The self in transition: Infancy to childhood*. Chicago: University of Chicago Press.

Radke-Yarrow, M., Campbell, J. D., & Burton, R. V. (1968). *Child rearing: An inquiry into research and methods*. San Francisco: Jossey-Bass.

Radke-Yarrow, M., & Kuczynski, L. (1983). Conceptions of environment in child-rearing interactions. In D. Magnusson & V. L. Allen (Eds.), *Human development: An interactional perspective*. New York: Academic Press.

Radke-Yarrow, M., & Zahn-Waxler, C. (1973). *Developmental studies of altruism* (NIMH Protocol, Clinical Project No. 73-M-02, J00.111).

Radke-Yarrow, M., & Zahn-Waxler, C. (1984). Roots, motives and patterning in children's prosocial behavior. In E. Staub, D. Bar-Tal, J. Karylowski, & J. Reykowski (Eds.), *The development and maintenance of prosocial behavior: International perspectives on positive morality*. New York: Plenum Press.

Radke-Yarrow, M., & Zahn-Waxler, C. (1986). The role of familial factors in the development of prosocial behavior: Research findings and questions. In D. Olweus, J. Block, & M. Radke-Yarrow (Eds.), *Development of antisocial and prosocial behavior: Research, theories, and issues*. New York: Academic Press.

Radke-Yarrow, M., Zahn-Waxler, C., & Chapman, M. (1983). Children's prosocial dispositions and behavior. In P. H. Mussen (Ed.), *Handbook of child psychology* (4th ed) (Vol. 4). New York: John Wiley.

Ricks, M. (1985). The social transmission of parental behavior: Attachment across generations. In I. Bretherton & E. Waters (Eds.), Growing points of attachment theory and research (pp. 211–227). *Monographs of the Society for Research in Child Development, 50* (1–2, Serial No. 209).

Rose, S. L., & Garske, J. (1987). Family environment, adjustment and coping among children of holocaust survivors: A comparative investigation. *American Journal of Orthopsychiatry, 57*(3), 332–344.

Rutter, M. (1988, May). *Age changes in depressive disorders: Some developmental considerations*. Paper presented at SRCD workshop on the development of affect regulation and dysregulation, Vanderbilt University.

Rutter, M., & Garmezy, N. (1983). Developmental psychopathology. In P. Mussen (Ed.), *Handbook of child psychology* (4th ed.) (Vol. 4). New York: John Wiley.

Schulman, A. H., & Kaplowitz, C. (1977). Mirror-image response during the first two years of life. *Developmental Psychology, 10*, 133; P1–142.

Sears, R. R., Maccoby, E. E., & Levin, H. (1957). *Patterns of child rearing*. Evanston, IL: Row, Peterson.

Seligman, M. E. P. (1975). *Helplessness: On depression, development and death*. San Francisco: Freeman.

Seligman, M. E. P., Peterson, C., Kaslow, N., Tanenbaum, R., Alloy, L., & Abramson, L. (1984). Attributional style and depressive symptoms among children. *Journal of Abnormal Psychology, 93*(2), 235–238.

Spitzer, R. L., & Endicott, J. (1978). *Schedule for affective disorders and schizophrenia—Lifetime version (SADS-L)*. New York: Biometrics Research Division, New York State Psychiatric Institute.

Staub, E. (1979). *Positive social behavior and morality: Vol. 2. Socialization and development*. New York: Academic Press.

Stern, D. N. (1985). *The interpersonal world of the infant.* New York: Basic Books.

Susman, E. J., Trickett, P. K., Iannotti, R. J., Hollenbeck, B. E., & Zahn-Waxler, C. (1985). Child-rearing patterns in depressed, abusive, and normal mothers. *American Journal of Orthopsychiatry, 55*(2), 237–251.

Thompson, R. A., & Hoffman, M. (1980). Empathy and the development of guilt in children. *Developmental Psychology, 16*(2), 155–156.

Trevarthen, C., & Hubley, P. (1979). Secondary intersubjectivity: Confidence, confiding and acts of meaning in the first year. In A. Lock (Ed.), *Action, gesture and symbol.* New York: Academic Press.

Tronick, E., & Field, T. (Eds.). (1986). *Maternal depression and infant disturbance* (New Directions for Child Development No. 34). San Francisco: Jossey-Bass.

Ushakov, G. K., & Girich, Y. P. (1972). Special features of psychogenic depressions in children and adolescents. In A. Annell (Ed.), *Depressive states in childhood and adolescence.* Stockholm: Almquist & Wiksell.

Vaughn, B. E., Kopp, C. B., & Krakow, J. B. (1984). The emergence and consolidation of self-control from eighteen to thirty months of age: Normative trends and individual differences. *Child Development, 55,* 990–1004.

Walker, L. J. (1984). Sex differences in the development of moral reasoning: A critical review. *Child Development, 55,* 677–691.

Weissman, M. M., & Paykel, E. S. (1974). *The depressed woman: A study of social relationships.* Chicago: University of Chicago Press.

Wenar, C. (1982). On negativism. *Human Development, 25,* 1–23.

Werner, H. (1948). *Comparative psychology of mental development.* New York: International Universities Press.

Werner, H. (1957). The concept of development from a comparative and organismic point of view. In D. Harris (Ed.), *The concept of development.* Minneapolis: University of Minnesota Press.

White, R. W. (1959). Motivation reconsidered: The concept of competence. *Psychological Review, 66*(5), 297–333.

Whiting, J. W. M., & Child, J. L. (1953). *Child training and personality.* New Haven: Yale University Press.

Wicklund, R. A. (1975). Objective self-awareness. In L. Berkowitz (Ed.), *Advances in experimental social psychology* (Vol. 7). New York: Academic Press.

Yarrow, M. R., Scott, P. M., & Waxler, C. Z. (1973). Learning concern for others. *Developmental Psychology, 8,* 240–260.

Zahn-Waxler, C., & Chapman, M. (1982). Immediate antecedents of caretakers' methods of discipline. *Child Psychiatry and Human Development, 12*(3), 179–192.

Zahn-Waxler, C., Chapman, M., & Cummings, E. M. (1984). Cognitive and social development in infants and toddlers with a bipolar parent. *Child Psychiatry and Human Development, 15*(2), 75–85.

Zahn-Waxler, C., Cummings, E. M., Iannotti, R. M., & Radke-Yarrow, M. (1984). Young offspring of depressed parents: A population at risk for affective problems. In D. Cicchetti & K. Schneider-Rosen (Eds.), *Childhood depression* (New Directions for Child Development No. 26). San Francisco: Jossey-Bass.

Zahn-Waxler, C., Kochanska, G., Krupnick, J., & McKnew, D. (1990). Patterns of guilt in children of depressed and well mothers. *Developmental Psychology*.

Zahn-Waxler, C., Mayfield, A., Radke-Yarrow, M., McKnew, D., Cytryn, L., & Davenport, Y. (1988). A follow-up investigation of offspring of bipolar parents. *American Journal of Psychiatry, 145*(4), 506–509.

Zahn-Waxler, C., McKnew, D., Cummings, E., Davenport, Y., & Radke-Yarrow, M. (1984). Problem behaviors and peer interactions of young children with a manic-depressive parent. *American Journal of Psychiatry, 141*(2), 236–240.

Zahn-Waxler, C., & Radke-Yarrow, M. (1982). The development of altruism: Alternative research strategies. In N. Eisenberg (Ed.), *The development of prosocial behavior*. New York: Academic Press.

Zahn-Waxler, C., Radke-Yarrow, M., & King, R. (1979). Child rearing and children's prosocial initiations toward victims of distress. *Child Development, 50*, 319–330.

Zahn-Waxler, C., Radke-Yarrow, M., Wagner, E., & Pyle, C. (1988). *The early development of prosocial behavior*. Paper presented at International Conference on Infant Studies, Washington, DC.

# The Organization and Coherence of Socioemotional, Cognitive, and Representational Development: Illustrations Through a Developmental Psychopathology Perspective on Down Syndrome and Child Maltreatment

## Dante Cicchetti
*University of Rochester and*
*Mt. Hope Family Center*

## Introduction

*T*hroughout history there have been attempts to acknowledge the role emotions play in an integrative developmental theory (see, e.g., Arnold, 1960; Darwin, 1872/1965; Kessen, 1971; Mischel, 1971; Piaget, 1954/1981; Tomkins, 1962, 1963). Nonetheless, it is only recently that systematic efforts have been made to address the traditional theoretical issues of developmental psychology as they pertain to the emotional domain and translate them into concrete research questions (see Campos, Barrett, Lamb, Goldsmith, & Stenberg, 1983; Cicchetti & Pogge-Hesse, 1981; Izard, 1977; and Sroufe, 1979a, for a discussion of the historical and contemporary factors underlying this state of affairs).

In an earlier paper (Hesse & Cicchetti, 1982) Hesse and I highlighted the distinctions between the domains of the mind and concluded that the emotions should be conceptualized as a separate developmental system (see also Izard, 1977, 1978; Malatesta, this volume). Furthermore, we delineated the theoretical and empirical contributions that were prerequisites for constructing a model of emotions and emotional development. Included were issues such as the definition and classification of the emotions, the course of nonverbal and verbal emotional ontogenesis, the development of social display roles and mechanisms of defense and the interrelations among the emotional, social, cognitive, linguistic, personality, and moral domains of ontogenesis (see also Bretherton & Beeghly, 1982; Bretherton, Fritz, Zahn-Waxler, & Ridgeway, 1986; Malatesta, this volume; Saarni, 1978 and this volume; and Selman, 1980, for an in-depth explication of these issues). Finally, we discussed the role of emotions in deviant development (Cicchetti & White, 1988; Izard, 1979; Zahn-Waxler & Kochanska, this volume). Our ultimate goal in these separate yet allied enterprises was to formulate a truly comprehensive developmental theory that would enable us not only to relate various domains of the human mind in their development across the life span, but also to integrate normal and atypical forms of ontogenesis.

## GOALS OF THIS CHAPTER

In this chapter I address the organization and coherence of socioemotional, cognitive, and representational development in two high-risk groups of children—those who have Down syndrome and those who have been maltreated. These conditions were chosen for several reasons. They occur frequently enough to warrant research and clinical attention. Together they define a continuum of the hypothesized contribution to maladaptation of reproductive (genetic and constitutional) and caretaking (parental and environmental) casualty factors (Sameroff & Chandler, 1975). That is, they vary in the relative significance that child-specific versus parent-specific influences have for ontogenesis.

Guided by an organizational perspective on development, I illustrate how studying the emotions in these atypical populations can contribute to our understanding of the organization and integration of normal emotional development. Conversely, I demonstrate how the developmental approach can enhance our understanding of these high-risk conditions. Finally, I suggest ways that our knowledge of emotional development in these populations can inform the design and timely provision of intervention services, thereby helping us remediate associated difficulties and make better decisions on policy.

## EMOTION AND PSYCHOPATHOLOGY: HISTORICAL ILLUSTRATIONS

Theoreticians, researchers, and clinicians from a variety of disciplines and areas of specialization have emphasized the importance of the emotions in the etiology, course, and sequelae of many forms of child and adult psychopathology (see, e.g., Arieti, 1955/1974; Bleuler, 1911/1950; Kanner, 1943). One such example is the work of Emil Kraepelin (1919/1971) who stressed the role of emotion in the development of schizophrenia and the relation of emotionality to the activities of the intellect and volition. Schizophrenia was characterized by a loss of the "inner unity" among emotion, cognition, and the will. Noting schizophrenics' tendency to cry or laugh without apparent reason, Kraepelin argued that without this underlying organization and integration, emotions did not correspond to ideas. According to Kraepelin, emotion and cognition were products of an underlying associational or connective process without which their normal integration was not possible.

Eugen Bleuler likewise (1911/1950) emphasized the role affectivity plays in the symptomatology of schizophrenia (see also Meehl, 1962, 1964). Noting that emotional deterioration stands at the forefront of the clinical picture of schizophrenia, Bleuler pointed out that the disappearance of affect signaled that an "acute curable psychosis" had become "chronic." According to Bleuler, affective indifference was characteristic of schizophrenia. Although in milder cases and in the beginning of the disease there might be affective oversensitivity, Bleuler contended that the affect lacks depth. He further noted the diagnostic power of the particular type of affect shown in acute episodes of the disease. He contrasted the deeply felt affective experience of the manic-depressive patient with the superficial, melodramatic, and disunifying aspects of affectivity in schizophrenics (cf. Kraepelin, 1921/1987). Unlike the case of the manic-depressive, where emotional lability and thought content are linked, the mood of the disturbed schizophrenic does not parallel the changing content of thought (Cicchetti, 1989). Bleuler believed that emotion in schizophrenia does not occur in response to thoughts but exists as an abnormal basic state of affectivity. This underlying affective rigidity can invest the expression of an entire range of moods. For example, he observed that schizophrenics seem to laugh and cry with the same affective expression.

Bleuler viewed schizophrenia as a breakdown in the relation between affect and cognition. He attributed the distortions of logic characteristic of schizophrenic thought to the way affectively charged associations replaced logical operations, and he believed that when reasoning weakened, the influence of the affects became stronger. Consequently, with the disintegration of the association pathways, the affects could connect any material to the split-off complexes of ideas so that any remaining logic served the affective needs.

A final illustration of the relation between affect and cognition can be found in Silvano Arieti's *The Intrapsychic Self* (1967), a compelling example of conceptualizing schizophrenia as a process of disintegration and dedifferentiation. Borrowing from Werner (1957), Arieti argues that in normal development primitive forms of emotions and cognitions become hierarchically integrated into increasingly advanced affective and cognitive forms. The earlier affective forms, or "protoemotions," decrease in importance as they gradually become transformed into higher types of emotion. This occurs through an evolution in interpersonal relations, particularly with regard to the mother. In psychopathology these primitive forms again become available to the psyche. According to Arieti, the schizophrenic resorts to an earlier level of emotional and cognitive development to reduce anxiety. However, this alternative is considered pathological or maladaptive because the patient originally functioned at a higher level and it is not possible to adapt to an earlier level of functioning.

Several themes emerge when one broadens historical accounts of the function of emotion in schizophrenia to address psychopathology more generally (Mora & Brand, 1970). According to one view, psychopathology is the result of unrestrained emotions, which thus play a dysregulating, negative role. A second theme is the regulating role of reason, which is seen as the check that can keep the emotions under control. From this viewpoint, psychopathology results from deficits in reason that allow the emotions to become unrestrained in a way deleterious to the individual. A third, albeit less frequent, theme is that psychopathology, which results from the imbalance between cognition and emotion, can best be alleviated by releasing the emotions. A final theme views emotion and reason (cognition) as two distinct domains.

Despite the long and rich history of work describing how emotion/cognition disequilibrium contributes to the unfolding of psychopathology, until the past few decades there has been a paucity of experimental research on emotion in high-risk conditions or in psychopathological disorders (see chapters in Izard, 1979). Spurred in part by major advances in our understanding of normal emotional development in infants and young children, researchers have increasingly focused on elucidating the organization of emotional development in at-risk youngsters and on uncovering the links between early adaptation/maladaptation and later psychobiological outcomes (Cicchetti & Beeghly, 1987a; Lewis, Feiring, McGuffog, & Jaskir, 1984; Rutter & Garmezy, 1983; Sameroff, Seifer, & Zax, 1982; Sroufe, 1979b, 1983; Zahn-Waxler & Kochanska, this volume). One of the major goals of these endeavors has been to identify nascent psychopathology and prevent such disturbances form undermining adaptive development (Cicchetti, Toth, & Bush, 1988; Greenspan et al., 1985; Provence & Naylor, 1983). Much of this recent work on atypical populations has been guided by the organizational or organismic developmental perspective (Cicchetti & Sroufe, 1978; Sroufe, 1979a; Sroufe & Waters, 1976; Werner & Kaplan, 1963) and has tried to enhance our knowledge of normal ontogenesis.

## ORIGINS OF ORGANISMIC THEORY

Before the eighteenth century, the concept of development as qualitative change over time was hardly fathomable. However, by approximately 1850 this idea had blossomed into a major viewpoint. Herbert Spencer's "developmental hypothesis" (Spencer, 1862/1900), which depicted development as a uniform process governed by universal laws and principles, was extremely influential in bringing about this dramatic shift. Most contemporary developmental models adhere to a similar organismic worldview, stressing the dynamic role of the individual and conceptualizing the individual as an organized whole (Kaplan, 1967; Mayr, 1982). Principles of behavior are accordingly seen in terms of the organization among parts and wholes and of the dynamic interplay between the person and the environment.

Each of the issues that are central foci of the organizational perspective on development has its roots in the beginnings of Western thought—in the works of Plato and Aristotle (Kaplan, 1967). The notion that multiple domains of behavior must be integrated to permit the harmonious functioning of the individual was anticipated by the Platonic conception of the triune character of the soul. In Plato one also can find the idea of hierarchically integrated domains of functioning in his concept of the dominance of reason (a higher function) over passion (a lower function). Moreover, in Plato's view of the dynamic role of the individual one discovers another historical precursor of the organismic perspective.

Likewise, Aristotle was one of the first to argue that individuation, differentiation, and self-actualization were characteristic aspects of developmental transformations (cf. Kaplan, 1967, 1983). Aristotle also stressed the interdependence between the individual and the environment. Believing in the multiple determination of behavior, Aristotle argued that humans had different levels of behavioral organization. Moreover, one also can find in Aristotle a holistic concept of behavior—to understand its true meaning, the part must be viewed in relation to the whole. Although neither Aristotle nor Plato focused on the relation between these ideas and the study of psychopathological disorders or high-risk conditions, nonetheless they built a potent theoretical foundation for the developmental approach to the study of all persons—normal and deviant.

## THE ORGANIZATIONAL PERSPECTIVE

The organizational approach to development (Cicchetti & Pogge-Hesse, 1982; Cicchetti & Sroufe, 1978; Sroufe, 1979a) comprises a set of regulative principles that can guide research and theorizing on human behavior (Werner, 1957; Werner & Kaplan, 1963). In referring to these principles as "regulative," I follow Werner (1948), who denied that they are themselves to be taken as empirical laws or that, in research and theory, one should necessarily attempt to find laws that can be seen as simple translations of these principles into empirical terms. Rather, these regulative principles are heuristic tools to help one find meaningful patterns in the great variety and quantity of data often accumulated in contemporary studies of human development and developmental psychopathology (Cicchetti, 1984; Sroufe & Rutter, 1984). With the aid of this heuristic, investigators may formulate empirical laws with greater confidence that they have uncovered true relations rather than coincidental correlations.

According to the organizational approach, development may be conceived as a series of qualitative reorganizations among and within behavioral and biological systems, which take place by differentiation and hierarchical integration (Atlan, 1981; Pattee, 1973; Simon, 1962; Varela, 1981). This orthogenetic principle (Werner, 1948) solves the problem of the individual's continuous adaptation to the environment and answers the question of how integrity of function may be maintained in the face of change (Dell, 1982; Guidano, 1987; Varela, 1976a, 1976b). Continuity in functioning can be maintained through hierarchical integration despite rapid constitutional changes and biobehavioral shifts (Block & Block, 1980; Sackett, Sameroff, Cairns, & Suomi, 1981; Sroufe, 1979b; Zahn-Waxler & Kochanska, this volume). Variables at many levels of analysis, including genetic, constitutional, neurobiological, biochemical, behavioral, psychological, environmental, and sociological, determine the character of these reorganizations. Moreover, these variables are conceived as being in dynamic transaction.

Normal development is defined in terms of a series of interlocking socioemotional, cognitive, and representational competencies. Competence at one period of development, which tends to make persons broadly adapted to their environments, prepares the way for competence at the next (Sroufe & Rutter, 1984). Moreover, normal development is marked by the integration of earlier competencies into later modes of functioning. It follows then that early adaptation promotes later adaptation and integration.

Pathological development, in contrast, may be conceived of as a lack of integration of the socioemotional, cognitive, and representational competencies that are important to adaptation at a particular developmental level (Cicchetti & Schneider-Rosen, 1986; Kaplan, 1966; Sroufe, 1979b). Because early structures often are incorporated into later ones, an early deviation or disturbance in functioning may ultimately lead to much larger disturbances.

In addition to orthogenesis, several related principles characterize the organizational framework: with development, there is change in structure-function relationships over time; the change that occurs is both qualitative and quantitative; and developmental change may best be conceived as a move toward increasing cortical control over the more diffuse, automatic behavioral centers (see Gottlieb, 1983).

The organizational perspective, with its emphasis on studying developing systems and uncovering the relation between normal and abnormal forms of ontogenesis, provides an excellent theoretical framework for conducting research on emotional development in high-risk populations. The empirical investigation of populations where differing patterns of development may be expected as a consequence of the pervasive and enduring influences that characterize the transaction between children and their environments—as is the case in Down syndrome and maltreatment—provides an appropriate basis for affirming and challenging our existing developmental theories.

## THE DISCIPLINE OF DEVELOPMENTAL PSYCHOPATHOLOGY

The discipline of developmental psychopathology has been built upon the assumption that a developmental approach can be applied to any unit of behavior or discipline and to all populations, normal or deviant (Werner, 1948; see also Cicchetti, in press; Kaplan, 1966, 1983). Developmental psychopathologists emphasize that we can learn more about an organism's normal functioning by studying its pathology and, likewise, more about its pathology by studying its normal condition (Cicchetti, 1984; Kaplan, 1966; Rutter, 1986). By virtue of their multidisciplinary perspective, developmental psychopathologists must study multiple domains of development, including perceptual-cognitive, socioemotional, linguistic-representational, and biological processes (Achenbach, in press; Cicchetti, 1984, in press; Mayr, 1982; Rutter & Garmezy, 1983).

Before developmental psychopathology could emerge as a distinct discipline, the science of normal development needed to mature, and a broader basis of firms results had to be acquired. Revolutionary advances have been made in cognition and cognitive science, including major contributions by theorists in cognitive development, linguistics, artificial intelligence, perception, and mental imagery (Fischer, 1980; Kosslyn, 1980; Miller & Wilson, 1979; Pribram, 1986; for a review of the history of the cognitive movement see Gardner, 1985).

During the past two decades, researchers and theoreticians have paid increasing attention to the noncognitive domains of development. Major advancements have occurred in a number of areas, including emotional development (Campos et al., 1983; Cicchetti & Hesse, 1982, 1983; Izard, 1977; Izard & Malatesta, 1987; Lewis & Michalson, 1983; Sroufe, 1979b), social development (Ainsworth, Blehar, Waters, & Wall, 1978; Bretherton, 1985, this volume; Damon, 1977; Greenberg, Cicchetti, & Cummings, in press; Hartup, 1983; Main, Kaplan, & Cassidy, 1985), social cognition (Kohlberg, 1981, 1984; Selman, 1980), motivation (Connell, 1985; Deci, 1975; Harter, 1978; Lepper, 1981), self-development (Bretherton, this volume, 1985; Cicchetti & Beeghly, in press; Damon & Hart, 1982; Harter, 1983; Lewis & Brooks-Gunn, 1979) and symbolization (Bates, Benigni, Bretherton, Camaioni, & Volterra, 1979; Bretherton, 1984; Cicchetti & Beeghly, 1987a; Rubin, Fein, & Vandenberg, 1983).

Accompanying the advancements in developmental knowledge, the 1970s witnessed an increasingly greater acceptance, among both researchers and clinicians, of the role that a variety of factors—for example, constitutional, genetic, biochemical, psychological, environmental, and sociological—play in the etiology, course, and sequelae of mental disorders. As a consequence, reductionistic notions of disease became less and less tenable (see, e.g., Cassell, 1986; Cicchetti & Schneider-Rosen, 1984b; Engel, 1977; Marmor, 1983; Meehl, 1972; Zubin & Spring, 1977). The increasing sophistication of the medical model employed by clinicians allowed for a more integrative understanding of disease than the "main effect" (Reese & Overton, 1970) Virchowian conceptions of disease had permitted. Moreover, incorporating the developmental perspective into other disciplines such as the neurosciences, psychobiology, and behavioral and molecular genetics promises exciting prospects for constructing an empirically and theoretically sound integrative developmental model of psychopathology (see, e.g., Goldman-Rakic, 1987; Greenough, Black, & Wallace, 1987; Hartlage & Telzrow, 1985; Jacobson, 1978; Plomin, 1986; Scarr & Kidd, 1983; Sulkowski, 1983; Weinberger, 1987; Wiggins, McCandless, & Enna, 1985).

Within the discipline of developmental psychopathology, exploring normal and atypical patterns of ontogenesis requires that we consider the different behavioral and biological systems within which advances are proceeding in parallel and influencing each other. To theorize about development without attending to the interaction among multiple domains would lead to a diminished view of the complexity of the developmental process. Likewise, to formulate a developmental theory without considering the deviations that might be expected from the prominent and wide-ranging intra-or extraorganismic disturbances, as well as the transactions among them, would result in incomplete or ambiguous accounts of ontogenesis that do not adequately consider individual differences, the continuity and quality of adaptation, and the different processes by which the same developmental outcome may be achieved (cf. E. Kaplan, 1983, and Werner, 1937, for lucid discussions of the process/achievement distinction).

Accordingly, any consideration of atypical patterns of early development needs to take into account the child's unique characteristics, age and stage level of functioning, experiences, and stability of environmental conditions. Additionally, we must consider the characteristics of the caregiving environment, the compatibility of the child-caregiver dyad, the continuity or discontinuity of adaptive or maladaptive behavior patterns, and the advances or lags in various behavioral and biological systems. To explore more fully the role these issues play in development, I now present the atypical populations I have chosen to focus on.

# Contributions That the Study of Children with Down Syndrome Can Make to Understanding Emotions and the Organization and Integration of Development

Children with Down syndrome are a particularly interesting population for developmentalists. As an "experiment in nature" (Bronfenbrenner, 1979), Down syndrome provides an excellent opportunity to address critical questions in developmental theory that on ethical grounds alone would be impossible to manipulate experimentally. In addition, unlike most mentally retarded youngsters, children with Down syndrome are an etiologically homogeneous group, their condition is detectable at birth, and therefore their developmental progress can be charted virtually from the beginning. Although their development unfolds at a slower pace, such children are cognitively quite heterogeneous, ranging from severe mental retardation to approximately normal intellectual functioning. This combination of delayed yet variable development permits a more careful examination of the nature of stages and sequences across developmental domains and of the relations between behavioral and biological systems at particular points in development. In essence, the study of Down syndrome, just as is true for cross-cultural research, can inform us about which stages, sequences, and structures are logically necessary, suggest what alternate pathways of ontogenesis are possible, and provide evidence on which factors contributing to the developmental process are most critical.

We have conducted research on children with Down syndrome that explores in detail several of the themes of the symposium: the development of emotion; the organization and coherence of socioemotional, cognitive, and representational development; the role emotion plays in relationships; and the relation between emotion and competent adaptation on the stage-salient developmental tasks of infancy and childhood (see Thompson, Introduction to this volume). These themes are addressed in the following sections.

One of the theoretical consequences of investigating emotional development in high-risk populations is that it underscores the importance of constructing a model of normal emotional development in order to distinguish between the abnormal and the well adjusted. Knowledge of the processes and mechanisms underlying normal emotional development will allow us to implement intervention strategies to aid children who manifest abnormalities. For example, now that we are beginning to learn more about the processes underlying the acquisition of emotion-related language (Bretherton, et al., 1986), we soon will be able to design therapeutic situations that will facilitate the development of emotional language and the control of acting-out behaviors (cf. Cicchetti, Toth, & Bush, 1988; Greenberg & Speltz, 1988). The theoretical and practical import of the investigation of emotional development also is relevant in formulating an integrated theory of development. Only if we know, for example, how emotions relate to other aspects of functioning will we be able to specify the necessary and sufficient conditions for altering the emotional domain.

Contemporary thought on the relation between emotion and cognition is based upon conceptualizations regarding the sequence of emergence of new cognitive or affective qualities or characteristics (Cicchetti & Hesse, 1983). Emotions may be regarded as developing ontogenetically earlier than cognition, thereby providing the context within which cognitive development may occur (*cognitive epiphenomenalism*). Conversely, the emergence of new emotions may depend upon cognitive advances that must occur before various emotions can be expressed (*emotional epiphenomenalism*). Emotions also may develop along a separate pathway from cognitive advances, so that the sequence, rate, and quality of change must be considered distinctly within each domain (*parallelism*). Finally, emotions may emerge in interaction with cognitive advances, a progression that requires us to consider developmental changes that occur across domains and that exert a reciprocal influence upon each other (*interactionism*).

In fact, children with Down syndrome provide an important test of the nature of the relation between emotional and cognitive development. Unlike normal development, where the rapid and simultaneous emergence of behaviors may be viewed as coincidental, the slower advance of children with Down syndrome through the same progression of stages as normal babies allows us to observe and demonstrate true convergences and discontinuities. The delayed rate of cognitive development in infants with Down syndrome enables us to separate the early prototypes of what will later be affective expression from genuine emotional reactions that are dependent on psychological processes (Cicchetti & Sroufe, 1978). Furthermore, their developmental heterogeneity lets us specify the interdependence of the relation between affect and cognition. Finally, their obvious autonomic and central nervous system deficits permit early statements both about the relation between brain and behavior and about how tension and affect promote development.

STUDIES OF POSITIVE AFFECT

The ontogenesis of smiling and laughter in infants with Down syndrome provides a good illustration of the intimate connection that underlies emotional and cognitive development. Previous research with several samples of nonretarded infants between the ages of 4 and 12 months revealed that changes in laughter accompanied advancing cognitive development (Sroufe & Wunsch, 1972). Whereas infants in the first half-year of life laughed mostly in situations that were physically intense or vigorous, during the second half-year infants laughed at progressively more subtle and complex social and visual stimulation and were less likely to laugh at simpler stimuli. Based on an organizational understanding of the interdependence of affect and cognition, one would predict that infants with Down syndrome who exhibit atypical cognitive development would show a parallel lag in their affective development. If affective development is a function of cognitive development and not merely an epiphenomenon of chronological age, then the affective stages should occur in the same sequence as that reported by Sroufe and Wunsch (1972), but at a rate corresponding to the child's degree of cognitive retardation.

To explore this issue, a study was conducted with 25 Down syndrome infants between 4 and 24 months of age (Cicchetti & Sroufe, 1976, 1978). Babies were presented with the standard series of 30 laughter items used in studies of normal infants. In addition, cognitive and motor assessments were made by persons unfamiliar with the infants' performance on the laughter items. These included the Uzgiris & Hunt (1975) ordinal scales of cognitive development, which were administered at 13, 16, 19, 21, and 24 months, and the Bayley (1969) Mental and Motor scales, given at 16, 19, and 24 months. Even though infants with Down syndrome showed a delayed onset of laughter, they laughed at these incongruous stimulus items in the same order as normal infants—initially to intrusive auditory and tactile items, later to the more complex social and visual items. This ordering suggests an intimate relation between cognitive and affective evelopment.

Differences in the onset and intensity of affective responses were related to the infants' degree of muscular hypotonia and to developmental level, as assessed by the Bayley Scales of Infant Development (Bayley, 1969). Down syndrome infants with the most flaccid muscle tone were the most delayed in smiling and laughing across all forms of stimulation. This relationship between motor control problems and delayed affect response has been supported by Gallagher, Jens, and O'Donnell (1983), who found that hypotonic and hypertonic infants demonstrate a restricted range of emotionality and responsiveness. Moreover, in general infants with Down syndrome smiled to situations where normal infants laughed. Because nearly all infants with Down syndrome are hypotonic to some degree (Cowie, 1970), the affect-intensity differences they display are at least partially related to motor problems and their underlying biological difficulties. Finally, Cicchetti and Sroufe (1976) contend that the diminution in laughter also may reflect deficits in information processing. Specifically, these investigators argue that infants with Down syndrome do not process the incongruity of the stimulus items quickly enough to generate the cognitively produced arousal necessary for laughter.

Furthermore, as schema formation becomes increasingly important in eliciting positive affect, it is no longer stimulation per se (Kagan, 1971; Strofe & Waters, 1976) that produces the tension necessary for smiling and laughter, but the infant's "effort" in processing stimulus content. Both infants with Down syndrome and nonretarded infants progress toward an ever more active participation in producing affectively effective stimulation. In this example of the development of smiling and laughter in infants, the similarity in the ordering of the responsiveness to the laughter items demonstrated by nonretarded and retarded infants suggests that the development of the emotional domain is inextricably interwoven with changes within the cognitive arena. Evidence from the cognitive tests strengthens this interactive conceptualization of the relation. The level of cognitive development as measured by performance on the Uzgiris-Hunt and Bayley scales correlated highly with the level of affective development as measured by the smiling and laughter items. Accordingly, it seems that motor ability and cognitive developmental level, not chronological age, are related to the capacity to express positive emotion. These results are consistent with findings of delayed or arrested neurological maturation in individuals with Down syndrome that may affect both motor control and cognitive development (cf. Cowie, 1970).

## STUDIES ON THE DEVELOPMENT OF NEGATIVE AFFECT

The organizational perspective assumes a close relation between strong positive and strong negative affect in that they are linked by the degree of cognitively produced arousal (Sroufe & Waters, 1976). Because the same event can produce the range of affective reactions, factors beyond information inherent in the event are viewed as influencing the direction of and thresholds for affective reactions (Cicchetti & Sroufe, 1976, 1978; Sroufe & Waters, 1976).

Two of the classic paradigms researchers use to assess the development of depth perception can provide valuable information on the relation between the ontogenesis of negative emotions and cognitive development. Specifically, the study of infants' reactions to "looming" objects (Bower, Broughton, & Moore, 1970) and of their prelocomotor and locomotor responses to the "visual cliff" (Campos, Hiatt, Ramsay, Henderson, & Svejda, 1978; Gibson & Walk, 1960) can enhance our understanding of the organization of emotional development in infants with Down syndrome. Using these paradigms, Cicchetti and Sroufe (1978) have compared the responses of infants with Down syndrome and of nonretarded infants to looming objects at 4, 8, and 12 months and studied the former's response at 16 months. Although there was no difference in the amount of crying at 4 months, significantly more normal infants cried at 8 and 12 months. It was not until 16 months that infants with Down syndrome showed any substantial crying. Moreover, those babies with Down syndrome who cried had significantly higher scores on the Bayley scales of mental and motor development than those who did not, thus showing more differentiation in their cognitive and emotional development.

A close relation between cognitive and negative emotional development also was found in reactions to the visual cliff. Far fewer infants with Down syndrome exhibited fear reactions (for example, crying, heart-rate acceleration, behavioral freezing) when placed directly atop the deep side. Just as was found for the looming data, the Down syndrome infants who manifested negative reactions on the visual cliff were more cognitively mature, with significantly higher scores on the Bayley scales of development, than those who did not exhibit fear.

## THE ORGANIZATION OF AFFECT, MOTIVATION, COGNITION, AND PLAY

Studies examining play behavior have revealed more about the nature of emotional development in children with Down syndrome. Moreover, these studies have provided valuable information about the organization of their development beyond the sensorimotor period. Researchers have noted that although emerging cognitive abilities may underlie the structure of children's play, the force behind play is often affective (Cicchetti & Hesse, 1983; Piaget, 1962). Studies of the play of nonretarded children have yielded information about the relations among affect, cognition, and symbolic development. Children's enthusiasm and persistence have been found to be significantly correlated with the complexity and maturity of their object play in these studies (Bretherton, 1984; Matas, Arend, & Sroufe, 1978). Similar relations between cognitive and affective dimensions of object play have been observed in children with Down syndrome.

For example, in a longitudinal study of 31 children with Down syndrome, Motti, Cicchetti, and Sroufe (1983) found that both symbolic play maturity and affective play behavior at 3 to 5 years were significantly correlated with indexes of affective and cognitive development assessed during their first and second years, respectively. Specifically, Motti and her colleagues found that children exhibiting higher levels of symbolic play were more likely to have had negative reactions to looming objects at 16 months and to have laughed to incongruous maternal stimuli (e.g., mother pretending to suck baby's bottle; mother walking like Charlie Chaplin) before 10 months. Furthermore, it was found that the higher the level of symbolic play, the earlier the children smiled to complex social and visual stimuli presented by the mother. Marked individual differences within the group of Down syndrome children also emerged; children with higher levels of cognitive development engaged in more mature levels of symbolic and social play, explored toys more actively and thoroughly, were more enthusiastic during play, and exhibited more positive affect than did less cognitively advanced children (cf. Hill & McCune-Nicolich, 1981).

In a study by Beeghly and Cicchetti (1987), correlational analyses revealed that affective/motivational play style (enthusiasm, persistence, positive affect) was correlated significantly both with level of cognitive development and with symbolic play maturity both in children with Down syndrome and in cognitively matched normal children. These findings indicate that the affective, motivational, and cognitive aspects of symbolic development apparent in the play of children with Down syndrome are organized similarly to those of normal children at a comparable level of cognitive development.

## THE RELATION BETWEEN EMOTION AND COGNITION

These studies of children with Down syndrome suggest that cognitive factors alone are not sufficient to account for their affective behavior. Analysis of the data indicates that the slower cognitive development of these youngsters accounts only partially for the reduced incidence of extreme forms of affect expression such as laughter and crying. In the laughter studies, even after these infants were matched in mental age with normal counterparts, less laughter was found than in the normal infants. Likewise, even when cognitive-developmental level was comparable between the groups, normal babies showed more negative reactions to the visual cliff and to looming objects. Fewer infants with Down syndrome were fearful when placed directly upon the deep side of the visual cliff than their cognitive-developmental level would have led us to predict. Even taking developmental level into account, infants with Down syndrome cried less than normal infants (Cicchetti & Sroufe, 1978).

I interpret these data as indicating that affect and cognition are indeed separate developmental systems and that both of the epiphenomenalist positions on the relation between them (Hesse & Cicchetti, 1982) are thus refuted in infants with Down syndrome. Furthermore, I think that the data on the development of positive and negative affect, in addition to the investigations on affect, motivation, and play, support an interactional interpretation of the relation between affect and cognition. Because cognitive factors alone are insufficient to explain these results, individual differences in the strength of external stimulation necessary to produce a given amount of physiological stimulation must be considered simultaneously. Perhaps the differing rates and levels of maturation of the neuroendocrinological system, combined with the slowed rate of cortical development, account in part for the decreased intensity and muted affect systems of children with Down syndrome (see Butterworth & Cicchetti, 1978).

When the results of studies on positive and negative affect are considered, quantitative differences in the expression of affect between children with Down syndrome and normal infants seem at least partially dependent upon cognitive status, motor ability, or perhaps more broadly, the maturation of abilities. Infants with Down syndrome frequently appear to demonstrate the same organization of affect and cognitive abilities and to undergo the same developmental processes as normal infants. The primary difference is that they develop more slowly.

However, children with Down syndrome also demonstrate some qualitative differences in responsiveness that cannot be accounted for by developmental level. Two such characteristics are multiple blinking in response to looming objects and diminished crying. Cicchetti and Sroufe (1978) describe blinking as a reflexive response to stimulation that comes under the control of forebrain inhibitory mechanisms early in development. Therefore they argue that increased blinking in infants with Down syndrome may reflect poorly developed inhibitory systems of the central nervous system. In addition, Cicchetti and Sroufe propose that their stimulation threshold may be higher than that of other infants owing to dysfunctions in the sympathetic nervous system. They argue that low-intensity responses to stimulation (such as smiling instead of laughter, gaze aversion or blinking instead of crying) may reflect dampened reactivity.

Accordingly, Cicchetti and Sroufe propose that it is not the true objective qualities of an object or event that prompt the expression of affect. Rather, one's ability to interpret an experience, reaction to stimulation, and ability to regulate a response will shape the expression of affect. At a basic level, reactivity of response systems will determine one's arousal level. However, further interpretation of a stimulus as pleasant or aversive may potentiate or diminish arousal. Likewise, self-regulatory abilities such as the inhibition of reflexes will affect the pairing of event appraisals with appropriate responses (see Thompson, this volume). If arousal is dampened from the beginning, one should expect lower-intensity responses, such as smiling instead of laughing. This effect may be accentuated by failure to fully appreciate the qualities of the stimulus, leading to either inappropriate or diminished affect, or by the interference of reflexes that cannot be controlled.

## CONTRIBUTIONS OF BIOLOGICAL/BIOCHEMICAL FACTORS TO THE RELATION BETWEEN EMOTION AND COGNITION

Our understanding of the relation between emotion and cognition can be enhanced by considering the role of biological/biochemical factors. Research has suggested that the Down syndrome genotype affects neurotransmitter systems that influence reactivity. For example, several studies with adults and children have proposed that Down syndrome is associated with decreased sympathetic nervous system activity. The sympathetic nervous system (SNS) mediates stress responses, heightening alertness and arousal in response to an event or a stimulus. Weinshilbaum, Thoa, Johnson, Kopin, and Axelrod (1971) found that dopamine-beta-hydroxylase, an enzyme that promotes the formation of noradrenaline, a neurotransmitter important in activating the SNS, is deficient in the blood of those with Down syndrome. Likewise, Keele, Richards, Brown, and Marshall (1969) found decreased levels of the metabolites of another neurotransmitter (adrenaline) that is usually released when the SNS is activated.

278

There is also evidence that both cholinergic and serotonergic systems are influenced by Down syndrome. These neurotransmitter systems influence two neurological systems important to a person's arousal levels: the parasympathetic nervous system and the reticular activating system. Consequently, differences in the functioning and activity of both systems affect reactivity. Casanova, Walker, Whitehouse, and Price (1985) and Yates, Simpson, Maloney, Gorden, and Reid (1980) present anatomical and chemical evidence of decreased cholinergic projections and activity in the brain in Down syndrome. Additionally, Scott, Becker, and Petit (1983) discuss several studies that indicate decreased serotonin activity within the central nervous system (see also Cicchetti & Sroufe, 1978).

If these neurochemical studies reflect meaningful differences in the functioning of the SNS as well as other arousal systems, persons with Down syndrome may possess dampened reactive systems that are less sensitive to the environment. Thus their thresholds to stimulation might be high while their sensitivity and arousability are inherently less than in normal infants. Behaviorally, as a group, they might seem placid and less easily disturbed by stimulation than infants who easily become physiologically aroused.

However, these characteristics do not completely define the temperament characteristics of the child with Down syndrome (Ganiban, Wagner, & Cicchetti, in press). Rothbart and Derryberry (1981) view temperament within a developmental framework in which reactivity and emotionality are increasingly regulated by thought and intention. Changes in temperament throughout the first years of life are apparent and depend upon neurological maturation and the development of self-regulatory skills that enable one to control reactivity. Once neurological tracts essential to the control of reactive systems are fully developed, behavior comes under the voluntary control of one's evaluations and appraisals of self and the environment. Given possible constitutional and maturational differences between Down syndrome and normal groups at different points in development, the inherent reactivity level of Down syndrome may affect the sensitivity to stimulation and the intensity of emotions as well (see, e.g., Cicchetti & Serafica, 1981; Cicchetti & Sroufe, 1976, 1978; Serafica & Cicchetti, 1976; Thompson, Cicchetti, Lamb, & Malkin, 1985). These relations among appraisal processes, reactivity, and constitution are central to Rothbart and Derryberry's (1981) conceptualization of temperament.

In addition to abnormalities in the activity of neurotransmitter systems, some studies also have found that Down syndrome affects the maturation of the brain (Becker, Armstrong, & Chan, 1986; Purpura, 1975; Takashima, Becker, Armstrong, & Chan, 1981). Essentially, these studies have examined the growth of neuronal networks throughout the brains of children with Down syndrome. Their basic findings suggest that after a short period of growth during the first few months of life, the maturation rate of their brains decreases relative to that of normally developing networks, and their neuronal networks appear to be less differentiated and elaborate.

The implications of decreases or cessations in the maturation and development of the brain are widespread. First, one would expect development in general to be delayed as the brain slowly develops the neuronal networks capable of quickly and efficiently synthesizing information. Second, decreased maturation also may interfere with the full development of important inhibitory tracts that control behavioral systems. This may account for the persistence of primitive reflexes beyond the neonatal period in Down syndrome (Cicchetti & Sroufe, 1978; Cowie, 1970). In addition, biological constraints upon the maturation of the brain may influence developmental changes in temperament (Rothbart & Derryberry, 1981; Wilson & Matheny, 1986). If changes in temperament across time reflect the maturation of the central nervous system (CNS), as prescribed by the qualities of the system, persons with Down syndrome would not be expected to demonstrate shifts or changes in temperament characteristics at the same time as the normal population. Further research must be conducted to determine whether these differences in dendritic maturation are a general effect of mental retardation or a specific consequence of Down syndrome.

## Emotion and Competence

### STAGE-SALIENT ISSUES OF EARLY DEVELOPMENT

We can enhance our understanding of the development of emotion by exploring it in relation to stage-salient issues. In recent years there has been considerable agreement that a series of such issues are characteristic of the early years of life (Sroufe, 1979b; see also Erikson, 1950). Rather than viewing ontogenesis as an unfolding series of tasks that are accomplished and then become insignificant, I construe development as consisting of a number of important age- and stage-appropriate tasks that remain critical to the child's adaptation throughout the life span. As new tasks emerge, old issues may decrease in relative salience. Nonetheless, each issue requires ongoing coordination with and integration into the child's adaptation to the environment and to the stage-salient developmental issue of the period (see Cicchetti, Cummings, Greenberg, & Marvin, in press, for an elaboration). Furthermore, there are corresponding roles for caregivers that increase the likelihood that children will successfully resolve each stage-salient issue (see Sander, 1962; Sroufe, 1979b).

### THE TRANSACTIONAL MODEL

Inherent in the organizational perspective on development and the notion of stage-salient issues is the recognition that genetic, constitutional, neurobiological, biochemical, psychological, environmental, and social factors are important in determining behavior (Sameroff, 1983). Proponents of the transactional model contend that the various factors operating in normal or pathological conditions do not occur in isolation but together influence development through a hierarchy of dispositions (Carnap, 1936; Sellars, 1958). According to Sameroff and Chandler (1975), the multiple transactions among parental, child, and environmental characteristics contribute to child development in a reciprocal, dynamic fashion. Consequently, a child who manifests pathological development over time is presumed to have been involved in a *continuous* maladaptive transactional process. The long-standing maladaptation is shaped by parental and environmental influences, while the child's characteristics help determine the nature of the "environment." Because the child and the environment are seen as reciprocally influencing each other, it follows that development at a later point reflects not only the quality of earlier adaptation, but also the intervening environmental input. As time elapses and the child develops, the match between child and parent, as well as salient parent characteristics, may change. In such a case declining quality of adaptation would demonstrate continuity of development. Moreover, adaptive or maladaptive outcomes may be influenced by long-term protective factors and transient buffers (cf. Cicchetti & Rizley, 1981).

It follows then that a transactional analysis incorporates the notions of stability and change over time while attempting to account for those factors that may maintain or alter the child's capacity to resolve developmentally salient tasks. In extending this analysis to the assessment of early competence (i.e., successful resolution of the stage-salient issues), several points need to be emphasized: (1) competence at one developmental period is a positive influence toward achieving competence at the next period; (2) early competence also exerts a subtle influence toward adaptation throughout the life span, since each developmental issue, although perhaps most salient at one period, is of continuing importance *throughout* the life cycle; (3) the failure to achieve adaptation at one period makes adaptation more difficult at the next period and, in a lesser way, throughout the life span; (4) many factors mediate between early and later adaptation or maladaptation and may permit alternative outcomes; that is, early problems or deviations in the successful resolution of a developmental task may be countered by major changes in the child's experience (e.g., positive changes in parenting; improvements in the environment) that could promote the successful negotiation of subsequent developmental tasks.

Now let us examine how infants and young children with Down syndrome negotiate these early stage-salient issues, which include: homeostatic regulation and the development of a reliable signaling system; management of tension and the differentiation of affect; development of a secure attachment relationship; development of an autonomous self; and symbolic representation and self/other differentiation.

## HOMEOSTATIC REGULATION AND THE DEVELOPMENT OF A RELIABLE SIGNALING SYSTEM (0–3 MONTHS)

The initial developmental task facing the newborn concerns neurophysiological organization, regulation, and homeostasis (Emde, Gaensbauer, & Harmon, 1976; Greenspan, 1981; Sander, 1962, 1975). During the first three months of life, the infant must establish basic cycles and rhythms of sleep and wakefulness, feeding and elimination. As these processes stabilize, the infant can interact more extensively with the outside world and begin to establish a reliable signaling system.

Caregivers play a critical role in the development of homeostasis, since they must provide a physical and emotional environment in which the infant can balance inner state and external stimuli. Adaptive patterns of homeostasis and a reliable signaling system emerge in a protective, predictable, and engaging environment. A chaotic, arbitrary, hypo/hyperstimulating environment contributes to problems in resolving this task.

Infants with Down syndrome have a variety of neurological, biochemical, physiological, and psychophysiological problems that may stress the caregiving system and result in homeostatic failure. For example, their slower maturation of reflexes and organ systems impairs the development of reliable sleep/wake patterns. Moreover, the confluence of neuromuscular hypotonia, poor eye contact, dampened affect intensity, higher arousal threshold, "noise" in the emotion-signaling system, and absence of crescendoing during face-to-face interaction significantly stress the caregiver-infant communication system (Berger, in press; Cicchetti & Sroufe, 1978; Emde, Katz, & Thorpe, 1978). Despite difficulties during the early months, most caregivers of infants with Down syndrome do accommodate to their behavioral and physiological anomalies and develop a mutually adaptive signaling system over the first year of life (Sorce & Emde, 1982).

MANAGEMENT OF "TENSION" (COGNITIVELY
PRODUCED AROUSAL) AND THE DIFFERENTIATION
OF AFFECT (4–6 MONTHS)

With the emergence of the social smile, a qualitatively new phase of development and behavioral organization surfaces (Emde et al., 1976). Mastery of homeostatic regulation and reliable patterns of signaling contribute to a capacity for more sustained attention to the environment. As a result, the infant begins to engage with both the animate and inanimate world in a more organized manner (Sroufe & Waters, 1976). Behaviors that were previously endogenously stimulated and primarily reflexive are replaced by contingent responses to exogenous stimulation. This state is characterized by increased intensity and differentiation in the expression of affect (Sroufe, 1979a, 1979b). During this stage the infant first laughs in response to vigorous stimulation and exhibits frustration or rage in response to unmet expectations. Both the infant's ability to elicit maternal response and the mother's sensitivity to infant cues are critical for successful negotiation of this issue.

Once again the biological system difficulties that exist in infants with Down syndrome present special challenges for the caregiver. As discussed earlier in this chapter, Cicchetti and Sroufe (1976) have documented that these infants are slower to laugh to a variety of stimuli and cannot process incongruity fast enough to generate the *tension* required for laughter (cf. Sroufe & Waters, 1976). Cicchetti and Sroufe (1978) have demonstrated similar delays in the emergence of full-blown fear expressions. The delayed appearance and diminished intensity of these affective responses may influence caregivers' cognitive perception or interpretation of the infants' cues, causing them to misread emotional messages or react to their babies with less affective involvement.

Because of the decreased responsiveness of infants with Down syndrome and their dampened affective tone, caregivers must use compensatory mechanisms to initiate or maintain interactions or to interpret and respond to affective states. As with homeostatic regulation, over time such caregivers negotiate patterns of communication that help accomplish this task (Sorce & Emde, 1982).

Cicchetti and Sroufe (1976, 1978) suggest that mothers of infants with Down syndrome appear to compensate for morphological and psychophysiological deviations by exerting themselves to initiate interaction and elicit affective responses. What may appear as over-stimulation or intrusiveness may actually be the manifestation of a sensitive and contingently responsive caregiver making compensatory adjustments to encourage the infant's interaction and adaptation.

Bridges and Cicchetti (1982) demonstrate that maternal ratings of infants with Down syndrome do not describe greater difficulty in interacting with them, although using Carey's (1973) criteria for assigning infants to different temperament categories reveals that more of these infants are difficult to manage relative to Carey's original standardization sample. This finding suggests that the caregiver can alter perceptions of, and attitudes toward, the infant to promote harmonious interaction within the dyad.

## THE DEVELOPMENT OF A SECURE ATTACHMENT RELATIONSHIP (6–12 MONTHS)

The development of a secure attachment relationship with the primary caregiver has generated considerable research (Ainsworth et al., 1978; Bowlby 1969; Lamb, Thompson, Gardner, & Charnov, 1985). It is marked by increased attention and attunement to interpersonal interaction (Stern, 1985). Although the capacity for attachment originates in earlier stages, overt manifestations of this issue reach ascendancy in the latter half of the first year of life (Sroufe, 1979a), when the infant learns to coordinate a broad variety of behavioral responses into an adaptive and flexible repertoire of goal-corrected responses. Dyadic interactions, marked by relatedness and synchrony, resiliency to stress, and appropriate affective interchange, are associated with successful adaptation during this stage (Sroufe, 1979b). The knowledge that a caregiver is reliable and responsive also is critical, since inadequate response-contingent stimulation is likely to exert a negative impact on the infant's ability to master the tasks of this stage. In the absence of regular contingent responses, neither infant nor caregiver develops feeling of efficacy, and the development of a secure attachment relationship may be impeded (Ainsworth et al., 1978; Belsky, Rovine, & Taylor, 1984; Lamb, Thompson, Gardner, Charnov, & Estes, 1984).

Despite their constitutional anomalies, the attachment system of infants with Down syndrome is organized much like that of non-handicapped youngsters matched in mental age. Most of these children form secure attachment relationships with their caregivers (Thompson et al., 1985). In addition, research on infants with Down syndrome demonstrates that a relationship similar to that in normal infants may be found between early attachment with the primary caregiver and the control of emotions. Cicchetti and Serafica (1981) found that attachment, affiliation, and fear/wariness systems in infants with Down syndrome were organized as in normal infants (Bretherton & Ainsworth, 1974). In particular, the intensity of their emotional responses varied with the context and the behaviors of both mother and stranger, suggesting an awareness of and sensitivity to eliciting conditions and a capacity to modulate and control emotional states.

Cicchetti and Serafica's (1981) analyses of qualitative and quantitative differences in responsiveness to mother and stranger for the fear/wariness, affiliation, and attachment behavioral systems broadened the potential conclusions about the emotional control of infants with Down syndrome. Thus, for example, their increased latency to crying during separation from the mother and the greater difficulty of soothing and calming them reflects their higher arousal threshold. This psychophysiological disturbance mediates the overt display of affective responsiveness but does not lessen the need for these children to learn to control their emotional displays. Berry, Gunn, and Andrews (1980) found that Down syndrome babies observed in a sequence of episodes similar, though not identical, to the "Strange Situation" (Ainsworth et al., 1978) displayed greater distress upon separation from the mother than those studied by Cicchetti and Serafica (1981). However, the infants studied by Berry and his colleagues were younger in mental and chronological age than those in Cicchetti and Serafica's (1981) sample, indicating that socialization experiences may influence the capacity for emotional control.

Although the organization of behavioral systems may be similar in normal infants and infants with Down syndrome, qualitative differences in the emotionality of the groups do exist. Although attachment and object-relations theorists agree that emotion is an important aspect of attachment relationships (Ainsworth et al., 1978; Engel, 1971; Sroufe, 1979b; Sroufe & Waters, 1977), the specific role of emotional arousal remains unclear. From this standpoint, impairment of cognitive appraisal processes (cf. Arnold, 1960; Sroufe, 1979b) should affect the speed, intensity, and variability of emotional reactions in social contexts such as the Strange Situation.

In a study of 19-month-olds, Thompson et al. (1985) focused upon the expression of affect during the Strange Situation (Ainsworth & Wittig, 1969) and its relation to cognitive-developmental level, comparing infants with Down syndrome and normal infants of the same chronological age and mental age (MA). In both comparisons the infants with Down syndrome were less intensely distressed and required more time to respond to separation than normal infants. In addition, the Down syndrome infants expressed only a limited range of emotions to separation and thus showed significantly less "emotional lability" than normal infants. Consistent with the results of prior studies, responsiveness and expressed affect in babies with Down syndrome are both delayed and qualitatively different than those in the normal population. These data provide further evidence that basic differences between Down syndrome and normal populations cannot be accounted for solely by cognitive delay. Although mental retardation may exert a large effect, underlying "constitutional" factors might limit the way those with Down syndrome can respond to the world. Again, this fundamental difference may lie in individual differences in biological reactive capacities (cf. Ganiban et al., in press).

## THE DEVELOPMENT OF AN AUTONOMOUS SELF (18– 24 MONTHS)

The acquisition of a sense of self, seen as encompassing both affective and cognitive dimensions, is a significant developmental task (Lewis & Brooks-Gunn, 1979; Stern, 1985) and enables the toddler to understand environmental occurrences more fully. Moreover, issues of body management begin to emerge from the context of the mother-infant relationship into the realm of autonomous function.

The toddler becomes increasingly invested in self-managing owing to new cognitive, representational, and motor achievements as well as to more sophisticated notions about self and other. Empathic acts also begin to emerge at this time as the child realizes that the self can have an impact on others (Zahn-Waxler & Radke-Yarrow, 1982). The caretaker's sensitivity and ability to tolerate the toddler's strivings for autonomy, as well as the capacity to set age-appropriate limits, are integral to the successful resolution of this issue. In contrast, intolerance for children's initiative may impede the development of autonomy. Caretakers who feel rejected owing to infants' increasing independence or overwhelmed by their actively initiated demands may inhibit the emergence of age-appropriate autonomy (Mahler, Pine, & Bergman, 1975).

Just like normal children, toddlers with Down syndrome evince visual self-recognition in the mirror-and-rouge paradigm (Lewis & Brooks-Gunn, 1979) when they reach a mental age of approximately 2 years (Hill & Tomlin, 1981; Loveland, 1987; Mans, Cicchetti, & Sroufe, 1978). In this procedure, infants see their reflections in a mirror for a brief period in the presence of their mothers and an experimenter. Then the experimenter surreptitiously dots rouge on the infants' noses. Visual self-recognition is inferred if the infants touch their noses while watching themselves in the mirror. In addition to self-recognition, toddlers with Down syndrome evince the same concomitant positive affect seen in cognitively equivalent nonhandicapped children, suggesting that they "feel positive" about themselves.

## SYMBOLIC REPRESENTATION AND FURTHER SELF/OTHER DIFFERENTIATION (24–36 MONTHS)

Between 24 and 36 months, toddlers learn to construct even more differentiated mental representations of animate and inanimate objects (Greenspan & Porges, 1984), and language and play become a way to represent the growing awareness of self and other. Children increasingly can label emotions, intentions, and cognitions, and they exhibit their growing social awareness through symbolic play (Beeghly & Cicchetti, 1987; Cicchetti & Beeghly, 1987b).

Investigations of play, language, and cognition have burgeoned in recent years (Bretherton, 1984; Rubin et al., 1983). Using language and play to represent early conceptions of relationships is an age-appropriate manifestation of growing awareness of self and other (Bretherton, 1984). In normally developing children this awareness typically emerges and is elaborated during the second and third years. For example, self-descriptive utterances are used more frequently as children provide verbal accompaniments to their ongoing behavior (Kagan, 1981). In addition, children increasingly can label the emotional states, intentions, and cognitions of both themselves and others (Bretherton & Beeghly, 1982), and they begin to use their own names and personal pronouns appropriately. Moreover, self-related language becomes increasingly decontextualized, with children first speaking primarily about themselves in the here and now and then discussing the actions and internal states of nonpresent others or hypothetical contexts.

Children also represent their growing social understanding in symbolic play. As in other forms of symbolization, the representation of self and other in play undergoes decentration, decontextualization, and integration (Fenson, 1984). Toddlers first play at being themselves and then project their own behavior onto other recipients, such as dolls. By the end of the third year children can represent the behavior of several interacting replicas in an integrated fashion and engage in sociodramatic play involving rudimentary role taking (Watson & Fischer, 1977).

Beeghly and Cicchetti (1987) found that children with Down syndrome showed similar but delayed sequences of development. In both language and play, they first represented themselves symbolically. With increasing age and cognitive maturity, their language and play became more decentered, integrated, and decontextualized. Only the most cognitively mature children used language and play to represent hypothetical situations involving self and other. Children with Down syndrome were significantly more advanced in symbolic play maturity than controls matched on mean length of utterance (MLU) (but not MA-matched controls). However, they did differ from their language controls when *linguistic* representations of self and other were analyzed. These results suggest that despite the similarity in developmental sequence in both domains, children with Down syndrome may be more advanced in nonlinguistic domains of symbolic representation. Both linguistic and nonlinguistic variables are correlated significantly with mental age for children with Down syndrome, attesting to the coherence of symbolic development in these children.

Finally, children with Down syndrome show increasingly differentiated concepts of self and other in play. During play, their self-related language (e.g., talking about their ongoing activities and internal states, using personal pronouns) was related to growth in both symbolic and cognitive development. In addition, parallel advances were found in their use of language as a communicative social tool (Beeghly & Cicchetti, 1987).

In summary, these findings on the development of children with Down syndrome are useful in elucidating principles related to the organization and coherence of development. I will continue by describing our work with children who have been maltreated.

## Contributions That the Study of Maltreated Children Can Make to Understanding Emotions and the Organization and Integration of Development

When prominent and pervasive disturbances exist in the parent-child-environment transaction, as often occurs when children are maltreated, the child is at heightened risk for the negative effects of the "continuum of caretaking casualty" (Sameroff & Chandler, 1975). Research on the socioemotional development of maltreated children and, more broadly, on the integration and organization of ontogenesis has both theoretical and practical relevance. It is essential for increasing our understanding of the developmental sequelae of maltreatment. Implicitly, research on the consequences of maltreatment permits us to learn how forms of parenting dysfunction more extreme than those typically studied in the normal parenting literature affect development and enable us to validate existing concepts of what constitutes "good," "average," and "poor" parenting, including the ecological and biological factors that may act as potentiating (risk) or compensating (buffering) factors (Belsky, 1984; Belsky & Vondra, 1989; Cicchetti & Rizley, 1981; Garbarino, 1977; Garbarino & Gilliam, 1980; King & Cicchetti, 1989; Rutter, 1989).

Furthermore, such research will contribute to a truly integrative developmental theory. For example, issues such as the effects of early experience, the continuity/discontinuity of adaptive and maladaptive functioning, and the interrelation among developmental domains all can be greatly informed through the study of child maltreatment. Likewise a developmental perspective will prove useful for delineating the roots, etiology, course, and nature of the maladaptation and the development of compensatory mechanisms in the face of adversity (Cicchetti & Rizley, 1981; Farber & Egeland, 1987).

In addition, intervention is being provided to these children and their families without sufficient empirical data on the developmental consequences of child maltreatment (Cicchetti & Aber, 1980; Cicchetti, Taraldson, & Egeland, 1978; Zigler, 1976). A developmental scheme is necessary if treatment is to be appropriately timed and guided (see, e.g., Cicchetti et al., 1978; Cicchetti, Toth, & Bush, 1988; Cicchetti, Toth, Bush, & Gillespie, 1988; Wald, Carlsmith, & Leiderman, 1988; Wolfe, 1987; Wolfe, Edwards, Manion, & Koverola, 1988).

Finally, given existing conditions such as the confusion over what constitutes maltreatment, the sharp rise in official reports of child maltreatment, and the real limitations of human and financial resources to address the issue, I believe that knowledge of the development of maltreated children can greatly assist clinicians, special educators, and policymakers who confront these problems daily (Aber, Allen, Carlson, & Cicchetti, 1989; Cicchetti, Toth, & Hennessey, 1989). One way this can occur is by validating existing definitions of the subtypes of maltreatment (Aber & Zigler, 1981; Besharov, 1981; Cicchetti & Aber, 1980; Cicchetti & Barnett, in press; Juvenile Justice Standards Project, 1977). As Aber and Zigler (1981) have discussed, while specifying actual physical harm is a relatively straightforward procedure, it is exceedingly difficult to document emotional damage such as depression, anxiety, or withdrawal. Studies such as those reported in this chapter begin to sketch ways to operationalize and dimensionalize emotional harm (see Cicchetti & Barnett, in press, for an elaboration of why we need a developmentally sensitive, scientifically sound nosology of child maltreatment).

## THEORETICAL MODELS OF MALTREATMENT

Child maltreatment is a heterogeneous problem. In mode of maltreatment, symptomatology, etiology, and sequelae, there are subtle and complex differences of type and severity (Cicchetti & Barnett, in press; Cicchetti & Rizley, 1981). The influx of developmental theorizing into this field has resulted in appropriately complex etiological models and a rich framework for conceptualizing the effects that maltreatment has upon adaptive and maladaptive ontogenetic processes (Cicchetti, 1987; Cicchetti & Olsen, 1990; Wolfe, 1987).

Rather than continuing the historical emphasis on single etiological factors such as parental psychopathology, abject poverty, situational stress, social isolation, or an unsupportive ecology (see Belsky, 1980; Cicchetti et al., 1978; Garbarino, 1977; and Parke & Collmer, 1975, for reviews), theorists and researchers increasingly define child maltreatment as multifactorial in origin (Cicchetti, 1987; Cicchetti & Rizley, 1981). Likewise, children's developmental outcomes are viewed as having multiple, interrelated causes rather than as being the direct outcomes of singular antecedents (Cicchetti & Rizley, 1981; Sameroff & Chandler, 1975). Consequently, an adequate model for conceptualizing maltreatment phenomena must be complex and developmental, allowing for multiple pathways to adaptive and maladaptive outcomes (see Bertalanffy, 1968; Weiss, 1969a, 1969b; Wilden, 1980).

The organizational approach and transactional model described earlier are again relevant. A transactional model of child maltreatment decries reductionism. In particular, it denies that either normal or pathological processes can be seen as emerging characteristics of, for example, some biological process or some history of reinforcement or some type of parental socialization *alone*. To apply a transactional model of development to child maltreatment, one must consider the specific risk factors associated with its occurrence. Focusing on the concept of "risk factors," Cicchetti and Rizley (1981) extended Sameroff and Chandler's (1975) transactional model to the etiology and intergenerational transmission of child maltreatment. Cicchetti and Rizley (1981) classify risk factors into two broad categories—*potentiating factors*, which increase the probability of maltreatment, and *compensatory factors*, which decrease it. Under each category, two subgroupings are distinguished—*transient*, fluctuating "state" factors and more permanent, *enduring* conditions or attributes.

Enduring vulnerability factors include all relatively long-term conditions or attributes that potentiate maltreatment. These may be biological (e.g., physical or behavioral anomalies that make child rearing unrewarding or difficult), historical (e.g., a parent with a history of being maltreated), psychological (e.g., parental or child psychopathology, personality attributes such as poor frustration tolerance or high trait levels of aggression and anger), or ecological (e.g., high stress levels, inadequate social networks or chaotic neighborhoods, or maltreatment-promoting societal values; see Belsky, 1980, and Gabarino, 1977). Transient challengers include the short-term conditions and stresses confronting families that may cause a predisposed parent to maltreat a child (e.g., physical injury or illness, legal difficulties, marital or family problems, discipline problems, or a child's entering a more difficult developmental period). Long-term protective factors comprise those relatively enduring or permanent conditions or attributes that decrease the risk of maltreatment or its transmission across generations (e.g., a parent's history of good parenting or a secure intimate relationship between the parental figures). Transient buffers include factors that may protect a family from stress, thereby reducing the probability of maltreatment and its transmission (e.g., sudden improvement in financial conditions, periods of marital harmony, a child's transition out of a difficult development period).

Cicchetti and Rizley (1981) contend that we must examine both positive and negative "risk factors" in order to understand the occurrence of maltreatment as well as the specific forms it will take (see Cicchetti & Barnett, in press). According to the transactional model, it is when potentiating factors override compensatory ones that an act of abuse is committed or maltreatment is allowed to begin. Furthermore, Cicchetti and Rizley (1981) state that the intergenerational transmission of maltreatment can best be understood by examining the transmission of risk factors. Cross-generational transmission must operate either by increasing vulnerability or by decreasing protective factors.

Cicchetti and Braunwald (1984) elaborated Cicchetti and Rizley's model to account for the processes leading to the formation of competence, defined as the use of internal and external resources to attain a satisfactory developmental outcome. Following the organizational perspective, adaptation at a particular point in the life course implies the successful resolution of the developmental task or tasks most salient for that period (Waters & Sroufe, 1983). Cicchetti and Braunwald's model, which can be applied more generally to the developmental sequelae of child maltreatment, underscores the ongoing transaction between a variety of factors that may support or inhibit competent behavior at any particular point during ontogenesis. Following Cicchetti and Rizley (1981), within this model two broad categories influence developmental outcome: *potentiating factors*, which increase the probability of manifesting incompetence, and *compensatory factors*, which increase the likelihood manifesting competence. Potentiating factors include the enduring influence of vulnerability factors (long-standing psychological, environmental, sociocultural, or biological factors that may inhibit competence) and the transient influence of challengers such as stressful life events. Similarly, compensatory factors include both enduring protective factors and transient buffers.

Researchers investigating child maltreatment increasingly use the transactional model to guide their work. Congruent with a basic tenet of developmental psychopathology, a normal developmental perspective can inform the study of a high-risk or atypical population (Cicchetti, 1984; Cicchetti & Sroufe, 1976; Rutter, 1986). Conversely, by extending this model to the developmental consequences of maltreatment, we can affirm, challenge, and elaborate our knowledge of normal ontogenesis.

## EMOTIONAL DEVELOPMENT IN MALTREATED CHILDREN

As is true of scientific investigations on the developmental sequelae of child maltreatment, empirical research on the emotional development of maltreated children has become the focus of systematic psychological study only during the past two decades (Cicchetti & Carlson, 1989). Studies of the consequences of maltreatment are crucial for improving the quality of clinical, legal, advocacy, and policymaking decisions for abused/neglected children (Aber, Allen, Carlson, & Cicchetti, 1989; Cicchetti & Aber, 1980; Juvenile Justice Standards Project, 1977; Wald, Carlsmith, & Leiderman, 1988). Decisions concerning such topics as confirming reports of child maltreatment, when to remove a child coercively from the home, how to develop and implement developmentally appropriate and sensitive interventions to meet the psychological needs of maltreated children, and how to evaluate these treatment efforts would all profit immeasurably from a more methodologically sound and comprehensive data base on the sequelae of maltreatment (Aber & Cicchetti, 1984; Cicchetti & Barnett, in press; Cicchetti et al., 1978; Goldstein, Freud, & Solnit, 1973, 1979; Wakefield & Underwager, 1988).

In their review and critique of the empirical literature on the consequences of maltreatment, Aber and Cicchetti (1984) concluded that the vast majority of research on the socioemotional and cognitive sequelae of child abuse and neglect that was published before the late 1970s was atheoretical, cross-sectional, and often seriously flawed both conceptually and methodologically. Recently, a similar conclusion was reached with respect to the early research literature on the language development of abused/neglected children (Cicchetti & Olsen, 1990). Beginning with work published over the past 10 to 15 years, significant gains have been made in our understanding of the developmental sequelae of child maltreatment.

Abnormalities in the development of affective communication between maltreated infants and their caretakers have been studied by Gaensbauer and his colleagues. Gaensbauer and Sands (1979) identified six patterns of distorted affective communications between infant and caretaker, including affective withdrawal, lack of pleasure, inconsistency/unpredictability, shallowness, ambivalence/ambiguity, and negative affective communications (e.g., distress, anger, sadness). In a subsequent study, Gaensbauer, Mrazek, and Harmon (1980) delineated four affective patterns that appeared to be relatively consistent and that could represent the predominant communicative pattern of a mother-infant dyad. These four groups were labeled *developmentally and affectively retarded* (characterized by lack of social responsiveness, emotional blunting, and inattentiveness to the environment); *depressed* (exhibiting inhibition, withdrawal, aimless quality of play, and sad and depressed facial expressions); *ambivalent/affectively labile* (showing sudden shifts from engagement and pleasure to withdrawal and anger); and *angry* (characterized by active, disorganized play and low frustration tolerance, with frequent angry outbursts). Although the direction of causality of these atypical communication patterns remains ambiguous, it is apparent that deviant styles of affective displays, decreased responsiveness and reciprocal interactions, aberrations in the patterns of initiating, maintaining, or terminating interaction, and deviations in the capacity to express emotional states tend to characterize the maltreating mother-infant dyad (Aber & Cicchetti, 1984; Crittenden, 1981, 1988; Crittenden & Ainsworth, 1989). The work of Frodi and Lamb (1980) reveals that maltreating parents have different psychophysiological responses to infants' cries, thereby suggesting that they may be less effective than nonmaltreating parents in responding to the affective expressions of their own children.

During the neonatal period, the infant's affective expression is immediate and unmodulated. At this point the infant's affect is sensorimotor, controlled by subcortical programs. Although socialization has not yet played a role in the expression of affect, the young infant has been neurally primed to be aware of and responsive to the emotional signals of its caretakers—to be affectively influenced by others. As Malatesta and Izard (1984) have stated, these underlying neural programs ensure that the basic components of emotional expression occur during normal development; however, it is only with input from a social partner that there is continuity in affective expression as well as increased modulation and affective regulation (see Thompson, this volume).

Caregivers can exert a major impact on the socialization of affect. Specifically, the types of affect a child is capable of expressing, the range, variation, intensity, and duration of affective expression, the contexts in which emotions are expressed, and the regulation of emotional displays all can be affected (Cicchetti & Schneider-Rosen, 1984a, 1986; see also Saarni, this volume; Thompson, this volume). An expanding area of inquiry on the interface between linguistic and emotional development, and one I believe holds great promise for augmenting our understanding of normal and abnormal emotional development, is internal-state language usage (Bretherton &

Beeghly, 1982). It has been suggested that emotional language helps one control nonverbal emotional expressions, which in turn enhances regulation of the emotions themselves (Hesse & Cicchetti, 1982). According to this view, then, parents who frequently use emotional language to interpret their own and others' (nonverbal) emotional expressions in effect provide their children with mechanisms to help control their nonverbal emotional expressions. In contrast, parents who use emotional language to intellectualize or defend against emotional experience may be exhibiting an over-controlled coping style. Thus, one can argue, they transfer their coping skills to their children through their use of emotional language (Hesse & Cicchetti, 1982; see also Thompson, this volume). One could hypothesize, then, that maltreating parents may transmit their emotional styles to their offspring in this way. Therefore we thought it important to study maltreating parents' emotional speech and their socialization of emotional language in their children. It also would be important to examine the parents' inappropriate or maladaptive labeling of emotion.

Sharing information about intentions, cognitions, and feelings is crucial to regulating human interaction. Although infants produce and comprehend nonverbal emotional signals by the end of the first year, it is only after mastering verbal internal-state labels that young children can communicate about past or anticipated feelings, goals, intentions, and cognitions. Moreover, internal-state language allows companions to clarify misunderstandings and misinterpretations during ongoing interactions.

Previous research with middle socioeconomic status (SES) samples has shown that internal-state words first emerge during the second year and become prevalent during the third. By 28 months, most children master verbal labels for perception (the five senses), physiological states, volition, and ability. More than half discuss emotions, moral conformity, and obligation, whereas only a few begin to talk about cognition (thought processes). Children also become increasingly able to use internal-state labels for both self and others, reflecting a growing awareness of self as distinct (Bretherton & Beeghly, 1982). Cicchetti and Beeghly (1987b) examined internal-state language in 30-month-old maltreated and nonmaltreated toddlers from welfare-dependent homes during interactions with their mothers in a laboratory setting. In addition, maternal reports of children's internal-state language were compared with similar reports by middle-SES mothers.

Although maltreated and nonmaltreated children did not differ significantly in receptive vocabulary, Cicchetti and Beeghly (1987b) found significant group differences on productive and internal-state language variables. Maltreated toddlers used proportionately fewer internal-state words, showed less differentiation in attributional focus, and were more context bound in their use of internal-state language. In contrast, with only two exceptions the maltreated and nonmaltreated children did not differ significantly in the categorical content of their internal-state language (e.g., words about perception and volition). However, nonmaltreated children produced proportionally more utterances about physiological states (e.g., hunger, thirst, state of consciousness) and about negative affect (e.g., hate, disgust, anger, bad feelings). For the most part the distribution of words in each category was markedly similar to that observed in middle-SES 28-month-olds. Children spoke most about volition and perception and least about cognition.

Analyses of the maternal interview data yielded similar patterns. Maltreating mothers reported that their 30-month-olds produced fewer internal-state words and attributed internal states to fewer social agents than reported for children of nonmaltreating mothers, corroborating the observational findings. In addition, mothers' reports concerning the categorical content of their children's language did not differ by child group. In support of the validity of the interview data for use with low-SES populations, mothers' reports of children's internal-state language were significantly correlated with observations of such language use.

The results of the maternal language interview revealed that, with very few exceptions, the maltreated toddlers produced far fewer internal-state words than did middle-SES nonmaltreated youngsters of the same age (Bretherton & Beeghly, 1982). In contrast, the percentages of *nonmaltreated* children reported to use different categories of internal-state language were markedly similar to the percentages of middle-SES children. Similar patterns were observed for children's ability to use internal-state words. That is, maltreated toddlers lagged far behind their nonmaltreated comparisons in using internal-state words about the self and others. The non-maltreated lower-SES children were very similar in this capacity to nonmaltreated middle-SES youngsters.

Maltreated toddlers may use fewer internal-state words because their parents disapprove of expressing affect or certain types of affect. In effect, these children may become "overcontrolled" as they try to meet parental demands. A recent study conducted by Kropp and Haynes (1987) supports this hypothesis. These authors found that abusive mothers had more difficulty decoding specific emotional signals. In particular, they were significantly more likely than comparison mothers to label negative affect as positive. Cicchetti and Beeghly's (1987b) results on emotional language usage fit nicely with these findings. Specifically, Cicchetti and Beeghly found that maltreated toddlers spoke less about negative emotions than did nonmaltreated comparison youngsters. One plausible interpretation is that maltreating mothers' socialization of affect interferes with certain affects, prevents maltreated children from being in touch with their true feelings, and leads to problems in developing emotional control. Two studies lend credence to our interpretations. Camras and her colleagues found that abused children were less able to decode facial expressions of emotion than a comparison group of nonmaltreated children (Camras, Grow, & Ribordy, 1983). Additionally, in our laboratory we discovered that upon reunion with their 12-month-old infants after two brief separations within the context of the Strange Situation, maltreating mothers used more attentional imperatives (e.g., "get the ball"; "go play") and less language about negative internal states than a demographically matched sample of nonmaltreating mothers (Cicchetti, Barnett, & Carlson, 1989). The nonmaltreating mothers dealt openly with their babies' feelings (e.g., "Are you okay?" "Are you sad?" "What's the matter?") and were more likely to have secure attachment relationships with their infants.

## THE INTEGRATION AND ORGANIZATION OF EMOTIONAL DEVELOPMENT

The integration and organization of emotional development in maltreated children have just begun to capture the attention of developmentalists. Such research is necessary not only to expand our knowledge of the developmental sequelae of maltreatment, but also to help us understand normal ontogenesis. For example, the investigation of emotional development in maltreated children has made significant contributions to our understanding of the relation between developmental domains (e.g., emotional and cognitive, socioemotional and linguistic) and has generated information critical to resolving the long-standing controversy over the role social factors play in language acquisition.

## THE RELATION BETWEEN EMOTION AND COGNITION IN MALTREATED CHILDREN

Schneider-Rosen and Cicchetti (1984) examined the affective responses of maltreated and nonmaltreated toddlers in response to their mirror images before and after a dot of rouge had been placed on their noses. These investigators found that only maltreated youngsters manifested impairment in their affective reaction to this event. Although there were no cognitive differences between the two groups of toddlers and no differences in visual self-recognition abilities per se, after seeing themselves in the mirror, a significantly greater percentage of the nonmaltreated comparison youngsters evinced an increase in positive affect following the application of rouge (74%), whereas a larger proportion of the maltreated toddlers displayed neutral or negative affect (78%). These findings suggest that maltreated toddlers attempt to mask their feelings or experience themselves primarily in negative ways (e.g., feel bad about themselves, feel shameful).

Earlier I noted that maltreated children used fewer internal-state words than demographically and cognitively matched nonmaltreated youngsters (Cicchetti & Beeghly, 1987b) and suggested that maltreated mothers may socialize their infants at an early age not to express or not to be in touch with their true feelings (Cicchetti, Barnett, & Carlson, 1989). In the present study, the absence of cognitive differences between the two groups suggests that cognition is necessary but not sufficient for the emergence of visual self-recognition. Consequently, it appears that emotion and cognition operate as separate, yet interactive, systems in maltreated youngsters and that such children may have a disequilibrium in the cognitive-emotional relation.

The interactive nature of emotional and cognitive processes also have been elucidated through the study of cognitive control development in maltreated children. To explore whether cognition plays differing organizing roles when acting upon various types of affect-arousing stimuli, Rieder and Cicchetti (1989) evaluated cognitive control development and cognitive-affective balance in maltreated children. Cognitive controls are viewed as coordinating the requirements of external stimuli with those of internal fantasies and affects (Santostefano, 1978, 1985). Cognitive activity is viewed as central to maintaining a balance between inner fantasies, affects, and needs and outer information. External stimuli and contexts, whether molar (e.g., a doctor's office) or molecular (e.g., a psychological test item), are viewed as containing "a call for action" (Sarason & Sarason, 1981), that is, a prescription for particular motor and cognitive responses and emotions. Similarly, fantasies, while condensing and representing past emotional and personal experiences, also call for action when imposed on and construing a situation or context. Cognitive controls register the call for action (requirements) embedded in a particular context; they simultaneously register the call for action (requirements) of the activated fantasies construing the stimuli and associated affects. Cognitive controls are viewed as coordinating the attributes and call for action of a context with those of the activated fantasy. The actions the child takes (whether motor, cognitive, or emotional) stem from the coordination achieved in dealing with the requirements of both external stimuli and inner fantasies and affects. Cognitive-affective balance refers to this coordinating process, which when successful fosters adaptation, psychological development, and learning.

Rieder and Cicchetti (1989) assessed the cognitive-affective balance maintained in maltreated and nonmaltreated children by two cognitive controls—field articulation and leveling/sharpening. Field articulation concerns how one deals with a visual field that contains information defined as relevant or irrelevant to the task at hand, from attending equally to relevant and irrelevant information to attending selectively. Leveling/sharpening concerns how one maintains images of past information and compares these images with present perceptions. This cognitive control ranges from constructing global images that are fused with present perceptions so that changes in information are not readily noticed to constructing articulate images that are distinguished from present perceptions so that similarities and differences between past and present information are highlighted. Conceptually, we chose to examine these particular cognitive controls because of their relevance to the maltreatment literature (e.g., maltreated children frequently are described as hypervigilant and prone to misinterpret the actions of others [Aber & Cicchetti, 1984]).

Maltreated and nonmaltreated children were presented with stimuli that did or did not pull for aggressive fantasies and affects. The aggressive versus nonaggressive stimuli elicited different patterns of cognitive control functioning for the entire group of children. When dealing with aggressive versus nonaggressive stimuli, all children, regardless of maltreatment status, exhibited a significant shift toward avoiding aggressive stimuli. With field articulation, attention was deployed selectively to avoid the aggressive distracting stimuli; with leveling/sharpening, cognition shifted toward leveling of aggressive stimuli, a result that corroborates previous findings (Santostefano & Rieder, 1984). Because children tend to experience aggressive fantasies when attending to aggressive stimuli, these findings suggest that for all children the call for action of aggressive fantasies prescribes avoiding aggressive stimuli, whether this results in greater or lesser task efficiency.

As predicted, a history of maltreatment was significantly related to cognitive control functioning. When presented with aggressive and nonaggressive test stimuli, cognitive controls reorganized responses differently in each group. When field articulation was assessed, maltreated children were more distracted by aggressive stimuli than were nonmaltreated children, as evidenced by the greater number of errors they made in response to such stimuli. In addition, maltreated children recalled a greater number of distracting aggressive stimuli than did nonmaltreated children. Essentially, the requirements (call for action) of aggressive fantasies of maltreated children prescribed a coordination/balance that called for the ready assimilation of aggressive stimuli, even though this resulted in less cognitive efficiency and impaired task performance. Conversely, the requirements of the aggressive fantasies of nonmal-treated children prescribed a coordination/balance between fantasy and stimuli that resulted in their avoiding aggressive stimuli, with attention being selectively withheld from aggressive information.

With leveling/sharpening, maltreated children showed less em-bellishment and distortion of aggressive information. When cogni-tive control development was examined independent of test stimuli, maltreated children showed developmental impairment in leveling/sharpening. That is, the cognitive organizations maltreated children employed insulated them from external information, such that ex-ternal stimuli were avoided, and memory images of outer informa-tion were global and undifferentiated.

In summary, this study demonstrates that all children, regard-less of maltreatment status, tend to avoid aggressive stimuli. When we explore cognitive control functioning in relation to maltreat-ment, maltreated children differ from nonmaltreated children re-gardless of the stimulus material. Finally, and perhaps most impor-tant, in terms of shifts manifested when coordinating aggressive versus nonaggressive stimuli, maltreated children assimilate ag-gressive stimuli more readily.

How might we understand these results? Perhaps hyper-vigilance and ready assimilation of aggressive stimuli initially de-velop as an adaptive coping strategy in the maltreating environ-ment, alerting the child to imminent danger and keeping affects from rising to a level that would impede adaptation. Efficient assimi-lation (sharpening) of aggressive stimuli might help the child iden-tify specific elements of the current situation (e.g., similarities and differences between this and past situations) and determine the most adaptive response.

The developmental impairment in leveling/sharpening ob-served in maltreated children also may well result from their history of maltreatment—a child exposed to an atypical environment may attempt to adapt by turning away from external stimuli so as to mini-mize their impact (Santostefano, 1978; see also Schneider-Rosen, Braunwald, Carlson, & Cicchetti, 1985). In this way, leveling as a cognitive strategy may originate adaptively in the maltreating envi-ronment but gradually rigidify, becoming maladaptive in more typi-cal settings. The leveling of nonaggressive information also may originate as an effort to gain protection from an onslaught of information. By carefully attending to (sharpening) aggressive cues in the environment and turning away from less significant input, the maltreated child may feel better prepared to deal with adversity.

The findings regarding cognitive-affective balance also may contribute to our understanding of various peer and socialization problems (e.g., heightened aggressiveness, physically assaulting peers, rejecting friendly overtures from peers) that have been observed in maltreated children (George & Main, 1979; Herrenkohl & Herrenkohl, 1981; Kaufman & Cicchetti, 1989; Kinard, 1980; Reidy, 1977). It seems reasonable that children who exhibit impairments in cognitive control functioning and who readily assimilate aggressive stimuli would be likely to have difficulty interacting with peers (Dodge, 1986; Dodge, Murphy, & Buchsbaum, 1984). The cognitive-affective balance they maintain may lead maltreated children to be overly attuned to the potentially aggressive components of the situation, to the extent that their peer relations become fraught with fear, tension, and defensive acting-out. Moreover, this stance also may adversely affect their interactions with adults.

There also is an interesting theoretical link between the present results and recent research on the attachment relationships of maltreated infants and toddlers. A number of investigators have found that these children tend to develop insecure attachments to their primary caregivers (Carlson, Cicchetti, Barnett, & Braunwald, 1989; Crittenden, 1988; Egeland & Sroufe, 1981; Schneider-Rosen et al., 1985; see the discussion below for an elaboration). Egeland and Sroufe (1981) also have found a subsequent decrease in the insecurely attached child's environmental exploration and attempts at independent mastery. They suggest that infants who have been unable to develop a secure attachment to their primary caregiver cannot, as toddlers, use the attachment relationship as a base of security from which to explore the world. Perhaps the differences in cognitive control functioning observed in maltreated children can best be viewed as developmental successors to earlier difficulties in forming secure attachments to primary caregivers.

Specifically, I am suggesting that the poor-quality working models (cf. Bretherton, 1985, this volume; Bowlby, 1980) that maltreated children develop early in life predispose them to the impairments in cognitive control and cognitive-affective balance described here. Bowlby describes working models as an individual's conscious or unconscious mental representations "of the world and of himself in it, with the aid of which he perceives events, forecasts the future, and constructs his plans" (Bowlby, 1973, p. 203). These working models are constructed out of children's own actions, the feedback they receive from these actions, and the actions of caregivers (see Bretherton, this volume). Children with sensitive caregivers learn to view themselves as worthy of care, whereas children with unresponsive caregivers come to see themselves as unlovable. Once organized, these internal working models tend to operate outside conscious awareness and to resist dramatic change (Bowlby, 1980).

In a related vein, Dodge and his colleagues (Dodge, 1986; Dodge et al., 1984) have argued that aberrant behaviors such as excessive aggression may result from a breakdown or deviation in social information processing. Moreover, Dodge (1986) has shown that a high percentage of aggressive behavior in children occurs in socially ambiguous situations. Camras et al. (1983) have demonstrated that maltreated children have problems in decoding nonverbal emotional expressions. Kropp and Haynes (1987) have provided similar results for maltreating adults. These data are consistent with those of Dodge and his colleagues, who posited deficits in the social information processing capacities of children who interpret ambiguous social stimuli as having aggressive intent. I believe that processing deficits, as well as immature cognitive control functioning, may be related to the poor-quality working models and negative expectations that maltreated children have formed about interpersonal relations (cf. Aber & Allen, 1987; Dean, Malik, Richards, & Stringer, 1986).

## THE RELATION BETWEEN SOCIOEMOTIONAL AND LINGUISTIC DEVELOPMENT

During the past several decades, much theoretical and empirical work has been directed toward identifying aspects of the social environment that contribute to the ontogenesis of language acquisition (Bruner, 1975; Golinkoff, 1983; Snow & Ferguson, 1977; Vygotsky,

1978; Werner & Kaplan, 1963). Most of this research falls into two categories. Several investigators have presented evidence that the course and outcome of communicative development in children may be affected by the type, quantity, and quality of verbal input they receive (e.g., Clarke-Stewart, 1973; Cross, 1978; McCartney, Scarr, Phillips, Grajek, & Schwartz, 1982; Nelson, 1977; Snow & Ferguson, 1977; Wells, 1980). Although there is some corroboration of the contention that language acquisition is enhanced by sensitive and contingent verbal feedback to children's signals that is heavily weighted to the here and now (Snow & Gilbreath, 1983), many of the assertions of sociolinguists have yet to be confirmed (Gleitman, Newport, & Gleitman, 1984).

Additionally, other researchers have stressed the specific importance of synchronous caregiver-infant interactions in achieving communicative competence (Bretherton, Bates, Benigni, Camaioni, & Volterra, 1979). Because differences in parental interactive styles have been related to individual differences in the quality of attachment relationships (Ainsworth et al., 1978; Goldsmith & Alansky, 1987; Lamb, Thompson, et al., 1985), one might expect that the linguistic development of the securely attached infant would be enhanced by the more sensitive and responsive social input received from the caregiver. Despite the logic of this assumption, few studies that have examined the links between quality of attachment and the child's linguistic growth have yielded statistically significant findings (see Bretherton et al., 1979, for a review).

This omission has resulted in arguments that language may be buffered against possible variations by the restricted range of maternal input found in the middle-class dyads who constituted the samples in most studies (Bates, Bretherton, Beeghly-Smith, & McNew, 1982). That is, it may be that a threshold level of input is provided by most middle-class samples. Bates et al. (1982) suggest that the relation between social experience and language may be observed more clearly in extreme cases and urge the study of naturally occurring atypical populations in which the threshold amounts of social and verbal input may not occur. Thus, perhaps the best way to demonstrate the relation between socioemotional experience and language acquisition is to study clinical populations who receive substantially different amounts or quality of social input. As yet another "experiment in nature," child maltreatment presents an opportunity to investigate this question empirically.

A growing body of literature on the characteristics of maltreating parent-child interactions indicates that many maltreated children are reared in atypical social environments. Observations both at home and in the laboratory reveal that the interaction patterns of abusive and neglectful mother-infant dyads often are typified by a low degree of reciprocity, minimal verbal interaction, limited playful exchanges, and the absence of harmony (Burgess & Conger, 1978; Crittenden, 1981; Egeland & Sroufe, 1981; Gaensbauer & Sands, 1979; Herrenkohl, Herrenkohl, Toedter, & Yanushevski, 1984; Wasserman, Green, & Allen, 1983). Moreover, a number of researchers have reported a higher incidence of insecure attachments among maltreated infants and toddlers, which they interpret as resulting from the inharmonious or inconsistent experience with the caregiver (Crittenden, 1988; Egeland & Sroufe, 1981; Schneider-Rosen et al., 1985; see below for an elaboration).

Observational studies of mother-child interaction in maltreating families suggest that maltreated children are raised in an unresponsive environment that fails to foster communicative exchanges. If communication is affected by the quality and quantity of conversational input, then maltreatment should have a deleterious effect upon linguistic development.

Whereas most investigations of the psycholinguistic sequelae of maltreatment have focused on deviations from the norm on standard linguistic measures (Blager & Martin, 1976), recent theoretical and empirical work in developmental psycholinguistics has emphasized the acquisition of pragmatic skills (e.g., Bates, 1976; Dore, 1979; Lieven, 1978). The observations reported earlier of maltreated children's deficient conversations suggest that pragmatic skills may be particularly at risk and that an investigation of communicative and discourse abilities might clarify how maltreatment affects communicative development.

Until recent years, few investigations have addressed how distortions in social and verbal interactions in maltreating families affect early language development. In one of the few studies relating maltreated toddlers' communicative development to their mothers' verbal style, Westerman and Haustead (1982) compared the conversations between an abused child and the natural mother with those of the same child and the foster mother. These investigators found that the abusive natural mother was less able than the foster mother to use linguistic forms that promote communication, thereby placing excessive burdens upon the child for managing the dialogue. Furthermore, Braunwald (1983) also reported that the two abused toddlers she observed were unable to initiate and sustain age-appropriate forms of communication.

Two recent studies in our laboratory have addressed the communicative development of maltreated youngsters, paying particular attention to pragmatics. Gersten, Coster, Schneider-Rosen, Carlson, and Cicchetti (1986) examined the syntactic maturity (mean length of utterance), vocabulary development, and categories of functional communication used by 25-month-old maltreated and comparison toddlers while they were engaged in two free-play interactions with their mothers in the laboratory. The children's quality of attachment to their mothers also was assessed using the Strange Situation (Ainsworth & Wittig, 1969). A modified, developmentally appropriate coding scheme for classifying attachment security in 2-year-olds was used (see Schneider-Rosen et al., 1985, for details). Gersten and her colleagues found a strong relation between quality of attachment and particular language-production variables. Specifically, securely attached maltreated and nonmaltreated toddlers were more likely to use complex syntax, an elaborate vocabulary, and more utterances that referred to objects, events, themselves, and others.

Despite the high frequency of insecure attachment in the maltreated subjects and the association of insecure attachment with less developed communicative behavior, no relation between maltreatment and language was found in these 25-month-olds. One possible explanation is that the toddlers were in such an early stage of language development that it was too soon to detect environmental variation. That is, the cumulative effects of adverse environmental influences may appear only after basic communication patterns have been established (Bretherton et al., 1979; Hardy-Brown, Plomin, & DeFries, 1981).

Consequently, Coster, Gersten, Beeghly, and Cicchetti (1989) chose to investigate a group of maltreated children who were at a more advanced stage of early language development to ascertain if these youngsters begin to manifest deviations in their pragmatic development. In addition to investigating the children's performance, they examined the mothers' communication to learn what concurrent input might be shaping the children's language. The literature on mother-child conversation has documented that adults' speech is usually modified in relation to children's developmental level (Bellinger, 1980; Snow, 1977). Many of these modifications are related to comprehension feedback from the child, suggesting they are designed to promote optimal communication with a still-immature partner. A number of researchers have stressed how greatly the mother's ability to respond appropriately to the child's cues influences language development and concept formation (e.g., Barnes, Gutfreund, Satterly, & Wells, 1983; Clarke-Stewart, 1973; Fowler & Swenson, 1979; Nelson, 1973). Others have identified specific ways mothers may help maintain connected discourse with their young partners, such as using many interrogatives (Brown, Bellugi, & Cazden, 1969; Corsaro, 1979; Holzman, 1972; Snow, 1977). This body of research on normal dyads, in conjunction with what we know about the interaction difficulties of maltreating parents, led us to hypothesize that maltreating parents also might display diminished contingent responsiveness to their children's communications and therefore be less likely to employ devices such as interrogatives to maintain dialogue. Coster and her colleagues also investigated the relation between the functional use of the mothers' communication and the toddlers' use of language to determine whether differences in the mothers' patterns might help explain any differences among the children.

Coster and her collaborators studied two new groups of twenty 31-month-old maltreated toddlers and twenty 31-month-old comparison toddlers and their mothers in the same interactional paradigms used by Gersten et al. (1986). Contrary to the results of Gersten et al. (1986) with 25-month-olds, Coster et al. (1989) found that 31-month-old maltreated toddlers had lower MLUs and were less advanced on all measures of expressive vocabulary as well as on total number of different words used. Because the maltreated and nonmaltreated youngsters did not differ on their total number of utterances, the expressive language differences obtained cannot be attributed to differences in linguistic output. These results are consistent with an organizational perspective in which advances and lags in one domain (e.g., the socioemotional) may have consequences for the emergence and development of functions in another domain (e.g., language; see also Cicchetti & Serafica, 1981; Cicchetti & Sroufe, 1978).

The maltreated toddlers' lags in MLU and in productive vocabulary may limit their ability to convey messages as clearly and fully as the comparison toddlers do. Furthermore, maltreated youngsters differed from the nonmaltreated toddlers in the kinds of messages they used in play interactions with their mothers. They were less likely to offer statements that described their own activities or features of objects in the environment and were less prone to seek information. Instead, they were more likely to give minimal replies and to use "fillers" such as "oh" and "um-hum" that acknowledged the conversation but did not add significant content to it. Their conversation also was more restricted to the immediate present rather than incorporating information beyond the current spatial and temporal context. This pattern of conversation clearly resembles the poverty of content described for the speech of older maltreated children (Blager & Martin, 1976; Elmer, 1981) and suggests that these maltreated toddlers are not using language as a means of positive social exchange.

In addition to limitations in the complexity and richness of their communication, the maltreated children showed a marked deviation in their maintenance of sustained and connected dialogue. They were much less likely to offer comments that were contingent on the current topic and were more likely to terminate a topic after a briefer exchange. Moreover, these children appeared to have less sophisticated mastery of how to use their emerging syntactic systems in social situations. Thus, when a command from the mother called for a specific syntactic form from the child (e.g., when mother says, "What is that?" child must reply with a nominal), maltreated toddlers were less likely to give the correct form of response.

It is noteworthy that these behaviors were observed in a context where measures of the mothers' contingent verbal exchanges did not differ between the two groups, suggesting a lack of skill in the maltreated toddlers that is somewhat independent of the mothers' current structuring of the verbal environment. This lack of conversational skill has particular implications for the toddlers' ability to use their available language skills effectively to negotiate with their environments in or outside the home. Inability to initiate or sustain conversation may limit participation in important social and learning situations and thus constitute a risk factor for failure or deviation in other domains (e.g., peer relations and adaptation to school). Furthermore, the limited complexity of the maltreated toddlers' language may elicit less complex verbal input from parents and other conversational partners, because this input is generally tailored to the perceived level of the child's speech (Bellinger, 1980; Snow, 1977). Even if this limited language at 31 months reflects a reluctance to engage rather than a competence deficit, the compensatory adjustments by conversational partners may eventually contribute to less adequate language skills.

The group differences between maltreated and nonmaltreated toddlers reflect the importance of variations in environmental input for communicative development. However, examining the mothers' concurrent communication failed to reveal any immediate evidence of this variation except in self-related language in the maltreated toddlers. As a group, the maltreating parents were not providing less contingent or elaborated communication during these sessions, suggesting that both groups of parents had the same language capacity and, in the laboratory, used this capacity equivalently. Clearly, if sources of variation in the toddlers' speech are to be traced to caretaker influences, other aspects of interaction must be examined.

Several potential influences deserve further investigation. One of the most important is the verbal and nonverbal affective and interactional features of the mothers' ongoing communication at home. A number of researchers have reported that maltreating parents evince more verbal aggression and offer praise less frequently (Bousha & Twentyman, 1984), ignore their children's communications more often (Wasserman et al., 1983), or use more utterances that convey a negative attitude toward their offspring (Salzinger, Wondolowski-Svensson, Kaplan, Kaplan, & Kristaul, 1984). These negative communications may act as potent deterrents to children's use of language for social exchange, particularly in speaking about their own activities and feelings or engaging in lengthy conversations. These factors also may mediate the previously noted relation between insecure attachment and less-developed communicative behavior in 25-month-olds (Gersten et al., 1986). This work currently is being conducted in our laboratory.

The confluence of findings emerging from these studies has contributed to our understanding of many of the most important theoretical questions on language acquisition. For example, as predicted by a number of attachment and object-relations theorists (Bowlby, 1969/1982; Bretherton, 1985, 1987; Cassidy, 1988; Cicchetti, Cummings, et al., in press; Mahler, Pine, & Bergman, 1975), securely attached youngsters show a more hierarchically organized and integrated "self system" (e.g., affective and cognitive indices reveal marked coherence). In addition, securely attached youngsters use more "self" language. Furthermore, maltreated toddlers use fewer internal-state words, another sign that their self systems are impaired from a very early age (see below under Emotion and Competence). By approximately 30 months there are striking differences in language performance between maltreated children and matched lower-SES nonmaltreated children.

Even though additional research must be conducted on the social bases of language, we believe that together these investigations provide compelling support for theorists who claim that social and emotional factors are important in language development. At present we are embarking on a series of cross-sectional; P1/longitudinal studies to advance our understanding of the development of representational processes and of the contributions that cognitive, language, play, and socioemotional development make to the domain of representation. For example, it has yet to be determined whether attachment status and maltreatment experience contribute differentially to communicative development. Likewise, it remains to be demonstrated whether maltreated children converse in the same way with other adults, both familiar and unfamiliar, as with their mothers. These and other studies of the relation between the existing developmental domains must be undertaken across the life span to provide more comprehensive information about the organization and coherence of development in maltreated children.

A final implication of the work on maltreatment and language deserves mention here. Historically, there has been a major debate on whether factors independent of those risk factors commonly associated with lower-SES membership differentiate maltreated from nonmaltreated children (cf. Aber & Cicchetti, 1984; Elmer, 1977). Studying the two groups' communication skills provides insight not only on this issue but on the impact poverty has on linguistic development (Feagans & Farran, 1982; Hess & Shipman, 1968). Another way of disentangling the effects of low SES and of maltreatment would be to compare groups of lower- and middle-SES maltreated and lower- and middle-SES nonmaltreated children.

## Emotion and Competence: The Effects of Maltreatment on Development

As I noted in the discussion of children with Down syndrome, there are a number of developmental tasks that are considered central at specific points in the life cycle. The investigation of maltreated children's ability to negotiate these stage-salient issues provides an interesting opportunity to test the underlying assumptions about how competent resolution of these tasks is fostered (see Sroufe, 1979b). Because research has not been conducted on how maltreated children resolve the first two stage-salient issues, this discussion will begin with the development of attachment relationships.

### THE DEVELOPMENT OF A SECURE ATTACHMENT RELATIONSHIP (6–12 MONTHS)

Bowlby's attachment theory articulates the functions and processes involved in establishing attachment relationships between parents and their offspring (Bowlby, 1969/1982). Bowlby stressed that, given the importance of the attachment bond to the offspring's survival, infants are able to form attachments to caregivers whose behavior spans a continuum of sensitivity and nurture. Based largely on evidence from animal studies (for reviews see Rajecki, Lamb, & Obmascher, 1978; Reite & Caine, 1983; and Ruppenthal, Arling, Harlow, Sackett, & Suomi, 1976), Bowlby stated that an attachment bond does form under conditions of maltreatment. However, the major compelling issues concern the quality of this attachment and the nature of the "working models" of the self and of the self in relation to others (e.g., caregivers, other adults, peers) that are established under such conditions (see Bretherton, this volume).

Recently a number of well-controlled studies have confirmed Bowlby's predictions and reinforced the findings of animal researchers. As discussed above, studies utilizing the strange situation (Ainsworth & Wittig, 1969) have demonstrated that maltreated children do form attachments to their caregivers but that these attachments are more likely to be insecure than are those of nonmaltreated children (Crittenden, 1988; Egeland & Sroufe, 1981; Lamb, Gaensbauer, Malkin, & Schultz, 1985; Schneider-Rosen et al., 1985).

Among investigators who have studied attachment in maltreated infants using the original ABC coding system, some have become unsettled because there were a number of securely rated attachments. Given the predictions of the Bowlby-Ainsworth attachment theory, secure attachment is not expected under conditions of insensitive caregiving such as would be likely with a maltreating caregiver (Ainsworth, 1980). Some researchers added qualifying comments to their reports of secure attachments among maltreated infants. Gaensbauer and Harmon (1982) noted that abused/neglected infants seen in their single-separation adaptation of the Strange Situation could be classified as secure but that upon more careful observation their behavior appeared to be different from that of nonmaltreated secure infants. Egeland and Sroufe (1981) chose to set some unclassifiable abuse and abuse/neglect cases aside from analyses, noting that the children seemed insecure but did not exhibit avoidance or resistance. Instead they were characterized by apathy or *disorganization*. Still other investigators noted unusual aspects in their maltreated subjects' behavior in the Strange Situation but decided to report the standard A, B, and C categories, leaving open the possibility of later reanalysis (Schneider-Rosen et al., 1985).

Uncertainties like these led investigators in several laboratories to reconsider the categorization process. They went back to their videotapes and carefully reviewed them, identifying new types or combinations of behavior not ordinarily found among A-, B-, and C-coded infants. Two new categories were proposed as a result.

**The avoidant/resistant category.** Given that the inconsistent and insensitive care maltreated children experience should promote insecure attachments, Crittenden (1988) conducted an extensive reevaluation of the videotapes of securely rated maltreated infants. Forty-three tapes of children aged 11 to 24 months were coded using the ABC system. Upon examining the data, Crittenden noticed that nine children who had experienced both abuse and neglect had been placed in the secure category. Because such a finding was almost impossible to explain theoretically, these tapes were carefully reviewed. It became apparent that the maltreated infants who had been rated secure did not demonstrate the appropriate mixture of low avoidance and low resistance mixed with moderate-to-high levels of proximity seeking and contact maintaining that typify secure attachment relationships under stress. Instead, they displayed the unusual combination of moderate-to-high avoidance and moderate-to-high resistance. The resistance was particularly likely to be in the form of persistent crankiness, noncontextual aggression, or both. In addition, most of the infants displaying this blend of responses also showed some stereotypical or maladaptive behaviors such as head cocking or huddling on the floor. Crittenden developed a coding scheme for this new category, which she labeled "A-C," and documented its reliability on a fresh sample (Crittenden, 1988). Again a strong relationship was obtained between the A-C classification and a history of both abuse and neglect.

A second laboratory also identified the need for an A-C category for infants who display both high avoidance and high resistance in the strange situation. Radke-Yarrow, Cummings, Kuczynski, and Chapman (1985) noted the same mix of insecure patterns in their study of the offspring of unipolar and bipolar depressed mothers. This important development revealed the need for a separate category for yet another population of high-risk infants.

**Development of the "disorganized/disoriented" or D category.** Main and Solomon (1986, in press) described the process by which the D category was developed. They carefully reexamined the 34 unclassifiable videotapes that had been set aside out of the 368 mother-infant and father-infant Strange Situations from the Berkeley Social Development Project (cf. Main & Weston, 1981). They had expected to discover a number of new categories, but instead of finding new organizations of behavior, they were struck with the overriding impression that the Strange Situation behavior of all 34 of these infants and toddlers was *disorganized and disoriented*. Evidence of coherent, organized strategies for dealing with the stresses inherent in the Strange Situation was consistently absent. Instead of new organizations, they discovered elements of the three major attachment patterns, combined in unusual ways. For example, they found the combination of moderate-to-high proximity seeking, moderate-to-high avoidance, and moderate-to-high resistance, which has been labeled A-C by Crittenden (1988), Radke-Yarrow et al. (1985), and Spieker and Booth (1988). In other cases proximity seeking was accompanied by avoidance, a combination first described in a study of physically abused toddlers conducted by George and Main (1979). Although that study involved toddlers' behavior in a day-care center with caregivers and peers rather than with mothers, the descriptions of oblique approaches, detours, and backing toward the other or approaching with head averted are very similar to the descriptions of avoidance mixed with proximity seeking in the unclassifiable cases.

In addition to manifesting these unusual combinations of behavior, infants with unclassifiable Strange Situations displayed other bizarre symptoms including incomplete, undirected, and interrupted movements and expressions; asymmetrical and mistimed movements; stereotyped and anomalous postures; stilling, slow movements, freezing, and depressed affect; and direct indices of apprehension (e.g., fear/wariness) toward the parent (see Main et al., 1985, and Main & Solomon, in press, for an elaboration of the D coding scheme and for a description of the construct-validation process).

After the publication of our traditionally coded Strange Situation results (Schneider-Rosen et al., 1985), my colleagues and I became interested in the descriptions of alternatives in coding, especially the work of Main and her colleagues on the disorganized/disoriented category. Congruent with the literature, we had found that the vast majority of maltreated youngsters formed anxious attachments with their mothers. Longitudinal assessments of these infant-mother dyads (e.g., from 12 to 18 months and from 18 to 24 months) revealed a striking movement toward the anxious-avoidant (type A) attachment category. Likewise, we found a relatively small percentage of "securely" attached maltreated infants; however, in making these "forced" classifications it was our strong clinical impression that several of the securely attached youngsters were false-positives.

When we reclassified our Strange Situations, using coders blind to group status and unaware of the earlier ABC ratings, we found that approximately 80% of our maltreated infants (18 of 22) fell into the disorganized/disoriented category (Carlson et al., 1989). In contrast, the matched comparison group of lower-SES nonmaltreated infants had a percentage of D attachments comparable to that reported in previous middle-class (Main et al., 1985) and high-risk samples (e.g., Spieker & Booth, 1988). Additionally, six of the maltreated infants we classified as type D had originally been classified as type B (securely attached). Even with the addition of the type D category, three of our maltreated infants were rated as securely attached.

Our finding that maltreated infants are particularly likely to demonstrate disorganized/disoriented attachments is not surprising given that they are reared in homes where parents often were maltreated in their childhoods or have maltreated other children in the home. Furthermore, because attachment is believed to have both affective and cognitive components (Ainsworth, 1973; Engel, 1971; Sroufe & Waters, 1977), it is informative to examine the emotional concomitants of type D attachments. Main and Hesse (in press) have suggested that introducing *fear* into the context of otherwise adequate caregiving is essential to developing a disorganized/disoriented attachment. Fear must certainly be a common experience for physically and emotionally abused children. It also is probable that there are frightening aspects to emotional and physical neglect. As Main and Hesse have described, the concurrent activation of the fear/wariness and attachment behavioral systems produces strong conflicting motivations to approach the caregiver for comfort and also to retreat to safety. Proximity seeking mixed with avoidance results as infants attempt to balance their conflicting tendencies. Freezing, dazing, and stilling may be the result of their mutual inhibition (Main & Solomon, 1986). Moreover, in other clinical populations, infants of depressed mothers have been found to be at increased risk for having avoidant/resistant attachment relationships (Radke-Yarrow et al., 1985). The mothers in our protective-service samples have higher levels of depression than do our comparison mothers. Depression thus could have contributed independently to the development of disorganized attachment in some of the infants in our sample (Gilbreath & Cicchetti, 1989).

In keeping with an organizational perspective, it is apparent that the relation between affect and cognition is impaired in maltreated infants' attachment systems. We believe that the fear/wariness, attachment, affiliation, and exploratory behavioral systems may be organized differently in such infants (Bischof, 1975; Bretherton & Ainsworth, 1974; Cicchetti & Serafica, 1981).

In addition to being a possible sequela of child maltreatment, attachment dysfunction also may be a prime etiological factor both for the occurrence of maltreatment and for its continuation across generations (Crittenden & Ainsworth, 1989). Main and Goldwyn (1984) have shown that adults who were maltreated as children may distort their early experiences and describe their caregivers in an exaggeratedly positive fashion—a form of defensive idealization. When viewed alongside Hunter and Kihlstrom's (1979) findings that adults who broke the cycle of maltreatment despite their own history of abuse were characterized by having open and appropriately angry recollections about their early childhood, one can readily see how continuing anomalies of attachment could play an influential role in the intergenerational transmission of child maltreatment. One interpretation of these results is that the adults who broke the cycle had better resolved ill feelings regarding their maltreatment, some of which may have included mourning the adequate parent they never had, to be able to parent their high-risk children more effectively. In a related vein, Main and Hesse (in press) found that parents who had successfully mourned the loss of a parent tended not to have infants with D attachments. Finally, a common underlying component of each of these interpretations may be the presence of a mood disorder (cf. Gilbreath & Cicchetti, 1989).

A recent prospective longitudinal study of the antecedents and consequences of child abuse and neglect further corroborates the role attachment quality and internal working models play in the intergenerational transmission of child maltreatment. Egeland, Jacobvitz, and Sroufe (1988) found that abusive mothers who were able to break the abusive cycle were significantly more likely to have received emotional support from a nonabusive adult during their childhood, to have participated in therapy at some point in their lives, and to have formed a nonabusive and more stable, emotionally supportive, and fulfilling relationship with a mate.

Parent-child role reversal suggests another important link between child maltreatment and the disorganized/disoriented attachment pattern. One of the most common characteristics of abused/ neglected children is that they seem to have traded roles with their caregivers (Dean et al., 1986; Morris & Gould, 1963). In such parent-child relationships the child appears to be the more sensitive and nurturing member of the dyad. Hence the role reversal of caregiving behaviors documented in 6-year-olds who were classified as type D at 12 months (Main et al., 1985) provides a new perspective on the etiology of this feature in abused and neglected children. The parentifying of the maltreated child may constitute a specific manifestation of a more generally disorganized attachment relationship.

Longitudinal studies of the processes by which maltreated children become parentified must be conducted. The confluence of findings described earlier suggests that maltreated children are taught to be over empathic to their parents' emotions (cf. Zahn-Waxler & Kochanska, this volume); are socialized not to recognize their own internal states; and often cope with chaotic parenting situations by assuming control (acting as parents) in an age-inappropriate fashion (see Main et al., 1985, for a description of the caregiving/controlling attachment relationship). One possible implication of these data is that though "caretaker/controlling" maltreated children may learn to take care of others, they may never learn to care for themselves, at least not adaptively. Clearly, even in the absence of the necessary longitudinal studies, knowledge about attachment relationships in maltreatment and of the concomitant disturbances in the self system should prove important in prevention and intervention (Cicchetti & Toth, 1987; Cicchetti, Toth & Bush, 1988; Egeland et al., 1988).

Bowlby (1980), Bretherton (1985, 1987), and Sroufe (in press) have all emphasized that "internal working models" of attachment figures can change. With the advent of formal operational thought, it is possible for adults to rerepresent their relationship experiences into more secure, hierarchically integrated models of attachment.

As Kaufman and Zigler (1989) have noted, not all abused children become abusive parents (see also Cicchetti & Aber, 1980). Altering maladaptive working models may be one mechanism for breaking the cycle of child abuse. Reworking poor-quality internal representations of attachment figures, either alone or in therapy (see Cicchetti, Toth, & Bush, 1988; Egeland et al., 1988; Guidano, 1987; Guidano & Liotti, 1983), seems like an effective way to prevent the occurrence, recurrence (within a family), and intergenerational transmission of child abuse and neglect. Of course, because the transactional approach emphasizes that extraorganismic factors also are important in the etiology and continuation of maltreatment (Cicchetti & Rizley, 1981), it is necessary that treatment programs for maltreating parents address ecological factors as well as internal self-perpetuating processes (Cicchetti & Toth, 1987; Cicchetti, Toth & Bush, 1988). Introducing compensatory factors, in concert with comprehensive child and adult interventions, should reduce the likelihood of recurrent maltreatment (see Cicchetti & Rizley, 1981; Cicchetti et al., 1978; Egeland et al., 1988; Kaufman & Zigler, 1989).

Clearly, it is essential that cross-sectional and longitudinal research be conducted on the development of attachment relationships beyond toddlerhood. Although there is some suggestive evidence that the organizational approach is a viable perspective for studying attachment past infancy (Aber & Allen, 1987; Cicchetti, Cummings, Greenberg, & Marvin, in press; Greenberg, Cicchetti, & Cummings, in press), important work remains to be done.

In our laboratory we are studying the development of representational models in maltreated and nonmaltreated preschool children using Bretherton's doll-play technique (Bretherton, Ridgeway, & Cassidy, in press). In conjunction with this study, we are assessing the maltreatment histories and attachment relationships of the parents of these children in an effort to understand the relation between maltreatment and parent-child internal working models of attachment figures. We also are independently investigating the attachment relationships of maltreating mothers using the Adult Attachment Interview (George, Kaplan, & Main, 1984). Again we are studying both middle-SES and lower-SES groups of nonmaltreating mothers and validating the adult attachment classifications against a

variety of adult (e.g., presence or absence of DSM-III-R psychopathology) and child (e.g., quality of attachment relationship; self-
development; peer relations) outcome measures. In addition, we
have developed a Childhood Attachment Interview (Cicchetti, 1988)
that we are administering to school-age maltreated children and
comparison groups of lower-SES and middle-SES children. We are
also doing extensive validation of this interview, including investigating its relationship to self-development, coping with background
anger, peer relations, and psychopathology.

## THE DEVELOPMENT OF AN AUTONOMOUS SELF (18–24 MONTHS)

In examining how early maltreatment affects subsequent adaptation, we must consider the specific systems that may be most at risk
for developmental deviations or delays at particular ages (cf. Cicchetti & Rizley, 1981). Consequently, it is crucial that we investigate
the effect of specific social experiences on the growing self-knowledge of toddlers.

One such relationship of major theoretical significance is between the quality of mother-child attachment and the emergence of
visual self-recognition (Lewis & Brooks-Gunn, 1979). Specifically,
the security of the attachment relationship promotes a movement
toward other objects and people and a developing sense of effectiveness and of mastery over the social and nonsocial environment
(Sroufe, 1979b). Youngsters who have developed a secure attachment to their caregivers will have a greater likelihood of exploring
the environment with confidence and trust in the caregivers' acces-
sibility (Ainsworth et al., 1978; Sroufe & Waters, 1977). Their exploration of new objects and persons and their affective growth will
promote the skills that underlie the capacity for visual self-recognition. Therefore securely attached toddlers should evince this capacity earlier than insecurely attached youngsters.

Examining a sample of maltreated and matched lower-SES toddlers, Schneider-Rosen and Cicchetti (1984) demonstrated the
importance of the quality of the early attachment relationship for explaining individual differences in the development of visual self-

recognition. Of the sample of 19-month-old youngsters, 41% displayed visual recognition as assessed by the standard mirror-and-rouge paradigm (Lewis & Brooks-Gunn, 1979). When data for the entire sample of infants were analyzed, we found that those infants who recognized themselves were significantly more likely to be securely attached to their mothers. However, a separate analysis of the maltreated and comparison groups revealed a different pattern. Of the comparison infants who recognized themselves, 90% were securely attached to their caregivers. In contrast, for maltreated infants there was no significant relation between recognizing themselves and the security of attachment. Recall also that maltreated youngsters displayed predominantly neutral or negative affect while inspecting their rouge-marked faces in the mirror.

In another study on self-differentiation in maltreated toddlers, Egeland and Sroufe (1981) employed a tool-use/problem-solving paradigm to assess 24-month-old toddlers' emerging autonomy, independent exploration of the environment, and ability to cope with frustration. These investigators found that physically abused children were more angry, frustrated with the mother, and noncompliant than controls as well as less enthusiastic. However, they exhibited more positive affect. In contrast, the neglected children expressed less positive and more negative affect and obtained higher noncompliance, frustration, and anger scores than the controls.

Longitudinal research also will help determine the developmental consequences of individual differences in visual self-recognition, self-regulation, and other early aspects of self development. Whether the relationship between security of attachment and visual self-recognition will influence the development, quality, or stability of emerging self cognitions is an empirical question that warrants investigation (Cummings & Cicchetti, in press). Will those toddlers who demonstrate visual self-recognition earlier develop a more stable and secure concept of the self? Will those toddlers with better self-regulatory skills be less likely to manifest problems in peer relations? Will the quality of early self cognitions affect later adaptation and adjustment? Future research should address these and related questions to clarify the effect that individual differences in the emergence of aspects of early self-system processes (cf. Connell, in press;

Harter, 1983) have on the subsequent development of self-knowledge and on later adaptation.

The early deviations in the "self system" of maltreated youngsters vividly illustrate the deleterious impact that a maltreating environment can have upon separation/individuation and demonstrate the importance of the "vicissitudes of parenting" (cf. Mahler et al., 1975) for promoting or undermining the successful resolution of this critical developmental task. Difficulties with separation/individuation are likely to result in future maladaptation. In particular, maltreated children are in grave danger of becoming enmeshed with their parents, perhaps in a "caretaker" relationship with their mothers, with resulting parentifying of the child (cf. Carlson et al., 1989; Main et al., 1985). Another possibility is that they may form a punitive/controlling relationship with their caretakers (Main et al., 1985). In becoming either controlling caretakers or punitive controlling, these children may come to expect that their future offspring should treat them similarly. Consequently, both these types of maltreated children may become intergenerational transmitters of maltreatment. These children also may one day choose mates who do not take care of them. Even if they do not become perpetrators of maltreatment, they may become "victimized" in their adult relationships (Sroufe & Fleeson, 1986). Moreover, many of these adults undoubtedly will form relationships that endanger the safety of their children—either because the children observe violence between spouses (Rosenberg, 1987) or because their partners may be physically or sexually abusive to one or more of the children (Daly & Wilson, 1981).

Although at present these control "caretaker" and "punitive" types of attachments cannot be assessed before the early years of life, they are associated with the disorganized/disoriented type D attachments (Main et al., 1985). Thus it may be noteworthy that Carlson et al. (1989) reported such a high base rate of these disorganized attachments in maltreated infants. These infants may be highly likely to become victims or victimizers or both in their future relationships.

## SYMBOLIC REPRESENTATION AND FURTHER SELF/ OTHER DIFFERENTIATION (24–36 MONTHS)

Piaget (1962) contended that symbolic competencies such as language acquisition or the unfolding of play proceed according to the exact rules that govern other domains of development—most notable cognition. Because Piaget imputed more causal power to the cognitive/maturational aspects of symbolization, he paid minimal attention to socioemotional or environmental influences. Moreover, he was not especially interested in individual differences in functioning, either across symbolic domains or across contexts.

In contrast to the Genevan viewpoint, the organismic-developmental theorists Werner and Kaplan (1963) stated that symbolization emerged within the context of the mother-child relationship, or what they referred to as the "interpersonal matrix." Guided by the orthogenetic principle (Werner, 1957), they theorized that with the child's development, the "primordial sharing experience" between the mother, child (self), and object of reference proceeded from a state of relative undifferentiation and globality to one of increasing differentiation and hierarchical integration. Furthermore, they claimed that the motivation to engage in symbolic activity emanated from the desire to share experiences with a social partner.

Bruner (1975) has argued along similar lines, stating that through dyadic interactions with the caregiver the child develops linguistic knowledge. The dual processes of joint action and joint reference between child and mother thus are viewed as critical in language acquisition because they help provide cognitive structure for the child (see also Vygotsky, 1978).

Another way the mother can contribute to the ontogenesis of the child's symbolic capacities is through her supportive presence (Matas, Arend, & Sroufe, 1978) or emotional availability (Egeland & Sroufe, 1981; Sorce & Emde, 1981). Through her sensitive responsiveness, the mother provides a sense of security that fosters exploration of the inanimate and animate object worlds (cf. Slade, 1987). The ability to explore while using the mother as a "secure base" enhances the child's autonomy (self/other differentiation) and the growth of representational thought. For example, Stern (1985) has described how the caregiver's attunement (or emotional-intensity calibration with the child) plays a crucial role in the unfolding and differentiation of the self system. Moreover, from different theoretical perspectives Ainsworth (1973) and Mahler (Mahler et al., 1975) both have theorized that infants and toddlers who can be confident of their mothers' availability will feel free to explore the world and to devote themselves more fully and enthusiastically to interacting with others. As a consequence, these children are expected to have a more highly differentiated sense of self.

In an important study described earlier, Gersten et al. (1986) found that attachment security was significantly related to communicative functioning for both maltreated and nonmaltreated toddlers. Most compellingly, even the small group of securely attached maltreated toddlers referred more often to themselves, to their ongoing activities, and to those of others than did a matched group of insecurely attached maltreated and nonmaltreated toddlers.

Additionally, in a longitudinal investigation Cicchetti, Beeghly, Carlson, and Toth (in press) found that securely attached youngsters continued to use more self- and other-related language, as well as proportionately more internal-state words, than insecurely attached children. With the passage of time, insecurely attached toddlers produced fewer emotional words, showed less differentiation in attribution, and were more focused on the present in their use of self- and emotion-related language. Again, even the small number of securely attached maltreated toddlers in this sample used more emotional language and self/other utterances than the insecurely attached maltreated and nonmaltreated youngsters.

## THE DEVELOPMENT OF EFFECTIVE PEER RELATIONS (3–5 YEARS)

The quality of children's peer relations has been associated with the quality of attachment relations in infancy (Sroufe, 1983; Waters, Wippman, & Sroufe, 1979), with measures of ego resiliency and empathy during the preschool period (Sroufe, 1983), and with emotional adjustment (Butler, 1979; Wagner, 1979) and school performance (Hartup, 1983) during childhood. Furthermore, the quality of peer relations has been associated with a variety of outcomes in adulthood. For example, difficulty with peers in childhood has been found to correlate with academic underachievement and educational failure (Roff, Sells, & Golden, 1972), delinquency and aggression (Robins, 1978), and mental health disorders later in life (Cowen, Pederson, Babigian, Izzo, & Trost, 1973; Janes & Hesselbrock, 1978).

To date, most studies on the peer relations of maltreated children have been conducted primarily with toddlers and preschoolers (Mueller & Silverman, 1989). In studies where global ratings were completed at the conclusion of an observation period, maltreated children exhibited less prosocial and more aggressive behavior than comparison groups (Herrenkohl & Herrenkohl, 1981; Hoffman-Plotkin & Twentyman, 1984). In investigations in which children's discrete social behaviors were recorded in relation to the interactions that preceded them, maltreated children were found to be avoidant (George & Main, 1979) or aggressive (Howes & Eldredge, 1985) in response to the friendly overtures of their peers and to respond aggressively to another classmate's distress (Howes & Espinosa, 1985; Main & George, 1985).

In the largest study of peer relations in school-age maltreated children conducted to date, Kaufman and Cicchetti (1989) assessed the impact of different forms of maltreatment on peer relations and self-esteem. As described above, existing theoretical conceptualizations of internal working models posit that mental representations of others and of the self are independent yet interacting systems. Because prior empirical research with nonmaltreated samples suggests that children with impaired peer relations also are deficient in self-esteem (Sroufe, 1983), we chose to examine the relation between self-esteem and peer relations.

For this purpose we designed and conducted a summer day camp. Camp counselors recorded their perceptions of the children's self-esteem. Additionally, both counselors and peers rated the children's prosocial, aggressive, and withdrawn behavior. Regardless of subgroup classification, maltreated children differed from the comparison group in a number of ways. They scored lower on the self-esteem and prosocial measures and higher on the withdrawn-behavior scales completed by counselors. When the effects of subtypes of maltreatment were considered, it was only with the aggressive peer-nomination ratings that significant maltreatment category effects appeared. The children who were physically abused scored significantly higher than the other maltreated children on the aggression ratings completed by their peers. These findings extend the results other investigators have obtained with younger children (George & Main, 1979; Hoffman-Plotkin & Twentyman, 1984; Howes & Espinosa, 1985) and suggest that both younger and older maltreated children have difficulty with peer relations. The strength of this study rests on the fact that multiple observations were conducted in a naturalistic setting over a far longer period than in previous research efforts.

Consistent with predictions based on attachment theory and on past empirical findings with nonmaltreated samples (Sroufe, 1983), maltreated children were found to be comparably impaired on measures of self-esteem and peer relations. The relationship between these two measures is most likely strengthened through a self-perpetuating negative feedback system, since negative expectations about the self and one's personal efficacy have been shown to promote unfavorable self-fulfilling prophecies (Bandura, 1982). Children who enter the peer world with low self-esteem are likely to have negative expectations about prospective social experiences. These expectations then increase the likelihood of unsuccessful encounters that, when realized, further diminish self-esteem.

Overall, in current level of adaptation the children in each of the maltreatment categories were less competent than their peers, and those who were physically abused were most adversely affected. In terms of prognosis, empirical findings (see Kohlberg, Snarey, & Ricks, 1984, for a review) suggest that the aggressive scale of the peer-nomination measure is the best predictor. Given the high ratings received on this measure by the children who experienced all three forms of maltreatment, it appears that these children may be considerably more likely than the others to have problems later in life.

To make meaningful predictions of later psychosocial adjustment, however, it is important to consider other possible influences on development (Cicchetti & Rizley, 1981). In this study, although all the children were of low SES, those who received the lowest ratings on the self-esteem measure were most likely to be from families receiving welfare. Even within this entirely low-income sample, gradations of poverty influenced child outcome. Because neglect and abuse occur most often within the context of poverty (Pelton, 1978) and the adverse effects of poverty observed in this study appear to be additive and independent of the impact of maltreatment, the effects of indigence must be considered in predicting the development of maltreated children.

## SUCCESSFUL ADAPTATION TO SCHOOL (5–10 YEARS)

To identify signs of incipient developmental failure and psychopathology, we need to assess maltreated children's adaptation across multiple contexts and in multiple areas of functioning. Successful adaptation to school—including integration into the peer group, acceptable performance in the classroom, and the appropriate motivational orientation for achievement—is a stage-salient developmental task for all children.

Based on theories of a hierarchical emergence of motives (Harter, 1978; Maslow, 1954), one would not expect maltreated children to be motivated to do well in school (McClelland, 1988; Murray, 1938). Considering their home environment, one would predict that physical needs, safety, and the quest for love and acceptance would almost certainly be more salient.

Motivational deficits may be a direct consequence of home experiences as well. The parent-child relationship and the child's working model of self are not the only self-system domains jeopardized by the caregiving attitudes and behaviors of maltreating parents. Trickett and Susman (1988), for example, found abusive parents to be higher than comparison parents on achievement orientation, but also higher on control and verbal prohibition. At the same time, these parents used less verbal reasoning, were less intellectually oriented, and were more dissatisfied with their children. This pattern of caregiving is highly reminiscent of Baumrind's (1967, 1968) descriptions of the authoritarian parent and is associated with less competence and lower school achievement among children. The combination of a controlling environment and high performance demands also has been linked to an extrinsic motivational orientation toward task performance (Koestner, Ryan, Bernieri, & Holt, 1984; Lepper, 1981), and is considered maladaptive for children's classroom performance (Harter, 1981; Ryan, Connell, & Deci, 1985).

Independent investigators operating from disparate theoretical orientations have found that maltreated children are more dependent on their teachers (Egeland, Sroufe, & Erickson, 1983), score lower on tests measuring cognitive maturity, perhaps for motivational reasons (Barahal, Waterman, & Martin, 1981), and are rated by both parents and their teachers as less ready to learn in school (Hoffman-Plotkin & Twentyman, 1984).

In a further negative transaction, the behavior problems that maltreated children manifest in school (Egeland et al., 1983) may necessitate the overcontrolling teaching styles that DeCharms (1968), Deci (1975), and Lepper (1981) found to undermine an intrinsic motivational orientation in school. If this finding is upheld with maltreated children, they will be further "at risk" for adopting an extrinsically motivated orientation toward their schoolwork.

Thus the maltreated child is at multiple risk for poor school functioning, stemming from deficits in the self system that include low self-esteem, impaired perceptions of competence, and an extrinsic motivational orientation. As noted earlier, children's expectations about adults' availability and responsiveness are thought to develop in infancy and toddlerhood through interactions with their primary attachment figures. These expectations concerning the availability and predictability of adults are carried forward via internal representations of self-in-relationships that in turn may influence both the construction of new relationships and the ability to explore and cope with the demands of new and stressful situations such as the adaptation to school (Aber et al., 1989).

Studies of maltreated infants and toddlers (George & Main, 1979), and of maltreated preschool and early-school-age children (Egeland et al., 1983) suggest impairments in maltreated children's relations with novel adults. In infancy and toddlerhood, physically abused children appear to experience greater approach/avoidance conflicts concerning novel adults (Carlson et al., 1989; Crittenden, 1988; George & Main, 1979; Schneider-Rosen et al., 1985). In the preschool and early school years, maltreated children appear to be especially dependent upon the social reinforcement of novel adults (Aber & Allen, 1987; Erickson, Egeland, & Pianta, 1989). These findings suggest that certain characteristics of maltreated children, like excessive dependency upon, wariness of, or avoidance of novel adults, may interfere with their effective entry into nursery school, kindergarten, and elementary school. Previous research by Zigler and his colleagues (Balla & Zigler, 1975; Yando, Seitz, & Zigler, 1978) indicates that social deprivation makes children both excessively dependent upon and wary of new adults.

Effectance motivation, described as the motive to deal competently with one's environment for the intrinsic pleasure of mastery, also is influenced by social history (Harter & Zigler, 1974) and may influence how the child adapts to the achievement and mastery demands of school (Dweck & Elliott, 1983; Harter, 1978). Zigler (1971), drawing upon Maslow's theory of a hierarchy of motives, has described effectance motivation as a "life fulfilling" rather than "life preserving" need and, consequently, as vulnerable to debilitating life experiences.

In our laboratory, Aber and Allen (1987) investigated whether maltreated preschool and early-school-age children were especially dependent upon or wary of novel adults as were other socially deprived children and whether they too subordinated effectance motivation to the need to establish secure social relationships with new adults. In effect, they conceptualized effectance motivation and successful relations with novel adults as components of the children's larger developmental task of adapting competently to their first major out-of-home environment and to the larger world that school represents.

Three samples of children between 4 and 8 years of age participated in this investigation: maltreated children, demographically matched nonmaltreated children from families receiving welfare, and nonmaltreated children from middle-class families. Aber and Allen (1987) factor analyzed children's scores on 10 dependent variables, and two theoretically meaningful factors emerged. Maltreated children scored lower than welfare children, who in turn scored lower than middle-class children, on a factor measuring secure readiness to learn in the company of novel adults. Maltreated children and welfare children also scored higher than middle-class children, but did not differ significantly from each other, on a factor measuring outer-directedness.

The secure readiness to learn factor was composed of high effectance motivation and low dependency. Similar to the organizational construct of security of attachment in infancy, secure readiness to learn can be conceptualized as an organizational construct of competence in early childhood. Like security of attachment, secure readiness to learn appears to represent a dynamic balance between establishing safe, secure relationships with adults and feeling free to venture out to explore the world in a manner likely to promote maturation of cognitive competencies. Furthermore, Aber and Allen's (1987) findings are especially compelling because they are congruent with prior empirical research on how maltreatment affects infants' and toddlers' development. At both developmental stages, maltreatment disrupts the dynamic balance between the motivation to establish safe, secure relationships with adults and the motivation to explore the world in a competency-promoting fashion.

The outer-directedness factor comprised verbal attention seeking, approval-seeking smiles, wariness with novel adults, and imitation. Theoretically, outer-directedness has been defined as an orientation to problem solving in which young children rely on external cues rather than on their own cognitive resources. Zigler believes that this dimension also taps the extent of their conformity or compliance with adults, especially for those from environments where a high degree of compliance has adaptive value (Zigler & Balla, 1982). Although both high-risk groups scored higher on outer-directedness than the middle-SES children, maltreatment does not appear to influence young children's outer-directedness beyond the effects attributable to lower SES.

In an effort to assess school adaptation within the context of their prospective longitudinal study of maltreatment, Egeland and his colleagues have followed their maltreated children from infancy through entry into kindergarten. Erickson et al. (1989) documented that maltreated children, including physically and sexually abused children, neglected children, and children of psychologically unavailable parents, performed poorly in kindergarten. Overall, they tended to have behavior problems and to do poorly academically. Moreover, they were generally unpopular with their peers.

More recently, Vondra, Barnett, and Cicchetti (1989) found that maltreated children perceive and describe themselves differently than do their low-income peers. Interestingly, these differences assumed the expected direction (with maltreated children describing themselves more negatively) only about the middle of elementary school. In earlier grades, maltreated children demonstrate a striking tendency to describe themselves in exaggeratedly positive terms. Importantly, Vondra, Barnett, and their colleagues have replicated this finding on two additional maltreatment samples (Vondra, Barnett, & Cicchetti, in press; Vondra, Barnett, Shonk, Toth, & Cicchetti, 1989). Furthermore, differences between maltreated and comparison children also appear in teachers' ratings of school functioning and competency (with maltreated children rated more negatively) as well as in terms of the need for special educational services during the elementary-school years. Thus, both self-perceptions and school functioning appear to be jeopardized by maltreatment (Vondra, Barnett, & Cicchetti, 1989, in press). Additionally, among older children self-perceptions are linked intimately with school functioning, and for all children relations between self-perceptions and some laboratory measures of mastery motivation and exploration can be discerned.

Vondra, Barnett, and their collaborators have argued that younger maltreated children presented themselves as more competent than they actually were (based on teacher ratings) because of defensive posturing (see Cassidy, 1988, and Vondra, Barnett, & Cicchetti, 1989, for an in-depth explanation). However, Vondra, Barnett, and their colleagues contend that as the reality of academic failure and peer rejection become increasingly evident and too difficult to ignore, self-perceptions decrease in middle childhood. While longitudinal studies are required in order to determine how far self-perceptions mediate the relation between maltreatment experiences and subsequent school and motivational functioning, nonetheless the findings of Vondra, Barnett, and their colleagues provide suggestive evidence for a causal chain extending from attachment relationships to self-perceptions to school functioning.

## Behavior Problems and Psychopathology

Developmental psychopathologists are interested in investigating deviant ontogenesis and uncovering the prototypes of, or precursors to, what may later become psychopathological disorder (Bowlby, 1988; Cicchetti, 1987; Cicchetti & Aber, 1986; Sroufe & Rutter, 1984). Moreover, they focus on charting the course of individual differences in adaptation, both normal and psychopathological. Additionally, they are concerned with identifying the circumstances that render certain individuals vulnerable and others protected with respect to life's vicissitudes (Garmezy, 1983; Rolf, Masten, Cicchetti, Neuchterlein, & Weintraub, in press). Finally, developmental psychopathologists seek to ascertain what factors underlie the organism's capacity to use environmental and inner resources (e.g., social supports, superior immune-system functioning, effective coping skills) in an adaptive and competent fashion (cf. Waters & Sroufe, 1983).

As we have seen, maltreated youngsters manifest disturbed functioning on each of the stage-salient developmental issues of the early years of life. Specifically, dysfunctional "internal working models" (Bowlby, 1980), both in relationships with primary attachment figures and with regard to the self, deviations in "self-system" processes (Harter, 1983), difficulties in the production and social usage of language, problematic peer relationships, and difficulty in adapting to school were found in maltreated children. These disruptions bode poorly for future adaptation.

Although not all maltreated children who have trouble resolving stage-salient issues will develop psychopathology, later disturbances in functioning are likely to occur. In addition, not all children who have difficulty with a particular issue (e.g., the formation of secure attachment) will exhibit any form of psychopathology, let alone the same psychopathological disorder (see Cummings & Cicchetti, in press). Prospective longitudinal studies are required to ascertain the relation between incompetence and the specific form of psychopathology that may eventuate, as well as the reasons psychopathology may not occur even against the backdrop of incompetent functioning.

Even though child maltreatment is not listed as a diagnostic entity in the DSM-III-R (American Psychiatric Association, 1987), I think it should be conceived as a "relational psychopathology"— that is, the result of a dysfunction in the parent-child-environment transactional system. Historically, a number of infant classification schemes have focused on such relational pathologies. For example, Spitz's (Spitz, 1951; Spitz & Wolf, 1946) classic research on hospital-ism and anaclitic depression, Bowlby's (1951) work on the effects of maternal deprivation (see also Rutter, 1972/1981), and Provence and Lipton's 1962) studies on the effects of institutionalization upon in-fant development each provide exemplars of how dysfunction within the caretaker-child-environment system may cause distur-bances in functioning. I believe that other than the pervasive devel-opmental disorders and the organic forms of mental retardation, the vast majority of the disorders of the early years of life can best be characterized as transactional "relational pathologies," not as endo-genous disorders arising solely "within the child" (cf. Cicchetti, 1987; Greenspan & Porges, 1984; Sroufe & Fleeson, 1986).

Proponents of attachment theory have claimed that many types of psychopathology may be brought about by deviations in the de-velopment of the attachment behavioral system (Bowlby, 1977a, 1977b; Guidano, 1987; Guidano & Liotti, 1983). Bowlby (1979) be-lieved that parents' threats to abandon a child and to commit suicide both would exert a pathogenic effect on the attachment system. Clearly, maltreated children, especially neglected and emotionally mistreated youngsters, are exposed to statements like these (cf. Rosenberg, 1987). In addition, advocates of the attachment theory perspective have argued that there are strong causal relations be-tween individuals' experiences with their parents and their later ca-pacity to form and sustain emotional bonds (Bowlby, 1944, 1977a, 1977b; Sroufe & Fleeson, 1986). Furthermore, a number of problems have been associated with poor-quality early parent-child relations, including marital difficulties, dysfunctional parenting, a variety of personality disorders (e.g., borderline and antisocial personality), neurotic symptoms, and depression and other types of severe psy-chopathology (Bowlby, 1977a, 1977b; Henderson, 1982; Kazdin, Mo-ser, Colbus, & Bell, 1985; Rutter, 1989; Sroufe & Fleeson, 1986).

In our laboratory, Aber, Allen, and Cicchetti (1988) examined the relation between parent-reported symptoms on the Achenbach Child Behavior Checklist (CBCL; Achenbach & Edelbrock, 1983) and the two experimentally assessed, theoretically derived constructs of secure readiness to learn and outer-directedness discussed above. Aber and his colleagues found that there was no difference between maltreated and demographically matched lower-SES preschool nonmaltreated children in levels of parent-reported symptoms; however, there were clear relations between these symptoms and the two developmental variables. Low secure readiness to learn predicted social withdrawal, aggression, and depression in maltreated preschoolers, whereas high outer-directedness predicted social withdrawal and aggression in the lower-SES nonmaltreated preschoolers.

These findings on different developmental correlates of symptomatology for maltreated and nonmaltreated preschool children may be understood as reflecting children's adaptations to the specific parenting styles of maltreating parents. For instance, Crittenden (1988) has described maltreated preschool children's compulsive compliance with their parents' demands. Our data are consistent with Crittenden's findings: whereas nonmaltreating parents perceive a link between their children's overcompliance (high outer-directedness) and their behavioral symptoms, children's compliance/outer-directedness is not linked to their symptoms by maltreating parents.

Conversely, maltreating parents have been described as "role reversing" and especially vulnerable to and upset by their children's dependency needs (Main & Goldwyn, 1984), with unrealistically high expectations of independence and autonomy. Consistent with this notion, maltreating parents' perceptions of their offspring's behavior are related to the children's insecurity/dependency (low secure readiness), whereas no such relationship existed for children of nonmaltreating parents. These results on differential developmental correlates of symptomatology suggest that although lower-SES maltreated and nonmaltreated children appear equally depressed, withdrawn, and aggressive, different underlying developmental processes may account for similar patterns in the phenotypic expression of symptoms. These different developmental processes appear to be congruent with differences in the child-rearing styles and family ecologies.

In contrast to the findings for preschoolers, during the early school years maltreated children were significantly more depressed and socially withdrawn as well as marginally more aggressive than nonmaltreated children; however, there were no relations between symptoms and developmental variables. Comparing these data with norms for clinic-referred and nonclinical samples of children indicated that maltreated children in both the preschool and early school years scored within the clinical range in symptoms.

This profile of maltreated school-age children as more depressed, more socially withdrawn, and somewhat more aggressive resembles the emerging picture of the psychological characteristics of maltreating parents. Although the earlier notion that maltreating parents differ from nonmaltreating parents in underlying personality attributes/traits has received little empirical support, evidence mounts that they do differ in levels of stress-related symptoms. In particular, maltreating parents have been found to be depressed (Gilbreath & Cicchetti, 1989; Kinard, 1982; Lahey, Conger, Atkeson, & Treiber, 1984; Mash, Johnston, & Kovitz, 1983), socially isolated and lacking in social supports (Garbarino, 1976, 1982; Salzinger, Kaplan, & Artemyeff, 1983), and lacking in impulse control, especially when emotionally aroused and stressed (Altemeier, O'Connor, Vietze, Sandler, & Sherrod, 1982; Brunquell, Crichton, & Egeland, 1981). Wolfe (1985) interprets these symptoms as indexes of failure in psychological functioning in handling stressful life events. Thus it appears that maltreated children may resemble their maltreating parents in psychological vulnerability to stress. This in turn raises the possibility that susceptibility to stress is one of the mediating mechanisms in the complex processes causing intergenerational transmission of child maltreatment within some families (Cicchetti & Aber, 1980; Cicchetti & Rizley, 1981; DeLozier, 1982; Kaufman & Zigler, 1989).

Finally, we found no relation between either secure readiness or outer-directedness and behavioral symptoms among the school-age children. Perhaps these constructs are less sensitive measures of adaptation at this developmental stage, or perhaps school-age children's levels of symptomatology are related to deficits in different areas of development, such as intention-cue detection skills (Dodge et al., 1984) or cognitive control functioning (Rieder & Cicchetti, 1989).

The consistent findings of variation by stage (preschool vs. early school age), both in group differences in symptomatology and in the relation of symptoms to developmental variables, suggest several explanations. First, the relative differences in symptomatology between maltreated and nonmaltreated children may increase with the children's developmental transition from home to school. This interpretation is consistent both with a stress-related theory of childhood symptoms and with the well-known clinical phenomenon of increased psychological problems among vulnerable children as they face the demands of formal schooling. Alternatively, children's absolute symptom levels may not increase from the preschool to the school years; rather, it may be parents' perceptions of their children's deviance that increase during this transition. Exposure to feedback from outside evaluators (e.g., teachers), developmental changes in the child (e.g., increased noncompliance), and a variety of other factors could change parents' perceptions of their children's symptoms. Of course these alternatives are not at all mutually exclusive.

On the basis of their findings, Aber and his colleagues hypothesized that lower-SES maltreated and nonmaltreated preschoolers become symptomatic via different developmental pathways: for maltreated children, by way of a low secure readiness to learn; for nonmaltreated children, through high outer-directedness. Longitudinal studies using repeated measures of behavioral symptomatology, developmental processes, and parent and family characteristics are needed to test directly their hypothesis that there are different pathways to symptomatology for different groups of children at risk. Such studies could prove useful in designing clinical and preventive intervention programs targeting the unique problems of specific subgroups of children at risk.

Finally, the similarity of the symptom profiles of maltreated children and maltreating parents deserves further exploration from a variety of theoretical perspectives such as cognitive-social learning theory and life-span attachment theory (Cicchetti, Cummings, Greenberg, & Marvin, in press; Crittenden & Ainsworth, 1989). Special attention needs to be addressed to identifying underlying processes that account for similarities in patterns of symptoms.

## Summary and Conclusions

In this chapter, I have used the organizational approach to development as a unifying framework for presenting our research in developmental psychopathology. The organizational perspective posits that development occurs through the reorganization and restructuring of competencies into new behavioral and biological structures. Such restructuring is thought to be guided by the orthogenetic principle (Werner, 1957), which describes development as proceeding from simple, undifferentiated forms to highly articulated structures and systems. A related line of inquiry has focused upon the extent to which the development and organization of behavioral systems in high-risk populations compare with those in normally developing, nonhandicapped individuals and, just as important, how the similarities and differences can contribute to our theories of development.

As we have seen, the development of children with Down syndrome across various ontogenetic domains follows a course similar to that for normal children. Although the pace of development is slower for children with Down syndrome, they demonstrate similar developmental trends, moving from states of low differentiation and simple interactions to the development of specific abilities, complex integrated thought, increasingly articulated conceptualizations, and a vast array of behaviors and schemes for interacting with the world.

Additionally, when developmental level is taken into consideration, children with Down syndrome generally appear to progress through the same stages of ontogenesis as normal children. Development occurs in an orderly fashion, with children from both populations acquiring increasingly complex skills.

In terms of the structuring and integration of competencies, children with Down syndrome demonstrate a coherence in development that in most cases parallels that of normally developing, nonhandicapped individuals. Underlying changes in ability to evaluate and to represent the world mentally are reflected concomitantly in socioemotional, cognitive, and representational systems, suggesting that their development is highly organized and coherent. Furthermore, children with Down syndrome successfully resolve each of the stage-salient areas of competence in early development.

However, despite these similarities, several differences also are apparent across developmental domains. First, the reactions of children with Down syndrome are less intense than those of normal children of the same chronological age or developmental level. Although the organization of affect and cognitive systems is similar for both populations, qualitative differences persist. These differences have been related to more fundamental differences at the level of the central nervous system.

Maltreated children, in contrast, manifest impairments in socioemotional, cognitive, and representational development and in the competent resolution of the stage-salient issues of childhood. Moreover, evidence is accumulating that there are different patterns of organization in their development compared with that of demographically matched groups of children of lower SES. Consequently, we view maltreated children as being at extremely high risk for a variety of maladaptive outcomes, including school failure, substance abuse, and personality disorders and psychopathology. In addition, future disturbances in interpersonal relationships are likely that, in the absence of reorganization, may adversely affect their own parenting abilities.

Although the scholarly relevance of the work described in this chapter is difficult to refute, all too often the application of such knowledge to the very populations from which it has been derived is overlooked. Unfortunately, academicians and clinicians often reside in very different worlds, minimizing productive communication. I believe that the discipline of developmental psychopathology holds great promise for bridging this knowledge gap. By its very nature, research in this area must employ clinical populations and settings, thereby applying practical information to the development of research paradigms. Equally important, researchers are thus in an excellent position to share results that can improve services to the populations being studied.

In several earlier papers, my colleagues and I illustrated how a transactional model of family intervention, in accord with the principles of the organizational perspective, could be applied fruitfully to children with Down syndrome and to maltreated children (Cicchetti & Toth, 1987; Cicchetti, Toth, & Bush, 1988; Cicchetti, Toth, Bush,

& Gillespie, 1988). Most relevant for these purposes, focusing on a unitary area of deficit (e.g., cognitive disability) may fail to uncover other problems or to elucidate areas of strength. In thinking about intervention strategies, we believe that a multidomain, multicontextual approach is indicated (Cicchetti & Toth, 1987). By gaining information related to transactions among parent-child-environment factors and to multiple domains of child functioning, we can identify the areas requiring intervention and provide the most developmentally appropriate treatment (Cicchetti, Toth, & Bush, 1988).

For example, a major goal of therapy with maltreated children is to find more adaptive ways of dealing with affective expression and regulation. Because many child-specific therapies deal with the expression of feelings, emotions, and affect, we need to understand a child's cognitive and representational developmental level in relation to the expression of affect. Accordingly, the development of cognitive controls is a rich area for intervention. Because maltreated children evince hypervigilance and assimilate aggressive stimuli more readily than do nonmaltreated children, they could be more likely to perceive ambiguous situations as threatening. This in turn could cause difficulty with interpersonal relations. Depending on the nature of the difficulty, cognitive control therapy (Santostefano, 1985), which strives to integrate cognition, inner experience, and the external environment, can be used to help maltreated children become either more externally or more internally focused. Similarly, because research has demonstrated that children with Down syndrome have muted affect signaling systems, intervention can be directed toward helping parents identify affect and respond synchronously to their infants.

Guided by the tenets of the organizational perspective, I believe that research on the developmental sequelae of high-risk children and the application of this work to developing interventions will improve our ability to influence clinical decision making and social policy (Aber et al., 1989; Cicchetti & Aber, 1980; Olds & Henderson, 1989; Spiker, in press; Wald et al., 1988). For example, policymakers who develop the standards for coercive state intervention routinely face difficult decisions that greatly influence the lives of maltreated children and their families. Empirical studies on the developmental sequelae of child maltreatment can provide clinicians and policymakers with a framework within which to target, design, and evaluate protective services (Aber et al., 1989). One major area that could benefit from such a basis for decision making is the removal from the home and subsequent foster-care placement of children who have been maltreated. Understanding the long-term effects of various forms of maltreatment (e.g., physical abuse versus physical neglect) and predicting the likelihood of *successfully* intervening with parents who differ in the chronicity and severity of maltreatment are critical to well-informed decisions (Cicchetti & Barnett, in press; King & Cicchetti, 1989). Moreover, it is necessary to assess parent-child attachment before deciding to sever this bond. While intuitively it seems that neglectful/abusing parents should have their children removed, the actual consequences for the children, with an often unending series of foster-care placements, have just begun to be compared systematically with the effects of maintaining them in the homes of their biological parents (Wald et al., 1988).

Furthermore, legal systems in many states continue to support the "rights" of parents, so that terminating parental custody may be rare even in severe and chronic cases of abuse. Unfortunately, the "rights" of children to a stable environment and the potential for reworking faulty attachment relationships assume secondary importance. A solid data base that evaluates the effect of differential decisions on child adaptation is necessary if current practices are to be modified in concert with children's needs as well as parents' rights. Until issues like these are confronted through rigorous empirical methods, we will continue to make uninformed decisions that affect, for better or worse, the lives of children and families. Because policymaking in the area of child maltreatment is likely to be affect laden, it is even more critical that those formulating policy and intervention strategies base their decisions on a body of sound scientific knowledge.

Although not as immediately apparent, research on children with Down syndrome also can contribute significantly to decision making. For example, it is critical that parents of children with organic impairments be helped to recognize the normality associated with aberrations. Although delayed cognitive functioning is a very real obstacle, children with Down syndrome have socioemotional needs, and a supportive environment can enhance the positive at-tributes they do possess. Rather than their feeling hopeless about their children's limitations, communicating knowledge about devel-opment in Down syndrome may encourage parents and motivate them to engage with their children in a positive fashion. Moreover, information like this may be critical to future decisions in the early stages of pregnancy when the child has Down syndrome. While these decisions are much more personal than the far-reaching soci-etal decisions made with respect to child maltreatment, they are equally difficult and powerful.

Another important implication of our work deserves mention here. Historically there has been a major debate on whether risk fac-tors independent of those commonly associated with lower SES dif-ferentiate maltreated from nonmaltreated children (Aber & Cic-chetti, 1984; Elmer, 1977). Because our samples of maltreated children were drawn largely from the lower-SES strata (cf. Pelton, 1978), our matched comparisons of necessity comprised high-risk poverty samples. That we found fairly uniform between-group dif-ferences in our studies demonstrates conclusively that maltreat-ment *does* adversely affect development beyond the deleterious ef-fects of poverty. Our findings underscore the importance of providing individually tailored intervention services to all children with a history of maltreatment. Contrary to the conceptions of some researchers, it is clear that maltreated children do exhibit maladapta-tions in development compared with other lower-SES children. Al-though evidence is emerging that persistent poverty also exerts an independent and significant negative impact on child adaptation be-yond child maltreatment (Kaufman & Cicchetti, 1989), the effects of maltreatment are significantly greater.

A final contribution our work can make to understanding nor-mal development lies in the effects of poverty. Currently there is far too little work on the development of children reared in poverty. Not only do our studies on how maltreated children negotiate stage-sa-lient tasks of development inform this issue, but the study of non-maltreated youngsters' attachment relationships, self development, communication skills, and peer relations also provides insight on the impact that poverty has on development (cf. Feagans & Farran, 1982; Hess & Shipman, 1968). The early results of this research suggest that most nonmaltreated children reared in poverty function adaptively despite the adversity they face. This suggests there are resilient children in this high-risk population (Pavenstedt, 1965) and encourages us to identify the processes by which this successful adaptation occurs.

## ACKNOWLEDGMENTS

The work described in this chapter was supported by grants from the Foundation for Child Development, the William T. Grant Foundation, the John D. and Catherine T. MacArthur Foundation, Network on Early Childhood, the A. L. Mailman Family Foundation, Inc., the March of Dimes, the Massachusetts Society for the Prevention of Cruelty to Children, the Monroe County Department of Social Services, the National Center on Child Abuse and Neglect, the National Institute of Mental Health Branch on Criminal and Violent Behavior, the New York State Department of Social Services, the New York State Department of Special Education, the Smith Richardson Foundation, Inc., the Spencer Foundation, and the Spunk Fund, Inc. I also would like to acknowledge the support I received from the Tishman family during my tenure as the Norman Tishman Associate Professor of Psychology and Social Relations at Harvard University. Special thanks go to my mentors and friends William Charlesworth, Norman Garmezy, Paul Meehl, Nina Murray, Alexander Siegel, Alan Sroufe, and Edward Zigler for their impeccable humane and scholarly example, as well as for their support, guidance, concern, and inspiration.

Additionally, I wish to thank my collaborators and students for the invaluable help on the projects described here. In particular, J. Lawrence Aber, Joseph Allen, Douglas Barnett, Marjorie Beeghly, Karen Braunwald, Vicki Carlson, Ann Churchill, Wendy Coster, E. Mark Cummings, Dorothy Dittman, Jody Ganiban, Michelle Gersten, Jan Gillespie, James Griffin, Kevin Hennessy, Joan Kaufman, Amber Keshishian, Carol Kottmeier, Michael Lynch, Linda Mans-Wagener, Laura McCloskey, Diana Meisburger, Kurt Olsen, Jerry Rabideau, Carolyn Rieder, Ross Rizley, Karen Schneider-Rosen, Susan Shonk, Ross Thompson, Jody Todd-Manly, Sheree Toth,

Mary Varanese, Joan Vondra, Sheldon Wagner, and Jennifer White deserve special recognition. I also extend my appreciation to Douglas Barnett, Susan Dickstein, Jody Ganiban, Donald Jensen, Ross Thompson, Sheree Toth, and Jennifer White for their valuable comments and to Victoria Gill for typing this manuscript. I wish to acknowledge the officials and especially the social workers of the Monroe County and New York State Department of Social Services and professionals of the New York State Department of Special Education for their dedicated effort in serving maltreated children and families. In particular, I would like to single out Diane Larter and Michelle Cournoyer Walsh. Finally, I dedicate this chapter to the memory of two friends who contributed so much to the well-being of others as well as to the development of scientific thought, Lawrence Kohlberg and Henry A. Murray. I will never forget their courage and vision. Their work and presence will live on forever.

## REFERENCES

Aber, J. L., & Allen, J. P. (1987). The effects of maltreatment on young children's socio-emotional development: An attachment theory perspective. *Developmental Psychology, 23*, 406–414.

Aber, J. L., Allen, J., Carlson, V., & Cicchetti, D. (1989). The effects of maltreatment on development during early childhood: Recent studies and their theoretical, clinical, and policy implications. In D. Cicchetti & V. Carlson (Eds.), *Child maltreatment: Theory and research on the causes and consequences of child abuse and neglect.* New York: Cambridge University Press.

Aber, J. L., Allen, J., & Cicchetti, D. (1988). The behavioral symptomatology of young maltreated children: A developmental analysis. Manuscript submitted for publication.

Aber, J. L. & Cicchetti, D. (1984). Socioemotional development in maltreated children: An empirical and theoretical analysis. In H. Fitzgerald, B. Lester, & M. Yogman (Eds.), *Theory and research in behavioral pediatrics* (Vol. 2). New York: Plenum Press.

Aber, J. L., & Zigler, E. (1981). Developmental considerations in the definition of child maltreatment. *New Directions for Child Development, 11*, 1–29.

Achenbach, T. (in press). What is "developmental" about developmental psychopathology? In J. Rolf, A. Masten, D. Cicchetti, K. Neuchterlein, & S. Weintraub (Eds.), *Risk and protective factors in the development of psychopathology.* New York: Cambridge University Press.

Achenbach, T. M., & Edelbrock, C. S. (1983). Taxonomic issues in child psychopathology. In T. H. Ollendick & M. Hersen, *Handbook of child psychopathology*. New York: Plenum Press.

Ainsworth, M. D. S. (1973). The development of infant-mother attachment. In B. Caldwell & H. Ricciutti (Eds.), *Review of child development research* (Vol. 3). Chicago: University of Chicago Press.

Ainsworth, M. D. S. (1908). Attachment and child abuse. In G. Gerbner, C. Ross, & E. Zigler (Eds.), *Child abuse: An agenda for action*. New York: Oxford University Press.

Ainsworth, M. D. S., Blehar, M. C., Waters, E., & Wall, S. (1978). *Patterns of attachment: A psychological study of the strange situation*. Hillsdale, NJ: Erlbaum.

Ainsworth, M., & Wittig, B. A. (1969). Attachment and exploratory behavior of 1-year-olds in a strange situation. In B. M. Foss (Ed.), *Determinants of infant behavior* (Vol. 4). New York: John Wiley.

Altemeier, W., O'Connor, S., Vietze, P., Sandler, H., & Sherrod, K. (1982). Antecedents of child abuse. *Journal of Pediatrics*, 100, 832–; P1830.

American Psychiatric Association. (1987). *Diagnostic and statistical manual of mental disorders* (3rd ed., rev.). Washington, DC: Author.

Arieti, S. (1967). *The intrapsychic self*. New York: Basic Books.

Arieti, S. (1974). *The interpretation of schizophrenia*. New York: Plenum Press. (Original work published 1955)

Arnold, M. (1960). *Emotion and personality* (2 vols.). New York: Columbia University Press.

Atlan, H. (1981). Hierarchical self-organization in living systems. In M. Zeleny (Ed.), *Autopoiesis: A theory of living organization*. New York: North-Holland.

Balla, D., & Zigler, E. (1975). Preinstitutional social deprivation and responsiveness to social reinforcement in institutionalized retarded individuals: A six-year follow-up study. *American Journal of Mental Deficiency, 80* 223–230.

Bandura, A. (1982). Self efficacy mechanisms in human agency. *American Psychologist, 32*, 122–147.

Barahal, R., Waterman, J., & Martin, H. (1981). The social-cognitive development of abused children. *Journal of Consulting and Clinical Psychology, 49*, 508–516.

Barnes, S., Gutfreund, M., Satterly, D., & Wells, G. (1983). Characteristics of adult speech which predict children's language development. *Journal of Child Language, 10*, 65; P1–84.

Bates, E. (1976). *Language and context: The acquisition of pragmatics*. New York: Academic Press.

Bates, E., Benigni, L., Bretherton, I., Camaioni, L., & Volterra, V. (1979). *The emergence of symbols: Cognition and communication in infancy*. New York: Academic Press.

Bates, E., Bretherton, I., Beeghly-Smith, M., & McNew, S. (1982). Social bases of language development: A reassessment. In H. Reese & L. Lipsitt

(Eds.), *Advances in child development and behavior* (Vol. 16). New York: Academic Press.

Baumrind, D. (1967). Childcare practices anteceding three patterns of preschool behavior. *Genetic Psychology Monographs, 75*, 43–88.

Baumrind, D. (1968). Authoritarian versus authoritative parental control. *Adolescence, 3*, 255–272.

Bayley, N. (1969). *The Bayley Scales of Infant Development.* New York: Psychological Corporation.

Becker, L., Armstrong, D., & Chan, F. (1986). Dendritic atrophy in children with Down's syndrome. *Annals of Neurology, 20*(4), 520–526.

Beeghly, M., & Cicchetti, D. (1987). An organizational approach to symbolic development in children with Down syndrome. *New Directions for Child Development, 36*, 5–29.

Bellinger, D. (1980). Consistency in the pattern of change in mothers' speech: Some discriminant analyses. *Journal of Child Language, 7*, 469–487.

Belsky, J. (1980). Child maltreatment: An ecological integration. *American Psychologist, 35*, 320–335.

Belsky, J. (1984). The determinants of parenting: A process model. *Child Development, 55*, 83–96.

Belsky, J., Rovine, M., & Taylor, D. G. (1984). The Pennsylvania infant and family development project: III. The origins of individual differences in infant-mother attachment: Maternal and infant contributions. *Child Development, 55*(3), 718–728.

Belsky, J., & Vondra, J. (1989). Lessons from child abuse: The determinants of parenting. In D. Cicchetti & V. Carlson (Eds.), *Child maltreatment: Theory and research on the causes and consequences of child abuse and neglect.* New York: Cambridge University Press.

Berger, J. (in press). Interactions between parents and their infants with Down syndrome. In D. Cicchetti & M. Beeghly (Eds.), *Children with Down syndrome: A developmental perspective.* New York: Cambridge University Press.

Berry, P., Gunn, P., & Andrews, R. (1980). Behavior of Down's syndrome infants in a strange situation. *American Journal of Mental Deficiency, 85*, 213–218.

Bertalanffy, L. von. (1968). *General system theory.* New York: George Braziller.

Besharov, D. (1981). Toward better research on child abuse and neglect: Making definitional issues an explicit methodological concern. *Child Abuse and Neglect, 5*, 383–390.

Bischof, N. (1975). A systems approach toward the functional connections of attachment and fear. *Child Development, 46*, 801–817.

Blager, F., & Martin, H. (1976). Speech and language of abused children. In H. P. Martin (Ed.), *The abused child.* Cambridge, MA: Ballinger.

Bleuler, E. (1950). *Dementia praecox or the group of schizophrenias.* New York: International Universities Press. (Original work published 1911)

Block, J. H., & Block, J. (1980). The role of ego-control and ego resiliency in the organization of behavior. In W. A. Collins (Ed.), *Minnesota symposia on child psychology* (Vol. 13). Hillsdale, NJ: Erlbaum.

Bousha, D. M., & Twentyman, C. T. (1984). Mother-child interactional style in abuse, neglect, and control groups: Naturalistic observations in the home. *Journal of Abnormal Psychology, 93*, 106–114.

Bower, T. G. R., Broughton, J., & Moore, M. K. (1970). Infant responses to approaching objects. *Perception and Psychophysics, 9*, 193–196.

Bowlby, J. (1944). Forty-four juvenile thieves: Their characters and home life. *International Journal of Psychoanalysis, 25*, 19–52, 107–127.

Bowlby, J. (1951) *Maternal care and mental health* (WHO Monograph No. 2). Geneva: World Health Organization.

Bowlby, J. (1973). *Attachment and loss. Vol. 2. Separation.* New York: Basic Books.

Bowlby, J. (1977a). The making and breaking of affectional bonds. *British Journal of Psychiatry, 130*, 201–210.

Bowlby, J. (1977b). The making and breaking of affectional bonds. *British Journal of Psychiatry, 130*, 421–431.

Bowlby, J. (1979). On knowing what you are not supposed to know and feeling what you are not supposed to feel. *Canadian Journal of Psychiatry, 24*, 403–; P1408.

Bowlby, J. (1980). *Attachment and loss. Vol. 3. Loss, sadness, and depression.* New York: Basic Books.

Bowlby, J. (1982). *Attachment and loss. Vol. 1. Attachment.* New York: Basic Books. (Original work published 1969).

Bowlby, J. (1988). Developmental psychiatry comes of age. *American Journal of Psychiatry, 145*, 1–10.

Braunwald, S. R. (1983). Why social interaction makes a difference: Insights from abused toddlers. In R. Golinkoff (Ed.), *The transition from prelinguistic to linguistic competence.* Hillsdale, NJ: Erlbaum.

Bretherton, I. (Ed.). (1984). *Symbolic play.* Orlando, FL: Academic Press.

Bretherton, I. (1985). Attachment theory: Retrospect and prospect. In I. Bretherton & E. Waters (Eds.), Growing points of attachment theory and research (pp. 3–35). *Monographs of the Society for Research in Child Development, 50* (1–2, Serial No. 209).

Bretherton, I. (1987). New perspectives on attachment relations. In J. Osofsky (Ed.), *Handbook of infancy* (2nd ed.) (pp. 1061–1100). New York: John Wiley.

Bretherton, I., and Ainsworth, M. (1974). Response of 1-year-olds to a stranger in a strange situation. In M. Lewis & L. Rosenblum (Eds.), *The origins of fear.* New York: John Wiley.

Bretherton, I., Bates, E., Benigni, L., Camaioni, D., & Volterra, V. (1979). Relationships between cognition, communication, and quality of attachment. In E. Bates, L. Benigni, I. Bretherton, L. Camaioni, & V. Volterra (Eds.), *The emergence of symbols*: *Cognitions and communication in infancy.* New York: Academic Press.

Bretherton, I., & Beeghly, M. (1982). Talking about internal states: The acquisition of an explicit theory of mind. *Developmental Psychology, 18*, 906–921.

Bretherton, I., Fritz, J., Zahn-Waxler, C., & Ridgeway, D. (1986). Learning to talk about emotion: A functionalist perspective. *Child Development, 57*, 530–548.

Bretherton, I., Ridgeway, D., & Cassidy, J. (in press). The role of internal working models in the attachment relationship: Theoretical, empirical, and developmental considerations. In M. Greenberg, D. Cicchetti, & M. Cummings (Eds.), *Attachment during the preschool years*. Chicago: University of Chicago Press.

Bridges, F. A., & Cicchetti, D. (1982). Mothers' ratings of the temperament characteristics of Down syndrome infants. *Developmental Psychology, 18*, 238–244.

Bronfenbrenner, U. (1979). *The ecology of human development: Experiments by nature and design*. Cambridge: Harvard University Press.

Brown, R., Bellugi, U., & Cazden, C. (1969). The child's grammar from 1 to 3. In J. P. Hill (Ed.), *Minnesota symposia on child psychology* (Vol. 2). Minneapolis: University of Minnesota Press.

Bruner, J. S. (1975). The ontogenesis of speech acts. *Journal of Child Language, 2*, 1–19.

Brunquell, D., Crichton, L., & Egeland, B. (1981). Maternal personality and attitude in disturbances of child rearing. *American Journal of Orthopsychiatry, 51*, 680–690.

Burgess, R., & Conger, R. (1978). Family interaction in abusive, neglectful and normal families. *Child Development, 19*, 1163–1173.

Butler, L. J. (1979, April). *Social and behavioral correlates of peer reputation*. Paper presented at the biennial meeting of the Society for Research in Child Development, San Francisco.

Butterworth, C., & Cicchetti, D. (1978). Visual calibration of posture in normal and motor retarded Down's syndrome infants. *Perception, 7*, 313–325.

Campos, J., Barrett, L., Lamb, M., Goldsmith, H. L., & Stenberg, C. (1983). Socioemotional development. In M. Haith & J. Campos (Eds.), *Handbook of child psychology. Vol. 2. Infancy and developmental psychology*. New York: John Wiley.

Campos, J., Hiatt, S., Ramsay, D., Henderson, C., & Svejda, M. (1978). The emergence of fear on the visual cliff. In M. Lewis & L. Rosenblum (Eds.), *The development of affect*. New York: Plenum Press.

Camras, L., Grow, J. G., & Ribordy, S. (1983). Recognition of emotional expression by abused children. *Journal of Clinical Child Psychology, 12*, 325–328.

Carey, W. (1973). Measurement of infant temperament in pediatric practice. In J. C. Westman (Ed.), *Individual differences in children* (pp. 298–304). New York: John Wiley.

Carlson, V., Cicchetti, D., Barnett, D., & Braunwald, K. (1989). Disorganized/disoriented attachment relationships in maltreated infants. *Developmental Psychology, 25*, 525–531.

Carnap, R. (1936). Testability and meaning. *Philosophy of Science, 3*, 420–471.

Casanova, M., Walker, L., Whitehouse, P., & Price, D. (1985). Abnormalities of the nucleus basalis in Down's syndrome. *Annals of Neurology, 18*, 310–313.

Cassell, E. J. (1986). Ideas in conflict: The rise and fall (and rise and fall) of new views of disease. *Daedalus*, 19–41.

Cassidy, J. (1988). Child-mother attachment and the self in six-year-olds. *Child Development, 59*, 121–134.

Cicchetti, D. (1984). The emergence of developmental psychopathology. *Child Development, 55*, 1–7.

Cicchetti, D. (1987). Developmental psychopathology in infancy: Illustration from the study of maltreated youngsters. *Journal of Consulting and Clinical Psychology, 55*, 837–845.

Cicchetti, D. (1988). *The child attachment interview.* Unpublished manuscript, University of Rochester.

Cicchetti, D. (1989). The developmental psychopathology of manic-depressive disease. (Manuscript in preparation.)

Cicchetti, D. (in press). An historical perspective on the discipline of developmental psychopathology. In J. Rolf, A. Masten, D. Cicchetti, K. Neuchterlein, & S. Weintraub (Eds.), *Risk and protective factors in the development of psychopathology.* New York: Cambridge University Press.

Cicchetti, D., & Aber, J. L. (1980). Abused children—abusive parents: An overstated case? *Harvard Educational Review, 50*, 244–255.

Cicchetti, D., & Aber, J. L. (1986). Early precursors to later depression: An organizational perspective. In L. Lipsitt & C. Rovee-Collier (Eds.), *Advances in infancy* (Vol. 4). Norwood, NJ: Ablex.

Cicchetti, D., & Barnett, D. (in press). Toward the development of a scientific nosology of child maltreatment. In D. Cicchetti & W. Grove (Eds.), *Thinking clearly about psychology: Essays in honor of Paul E. Meehl.* Minneapolis: University of Minnesota Press.

Cicchetti, D., Barnett, D., & Carlson, V. (1989). *The relation between maternal socialization of affect and the subsequent usage of emotion language: Evidence from maltreating and nonmaltreating dyads.* Manuscript submitted for publication.

Cicchetti, D., & Beeghly, M. (Eds.). (1987a). *Symbolic development in atypical children.* San Francisco: Jossey-Bass.

Cicchetti, D., & Beeghly, M. (1987b). Symbolic development in maltreated youngsters: An organizational perspective. *New Directions for Child Development, 36*, 47–68.

Cicchetti, D. & Beeghly, M. (Eds.). (in press). *The self in transition: Infancy to childhood.* Chicago: University of Chicago Press.

Cicchetti, D., Beeghly, M., Carlson, V., & Toth, S. (in press). An organizational developmental psychopathology perspective on the study of the self in atypical populations. In D. Cicchetti & M. Beeghly (Eds.), *The self in transition: Infancy to childhood*. Chicago: University of Chicago Press.

Cicchetti, D., & Braunwald, K. (1984). An organizational approach to the study of emotional development in maltreated infants. *Infant Mental Health Journal, 5*, 172–182

Cicchetti, D., & Carlson, V. (Eds.). (1989). *Child maltreatment: Theory and research on the causes and consequences of child abuse and neglect*. New York: Cambridge University Press.

Cicchetti, D., Carlson, V., Braunwald, K., & Aber, J. L. (1987). The Harvard Child Maltreatment Project: A context for research on the sequelae of child maltreatment. In R. Gelles & J. Lancaster (Eds.), *Research in child abuse: Biosocial perspectives*. New York: Aldine-DeGruyter.

Cicchetti, D., Cummings, E. M., Greenberg, M., & Marvin, R. (in press). An organizational perspective on attachment beyond infancy: Implications for theory, measurement, and research. In M. Greenberg, D. Cicchetti, & M. Cummings (Eds.), *Attachment during the preschool years*. Chicago: University of Chicago Press.

Cicchetti, D., & Hesse, P. (Eds.). (1982). *Emotional development*. San Francisco: Jossey-Bass.

Cicchetti, D., & Hesse, P. (1983). Affect and intellect: Piaget's contributions to the study of infant emotional development. In R. Plutchik & H. Kellerman (Eds.), *Emotion: Theory, research and experience* (Vol. 2). New York: Academic Press.

Cicchetti, D., & Olsen, K. (1990). The developmental psychopathology of child maltreatment. In M. Lewis & S. Miller (Eds.), *Handbook of developmental psychopathology*. New York: Plenum Press.

Cicchetti, D., & Pogge-Hesse, P. (1981). The relation between emotion and cognition in infant development: Past, present, and future perspectives. In M. Lamb & L. Sherrod (Eds.), *Infant social cognition: Empirical and theoretical considerations*. Hillsdale, NJ: Erlbaum.

Cicchetti, D., & Pogge-Hesse, P. (1982). Possible contributions of the study of organically retarded persons to developmental theory. In E. Zigler & D. Balla (Eds.), *Mental retardation: The developmental-difference controversy*. Hillsdale, NJ: Erlbaum.

Cicchetti, D., & Rizley, R. (1981). Developmental perspectives on the etiology, intergenerational transmission, and sequelae of child maltreatment. *New Directions for Child Development, 11*, 31–55.

Cicchetti, D., & Schneider-Rosen, K. (1984a). Theoretical and empirical considerations in the investigation of the relationship between affect and cognition in atypical populations of infants: Contributions to the formulation of an integrative theory of development. In C. Izard, J. Kagan, & R. Zajonc (Eds.), *Emotions, cognition and behavior*. New York: Cambridge University Press.

Cicchetti, D., & Schneider-Rosen, K. (1984b). Toward a developmental model of the depressive disorders. *New Directions for Child Development*, 26, 5–27.

Cicchetti, D., & Schneider-Rosen, K. (1986). An organizational approach to childhood depression. In M. Rutter, C. Izard, & P. Read (Eds.), *Depression in young people: Clinical and developmental perspectives*. New York: Guilford Press.

Cicchetti, D., & Serafica, F. (1981). The interplay among behavioral systems: Illustrations from the study of attachment, affiliation and manners in young Down syndrome children. *Developmental Psychology, 17*, 36–49.

Cicchetti, D., & Sroufe, L. A. (1976). The relationship between affective and cognitive development in Down syndrome infants. *Child Development, 47*, 920–929.

Cicchetti, D., & Sroufe, L. A. (1978). An organizational view of affect: Illustration from the study of Down's syndrome infants. In M. Lewis & L. Rosenblum (Eds.), *The development of affect*. New York: Plenum Press.

Cicchetti, D., Taraldson, B., & Egeland, B. (1978). Perspectives in the treatment and understanding of child abuse. In A. Goldstein (Ed.), *Perspectives for child mental health and education*. New York: Pergamon Press.

Cicchetti, D., & Toth, S. (1987). The application of a transactional risk model to intervention with multi-risk maltreating families. *Zero to Three, 7*, 1–8.

Cicchetti, D., Toth, S., & Bush, M. (1988). Developmental psychopathology and incompetence in childhood: Suggestions for intervention. In B. Lahey & A. Kazdin (Eds.), *Advances in clinical child psychology*. New York: Plenum Press.

Cicchetti, D., Toth, S., Bush, M. A., & Gillespie, J. F. (1988). Stage-salient issues: A transactional model of intervention. *New Directions for Child Development, 39*, 123–145.

Cicchetti, D., Toth, S., & Hennessy, K. (1989). Research on the consequences of child maltreatment and its application to educational settings. *Topics in Early Childhood Special Education, 9*, 33–55.

Cicchetti, D., & White, J. (1988). Emotional development and the affective disorders. In W. Damon (Ed.), *Child development: Today and tomorrow*. San Francisco: Jossey-Bass.

Clarke-Stewart, K. A. (1973). Interactions between mothers and their young children: Characteristics and consequences. *Monographs of the Society for Research in Child Development, 38* (Serial No. 153).

Connell, J. P. (1985). A new multidimensional measure of children's perceptions of control. *Child Development, 56*, 1018–1041.

Connell, J. P. (in press). Context, self, and action: A motivational analysis of self-system processes across the life-span. In D. Cicchetti & M. Beeghly (Eds.), *The self in transition: Infancy to childhood*. Chicago: University of Chicago Press.

Corsaro, W. A. (1979). Sociolinguistic patterns in adult-child interaction. In

E. Ochs & B. Shieffelin (Eds.), *Developmental pragmatics*. New York: Academic Press.

Coster, W. J., Gersten, M. S., Beeghly, M., & Cicchetti, D. (1989). Communicative functioning in maltreated toddlers. *Developmental Psychology, 25*.

Cowen, E., Pederson, A., Babigian, H., Izzo, L., & Trost, M. (1973). Long-term follow-up of early detected vulnerable children. *Journal of Consulting and Clinical Psychology, 41*, 438–446.

Cowie, V. (1970). *A study of the early development of mongols*. Oxford: Pergamon Press.

Crittenden, P. M. (1981). Abusing, neglecting, problematic, and adequate dyads: Differentiating by patterns of interaction. *Merrill-Palmer Quarterly, 27*, 201–208.

Crittenden, P. M. (1988). Relationships at risk. In J. Belsky & T. Nezworski (Eds.), *Clinical implications of attachment theory*. Hillsdale, NJ: Erlbaum.

Crittenden, P., & Ainsworth, M. (1989). Attachment and child abuse. In D. Cicchetti & V. Carlson (Eds.), *Child maltreatment: Theory and research on the consequences of child abuse and neglect*. New York: Cambridge University Press.

Cross, T. G. (1978). Motherese: Its association with rate of syntactic acquisition in young children. In N. Waterson & C. Snow (Eds.), *The development of communication: Social and pragmatic factors in language acquisition*. New York: John Wiley.

Cummings, E. M., & Cicchetti, D. (in press). Attachment, depression, and the transmission of depression. In M. T. Greenberg, D. Cicchetti, & E. M. Cummings (Eds.), *Attachment during the preschool years*. Chicago: University of Chicago Press.

Daly, M., and Wilson, M. (1981). Child maltreatment from a sociobiological perspective. *New Directions for Child Development, 11*, 93–112.

Damon, W. (1977). *The social world of the child*. San Francisco: Jossey-Bass.

Damon, W., and Hart, D. (1982). The development of self-understanding from infancy through adolescence. *Child Development, 53*, 841–864.

Darwin, C. (1965). *The expression of the emotions in man and animals*. Chicago: University of Chicago Press. (Original work published 1872)

Dean, A., Malik, M., Richards, W., & Stringer, S. (1986). Effects of parental maltreatment on children's conceptions of interpersonal relationships. *Developmental Psychology, 22*, 617–626.

DeCharms, R. (1968). *Personal causation: The internal affective determinants of behavior*. New York: Academic Press.

Deci, E. L. (1975). *Intrinsic motivation*. New York: Plenum Press.

Dell, P. F. (1982). Beyond homeostasis: Toward a concept of coherence. *Family Process, 21*, 21–41.

DeLozier, P. P. (1982). Attachment theory and child abuse. In C. M. Parkes & J. Stevenson-Hinde (Eds.), *The place of attachment in human behavior* (pp. 95–117). New York: Basic Books.

Dodge, K. A. (1986). A social information processing model of social competence in children. In M. Perlmutter (Ed.), *Minnesota symposia on child psychology* (Vol. 18, pp. 77–125). Hillsdale, NJ: Erlbaum.

Dodge, K. A., Murphy, R. R., & Buchsbaum, K. (1984). The assessment of intention-cue detection skills in children: Implications for developmental psychopathology. *Child Development, 55,* 163–173.

Dore, J. (1979). Children's illocutionary acts. In R. Freedle (Ed.), *Discourse processes: Advances in research and theory.* Norwood, NJ: Ablex.

Dweck, C. S., & Elliot, E. S. (1983). Achievement motivation. In P. H. Mussen (Ed.), *Handbook of child psychology. Vol. 4. Socialization, personality and social development* (pp. 643–691). New York: John Wiley.

Egeland, B., Jacobvitz, D., & Sroufe, L. A. (1988). Breaking the cycle of abuse. *Child Development, 59,* 1080–1088.

Egeland, B., & Sroufe, L. A. (1981). Developmental sequelae of maltreatment in infancy. *New Directions for Child Development, 11,* 77–92.

Egeland, B., Sroufe, L. A., & Erickson, M. (1983). The developmental consequences of different patterns of maltreatment. *Journal of Child Abuse and Neglect, 7,* 459–469.

Elmer, E. (1977). *Fragile families, troubled children.* Pittsburgh: University of Pittsburgh Press.

Elmer, E. (1981). Traumatized children, chronic illness, and poverty. In L. Pelton (Ed.), *The social context of child abuse and neglect.* New York: Human Sciences Press.

Emde, R. N., Gaensbauer, T., & Harmon, R. (1976). *Emotional expression in infancy: A biobehavioral study.* New York: International Universities Press.

Emde, R. N., Katz, E. L., & Thorpe, J. K. (1978). Emotional expression in infancy: II. Early deviations in Down syndrome. In M. Lewis and L. A. Rosenblum (Eds.), *The development of affect.* New York: Plenum Press.

Engel, G. (1971). Attachment behavior, object relations and the dynamic-economic points of view. *International Journal of Psychoanalysis, 52,* 183–196.

Engel, G. (1977). The need for a new medical model: A challenge for biomedicine. *Science, 196,* 129–135.

Erickson, M., Egeland, B., & Pianta, R. (1989). The effects of maltreatment on the development of young children. In D. Cicchetti & V. Carlson (Eds.), *Child maltreatment: Theory and research on the causes and consequences of child abuse and neglect.* New York: Cambridge University Press.

Erikson, E. (1950). *Childhood and society.* New York: W. W. Norton.

Farber, E. & Egeland, B. (1987). Invulnerability among abused and neglected children. In E. J. Anthony & B. Cohler (Eds.), *The invulnerable child.* New York: Guilford Press.

Feagans, L., & Farran, D. (Eds.). (1982). *The language of children reared in poverty.* New York: Academic Press.

Fenson, L. (1984). Developmental trends for action and speech in pretend play. In I. Bretherton (Ed.), *Symbolic play.* Orlando, FL. Academic Press.

Fischer, K. W. (1980). A theory of cognitive development: Control and construction of hierarchies of skills. *Psychological Review, 87*, 477–531.

Fowler, W., & Swenson, A. (1979). The influence of early language stimulation on development: Four studies. *Genetic Psychology Monographs, 100*, 73–109.

Frodi, A., & Lamb, M. (1980). Child abusers' responses to infant smiles and cries. *Child Development, 51*, 238–241.

Gaensbauer, T., & Harmon, R. (1982). Attachment behavior in abused/neglected and premature infants: Implications for the concept of attachment. In R. N. Emde & R. J. Harmon (Eds.), *Attachment and affiliative systems* (pp. 245–279). New York: Plenum Press.

Gaensbauer, T., Mrazek, D., & Harmon, R. (1980). Affective behavior patterns in abused and/or neglected infants. In N. Frude (Ed.), *The understanding and prevention of child abuse: Psychological approaches*. London: Concord Press.

Gaensbauer, T., & Sands, S. K. (1979). Distorted affective communications in abused/neglected infants and their potential impact on caretakers. *Journal of the American Academy of Child Psychiatry, 18*, 236–250.

Gallagher, R., Jens, K., & O'Donnell, K. (1983). The effect of physical status on the affective expressions of handicapped infants. *Infant Behavior and Development, 6*, 73–77.

Ganiban, J., Wagner, S., & Cicchetti, D. (in press). Temperament and Down syndrome. In D. Cicchetti & M. Beeghly (Eds.), *Children with Down syndrome: A developmental perspective*. New York: Cambridge University Press.

Garbarino, J. (1976). A preliminary study of some ecological correlates of child abuse: The impact of socioeconomic stress on mothers. *American Journal of Orthopsychiatry, 47*, 372–381.

Garbarino, J. (1977). The human ecology of child maltreatment: A conceptual model for research. *Journal of Marriage and the Family, 39*, 721–732.

Garbarino, J. (1982). *Children and families in the social environment*. Hawthorne, NY: Aldine.

Garbarino, J., & Gilliam, G. (1980). *Understanding abusive families*. Lexington, MA: Lexington Books.

Gardner, H. (1985). *The mind's new science*. New York: Basic Books.

Garmezy, N. (1983). Stressors of childhood. In N. Garmezy & M. Rutter (Eds.), *Stress, coping, and development in children*. New York: McGraw-Hill.

George, C., Kaplan, N., & Main, M. (1984). *Attachment interview for adults*. Unpublished manuscript, University of California, Berkeley.

George, C., & Main, M. (1979). Social interactions of young abused children: Approach, avoidance, and aggression. *Child Development, 50*, 306–318.

Gersten, M., Coster, W., Schneider-Rosen, K., Carlson, V., & Cicchetti, D. (1986). The socio-emotional bases of communicative functioning: Quality of attachment, language development, and early maltreatment. In M. E.

Lamb, A. L. Brown, & B. Rogoff (Eds.), *Advances in developmental psychology* (Vol. 4). Hillsdale, NJ: Erlbaum.

Gibson, E. J., & Walk, R. (1960). The "visual cliff." *Scientific American, 202*, 2–9.

Gilbreath, B., & Cicchetti, D. (1989). *Psychopathology in maltreating mothers.* Manuscript in preparation.

Gleitman, L. R., Newport, E. L., & Gleitman, H. (1984). The current status of the motherese hypothesis. *Journal of Child Language, 11*, 43–79.

Goldman-Rakic, P. (1987). Development of cortical circuitry and cognitive function. *Child Development, 58*, 601–622.

Goldsmith, H. H., & Alansky, J. (1987). Maternal and infant temperamental predictors of attachment: A meta-analytic review. *Journal of Consulting and Clinical Psychology, 55*, 805–816.

Goldstein, J., Freud, A., & Solnit, A. (1973). *Beyond the best interests of the child.* New York: Free Press.

Goldstein, J., Freud, A., & Solnit, A. (1979). *Before the best interests of the child.* New York: Free Press.

Golinkoff, R. (1983). *The transition from prelinguistic to linguistic communication.* Hillsdale, NJ: Erlbaum.

Gottesman, I. I., & Shields, J. (1972). *Schizophrenia and genetics: A twin study vantage point.* New York: Academic Press.

Gottlieb, G. (1983). The psychobiological approach to developmental issues. In P. Mussen (Ed.), *Handbook of child psychology.* New York: John Wiley.

Greenberg, M., Cicchetti, D., & Cummings, E. M. (Eds.). (in press). *Attachment beyond infancy.* Chicago: University of Chicago Press.

Greenberg, M., & Speltz, M. (1988). Attachment and the ontogeny of conduct problems. In J. Belsky and T. Nezworski (Eds.), *Clinical implications of attachment* (pp. 177–218). Hillsdale, NJ: Erlbaum.

Greenough, W., Black, J., & Wallace, C. (1987). Experience and brain development. *Child Development, 58*, 539–559.

Greenspan, S. I. (1981). *Psychopathology and adaptation in infancy and early childhood.* New York: International Universities Press.

Greenspan, S. I., & Porges, S. (1984). Psychopathology in infancy and early childhood: Clinical perspectives on the organization of sensory and affective-thematic experience. *Child Development, 55*, 49–70.

Greenspan, S. I., Weider, S., Lieberman, A., Nover, R., Lourie, R., & Robinson, M. (1985). *Infants in multi-risk families: Case studies in preventive intervention.* New York: International Universities Press.

Guidano, V. F. (1987). *Complexity of the self.* New York: Guilford Press.

Guidano, V. F., & Liotti, G. (1983). *Cognitive processes and emotional disorders: A structural approach to psychotherapy.* New York: Guilford Press.

Hardy-Brown, K., Plomin, R., & DeFries, J. C. (1981). Genetic and environmental influences on rate of communicative development in the first year of life. *Developmental Psychology, 17*, 704–717.

Harter, S. (1978). Effectance motivation reconsidered: Toward a developmental model. *Human Development, 21,* 34–64.

Harter, S. (1981). A model of intrinsic mastery motivation in children: Individual differences and developmental change. In A. Collins (Ed.), *Minnesota symposia on child psychology* (Vol. 14, pp. 215–255). Hillsdale, NJ: Erlbaum.

Harter, S. (1983). Developmental perspectives on the self system. In P. Mussen (Ed.), *Handbook of child psychology.* New York: John Wiley.

Harter, S., & Zigler, E. (1974). The assessment of effectance motivation in normal and retarded children. *Developmental Psychology, 10,* 169–180.

Hartlage, L. C., & Telzrow, C. F. (Eds.). (1985). *The neuropsychology of individual differences: A developmental perspective.* New York: Plenum Press.

Hartup, W. (1983). Peer relations. In P. Mussen (Ed.), *Carmichael's manual of child psychology.* New York: John Wiley.

Henderson, S. (1982). The significance of social relationships in the etiology of neurosis. In C. M. Parkes & J. Stevenson-Hinde (Eds.), *The place of attachment in human behavior.* London: Tavistock.

Herrenkohl, R. C., & Herrenkohl, E. C. (1981). Some antecedents and developmental consequences of child maltreatment. *New Directions for Child Development, 11,* 57–76.

Herrenkohl, E. C., Herrenkohl, R. C., Toedter, L., & Yanushevski, M. (1984). Parent-child interactions in abusive and nonabusive families. *Journal of the American Academy of Child Psychiatry, 23,* 641–648.

Hess, R., & Shipman, V. (1968). Maternal influences upon early learning: The cognitive environments of urban preschool children. In R. Hess & R. Bear (Eds.), *Early education: Current theory, research and action.* Chicago: Aldine.

Hesse, P., & Cicchetti, D. (1982). Toward an integrative theory of emotional development. *New Directions for Child Development, 16,* 3–48.

Hill, P., & McCune-Nicolich, L. (1981). Pretend play and patterns of cognition in Down's syndrome infants. *Child Development, 23,* 43–60.

Hill, S., & Tomlin, C. (1981). Self recognition in retarded children. *Child Development, 52,* 145–150.

Hoffman-Plotkin, D., & Twentyman, C. T. (1984). A multimodal assessment of behavioral and cognitive deficits in abused and neglected preschoolers. *Child Development, 55,* 794–802.

Holzman, M. (1972). The use of interrogative forms in the verbal interaction of three mothers and their children. *Journal of Psycholinguistic Research, 1,* 311–336.

Howes, C., & Eldredge, R. (1985). Responses of abused, neglected, and nonmaltreated children to the behavior of their peers. *Journal of Applied Developmental Psychology, 6,* 261–270.

Howes, C., & Espinosa, M. P. (1985). The consequences of child abuse for the formation of relationships with peers. *Child Abuse and Neglect, 9,* 397–404.

Hunter, R. S., & Kihlstrom, N. (1979). Breaking the cycle in abusive families. *American Journal of Psychiatry, 136*, 1320–1322.

Izard, C. (1977). *Human emotions.* New York: Plenum Press.

Izard, C. (1978). On the ontogenesis of emotions and emotion-cognition relationships in infancy. In M. Lewis & L. Rosenblum (Eds.), *The development of affect.* New York: Plenum Press.

Izard, C. (Ed.). (1979). *Emotions in personality and psychopathology.* New York: Plenum Press.

Izard, C. & Malatesta, C. (1987). Perspectives on emotional development: 1. Differential emotions theory of early emotional development. In J. D. Osofsky (Ed.), *Handbook of infant development* (2d edition, pp. 494–594). New York: Wiley.

Jacobsen, M. (1978). *Developmental neurobiology.* New York: Plenum Press.

Janes, C. L., & Hesselbrock, V. (1978). Problem children's adult adjustment predicted from teacher's ratings. *American Journal of Orthopsychiatry, 48*, 300; P1–309.

Juvenile Justice Standards Project. (1977). *Standards relating to abuse and neglect.* Cambridge, MA: Ballinger.

Kagan, J. (1971). *Change and continuity in infancy.* New York: John Wiley.

Kagan, J. (1981). *The second year: The emergence of self-awareness.* Cambridge: Harvard University Press.

Kanner, L. (1943). Autistic disturbances of affective contact. *Nervous Child, 2*, 217–250.

Kaplan, B. (1966). The study of language in psychiatry: The comparative developmental approach and its application to symbolization and language in psychopathology. In S. Arieti (Ed.), *American handbook of psychiatry.* New York: Basic Books.

Kaplan, B. (1967). Meditations on genesis. *Human Development, 10*, 65–87.

Kaplan, B. (1983). Genetic-dramatism: Old wine in new bottles. In S. Wapner & B. Kaplan (Eds.), *Toward a holistic developmental psychology.* Hillsdale, NJ: Erlbaum.

Kaplan, E. (1983). Process and achievement revisited. In S. Wapner & B. Kaplan (Eds.), *Toward a holistic developmental psychology.* Hillsdale, NJ: Erlbaum.

Kaufman, J., & Cicchetti, D. (1989). The effects of maltreatment on school-aged children's socioemotional development: Assessments in a day camp setting. *Developmental Psychology, 25*, 516–524.

Kaufman, J., & Zigler, E. (1989). The intergenerational transmission of child abuse and the prospect of predicting future abusers. In D. Cicchetti & V. Carlson (Eds.), *Child maltreatment: Theory and research on the causes and consequences of child abuse and neglect.* New York: Cambridge University Press.

Kazdin, A. E., Moser, J., Colbus, D., & Bell, R. (1985). Depressive symptoms among physically abused and psychiatrically disturbed children. *Journal of Abnormal Psychology, 94*, 298–307.

Keele, D., Richards, C., Brown, J., & Marshall, J. 1969). Catecholamine metabolism in Down's syndrome. *American Journal of Mental Deficiency, 74,* 125–129.

Kessen, W. (1971). Early cognitive development: Hot or cold? In T. Mischel (Ed.), *Cognitive development and epistemology*. New York: Academic Press.

Kinard, E. M. (1980). Emotional development in physically abused children. *American Journal of Orthopsychiatry, 50,* 686–696.

Kinard, E. M. (1982). Child abuse and depression: Cause or consequence? *Child Welfare, 61,* 403–413.

King, K., & Cicchetti, D. (1989). *Nosological distinction between chronic and acute, active and nonactive, maltreating parents: The role of stress, supports, and perceptions of child rearing hassles.* Manuscript submitted for publication.

Koestner, R., Ryan, R. M., Bernieri, F., & Holt, K. (1984). Setting limits on children's behavior: The differential effects of controlling versus informational styles on intrinsic motivation and creativity. *Journal of Personality, 52,* 233–248.

Kohlberg, L. (1981). *Essays on moral development. Vol. 1. The philosophy of moral development*. San Francisco: Harper & Row.

Kohlberg, L. (1984). *Essays on moral development. Vol. 2. The psychology of moral development*. San Francisco: Harper & Row.

Kohlberg, L., Snarey, W., & Ricks, D. (1984). The predictability of adult mental health. *Genetic Psychology Monographs*.

Kosslyn, S. (1980). *Image and mind*. Cambridge: Harvard University Press.

Kraepelin, E. (1971). *Dementia praecox and paraphrenia*. New York: Robert E. Krieger. (Original work published 1919)

Kraepelin, E. (1987). *Manic-depressive insanity and paranoia*. Edinburgh: Livingston. (Original work published 1921)

Kropp, J., & Haynes, O. M. (1987). Abusive and nonabusive mothers' ability to identify general and specific emotion signals of infants. *Child Development, 58,* 187–190.

Lahey, B., Conger, R., Atkeson, B., & Treiber, F. (1984). Parenting behavior and emotional status of physically abusive mothers. *Journal of Consulting and Clinical Psychology, 52,* 1062–1071.

Lamb, M., Gaensbauer, T. J., Malkin, C. M., & Schultz, L. A. (1985). The effects of child maltreatment on security of infant-adult attachment. *Infant Behavior and Development, 8,* 35–45.

Lamb, M., Thompson, R., Gardner, W., & Charnov, E. (1985). *Infant-mother attachment*. Hillsdale, NJ: Erlbaum.

Lamb, M., Thompson, R., Gardner, W., Charnov, E., & Estes, D. (1984). Security of infantile attachment as assessed in the strange situation: Its study and biological interpretation. *Behavioral and Brain Sciences, 7,* 124–147.

Lepper, M. R. (1981). Intrinsic and extrinsic motivation in children: Detrimental effects of superfluous social controls. In W. A. Collins (Ed.), *Minnesota symposia on Child Psychology* (Vol. 14). Hillsdale, NJ: Erlbaum.

Lewis, M., & Brooks-Gunn, J. (1979). *Social cognition and the acquisition of self*. New York: Plenum Press.

Lewis, M., Feiring, C., McGuffog, C., & Jaskir, J. (1984). Predicting psychopathology in six-year-olds from early social relations. *Child Development, 55*, 123–136.

Lewis, M., & Michalson, L. (1983). *Children's emotions and moods: Developmental theory and measurement*. New York: Plenum Press.

Lieven, E. (1978). Conversations between mothers and young children: Individual differences and their possible implications for the study of language learning. In N. Waterson & C. Snow (Eds.), *The development of communication*. New York: John Wiley.

Loveland, K. (1987). Behavior of young children with Down syndrome before the mirror: Finding things reflected. *Child Development, 58*, 928–936.

Maccoby, E. M., & Jacklin, C. M. (1974). *The psychology of sex differences*. Stanford: Stanford University Press.

Mahler, M., Pine, F., & Bergman, A. (1975). *The psychological birth of the human infant*. New York: Basic Books.

Main, M., & George, C. (1985). Response of abused and disadvantaged toddlers to distress in agemates: A study in the day care setting. *Developmental Psychology, 21*, 407–412.

Main, M., & Goldwyn, R. (1984). Predicting rejecting of her infant from mother's representation of her own experience: Implications for the abused-abusing intergenerational cycle. *Child Abuse and Neglect, 8*, 203–217.

Main, M., & Hesse, P. (in press). Lack of resolution of mourning in adulthood and its relationship to infant disorganization: Some speculations regarding causal mechanisms. In M. Greenberg, D. Cicchetti, & M. Cummings (Eds.), *Attachment during the preschool years*. Chicago: University of Chicago Press.

Main, M., Kaplan, N., & Cassidy, J. C. (1985). Security in infancy, childhood and adulthood: A move to the level of representation. In I. Bretherton & E. Waters (Eds.), Growing points of attachment theory and research (pp. 66–104). *Monographs of the Society for Research in Child Development, 50*, (1–2, Serial No. 209).

Main, M., & Solomon, J. (1986). Discovery of a disorganized disoriented attachment pattern. In T. B. Brazelton & M. W. Yogman (Eds.), *Affective development in infancy*. Norwood, NJ: Ablex.

Main, M., & Solomon, J. (in press). Procedures for identifying infants as disorganized/disoriented during the Ainsworth strange situation. In M. Greenberg, D. Cicchetti, & M. Cummings (Eds.), *Attachment during the preschool years*. Chicago: University of Chicago Press.

Main, M., & Weston, D. (1981). The quality of the toddler's relationship to mother and father. *Child Development, 53*, 932–940.

Malatesta, C., & Izard, C. (1984). The ontogenesis of human social signals: From biological imperatives to symbol utilization. In N. A. Fox & R. J.

Davidson (Eds.), *The psychobiology of affective development* (pp. 161–206). Hillsdale, NJ: Erlbaum.

Mans, L., Cicchetti, D., & Sroufe, L. A. (1978). Mirror reactions of Down's syndrome infants and toddlers: Cognitive underpinnings of self-recognition. *Child Development, 49,* 1247–1250.

Marmor, J. (1983). Systems thinking in psychiatry: Some theoretical and clinical implications. *American Journal of Psychiatry, 140,* 833–838.

Mash, E. J., Johnston, C., & Kovitz, K. (1983). A comparison of the mother-child interactions of physically abused and non-abused children during play and task situations. *Journal of Clinical Child Psychology, 12,* 337–346.

Maslow, A. (1954). *Motivation and personality.* New York: Harper & Row.

Matas, L., Arend, R., & Sroufe, L. A. (1978). Continuity in adaptation in the second year: The relationship between quality of attachment and later competence. *Child Development, 49,* 547–556.

Mayr, E. (1982). *The growth of biological thought.* Cambridge: Harvard University Press.

McCartney, K., Scarr, S., Phillips, D., Grajek, S., & Schwartz, J. C. (1982). Environmental differences among day care centers and their effects on children's development. In E. Zigler & E. Gordon (Eds.), *Day care: Scientific and social policy issues.* Boston: Auburn House.

McClelland, D. (1988). *Human motivation.* New York: Cambridge University Press.

Meehl, P. E. (1962). Schizotaxia, schizotypy, schizophrenia. *American Psychologist, 17,* 827–838.

Meehl, P. E. (1964). *Manual for use with a checklist of schizotypic signs.* Unpublished manuscript, University of Minnesota.

Meehl, P. E. (1972). Specific genetic etiology, psychodynamics, and therapeutic nihilism. *International Journal of Mental Health, 1,* 10–27.

Miller, A., & Wilson, P. (1979). Cognitive differentiation and integration: A conceptual analysis. *Genetic Psychology Monographs, 99,* 3–; P140.

Mischel, T. (1971). Piaget: Cognitive conflict and the motivation of thought. In T. Mischel (Ed.), *Cognitive development and epistemology.* New York: Academic Press.

Mora, G., & Brand, J. (Eds.). (1970). *Psychiatry and its history.* Springfield, IL: Charles C. Thomas.

Morris, M. G., & Gould, R. W. (1963). Role reversal: A necessary concept in dealing with the battered-child syndrome. *American Journal of Orthopsychiatry, 33,* 298–299.

Motti, F., Cicchetti, D., & Sroufe, L. A. (1983). From infant affect expression to symbolic play: The coherence of development in Down syndrome children. *Child Development, 54,* 1168–1175.

Mueller, N., & Silverman, N. (1989). Peer relations in maltreated children. In D. Cicchetti & V. Carlson (Eds.), *Child maltreatment: Theory and research on the causes and consequences of child abuse and neglect.* New York: Cambridge University Press.

Murray, H. A. (1938). *Explorations in personality*. New York: Oxford University Press.

Nelson, K. (1973). Structure and strategy in learning to talk. *Monographs of the Society for Research in Child Development, 38* (Serial No. 149).

Nelson, K. (1977). Facilitating children's syntax acquisition. *Developmental Psychopathology, 13*, 101–107.

Olds, D. L., & Henderson, C. (1989). The prevention of maltreatment. In D. Cicchetti & V. Carlson (Eds.), *Child maltreatment: Theory and research on the causes and consequences of child abuse and neglect*. New York: Cambridge University Press.

Pap, A. (1958). Disposition concepts and extension logic. In H. Feigl, M. Scriven, & G. Maxwell (Eds.), *Minnesota studies in the philosophy of science* (Vol. 2, pp. 196–224). Minneapolis: University of Minnesota Press.

Parke, R. D., & Collmer, C. W. (1975). Child abuse: An interdisciplinary analysis. In E. M. Hetherington (Ed.), *Review of child development research* (Vol. 5, 509–590). Chicago: University of Chicago Press.

Pattee, H. (Ed.). (1973). *Hierarchy theory: The challenge of complex systems*. New York: George Braziller.

Pavenstedt, E. (1965). A comparison of the child-rearing environment of upper-lower and very low-lower class families. *American Journal of Orthopsychiatry, 35*, 89–98.

Pelton, L. (1978). Child abuse and neglect: The myth of classlessness. *American Journal of Orthopsychiatry, 48*, 608–; P1617.

Piaget, J. (1962). *Play, dreams and imitation in childhood*. New York: W. W. Norton.

Piaget, J. (1981). *Intelligence and affectivity: Their relationship during child development*. Palo Alto, CA: Annual Reviews. (Original work published 1954)

Plomin, R. (1986). *Development, genetics and psychology*. Hillsdale, NJ: Erlbaum.

Pribram, K. H. (1986). The cognitive revolution and mind/brain issues. *American Psychologist, 41*, 507–520.

Provence, S., & Lipton, R. (1962). *Infants in institutions*. New York: International Universities Press.

Provence, S., & Naylor, A. (1983). *Working with disadvantaged parents and their children*. New Haven: Yale University Press.

Purpura, D. (1975). Dendritic differentiation in human cerebral cortex: Normal and aberrant developmental patterns. In G. Kretzberg (Ed.), *Advances in neurology* (Vol. 12, pp. 91–116). New York: Raven Press.

Radke-Yarrow, M., Cummings, E. M., Kuczynski, L., & Chapman, M. (1985). Patterns of attachment in two- and three-year-olds in normal families and families with parental depression. *Child Development, 56*, 884–893.

Rajecki, D. W., Lamb, M. E., & Obmascher, P. (1978). Toward a general theory of infantile attachment: A comparative review of aspects of the social bond. *Behavioral and Brain Sciences, 1*, 417–464.

Reese, H., & Overton, W. (1970). Models of development and theories of development. In L. R. Goulet & P. Baltes (Eds.), *Life span developmental psychology: Research and theory.* New York: Academic Press.

Reidy, T. J. (1977). The aggressive characteristics of abused and neglected children. *Journal of Clinical Psychology, 33,* 1140–1145.

Reite, M., & Caine, N. (Eds.). (1983). *Child abuse: The nonhuman primate data.* New York: Alan R. Liss.

Rieder, C., & Cicchetti, D. (1989). An organizational perspective on cognitive control functioning and cognitive-affective balance in maltreated children. *Developmental Psychology, 25,* 482–493.

Robins, L. N. (1978). Sturdy childhood predictors of adult anti-social behavior: Replications from longitudinal studies. *Psychological Medicine, 8,* 611–622.

Roff, M., Sells, B., & Golden, M. M. (1972). *Social adjustment and personality development in children.* Minneapolis: University of Minnesota Press.

Rolf, J., Masten, A., Cicchetti, D., Neuchterlein, K., & Weintraub, S. (Eds.). (in press). *Risk and protective factors in the development of psychopathology.* New York: Cambridge University Press.

Rosenberg, M. S. (1987). New directions for research on the psychological maltreatment of children. *American Psychologist, 42,* 166–171.

Rothbart, M., & Derryberry, D. (1981). The development of individual differences in temperament. In M. Lamb & A. L. Brown (Eds.), *Advances in developmental psychology* (Vol. 1, pp. 37–86). Hillsdale, NJ: Erlbaum.

Rubin, K., Fein, G., & Vandenberg, B. (1983). Play. In P. Mussen (Ed.), *Handbook of child psychology. Vol. 4. Socialization.* New York: John Wiley.

Ruppenthal, G. C., Arling, G. L., Harlow, H. F., Sackett, G. P., & Suomi, S. J. (1976). A 10-year perspective of motherless mother monkey behavior. *Journal of Abnormal Psychology, 85,* 341–349.

Rutter, M. (1981). *Maternal deprivation reassessed.* Harmondsworth, Middlesex: Penguin Books. (Original work published 1972)

Rutter, M. (1986). The developmental psychopathology of depression: Issues and perspectives. In M. Rutter, C. Izard, & P. Read (Eds.), *Depression in children: Developmental perspectives.* New York: Guilford Press.

Rutter, M. (1989). Intergenerational continuities and discontinuities in serious parenting difficulties. In D. Cicchetti & V. Carlson (Eds.), *Child maltreatment: Theory and research on the causes and consequences of child abuse and neglect.* New York: Cambridge University Press.

Rutter, M., & Garmezy, N. (1983). Developmental psychopathology. In P. Mussen (Ed.), *Handbook of child psychology.* (Vol. 4, pp. 775–911). New York: John Wiley.

Ryan, R. M., Connell, J. P., & Deci, E. L. (1985). A motivational analysis of self-determination and self-regulation in education. In C. Ames & P. E. Ames (Eds.), *Research on motivation in education: The classroom milieu.* New York: Academic Press.

Saarni, C. (1978). Cognitive and communicative features of emotional experience, or Do you show what you think you feel? In M. Lewis & L. Rosenblum (Eds.), *The development of affect.* New York: Plenum Press.

Sackett, G., Sameroff, A., Cairns, R., & Suomi, S. (1981). Continuity in behavioral development: Theoretical and empirical issues. In K. Immelmann, G. Garlow, L. Petrinovich, & M. Main (Eds.), *Behavioral development*. Cambridge: Cambridge University Press.

Salzinger, S., Kaplan, S., & Artemyeff, C. (1983). Mothers' personal social networks and child maltreatment. *Journal of Abnormal Psychology, 92*, 68–76.

Salzinger, S., Wondolowsky-Svensson, S., Kaplan, T., Kaplan, S., & Kristaul, J. (1984). *A discourse analysis of the conversations between maltreated children and their mothers*. Paper presented at the meeting of the Society for Research in Child Development, Toronto.

Sameroff, A. (1983). Developmental systems: Contexts and evolution. In P. Mussen (Ed.), *Handbook of child psychology* (Vol. 1, pp. 237–294). New York: John Wiley.

Sameroff, A., & Chandler, M. (1975). Reproductive risk and the continuum of caretaking casualty. In F. Horowitz, M. Hetherington, S. Scarr-Salapatek, & G. Siegel (Eds.), *Review of child development research* (Vol. 4). Chicago: University of Chicago Press.

Sameroff, A., Seifer, R., & Zax, M. (1982). Early development of children at risk for emotional disorder. *Monographs of the Society for Research in Child Development, 47*.

Sander, L. (1962). Issues in early mother-child interaction. *Journal of the American Academy of Child Psychiatry, 1*, 141–166.

Sander, L. (1975). Infant and caretaking environment: Investigation and conceptualization of adaptive behavior in systems of increasing complexity. In E. J. Anthony (Ed.), *Exploration in child psychiatry*. New York: Plenum Press.

Santostefano, S. (1978). *A bio-developmental approach to clinical child psychology*. New York: John Wiley.

Santostefano, S. (1985). *Cognitive control therapy with children and adolescents*. Elmsford, NY: Pergamon Press.

Santostefano, S., & Rieder, C. (1984). Cognitive controls and aggression in children: The concept of cognitive-affective balance. *Journal of Consulting and Clinical Psychology, 52* (1), 46–56.

Sarason, I. G., & Sarason, B. R. (1981). The importance of cognition and moderator variables. In D. Magnusson (Ed.), *Toward a psychology of situations: An interpersonal perspective*. Hillsdale, NJ: Erlbaum.

Scarr, S., & Kidd, K. (1983). Developmental behavior genetics. In M. Haith & J. Campos (Eds.), *Carmichael's manual of child psychology* (Vol. 2, pp. 345–434). New York: John Wiley.

Schneider-Rosen, K., Braunwald, K., Carlson, V., & Cicchetti, D. (1985). Current perspectives in attachment theory: Illustration from the study of maltreated infants. In I. Bretherton & E. Waters (Eds.), Growing points of attachment theory and research (pp. 194–210). *Monographs of the Society for Research in Child Development, 50* (1–2 Serial No. 209).

Schneider-Rosen, K., & Cicchetti, D. (1984). The relationship between affect and cognition in maltreated infants: Quality of attachment and the development of visual self-recognition. *Child Development, 55,* 648–658.

Scott, B., Becker, L., & Petit, T. (1983). Neurobiology of Down's syndrome. *Progress in Neurobiology, 21,* 199–237.

Sellars, W. S. (1958). Counterfactuals, dispositions, and the causal modalities. In H. Feigl, M. Scriven, & G. Maxwell (Eds.), *Minnesota studies in the philosophy of science* (Vol. 2, pp. 225–308). Minneapolis: University of Minnesota Press.

Selman, R. (1980). *The growth of interpersonal understanding: Developmental and clinical analyses.* New York: Academic Press.

Serafica, F. C., & Cicchetti, D. (1976). Down's syndrome children in a strange situation: Attachment and exploratory behaviors. *Merrill-Palmer Quarterly, 21,* 137–150.

Simon, H. (1962). The architecture of complexity. *Proceedings of the American Philosophical Society, 106,* 467–482.

Slade, A. (1987). A longitudinal study of maternal involvement and symbolic play during the toddler period. *Child Development, 58,* 367–375.

Snow, C. E. (1977). The development of conversation between mothers and babies. *Journal of Child Language, 4,* 1–2.

Snow, C. E., & Ferguson, C. (1977). *Talking to children.* Cambridge: Cambridge University Press.

Snow, C. E., & Gilbreath, B. J. (1983). Explaining transitions. In R. M. Golinkoff (Ed.), *The transition from prelinguistic to linguistic communication.* Hillsdale, NJ: Erlbaum.

Sorce, J., & Emde, R. (1981). Mother's presence is not enough: Effect of emotional availability on infant exploration. *Developmental Psychology, 17,* 737–745.

Sorce, J., & Emde, R. (1982). The meaning of infant emotional expressions: Regularities in caregiving responses in normal and Down's syndrome infants. *Journal of Child Psychology and Psychiatry, 23,* 145–158.

Spencer, H. (1900). *First principles* (6th ed.). New York: Appleton. (Original work published 1862)

Spieker, S. J., & Booth, C. (1988). Family risk typologies and patterns of insecure attachment. In J. Belsky & T. Nezworski (Eds.), *Clinical implications of attachment* (pp. 95–135). Hillsdale, NJ: Erlbaum.

Spiker, D. (in press). Early intervention from a developmental perspective. In D. Cicchetti & M. Beeghly (Eds.), *Children with Down syndrome: A developmental perspective.* New York: Cambridge University Press.

Spiker, D., & Ricks, M. (1984). Visual self-recognition in autistic children: Developmental relationships. *Child Development, 55,* 214; P1–225.

Spitz, R. (1951). The psychogenic diseases of infancy: An attempt at their etiologic classification. *Psychoanalytic Study of the Child, 6,* 255–275.

Spitz, R., & Wolf, K. (1946). Anaclitic depression: An inquiry into the genesis of psychiatric conditions in early childhood, II. *Psychoanalytic Study of the Child, 2,* 313–342.

Sroufe, L. A. (1979a). The coherence of individual development. *American Psychologist, 34*, 834–841.

Sroufe, L. A. (1979b). Socioemotional development. In J. Osofsky (Ed.), *Handbook of infant development*. New York: John Wiley.

Sroufe, L. A. (1983). Infant-caregiver attachment and patterns of adaptation in preschool: The roots of maladaptation and competence. In M. Perlmutter (Ed.), *Minnesota symposium on child psychology* (Vol. 16). Hillsdale, NJ: Erlbaum.

Sroufe, L. A. (in press). An organizational perspective on the self. In D. Cicchetti & M. Beeghly (Eds.), *The self in transition: Infancy to childhood*. Chicago: University of Chicago Press.

Sroufe, L. A., & Fleeson, J. (1986). Attachment and the construction of relationships. In W. Hartup & Z. Rubin (Eds.), *Relationships and development*. Hillsdale, NJ: Erlbaum.

Sroufe, L. A., & Rutter, M. (1984). The domain of developmental psychopathology. *Child Development, 55*, 17–29.

Sroufe, L. A., & Waters, E. (1976). The ontogenesis of smiling and laughter: A perspective on the organization of development in infancy. *Psychological Review, 83*, 173–189.

Sroufe, L. A., & Waters, E. (1977). Attachment as an organizational construct. *Child Development, 48*, 1184–1199.

Sroufe, L. A., & Wunsch, J. (1972). The development of laughter in the first year of life. *Child Development, 43*, 1326; P1–1344.

Stern, D. (1985). *The interpersonal world of the infant: A view from psychoanalysis and developmental psychology*. New York: Basic Books.

Sulkowski, A. (1983). Psychobiology of schizophrenia: A neo-Jacksonian detour. *Perspectives in Biology and Medicine, 26*, 205; P1–218.

Takashima, S., Becker, L., Armstrong, D., & Chan, F. (1981). Abnormal neuronal development in the visual cortex of the human fetus and infant with Down's syndrome: A quantitative and qualitative Golgi study. *Brain Research, 225*, 1–21.

Thompson, R., Cicchetti, D., Lamb, M., & Malkin, C. (1985). The emotional responses of Down syndrome and normal infants in the strange situation: The organization of affective behavior in infants. *Developmental Psychology, 21*, 828–841.

Tomkins, S. (1963). *Affect, imagery, consciousness. Vol. 1. Positive affects*. New York: Springer.

Tomkins, S. (1962). *Affect, imagery, consciousness. Vol. 2. Negative affects*. New York: Springer.

Trickett, P. K., & Susman, E. J. (1988). Parental perceptions of childrearing practices in physically abusive and nonabusive families. *Developmental Psychology, 24*, 270–276.

Uzgiris, I., & Hunt, J. (1975). *Assessment in infancy*. Urbana: University of Illinois Press.

Varela, F. J. (1976a). On observing natural systems. *CoEvolution Quarterly*, Summer.

*Socioemotional, Cognitive, and Representational Development*

Varela, F. J. (1976b). Not one, not two. *CoEvolution Quarterly,* Fall.

Varela, F. J. (1981). Describing the logic of the living. In M. Zeleny (Ed.), *Autopoisesis: A theory of living organization.* New York: North-Holland.

Vondra, J., Barnett, D., & Cicchetti, D. (1989). *Perceived and actual competence among maltreated and comparison school children. Development and Psychopathology, 1,* 237–255.

Vondra, J., Barnett, D., & Cicchetti, D. (in press). Self-concept, motivation, and competence among preschoolers from maltreating and comparison families. *Child Abuse and Neglect.*

Vondra, J., Barnett, D., Shonk, S., Toth, S., & Cicchetti, D. (1989). *Self, parent and teacher perceptions of competence in maltreated and nonmaltreated school children.* Manuscript submitted for publication.

Vygotsky, L. S. (1978). *Mind in society.* Cambridge: Harvard University Press.

Wagner, E. (1979, March). *Interpersonal behavior and peer status.* Paper presented at the biennial meeting of the Society for Research in Child Development, San Francisco.

Wakefield, H., & Underwager, R. (1988). *Accusations of child sexual abuse.* Springfield, IL: Charles C. Thomas.

Wald, M., Carlsmith, J., & Leiderman, P. H. (Eds.). (1988). *Protecting abused/ neglected children: A comparison of home and foster placement.* Stanford: Stanford University Press.

Wasserman, G., Green, A., & Allen, R. (1983). Going beyond abuse: Maladaptive patterns of interaction in abusing mother-infant pairs. *Journal of the American Academy of Child Psychiatry, 22,* 245–252.

Waters, E., & Sroufe, L. A. (1983). Competence as a developmental construct. *Developmental Review, 3,* 79–97.

Waters, E., Wippman, J., & Sroufe, L. A. (1979). Attachment, positive affect, and competence in the peer group: Two studies in construct validation. *Child Development, 50,* 821–829.

Watson, M., & Fischer, K. (1977). A developmental sequence of agent use in late infancy. *Child Development, 48,* 828–836.

Wechsler, J. (1981). *National study of the incidence and severity of child abuse and neglect.* Washington, DC: U.S. Department of Health and Human Services, National Center on Child Abuse and Neglect.

Weinberger, D. R. (1987). Implications of normal brain development for the pathogenesis of schizophrenia. *Archives of General Psychiatry, 44,* 660–669.

Weinshilbaum, R., Thoa, N., Johnson, D., Kopin, I., & Axelrod, J. (1971). Proportional release of norepinephrine and dopamine-beta-hydroxylase from sympathetic nerves. *Science, 174,* 1349–1351.

Weiss, P. A. (1969a). The living system: Determinism stratified. In A. Koestler & J. Smythies (Eds.), *Beyond reductionism.* Boston: Beacon Press.

Weiss, P. (1969b). *Principles of development.* New York: Hafner.

Wells, G. (1980). Apprenticeship in meaning. In K. W. Nelson (Ed.), *Children's language* (Vol. 2). New York: Gardner.

Werner, H. (1937). Process and achievement: A basic problem of education and developmental psychology. *Harvard Educational Review, 7*, 353–368.

Werner, H. (1948). *Comparative psychology of mental development.* New York: International Universities Press.

Werner, H. (1957). The concept of development from a comparative and organismic point of view. In D. B. Harris (Ed.), *The concept of development.* Minneapolis: University of Minnesota Press.

Werner, H., & Kaplan, B. (1963). *Symbol formation: An organismic-developmental approach to language and the expression of thought.* New York: John Wiley.

Westerman, M., & Haustead, L. F. (1982). The role of adult speech in language development. In C. Fraser & K. Scherer (Eds.), *The social psychology of language.* Cambridge: Cambridge University Press.

Wiggins, R., McCandless, D., & Enna, S. (1985). *Developmental neurochemistry.* Austin: University of Texas Press.

Wilden, A. (1980). *System and structure.* London: Tavistock.

Wilson, R., & Matheny, A. (1986). Behavior-genetics research in infant temperament: The Louisville Twin Study. In R. Plomin & J. Dunn (Eds.), *The study of temperament: Continuities and challenges.* Hillsdale, NJ: Erlbaum.

Wolfe, D. A. (1985). Child abusive parents: An empirical review and analysis. *Psychological Bulletin, 97*, 462–482.

Wolfe, D. A. (1987). *Child abuse.* Newbury Park, CA: Sage.

Wolfe, D. A., Edwards, B., Manion, I., & Koverola, C. (1988). Early intervention for child abuse and neglect: A preliminary investigation. *Journal of Consulting and Clinical Psychology, 56*, 40–47.

Yando, R., Seitz, V., & Zigler, E. (1978). *Imitation: A developmental perspective.* Hillsdale, NJ: Erlbaum.

Yates, C., Simpson, J., Maloney, A., Gorden, A., & Reid, A. (1980). Alzheimer-like cholinergic deficiency in Down's syndrome. *Lancet, 2,* 979.

Zahn-Waxler, C., & Radke-Yarrow, M. (1982). The development of altruism: Alternative research strategies. In N. Eisenberg (Ed.), *Development of social behavior.* New York: Academic Press.

Zigler, E. (1971). The retarded child as a whole person. In H. E. Adams & W. K. Boardman (Eds.), *Advances in experimental clinical psychology* (Vol. 1). New York: Pergamon Press.

Zigler, E. (1976). Controlling child abuse: An effort doomed to failure? *Newsletter of the Division on Developmental Psychology, American Psychological Association,* February, 17–30.

Zigler, E., & Balla, D. (1982). Atypical development: Personality determinants in the behavior of the retarded. In E. Zigler, M. Lamb, & I. Child (Eds.), *Socialization and personality development* (pp. 238–245). New York: Oxford University Press.

Zubin, J., & Spring, B. (1977). Vulnerability: A new view of schizophrenia. *Journal of Abnormal Psychology, 56*, 103–126.

# Emotion and Self-Regulation

## Ross A. Thompson
*University of Nebraska–Lincoln*

*E*motions are important to developmental study because they shape the experience of developing individuals. Consider the following examples:

> During a routine laboratory procedure, 12-month-old Joey watched his mother unexpectedly leave the room. He immediately erupted into loud sobs and would not be comforted by the research assistant. Indeed, his crying became more intense and angry—fists clenched and back arched—the more she tried to soothe him. When his mother returned, Joey quieted immediately and quickly turned to her with the raised-arms "pick me up" gesture. After a few moments, he returned to playing with the toys at her feet.

> Sarah, a 4-year-old, was busily building a tower of blocks at her day-care center. Suddenly another preschooler crashed into her tower while playing a running game. Sarah stood up and

The new research reported in this chapter on developmental changes in emotional dynamics was supported by a grant from the Foundation for Child Development as part of my recognition as a Young Scholar in Social and Affective Development, and I also received a small supplementary grant from the same foundation for the cross-cultural work on emotion and attachment. The Foundation's support of this work is deeply appreciated. The financial support of the University of Nebraska Research Council for the purchase of video equipment and release time for two summers of research work is also gratefully acknowledged. This chapter is for Janet, Scott, and Brian, my educators in emotion.

raised her fist to strike the offender, but instead she shouted, "I HATE IT WHEN YOU DO THAT!" Soon afterward she retreated to the reading corner, where she began looking at books with a teacher, thumb in mouth.

Mike was sitting in the roller-coaster car that would soon have him hurtling through the air. He had been unsure whether he wanted to go on this ride, but the challenges of the older boys he was with compelled him to buy a ticket. As the car moved faster and faster, Mike could feel his heart beating rapidly and his palms getting sweaty, so he closed his eyes and began to think about his birthday party last week. When the ride ended, he turned to his friends and said, "That was neat—let's do it again!"

As parents and practitioners have long recognized, emotional reactions are a prominent feature of everyday life for children. But the systematic study of emotional development has waned until recently because theorists have lacked good models for describing the functional value of emotion in the organization of psychologically adaptive behavior. These vignettes illustrate two features of emotion that have rekindled the interest of developmental researchers and that constitute the dual themes for this chapter.

The first concerns emotion as a behavioral regulator. Contrary to some earlier views of emotions as disorganizing, as extraneous, or as epiphenomena of more significant cognitive or social accomplishments, current views of emotion underscore their biologically adaptive and psychologically constructive functions (see, for example, Barrett & Campos, 1987; Campos, Barrett, Lamb, Goldsmith, & Stenberg, 1983; Izard & Malatesta, 1987; Lewis & Michalson, 1985; Sroufe, 1979). Developmental researchers have discovered that emotions assume a significant role in social communication, personality functioning, goal achievement, and even cognitive processing and are particularly important in social interactions with parents and peers (as the examples above illustrate). Although emotions retain a capacity to disorganize or undermine healthy functioning, their capacity to motivate, organize, and direct more adaptive behavioral processes has contributed to a reappraisal of their role in development and behavior. This reappraisal has sparked considerable research—much of it reflected in the contributions to this symposium—and the first part of this chapter is devoted to a brief summary of our own laboratory's recent contributions to this emergent view.

The second theme concerns emotion as a regulated phenomenon. In the examples above, emotional reactions are dynamic processes that vary over time according to the efforts of familiar caregivers (as with Joey), the use of a repertoire of expressive modes and self-soothing behaviors (as with Sarah), or the strategic efforts of the individual (as with Mike). Emotion is initially regulated by others, but over the course of early development it becomes increasingly self-regulated as a result of neurophysiological development, the growth of cognition and language, and the emergence of emotional and self-understanding. As a consequence, whereas the newborn infant may cry uncontrollably, the toddler is capable of seeking assistance, the preschooler can reflect upon and talk about her feelings, the school-age child can redirect attention and use other deliberate strategies to reduce distress or anxiety, and the adolescent has sufficient self-understanding to evoke more idiosyncratic self-regulatory strategies. As a consequence, the enlistment of emotion in the organization of higher-order behavioral processes increases through the use of emotional regulation.

Emotional regulation is different from, but related to, the regulation of emotional displays (cf. Saarni, 1979, 1989, this volume). Whereas the latter concerns the management of emotional expressions in social situations, the former concerns the regulation of underlying experiences of emotional arousal, whether or not they are socially dissembled. To be sure, the two are often linked. For example, one way of altering emotional experience is to behave in an inconsistent manner (e.g., "whistling in the dark" or appearing happy while distressed), although this may be ineffective when underlying arousal is strong. Conversely, emotional display rules sometimes require the management of one's emotion (e.g., standing up to a bully). They are distinguished, however, both in their developmental antecedents (with early emotional regulatory processes preceding the socialization of display rules) and in some of their motivational bases (with individuals striving for emotional homeostasis in both nonsocial and social situations). Consequently, the focus of this chapter is on the development of emotional regulation, although children's strategic management of emotional displays will be considered as part of this regulatory process.

The regulation of emotion has received little systematic attention thus far, but it is an important aspect of emotional development for several reasons. First, many significant developmental changes in emotional experience are related to the growth of emotional regulation. As infants respond to caregivers' regulatory efforts and as children develop more effective modes of emotional modulation, emotional experience is socialized, acquires new meaning, can be self-controlled and used purposively, and is increasingly integrated into the organized network of behavioral functioning. Thus, although the core experience of the primary emotions may be relatively consistent across individuals owing to their evolutionary origins (Izard & Malatesta, 1987), with development it is modified considerably by the diverse influences through which emotion is externally modulated, and as it becomes increasingly self-regulated.

Second, the study of emotional regulation also provides a window into the growth of individual differences in emotionality and its links to personality development. The study of adult personality traits (e.g., warmth, emotional stability, extraversion/introversion) as well as childhood personality dimensions (e.g., dominant mood, approach/withdrawal, threshold of responsiveness) suggests that individual differences in emotional regulation are core components of personality organization. If the development of emotional regulation changes the meaning of emotional experience, then variations in regulatory processes may also account for differences in the personal meaning of emotional arousal between individuals at various ages. Studying the developmental emergence of these differences in emotional regulation may thus provide insight into broader aspects of personality development.

Finally, the study of emotional regulation is important because of its influence on social behavior, as the examples above suggest. Indeed, early in life, individual differences in attachment, reactions to strangers, and peer relations are indexed primarily by variations in emotionality (e.g., see Lamb, Thompson, & Frodi, 1982; Thompson & Limber, in press; and below), and the regulation of affective processes continues to exert a profound influence on sociability at later ages. For example, difficulties in peer relations can often be traced to problems with emotional self-regulation, such as with children whose anger and social inferences lead to aggression (Dodge, Pettit, McClaskey, & Brown, 1986) or children who are socially withdrawn because of shyness (Kagan, Reznick, & Snidman, 1987). Contrary to the more traditional view that emotional reactions in social situations are by-products of variations in social competence, therefore, the growth of emotional regulation may provide a foundation for the development of social skills.

Thus the dual themes of this chapter are complementary: emotion as a behavioral regulator and emotion as a developmentally regulated phenomenon. Taken together, these themes underscore the emergent view of emotional processes as wholly integrated into the stream of adaptive functioning. The biologically adaptive functions of emotions as social signals and survival-enhancing behavioral catalysts are present from birth. But the enlistment of these emotional processes into the organization and control of higher-order behavioral systems depends on the growth of emotional regulatory processes that provide flexibility, efficiency, and greater homeostasis to our innate emotive systems. The story of emotional development is thus, in part, the story of the growth of regulatory processes by which emotional reactions continue to guide, motivate, and direct adaptive functioning in more sophisticated ways with increasing age. In this manner, emotional regulation fosters the continuing role of emotion as a behavioral regulator throughout ontogenesis.

## The Dynamics of Emotion

The study of emotion and its links to self-regulation requires new ways of studying emotional behavior because of the rich variability in emotional reactions that may index diverse regulatory processes. Casual observation of infants at a play group, for example, reveals that some are characterized by intense, animated expressions of distress or pleasure that rapidly escalate and decline, while others seem characteristically more subdued and gradual in their reactivity. By the preschool years, some children display considerable range and lability in their emotional expressions, while others show a more limited emotional repertoire. The task of a developmental analysis is to understand the origins of these individual and developmental differences and their effects on other aspects of functioning.

Two characteristics of emotional behavior seem necessary to describe these variations. The first concerns *emotional tone*: the specific emotion that characterizes an individual's response or enduring mood. We know that from early in life children can feel and express a variety of discrete emotions, including joy, interest, surprise, fear, anger, sadness, and disgust, and considerable attention has been devoted to developmental changes in the conditions eliciting these emotions and the factors that may contribute to more enduring "affective biases" (Malatesta, this volume) in individuals (see Barrett & Campos, 1987; Campos et al., 1983; Izard & Malatesta, 1987; Sroufe, 1979).

A second characteristic of emotional behavior is the *emotional dynamics* of the response. Emotional dynamics are response parame-

**Table 1**

*Emotional Dynamics*

---

- *Intensity* of an emotional reaction (either positive or negative). Intensity can be appraised either as *onset intensity* or as *peak intensity* of emotion.
- *Range* of emotional responses observed over an assessment period. Range can be indexed in terms of variations in emotional intensity or tone.
- *Lability* of emotional responsiveness, reflecting the frequency of changes from one form of emotional reaction to another. Lability can be indexed in terms of fluctuations between positive and negative hedonic tone, variations in discrete emotions, or variations in emotional intensity.
- *Latency* between the onset of an eliciting stimulus and the emotional reaction. Latency can be appraised either as *onset latency* or as *peak latency*.
- *Rise time* between the initial emotional response and the attainment of peak intensity.
- *Recovery* from the time of stimulus offset until emotional responses return to baseline.
- *Persistence* of the emotional response throughout the assessment period.

---

ters that define the quality of emotional behavior regardless of its tone, and that often reflect the influence of diverse emotional regulatory processes. In a sense they resemble the dynamic markings of a musical score concerning the intensive and temporal features of the composition: to extend the metaphor, while emotional tone may "play the tune" of a person's emotional response, emotional dynamics affect its quality and changes over time. Emotional dynamics are described in several ways (see Table 1). They can be indexed by variations in the *range* or *lability* of responding over a period of time (either episodic or long term). They can include variations in the onset or peak *intensity* of emotional reactions. Emotional dynamics are also indexed by the temporal features of emotional responding: the *latency* between the eliciting event and the onset or peak of an emotional response, for example, or the *rise time* from the onset to the attainment of peak intensity, or the *persistence* of emotional behavior over time. Temporal features related to the decline of an emotional response—or its *recovery*—are also relevant.

The importance of emotional dynamics can be appreciated by considering their role in behavioral organization and the importance of the regulatory processes they reflect. Consider two toddlers who become angry because an attractive toy is denied them. One child's fussing gradually escalates into angry screams that eventually subside as he becomes interested in alternate activities (by himself or perhaps with the assistance of a caregiver). Another child immediately erupts into full-blown shouting that persists at length until she finally becomes exhausted, despite the soothing of an adult. Each child's experience of anger is significantly affected by its dynamics (specifically, its intensive and temporal features) in ways that either foster or undermine effective behavioral organization. Ideally, well-regulated emotional experiences are sufficiently intense to motivate a suitable, organized behavioral response (and to convey meaningful signals to others), occur promptly enough to affect elicitors of emotion, persist until the individual's goals are achieved, flexibly change in response to changing conditions, and rise and fall in intensity in a manner that permits a productive accommodation to changing situational demands. As this characterization implies, the emotional dynamics that reflect well-regulated emotional experiences can never be defined in an absolute sense but depend on situational demands, goals, and the internal characteristics of the individual. Moreover, these dynamics themselves reflect diverse regulatory influences.

Although emotional dynamics have not received as much research attention as emotional tone, they have been of considerable theoretical interest to developmental and clinical investigators. Students of early temperament—who are concerned with the "how" of a behavioral response (cf. Thomas & Chess, 1977)—commonly focus on such dimensions as reactivity, intensity, threshold of response, soothability, and general mood (e.g., Buss & Plomin, 1984; Goldsmith & Campos, 1982; Rothbart & Derryberry, 1981; Thomas & Chess, 1977; see Bates, 1987). These dimensions relate to emotional dynamics, especially because most temperament theories explicitly include emotionality in their conceptualizations of temperament (indeed, for Goldsmith & Campos, 1982, it is central). Clinical investigators who are concerned with issues of infant mental health (see Fraiberg, 1980), parent-child disorders (e.g., Gaensbauer & Sands, 1979), and congenital abnormalities (e.g., Down syndrome: Emde, Katz, & Thorpe, 1978; Thompson, Cicchetti, Lamb, & Malkin, 1985; blindness: Fraiberg, 1977; prematurity: Field, 1982; Goldberg, 1978; Stiefel, Plunkett, & Meisels, 1987) are typically concerned with the quality of emotional responses, including evidence for subdued or blunted affective expressions, diminished range or lability of emotional responding, or lack of soothability.

From the standpoint of developmental study, serious attention to emotional dynamics can also be informative. The influence of appraisal models of emotional evocation leads naturally to interest in how developmental changes in the child's cognitive and information-processing skills affect emotional development (cf. Campos et al., 1983; Sroufe, 1979). Some theoretical models posit that emotion is evoked, in part, through a build-up of "tension" (e.g., Field, 1981; Sroufe, 1979; Sroufe & Waters, 1976; Sroufe & Wunsch, 1972) or an "arousal jag" (cf. Berlyne, 1960, 1969), in which the speed and efficiency of the child's processing of situational events may be especially important. These dynamic processes related to emotion can be indexed by examining the temporal features of the emotional response, as well as episodic changes in its intensity, and thus can contribute to greater insight into developmental changes in cognition/emotion interrelationships. Furthermore, developmental changes in early neurophysiological organization, social experience, and social information processing may each be related to changes in the emotional dynamics of certain responses. For example, soothability increases over the first year as infants learn to anticipate the caregiver's ministrations when hearing her approach (Gekoski, Rovee-Collier, & Carulli-Rabinowitz, 1983; Lamb & Malkin, 1986), and preschoolers are aware that distress can be blunted by restricting information intake (e.g., Bretherton, Fritz, Zahn-Waxler, & Ridgeway, 1986). Emotional dynamics are thus likely to reflect important developmental changes in emotional functioning and emotional regulation.

## DEVELOPMENTAL RESEARCH

Unfortunately, there has been very little systematic developmental study of emotional dynamics. Despite common observation that early emotional reactions assume an unmodulated, all-or-none quality and become progressively more differentiated, subtle, and situationally responsive with increasing age, few research studies assess these emotional parameters. In their developmental studies of separation protest in day-care and home-reared infants, Kagan, Kearsley, and Zelazo (1978) indexed the latency of separation distress as well as its duration (or persistence) and found that infants reacted more rapidly and intensely to the mother's departure over the course of the first two years of life. Hyson and Izard (1985) found that individual differences in emotional lability ("expression change rate") during separation episodes at 13 and 18 months were significantly stable and that lability increased with age for the sample as a whole. Similarly, in their longitudinal study of infants' reactions to routine inoculations from 2 to 18 months, Izard, Hembree, and Huebner (1987) found that with increasing age, infants soothed more quickly but did not vary in the latency to distress onset. Interestingly, individual differences in these emotional dynamics were not consistent over this period. Unfortunately, in these and the few other studies in which these emotion parameters were appraised there has been relatively little interest in the meaning of these differences for the nature of emotional experience in infancy.

To extend our understanding of developmental changes in emotional dynamics to positive as well as negative emotions, my students and I have recently completed a short-term longitudinal investigation of these emotion parameters in the first year of life (Thompson, in preparation). A sample of 58 infants and their mothers was observed in identical assessments when the babies were 6, 9, and 12 months old. The assessment procedure began with 1½ minutes of a standardized peek-a-boo game, after which the mother ceased play and simply looked at her baby. This was followed by a puppet game, in which the mother entertained the baby with a furry hand-held puppet for 1½ minutes, followed by another brief looking period. After a brief interlude of low-key play, the infant was seated on mother's lap while a female adult stranger gradually approached and interacted with the baby. This stranger episode was followed by another brief play interlude, after which the mother left the room for a 3-minute separation episode. We continued observing them after the mother returned to the room to play with and (if necessary) comfort the baby.

These episodes were chosen because of their emotionally arousing potential for the baby and because the affective response systems they elicited were developmentally in place. By 6 months of age, for example, infants have had considerable experience with peek-a-boo (Field, 1979; Sroufe & Wunsch, 1972), as well as with the more flexible, nonconventional types of play reflected in the puppet game. Moreover, by this age infants are beginning to show signs of stranger wariness and separation distress (see Thompson & Limber, in press). Our interest was not in *whether* infants at each age would respond positively to the two mother-infant games or negatively to the stranger and separation episodes, because these vignettes were chosen with the expectation that they were age-appropriate for eliciting the specified emotional responses. Rather, we were interested in examining developmental changes in the *quality*—or emotional dynamics—of infants' responses to them.

To analyze these dynamics, videotaped records of the sessions at each age were rated in a highly detailed fashion. Continuous time-sampled ratings (every 5 seconds) of positive and negative facial and vocal expressions of emotion were conducted throughout each of the four assessment vignettes (i.e., peek-a-boo, puppet play, stranger encounter, and separation episode). We also rated infant behavior during each of the recovery periods (e.g., when the mother ceased play and looked at the baby), because we were also interested in the decline in infant emotionality after the emotionally arousing event ceased. From these ratings, we constructed summary measures for the primary emotion parameters: onset and peak intensity of emotion, latency to onset and peak intensity, rise time, persistence of emotion, and recovery following the end of the vignette (measures of lability and range were not included because of the brevity of the assessment procedures). Both facial and vocal response measures were used because of the differential sensitivity of each to various aspects of emotionality: vocal expressions are much more sensitive to the intensive features of emotion, for example, while the progressive escalation of arousal can be better indexed using facial measures.

Consistent with earlier research and our own review of the literature on emotional regulation (see below), we anticipated that with increasing age infants would exhibit—across positive and negative emotion assessments—increasing response intensity, decreasing response latency, and increases in persistence. In short, we expected that infants would evince greater *vitality* in their emotional reactions, regardless of its hedonic tone. This is, in fact, what our findings indicated. For each of the four assessment vignettes there were increases with age in onset intensity and peak intensity and decreases in onset latency and peak latency, especially on vocal measures of emotion. For example, older infants responded with greater positive emotion in the mother-infant games, but also with greater negative emotion during the stranger and separation episodes, and they responded throughout more quickly than did younger babies (see Figures 1 and 2). We also found increases with age in the persistence of distress in assessments of stranger wariness and separation distress, but these developmental trends were not apparent in measures of persistence from the two mother-infant games. There were no developmental changes on measures of recovery.

To refine these findings, we used convergent behavioral measures to index whether the infants were in fact responding in the expected fashion to the stranger and separation vignettes (very few infants at any age failed to exhibit pleasure during the two social games with the mother). Our reason for doing so was to ensure that these developmental changes in emotion parameters were not simply due to the fact that a high proportion of the youngest infants did not exhibit any stranger wariness or separation distress at all. We thus eliminated from longitudinal comparison those infants who

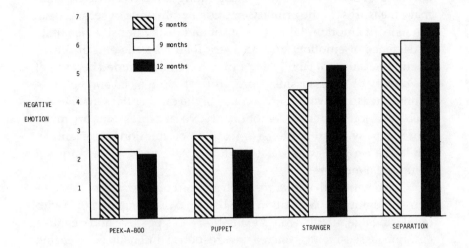

FIGURE 1. Developmental changes in the peak intensity of emotional responses to the four assessments (vocal measures). Note that lower scores on the emotion measure reflect positive vocalizations, with a score of 4 as a neutral midpoint rating.

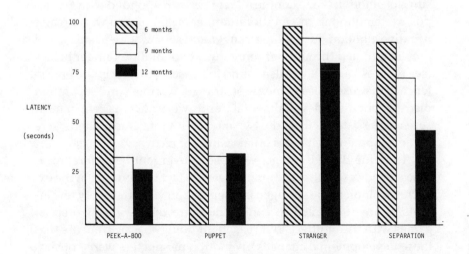

FIGURE 2. Developmental changes in the onset latency of emotional responding to the four assessments (vocal measures).

did not show, at each age, behavioral indications of stranger wariness (e.g., gaze avoidance, behavioral avoidance, or resistance to
the stranger's overtures) or separation distress (i.e., search behavior) to ensure that infants' emotional reactions reflected the
expected response systems. With this subsample of infants, the
developmental changes indicated above remained robust: infants
showed more intense emotional reactions, quicker reactions, and
more persistent reactions with increasing age across all four assessment vignettes.

Taken together, these developmental changes in emotional dynamics suggest that some of the developmental processes regulating emotional arousal in infancy are generalized across different discrete emotional experiences. As the research reviewed below
indicates, some of these developmental processes may be neurocor-
tical, with growing interhemispheric interconnectivity fostering
greater modulation of many emotional states over the first year. In
addition, cognitive changes over this period permit a more refined,
experience-based appraisal of social situations with the growth of
social expectations, an emergent understanding of means-ends relations, and more efficient memory skills. As a consequence, the 12-
month-old approaches social play and separation episodes with a
capacity to draw on an experiential history that affects emotional responding (especially its temporal and intensive features) in a manner unequaled in the 6-month-old. For these reasons, among others,
certain parameters of emotional responding are likely to change developmentally in a manner independent of the discrete emotion underlying the response.

On the other hand, we also discovered that the organization of
these emotion parameters varied for positive and negative emotion
assessments, and in a manner that did *not* change developmentally.
Figures 3 and 4 illustrate the significant correlations among emotion
parameters that appeared in assessments of negative emotion
(stranger and separation episodes) and positive emotion (peek-
a-boo and puppet play) at each age. When infants were negatively
aroused (Figure 3), the intensity of emotion was negatively correlated with its latency: babies who were most distressed reacted most
quickly, although they also required a somewhat longer escalation
(rise time). Moreover, high-intensity reactions also tended to persist
over time. This pattern of emotional reactivity permits a relatively

rapid mobilization of the baby's resources to meet a threatening event once it has been appraised as such, and this has adaptive value both as a social signal and as a stress response. Whether the threat consists of an approaching stranger or the mother's departure, a rapid and intense emotional response can increase the likelihood of removing the threat. It is noteworthy also that these intercorrelations (which replicate a previous analysis of separation distress by Thompson & Lamb, 1984) are very strong, suggesting

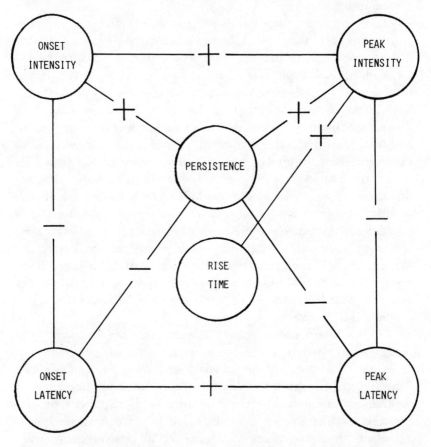

FIGURE 3. Significant positive and negative intercorrelations among emotional dynamics for assessments of negative emotion at each age (stranger encounter and separation episode). Cross-diagonal relations are not shown.

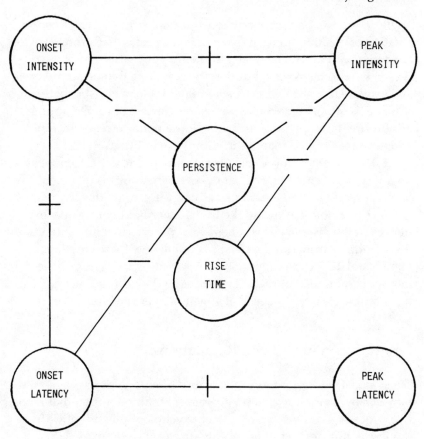

FIGURE 4. Significant positive and negative intercorrelations among emotional dynamics for assessments of positive emotion at each age (peak-a-boo and puppet games with mother). Cross-diagonal relations are not shown.

that this preemptory "emergency reaction" is a deeply rooted emotional response system.

By contrast, the intercorrelations among emotional dynamics for positive reactions were much weaker and assumed a different pattern (Figure 4). High-intensity pleasure reactions did not occur immediately at stimulus onset but had a longer latency, and they did not tend to persist over time when compared with milder pleasure reactions. Moreover, high-intensity expressions were preceded by a briefer rise time than were milder expressions. In a sense, the organization of positive emotional dynamics suggests that stronger reactions involve a more sustained period of appraisal as part of the process of emotional arousal but that the reactions that occur are brief and escalate rapidly. These are also valuable characteristics of the organization of positive arousal, since they foster continued appraisal of nonthreatening events and enable the child to respond rapidly and appropriately to changes in stimulus conditions.

Taken together, this exploratory study of the development and organization of emotional dynamics in infancy affirms that these dynamic processes can be informative concerning developmental changes in emotionality and the functional roles of emotional experiences in the organization of behavior. We are currently extending these findings from this data set to examine how these emotional dynamics relate developmentally to parent-report temperamental measures (obtained at each age) and how they can predict individual differences in the security of attachment at age one.

## Emotion and Behavioral Regulation

These questions are important because of emergent views of emotion as a behavioral regulator. To some extent the notion that emotive processes can guide and direct psychologically adaptive functioning is not new: studies of empathy (e.g., Hoffman, 1982), for example, attest to the catalytic role of emotion as a prosocial behavioral regulator. But even more intriguing is the view that emotions assume this function very early in life. Rather than being exclusively disorganizing or maladaptive in the construction of mature thinking and behaving, in other words, emotions may play a valuable role in this constructive process even in infancy. And in studies of phenomena as diverse as memory retrieval (Fagan, Ohr, Fleckenstein, & Ribner, 1985), parent-infant interaction (Gianino & Tronick, 1988) and understanding of self and others (Bretherton, McNew, & Beeghly-Smith, 1981), there is considerable evidence that emotion can serve psychologically adaptive purposes in very young children.

Even distress—which is classically regarded as disorganizing—can function as a behavioral regulator in infancy, especially in social interaction. This is particularly apparent when distress responses can motivate psychologically adaptive social responses and when the child can enlist others (or use self-soothing behaviors) to exercise rudimentary regulation of distress. For several years my colleagues and I have been studying the dynamics of distress responses in infants, and their potential roles as organizers of infant-mother attachment behavior, to elucidate the functions of emotions as early behavioral regulators.

## EMOTION AND ATTACHMENT

There are several reasons for our interest in emotion and attachment. First, attachment is a crucial aspect of early sociopersonality development, and emotion occupies a central theoretical role in classic portrayals of attachment system functioning. In the first volume of his *Attachment and Loss* trilogy, Bowlby (1969) portrayed emotion as central to the appraisal processes by which attachment behavior is instigated, monitored, and later terminated. Moreover, the behavioral systems perspective with which attachment theory is closely associated (e.g., Bretherton & Ainsworth, 1974) also portrays emotions as central motivational processes by which the four behavioral systems governing early social functioning (i.e., attachment, fear/wariness, affiliative, and exploratory) are regulated and controlled. Thus emotion is regarded as central to attachment system functioning in major theoretical viewpoints. More generally, in studying emotion and attachment we gain added insight into the role of emotional reactions in early social behavior and personality functioning.

Second, the typical assessment of attachment in the Strange Situation procedure relies heavily on emotional reactions (see Ainsworth, Blehar, Waters, & Wall, 1978). The Strange Situation is explicitly designed to create moderately escalating stress for a baby by observing the child with the mother in an unfamiliar laboratory playroom (episodes 1 and 2), then progressively introducing a stranger (episode 3) and a separation from the mother (episode 4) and then—after mother and baby have been reunited (episode 5)—again introducing the stranger (episode 6) and a maternal separation (episode 7) before the final reunion episode (episode 8) (see Bretherton, this volume, for procedural details). Attachment theorists believe that by studying the infant's responses during the reunion episodes, individual differences in attachment security will be revealed most clearly because the baby must seek the support of the attachment figure. This procedure has proved insightful (see Lamb, Thompson, Gardner, & Charnov, 1985, for a comprehensive review of this research literature), and its design invites questions concerning the organizational and motivational roles of emotional reactions to these episodes.

Finally, our interest in emotion and attachment derives also from the fact that many of the current issues in attachment theory pertain to the role of emotion in the organization of attachment behavior (see Lamb et al., 1985). These include the influence of temperament on attachment, how to interpret the Strange Situation behavior of infants from different cultural or subcultural backgrounds, and new ways of assessing attachment. In each case, there are important questions concerning how variations in the emotional reactions of infants to the stress created by the Strange Situation may account for the diverse reunion responses shown toward the mother, and their interpretation.

In a series of studies, we have sought to address three central questions. First, what are the links between the secure and insecure attachment classifications and individual differences in the emotion dynamics exhibited by infants in the Strange Situation? Based on their reunion responses, infants are classified as either securely attached (Group B), insecure-avoidant (Group A), or insecure-resistant (Group C) (although in recent studies a fourth classification has emerged, Group D) (see Ainsworth et al., 1978). Can these groups be distinguished by their earlier separation-related distress dynamics? If so, it would suggest that emotive processes may organize this important aspect of early sociopersonality development. Second, in what *specific* ways does distress influence the child's subsequent reunion behavior toward the mother? Can we identify how emotion functions as a behavioral regulator of attachment processes within this procedure? And third, what role does temperament assume in this process?

## EMOTION AND ATTACHMENT CLASSIFICATION

Several studies have now been completed that examine the links between individual differences in distress dynamics within the
Strange Situation and the A, B, and C attachment classifications
(e.g., Frodi & Thompson, 1985; Thompson & Lamb, 1984). While
confirming that the two insecurely attached classification groups (A
and C) exhibit unique features of separation distress, these studies
have also revealed surprising heterogeneity *within* the securely attached group, with infants in secure subclassifications B1 and B2 differing emotionally from those in subclassifications B3 and B4 (see
Table 2). Infants in the B1 and B2 subgroups—whose reunion responses to the mother entail distance interaction and some proximity seeking—resemble the insecure-avoidant (Group A) infants in
their subdued distress intensity, gradual escalation, quick recovery,
and relatively high emotional lability. By contrast, infants in the B3
and B4 subgroups—who seek greater contact with the mother upon
reunion—resemble the insecure-resistant (Group C) infants in their
heightened distress intensity, quick escalation, and prolonged time
required for soothing. In a sense, therefore, the dynamics of separation distress within the Strange Situation are consistent with the
threefold attachment classification system but also cut across the
insecure-secure distinction. Variations in emotional dynamics underlie a distal-interactive versus contact-maintaining dimension of
attachment behavior toward the mother, with more highly dis-

**Table 2**

*Emotional Dynamics of Attachment Classification Groups*

| Parameter | A | B1, B2 | B3, B4 | C |
| --- | --- | --- | --- | --- |
| Preseparation distress *intensity* | low | low | low | moderate |
| Separation distress *intensity* | moderate | moderate | high | high |
| Reunion distress *intensity* | low | low | moderate | high |
| Separation distress *latency* | long | long | short | short |
| Separation distress *rise time* | long | long | short | short |
| Distress *recovery* (stranger) | short | short | long | long |
| Reunion distress *recovery* (mother) | short | short | moderate | long |
| General emotional *lability* | high | moderate | low | low |

tressed babies requiring greater contact with their mothers upon reunion.

Based on these findings, it appears that the quality and intensity of separation distress defines what the infant requires psychologically of the mother during reunion, and security derives from how well this assistance is provided. Infants who respond to their mothers' departure with the imperative "emergency" reaction of rapid escalation/high intensity/low lability distress require a similarly immediate and effective response from the mother to regulate this arousal, and these emotion dynamics motivate attachment behaviors (heightened contact seeking) that can help elicit the mother's assistance. Attachment studies suggest that infants who are securely attached (subgroups B3 and B4) are more likely to receive this assistance from their caregivers than are those who are insecurely attached (Group C) (see Lamb et al., 1985). By contrast, infants whose separation reactions are more subdued (gradual escalation/low intensity/higher lability) can cope better with distress individually through search, toy play, or automanipulation (e.g., thumb sucking). The reunion responses that these emotional dynamics underlie either foster the caregiver's involvement in these modes of distress regulation (through positive distance interaction for B1 and B2 subgroups) or do not (through avoidance for Group A infants), perhaps because of differences in infants' expectations for their caregivers' assistance. Taken together, these findings suggest that theoretical efforts to portray the organization of attachment behavior in terms of variations in "felt security" (cf. Sroufe & Waters, 1977) are useful approaches insofar as they underscore the affective bases of the regulation of attachment behavior, because these variation in separation distress dynamics appear to define what the baby requires of the parent psychologically in terms of emotional regulation and reestablishing affective homeostasis upon reunion.

There is some evidence that differences in these separation distress dynamics also have a temperamental basis (Belsky & Rovine, 1987), and we shall examine temperamental influences below. There is also evidence that they may derive from an interaction between intrinsic features of infants' reactions to challenge and stress (indexed in part by adrenocortical activity) and the demands of specific Strange Situation episodes (Gunnar, Mangelsdorf, Kestenbaum,

Lang, Larson, & Andreas, in press). This "infant × situation inter-action" suggests that intrinsic differences between infants are mani-fested in situation-specific ways in the Strange Situation, partly due to the demands they impose on infants' coping and emotional self-regulation. These studies thus affirm that intrinsic features of the baby considerably influence the emotion dynamics of separation distress within this procedure.

These dynamic differences are also influenced by the cultural conditions of child care. In a cross-cultural collaborative study, Avi Sagi and I examined these emotional dynamics for samples of in-fants from traditional Israeli kibbutzim (where infants received daily and evening care in communal centers), Israeli day-care centers (which are comparable to American centers), and American middle-class homes (a small minority employing full-time day care) (Thompson & Sagi, in preparation). We discovered that for many Strange Situation episodes, kibbutz-reared infants displayed heightened distress intensity and diminished soothability com-pared with Israeli day-care and American babies. Perhaps for this reason, a higher proportion of kibbutz infants were found to be inse-cure-resistant in this procedure (see Sagi, Lamb, Lewkowicz, Shoham, Dvir, & Estes, 1985). Their emotion dynamics during sep-aration distress, and their consequent insecure attachments, may have been due to their conditions of care, which involved regular and repeated separations from caregivers (Sagi et al., 1985). (Inter-estingly, the same group differences were apparent when attach-ment classification was controlled by comparing only infants from B1 and B2 classifications for each sample. This suggests that attach-ment raters from different cultural settings also intuitively con-trolled for variations in normative distress intensity between cul-tural groups when assigning attachment classifications.)

The baby's congenital characteristics are also influential. In a comparative study of Down syndrome and normal infants, for ex-ample, we discovered that although the links between separation distress dynamics and attachment behavior were highly compara-ble, Down syndrome infants displayed a diminished range and la-bility of emotional responding, showed less intense and more de-layed separation reactions, and recovered more quickly than matched normals (Thompson et al., 1985). These may derive from the physiological characteristics of Down syndrome as well as from their cognitive retardation (see Thompson et al., 1985). However, among these affectively more subdued Down syndrome infants, heightened distress also provoked angry as well as positive contact seeking toward the mother during reunion episodes, perhaps because of their physiologically based arousal-modulation deficits. Similarly, Stiefel, Plunkett, and Meisels (1987) found that high-risk premature infants exhibited not only heightened attachment insecurity, but also greater distress and limited soothability than matched moderate-risk and low-risk premature samples (see also Frodi & Thompson, 1985).

Taken together, these findings provide the strongest evidence to date for the motivational and organizational roles of emotion in early social interaction. Variations in the baby's distress dynamics derive both from intrinsic characteristics and from a history of prior care, and they instigate attachment behavior that is well suited either to eliciting the caregiver's assistance or to fostering self-regulation of emotional arousal (or both). For some infants, however, arousal-modulation deficits undermine effective social functioning. In each case, emotional dynamics shape the quality of mother-infant interaction and elements of the child's emerging personality. By underscoring the links between the dynamics of separation distress and attachment behavior within the Strange Situation and elucidating the diverse origins of individual differences in these emotional dynamics, these studies clarify the role of emotion in attachment system functioning in a manner that extends theoretical work in this area (e.g., Bowlby, 1969).

EMOTION AND SOCIAL INTERACTION

Further work remained, however, to specify more precisely *how* separation distress dynamics influence the baby's attachment behavior. Because the threefold attachment classifications are so inclusive, we adopted an alternative component-process analytic strategy to better understand infant behavior within the Strange Situation (see Connell, 1985; Connell & Thompson, 1986; Thompson, Connell, & Bridges, 1988). Rather than relying on summary attachment classifications (i.e., A, B, C groups), this strategy instead focuses on the component measures of social interactive behavior that form the basis for attachment classifications and are rated episode by episode (the baby's proximity seeking, contact maintenance, resistance, avoidance, and distance interaction). These measures were factor analyzed for each Strange Situation episode to yield two dimensions of social interactive behavior per episode. Similarly, measures of distress dynamics were also factor analyzed to yield a single dimension of distress for each episode. Using this procedure, we could examine more carefully the interrelationships between social interactive and distress dimensions both within and across Strange Situation episodes, treating the Strange Situation as a mini-longitudinal study, in order to elucidate their mutual and predictive relationships.

Our findings indicated that emotion assumed a strong causal role in the child's social behavior within this procedure (Connell & Thompson, 1986; see Bridges, Connell, & Belsky, 1988, and Thompson & Connell, 1985, for replications with independent samples). In partial correlational analyses, for example, we found that separation distress significantly predicted the child's later reunion behavior with the mother, even with the effects of prior social interaction held constant. Thus emotion and its regulation had a unique influence on later social behavior, an influence that was not replicated when we sought to predict emotion from prior social interaction. This asymmetric influence of emotion on later social behavior should not be surprising, because we also found that individual differences in emotion with the Strange Situation were far more consistent across episodes than were variations in social interactive behavior. In short, variations in emotion were a more consistent baseline of individual socioemotional functioning within the Strange Situation than were variations in social behavior, even though this procedure is explicitly designed to manipulate the baby's emotional state across the episodes.

Even more striking, variations in emotion were powerful predictors of social behavior over much longer temporal periods. In our study, infants were observed in the Strange Situation at both 12½ and 19½ months. When we selected a subsample of infants whose emotional reactions to this procedure were consistent at each age, there was also striking consistency in their social behavior on each occasion (with nearly 90% shared variance between the two assessments on social measures). This was not duplicated when infants were selected based on consistency in their social behavior: for these babies, emotional reactions varied between the two assessments. Thus simply by knowing whether a baby showed a consistent pattern of emotion during two assessments separated by a seven-month period, we could predict with high accuracy whether patterns of social behavior would also be maintained over this period. A baby that showed a consistent emotional response to each Strange Situation was highly likely to show consistent patterns of social behavior also.

On the basis of these findings, therefore, not only do we know what patterns of attachment are predicted by variations in separation distress, but we also know how separation reactions have this influence. Individual differences in emotionality establish a baseline of socioemotional functioning within the Strange Situation, and it is from this baseline that infants react psychologically to elements of the procedure and require assistance from the caregiver. This individual baseline is maintained even though the child's ambient emotional state changes during the Strange Situation, and this baseline of emotionality underlies attachment and social functioning, even over long temporal spans. We will consider further below the origins of this individual emotional baseline. Interestingly, the only notable developmental changes we found between 12½ and 19½ months concerned the diminished consistency of emotional behavior across episodes at the older age, and also the increased power of emotion in predicting later social behavior (Connell & Thompson, 1986). We suspect this might be due to the toddler's growing ability to exercise rudimentary emotional self-regulatory skills, which both alter the consistency of emotionality over this assessment and also strengthen its role in later sociability. Quite remarkably, emotional dynamics are predictively powerful not only within the Strange Situation, but also across longer time spans. This suggests that individual differences in emotion and its regulation may have early and significant influences on social behavior and personality in infancy.

EMOTION, ATTACHMENT, AND TEMPERAMENT

Given these findings, it was reasonable to suspect that a large share of the influence of emotion within the Strange Situation might be due to temperament because temperament is commonly regarded as an enduring and influential aspect of individual emotional reactivity. To explore this possibility, we focused on one important temperament dimension obtained from maternal responses to the Infant Behavior Questionnaire (Rothbart, 1981), which was *fear*. We focused on the fear dimension because this temperamental attribute is implicated most frequently in attachment system functioning because of the novel setting, unfamiliar adult, and unusual sequence of events that characterize the Strange Situation procedure. Do variations in temperamental fear underlie both the consistency of emotional behavior within the Strange Situation and its predictive power within and across assessments?

To address this question, we conducted a series of multiple regression analyses to examine both the direct and the indirect influences of temperamental fear on the child's social interactive behavior during reunions (episodes 5 and 8) (see Thompson et al., 1988). Temperamental fear would, we hypothesized, be indirectly influential as its influence was mediated by the quality of distress during the preceding separation episodes (episode 4 or 7). The resulting path-analytic models are shown in Figure 5 (with standardized regression coefficients representing the unique contribution of each predictor). Our findings indicate that there were both direct and indirect effects of temperamental fear on each dimension of reunion-episode social behavior, but that only the indirect effects were statistically significant. Thus, as we expected, temperament influenced attachment behavior, especially as it was mediated by distress dynamics during the preceding separation episode. This is contrary to the conclusions of prior studies that have focused only on direct temperamental effects (e.g, by correlating temperamental dimensions with attachment classifications), and it suggests that more complex models of indirect influence are necessary to specify temperamental effects more clearly (see Lamb et al., 1985; Thompson et al., 1988).

NEBRASKA SYMPOSIUM ON MOTIVATION 1988

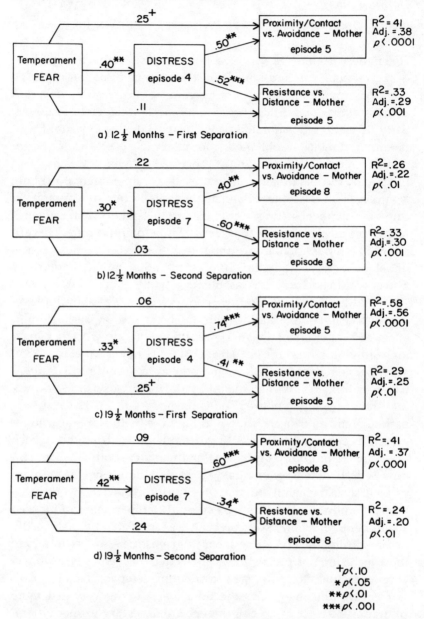

FIGURE 5. Path-analytic models of the contributions of temperament to Strange Situation behavior in assessments at 12½ and 19½ months. From Thompson, Connell, and Bridges (1988), © the Society for Research in Child Development. Reprinted by permission.

However, the path-analytic models in Figure 5 also indicated that distress continued to have a strong, direct influence on reunion-episode attachment behavior *independent* of temperament. Temperamental fear alone could not account for the strong effects of emotionality on subsequent social behavior within the Strange Situation. To confirm this, we residualized the distress measures for temperamental variance to create new measures of nontemperamentally based distress that we called "context-specific distress," and we discovered that these new measures remained highly consistent across Strange Situation episodes and powerfully predictive of later social behavior across assessments at 12½ and 19½ months (Thompson et al., 1988). In short, even though temperament is widely regarded as a stable aspect of individual emotional functioning, our measures of emotional dynamics continued to underlie variations in social behavior within the Strange Situation even with temperamental variance removed.

Clearly, these emotional influences are more than temperament or mere random mood fluctuations. But what is their origin? There are at least two possibilities. First, infants may be reacting emotionally to the behavior of the parent within this procedure, and parental behavior may be regulating the infant's emotional reactions. A considerable amount of the "secure base behavior" of infants in the Strange Situation involves visually checking back with the parent to obtain reassuring emotional cues. We have evidence from this sample of significant amounts of this kind of "social referencing" during the Strange Situation, and children who were securely and insecurely attached received different kinds of verbal cues from their caregivers (Dickstein, Thompson, Estes, Malkin, & Lamb, 1984). Clearly, the kinds of emotional messages received from the parent may influence not only the baby's emotional reactions but also subsequent social behavior. Thus one basis for the infant's emotional regulation in the Strange Situation may be the emotional messages received from a parent, functioning as a kind of extrinsic form of emotional management.

Second, infants also contribute independently to the management of their own emotional arousal: distressed babies can use a rudimentary repertoire of coping behaviors (e.g., hand-to-mouth and other automanipulative behaviors, playing with a familiar toy) as well as seeking the assistance of the stranger. These nascent self-regulatory strategies may provide the infant with a more or less competent psychological foundation on which to renew positive social interaction with the caregiver during reunions, and this could help to explain the unique and asymmetric links between emotion and subsequent sociability. Moreover, as indicated earlier, developmental changes in the role of emotionality in the Strange Situation may be explained in part by the growing self-regulatory repertoire infants employ during the second year.

In short, the emotional influences within the Strange Situation cannot be reduced simply to temperamental attributes and may derive from the way the baby's reactions to separation are managed within this procedure, either intrinsically or extrinsically. Yet these emotional influences are extremely powerful not only in providing a baseline of socioemotional functioning for the child, but also in motivating patterns of attachment behavior that have psychologically adaptive consequences. Thus the study of emotion as a behavioral regulator of attachment functioning turns to the study of emotion as a developmentally regulated phenomenon. I now turn to a review of research concerning the latter.

## The Regulation of Emotion

Emotion can energize, motivate, and guide adaptive functioning, but its capacity to do so depends on the diverse processes by which emotion is regulated. Emotional regulation is required both to provide flexibility (rather than stereotypy) to the behavioral processes that emotions help to motivate and direct and also to enable organisms to respond quickly and efficiently to changes in their conditions by maintaining internal arousal within performance-enhancing limits. The importance of arousal-regulating neurophysiological processes is reflected in nervous system organization (in which sympathetic activating systems are coupled with parasympathetic inhibitory processes) and in the influence of frontal inhibitory centers in the cerebral cortex. Indeed, in higher organisms the evolution of higher-order cortical functions appears to have fostered the emergence of inhibitory control over subcortical emotive processes (Panksepp, in press). These neurophysiological principles reflect the fact that arousal is a valuable behavioral catalyst and organizer but that heightened and prolonged arousal can be disorganizing and maladaptive. In essence, emotional regulation is essential to enlisting emotive processes into the organized and psychologically adaptive higher-order control of behavior.

This is nowhere clearer than in ontogenesis. At birth, emotions have biologically adaptive functions as social signals and as survival-enhancing behavioral catalysts. But the newborn infant cannot consistently regulate emotional arousal without the assistance of caregivers and frequently becomes overaroused and disorganized. The slow growth of endogenous regulatory capacities in the early years is assisted by the growth of constituent neurophysiological, cognitive, and self-reflective capacities detailed below. This is a painstaking process because emotional regulation means intervening in phylogenetically deeply rooted affect systems with psychologically complex control mechanisms. Nevertheless, the mature capacity to regulate internal states of emotional arousal and their expression is an important step toward sophisticated behavioral functioning. Indeed, central to the concepts of "emotional maturity" (Jersild, 1954) and "emotional competence" (Gordon, in press; Saarni, this volume) is a capacity to regulate emotion in productive and complex ways. Similarly, Zivin's (1986) developmental model of emotional expression emphasizes changes with age in the complexity and integrated processes of the "editor," a system component in her model that regulates emotion.

The following pages outline the growth of emotional regulation in infancy and childhood. I begin with a discussion of exogenous sources of emotional regulation because these are foremost early in development, although they maintain a pervasive coregulatory influence throughout ontogenesis. Following this, I consider various emergent capacities related to intrinsic processes of emotional regulation that unfold with the growth of neurophysiological, cognitive, and self-reflective skills. A focus on "emergent capacities" is intended to reflect the gradual integration of new regulatory capacities into the regulatory repertoire that has already been established and the resulting transformation of emotional management that results. Although these emergent capacities are considered in age-graded fashion, any stagelike portrayal of the unfolding of these processes is unintended.

EXOGENOUS INFLUENCES ON EMOTIONAL
REGULATION

Early in life, infants are equipped with a rudimentary repertoire of
behaviors (many of them reflexive) that can alter or modulate states
of heightened arousal. These include automanipulative activity
(e.g., hand-to-mouth), sucking on the tongue, finger, pacifier, or another object, looking or turning away, and rocking (Brazelton,
Koslowski, & Main, 1974; Gianino & Tronick, 1988; Kessen & Mandler, 1961). Behaviors such as these have a regulatory effect on
arousal even though the baby uses them fortuitously rather than intentionally. But even the casual observer of young infants is impressed with the limits of this regulatory repertoire: infants are easily
and frequently overaroused when elicitors persist or when arousal
rises above a very low threshold, and disorganization commonly results. Indeed, as Fogel (1982) has noted, infants must cope with conditions of heightened (and potentially overwhelming) arousal more
frequently than do individuals at any later period of the life span.
Their coping is aided by the active efforts of caregivers to modulate
and buffer the child's arousal.

Exogenous influences on emotional regulation thus com-
mence virtually from birth and continue to affect a child's emotional experience even after self-regulatory processes have begun
to develop. In this sense emotional regulation can be regarded as a
developmental endeavor to which the child and social agents
(both immediate and distal) jointly contribute and that helps socialize emotional experience. This is because caregivers and other
adults guide the child's emotional regulation in accordance with
personal beliefs about emotion and cultural prescriptions related
to emotion and its display as well as values concerning children
and their present and future needs (see Gordon, in press; Miller &
Sperry, 1987; Super & Harkness, 1982). Whether these prescriptions concern the emotions that it is suitable to express in public
(toward whom, and in what contexts), the intensity and range of
emotional expressions that are appropriate for individuals of different ages, or gender differences in the range and lability of emotional expressions, these beliefs constitute the "emotional culture" in which a child is raised (Gordon, in press). From the

outset, therefore, many elements of emotional regulatory processes are socially constructed.

**Modeling, reinforcement, and affective induction: The example of mother-infant interaction.** There is considerable evidence that this socialization process begins early in infancy. Researchers interested in the origins of emotional regulation have focused on early mother-infant face-to-face interaction as an important context in which a baby's emotional responses are shaped and organized. One reason for this focus derives from a long theoretical legacy—largely within psychoanalytic and neoanalytic viewpoints—emphasizing the "affective climate" of the mother-infant relationship and their shared "dialogue" as a formative influence on early socioemotional development (e.g., Spitz, 1965). Certainly in the sharing of gaze and smiling and the back-and-forth exchanges of animated vocal expressions, it has been easy for students of early development to observe in mother-infant play the baby's earliest experience of delight in a human partner. More recently, developmentalists have refined this viewpoint to explore how patterns of face-to-face play affect a baby's emergent capacity to cope with the heightened excitement engendered by play activity—or, in the words of one researcher, to develop "affective tolerance" (Fogel, 1982).

Guiding much of this recent research is the portrayal of mother-infant interaction as a jointly regulated process in which maintaining mutual pleasure is an overriding goal (e.g., Gianino & Tronick, 1988; Tronick, Cohn, & Shea, 1986). As a consequence, the mother's task is both to arouse pleasure in the baby through her own entertaining activities and to maintain sensitivity to infant cues that may require a change in her activity. These infant cues include gazing and gaze aversion, motor activity, and positive and negative emotional reactions that indicate engagement, lack of interest, overarousal, or rejection of the mother's social bids. By modifying the pace of her activity in light of these cues, according to researchers, the mother is capable of maintaining the baby within an optimal level of arousal that is manifested in the infant's sustained interest and pleasure in play interaction. Thus when infants show signs of overarousal, for example, sensitive partners reduce their activity to allow for a time-out from active play. By contrast, insensitive or unanimated maternal behavior may result in the baby's lack of interest, avoidance, or distress. In this manner, mother and baby are co-contributors to the success of their interactions: the infant through a rudimentary signaling system, and the mother through her play activity and responsiveness to these signals (see Brazelton et al., 1974; Field, 1981; Stern, 1974, 1977; Thompson & Lamb, 1983; Tronick, Als, & Adamson, 1978).

Although the concept of "optimal arousal" as a goal of play behavior is hard to define and the mutuality of this activity is open to debate (Kaye, 1982), this portrayal of face-to-face interaction accurately underscores the regulation of infant emotion through maternal behavior. Indeed, since the purpose of social play is sheer enjoyment and young infants have difficulty regulating or sustaining the heightened emotion generated by such encounters, it would be surprising if emotional regulation was not a central maternal goal. Importantly, this kind of regulation is likely to affect diverse dynamics of the baby's immediate emotional reactions. By these accounts, for example, infants are most likely to respond positively when the mother fosters a gradual increase in their arousal at the beginning of the play session (slow rise time), modulates the intensity and range of arousal by alternating periods of animated play activity with "time-out" periods of more subdued activity, and allows for a gradual decline in the pace of interaction when they show signs of flagging interest (slow recovery). Regulated in this manner, the child's emotional experience during face-to-face play is likely to remain within the parameters of a young infant's tolerance for stimulation, which fosters continued engagement in play as the mother paces interactive activity in a manner suitable to the baby's information-processing capability.

How do mothers regulate their babies' emotional experience in this manner? Selective modeling and reinforcement of emotional expressions may be one way. In microanalyses of mother-infant interaction throughout the first year, Malatesta and her colleagues (Malatesta, Grigoryev, Lamb, Albin, & Culver, 1986; Malatesta & Haviland, 1982; see Malatesta, this volume) examined patterns of maternal and infant facial expressions and their interrelationships. They found that mothers restricted their expressions to positive emotions (primarily enjoyment, interest, and surprise) to promote their babies' pleasure. Mothers also imitated or "matched" many infant facial expressions, especially those of positive emotion. In short, mothers appeared to be actively modeling the desired emotional behavior in the infants and selectively reinforcing (through contingent matching) the babies' positive emotional expressions, perhaps in an effort to accentuate, modulate, and regulate the infants' positive emotional experience. Thus infants who smiled were greeted with mothers who smiled in reply; those who fussed had mothers who quickly acted in a manner that redirected the babies' emotional response more positively. These influences may be partly responsible for the linear increase in positive emotional expressions noted in babies as they became older (Malatesta & Haviland, 1982). It may also help to explain the similarity between mothers and infants in their facial expressive styles (see Malatesta & Izard, 1984).

Modeling and selective reinforcement may not alone be responsible for these influences. Haviland and Lelwica (1987) and Termine and Izard (1988) have reported that infants as young as 10 weeks respond discriminatingly to maternal expressions of affect, occasionally spontaneously matching them in affective tone. Convergent behavioral data supported each research groups' suggestion that mothers' expressions may have directly *induced* affect in their young babies.

What long-term effects do these experiences have on babies? Insofar as infants experience a consistent history of play interactions with their mothers that are emotionally well regulated, their tolerance for heightened arousal in similar contexts may be increased. As Berlyne's (1960, 1969) concept of the "arousal jag" in humor and laughter suggests, gradual increases in excitement and arousal can become pleasurable in their own right because the individual anticipates a decline in arousal once peak intensity has been achieved, and this is likely to be the baby's experience during well-regulated episodes of face-to-face play. More generally, with the development of rudimentary social expectations at the end of the first trimester, infants may arrive at play interactions with an expectation of positive arousal that further fosters their tolerance of heightened emotion. As a consequence, the range and intensity of tolerable conditions of arousal may be broadened (Fogel, 1982), and there may be a lowering of the threshold for positive arousal under similar conditions. As a consequence, maternal behavioral strategies that are intended to socially regulate the baby's immediate emotional experience may have long-term effects by influencing the child's emergent self-regulatory tendencies.

Moreover, as mothers adjust their interactive strategies over time in accord with their changing expectations for the baby's behavior, their activities may further help to foster the changes in emotion they anticipate. In an observational study of changes in mother-infant interaction over the first three years of life, Brooks-Gunn and Lewis (1982) noted that with their babies' increasing age, mothers became significantly more responsive to smiles, less responsive to frets and cries, and more responsive to nondistressed vocalizations. Over the same period, infants' smiles and vocalizations increased and fretting decreased. These researchers suggested that changes in maternal behavior resulted, in part, from changing expectations for the children's behavior resulting from social rules governing positive and negative emotional expressions (see Lewis & Michalson, 1983). In other words, the emotional regulatory strategies of parents changed as part of their early efforts to socialize emotion in their children.

The portrayal of mother-infant play as an early arena for the regulation of infant emotion is complicated, however, by two conclusions from recent research. The first is that any child's "optimal arousal" level is significantly influenced by developmental competencies and individual characteristics. In her own reformulation of the mutual regulation model, for example, Field (1981) has proposed that the range of tolerable arousal in play broadens with increasing age owing to the growth of state regulation, decreasing sensory thresholds, and an increased speed and efficiency in information processing. Moreover, individual characteristics may also affect the range of emotional arousal infants can tolerate in face-to-face play. For example, preterm infants are more passive and unresponsive during the early months but also show more fussing and irritability (Brown & Bakeman, 1980; Field, 1977), suggesting a more restricted range of optimal arousal during early interactions. Perhaps for this reason, mothers of preterm infants tend to behave more intrusively and less contingently when interacting with them, and problems in mother-infant interaction often result (see Goldberg, 1978). Taken together, observations of developmental changes as well as considerable idiosyncrasy in a baby's arousal threshold indicate that the maternal behaviors fostering well-regulated emotion in face-to-face play must be finely tuned but also dynamic, accommodating to the changing, developing child.

A second conclusion from this research, consistent with the first, is that well-regulated interactions involving a good match between maternal behavior and infant arousal are the exception rather than the rule. According to Gianino and Tronick (1988), for example, infants and mothers are out of synchrony more than two-thirds of the time owing to misreading of behavior, different goals of each partner, or the mother's efforts to expand the baby's interactive capabilities. They propose that these frequently occurring "mismatches" between mother and baby foster the development of the child's own emotional self-regulatory skills, independent of external supports, including behaviors such as gaze aversion, redirecting attention to an object, and self-comforting (e.g., oral or automanipulative) activity. In one empirical investigation, they reported that babies' repertoire of regulatory skills broadened significantly from 3 to 9 months of age; these capabilities were limited, however, since the same infants also exhibited considerable amounts of distressed behavior in face-to-face play. Further research is thus required to determine whether such behaviors are genuinely used in a self-regulatory fashion by infants or are behavioral reactions to characteristics of maternal activity (e.g., maternal withdrawal) that have the fortuitous effect of modulating arousal.

Taken together, these studies of the regulation of a baby's emotion in face-to-face play indicate that the earliest origins of emotional regulation may occur in a mother's strategic efforts to maintain her baby's arousal within limits that foster positive, animated play exchanges and that shape a child's earliest capacities for affective tolerance. The use of modeling, selective reinforcement, and direct affective induction as regulatory strategies at this early age sets the stage for their ongoing use by socialization agents as a child grows up. Indeed, observational learning and selective reinforcement may be among the most important influences by which a child's emotional regulatory style is shaped within the family, as children imitate the emotional behavior of parents and other adults and are reinforced for conforming to parental expectations for emotional regulation. For example, parents' modeling and their expectations for the management of anger by family members may lead some children to voice angry feelings with explosive words and gestures, others to minimize the direct expression of anger, and still others to lose control in temper tantrums and other outbursts. Similar processes are likely to apply to how children learn to cope with feelings of disappointment, frustration, and other emotions. Furthermore, as the findings of Brooks-Gunn and Lewis (1982) suggest, parents' regulatory strategies change with the child's age, fostering different regulatory patterns in offspring that increasingly conform to social rules governing emotional behavior. The extent to which this reflects a deliberate socialization strategy by the parent is an important topic for future research. Considerably more research is also required to determine the consistency and the long-term importance of individual variations in the regulatory processes exhibited in face-to-face play.

**Direct intervention strategies: The example of distress-relief sequences.** Although the regulation of emotion in face-to-face play undoubtedly influences early emotional development, researchers have probably overemphasized its significance. It is doubtful that play interactions occupy a substantial proportion of the daily time that infants and caregivers are together (particularly if there are siblings), especially in view of recent trends toward maternal employment and early day-care experience. Multiple caregivers may not foster consistent styles of emotional regulation through their interactive behavior (although this remains an empirical question), and thus it is uncertain whether early influences through play with different partners are redundant or inconsistent, and what their effects are. Furthermore, face-to-face play is an important interactive context for infants and parents for only a limited period in the first year. It typically begins to occur with the growth of rudimentary interactive skills at about 3 months of age, but it declines in frequency between 6 and 9 months as infants become more mobile and develop greater interest in object play (Malatesta & Izard, 1984).

The early months also witness, however, the emergence of several other processes relevant to emotional regulation, and their influence may be more pervasive. One of these concerns the caregiver's behavior during distress-relief sequences, which constitute another important interactive context involving emotion in infancy (Lamb, 1981a, 1981b). Distress-relief sequences are important because young infants require external assistance in regulating states of negative as well as positive emotion, and this remains true throughout the early years of life. As Lamb (1981a) has argued, instances of infant distress and soothing involve repetitive, highly salient associations between infants' emotions and an environmental response. This makes it easy as well as adaptive for babies to learn a conditioned association between soothing interventions and the cues of the caregiver. Furthermore, the typical response of caregivers—picking up the distressed baby—produces quiet alertness that can foster this learning process (see Korner & Thoman, 1970, 1972). As a consequence, according to Lamb, infants are provided a predictable, salient early opportunity to associate, through classical conditioning, the caregiver's cues with the relief of distress. In research bearing on this formulation, Gekoski and colleagues (1983) and Lamb and Malkin (1986) both observed anticipatory quieting in distressed 1- and 2-month-olds to the sight or sound of a caregiver's approach *before* being picked up. Anticipatory quieting increased from 1 to 6 months of age, and there were also increases in infant protest and aversion when the caregiver approached but did not pick up the baby. Both findings would be expected if social expectations concerning the adult's soothing interventions were developing over this period.

Distress-relief sequences are thus another important early context in which caregivers strategically regulate infants' emotions through direct intervention. The quality of the caregiver's responsiveness—acting quickly to soothe the baby, for example, rather than after a delay (perhaps to allow the baby to "cry it out"); intervening with effective or ineffective ministrations; soothing until the baby is fully quiet rather than temporarily subdued—is likely to have a profound influence on the regulatory dynamics of infants' distress. Prompt and effective interventions, for example, may restrict the intensity of distress while permitting a progressive recovery and resumption of interest in other activities. Insofar as infants have a reasonably consistent experiential history of this kind, these patterns of responsiveness by caregivers may reinforce a more generalized emotional style in the child. For example, infants who receive attention only after their distress has reached high intensity may be reinforced for escalating rapidly (rather than gradually) into full-blown crying. This may, in fact, be one of the experiential bases for infants' behavioral difficulty, because it likely contributes also to problems with soothability (or recovery), since highly distressed babies are more difficult to comfort.

Furthermore, if Lamb's formulation is correct, these episodes may not only directly regulate the baby's immediate emotional state, but also contribute to the development of social expectations that are pertinent to emotional regulation. A baby's confidence in the caregiver's prompt helpfulness can make heightened distress easier to tolerate since assistance is anticipated, and it may thus be easier for the child to maintain behavioral organization under stress. Moreover, these expectations also make the adult's presence a source of support (a "secure base") in distressing or frightening circumstances. As a consequence, young children are likely to turn increasingly to trusted caregivers for assistance in the relief of their own distress (e.g., Van Lieshout, 1975).

More generally, and with increasing age, adult interventions help to regulate a broader range of emotional experiences in older children—including anger, grief, and frustration—and adult regulatory strategies are likely to become more diverse as the child's age increases. As children get older, for example, it is not only the promptness and effectiveness of the caregiver's ministrations that shape social expectations; the metaemotive messages the adult conveys influence the child's immediate emotional condition and may also affect emergent self-regulatory capacities (e.g., an adult's declaring, "Big kids don't cry!"). These proposals must remain speculative, however, until further research is done on how parents' intervention strategies affect children's emotional regulation and the relevant longitudinal study is conducted on the effects of variations in caregiver responsiveness during distress-relief sequences in the early years.

**Affective contagion as emotional regulation: Affective attunement and social referencing.** Parents regulate a child's emotional experience not only through direct interventions, but also through distal cues that shape a child's experience and appraisal of events. For example, when a baby exuberantly bangs a toy on the floor to make a loud noise, parents sometimes mirror the vitality of the baby's actions in their own resonant response (e.g., saying "yes!" each time the toy is banged or moving in time to the baby's actions). This kind of intermodal resonance by a caregiver has been described by Stern (1985; Stern, Hofer, Haft, & Dore, 1985) as *affective attunement*. Affective attunement is used (both deliberately and nonconsciously) by caregivers to create a kind of "feeling-connectedness" with the child, but Stern's research has revealed that it is also used to "tune" the child's emotion; to increase or decrease the infant's arousal to a more desirable level. A resounding "yeah!" by the adult when the child encounters some pleasant surprise may be intended to increment the child's own delight, for example. In this manner, then, affective attunement may be another early form of exogenous emotional regulation fostered, in part, by the contagion of the adult's own affective expressions.

In addition, when feeling uncertain about a situation, children frequently look to familiar adults for cues about how to respond. This can be observed, for example, when children are approached by strangers in unfamiliar circumstances or when they encounter unfamiliar procedures (e.g., in a dentist's office). This constitutes a kind of secondary appraisal to facilitate the child's own assessment of events, and the socioemotional messages children receive may contribute to accentuating, dampening, redirecting, delaying, or otherwise altering their initial emotional reaction to these circumstances. This phenomenon has been called *social referencing* (Campos & Stenberg, 1981; Feinman, 1982, 1985; Klinnert, Campos, Sorce, Emde, & Svejda, 1983), and it constitutes another important way emotional behavior can be regulated by others.

Social referencing has been observed in infants as young as 7 months (Sorce, Emde, & Frank, 1982), but it is more commonly observed beginning at 10 to 12 months of age, after the infant can interpret facial expressions as emotionally meaningful (Klinnert et al., 1983). In a number of studies, researchers have demonstrated that the mother's posed facial expressions of emotion have a powerful effect on a baby's behavior when infants engage in social referencing (see Feinman, 1985, for a review). For example, infants are more likely to approach unusual objects when mothers are smiling rather than showing fearful expressions (Klinnert, 1984). One reason for this influence is that these expressions arouse resonant emotion in the child: a mother's clear display of negative emotion may elicit wariness in a child, which fosters behavioral inhibition, while maternal expressions of positive affect produce resonant feelings of well-being that facilitate approach and exploration (Thompson, 1987a; see Klinnert et al., 1983, and Sorce, Emde, Campos, & Klinnert, 1985, for supportive data). Moreover, it appears that not only parents but also familiar adults can have this influence on infant emotionality (Klinnert, Emde, & Butterfield, 1983).

Our own research on social referencing indicates that parents are naturally aware of the influence of referencing and deliberately alter their facial expressions to provide specific emotional messages when infants look to them (Benson & Thompson, in preparation). This should not be surprising: parents often strive to "look supportive" when their offspring encounter stressful but not dangerous circumstances (e.g., a medical exam), as if to foster effective coping by altering the child's emotional appraisal of the situation. They also accentuate their positive emotional expressions in appropriate circumstances to overcome a child's initial uncertainty and contribute to pleasure in the event (e.g., a carnival ride). The generality of social referencing processes is reflected in Feinman's (1982, 1985) argument that they are involved in diverse phenomena—such as social comparison, conformity, and modeling—that together contribute to the social construction of reality throughout development. For present purposes, however, it is clear that from an early age a child's emotional experience may be altered and regulated in significant ways by the emotional cues provided by parents and other socialization agents. Moreover, it is likely that more sophisticated forms of social referencing exert a continuing influence on emotional regulation throughout the life span. As adults, our immediate emotional reactions are intensified, dampened, or redirected as a consequence of our reappraisal of events based on the emotional reactions of those around us (consider, for example, reactions to rallies or at cocktail parties).

Phenomena like affective attunement and social referencing—as well as vicarious distress and group glee (Sherman, 1975)—alert us to the fact that a considerable part of one's emotional life is affected in a resonant or contagious fashion by the emotional expressions of others. These quasi-empathic processes affect not only a child's immediate emotional reactions, but also regulatory features such as the threshold, lability, and intensity of emotional responding. For example, a child's threshold of distress may be lowered in the presence of other distressed individuals. Importantly, affective contagion may influence emotional regulation whether it is an intended or unintended facet of the social management of emotion. As noted above, parents and other caregivers often deliberately enact emotional expressions that are intended to accentuate a child's positive experience or dampen a fearful or distressed response. On other occasions, however, resonant or contagious emotional influences may unintentionally undermine effective emotional regulation in children. In a series of naturalistic home observations and laboratory studies, Cummings and his colleagues (Cummings, 1987; Cummings, Iannotti, & Zahn-Waxler, 1985; Cummings, Zahn-Waxler, & Radke-Yarrow, 1981, 1984; see Zahn-Waxler and Kochanska, this volume) have shown that toddlers respond with distress, anger, and anxiety against a backdrop of adult expressions of anger. In one experimental study, for example, aggression toward an innocent peer increased when adults argued in the background, presumably owing to the influence of adult anger on the child's ongoing emotional experience (Cummings et al., 1985). Such findings suggest that the "emotional climate" of the home may significantly affect a child's ambient emotional condition through processes of affective contagion similar to those described above. This emotional climate may exert long-term influences on a child's general emotional regulatory style if this climate persists over time.

**Control of opportunity.** Over the path of early development, of course, children have many experiences of heightened emotion in their encounters with frightening or distressing events, experiences of exuberant social play, and animated (or frustrated) engagement with toys and other objects. The frequency, regularity, persistence, and intensity of these arousal experiences depends to a great extent on caregiving conditions, which are shaped both by adults' active efforts to regulate children's emotional experiences and also by the physical and social ecology. In a sense, adults control many of the opportunities children have to experience and learn to cope successfully with the heightened emotion through the caregiving conditions adults create, and these conditions are likely to be especially important contributors to individual differences in emotional regulation in the early years, before children can exert significant control over their own settings.

Cross-cultural studies of early development are especially pertinent to an appreciation of how caregivers control opportunities for emotional arousal and its regulation. Culturally normative child-rearing beliefs prescribe, among other things, (a) the amount of distance typically maintained between parents and infants (and thus the frequency of separation as well as the promptness of parental responses to distress signals), (b) the use of disruptive or upsetting child-rearing procedures (e.g., related to circumcision, rapid weaning, early independence training, and rites of passage), (c) the interpretation of children's needs and emotions (portraying children as innocent or demanding, for example, which can affect parental responsiveness), (d) the amount of stimulation provided young children (e.g., through practices such as swaddling or cradleboards), (e) the interpersonal density of the child's ecology (which affects the amount of social stimulation), as well as defining more generally the appropriate repertoire of emotional expressions for children of various ages. The institutionalization of children in day-care centers and schools provides normative experiences that also affect the growth of emotion and of emotional regulation. Day-care centers and schools provide incentives for the growth of emotional management through social comparison processes with peers, for example, as well as norms for the regulation of specific emotions (e.g., related to achievement and morality). In many ways, therefore, children develop emotionally in settings that are created for them by adults, and these settings affect their opportunities to learn to cope successfully and regulate states of heightened emotion.

Exemplary of this is Caudill's classic research (Caudill & Frost, 1975; Caudill & Weinstein, 1969), in which the soothing, pacifying style of Japanese mothers was contrasted with the more active, stimulating child-rearing approaches Americans adopted. Behavioral differences in their offspring appeared to reflect the influence of these caregiving differences: American infants were more emotionally expressive and labile than their Japanese counterparts. But recent commentators have noted that not only child-rearing practices but also ecological conditions may have contributed to the differences Caudill noted between American and Japanese infants. The size and layout of the Japanese house, for example, promote much greater proximity between mother and baby than in America, and mothers and infants bathe together, sleep together, and engage in other physically intimate behavior. Furthermore, the American custom of baby-sitting is practiced infrequently in Japan (see Miyake, Campos, Kagan, & Bradshaw, 1986; Chen & Miyake, 1986). As a consequence, a constellation of ecological and caregiving conditions restricts the opportunities Japanese infants have to experience many of the stresses (e.g., of physical separation from the mother) that are more common to the experience of American babies. As a further contrast, infants raised on traditional Israeli kibbutzim are, from 6 to 12 weeks postpartum, tended by one or more communal caregivers while mothers work, and babies are reassigned to another caregiver after the end of the first year. The heightened distress exhibited by infants from these settings (compared with American infants) during routine encounters with strangers and separations from mother noted earlier is consistent with their experience of frequently changing care in this small, enclosed community (see Sagi et al., 1985; Thompson & Sagi, in preparation).

By controlling the ecology of child development and the opportunities it affords for certain experiences of emotional arousal, caregivers may (often unintentionally) influence the development of emotional regulation in young children. In many circumstances, a child's capacity to maintain behavioral organization in conditions of heightened emotional arousal is related to the amount of prior experience with successful self-regulation in similar situations, and these opportunities are strongly influenced by the range of experiences caregiving conditions normatively afford. Although children obviously do not benefit psychologically from recurrent and overwhelming stress, it may be true that a range of emotional experiences (especially when self-regulation is fostered by exogenous sources) contributes to the acquisition of broad resources for effective coping, especially in young children. And there is some evidence that the physiological concomitants of regular experiences of peripheral arousal (of which emotional arousal is one kind) contribute to a kind of "physiological toughness" that also fosters psychological coping (see Dienstbier, in press and below).

**Discourse about emotion.** Once children begin to master basic language skills, other avenues for exogenous emotional regulation arise in parent-child conversations about emotion. In these conversations, children receive influential verbal messages from adults concerning the need for emotional regulation, the benefits of regulated emotion, strategies by which emotion may be regulated, the social rules governing emotional displays, and other information relevant to emotional understanding and the control of emotion. Language may be an especially powerful mode of emotional regulation for children because of its explicitness, its capacity for past and future reference (allowing adults to draw on a history of shared experiences as well as to anticipate future experiences when conveying messages about emotion), and its multifaceted character. The latter contributes to multiple modes of emotional communication (e.g., through specific words, intonation, and indirect discourse) that, together with nonverbal communicative modes, can contribute to redundant messages about emotion and its regulation (or at times inconsistent messages) (Miller & Sperry, 1988). Although language serves other purposes in the child's own regulatory efforts (which are discussed below), it also provides a significant conduit for exogenous emotional regulation.

It appears that these influences begin surprisingly early, as soon as children have constructed a basic vocabulary of emotion terms and are capable of receptive understanding of emotion-based messages from adults. In a series of provocative studies of parent-child conversation, Bretherton and her colleagues (Bretherton & Beeghly, 1982; Bretherton et al., 1986; Bretherton et al., 1981; Dunn, Bretherton, & Munn, 1987) found that explicit reference to emotional experiences mushrooms after 18 months of age. By early in the third year, children make relatively frequent reference to internal states related to emotion. Interestingly, although explicit reference to emotion is less common at this age than reference to other internal states, causal utterances concerning emotion are most frequent (Bretherton

& Beeghly, 1982). This suggests that the relative salience of emotional arousal leads young children to a more active effort to understand the origins and consequences of emotional experiences. Consistent with this, Bretherton and her colleagues also documented early utterances related to the regulation and control of emotion beginning in the third year (e.g., "I scared of the shark. Close my eyes" [Bretherton & Beeghly, 1982, p. 917]) that increased in scope and sophistication at later ages (see Bretherton et al., 1986). In short, a considerable amount of verbal interaction concerning emotion and its bases occurs in the toddler and early preschool years (see also Miller & Sperry, 1987). As Bretherton and her colleagues have argued, these conversations can help to clarify, interpret, and regulate young children's understanding of their own emotional states as well as those of others, while also channeling emotion knowledge into the interpretive structures of the culture and language system.

There are several ways caregivers can foster emotional regulation through conversation with the child. First, parents actively direct regulatory processes through verbal commands and instructions. "Will you please calm down!" is a familiar parental cry for emotional control by the child, but in more specific circumstances parents instruct offspring concerning appropriate modes of emotional expression, especially in public places. This can occur directly by instruction ("We don't laugh out loud in church!"), disapproval ("I thought you were a big boy. Big boys don't have tantrums"), or threats ("You'll go to your room if you don't stop crying!"), or indirectly by warning children of the consequences of unregulated emotional displays ("You'll get hiccups if you keep laughing so hard"). Discourse of this kind contributes to the development of emotional understanding that guides the child's own self-regulatory efforts, but it also has direct effects on the child's ongoing emotional experience. Indeed, it seems likely that distinct emotional regulatory styles arise in offspring in part because of a history of family experiences in which parents actively seek to regulate the child's emotional experience and expressions through direct instructions. These regulatory efforts of parents reflect attempts to conform the child's emotional behavior to cultural rules for emotional displays as well as to family rules based on parental values and child-rearing goals. According to Saarni (this volume), by the early elementary-school years children not only are keenly aware of the situations in which parents actively exert regulatory influence over their emotional expressions, but they can also justify the parents' actions in remarkably sophisticated ways.

A second way that parent-child discourse can affect the child's emotional regulation is through the adult's management of information provided the child. Especially when children encounter threatening or stressful circumstances, parents often shape their offspring's appraisal of emotionally arousing conditions through the kinds of information they provide and how this information is presented. For example, before an intrusive or painful medical examination, parents often help the child anticipate the procedures. This information may be presented in a manner that minimizes its stressful aspects (e.g., by focusing on how much better the child will feel afterward), reinterprets the nature of the procedures (e.g., describing them as "tickling"), or dispassionately intellectualizes what will occur. Alternatively, parents may intentionally distract the child with conversation about more pleasant topics and minimize information that relates to the stresses that will occur. In these ways parents often deliberately try to regulate the child's emotional experience through the kinds of information they make available.

This manner of exogenous emotional regulation is potentially risky, however, because it requires an astute evaluation of children's own assessment of threatening or stressful circumstances and the kinds of information that will best assist their coping. Children, like adults, often experience greater (not less) anxiety when provided with explicit information about aversive circumstances, and they benefit from cognitive strategies that can blunt the impact of threat-related information (Miller & Green, 1985). Thus it is often difficult to estimate how much information is necessary to help the child anticipate difficult events without undermining effective coping. There are also individual differences in the effects of information management: as Miller and Green (1985) have noted in a comprehensive review of this literature, younger children and those who have experienced a stressful condition are more fearful of these conditions than those who are older or inexperienced, and these children may be more adversely affected by receiving additional information about what to expect. Furthermore, if parents are unrealistically reassuring when children have reason to expect discomfort, parent-child conversations may not be especially helpful to the child's coping efforts. Thus, while information management by parents can be one significant mode of emotional regulation in offspring, it can potentially undermine rather than support the child's own self-regulatory efforts.

A third way parent-child discourse can affect emotional regulation is through the parent's suggesting explicit regulatory strategies. Parents are not only models but also teachers of emotional regulation: they can suggest, for example, the value of distracting or pleasant mental imagery, comforting self-talk, closing one's eyes when encountering threatening or scary events, redirecting thoughts, using external distractors, redefining goals or outcomes, or other specific strategies for regulating emotion. In immediate situations of emotional arousal, parents' suggestions of this kind can provide one valuable source of exogenous management of emotion. There is considerable evidence that children can benefit from instructed strategies for emotional regulation of this kind (Miller & Green, 1985), and parent-child discourse may be one important avenue for acquiring such strategies.

Finally, language influences emotional regulation indirectly through parental discussions that affect children's conceptions of emotion and its management. What do you do when you feel angry toward someone? How should affection be expressed? Is it wise to let others know when you are fearful or anxious? Although children derive answers to such questions from the parents' specific instructions, they also develop expectations about emotion indirectly from how parents comment on their own emotional experiences and those of others. Adults who frequently verbalize their angry feelings about co-workers or authorities provide salient cues to offspring about the normative occurrence of anger as well as modeling how it should be expressed or regulated (Miller & Sperry, 1987). When parents portray a sibling as "shy" and initiate strategies to overcome this tendency, they provide important cues about how shyness is regarded and can be managed. And in overhearing conversations between parents and other adults, children often learn a great deal about how certain emotions are socially appraised, valued, and regulated. Through such indirect means, parents can influence how children think about emotion and its management.

In these ways, therefore, discourse about emotion can have a profound influence on the regulation of emotion in children. But there are two additional reasons for its significance as an exogenous influence on emotional regulation. First, parent-child discourse begins to be influential developmentally at a time when children are acquiring a conceptual network of emotion terms, concepts, and ideas, and thus the substance of parent-child conversations about emotion and its regulation can shape the burgeoning social-cognitive understanding of emotion that is emerging at this time. Second, language systems are intimately linked to cultural meaning, and as language ability provides additional conduits of exogenous emotional regulation, children's emotion becomes increasingly socialized. Thus as language constructions infuse the child's growing social-cognitive network of emotion concepts, language provides yet another avenue for cultural values to influence children's emotion management. It is perhaps with the advent of language and discourse concerning emotion, therefore, that emotional regulation is most clearly a social construction.

**Beyond the family.** Consistent with traditional developmental perspectives, most of this discussion of exogenous influences on the development of emotional regulation has focused on processes within the family. But it is important to note that few of the influence modes considered thus far are confined to parent-child interaction, and with the growing institutionalization of child development (e.g., in out-of-home caregiving arrangements in the early years and educational institutions through adolescence), a growing variety of social agents are likely to influence the child's emerging capacity for emotion management. Extrafamilial influences may be redundant to those of parents, may be inconsistent with family influences, or may contribute to the development of regulatory capacities independent of those fostered within the home. A regular day-care worker may, for example, respond to a young baby's cries more slowly and more briefly than the parents do, making the development of emotional regulation in distress-relief sequences an inconsistent experience at home and in day care (and possibly leading to context-dependent social expectations as the child grows older). The same caregiver may, on the other hand, reinforce positive expressive modes in face-to-face play previously acquired in parent-infant play. At present, developmental study of emotion and emotional regulation has not progressed far enough to embrace this diversity in external influences on individual development.

With increasing age, of course, the child is influenced by a greater variety of social ecologies outside the home. Among the most important of these is the school system, in which, as noted earlier, unique forms of emotional regulation may develop in the achievement-oriented, social-comparison context of most formal school environments. Thus at school children encounter strong incentives to acquire skills related to the management of emotions like pride, shame, and embarrassment—and their display—especially in the context of peer interactions. Teachers may also assume a significant role in the development of these skills as well as shaping the constituent attributional processes by which children experience these emotions. The school environment also broadens a child's opportunities for observational learning of emotional regulatory strategies from peers, both within and outside the classroom.

Two other extrafamilial influences on emotional regulation should also be noted (although these do not exhaust the range of influences). First, watching television is one of a variety of "framed" experiences of emotion that provide children with highly salient opportunities for observational learning of emotion management, as well as direct experiences of regulating the emotion engendered by the medium itself (Dorr, 1985). Although television is one of a variety of such experiences (others include theater and radio), it is probably the most influential given the astonishing amount of time children are exposed to it. Some children's television programming is directly oriented toward fostering emotional regulatory skills (e.g., "Mister Rogers' Neighborhood" and "Sesame Street"); other programs present salient role models who themselves manage emotional arousal in explicit ways (e.g., children's cartoons and other programs); still other television presentations arouse emotion directly in children and require self-management of arousal (e.g., adult programming that includes explicit violence). At present little is known about the role of television exposure in the development of emotional regulation.

Second, children's stories are increasingly focused on emotional themes, and thus children are provided with additional opportunities to acquire skills of emotional regulation from these sources. Books and stories are important because they provide a forum for parent-child interaction and thus further instruction in emotional regulation (Greif, Alvarez, & Ulman, 1981). Exemplary of the opportunities afforded by children's stories is Aliki Brandenberg's (1984) *Feelings*, which explicitly describes the management of emotions as diverse as anger, fear, grief, jealousy, delight (and even boredom!).

**Summary.** In this long section, I have outlined the diverse processes by which emotional experience is shaped and regulated by individuals in the social environment. The purpose of doing so is to reveal how much the phylogenetically deeply rooted experience of emotion can be developmentally transformed by the socialization of emotional regulation. Beginning virtually from birth, these regulatory processes include (a) the selective reinforcement of certain expressions or expressive styles in the child, (b) modeling emotive behaviors and fostering their progressive imitation, (c) direct affective induction as a way of redirecting or otherwise regulating the child's ambient emotional state, (d) fostering emotion-relevant social expectations through caregiver responsiveness, (e) affective contagion as a way of influencing the child's immediate appraisal of emotionally arousing events, (f) the control of opportunities to acquire successful regulatory capacities based on the ecological and caregiving conditions created for a child, (g) the influence of discourse about emotion that can directly affect children's emotional regulation as well as their conceptions of emotion and its management, and (h) exposure to extrafamilial influences like television. These modes of influence have both immediate consequences (they contribute to a short-term change in the intensity or threshold of a child's ongoing emotional state) and long-term effects (they contribute to the development of more enduring regulatory styles in children).

The reasons caregivers and other adults seek to regulate a child's emotional experience are equally diverse: to promote positive social interactions with the child, to make the child's emotional expressions conform to cultural and familial display rules, to support the child's own coping efforts, or to broaden the child's emotional repertoire (e.g., "affective tolerance"). As we have seen, these forms of exogenous regulation are applied to positive as well as to negative emotional experiences, and they sometimes require a dissociation of the components of emotional experience (e.g., expressing an emotion that is inconsistent with one's internal experience in order to conform to parental demands) (Lewis & Michalson, 1983). Although many of these processes contribute to idiosyncratic styles of emotional regulation among children of a given age, many of these processes are also age-graded, resulting in normative progressive changes in regulatory capacities. For example, there is evidence that caregivers alter their expectations for positive and negative emotional expressions as their infants grow older (Brooks-Gunn & Lewis, 1982), parental discourse concerning emotion increases in complexity and scope as children's receptive language abilities increase (Dunn et al., 1987), and the diversity of ecological contexts for children typically broadens with increasing age, contributing to greater demands (and opportunities) for the development of regulatory capacities.

The complexity of these processes, and their integration as socializing influences, is nicely illustrated in Miller and Sperry's (1987) provocative ethnographic description of the socialization of anger and aggression by the mothers of three 2½-year-old girls growing up in a blue-collar neighborhood in South Baltimore. As the authors noted, fundamental values concerning the expression of anger not only were part of the child-rearing values of these mothers but were also part of their life experience: assertiveness and self-defense were necessary aspects of their survival and self-esteem in this environment as well as of their daughters'. As a consequence, these mothers actively sought to "toughen" their young children by modeling assertive/aggressive behavior (often in the context of evocative verbal accounts to others in the children's presence), selective reinforcement of justified aggressive outbursts by their offspring, teasing their daughters to provide mock "practice" aggressive episodes, using social referencing processes to heighten the children's anger when self-defense seemed warranted, rewarding self-control when aggression was unjustified or inappropriate, and using verbal discourse to interpret, comment, threaten, challenge, warn, or pacify their children. All these practices reflect exogenous modes of emotional regulation discussed in this section.

What were the effects of these practices on the children? According to Miller and Sperry (1987), by the age of 2½ the daughters possessed a rich repertoire of expressive modes for conveying anger, but they were also capable of regulating its expression in conformity with rules of the subculture. But as Saarni (1987) has noted, the association of anger with self-protective retaliation and the orientation toward anger rather than sadness in situations of wrongdoing are subculturally prescribed socialization norms that may not be consistently functional for these children. In different contexts (e.g., in school), or when presented with unexpected demands (e.g., in authority relations), this style of emotional regulation may be unhelpful and indeed dysfunctional.

Taken together, it is crucial to recognize the pervasive and systematic influences on emotional regulation arising from exogenous sources if we are to appreciate how the core experience of emotion becomes progressively shaped, altered, and managed by social partners throughout development. The social construction of emotional development becomes most apparent when these exogenous regulatory influences are taken seriously. But these influences occur hand in hand with the child's own emergent capacities, of course, and thus we now turn to these intrinsic influences.

## INTRINSIC INFLUENCES ON EMOTIONAL REGULATION

In a sense, the child's own emergent capacities for regulating and managing emotion impose limits on the social influences discussed above. Before the maturation of cortical inhibitory processes that affect emotionality, for example, the parents of young infants often find that they have little influence on their newborns' states of arousal. Until rudimentary social expectations have developed, parental behavior in face-to-face play or distress-relief sequences has more limited long-term consequences for the child. And with the growth of sophisticated social-cognitive understanding, children can begin to construct complex networks of emotional understanding and self-awareness that contribute to more subtle—and effective—modes of emotional self-regulation. Consistent with a truly transactional view of development, therefore, it is also essential that we consider how the child's emergent intrinsic capacities related to emotional regulation not only make direct contributions to emotion management but also interact with the exogenous influences described above.

**Neurophysiological constituents.** Whether regulation is through exogenous or endogenous influences, a capacity for emotional regulation depends on the neurophysiological processes by which the organism can control or inhibit emotion. If these control processes are inoperative, dysfunctional, or immature, emotional regulation is likely to be limited regardless of external supports. There is considerable evidence that many of these neurophysiological control mechanisms are functionally immature in the newborn. Parents of young infants discover this when, despite their concerted efforts to regulate arousal states, the newborn shifts unpredictably and erratically from quiescence to heightened distress and back again. It is partly due to their inability to regulate infantile fussing and crying, as well as the limited amounts of positive affect their babies exhibit, that many parents describe their newborns as being like animals or dolls, lacking distinctly human qualities of emotional responsiveness (Robson & Moss, 1970).

Arousal is difficult to regulate in the early months of life because of the immaturity of nervous system organization, and the postnatal period is one of progressive consolidation and integration of excitatory/inhibitory processes. Diffuse excitatory processes—such as those related to the sympathetic nervous system and subcortical structures—are functionally active from birth, partly because of their relevance to organismic survival. But many of the more finely tuned inhibitory systems—which include parasympathetic nervous system activity and higher-order cortical processes, especially in the frontal lobes—are slower to develop and myelinate, and their influence emerges more slowly in the postnatal period. Indeed, the growth of cortical inhibitory control over subcortically mediated excitatory systems like emotion is a significant but gradually emerging developmental achievement, and as a consequence the fully mature inhibitory processes that assist in the regulation of emotional arousal do not become functional until long after birth. In the paragraphs that follow, we will consider the developmental organization of excitatory and inhibitory systems.

1. Consider first the progressive organization of excitatory systems that govern organismic arousal, such as during emotional experiences. Emotional arousal is linked to activation of the hypothalamic-pituitary-adrenocortical (HPAC) system, which has traditionally been regarded as responsive to aversive, stressful stimulation. (This system interacts with the sympatho-adrenomedullary [SAM] system, which also fosters coping in stressful circumstances). Recent research on the HPAC system underscores a complex portrayal of adrenocortical activation as reactive to uncertainty, novelty, and "significant changes in demands that the organism is not immediately prepared to meet" (Gunnar, Marvinney, Isensee, & Fisch, in press), and from this perspective activation is complexly tied to organismic state, ongoing intrinsic and extrinsic demands, and developmental changes in coping resources (see Tennes & Mason, 1982). Gunnar's research with neonates indicates that the HPAC system is functional from birth but may be more reactive and labile than later in the first year (Gunnar, 1986; Gunnar, Malone, & Fisch, 1985; Gunnar, Mangelsdorf, Kestenbaum, Lang, Larson, & Andreas, in press; Gunnar, Mangelsdorf, Larson, & Hertzgaard, in press; Gunnar, Marvinney, Isensee, & Fisch, in press). As a consequence, organismic arousal gradually assumes less of the reactive, all-or-none character of the immediate postnatal period.

There is also evidence that early individual differences in adrenocortical reactivity are related to differences in emotional and coping behavior. Tennes, Downey, and Vernadakis (1977), for example, found modest associations between ratings of separation anxiety and urinary cortisol levels in a sample of 1-year-olds. They noted that cortisol levels were similarly associated with ratings of the child's postseparation reunion responses and fearfulness with a stranger: infants with elevated urinary cortisol exhibited more separation distress, more negative reunion greetings, and greater stranger wariness (see Tennes, 1982; Tennes & Mason, 1982). Individual differences in cortisol levels also remained consistent over several years (Tennes, 1982). More generally, if activation of the HPAC system is related to novelty, uncertainty, and unexpected demands, then variations in HPAC activity are likely to be associated with developmental changes in how children interpret uncertain and potentially demanding circumstances, and there is some evidence for this (Gunnar, Marvinney, Isensee, & Fisch, 1989).

Individual differences in the functioning of the HPAC and SAM systems may also be informative about differences between normal and atypical populations in emotional arousal and its regulation. In a comparative study of emotional regulation of normal and Down syndrome infants during separation from their mothers, we (Thompson et al., 1985) found that Down syndrome infants exhibited a diminished range and lability of emotion, lower intensity of distress, with a longer latency to react emotionally and a quicker recovery than normal infants who were comparable either in chronological age or in mental age. These differences are consistent with research indicating that Down syndrome is characterized by decreased sympathetic nervous system activity as well as dampened cholinergic and serotonergic regulatory systems (see Cicchetti, this volume). As a consequence, Down syndrome children exhibit a higher arousal threshold, diminished intensity of emotional reactions, and dampened reactivity reflected in these temporal characteristics of emotion.

In sum, although excitatory arousal systems are functional from birth, important changes occur in their organization during the first year that contribute to less labile, better modulated arousal reactions. Moreover, individual differences in sympathetic nervous system reactivity have predictable links to the quality and intensity of emotional behavior as well as to its regulatory features (e.g., arousal thresholds, temporal features related to onset and offset, lability). The organization of excitatory arousal systems thus underlies important dimensions of emotional regulation.

2. Now consider the growing influence of inhibitory processes related to emotional arousal, especially those involving cortical control mechanisms. There appear to be two important transitions in the development of cortical inhibitory processes in infancy. The first occurs at 2–4 months of age with the gradual disappearance (or suppression) of transitory neonatal reflexes, the emergence of more regular sleep/wake patterns and a change in neural activity during sleep, and greater regularity and control of behavioral state, all indicating the growth of forebrain inhibitory centers (e.g., Emde,

Gaensbauer, & Harmon, 1976). The emotional correlates of these be-havioral changes may also relate to the growth of cortical inhibitory processes: a decrease in the incidence of endogenous smiling and an increase in smiling that is responsive to external stimulation, to-gether with a decline in unexplained fussiness (Emde et al., 1976), increases in emotional responsiveness to contingent stimulation (Watson, 1982; Watson & Ramey, 1977), and an emerging capacity for laughter in response to environmental events (Sroufe & Wunsch, 1972). This is also the time when parents begin to report perceiving their infants as more human and emotionally responsive (Robson & Moss, 1970). Rudimentary forebrain inhibitory processes may ac-count for the increasing environmental responsiveness of these early emotional reactions.

The second transition occurs at about 9–10 months of age and is associated with changes in the functioning of the frontal lobe, which is evolutionarily one of the newest structures of the cerebral cortex and among the last to be myelinated. In a series of provocative studies with infants and nonhuman primates, Diamond (1988a, 1988b) and Goldman-Rakic (1987) have suggested that the capacity for response inhibition at this time is linked to maturation of the frontal cortex (specifically the dorsal-lateral prefrontal cortex), which facilitates performance in problem-solving tasks by 9–12 months of age by permitting a memory-based overriding of habit-based tendencies. Thus in cognitive processing the maturation of frontal activity may be influential in exerting higher-order inhibition over initial response tendencies. With respect to emotion, the same frontally mediated inhibitory processes may also regulate excitatory processes related to emotional arousal.

In understanding these emergent inhibitory processes, the lat-eralization of hemispheric functioning related to emotion must be considered. Although researchers no longer distinguish so simply between the "emotional" right hemisphere and the "rational" left hemisphere, the delineation of the specific functions associated with each is not so clear. Many current conceptualizations now por-tray the right hemisphere as more attuned to the perception and processing of negative emotion, while the left hemisphere is more dominant with respect to positively valenced emotion. But a some-what more generalized delineation may be truer to current research evidence: the left hemisphere is dominant with respect to approach behavior, and the right hemisphere is more strongly related to withdrawal/avoidance (see Davidson & Fox, 1988; Fox, 1985a; Fox & Davidson, 1984; and Kinsbourne & Bemporad, 1984 for a review of this evidence). Although this approach/withdrawal distinction maps onto the positive/negative valence distinction in many respects, it may provide a more accurate portrayal of hemispheric contributions to certain emotional states that entail mingled approach/withdrawal tendencies (such as sadness).

There is considerable evidence that hemispheric specialization for many cognitive and affective functions is apparent from an early age (see Kinsbourne & Hiscock, 1983). For example, Davidson and Fox (1982) found that 10-month-olds who watched a filmed actress displaying happiness showed greater relative activation of the left over the right frontal region. In another study, Fox and Davidson 1987) showed that infants of the same age who cried during a brief separation from their mothers showed greater relative right frontal activation, while noncriers showed relatively greater left frontal activity. Similar asymmetries in frontal activation paralleled other facial expressions of discrete emotion (Fox & Davidson, 1988, in press). There is also evidence for asymmetries in frontal activity in newborn infants who respond to emotionally arousing stimulation (Fox & Davidson, 1986), although these are not as clear-cut because of some of the maturational processes outlined earlier.

According to these researchers, a capacity for emotional regulation emerges late in infancy because of developing *interconnectivity* between different regions within and between each cerebral hemisphere, with right and left *frontal* lobes assuming specialized inhibitory roles in emotional arousal (e.g., Tucker & Frederick, in press), consistent with the findings of Diamond and Goldman-Rakic discussed earlier. For example, Kinsbourne and Bemporad (1984) have argued that the right frontotemporal cortex exerts emotional inhibitory control over internal emotional arousal, partly by regulating posterior areas of the right hemisphere related to emotion. They also suggest—and Fox and Davidson (1984) elaborate on this view—that right and left frontal lobes may also exert *mutual* regulatory control, with the left frontal cortex assisting in the management of right hemispheric activation related to negative emotion/withdrawal tendencies. The latter is a slow developmental process because it depends on the maturation of the cerebral commissures, but Fox and Davidson (1984) argue that evidence for greater interhemispheric interconnectivity appears during the 9–12-month period in certain cognitive, affective, and motor achievements, and this view is consistent with the findings of Diamond and her colleagues outlined above. Fox and Davidson (1984) suggest, therefore, that during this period there is a developing neurophysiological capacity to inhibit or regulate negative emotional arousal both because of the increased functional activity of the left frontal area and also because of the maturation of transcollosal fibers. This is manifested in emotional reactions that include response inhibition (for example, the noncriers in the Fox and Davidson [1987] study described earlier showed greater relative left frontal activation, perhaps reflecting a suppression of distress arousal), the emergence of more complex affective reactions like fear and sadness, and the sophistication of primary and secondary appraisal processes that contribute to emotional reactions (e.g., social referencing and other processes described above).

These arguments are speculative, of course, and require further developmental study of neurophysiological inhibitory processes. Yet they point to the importance of the maturation of frontal inhibitory processes that may contribute, in the first two years of life, to an emergent capacity for the modulation, regulation, and fine-tuning of emotional reactions (especially negative emotions). Considering also the developing refinement of neurophysiological excitatory processes described earlier, these studies point to the early years of life as a period of increasing consolidation and integration of excitatory/inhibitory processes that foster the transition from the reflexive, all-or-none arousal states of the newborn to the environmentally sensitive, more self-controlled emotions of the toddler.

**Biogenetic differences.** Although the preceding discussion of the neurophysiological constituents of emotional regulation has already highlighted the importance of individual differences that may have a biological basis, considerable additional research has been devoted to describing and studying these differences in emotion and regulation. The conceptual rubric for most of this work is temperament: individual differences in behavioral style that are presumed to have a constitutional or hereditary basis. Although there are significant differences in how theories define temperament and the dimensions of temperamental variability (see Bates, 1987, and Goldsmith et al., 1987, for reviews), most temperamental theories underscore individual differences in emotionality (e.g., Buss & Plomin, 1984; Campos et al., 1983; Derryberry & Rothbart, 1984; Goldsmith & Campos, 1982, 1986; Rothbart & Derryberry, 1981), and at least one emphasizes the self-regulatory aspects of temperament (Rothbart & Derryberry, 1981). Moreover, temperamental variability is often assessed in terms of response characteristics similar to those involved in emotional regulation, such as the threshold of responsiveness, lability and intensity of reactions, the latency and rise time of a response, and general mood (e.g., Rothbart, 1981; Thomas & Chess, 1977). For all these reasons—and because these behavioral variations are thought to be grounded in biogenetic or constitutional differences—temperamental theory provides another important perspective on the study of emotion and self-regulation.

Rothbart's temperamental theory provides the most provocative viewpoint on the growth of self-regulation and its emotional components (see Derryberry & Rothbart, 1984; Rothbart & Derryberry, 1981; Rothbart & Posner, 1985). In this view, temperament is defined as "constitutional differences in reactivity and self-regulation" (Derryberry & Rothbart, 1984, p. 132), in which "reactivity" refers to the excitability or arousability of the organism's response systems and "self-regulation" refers to the higher-order regulatory processes that modulate these reactions. The former are reflected in response parameters such as threshold, latency, intensity, rise time, and recovery; the latter involve attentional, approach/avoidance, and inhibitory mechanisms. Because emotional processes are relevant to both the reactivity and self-regulatory aspects of temperament, emotion constructs figure prominently in Rothbart's dimensions of temperamental variability, which include positive and negative reactivity as well as behavioral inhibition and attentional orienting/focusing (see Goldsmith et al., 1987). These are appraised through fine-grained assessments of infantile activity level, smiling/laughter, fear, distress to limitations (i.e., anger and frustration), soothability, and duration of orienting (Rothbart, 1981). Although Rothbart and her collaborators emphasize the neurophysiological, endocrinological, and other biological bases of temperamental individuality (see Rothbart & Posner, 1985), they also underscore developmental changes in temperament as these systems mature and reorganize throughout the life span.

The potential value of such biogenetic models of temperamental individuality lies, in part, in the capacity of researchers to identify the specific physiological processes by which constitutional or hereditary tendencies are translated into different emotional regulatory styles. Recent research in several laboratories indicates that some of this promise is currently being realized. In Kagan's research, large numbers of preschoolers were screened to yield groups of consistently inhibited and uninhibited children, who were then compared longitudinally on a variety of behavioral and physiological measures. He and his colleagues found that inhibited and uninhibited children differed within and across assessments not only on behaviors reflecting shyness and fearfulness, but also on a range of autonomic measures. Inhibited children, for example, had higher and more stable heart rates at every age of evaluation, had higher levels of urinary norepinephrine and salivary cortisol at age 5½, and exhibited other behaviors reflecting higher tonic levels in hypothalamic-pituitary-adrenocortical (HPAC) system activity (see Garcia Coll, Kagan, & Reznick, 1984; Kagan, Reznick, Clarke, & Snidman, 1984; Reznick, Kagan, Snidman, Gersten, Baak, & Rosenberg, 1986; see Kagan et al., 1987, for a review). Kagan and his colleagues have suggested that these inhibited children have a generally lower threshold of reactivity in limbic structures mediating fear and defense (i.e., the amygdala, the hypothalamus, or both), while the uninhibited children have a higher threshold of reactivity. As a consequence, inhibited children show greater fearful, wary, and shy behavior, while the uninhibited children are generally more outgoing and emotionally more labile.

In Fox's (in press a, in press b) research, measures of heart rate and heart-period variance, together with measures of vagal tone, were used to index parasympathetic nervous system influences on stress reactions in young infants. As in Kagan's research, two selected groups of infants were compared: one group that displayed consistently high heart rate and low heart-period variance and vagal tone at 14 months (comparable to Kagan's inhibited children), and another group that showed consistently low heart rate and high variance and vagal tone (like the uninhibited children). Although these groups did not differ on various newborn behavioral measures, at 5 months of age the infants with higher/stable heart rate were emotionally less reactive (e.g., little crying to a frustration task), and at 14 months they were slower to approach a stranger and a strange toy than infants with lower/variable heart rates. Conversely, those infants with lower/variable heart rates reacted with greater crying but also greater self-regulatory efforts at 5 months and greater stranger sociability and toy interest at 14 months. Thus, as in Kagan's research, indexes of autonomic reactivity were related in a predictable manner to behavioral measures of wariness, inhibition, and emotional regulation. Contrary to Kagan, Fox and his colleagues have emphasized the differences in parasympathetic regulation (rather than sympathetic activation), arguing that infants with lower/variable heart rates are better organized behaviorally and are more responsive to the environment, partly because of their use of attentional strategies (which are partly parasympathetically mediated) to regulate their emotional reactions (see Fox, 1985b).

Research findings like these add credence to Rothbart's portrayal of temperamental variability in terms of inhibition and positive/negative emotionality and suggest that individual differences in physiological reactivity and regulation mediate these behavioral differences. These differences may have a constitutional or hereditary basis, and this view is buttressed by findings from each laboratory indicating impressive individual consistency in these physiological indexes over periods of months or years and significant heritability in one twin study (Healy, Fox, & Porges, 1988). Thus, insofar as genetic potential becomes translated into the kinds of physiological processes underlying emotional regulation identified in these studies, individual differences in regulatory processes may have an important hereditary foundation (see also Buss & Plomin, 1984).

Even so, temperamental theory is potentially misleading if we therefore assume that these individual differences are unchanging or immutable. Indeed, recent empirical work in developmental behavioral genetics and molecular genetics has revealed that genes are themselves the sources of change as well as continuity in behavior (see Plomin, 1983, 1986; Plomin & Thompson, 1988; Scarr & Kidd,

1983, for reviews). Genes "turn on and off" during development, gene expression based on DNA transcription changes over time, there are developmental changes in the heritability of many characteristics, and many genetically based differences are not early emerging but appear at different periods of the life span (e.g., the timing of puberty). Moreover, the phenotypic expression of an individual genotype depends in part on the "goodness of fit" (Lerner & Lerner, 1983) or "match" (Buss & Plomin, 1984) between genotypical characteristics and environmental demands. This is especially likely for the manifestation of genotypes within the normal range; more extreme genotypes, by contrast, may be more resilient in their phenotypical expression. (Indeed, part of the power of the research strategies of Kagan and Fox is their focus on extreme contrast groups [each representing no more than 10% of the population], although even in Kagan's study the consistency of individual differences in inhibition was affected by mothers' concerted efforts to modify this behavioral characteristic in offspring [Kagan et al., 1987].)

Moreover, Dienstbier (in press) has argued that experiences of intermittent stress (including mental challenges and aerobic exercise) can modify the HPAC and SAM physiological systems governing stress reactions in humans by promoting resistance to neuroendocrine depletion and enhancing catecholamine capacity. According to Dienstbier, this results in a kind of physiological "toughening" that fosters better performance in stressful conditions and may have indirect effects on emotional and personality functioning. In this formulation, therefore, environmental experiences related to stress regulation (largely under parental control early in life, but increasingly self-selected) can modify the phenotypic expression of genotypical differences by altering the physiological systems they influence.

Biogenetic differences thus assume an important role in individual variability in emotional regulatory processes. According to the studies of Kagan and Fox, they can influence the sympathetic/parasympathetic balance within individuals, contributing either to lower stress thresholds or, alternatively, to greater attentional regulation and control of emotional reactions. Although individual differences in excitatory/inhibitory thresholds appear to influence a wide range of behavioral characteristics from an early age, their potential modifiability is also revealed not only in these studies, but also in other research in behavioral genetics. In this manner, therefore, genotypical variability related to emotion and its regulation provides parameters within which environmental influences affect the processes of emotion management throughout development.

**Cognitive constituents.** Cognitive development provides a framework for the growth of emotion and emotional regulation, but its influence is general rather than specific (Case, Hayward, Lewis, & Hurst, 1988; Piaget, 1954/1981; see Kopp, 1982, 1987, in press, for excellent analyses). With the emergence of new intellectual capabilities, the appraisal processes (both primary and secondary) underlying emotional arousal increase in sophistication and scope, the capacities of the individual to respond adaptively to emotionally arousing events become more subtle and complex, emotional experiences become represented and cognized in more abstract ways, and emotional regulatory efforts increasingly draw upon a system of social-cognitive understanding of emotion, its antecedents, and its management. Moreover, the growth of language and communicative competencies dramatically increases the individual's susceptibility to extrinsic regulatory influences and also contributes to early self-regulatory efforts (see below). But in providing a framework for the growth of emotional regulation, cognitive capabilities neither direct nor guarantee their emergence, but rather set the stage for the unfolding of regulatory skills that are responsive to the specific demands upon the individual (Fischer, 1980).

Cognitive developmental processes influence both the child's susceptibility to extrinsic modes of emotional regulation and the growth of emotional self-regulation. On one hand, the effects of many extrinsic influences are mediated by the child's emerging cognitive capabilities. As noted earlier, for example, the effects of parental interventions during distress-relief sequences and social play increase during the first six months of life as infants develop rudimentary social expectations for the behavior of familiar partners (Lamb, 1981b). Consequently, infants increasingly approach these social encounters with person-specific affective biases that color their thresholds for positive arousal in social play and speed of recovery (soothability) in distress-relief sequences (Thompson &

Lamb, 1983). The more differentiated social expectations of older children may also have significant effects on their emotional behavior (this is, in some respects, what is meant by a child's being "secure" or "insecure").

Other cognitive achievements also affect extrinsic regulatory influences. Once infants can interpret facial expressions as emotionally meaningful late in the first year, for example, social referencing becomes an external regulator of emotion (Klinnert et al., 1983). The growth of evocative memory skills (Kagan, Kearsley, & Zelazo, 1978) and means-ends understanding during this period also fosters the ability to spontaneously anticipate emotionally arousing events and to respond accordingly. Anticipatory cognitions probably lower the threshold (and increase the intensity) of emotional arousal in situations as diverse as peek-a-boo games (Sroufe & Wunsch, 1972) and separation distress (Thompson & Limber, in press), as noted earlier in the discussion of developmental changes in emotion dynamics. Moreover, the enlistment of means-ends understanding with the emergence of intersubjectivity and intentionality in communicative efforts toward the end of the first year (e.g., Bretherton et al., 1981; Harding & Golinkoff, 1979; Trevarthen & Hubley, 1978) fosters the use of social signals to obtain nurturance, assistance, and other emotionally regulatory social interventions (as reflected in the classic example of the child who falls, looks around to see whether adults are watching, and then cries loudly when an audience appears). These skills increase in sophistication and scope during the second year of life (cf. Bretherton et al., 1986).

With the growth of representational skills during the second year, however, the child's nascent capacities for emotional *self*-regulation begin to emerge more fully. The symbolic representations of earlier experiences in memory provide the child with greater access to past experiences of emotion and its management, fostering more sophisticated emotional anticipations, more differentiated social expectations, and rudimentary strategies for emotional self-management based on these earlier experiences. Language ability increases the child's consciousness of emotional experiences through communication with others, as well as giving the child access to the verbal guidance of others (see below). Pretend play offers the opportunity to rehearse the management of emotion in evocative but imaginary contexts, often accompanied by peers or siblings (Dunn, 1987; Gottman & Mettetal, 1986). In these contexts, salient feelings can be safely replayed to understand their causes, consequences, and management and can be projected onto others to examine how one can assist in another's emotional regulation. Emotion dynamics figure prominently in these play episodes because children experiment not only with discrete emotions but also with their intensive and temporal features. Moreover, when such play is social in nature, emotional self-regulation is required to ensure the smooth coordination of different goals, interests, and approaches to play and thus to promote positive interaction with a play partner.

With increasing age, emotive processes themselves become the object of explicit reflection and analysis, and important cognitive constituents contribute to a developing understanding of emotion and its management. For example, as children increasingly distinguish the behavioral manifestations of emotional displays from their underlying psychological origins in the late preschool years, the internal antecedents of emotional arousal (e.g., mental imagery, attributions, goals) can become targets for deliberate intervention in self-regulatory efforts. The growth of children's understanding of the appearance/reality distinction (Flavell, Flavell, & Green, 1983) may underlie their understanding of emotional display rules, which guide the distinction between how one appears and how one actually feels (e.g., Saarni, this volume). A growing cognitive capacity to coordinate multiple perspectives on a task may contribute to children's emergent appreciation of the multiple dimensions of emotional experience (e.g., subjective experience, behavior, expression) and the simultaneity of different emotions (Harter, 1982a, 1982b). The growth of perspective-taking and role-taking skills and the development of recursive thought in middle childhood may contribute to children's ability to anticipate others' reactions to their emotional displays and to strategically enlist these reactions in their emotional self-regulatory efforts (Harter & Whitesell, 1989). And with the growth of self-reflection and self-understanding (Damon & Hart, 1982; Harter, 1983), emotion in oneself and one's own idiosyncratic emotive processes can also become objects of reflective analysis.

At times the growth of cognitive abilities may transform early-emerging self-regulatory capabilities into more sophisticated forms.

Consider the management of attentional processes, which is at the root of many forms of emotional regulation. Newborns are deficient in attentional self-control (reflected in the "obligatory attention" devoted to compelling visual stimuli; see Stechler & Latz, 1966), but by 2 to 3 months of age infants are more proficient at shifting their attention away from unpleasant events and toward more positive, engaging stimuli, and this can have an emotionally regulating effect (Derryberry & Rothbart, 1984). Caregivers enlist this capacity by providing distracting stimuli when infants are distressed, and toddlers can use deliberate self-distraction as a means of emotional management (Gunnar & Hornik, 1987). By the preschool years, the diversion of attention away from events that arouse negative emotion is a cognized strategy of emotional regulation (Bretherton et al., 1986), and with increasing age attention may be diverted by psychological means as well (e.g., relaxing mental imagery, redirection of thoughts, reevoking past memories; see below). Thus new cognitive capabilities not only introduce new means of emotional regulation into an individual's repertoire, but can transform early-emerging regulatory abilities into more sophisticated modes.

As noted earlier in this chapter, the developing speed and efficiency of information-processing capabilities (fostered by the routinization of mental subroutines, changes in short-term memory capacity, and other cognitive changes) may also affect emotional regulation through its effects on the child's appraisals of changing situational events (e.g., related to distress relief). Indeed, one important catalyst to the maturity of emotional management strategies is the flexible efficiency of mental processes that permit rapid shifts between different appraisals of the situation within a broad temporal context. But by and large these cognitive constituents of emotional regulation have been minimally explored by developmental researchers, and considerable research effort is required to elucidate their effects and the broader role of cognitive development in the growth of emotional management.

**Communicative and language ability.** Among the most important cognitive constituents of emotional regulation is the growth of communicative skills and language ability. We have already considered some of the reasons. Discourse about emotion assumes a significant role in the socialization of emotional regulation. Caregivers use language to direct regulatory processes in children (primarily through exhortatory messages) and to suggest regulatory strategies. They also influence emotional regulation indirectly through the management of information to the child and their discussions of their own efforts at emotion management. In short, language ability heightens the social construction of emotional regulatory processes.

As a mode of self-reflection, language ability also fosters the child's consciousness of emotion as children can better consider the events that elicit emotion and the experience of emotion itself. As Bretherton and her colleagues have noted, toddlers and young preschoolers devote considerable effort to understanding the causes of emotion, and language enables caregivers to label, interpret, and guide the understanding and management of emotional arousal through verbal discourse as children inquire about the origins of their emotions, request reassurance, and discuss other elements of their feelings (Bretherton & Beeghly, 1982; Bretherton et al., 1986; Dunn et al., 1987). Moreover, because language can enlist reference to past events as well as anticipations of future events, caregivers can further assist in emotional regulation by establishing temporal connections in self-regulatory strategies for the child (e.g., "Yesterday, you felt better when you did . . . you might try that again later"). At somewhat older ages, peer interactions assume similar functions by enabling children to clarify, understand, and regulate their emotions through discourse (cf. Gottman & Mettetal, 1986). Moreover, as an avenue of self-expression, language enables children to manage emotional arousal by venting that arousal through words as well as actions.

The emergent role of language in the child's emotional self-regulation has received considerable theoretical attention. As noted by Kopp (1982, 1987), Vygotskian perspectives portray the development of interiorized speech as an important contributor to self-regulation (cf. Luria, 1961; Vygotsky, 1962), while psychodynamic perspectives portray language as an ego-related constituent of impulse control. Neither perspective has received considerable empirical support, however, and neither has been tested directly with respect to emotional self-regulatory efforts. This is an important shortcoming, because young children often spontaneously use language in their efforts to manage emotion in a manner that resembles the emotional self-coaching of adults: it is not uncommon, for example, to overhear preschoolers reassuring themselves (or a doll or playmate) of Mommy's anticipated return during a separation (cf. Smolek & Weinraub, 1979). (One colleague reported overhearing his 3-year-old grandson saying to himself during a stressful moment, "I don't need a bottle! Big boys don't need bottles.") It seems likely that such language use is efficacious not as a prelude to interiorized speech, but rather as an evoking of supportive words provided earlier by caregivers. In this context, for both young children and adults, language may foster emotional self-regulation as reassuring or exhortatory self-talk.

However, there is intriguing recent evidence that language production itself may affect emotionality, especially during the early period of language acquisition. Bloom and her colleagues (Bloom, in press; Bloom & Beckwith, in press; Bloom, Beckwith, & Capatides, 1988; Bloom & Capatides, 1987) have reported that major advances in language development early in the second year were accompanied by diminished emotionality and greater time in neutral affect when children were observed longitudinally in play sessions. She has argued that neutral affect promotes the reflectivity required for early language use, and this conclusion is supported by microanalyses of early word usage, in which the onset of a spoken word was found to be preceded by diminished emotion in the moments immediately before (Bloom & Beckwith, in press). Thus, both in microanalyses of early word usage and in developmental trends in early language development, emotion and language seem to be relatively independent expressive systems with mutual influences: they compete, in a sense, for the young child's cognitive resources. Further study is needed to elucidate how these systems are related at later ages and the extent to which language production has an emotional regulatory influence.

**The growth of metaemotive understanding.** With the emergence of representational skills in the second year of life, the child's capacities for emotional self-regulation broaden dramatically. Although rudimentary behavioral self-regulatory capacities obviously exist before this time (e.g., attentional shifts, self-soothing behaviors), as noted earlier, they are limited in their flexibility, goal directedness, and range of applicability by the constraints of sensorimotor cognition. By contrast, when emotion itself can become an object of reflective analysis by the child, the emotional understanding that develops fosters the emergence of self-regulatory processes that can be used in a variety of conditions, more efficiently adapted to present circumstances, employed deliberately and with strategic purposes, and incorporated into a broader representational network of social-cognitive understanding. Emotional understanding gives the child conscious access to emotive processes and their regulation, and even though these emotive (and to some extent regulatory) processes often predate the emergence of cognitions about them, representational understanding makes them targets of reflective thought and thus of greater conscious control. Moreover, the emergence of emotional understanding also sensitizes the child to relevant regulatory influences (e.g., others' reactions, personal goals and values, anticipations, psychological processes in oneself and others) that can become systematically incorporated into self-regulatory efforts for the first time. Thus the growth of emotional understanding and emotional self-regulation occur hand in hand, and because many elements of emotional understanding are enlisted in the child's emergent self-regulatory efforts, this understanding is *metaemotive* in nature, defined as the individual's awareness and understanding of processes concerning the strategic regulation of emotion.

As Meerum Terwogt and Olthof (1989) have noted, there are several components to this emergent metaemotive understanding. First is the child's knowledge of the antecedents of emotion, or the linkages between situations and emotional responses. Because of its importance for the child's everyday social transactions, this kind of emotional understanding emerges early. Before the age of 3 ½ years, for example, children can accurately identify situations that elicit simple emotional reactions like happiness, sadness, anger, and fear (Borke, 1971; Harter, 1982a; Mood, Johnson, & Shantz, 1978; Trabasso, Stein, & Johnson, 1981; see also Barden, Zelko, Duncan, & Masters, 1980; Harris, Olthof, Meerum Terwogt, & Hardman, 1987). In succeeding years their emotional lexicons expand significantly (Harter, 1982a; Ridgeway, Waters, & Kuczaj, 1985; Russell & Ridgeway, 1983; Schwartz & Trabasso, 1984), they increasingly discriminate between the different causal conditions that evoke emotion (e.g., Graham & Weiner, 1986; Thompson, 1987b, 1989; Weiner & Graham, 1984), and they better appreciate the idiosyncratic psychological as well as situational determinants of emotional arousal (e.g., Gnepp & Chilamkurti, 1988; Gnepp & Gould, 1985; Harris, 1983; Stein & Trabasso, 1989). Thus from early preschool to early adolescence children progress from a shallow appreciation of the antecedents of a limited range of emotions to deeper processing of the situations giving rise to a broader array of emotional reactions.

A second component of metaemotive understanding is knowledge of the consequences of an emotional response. In a sense, children's awareness of the consequences of their unregulated emotional behavior provides the motivational basis for emotional self-regulation. Much of this awareness is, of course, intuitive: we are motivated to regulate experiences of negative arousal because these experiences are subjectively uncomfortable, especially at high intensity (the same is sometimes true of heightened positive arousal). This form of intuitive knowledge motivates self-regulatory efforts from an early age. Later, children acquire standards for the expression of emotion from the social surround and thus learn that the unregulated expression of certain emotions in some situations provokes negative reactions from others (see Saarni, this volume). The internalization of cultural standards of emotional conduct also fosters children's emotional self-management.

But children also are motivated to regulate emotional experiences because of their growing knowledge of the *personal* consequences of doing so. For example, from the age of 6 (the earliest age studied) children are aware that they perceive others more positively when they are in a positive mood, and that negative emotion impairs task performance (Harris, Olthof, & Meerum Terwogt, 1981). They are also aware, from the late preschool years, that happiness instills generosity, anger diminishes self-control, and sadness as well as anger dampens self-gratification (see Masters & Carlson, 1984). Children are also cognizant of the interpersonal effects of emotional behavior: as Saarni's (1979, 1989, this volume) provocative studies have shown, children in the grade-school years increasingly appreciate that emotional experience and its expression should be regulated to avoid derision or embarrassment, get attention, elicit sympathy, obtain help, or preserve others' feelings when direct emotional displays would exploit others' vulnerability or one's own. Thus one of the purposes of regulating emotional expressions is to affect others' behavior and, as a consequence of their actions, alter one's underlying emotional experience (e.g., reduce embarrassment or distress). Much of this understanding of the personal consequences of emotional self-regulation emerges because it is functionally valuable: acting on emotion knowledge of this kind improves the child's own emotional well-being and homeostasis. Thus there are strong incentives for acquiring some understanding of the consequences of an emotional response.

A third component of metaemotive understanding concerns children's knowledge of the strategies of emotional self-regulation. Obviously, knowledge of the consequences of regulated or unregulated emotional experiences is of little value to emotional management unless the child possesses a rudimentary repertoire of emotional self-regulatory strategies. Fortunately, investigators have devoted considerable attention to children's knowledge of emotion and emotional regulation, and Table 3 presents a partial taxonomy of children's understanding of processes related to emotional self-regulation.

There are several noteworthy features of children's emergent knowledge of emotion and its management. In addition to the diverse strategies that older children are aware of (e.g., internal affective redirection, altering the situation, changing causal attributions, self-coaching), the emergence of this strategic understanding is age graded in a manner that reflects children's growing appreciation of emotion and its antecedents. Thus the earliest kinds of strategic understanding, apparent at the end of the second year, consist simply of regulating sensory intake by closing the eyes or covering the ears (Bretherton et al., 1986) or eliciting nurture from others (e.g., Smolek & Weinraub, 1979). During the years that follow children increasingly apprehend that emotion diminishes over time (and thus that "time heals all ills"), that one can alter the situation to change emotion, that emotionally arousing stimuli can be removed or avoided, that goal substitution is one means of coping with negative emotional experiences, and that emotion can be renewed by evoking memories of an earlier emotional experience. It is not until later childhood that psychologically more sophisticated emotional regu-

**Table 3**

*Elements of Metaemotional Understanding: The Strategies of Emotional Regulation*

---

### Early Childhood

- Emotion can be blunted by restricting sensory input (e.g., covering the eyes or ears), ignoring emotionally arousing stimuli, leaving the situation, or otherwise restricting information intake.[a]
- Eliciting nurture can reduce negative emotional experiences.[b]
- Emotion can be regulated by encouraging or reassuring self-talk.[c]
- Emotion can be altered by removing emotionally arousing stimuli.[d]
- Changing or substituting goals is one way of coping with the negative emotion generated by a failure in goal attainment (e.g., "I didn't want to play anyway!").[e]
- An earlier emotional experience can be renewed by evoking memories of that experience.[f]
- The intensity of emotion wanes over time, but emotion can nevertheless have long-term effects that depend in part on the initial intensity of emotional arousal. The waning of emotion can derive either from changes in emotionally arousing conditions or from changes in one's psychological processes (e.g., ceasing to think about emotionally arousing events).[g]

### Middle Childhood

- Redefining or reinterpreting the situation can be used to dampen or increase emotional arousal (e.g., thinking "it's just a story" when listening to a sad account).[h]
- Emotions can be altered through internal affective redirection (e.g., thinking happy thoughts in a sad situation), emotion-blunting ideation, or deliberate distraction or redirection of attention.[i]
- Emotions can be changed by acting in a manner that fosters a competing emotional experience.[j]
- Emotional self-regulation can be fostered by concentrating on the potential benefits of regulated emotion or the costs of unregulated emotion.[k]
- Emotional expressions to others can be dissociated from internal emotional experience. These expressions can be deliberately controlled to alter others' reactions to oneself.[l]

- Different emotions can be experienced either sequentially or simultaneously. When the emotions are of a different valence, they can be mutually influential (and sometimes may produce ambivalence or emotional conflict).[m]
- Emotion is related not only to one's goals but also to one's causal attributions for success or failure. Changing attributions of causality can have different emotional consequences (e.g., "You shouldn't be mad at your little brother: he didn't mean it!").[n]

---

Reference notes:

[a]Bretherton et al., 1986; Cummings, 1987

[b]Masters, Ford, & Arend, 1983; McCoy & Masters, 1985; Smolek & Weinraub, 1979

[c]Smolek & Weinraub, 1979

[d]Mischel & Mischel, 1983; Yates & Mischel, 1979

[e]Stein & Levine, in press; Stein & Trabasso, 1989

[f]Harris, Guz, Lipian, & Man-Shu, 1985

[g]Harris, 1983; Harris, Guz, Lipian, & Man-Shu, 1985; Taylor & Harris, 1983

[h]Meerum Terwogt, Schene, & Harris, 1986

[i]Carroll & Steward, 1984; Harris & Lipian, 1989; Harris, Olthof, & Meerum Terwogt, 1981; Mischel & Mischel, 1983; Yates & Mischel, 1979

[j]Harris & Lipian, 1989; Harris & Olthof, 1982; Harris, Olthof, & Meerum Terwogt, 1981

[k]Mischel & Mischel, 1977, 1983

[l]Harris, Donnelly, Guz, & Pitt-Watson, 1986; Harris & Lipian, 1989; Harris, Olthof, & Meerum Terwogt, 1981; Saarni, 1979, 1984, 1985; Selman, 1981; Taylor & Harris, 1984; there may be antecedents of this awareness at earlier ages: see Gardner, Harris, Ohmoto, & Hamazaki, 1988; Gross & Harris, 1988; Harris & Gross, 1989

[m]Carroll & Steward, 1984; Donaldson & Westerman, 1986; Harris, 1983; Harris & Lipian, 1989; Harter, 1982a, 1982b; Harter & Buddin, 1987; Meerum Terwogt, Koops, Oosterhoff, & Olthof, 1986

[n]Graham & Weiner, 1986; Thompson, 1987b, 1989; Weiner & Graham, 1984

latory strategies become cognized, such as using thought processes to distract or ideate in emotionally regulating ways, changing ascriptions of causality that provoke different emotional reactions, understanding the dissociation of emotional experience from its expression (and thus altering others' reactions to oneself in emotionally influential ways), and redefining the situation to alter emotional experience. At this time children's appreciation of multidimensional emotional experience also increases, fostering not only an awareness that people can feel different emotions simultaneously, but also an understanding of how simultaneous emotions can be mutually influential.

Thus an understanding of emotion and its management proceeds from an early focus on simple, behaviorally oriented approaches to more complex strategies that depend on a rudimentary understanding of the internal cognitive, attributional, and goal-directed motivational processes by which emotion is instigated, directed, and altered. In this respect the growth of children's understanding of emotional self-regulation parallels the emergence of psychologically oriented conceptions of self and other (e.g., Damon & Hart, 1982; Shantz, 1983). But another catalyst for the growth of regulatory strategies comes from children's increasingly flexible representations of emotion and its antecedents. It seems likely that when children have become sufficiently conversant with the links between different situations and the emotions they provoke, these associations can become targets of intervention: one can influence one's emotional experience by altering its antecedents, whether circumstantial or psychological. This representational flexibility appears to be a middle-childhood achievement: in terms of Fischer's (1980) skill theory, children of this age have begun to master representational *systems* related to emotion and its antecedents (see Fischer, Shaver, & Carnochan, in press). Thus, in the early school-age years understanding of a variety of emotional management strategies may unfold not only because of the growing psychologically oriented understanding of emotion and its antecedents, but also because of the emerging representational flexibility that enables children to devise strategies for intervening and altering these associations in their own experience.

Another reason the strategic understanding of emotional self-regulation unfolds in middle childhood is that such skills become enlisted in peer interactions. As Gottman and Mettetal (1986) have noted, as friendships become oriented toward psychological intimacy during this period, one of the primary objectives of conversations between peers is to avoid embarrassment—the feeling of being noticed and socially exposed. As a consequence, children acquire and enlist a broad variety of self-regulatory strategies for managing immediate emotional reactions to potentially embarrassing situations and for managing emotional reactions during conversations about these situations. Thus children's emergent cognitive skills during middle childhood dovetail with the demands of friendship to foster the acquisition of a broad repertoire of strategies for emotional self-regulation.

However, this research portrayal of children's awareness of emotional self-regulatory strategies may underestimate both their true understanding of these strategies and their ability to implement them. One reason is that nearly all of the studies cited in Table 3 relied on children's interview responses to hypothetical story situations in which the child was required either to nominate an emotional regulatory strategy or to justify a strategy the story character used. As is often true in social-cognitive research, requiring young children to verbalize complex psychological processes risks underestimating their true understanding of them, and there is some evidence that this is true with respect to strategies of emotional management. For example, Cole (1986) reported that children as young as 4 years spontaneously assumed an emotional display that was incongruent with their underlying feelings (i.e., expressing pleasure with a disappointing gift), even though very few of them could justify their actions or verbally articulate this control strategy. Similarly, Mischel's (1981) work on delay of gratification suggests that by age 4½ children can use behavioral strategies while waiting for a preferred reward (e.g., redirecting attention or distraction; see Mischel & Ebbesen, 1970), but they cannot verbally describe this regulatory strategy until at least age 6 (Mischel & Mischel, 1983; but see Yates & Mischel, 1979). And Cummings (1987) has reported that 5-year-old children who were behaviorally unresponsive during a simulated adult argument nevertheless reported feeling angry while trying to ignore the fight—a rather sophisticated mixture of affect, display, and self-regulation.

Thus it appears that children can employ certain forms of emotional regulation—especially related to expressive display rules—before they conceptually understand them (Meerum Terwogt & Olthof, 1989). It is not difficult to understand why. Parents and other caregivers devote concerted efforts to socializing emotional displays in young children, especially in social situations when others could be hurt by unregulated emotional expression. Thus, through direct instruction, modeling, and reinforcement (supplemented perhaps by trial-and-error learning), children master many of the rudiments of display rules from a relatively early age, even before they can articulate or justify them. If this is true, it is possible that another catalyst to their conceptual understanding of emotional self-regulatory strategies derives from their dawning awareness of the occasional dissonance between their subjective emotional experience and others' reactions to them based on children's deliberately managed (and well-socialized) emotional displays (Harris & Gross, 1989). An awareness of the dissociation between internal emotional experience and emotional expression in such situations probably provides children with some of their earliest recognizable experiences of the benefits of emotional self-regulation: they conceptualize, in other words, the advantages of managing how you feel.

In most of the studies reviewed above, strategies for emotional management were assessed in situations involving relatively mild arousal. What about when emotional arousal is intense? There is evidence that in such situations children may be more limited in their capacity to evoke self-regulatory strategies that they are conceptually capable of understanding—a classic instance of a competence-performance dissonance. Harris and Lipian (1989) interviewed 10-year-olds who were hospitalized for a variety of acute conditions and discovered that their evocation of emotional regulatory strategies was impoverished compared with that of non-hospitalized children of the same age. Because there were no other reasons for expecting these children to be cognitively incapable of understanding emotional processes, Harris and Lipian concluded that the negative emotion associated with hospitalization flooded children's perceptions of their circumstances, blunting their capacity to regulate negative affect and accounting for the "slippage" the investigators saw in the children's emotional understanding. Gunnar, Marvinney, Isensee, and Fisch (1989) detected similar deficits in the understanding of emotional management strategies by children with phenylketonuria who experience routine clinic visits for blood sampling. Taken together, these studies suggest that the intensity of negative emotion may affect not only children's self-regulatory efforts but also their capacity to spontaneously evoke the needed strategies of emotion management.

As these studies suggest, the valence of emotion also influences self-regulatory understanding because children experience different demands for the regulation of positive and negative arousal. Four-year-olds have some understanding of how to manage displays of negative emotion, for example, but appreciation of positive emotional display rules does not appear until age 6 (Harris, Donnelly, Guz, & Pitt-Watson, 1986). Four-year-olds also know that positive emotional experiences can be renewed if one remembers an earlier satisfying experience, but appreciation that negative emotion can be similarly reevoked does not appear until age 6 (Harris, Guz, Lipian, & Man-Shu, 1985). These differences may be attributable not just to the social demands of regulating emotion, but also to young children's efforts to create and maintain satisfying emotional homeostasis. Cole (1985) noted that preschoolers are often reluctant to generate negative facial expressions for a researcher because they are afraid of generating consonant emotional experiences, and Glasberg and Aboud (1982) reported that 5-year-olds are more likely to deny the experience of sadness than are older children. It appears that early elements of emotional understanding are predicated, in part, on young children's efforts to maintain a positive emotional experience as much as possible, and this may also influence the development of strategies of emotional management.

With increasing age, these emotional self-regulatory strategies become more differentiated and more flexibly applied to different situations. Whereas young children may strive to blunt emotional arousal by restricting information intake (e.g., covering the eyes), for example, adults can more actively restructure their settings to cope with aversive arousal (e.g., clearing the schedule for a "time out"). Whereas younger children turn to those near them to elicit nurture, adults can enlist a broader range of social supports from various settings. And adults may develop emotional regulatory strategies that are affect specific (e.g., techniques for managing anger). These developmental changes are attributable not only to adults' greater conceptual mastery of emotive processes, of course, but also to their control over the settings and circumstances that evoke emotion or may assist in its management.

With increasing age, individual differences in emotional self-regulatory styles are also likely to emerge and become consolidated. People vary in their preferred modes of emotional management (e.g., using distracting ideation, intellectualization, or escape/avoidance), but because these strategies emerge slowly throughout childhood it is unlikely that distinct self-regulatory styles become consolidated until well into adolescence. This issue is considered further below. A person's distinctive attributional tendencies may also become enlisted in emotional management (one way of blunting guilt arousal, for example, is to blame the victim), and there is some evidence that these idiosyncratic attributional tendencies emerge during the grade-school years (see Dodge, 1986; Dodge et al., 1986, for reviews). Because there has been little study of individual differences in emotional self-regulatory styles and their developmental origins, however, this area remains ripe for further exploration.

Clearly, these early elements of metaemotive understanding form the constituents of more mature forms of emotional understanding and self-regulation. An understanding of the antecedents of emotion, the consequences of an emotional response, and strategies of emotional self-regulation are central components of emotion prototypes, or scripts, around which mature emotional understanding is organized (see Fischer et al., in press; Shaver, Schwartz, Kirson, & O'Connor, 1987). Moreover, many of the self-regulatory strategies outlined here are components of the secondary appraisal processes mature individuals enlist when coping with challenging or threatening events (cf. Lazarus, 1975). The systematic developmental study of these processes offers the potential of understanding how these elements of metaemotive understanding are constructed out of a complex matrix of socialization influences, growing self-understanding, and the child's ongoing efforts to preserve a sense of emotional well-being. As the preceding review suggests, a promising beginning to this study has been achieved.

**A theory of personal emotion.** Of course, throughout this developmental process, children not only are acquiring general knowledge about emotive processes but (perhaps more important) are also learning how emotion functions within themselves. The two are not always the same. Children may be aware, for example, that some of their friends can comfortably manage the emotional arousal engendered by horror films or roller-coaster rides yet may acknowledge that this is not true for themselves. Moreover, they are also likely to appreciate that certain emotional regulatory strategies function well for them while others do not. In short, concurrent with the development of metaemotive understanding, children are also developing a *theory of personal emotion*—that is, an understanding of how emotion functions and is managed within themselves as idiosyncratic emotive beings. In many respects a developing theory of personal emotion consists of applying metaemotive understanding to oneself, taking into account one's awareness of one's emotional idiosyncrasies.

On the face of it, this kind of personal understanding would appear to emerge late, coinciding with the growth of other forms of psychological self-understanding in late childhood and early adolescence (cf. Damon & Hart, 1982; Harter, 1983). Yet there are occasional clues in the literature that rudimentary forms of a theory of personal emotion emerge much earlier. For example, Kagan and colleagues (1987) quote one of their inhibited children at 5½ years as saying to his mother, "I know I am afraid, but I'm trying not to be"— an effort to manage self-aware idiosyncratic emotional experiences. Anecdotal evidence also contributes to the view that rudiments of this personal theory emerge early. Anticipating the first session of his tumbling class, my son Scott at age 4 spontaneously said to me, "You know, Daddy, sometimes the first time I do things it seems kind of scary. But after I get used to them, they're funner." In this case, his reflections on his own past emotional experiences provided reassurance when facing another challenging situation and helped him to manage his emotions.

If children establish rudimentary forms of a theory of personal emotion during the preschool years, it is not difficult to understand why. Owing to the salience of emotional experiences and the benefits from managing them, children are highly motivated to acquire whatever understanding they can of their own emotive processes to enlist in this regulatory effort. Quite likely, much of this early emotional self-understanding is socially constructed: children probably attribute to themselves emotive processes that their parents comment on verbally. But it is also likely that self-reflection contributes to this understanding, because emotional experiences provoke considerable thought, inquiry, and analysis from very early ages (Bretherton et al., 1986).

However, the term "theory" is appropriate to describe this form of self-understanding, because the child's emerging notions of personal emotion become progressively revised with increasing age and with the growth of more sophisticated forms of self-understanding. Thus, although a theory of personal emotion does not originate with the advanced kinds of psychological self-understanding characteristic of late childhood, it is certainly affected by them. And as it becomes progressively more differentiated and complex, the theory of personal emotion becomes a significant component of the self-system in mature individuals. Indeed, it seems likely that the emotive self-understanding encompassed within this theory is a significant component of the self-schemas (e.g., Markus, 1977) that interest students of personality and that begin to take mature form in late childhood and early adolescence.

**Summary.** Taken together, developmental changes in the child's characteristics and abilities contribute emergent capacities that assist in the external management of emotion and eventually in emotional self-regulation. With early changes in neurophysiological functioning, emotional regulation is fostered by the growth of cortical inhibitory processes and stability in biological excitatory processes. The growth of representational and reasoning skills helps in the extrinsic management of emotion, and children become increasingly capable of regulating their emotive processes as emotion becomes an object of analysis and intervention. This is reflected especially in the emergence of metaemotive understanding, and through their conscious awareness of procedures for regulating emotion children can increasingly approach emotional management in a planned, intentional, and strategic fashion. This cognized awareness of the skills of emotion management is fostered by the representational and discoursive capacities involved in language, which provide access to a rich variety of social influences regulating emotion as well as heightening consciousness of emotion and its origins. Finally, commingling with these are the effects of biogenetic processes that confer individuality to self-regulatory processes from a very early age.

Within this developmental portrayal, these emergent capacities both impose limits on the extrinsic regulation of emotion and are themselves influenced by social processes. As earlier noted, before the maturation of cortical inhibitory processes and rudimentary conceptual structures, the regulatory efforts of parents and other caregivers are more limited in efficacy and scope, and with the growth of language and representational skills children can benefit from caregivers' interventions in unprecedented ways. Thus the extrinsic regulation of emotion is constrained by the emergent capacities outlined above. On the other hand, many features of these emergent capacities are themselves socially constructed. As Miller and Sperry's (1987) ethnographic study indicates, many elements of the young child's metaemotive understanding are shaped (in both deliberate and unintentional ways) by caregivers, whose verbal guidance, exhortations, challenges, and interpretations of emotionally arousing situations provide salient messages concerning the regulation of children's emotional experiences. Moreover, children's emergent theories of personal emotion likely are also influenced by these socialization efforts. Thus their growing self-regulatory capacities are influenced, in large measure, by the social context in which these capacities emerge and are constructed.

This suggests that it is wisest to regard emotional management as a coregulatory process in which the social setting and the individual (equipped with emergent intrinsic capacities) jointly manage emotional arousal and its display. Although the relative influence of extrinsic and intrinsic processes changes significantly with development, there is no period in the life span when each is not important. Even for adults, an ability to maintain satisfying emotional homeostasis through self-regulatory efforts is influenced by the demands of the social setting, the influences of proximate social partners, and myriad other extrinsic influences. As a consequence of this coregulatory functioning, processes of emotional management maintain considerable plasticity throughout ontogenesis. I now turn to a brief consideration of that plasticity.

## A Perspective on Developmental Continuity

As the foregoing research review suggests, emotional regulation has strong ties to socioemotional and personality functioning, and this review has considered two aspects of the growth of emotional regulation that have also been of long-standing interest to students of personality development: normative developmental changes and the growth of individual differences. Throughout this review, I have considered both intrinsic and extrinsic processes that contribute to (a) the normative emergence of new emotional regulatory capacities for most children throughout ontogenesis, as well as (b) the growth of characteristics that distinguish the regulatory capacities of one child from those of another.

The developmental links between emotional regulatory processes and personality organization lead naturally to inquiries concerning the importance of early influences on individual differences in mature patterns of emotional management. Are the adult's anxiety proneness and disorganized thinking under stress foreshadowed in the young child's congenital or temperamental characteristics? Can the mature person's explosive temper be predicted on the basis of early infant-parent interactions and the security of their attachment relationship? Is the adult's capacity to maintain satisfying emotional homeostasis built upon a foundation of early socialization influences beginning in infancy? It is natural to expect such long-range developmental continuity because the formative processes influencing the growth of emotional regulatory capacities are organized along highly predictable, stable developmental pathways. Perhaps because of their biomaturational or bioevolutionary underpinnings, the normative pathways guiding the growth of neurophysiological organization, cognitive and language abilities, and early social discriminations are rather consistent for children growing up in species-typical rearing environments (see Thompson, 1988, for a review), so it is reasonable to expect that individual differences that emerge along these pathways would similarly have stable, long-term effects on individual development. This view is further affirmed by theoretical perspectives that underscore the importance of early influences in emergent personality organization and the pervasive and persisting effects of temperamental individuality throughout the life span.

Yet it is important, in considering issues of developmental continuity, to distinguish normative developmental processes from individual-difference phenomena (cf. McCall, 1979, 1981; Thompson, 1988). As McCall (1981) has shown with respect to intellectual development and Thompson (1988) has elaborated with respect to other developmental domains, the processes fostering continuity and change in these two aspects of individual growth are much different. In many domains of development, in fact, the sequence and timetable for normative growth processes are highly consistent for most children, perhaps because they are constrained (or "canalized") by biomaturational or evolutionary processes. By contrast, in the same developmental domains, individual differences in developmental pathways are malleable and plastic; individuals who show spurts in their growth curves early in life may not maintain them, while others who show early lags also do not exhibit their long-term consequences. In short, considerable research evidence indicates that though normative developmental pathways are maturationally constrained and thus highly consistent in most rearing conditions, individual differences along these pathways tend not to show much stability over time.

With respect to emotional regulatory processes, a similar portrayal may apply. Clearly, many of the normative growth processes affecting the emergent capacities of emotional regulation are highly stable: the development of neocortical organization, cognitive and linguistic achievements, and early social discriminations occur according to a rather consistent sequence and timetable for most individuals. But individual differences in emotional regulation that arise early in life may not necessarily foreshadow later differences in mature forms of emotional regulation. This research review indicates several reasons why.

First, early forms of emotional regulation are highly influenced by extrinsic, social influences. Caregivers manage emotion in offspring by modeling, selective reinforcing, inducing affect, fostering emotional contagion, shaping social expectations, providing discourse concerning emotional regulation, controlling opportunities to exercise regulatory capacities, and acting in other ways that have a pervasive influence on early experiences—and because intrinsic self-regulatory capacities are immature, nascent, or ill-formed early in life, reliance on extrinsic influences is even more profound. As a consequence, early individual differences in emotional regulation are likely to be socially constructed to a significant degree, built upon repeated social experiences provided (deliberately or unintentionally) by proximate partners. Early variations in emotional regulation may thus change—sometimes significantly—with the growing influence of intrinsic regulatory capacities or with changes in social influences (e.g., transitions to new caregiving arrangements, entry into school, etc.).

Second, mature forms of emotional self-regulation are based on sophisticated self-referent belief systems, a complex network of social-cognitive understanding, and a broad experiential history, and these constituents exist only in rudimentary form early in life. Moreover, the development of these mature constituents is likely to involve the progressive reconstruction of earlier self-regulatory skills and tendencies as new capacities emerge (as illustrated earlier with respect to attentional processes of emotional regulation). Thus early individual differences in emotional self-regulation are likely to be more provisional and flexible than are later differences because they have not yet become consolidated into a mature network of intrinsic self-regulatory skills. It is, in fact, the adult's sophisticated and reflective self-system that contributes to the consistency of personal attributes over time, together with the self-selection of settings, relationships, and environmental demands that are consistent with, and thereby preserve, these attributes. Since infants and young children lack both the sophisticated self-reflection and self-understanding of older individuals and the capacity to exert significant control over the settings that affect them, individual differences in emotional self-regulation are likely to be more malleable and plastic in early life than at later ages.

Taken together, the young child's dependence on extrinsic forms of emotional regulation and the rudimentary quality of early intrinsic self-regulatory processes suggest that when we observe significant stability in early individual differences in emotional management, it may be due to consistency over time in the social processes guiding the child's emotive experiences (e.g., Thompson, in press). To be sure, individual differences in temperament or congenital characteristics are also significant influences on early emotionality that can potentially have long-term consequences. But as noted earlier, social influences can also modify the expression or sequelae of these differences by shaping the contexts in which they are manifested, the responses they receive, and the physiological systems they influence (cf. Dienstbier, in press; Lerner & Lerner, 1983; Meisels & Anastasiow, 1982). Thus early emotive experiences are primarily socially guided and managed through the early years of life.

The view that early individual differences in emotional regulation do not necessarily foreshadow later differences is an unorthodox one (at least for a specialist in infancy like myself) because it implies that our concern with early differences should focus on their contemporary, rather than predictive, significance. Yet it is an optimistic view with respect to the flexibility of early individual characteristics and the young organism's openness to intervention. While underscoring that infants and young children do contribute to emotional regulatory processes from an early age, this coregulatory portrayal affirms that with increasing age and growth, intrinsic self-regulatory processes assume increasing importance in the emergent capacities that contribute to the management of emotion. Indeed, the early plasticity of individual differences in emotional self-regulation derives from the fact that the ability to manage one's emotional experiences develops slowly and is subject to the rich diversity of growth processes that makes the study of human development such a challenging enterprise.

## Conclusion

The complementary themes of this chapter—emotion as a behavioral regulator and the developmental regulation of emotion—underscore that emotive processes are well integrated into the organization and development of adaptive behavior throughout the life span. By focusing not on discrete emotions but rather on emotional dynamics, we can explore the rich variety of processes that transform emotional experience—over development and idiosyncratically—and can elucidate the influence of these dynamics on other behavioral processes. In the end, it should be clear that a considerable research agenda remains for further study of these dual themes but that a promising and provocative foundation for this work has been established in research thus far.

## REFERENCES

Ainsworth, M. D. S., Blehar, M. C., Waters, E., & Wall, S. (1978). *Patterns of attachment*. Hillsdale, NJ: Erlbaum.
Barden, R. C., Zelko, F. A., Duncan, S. W., & Masters, J. C. (1980). Children's consensual knowledge about the experiential determinants of emotion. *Journal of Personality and Social Psychology, 39*, 968–976.
Barrett, K. C., & Campos, J. J. (1987). Perspectives on emotional development II: A functionalist approach to emotions. In J. D. Osofsky (Ed.), *Handbook of infant development* (2nd ed.) (pp. 555–578). New York: John Wiley.
Bates, J. E. (1987). Temperament in infancy. In J. D. Osofsky (Ed.), *Handbook of infant development* (2nd ed.) (pp. 1101–1169). New York: John Wiley.
Belsky, J., & Rovine, M. (1987). Temperament and attachment security in the Strange Situation: An empirical rapprochement. *Child Development, 58*, 787–795.
Benson, S. A., & Thompson, R. A. (in preparation). *Social referencing and secure-base behaviors: A comparison of infants from maltreating, low-income and middle-income families.*
Berlyne, D. E. (1960). *Conflict, arousal and curiosity.* New York: McGraw-Hill.
Berlyne, D. E. (1969). Laughter, humor and play. In G. Lindzey & E. Aronson (Eds.), *Handbook of social psychology* (2nd ed.) (Vol. 3, pp. 795–852). Reading, MA: Addison-Wesley.
Bloom, L. (in press). Developments in expression: Affect and speech. In N. L. Stein, B. Leventhal, & T. Trabasso (Eds.), *Psychological and biological approaches to emotion*. Hillsdale, NJ: Erlbaum.
Bloom, L., & Beckwith, R. (in press). Talking with feeling: Integrating affective and linguistic expression in early language development. *Cognition and Emotion*.
Bloom, L., Beckwith, R., & Capatides, J. B. (1988). Developments in the expression of affect. *Infant Behavior and Development, 11*, 169–186.
Bloom, L., & Capatides, J. B. (1987). Expression of affect and the emergence of language. *Child Development, 58*, 1513–1522.
Borke, H. (1971). Interpersonal perception of young children: Egocentrism or empathy? *Developmental Psychology, 5*, 263–269.
Bowlby, J. (1969). *Attachment and loss: Vol. 1. Attachment.* New York: Basic Books.
Brandenberg, A. (1984). *Feelings.* New York: Mulberry Books.

Brazelton, T. B., Koslowski, B., & Main, M. (1974). The origins of reciprocity: The early mother-infant interaction. In M. Lewis & L. Rosenblum (Eds.), *The effects of the infant on its caregiver* (pp. 49–76). New York: John Wiley.

Bretherton, I., & Ainsworth, M. D. S. (1974). Responses of one-year-olds to a stranger in a strange situation. In M. Lewis & L. Rosenblum (Eds.), *The origins of fear* (pp. 131–164). New York: John Wiley.

Bretherton, I., & Beeghly, M. (1982). Talking about internal states: The acquisition of an explicit theory of mind. *Developmental Psychology, 18*, 906–921.

Bretherton, I., Fritz, J., Zahn-Waxler, C., & Ridgeway, D. (1986). Learning to talk about emotions: A functionalist perspective. *Child Development, 57*, 529–548.

Bretherton, I., McNew, S., & Beeghly-Smith, M. (1981). Early person knowledge as expressed in gestural and verbal communication: When do infants acquire a "theory of mind"? In M. E. Lamb & L. R. Sherrod (Eds.), *Infant social cognition* (pp. 333–373). Hillsdale, NJ: Erlbaum.

Bridges, L. J., Connell, J. P., & Belsky, J. (1988). Similarities and differences in infant-mother and infant-father interaction in the Strange Situation: A component process analysis. *Developmental Psychology, 24*, 92–100.

Brooks-Gunn, J., & Lewis, M. (1982). Affective exchanges between normal and handicapped infants and their mothers. In T. Field & A. Fogel (Eds.), *Emotion and early interaction* (pp. 161–188). Hillsdale, NJ: Erlbaum.

Brown, J., & Bakeman, R. (1980). Relationships of human mothers with their infants during the first year of life: Effects of prematurity. In R. W. Bell & W. P. Smotherman (Eds.), *Maternal influences and early behavior* (pp. 353–373). Holliswood, NY: Spectrum.

Buss, A. H., & Plomin, R. (1984). *Temperament: Early developing personality traits*. Hillsdale, NJ: Erlbaum.

Campos, J. J., Barrett, K. C., Lamb, M. E., Goldsmith, H. H., & Stenberg, C. (1983). Socioemotional development. In P. H. Mussen (Ed.), M. M. Haith & J. J. Campos (Vol. Eds.), *Handbook of child psychology: Vol. 2. Infancy and developmental psychobiology* (pp. 783–915). New York: John Wiley.

Campos, J. J., & Stenberg, C. R. (1981). Perception, appraisal and emotion: The onset of social referencing. In M. E. Lamb & L. R. Sherrod (Eds.), *Infant social cognition* (pp. 273–314). Hillsdale, NJ: Erlbaum.

Carroll, J. J., & Steward, M. S. (1984). The role of cognitive development in children's understandings of their own feelings. *Child Development, 55*, 1486–1492.

Case, R., Hayward, S., Lewis, M., & Hurst, P. (1988). Toward a neo-Piagetian theory of cognitive and emotional development. *Developmental Review, 8*, 1–51.

Caudill, W., & Frost, L. (1975). A comparison of maternal care and infant behavior in Japanese-American, American, and Japanese families. In U. Bronfenbrenner & M. A. Mahoney (Eds.), *Influences on human development* (2nd ed.) (pp. 329–342). Hinsdale, IL: Dryden.

Caudill, W., & Weinstein, H. (1969). Maternal care and infant behavior in Japan and America. *Psychiatry, 32*, 12–43.

Chen, S.-J., & Miyake, K. (1986). Japanese studies of infant development. In H. Stevenson, H. Azuma, & K. Hakuta (Eds.), *Child development and education in Japan* (pp. 135–146). New York: Freeman.

Cole, P. M. (1985). Display rules and socialization. In G. Zivin (Ed.), *The development of expressive behavior* (pp. 269–290). New York: Academic Press.

Cole, P. M. (1986). Children's spontaneous control of facial expression. *Child Development, 57*, 1309–1321.

Connell, J. P. (1985). A component process approach to the study of individual differences and developmental change in attachment system functioning. In M. E. Lamb, R. A. Thompson, W. P. Gardner, & E. L. Charnov, *Infant-mother attachment* (pp. 223–247). Hillsdale, NJ: Erlbaum.

Connell, J. P., & Thompson, R. A. (1986). Emotion and social interaction in the Strange Situation: Consistencies and asymmetric influences in the second year. *Child Development, 57*, 733–745.

Cummings, E. M. (1987). Coping with background anger in early childhood. *Child Development, 58*, 976–984.

Cummings, E. M., Iannotti, R. J., & Zahn-Waxler, C. (1985). Influence of conflict between adults on the emotions and aggression of young children. *Developmental Psychology, 21*, 495–507.

Cummings, E. M., Zahn-Waxler, C., & Radke-Yarrow, M. (1981). Young children's responses to expressions of anger and affection by others in the family. *Child Development, 52*, 1274–1282.

Cummings, E. M., Zahn-Waxler, C., & Radke-Yarrow, M. (1984). Developmental changes in children's reactions to anger in the home. *Journal of Child Psychology and Psychiatry, 25*, 63–74.

Damon, W., & Hart, D. (1982). The development of self-understanding from infancy through adolescence. *Child Development, 53*, 841–864.

Davidson, R. J., & Fox, N. A. (1982). Asymmetrical brain activity discriminates between positive and negative affective stimuli in human infants. *Science, 218*, 1235–1237.

Davidson, R. J., & Fox, N. A. (1988). Cerebral asymmetry and emotion: Developmental and individual differences. In S. Segalowitz & D. Molfese (Eds.), *Developmental implications of brain lateralization* (pp. 191–206). New York: Guilford.

Derryberry, D., & Rothbart, M. K. (1984). Emotion, attention, and temperament. In C. E. Izard, J. Kagan, & R. B. Zajonc (Eds.), *Emotions, cognition and behavior* (pp. 132–166). Cambridge: Cambridge University Press.

Diamond, A. (1988a). Abilities and neural mechanisms underlying AB performance. *Child Development, 59*, 523–527.

Diamond, A. (1988b). Differences between adult and infant cognition: Is the crucial variable presence or absence of language? In L. Weiskrantz (Ed.), *Thought without language* (pp. 337–370). Oxford: Oxford University Press.

Dickstein, S., Thompson, R. A., Estes, D., Malkin, C., & Lamb, M. E.

(1984). Social referencing and the security of attachment. *Infant Behavior and Development, 7*, 507–516.

Dienstbier, R. A. (in press). Arousal and physiological toughness: Implications for mental and physical health. *Psychological Review.*

Dodge, K. A. (1986). A social information processing model of social competence in children. In M. Perlmutter (Ed.), *Cognitive perspectives on children's social and behavioral development. Minnesota Symposium on Child Psychology* (Vol. 18, pp. 77–125). Hillsdale, NJ: Erlbaum.

Dodge, K. A., Pettit, G. S., McClaskey, C. L., & Brown, M. M. (1986). Social competence in children. *Monographs of the Society for Research in Child Development, 51* (Serial No. 213).

Donaldson, S. K., & Westerman, M. A. (1986). Development of children's understanding of ambivalence and causal theories of emotions. *Developmental Psychology, 22*, 655–662.

Dorr, A. (1985). Contexts for experience with emotion, with special attention to television. In M. Lewis & C. Saarni (Eds.), *The socialization of emotion* (pp. 55–85). New York: Plenum Press.

Dunn, J. (1987). Understanding feelings: The early stages. In J. Bruner & H. Haste (Eds.), *Making sense: The child's construction of the world* (pp. 26–40). London: Methuen.

Dunn, J., Bretherton, I., & Munn, P. (1987). Conversations about feeling states between mothers and their young children. *Developmental Psychology, 23*, 132–139.

Emde, R. N., Gaensbauer, T. J., & Harmon, R. J. (1976). *Emotional expression in infancy: A biobehavioral study. Psychological Issues, 10*, Monograph 37.

Emde, R. N., Katz, E. L., & Thorpe, J. K. (1978). Emotional expression in infancy: 2. Early deviations in Down's syndrome. In M. Lewis & L. A. Rosenblum (Eds.), *The development of affect* (pp. 351–360). New York: Plenum Press.

Fagan, J. W., Ohr, P. S., Fleckenstein, L. K., & Ribner, D. R. (1985). The effect of crying on long-term memory in infancy. *Child Development, 56*, 1584–1592.

Feinman, S. (1982). Social referencing in infancy. *Merrill-Palmer Quarterly, 28*, 445–470.

Feinman, S. (1985). Emotional expression, social referencing, and preparedness for learning in infancy—Mother knows best, but sometimes I know better. In G. Zivin (Ed.), *The development of expressive behavior* (pp. 291–318). Orlando, FL: Academic Press.

Field, T. (1977). Effects of early separation, interactive deficits, and experimental manipulations on infant-mother face-to-face interaction. *Child Development, 48*, 763–771.

Field, T. (1979). Games parents play with normal and high-risk infants. *Child Psychiatry and Human Development, 10*, 41–48.

Field, T. (1981). Infant arousal, attention and affect during early interactions. In L. P. Lipsitt (Ed.), *Advances in infancy research* (Vol. 1, pp. 57–100). Norwood, NJ: Ablex.

Field, T. (1982). Affective displays of high-risk infants during early interactions. In T. Field & A. Fogel (Eds.), *Emotion and early interaction* (pp. 101–
125). Hillsdale, NJ: Erlbaum.

Fischer, K. W. (1980). A theory of cognitive development: The control and
construction of hierarchies of skills. *Psychological Review, 87*, 477–531.

Fischer, K. W., Shaver, P., & Carnochan, P. (in press). From basic- to subordinate-category emotions: A skill approach to emotional development.
In W. Damon (Ed.), *Child development today and tomorrow* (New Directions
for Child Development series, no. 40; W. Damon, Gen. Ed.). San Francisco: Jossey-Bass.

Flavell, J. H., Flavell, E. R., & Green, F. L. (1983). Development of the appearance-reality distinction. *Cognitive Psychology, 15*, 95–120.

Fogel, A. (1982). Affect dynamics in early infancy: Affective tolerance. In T.
Field & A. Fogel (Eds.), *Emotion and early interaction* (pp. 25–56). Hillsdale, NJ: Erlbaum.

Fox, N. A. (1985a). Sweet/sour—interest/disgust: The role of approach-
withdrawal in the development of emotions. In T. M. Field & N. A. Fox
(Eds.), *Social perception in infants* (pp. 53–71). Norwood, NJ: Ablex.

Fox, N. A. (1985b). Behavioral and autonomic antecedents of attachment in
high-risk infants. In M. Reite & T. Field (Eds.), *The psychobiology of attachment and separation* (pp. 389–414). New York: Academic Press.

Fox, N. A. (in press a). The biological basis of emotional reactivity during
the first year of life. *Developmental Psychology*.

Fox, N. A. (in press b). Heart rate variability and self-regulation: Individual
differences in autonomic patterning and their relation to infant and child
temperament. In S. Reznick & J. Kagan (Eds.), *Perspectives on behavioral
inhibition*. Chicago: University of Chicago Press.

Fox, N. A., & Davidson, R. J. (1984). Hemispheric substrates of affect: A developmental model. In N. A. Fox & R. J. Davidson (Eds.), *The psychobiology of affective development* (pp. 353–381). Hillsdale, NJ: Erlbaum.

Fox, N. A., & Davidson, R. J. (1986). Taste-elicited changes in facial signs of
emotion and the asymmetry of brain electrical activity in human newborns. *Neuropsychologia, 24*, 417–422.

Fox, N. A., & Davidson, R. J. (1987). Electroencephalogram asymmetry in
response to the approach of a stranger and maternal separation in 10-
month-old infants. *Developmental Psychology, 23*, 233–240.

Fox, N. A., & Davidson, R. J. (1988). Patterns of brain electrical activity during facial signs of emotion in 10-month-old infants. *Developmental Psychology, 24*, 230–236.

Fox, N. A., & Davidson, R. J. (in press). Hemispheric specialization and
separation protest behavior: Developmental processes and individual
differences. In J. L. Gewirtz & W. Kurtines (Eds.), *Intersection points in attachment research*. New York: Plenum Press.

Fraiberg, S. (1977). *Insights from the blind*. New York: Basic Books.

Fraiberg, S. (Ed.). (1980). *Clinical studies in infant mental health*. New York: Basic Books.

Frodi, A., & Thompson, R. A. (1985). Infants' affective responses in the Strange Situation: Effects of prematurity and of quality of attachment. *Child Development, 56*, 1280–1290.

Gaensbauer, T. J., & Sands, K. (1979). Distorted affective communications in abused/neglected infants and their potential impact on caretakers. *Journal of the American Academy of Child Psychiatry, 18*, 236–250.

Garcia Coll, C., Kagan, J., & Reznick, J. S. (1984). Behavioral inhibition in young children. *Child Development, 55*, 1005–1019.

Gardner, D., Harris, P. L., Ohmoto, M., & Hamazaki, T. (1988). Japanese children's understanding of the distinction between real and apparent emotion. *International Journal of Behavioral Development, 11*, 203–218.

Gekoski, M. J., Rovee-Collier, C. K., & Carulli-Rabinowitz, V. (1983). A longitudinal analysis of inhibition of infant distress: The origins of social expectations? *Infant Behavior and Development, 6*, 339–351.

Gianino, A., & Tronick, E. (1988). The mutual regulation model: The infant's self and interactive regulation and coping and defensive capacities. In T. Field, P. McCabe, & N. Schneiderman (Eds.), *Stress and coping* (Vol. 2, pp. 47–68). Hillsdale, NJ: Erlbaum.

Glasberg, R., & Aboud, F. (1982). Keeping one's distance from sadness: Children's self-reports of emotional experience. *Developmental Psychology, 18*, 287–293.

Gnepp, J., & Chilamkurti, C. (1988). Children's use of personality attributions to predict other people's emotional and behavioral reactions. *Child Development, 59*, 743–754.

Gnepp, J., & Gould, M. E. (1985). The development of personalized inferences: Understanding other people's emotional reactions in light of their prior experiences. *Child Development, 56*, 1455–1464.

Goldberg, S. (1978). Prematurity: Effects on parent-infant interaction. *Journal of Pediatric Psychology, 3*, 137–144.

Goldman-Rakic, P. S. (1987). Development of cortical circuitry and cognitive function. *Child Development, 58*, 601–622.

Goldsmith, H. H., Buss, A. H., Plomin, R., Rothbart, M. K., Thomas, A., Chess, S., Hinde, R. A., & McCall, R. B. (1987). Roundtable: What is temperament? Four approaches. *Child Development, 58*, 505–529.

Goldsmith, H. H., & Campos, J. J. (1982). Toward a theory of infant temperament. In R. N. Emde & R. J. Harmon (Eds.), *The development of attachment and affiliative systems* (pp. 161–193). New York: Plenum Press.

Goldsmith, H. H., & Campos, J. J. (1986). Fundamental issues in the study of early temperament: The Denver twin temperament study. In M. E. Lamb, A. L. Brown, & B. Rogoff (Eds.), *Advances in developmental psychology* (Vol. 4, pp. 231–283). Hillsdale, NJ: Erlbaum.

Gordon, S. L. (in press). The socialization of children's emotions: Emotional culture, competence, and exposure. In C. Saarni & P. Harris (Eds.), *Children's understanding of emotion*. Cambridge: Cambridge University Press.

Gottman, J., & Mettetal, G. (1986). Speculations about social and affective development: Friendship and acquaintanceship through adolescence. In J. M. Gottman & J. G. Parker (Eds.), *Conversations of friends: Speculations on affective development* (pp. 192–237). Cambridge: Cambridge University Press.

Graham, S., & Weiner, B. (1986). From an attributional theory of emotion to developmental psychology: A round-trip ticket? *Social Cognition, 6,* 152–179.

Greif, E. B., Alvarez, M. M., & Ulman, K. (1981, April). *Recognizing emotions in other people: Sex differences in socialization.* Paper presented to the meeting of the Society for Research in Child Development, Boston, MA.

Gross, D., & Harris, P. L. (1988). False beliefs about emotion: Children's understanding of misleading emotional displays. *International Journal of Behavioral Development, 11,* 475–488.

Gunnar, M. R. (1986). Human developmental psychoneuroendocrinology: A review of research on neuroendocrine responses to challenge and threat in infancy and childhood. In M. Lamb, A. Brown, & B. Rogoff (Eds.), *Advances in developmental psychology* (Vol. 4, pp. 51–103). Hillsdale, NJ: Erlbaum.

Gunnar, M. R., & Hornik, R. (1987). *Toward a taxonomy of toddler coping strategies.* Unpublished manuscript, University of Minnesota, Minneapolis, MN.

Gunnar, M. R., Malone, S., & Fisch, R. O. (1985). The psychology of stress and coping in the human neonate: Studies of adrenocortical activity in response to aversive stimulation. In T. M. Field, P. M. McCabe, & N. Schneiderman (Eds.), *Stress and coping* (pp. 179–196). Hillsdale, NJ: Erlbaum.

Gunnar, M. R., Mangelsdorf, S., Kestenbaum, R., Lang, S., Larson, M., & Andreas, D. (in press). Temperament, attachment and neuroendocrine reactivity: A systemic approach to the study of stress in normal infants. In D. Cicchetti (Ed.), *Process and psychopathology.* Cambridge: Cambridge University Press.

Gunnar, M. R., Mangelsdorf, S., Larson, M., & Hertzgaard, L. (in press). Attachment, temperament and adrenocortical activity in infancy: A study of psychoendocrine regulation. *Developmental Psychology.*

Gunnar, M. R., Marvinney, D., Isensee, J., & Fisch, R. O. (1989). *Stress and distress among children with a chronic condition.* Unpublished manuscript, University of Minnesota, Minneapolis, MN.

Gunnar, M. R., Marvinney, D., Isensee, J., & Fisch, R. O. (in press). Coping with uncertainty: New models of the relations between hormonal, behavioral and cognitive processes. In D. Palermo (Ed.), *Coping with uncertainty.* Hillsdale, NJ: Erlbaum.

Harding, C. G., & Golinkoff, R. M. (1979). The origins of intentional vocalizations in prelinguistic infants. *Child Development, 50,* 33–40.

Harris, P. L. (1983). Children's understanding of the link between situation and emotion. *Journal of Experimental Child Psychology, 36,* 490–509.

Harris, P. L., Donnelly, K., Guz, G. R., & Pitt-Watson, R. (1986). Children's understanding of the distinction between real and apparent emotion. *Child Development, 57,* 895–909.

Harris, P. L., & Gross, D. (1989). Children's understanding of real and apparent emotion. In J. W. Astington, P. L. Harris, & D. R. Olson (Eds.), *Developing theories of mind* (pp. 295–314). New York: Cambridge University Press.

Harris, P. L., Guz, G. R., Lipian, M. S., & Man-Shu, Z. (1985). Insight into the time course of emotion among Western and Chinese children. *Child Development, 56,* 972–988.

Harris, P. L., & Lipian, M. S. (1989). Understanding emotion and experiencing emotion. In C. Saarni & P. L. Harris (Eds.), *Children's understanding of emotion.* New York: Cambridge University Press.

Harris, P. L., & Olthof, T. (1982). This child's concept of emotion. In G. Butterworth & P. Light (Eds.), *Social cognition: Studies in the development of understanding* (pp. 188–209). Chicago: University of Chicago Press.

Harris, P. L., Olthof, T., & Meerum Terwogt, M. (1981). Children's knowledge of emotion. *Journal of Child Psychology and Psychiatry, 22,* 247–261.

Harris, P. L., Olthof, T., Meerum Terwogt, M., & Hardman, C. E. (1987). Children's knowledge of the situations that provoke emotion. *International Journal of Behavioral Development, 10,* 319–343.

Harter, S. (1982a). A cognitive-developmental approach to children's understanding of affect and trait labels. In F. C. Serafica (Ed.), *Social-cognitive development in context* (pp. 27–61). New York: Guilford.

Harter, S. (1982b). Children's understanding of multiple emotions: A cognitive-developmental approach. In W. F. Overton (Ed.), *The relationship between social and cognitive development* (pp. 147–194). Hillsdale, NJ: Erlbaum.

Harter, S. (1983). Developmental perspectives on the self-system. In P. H. Mussen (Ed.), E. M. Hetherington (Vol. Ed.) *Handbook of child psychology: Vol. 4. Socialization, personality, and social development* (pp. 275–385). New York: Wiley.

Harter, S., & Buddin, B. J. (1987). Children's understanding of the simultaneity of two emotions: A five-stage developmental acquisition sequence. *Developmental Psychology, 23,* 388–399.

Harter, S., & Whitesell, N. (1989). Developmental changes in children's emotion concepts. In C. Saarni & P. L. Harris (Eds.), *Children's understanding of emotion.* Cambridge: Cambridge University Press.

Haviland, J. M., & Lelwica, M. (1987). The induced affect response: 10-week-old infants' responses to three emotion expressions. *Developmental Psychology, 23,* 97–104.

Healey, B. T., Fox, N. A., & Porges, S. W. (1988). *The heritability of autonomic patterns and social behavior in young twins.* Manuscript submitted for publication, University of Miami Medical School.

Hoffman, M. L. (1982). Development of prosocial motivation: Empathy and guilt. In N. Eisenberg (Ed.), *The development of prosocial behavior* (pp. 281–313). New York: Academic Press.

Hyson, M. C., & Izard, C. E. (1985). Continuities and changes in emotion expressions during brief separation at 13 and 18 months. *Developmental Psychology, 21,* 1165–1170.

Izard, C. E., Hembree, E. A., & Huebner, R. R. (1987). Infants' emotional expressions to acute pain: Developmental change and stability of individual differences. *Developmental Psychology, 23*, 105–113.

Izard, C. E., & Malatesta, C. Z. (1987). Perspectives on emotional development I: Differential emotions theory of early emotional development. In J. D. Osofsky (Ed.), *Handbook of infant development* (2nd ed.) (pp. 494–554). New York: John Wiley.

Jersild, A. T. (1954). Emotional development. In L. Carmichael (Ed.), *Manual of child psychology* (2nd ed.) (pp. 833–917). New York: John Wiley.

Kagan, J., Kearsley, R. B., & Zelazo, P. R. (1978). *Infancy: Its place in human development*. Cambridge: Harvard University Press.

Kagan, J., Reznick, J. S., Clarke, C., & Snidman, N. (1984). Behavioral inhibition to the unfamiliar. *Child Development, 55*, 2212–2225.

Kagan, J., Reznick, J. S., & Snidman, N. (1987). The physiology and psychology of behavioral inhibition in children. *Child Development, 58*, 1459–1473.

Kaye, K. (1982). *The mental and social life of babies: How parents create persons.* Chicago: University of Chicago Press.

Kessen, W., & Mandler, G. (1961). Anxiety, pain, and the inhibition of distress. *Psychological Review, 68*, 396–404.

Kinsbourne, M., & Bemporad, B. (1984). Lateralization of emotion: A model and the evidence. In N. A. Fox & R. J. Davidson (Eds.), *The psychobiology of affective development* (pp. 259–291). Hillsdale, NJ: Erlbaum.

Kinsbourne, M., & Hiscock, M. (1983). The normal and deviant development of functional lateralization of the brain. In P. H. Mussen (Ed.), M. M. Haith & J. J. Campos (Vol. Eds.), *Handbook of child psychology: Vol. 2. Infancy and developmental psychobiology* (pp. 157–280). New York: John Wiley.

Klinnert, M. D. (1984). The regulation of infant behavior by maternal facial expression. *Infant Behavior and Development, 7*, 447–465.

Klinnert, M. D., Campos, J. J., Sorce, J. F., Emde, R. N., & Svejda, M. (1983). Emotions as behavior regulators: Social referencing in infancy. In R. Plutchik & H. Kellerman (Eds.), *Emotion: Theory, research, and experience: Vol. 2. Emotions in early development* (pp. 57–86). New York: Academic Press.

Klinnert, M. D., Emde, R. N., & Butterfield, P. (1983, April). *Social referencing: The infant's use of emotional signals from a friendly adult with mother present.* Paper presented to the meeting of the Society for Research in Child Development, Detroit, MI.

Kopp, C. B. (1982). Antecedents of self-regulation: A developmental perspective. *Developmental Psychology, 18*, 199–214.

Kopp, C. B. (1987). The growth of self-regulation: Caregivers and children. In N. Eisenberg (Ed.), *Contemporary topics in developmental psychology* (pp. 34–55). New York: John Wiley.

Kopp, C. B. (in press). Regulation of distress and negative emotions: A developmental view. *Developmental Psychology*.

Korner, A. F., & Thoman, E. B. (1970). Visual alertness in neonates as evoked by maternal care. *Journal of Experimental Child Psychology, 10,* 67–78.

Korner, A. F., & Thoman, E. B. (1972). The relative efficacy of contact and vestibular-proprioceptive stimulation in soothing neonates. *Child Development, 43,* 443–453.

Lamb, M. E. (1981a). Developing trust and perceived effectance in infancy. In L. P. Lipsitt (Ed.), *Advances in infancy research* (Vol. 2, pp. 101–127). Norwood, NJ: Ablex.

Lamb, M. E. (1981b). The development of social expectations in the first year of life. In M. E. Lamb & L. Sherrod (Eds.), *Infant social cognition* (pp. 155–175). Hillsdale, NJ: Erlbaum.

Lamb, M. E., & Malkin, C. M. (1986). The development of social expectations in distress-relief sequences: A longitudinal study. *International Journal of Behavioral Development, 9,* 235–249.

Lamb, M. E., Thompson, R. A., & Frodi, A. (1982). Early social development: Issues, paradigms and approaches. In R. Vasta (Ed.), *Strategies and techniques of child study* (pp. 49–81). New York: Academic Press.

Lamb, M. E., Thompson, R. A., Gardner, W. P., & Charnov, E. L. (1985). *Infant-mother attachment.* Hillsdale, NJ: Erlbaum.

Lazarus, R. (1975). The self-regulation of emotion. In L. Levi (Ed.), *Emotions: Their parameters and measurement* (pp. 47–67). New York: Raven Press.

Lerner, J. V., & Lerner, R. M. (1983). Temperament and adaptation across life: Theoretical and empirical issues. In P. B. Baltes & O. G. Brim, Jr. (Eds.), *Life-span development and behavior* (Vol. 5, pp. 197–231). New York: Academic Press.

Lewis, M., & Michalson, L. (1985). *Children's emotions and moods: Developmental theory and measurement.* New York: Plenum Press.

Luria, A. R. (1961). *The role of speech in the regulation of normal and abnormal behavior.* New York: Pergamon Press.

Malatesta, C. Z., Grigoryev, P., Lamb, C., Albin, M., & Culver, C. (1986). Emotion socialization and expressive development in preterm and full-term infants. *Child Development, 57,* 316–330.

Malatesta, C. Z., & Haviland, J. M. (1982). Learning display rules: The socialization of emotion expression in infancy. *Child Development, 53,* 991–1003.

Malatesta, C. Z., & Izard, C. E. (1984). The ontogenesis of human social signals: From biological imperative to symbol utilization. In N. A. Fox & R. J. Davidson (Eds.), *The psychobiology of affective development* (pp. 161–206). Hillsdale, NJ: Erlbaum.

Markus, H. (1977). Self-schemata and processing information about the self. *Journal of Personality and Social Psychology, 35,* 63–78.

Masters, J. C., & Carlson, C. R. (1984). Children's and adults' understanding of the causes and consequences of emotional states. In C. E. Izard, J. Kagan, & R. B. Zajonc (Eds.), *Emotions, cognition, and behavior* (pp. 438–463). Cambridge: Cambridge University Press.

Masters, J. C., Ford, M. E., & Arend, R. A. (1983). Children's strategies for controlling affective responses to aversive social experience. *Motivation and Emotion, 7,* 103–116.

McCall, R. B. (1979). The development of intellectual functioning in infancy and the prediction of later IQ. In J. D. Osofsky (Ed.), *Handbook of infant development* (pp. 707–741). New York: John Wiley.

McCall, R. B. (1981). Nature-nurture and the two realms of development: A proposed integration with respect to mental development. *Child Development, 52,* 1–12.

McCoy, C. L., & Masters, J. C. (1985). The development of children's strategies for the social control of emotion. *Child Development, 56,* 1214–1222.

Meerum Terwogt, M., Koops, W., Oosterhoff, T., & Olthof, T. (1986). Development in processing of multiple emotional situations. *Journal of General Psychology, 113,* 109–119.

Meerum Terwogt, M., & Olthof, T. (1989). Awareness and self-regulation of emotion in young children. In C. Saarni & P. L. Harris (Eds.), *Children's understanding of emotion.* New York: Cambridge University Press.

Meerum Terwogt, M., Schene, J., & Harris, P. L. (1986). Self-control of emotional reactions by young children. *Journal of Child Psychology and Psychiatry, 27,* 357–366.

Meisels, S. J., & Anastasiow, N. J. (1982). The risks of prediction: Relationships between etiology, handicapping conditions, and developmental outcomes. In S. G. Moore & C. R. Cooper (Eds.), *The young child: Reviews of research* (Vol. 3). Washington, DC: National Association for the Education of Young Children.

Miller, P. J., & Sperry, L. L. (1987). The socialization of anger and aggression. *Merrill-Palmer Quarterly, 33,* 1–31.

Miller, P. J., & Sperry, L. L. (1988). The socialization and acquisition of emotional meanings, with special reference to language: A reply to Saarni. *Merrill-Palmer Quarterly, 34,* 217–222.

Miller, S. M., & Green, M. L. (1985). Coping with stress and frustration: Origins, nature, and development. In M. Lewis & C. Saarni (Eds.), *The socialization of emotions* (pp. 263–314). New York: Plenum Press.

Mischel, H. N., & Mischel, W. (1983). The development of children's knowledge of self-control strategies. *Child Development, 54,* 603–619.

Mischel, W. (1981). Metacognition and the rules of delay. In J. H. Flavell & L. Ross (Eds.), *Social cognitive development* (pp. 240–271). Cambridge: Cambridge University Press.

Mischel, W., & Ebbesen, E. B. (1970). Attention in delay of gratification. *Journal of Personality and Social Psychology, 16,* 329–337.

Mischel, W., & Mischel, H. N. (1977). Self-control and the self. In T. Mischel (Ed.), *The self: Psychological and philosophical issues* (pp. 31–64). Oxford: Basil Blackwell.

Miyake, K., Campos, J. J., Kagan, J., & Bradshaw, D. L. (1986). Issues in socioemotional development. In H. Stevenson, H. Azuma, & K. Hakuta (Eds.), *Child development and education in Japan* (pp. 239–261). New York: Freeman.

Mood, D. W., Johnson, J. E., & Shantz, C. U. (1978). Social comprehension and affect-matching in young children. *Merrill-Palmer Quarterly, 24*, 63–66.

Panksepp, J. (in press). The neurobiology of emotions: Of animal brains and human feelings. In H. Wagner & T. Manstead (Eds.), *Handbook of psychophysiology.* New York: Plenum Press.

Piaget, J. (1954/1981). *Intelligence and affectivity.* Palo Alto, CA: Annual Reviews. (Originally published 1954)

Plomin, R. (1983). Developmental behavioral genetics. *Child Development, 54*, 253–259.

Plomin, R. (1986). *Development, genetics, and psychology.* Hillsdale, NJ: Erlbaum.

Plomin, R., & Thompson, L. (1988). Life-span developmental behavioral genetics. In P. B. Baltes, D. L. Featherman, & R. M. Lerner (Eds.), *Life-span development and behavior* (Vol. 8, pp. 1–31). Hillsdale, NJ: Erlbaum.

Reznick, J. S., Kagan, J., Snidman, N., Gersten, M., Baak, K., & Rosenberg, A. (1986). Inhibited and uninhibited children: A follow-up study. *Child Development, 57*, 660–680.

Ridgeway, D., Waters, E., & Kuczaj, S. A. (1985). Acquisition of emotion-descriptive language: Receptive and productive vocabulary norms for ages 18 months to 6 years. *Developmental Psychology, 21*, 901–908.

Robson, K. S., & Moss, H. A. (1970). Patterns and determinants of maternal attachment. *Journal of Pediatrics, 77*, 976–985.

Rothbart, M. K. (1981). Measurement of temperament in infancy. *Child Development, 52*, 569–578.

Rothbart, M. K., & Derryberry, D. (1981). Development of individual differences in temperament. In M. E. Lamb & A. L. Brown (Eds.), *Advances in developmental psychology* (Vol. 1, pp. 37–86). Hillsdale, NJ: Erlbaum.

Rothbart, M. K., & Posner, M. I. (1985). Temperament and the development of self-regulation. In L. C. Hartlage & C. F. Telzrow (Eds.), *The neuropsychology of individual differences: A developmental perspective* (pp. 93–123). New York: Plenum Press.

Russell, J. A., & Ridgeway, D. (1983). Dimensions underlying children's emotion concepts. *Developmental Psychology, 19*, 795–804.

Saarni, C. (1979). Children's understanding of display rules for expressive behavior. *Developmental Psychology, 15*, 424–429.

Saarni, C. (1984). An observational study of children's attempts to monitor their expressive behavior. *Child Development, 55*, 1504–1513.

Saarni, C. (1985). Indirect processes in affect socialization. In M. Lewis & C. Saarni (Eds.), *The socialization of emotions* (pp. 187–209). New York: Plenum Press.

Saarni, C. (1987). Cultural rules of emotional experience: A commentary on Miller and Sperry's study. *Merrill-Palmer Quarterly, 33*, 535–540.

Saarni, C. (1989). Children's understanding of strategic control of emotional expression in social transactions. In C. Saarni & P. L. Harris (Eds.), *Children's understanding of emotion.* New York: Cambridge University Press.

Sagi, A., Lamb, M. E., Lewkowicz, K. S., Shoham, R., Dvir, R., & Estes, D.

(1985). Security of infant-mother, -father, and -metapelet attachments among kibbutz-reared Israeli children. In I Bretherton & E. Waters (Eds.), *Growing points in attachment theory and research. Monographs of the Society for Research in Child Development, 50* (1–2, Serial No. 209).

Scarr, S., & Kidd, K. K. (1983). Developmental behavior genetics. In P. H. Mussen (Ed.), M. M. Haith, & J. J. Campos (Vol. Eds.), *Handbook of child psychology: Vol. 2. Infancy and developmental psychobiology* (pp. 345–433). New York: John Wiley.

Schwartz, R. M., & Trabasso, T. (1984). Children's understanding of emotions. In C. E. Izard, J. Kagan, & R. Zajonc (Eds.), *Emotions, cognition, and behavior* (pp. 409–437). New York: Cambridge University Press.

Selman, R. L. (1981). What children understand of intrapsychic processes: The child as a budding personality theorist. In E. K. Shapiro & E. Weber (Eds.), *Cognitive and affective growth* (pp. 187–215). Hillsdale, NJ: Erlbaum.

Shantz, C. U. (1983). Social cognition. In P. H. Mussen (Ed.), J. H. Flavell & E. M. Markman (Vol. Eds.) *Handbook of child psychology: Vol. 3. Cognitive development* (pp. 495–555). New York: John Wiley.

Shaver, P., Schwartz, J., Kirson, D., & O'Connor, C. (1987). Emotion knowledge: Further exploration of a prototype approach. *Journal of Personality and Social Psychology, 52,* 1061–1086.

Sherman, L. W. (1975). An ecological study of glee in small groups of preschool children. *Child Development, 46,* 53–61.

Smolek, L., & Weinraub, M. (1979, March). *Separation distress and representational development.* Paper presented at the annual meeting of the Society for Research in Child Development, San Francisco, CA.

Sorce, J. F., Emde, R. N., Campos, J. J., & Klinnert, M. D. (1985). Maternal emotional signaling: Its effects on the visual cliff behavior of 1-year-olds. *Developmental Psychology, 17,* 737–745.

Sorce, J. F., Emde, R. N., & Frank, M. (1982). Maternal referencing in normal and Down's syndrome infants: A longitudinal analysis. In R. N. Emde & R. Harmon (Eds.), *The development of attachment and affiliative systems* (pp. 281–292). New York: Plenum Press.

Spitz, R. A. (1965). *The first year of life.* New York: International Universities Press.

Sroufe, L. A. (1979). Socioemotional development. In J. D. Osofsky (Ed.), *Handbook of infant development* (pp. 462–516). New York: John Wiley.

Sroufe, L. A., & Waters, E. (1976). The ontogenesis of smiling and laughter: A perspective on the organization of development in infancy. *Psychological Review, 83,* 173–189.

Sroufe, L. A., & Waters, E. (1977). Attachment as an organizational construct. *Child Development, 48,* 1184–1199.

Sroufe, L. A., & Wunsch, J. P. (1972). The development of laughter in the first year of life. *Child Development, 43,* 1326–1344.

Stechler, G., & Latz, E. (1966). Some observations on attention and arousal in the human infant. *Journal of the American Academy of Child Psychiatry, 5,* 517–525.

Stein, N. L., & Levine, L. J. (in press). The causal organization of emotional knowledge: A developmental study. *Cognition and Emotion.*

Stein, N. L., & Trabasso, T. (1989). Children's understanding of changing emotional states. In C. Saarni & P. L. Harris (Eds.), *Children's understanding of emotion.* New York: Cambridge University Press.

Stern, D. N. (1974). The goal and structure of mother-infant play. *Journal of the American Academy of Child Psychiatry, 13,* 402–421.

Stern, D. N. (1977). *The first relationship.* Cambridge: Harvard University Press.

Stern, D. N. (1985). *The interpersonal world of the infant.* New York: Basic Books.

Stern, D. N., Hofer, L., Haft, W., & Dore, J. (1985). Affect attunement: The sharing of feeling states between mother and infant by means of intermodal fluency. In T. M. Field & N. A. Fox (Eds.), *Social perception in infants* (pp. 249–268). Norwood, NJ: Ablex.

Stiefel, G. S., Plunkett, J. W., & Meisels, S. J. (1987). Affective expression among preterm infants of varying levels of biological risk. *Infant Behavior and Development, 10,* 151–164.

Super, C. M., & Harkness, S. (1982). The development of affect in infancy and early childhood. In D. A. Wagner & H. W. Stevenson (Eds.), *Cultural perspectives on child development* (pp. 1–19). San Francisco: Freeman.

Taylor, D. A., & Harris, P. L. (1983). Knowledge of the link between emotion and memory among normal and maladjusted boys. *Developmental Psychology, 19,* 832–838.

Taylor, D. A., & Harris, P. L. (1984). Knowledge of strategies for the expression of emotion among normal and maladjusted boys: A research note. *Journal of Child Psychology and Psychiatry, 24,* 141–145.

Tennes, K. (1982). The role of hormones in mother-infant transactions. In R. N. Emde & R. J. Harmon (Eds.), *The development of attachment and affiliative systems* (pp. 75–80). New York: Plenum Press.

Tennes, K., Downey, K., & Vernadakis, A. (1977). Urinary cortisol excretion rates and anxiety in normal 1-year-old infants. *Psychosomatic Medicine, 39,* 178–187.

Tennes, K. H., & Mason J. W. (1982). Developmental psychoendocrinology: An approach to the study of emotions. In C. E. Izard (Ed.), *Measuring emotions in infants and children* (pp. 21–37). Cambridge: Cambridge University Press.

Termine, N. T., & Izard, C. E. (1988). Infants' responses to their mothers' expressions of joy and sadness. *Developmental Psychology, 24,* 223–229.

Thomas, A., & Chess, S. (1977). *Temperament and development.* New York: Brunner/Mazel.

Thompson, R. A. (1987a). Empathy and emotional understanding: The early development of empathy. In N. Eisenberg & J. Strayer (Eds.), *Empathy and its development* (pp. 119–145). Cambridge: Cambridge University Press.

Thompson, R. A. (1987b). Development of children's inferences of the emotions of others. *Developmental Psychology, 23,* 124–131.

Thompson, R. A. (1988). Early development in life-span perspective. In P. B. Baltes, D. L. Featherman, & R. M. Lerner (Eds.), *Life-span development and behavior* (Vol. 9, pp. 129–172). Hillsdale, NJ: Erlbaum.

Thompson, R. A. (1989). Causal attributions and children's emotional understanding. In C. Saarni & P. L. Harris (Eds.), *Children's understanding of emotion* (pp. 117–150). Cambridge: Cambridge University Press.

Thompson, R. A. (in press). Construction and reconstruction of early attachments: Taking perspective on attachment theory and research. In D. P. Keating & H. Rosen (Eds.), *Constructivist perspectives on atypical development and developmental psychopathology*. Hillsdale, NJ: Erlbaum.

Thompson, R. A. (in preparation). *Developmental changes in emotional dynamics in infancy*. University of Nebraska, Lincoln, NE.

Thompson, R. A., Cicchetti, D., Lamb, M. E., & Malkin, C. (1985). Emotional responses of Down syndrome and normal infants in the Strange Situation: The organization of affective behavior in infants. *Developmental Psychology, 21*, 828–841.

Thompson, R. A., & Connell, J. P. (1985, April). *The role of emotion in social interaction in the second year: Short-term longitudinal studies*. Paper presented to the meeting of the Society for Research in Child Development, Toronto, Ontario, Canada.

Thompson, R. A., Connell, J. P., & Bridges, L. (1988). Temperament, emotion, and social interactive behavior in the Strange Situation: A component process analysis of attachment system functioning. *Child Development, 59*, 1102–1110.

Thompson, R. A., & Lamb, M. E. (1983). Individual differences in dimensions of socioemotional development in infancy. In R. Plutchik & H. Kellerman (Eds.), *Emotion: Theory, research, and experience: Vol. 2. Emotions in early development* (pp. 87–114). New York: Academic Press.

Thompson, R. A., & Lamb, M. E. (1984). Assessing qualitative dimensions of emotional responsiveness in infants: Separation reactions in the Strange Situation. *Infant Behavior and Development, 7*, 423–445.

Thompson, R. A., & Limber, S. (in press). "Social anxiety" in infancy: Stranger wariness and separation distress. In H. Leitenberg (Ed.), *Handbook of Social and Evaluation Anxiety*. New York: Plenum Press.

Thompson, R. A., & Sagi, A. (in preparation). *Emotional reactions in the Strange Situation: A comparison of Israeli kibbutz, Israeli day care, and American infants*.

Trabasso, T., Stein, N. L., & Johnson, L. R. (1981). Children's knowledge of events: A causal analysis of story structure. In G. Bower (Ed.), *The psychology of learning and motivation* (pp. 237–282). New York: Academic Press.

Trevarthan, C., & Hubley, P. (1978). Secondary intersubjectivity: Confidence, confiding and acts of meaning in the first year. In A. Lock (Ed.), *Action, gesture and symbol: The emergence of language* (pp. 183–229). New York: Academic Press.

Tronick, E. Z., Als, H., & Adamson, L. (1978). Structure of early face-to-face communicative interactions. In M. Bullowa (Ed.), *Before speech* (pp. 349–372). Cambridge: Cambridge University Press.

Tronick, E. Z., Cohn, J., & Shea, E. (1986). The transfer of affect between mothers and infants. In T. B. Brazelton & M. W. Yogman (Eds.), *Affective development in infancy* (pp. 11–25). Norwood, NJ: Ablex.

Tucker, D. M., & Frederick, S. L. (in press). Emotion and brain lateralization. In H. Wagner & T. Manstead (Eds.), *Handbook of psychophysiology: Emotion and social behaviour*. New York: John Wiley.

Van Lieshout, C. F. M. (1975). Young children's reactions to barriers placed by their mothers. *Child Development, 46*, 879–886.

Vygotsky, L. S. (1962). *Thought and language*. Cambridge: MIT Press.

Watson, J. S. (1972). Smiling, cooing, and "the game." *Merrill-Palmer Quarterly, 18*, 323–339.

Watson, J. S., & Ramey, C. T. (1972). Reactions to response-contingent stimulation in early infancy. *Merrill-Palmer Quarterly, 18*, 219–227.

Weiner, B., & Graham, S. (1984). An attributional approach to emotional development. In C. E. Izard, J. Kagan, & R. Zajonc (Eds.), *Emotions, cognition, and behavior* (pp. 167–191). New York: Cambridge University Press.

Yates, B. T., & Mischel, W. (1979). Young children's preferred attentional strategies for delaying gratification. *Journal of Personality and Social Psychology, 37*, 286–300.

Zivin, G. (1986). Processes of expressive behavior development. *Merrill-Palmer Quarterly, 32*, 103–140.

# Subject Index

# Author Index

484

Goodwin, F. K., 208
Gopnik, A., 92
Gorden, A., 278
Gordon, S. L., 115, 130, 395, 396
Gotlib, I., 211
Gottlieb, G., 266
Gottman, J., 431, 441, 433
Gould, M. E., 159, 436
Gould, R. W., 318
Gove, F. L., 6, 92
Graham, S., 93, 165–166, 168, 201, 436, 439
Grajek, S., 305
Grayson, M., 149, 173
Green, A., 306
Green, F. L., 92, 431
Green, M. L., 128, 168, 412–413
Greenberg, M. T., 85, 94, 267, 270, 280, 319, 336
Greenfield, P. M., 82, 88
Greenough, W., 268
Greenspan, S. I., 263, 282, 287, 333
Greif, E. B., 416
Grigoryev, P., 32, 398
Gross, D., 137, 156, 439, 442
Grossmann, K., 6, 37, 64–66, 73, 88, 100, 101, 165
Grossmann, K. E., 6, 37, 64–66, 73, 88, 100, 165
Grow, J. G., 150, 298
Gruendel, J., 79, 81, 82
Grusec, J., 198, 199
Guardo, C. J., 96
Guarino, P. A., 201
Guidano, V. F., 102, 265, 319, 333
Gunn, P., 285
Gunnar, M. R., 386, 420, 421, 432, 442
Gustafson, J. P., 98, 102
Gutfreund, M., 308
Guz, G. R., 439, 443

Haft, W., 405
Hall, J. A., 193
Hamazaki, T., 439

Hand, H., 96
Handel, S., 145
Handsburg, H. G., 69
Harding, C. G., 430
Hardman, C. E., 435
Hardy-Brown, K., 307
Harkness, S., 396
Harlow, H. F., 312
Harmon, R. J., 124, 282, 294, 313, 422
Harris, P. L., 48, 93, 126, 130, 137, 145, 156, 163, 164, 165, 167–169, 173, 435, 436, 439, 442, 443
Hart, D., 267, 431, 440, 445
Harter, S., 84, 96, 116, 148–149, 173–174, 267, 322, 327, 328, 329, 332, 431, 435, 439, 445
Hartlage, L. C., 268
Hartmann, H., 77
Hartup, W., 267, 324
Haustead, L. F., 306
Haviland, J. M., 27, 41, 42–43, 45, 195, 398–399
Hay, D. F., 203
Hayes, A., 164
Haynes, O. M., 298, 304
Hayward, S., 429
Healey, B. T., 427
Heidegger, M., 9–10, 48
Heinicke, C. M., 190
Hembree, E. A., 25, 34, 375
Henderson, C., 273, 339
Henderson, S., 333
Hennessey, K., 290
Herrenkohl, E. C., 303, 306, 325
Herrenkohl, R. C., 303, 306, 325
Hertzgaard, L., 420
Hess, R., 312, 342
Hesse, E., 59, 61, 70
Hesse, P., 259, 267, 270, 274, 276, 296, 316, 317
Hesselbrock, V., 325
Hiatt, S., 273
Hill, P., 275
Hill, S., 287

488